# The Social Forces
# in Later Life

## Lifetime Series in Aging

Available now from Wadsworth:

*The Social Forces in Later Life: An Introduction to Social Gerontology,
Second Edition*
by Robert C. Atchley, Miami University

*The Sociology of Aging: Selected Readings*
by Robert C. Atchley and Mildred M. Seltzer, Miami University

*Social Problems of the Aging: Readings*
by Mildred M. Seltzer, Sherry L. Corbett, and Robert C. Atchley,
Miami University

*The Economics of Aging*
by James H. Schulz, Brandeis University

Available now from Brooks/Cole:

*Early and Middle Adulthood: The Best Is Yet to Be—Maybe*
by Lillian E. Troll, Rutgers University

*Late Adulthood: Perspectives on Human Development*
by Richard A. Kalish, Berkeley, California

*The Later Years: Social Applications of Gerontology*
by Richard A. Kalish, Berkeley, California

*Life-Span Developmental Psychology: Introduction to Research Methods*
by Paul B. Baltes, Hayne W. Reese, and John R. Nesselroade, The Pennsylvania State University and West Virginia University

Forthcoming titles from Wadsworth:

*The Family in Later Life*
by Lillian E. Troll, Sheila J. Miller, and Robert C. Atchley, Rutgers University
and Miami University

*Aging: Politics and Policies*
by Robert H. Binstock, Brandeis University

*Comparative Gerontology: Aging in Various Societies*
by Donald O. Cowgill, University of Missouri, Columbia

*Minorities and Aging*
by Jacquelyne J. Jackson, Duke University

# The Social Forces in Later Life

An Introduction to Social Gerontology

SECOND EDITION

**Robert C. Atchley**

Scripps Foundation Gerontology Center
Miami University

Wadsworth Publishing Company, Inc.
Belmont, California

*Sociology Editor*: Stephen Rutter

PRINTED IN THE UNITED STATES OF AMERICA

3 4 5 6 7 8 9 10—81 80 79 78

**Library of Congress Cataloging in Publication Data**

Atchley, Robert C
    The social forces in later life.

    Bibliography:  p.
    Includes index.
    1.  Gerontology.  2.  Aged—United States.  3.  Retire-
ment—United States.  I.  Title.
HQ1061.A78  1977        301.43′5         76-18902
ISBN 0-534-00463-6

# Preface

The intent of this book is to provide a brief but comprehensive introduction to the subject of human aging, with particular emphasis on its social and sociopsychological aspects. The book begins with an orientation to social gerontology as a multidisciplinary field of social science. Part Two of the book briefly summarizes what we know about the impact of aging on biological and psychological functioning. This basic information is necessary background in order to be able to put the social aspects of aging into a realistic context. Part Three deals with situations that usually face aging individuals. Part Four discusses how society treats its older members.

The second edition has several improvements in addition to general updating and reorganization.

- ☐ The section on theory is better organized to give the reader an overview of the various theories in social gerontology.
- ☐ Material on the life course and age stratification is given more prominent coverage.
- ☐ The range of coverage has been considerably expanded for the chapters on social situation, personal adaptation, and family and friends.
- ☐ A new chapter has been added on death, dying, bereavement, and widowhood.
- ☐ A new reference format has been developed that will allow easier cross- referencing and bibliography development.
- ☐ An expanded instructor's manual includes an annotated film guide.

No one can do a basic book in a multidisciplinary field without a great deal of help. For their comments on specific chapters, I owe thanks to Bernice Neugarten, Ethel Shanas, Hiram Friedsam, Jerome Kaplan, Nancy Datan, Paul Maves, David Moberg,

Richard Kalish, Kathy Gribbin, James Schulz, Nathan Shock, Takashi Makinodan, Jon Hendricks, and Calvin Lang. The revision of the chapter on the family in particular benefited from the thorough criticisms of Sheila Miller. Lillian Troll provided hundreds of suggestions that greatly influenced the first edition. The second edition was greatly helped by detailed suggestions on the overall manuscript from Stephen Cutler and Vivian Wood. I also received numerous helpful suggestions from students and teachers who used the first edition, and I will continue to appreciate the same invaluable comments from those who work with this second edition. Finally, I owe a special debt to David T. Lewis, whose inspiring classes and keen interest in students attracted me to the profession of sociology in the first place, and gratitude to Fred Cottrell, who has taught me more than I used to think there was to know.

# Contents in Brief

PART ONE    **INTRODUCTION**

   Chapter 1    **The Field of Social Gerontology**   3

PART TWO    **THE AGING INDIVIDUAL**

   Chapter 2    **Biological Aging**   33

   Chapter 3    **The Psychology of Aging**   40

   Chapter 4    **The Social Psychology of the Aging Individual**   67

PART THREE    **AGE CHANGES IN SITUATIONAL CONTEXT**

   Chapter 5    **The Changing Social Context of Later Life**   87

   Chapter 6    **Health**   104

   Chapter 7    **Finances**   125

   Chapter 8    **Retirement**   139

   Chapter 9    **Leisure**   168

   Chapter 10    **Death, Dying, Bereavement, and Widowhood**   179

Chapter 11     **Independence and Dependency**   197

Chapter 12     **Personal Adaptation to Aging**   207

PART FOUR     **SOCIETAL RESPONSE TO OLDER PEOPLE**

Chapter 13     **Societal Disengagement**   227

Chapter 14     **The Economy**   234

Chapter 15     **Politics and Government**   245

Chapter 16     **Community**   261

Chapter 17     **Moorings in the Community:
               Religion and Voluntary Associations**   279

Chapter 18     **Interpersonal Relationships: Family, Friends,
               and Neighbors**   289

Chapter 19     **Epilogue: What Does It All Mean?**   316

               **Appendix on Methodology**   325

               **Glossary**   329

               **References**   333

               **Index**   407

# Contents in Detail

PART ONE    **INTRODUCTION**

Chapter 1 • **The Scope of Social Gerontology**   3
Gerontology defined, 4    Social gerontology, 5    Age changes, age
differences, and period effects, 8    The stages of later life, 10    What
makes aging an important area for study? 11    The rise of aging as a social
problem, 12    RESEARCH ILLUSTRATION 1, 20    Approaches to the
study of aging, 23    Summary, 28

PART TWO    **THE AGING INDIVIDUAL**

Chapter 2 • **Biological Aging**   33
Results of senescence, 37    Summary, 38

Chapter 3 • **The Psychology of Aging**   40
Sensory processes, 40    The perceptual process, 45    Psychomotor
performance, 46    Mental functioning, 49    RESEARCH
ILLUSTRATION 2, 52    Drives, 58    Motives, 60    Emotions, 61
Practical implications, 61    RESEARCH ILLUSTRATION 3, 62
Summary, 63    RESEARCH ILLUSTRATION 4, 64

Chapter 4 • **The Social Psychology of the Aging Individual**   67
Socialization, 67    Personality, 73    RESEARCH ILLUSTRATION 5,
74    Summary, 82

PART THREE    AGE CHANGES IN SITUATIONAL CONTEXT

Chapter 5 • **The Changing Social Context of Later Life**  87
The life course, 88    Social roles, 91    RESEARCH ILLUSTRATION 6,
92   Summary, 102

Chapter 6 • **Health**  104
RESEARCH ILLUSTRATION 7, 110    Treatment, 112    Institutionalization, 116    The continuum of health care, 121    Summary, 122

Chapter 7   **Finances**  125
The financial need, 125    Direct income sources, 127    Indirect income
sources, 134    Level of living, 134    The future, 136    Summary, 137

Chapter 8   **Retirement**  139
The link between people and their jobs, 141    The evolution and
institutionalization of retirement, 141    The retirement process, 143
RESEARCH ILLUSTRATION 8, 152    The consequences of retirement,
155    RESEARCH ILLUSTRATION 9, 160    The future of retirement,
164    Summary, 164

Chapter 9   **Leisure**  168
Identity crisis and leisure participation, 169    Identity continuity and
leisure participation, 170    Leisure competence, 174    Variety in leisure
roles, 175    Summary, 178

Chapter 10   **Death, Dying, Bereavement, and Widowhood**  179
Defining death, 179    The demography of death, 180    The meaning of
death, 181    Losing a spouse, 186    Summary, 194

Chapter 11   **Independence and Dependency**  197
Learning to be independent, 198    Types of independence, 200
Maintaining independence, 202    Dependency, 203    Summary, 205

Chapter 12   **Personal Adaptation to Aging**  207
Disengagement, 209    Substitution, 212    Consolidation, 212    Life-
style solutions, 212    Adaptive tasks, 214    Maintaining competence,
217    Varieties of escape, 217    Successful aging, 219    Summary, 223

PART FOUR    SOCIETAL RESPONSE TO OLDER PEOPLE

Chapter 13   **Societal Disengagement**  227
Role loss, 228    Atrophy of opportunity, 229    Summary, 232

Chapter 14   **The Economy**  234
Older people as jobholders, 235    Older people as consumers, 239
Other economic roles, 243    Summary

Chapter 15    **Politics and Government**   245
Political participation, 245    Political power, 250    Government and
older people, 254    Summary, 259

Chapter 16    **Community**   261
Social structure, 262    Community facilities, 263    Social services, 264
Coordination of services, 269    Transportation, 271    Housing, 272
Education, 275    Planned retirement communities, 276    Summary, 277

Chapter 17    **Moorings in the Community:**
**Religion and Voluntary Associations**   279
Religion, 279    Voluntary associations, 285    Summary, 287

Chapter 18    **Primary Relationships: Family, Friends,**
**and Neighbors**   289
The older couple, 291    Widows and widowers, 295    Never-married
older people, 296    Divorced older people, 296    Trends in marital
status, 297    Sexuality in older people, 297    The older parent role,
299  The grandparent role, 301    The great-grandparent role, 301
RESEARCH ILLUSTRATION 10, 302    The sibling role, 304    Family
structure, 304    Family values, 305    Family dynamics, 307    Friends
and neighbors, 309    RESEARCH ILLUSTRATION 11, 310
Summary, 312

Chapter 19    **Epilogue: What Does It All Mean?**   316
Research, 316    Training, 319    Policy and planning, 319    The future
of social gerontology, 322

**Appendix on Methodology**   325
Methodological problems in social gerontology, 325

**Glossary**   329

**References**   333

**Index**   407

# Part One
# Introduction

The introductory chapter in Part I deals with the *discipline* of social gerontology. Chapter 1 defines social gerontology and provides the background essential for understanding the emergence of human aging as an important field within social science. It also gives the characteristics of the discipline—its various types of knowledge, the methodology for learning about aging, and some of the prominent approaches that form the nucleus for research on the social aspects of aging.

# 1

# The Scope
# of Social Gerontology

The following case histories have been adapted from the Kansas City Study of Adult Life:

### Case 1

This retired semiskilled government employee was 70 at the beginning of the study. He lived with his wife and had grown children and several grandchildren. He mentioned his wife as a most admired person, wonderful, congenial, and pleasing; the only thing wrong, he indicated with a chuckle, was that she kept him working around the house.

He thoroughly enjoyed being retired and did not miss his work. He had worked hard and worried a lot, and liked being free of all that. He thought of himself as "more mellow, more settled and less tempted." He loved his children and grandchildren and enjoyed *short* visits from them. One neighbor said she felt toward him as a daughter toward a father. He had lived in the same house for more than 20 years, knew several neighbors, considered a few of them as friends, but did very little visiting. His nights were almost always dreamless in the last half of his life. He had absolutely no telephone calls.

The clinical psychologist found no evidence of anxiety or depression. His family and close friends spoke of him with real affection, and expressed concern for his health, about which he himself never complained. He was in no way alienated, anomic, or isolated, and he coped extremely well. The exchange of energy between

**3**

himself and his wife appeared in good balance, and certainly he gave as much or more into his social system than he took out of it.[1]

### Case 2

Dependency is not always a voluntary state—it can be forced on an aging person most cruelly. This 80-year-old widow is a good example of what can happen when older people become physically incapable of caring for themselves and are left emotionally to their own devices because everyone else is too busy or too bored to care.

At the beginning of the study, this woman was far from being in this position. She lived with her widowed daughter, mothered the daughter's 17-year-old son, and did her share of keeping house. At the time of the first interview, she was bright and hardworking and looked rather young for her age. She found it hard to think of herself as 80, and yet, except for one physically disabled sister on the West Coast, she was the only one of her generation left.

The last inverview, 4 years after the initial one, showed that the respondent had failed drastically. She had sprained her back and was confined to a chair or bed. A niece and a granddaughter were also living in the apartment, as well as a great-granddaughter, making a total of five in the rather small quarters. Noise and confusion abounded, and the respondent was left sitting helplessly in the midst of this bedlam. Her own role was clearly that of a nonparticipant. Occasionally she was able to hold the baby and feed it or wash a few dishes, but there her services ended, of necessity. Everyone else was too busy or too bored with her to give her more than nominal attention, and she was dying of loneliness in this mass of people.

She described her daily round as one of deadly monotony—nothing to do, nothing she could do, just sit from meal to meal and then to bed for a poor night's sleep. They were all too occupied to take her visiting or to church, and although she did not want to resent this neglect, she did. She did not want to be a "crank" and tried to guard her tongue, but found it hard to do so, as she still was mentally alert to what was going on. For this reason, she really welcomed the interviewers. They were someone to talk to, they were interested in her, and at least they relieved the boredom (Williams and Wirths, 1965:48–49).

## GERONTOLOGY DEFINED

These two short vignettes illustrate the substance of **gerontology**. It is a complex subject, wandering far and wide across the traditional lines of academic study. Yet it never strays from a basic concern with **older persons** and with the processes of physical and social **aging**. Doctors study the illnesses of older people;[2] biologists study the physical changes that aging brings to the cells of the body; psychiatrists study

---

[1]Adapted by permission from Williams and Wirths (1965:37–39).

[2]*Geriatrics* is the practice of medicine with specialization in conditions prevalent among older people, just as *pediatrics* is specialization in the treatment of conditions common to children.

mental illness among older people; psychologists study age changes in sensory perception; economists study the income requirements of older people; architects design special housing for older people; and sociologists study the relationships between older people and their society and culture. Almost every area of study dealing with people or their needs has a branch that deals with older humans. All of these tiny branches of these many fields come together under the name of *gerontology*—literally, "the logic of aging."

There are four related but separate aspects to the study of aging. The biological aspect deals with physical aging—the body's gradual loss of the ability to renew itself. The psychological aspect deals with the sensory processes, perceptions, motor skills, intelligence, problem-solving ability, understanding, learning processes, drives, and emotions of the aging individual. The biological and psychological changes that occur with advancing age are coupled with the social environment of the individual to produce a third aspect—the behavioral. This aspect of aging deals with the aged person's attitudes, expectancies, motives, self-image, social roles, personality, and psychological adjustment to aging. Finally, the sociological aspect of aging deals with the society in which aging occurs, the influence this society has on aging individuals, and the influence they have on society. The health, income, work, and leisure of older people as these areas relate to their families, friends, voluntary associations, and religious groups, as well as to society in general, the economy, the government, and the community, are all part of the sociology of aging.

These four aspects of aging—biological, psychological, behavioral, and sociological—are all interrelated in the lives of older people.

## SOCIAL GERONTOLOGY

**Social gerontology** is the subfield of gerontology that deals primarily with the nonphysical aspects of aging. Clark Tibbitts, one of the founders of social gerontology, describes it as "concerned with the developmental and group behavior of adults following maturation and with the social phenomena which give rise to and arise out of the presence of older people in the population" (Tibbitts, 1964:139).

Biological and psychological aspects of aging interest the social gerontologist only insofar as they influence the ways in which the individual and society adapt to each other. Yet because biology and psychology are at the root of the social aspects of aging, social gerontologists must understand as much as they can about these areas.

### Characteristics of Social Gerontology As a Discipline

There are two essential areas within any discipline: language and knowledge. Language provides a set of symbols that promotes efficient communication and allows adequate description of what people see. Language also contains systems of classification that can be used to diagnose and to attach labels to the phenomena people observe. An area of study that is a subfield of a larger discipline usually will employ all of the language of the larger field, as well as a specialized language of its own. Social gerontologists, for example, use the term *social role*, from sociology, but they also use the term *disengagement*, which as a term is not well-known outside social gerontology.

Language also tells us where to look for additional factors of interest. For example, an observer who sees an object that he or she labels as "retired man" will also probably look for an object to label "working man," since his or her language provides a relationship between the symbols "retired man" and "working man." The language of a discipline thus can be expected to provide a group of *definitions* and a *system of classification* that connects these definitions.

As with language, knowledge has many facets. In its simplest form, knowledge is the *systematic description* of the world we live in. This type of knowledge answers the questions "What?" "When?" and "Where?" An example of this type of knowledge is the statement, "When an employee reaches 35 years of service with the company, he or she retires." "An employee retires" tells *what* happens; "when he or she reaches 35 years of service" tells *when* it happens; and "with the company" tells *where* (in what context) it happens.

As you have no doubt noticed, two important questions—"How?" and "Why?"—are omitted. Answers to these questions involve a more complex aspect of knowledge, called *explanation*. Explanation builds on description, for in order to explain a phenomenon, something must be known about it and other, surrounding phenomena. To expand our earlier description into explanation we might say, "*In order to make room for incoming personnel and to expand opportunities for promotion*, when an employee reaches 35 years of service with the company, he or she is *forced* to retire." Of course, a single, short statement of this type is seldom a complete description or explanation.

In social gerontology, *knowledge* thus aims at making *explicit* the systematic and predictable elements of the world around us. It seeks to describe and explain the structure of the social world of older people and how they are influenced by that structure. The ideas that make up social gerontology are a hodgepodge of social criticism, impressionistic observations, and scientifically developed facts and theories. The test of any particular idea is not its source or the prestige of its proponents, but its ability to help people understand and cope better with their world.

At the outset it should be understood that we are not concerned with every idea about the how and why of the social world of older people. We are concerned only with explanations and descriptions that can be *empirically verified*. This limitation automatically rules out many magical, mystical, and religious explanations, not because these ideas are necessarily wrong, but because they cannot be *proved* one way or the other, according to traditional scientific tests of congruence. Thus, an important criterion for evaluating a proposed explanation or description is whether it can be established or refuted by direct observation. If so, then it can be evaluated. If not, then it must simply be accepted or rejected as a matter of belief or faith.

Because the discipline includes only ideas that can be tested, it is possible to set up procedures for refining and accumulating both descriptions and explanations, all firmly grounded in the world of concrete observation. Thus, social gerontologists use observations and ideas about society to invent explanations for what they observe. But they use still more observations to try to disprove the explanations they have invented.

The more times they have tried to disprove an explanation and failed, the more confident they can be that it will lead to successful decisions, predictions about what will happen. A description or explanation of a social setting that has not yet been widely tested is not necessarily false. But we should expect less accurate results from untested facts and theories than from tested ones. Whenever possible, we will rely on descriptions and explanations developed from controlled observation, because, like everyone else, we play the percentages. Moral philosophy may lead to some right answers, but it is effective much less often than is controlled observation.

$T$ $104$

By definition, *scientific* ideas are developed from structured, direct observation. By *structured, direct observation* we mean that the procedures used to make the observations are explicit enough that they can be exactly repeated and thus compared.

Scientific knowledge relies for description on observations that can be repeated, the development of explanations only from empirically grounded description, and the use of observation to verify and refine scientific explanations and predictions.

Scientific ideas are also characterized by what happens to them after they are developed. Whereas mystical ideas are accepted on faith and tend to remain static, scientific ideas are continually being classified, tentatively substantiated, reconsidered, and corrected. This tentative nature of scientific ideas means that they are seldom viewed as "truths" but are more like road maps—they'll do for the present, but when better ones come along we don't hesitate to use them.

Although the greatest emphasis may be placed on scientific ideas, *impressionistic* ideas are also quite common in social gerontology. Whereas scientific ideas are developed from direct and repeated observations, impressionistic ideas are often based on the unverified work of a single observer. Because each of us has unique biases, no two people see exactly the same thing when they observe the world; and while scientific training stresses unbiased observation, a certain amount of bias is unavoidable. Thus, the more observers who give the same report, the more sure we can be that we are getting an accurate picture. Impressionistic ideas are not necessarily wrong. They may produce useful decisions. And there are many areas of social life that can only be studied by a sensitive and experienced observer in an ongoing social setting. Scientific ideas are preferable only because they generally can be more easily evaluated.

In social gerontology, *social criticism* arises from the fact that scientists also have roles other than that of scientist. They are also fathers or mothers; children of their parents; members of a political party, church, or civic association; amateur artists; music lovers; and so on. As full-fledged members of society, scientists take on certain values and share most of them with the people around them. The dominant values, those that people are willing to base decisions on, are usually widely shared and serve as the basis for defining what is good, true, and beautiful. Thus, values are translated into behavior and serve as the underpinnings for society. People want to know if their values are being served by the social world in which they are participating. Social scientists are in a good position to tell them because they themselves understand and often hold these same values, and they know how to find out if social reality is matching up to social values. Furthermore, because they are armed with explanations for some of the things that happen in the social world, social scientists can often explain how reality may fall short of desirable goals and can suggest changes in society that might improve society's direction toward these goals.

Social scientists disagree over just how much they should get involved in social criticism. Some say that any social criticism is inappropriate, because it takes the social scientist away from an "objective" search for "truth" and because the public may misunderstand and hold all social science responsible for inept criticisms. Opponents of this view reply that objectivity and truth are relative concepts that can be used in social criticism as well as in "hard science"; that social science knowledge will get into the public domain anyway, and that it is to the advantage of social scientists to make such suggestions themselves, since they are the most qualified to do so.

Social criticism is here to stay because it is *valued*. Not only does it perform a valuable function of self-analysis for the society as a whole, but it also indicates areas of social life in need of more rigorous inquiry. Social criticism can be very useful to gerontologists, provided they keep in mind that social critics have messages to deliver that may interfere with the accuracy of their analyses.

## AGE CHANGES, AGE DIFFERENCES, AND PERIOD EFFECTS

It is one thing to say that people change in certain ways as they age. It is quite another to say that people of different ages have different characteristics. It is still another to say that what it means to be a given age depends to some extent on when in historical time one experiences that age. In evaluating the ideas that comprise social gerontology, it is *essential* to distinguish statements of age change from statements of age difference and, in turn, from statements of period effect.

**Age change** refers to biological, psychological, and social maturation and aging. **Age difference** refers to differences among people who are different ages at a given point in time. In this context, *age* refers to chronological age. Two other terms, **cohort** and *time of measurement*, are necessary to distinguish studies of age differences from studies of age change. A *cohort* is a group of people who were born during a given interval and thus are in the same general chronological age category. Thus, everyone born in 1900 constitutes a cohort. The term *time of measurement* refers, of course, to the calendar date of measurement.

Most studies of aging have been **cross-sectional studies** of age differences. Cross-sectional studies look at people of different ages at the same point in time. For example, in Table 1-1, Samples A, B, and C represent people who were 55 in 1955, 60 in 1955, and 65 in 1955. If we found that the median annual income of Sample A was $5,600, and of Sample C was $4,800,[3] we could say there was an *age difference* of $800.

Unfortunately, social gerontologists have tended to *infer* age changes from data on age differences. For example, if we infer from the data above that annual income (adjusted for inflation) drops an average of $800 from age 55 to age 65, we are taking an unwarranted liberty with the information we have in hand. Age differences may, in

---

[3]The figures used here are for illustrative purposes only and are entirely fictitious.

**TABLE 1-1**
**Various Possible Cohorts and Times of Measurement**

| | | Time of Measurement | | | |
|---|---|---|---|---|---|
| | | *1955* | *1960* | *1965* | *1970* |
| Time of Birth (Cohort) | 1900 | Sample A Age 55 | Sample D Age 60 | Sample G Age 65 | Sample I Age 70 |
| | 1895 | Sample B Age 60 | Sample E Age 65 | Sample H Age 70 | |
| | 1890 | Sample C Age 65 | Sample F Age 70 | | |

*Source:* Adapted from Schaie (1967).

fact, result from age changes, but they are also quite likely to result from *life experiences* that differ because the people studied were born at different points in historical time. The age difference of $800 could result from a decline with age in earnings, but it could just as easily result from a tendency for people who entered the labor market in 1915 to have gotten into better-paying careers than did those who entered in 1905.

Valid measures of *age change* require measuring a given birth cohort at several points in time. If measures are taken on different samples from the same cohort, the research is called **cohort analysis**. If measures are taken on the same sample at different points in time, the research is called **longitudinal**. Thus, Samples A, D, and G represent the *same birth cohort* at ages 55, 60, and 65. If the median annual incomes (adjusted for inflation) of the three samples were $5,600, $5,600, and $5,200, we could say that between age 55 and age 65 the median income of the cohort born in 1900 dropped $400.

The historical point in time at which a person is a given age sometimes has a bearing on what it is like to be that age. This is called **period effect**. Samples C, E, and G in Table 1-1 represent people who were all 65 at different points in historical time. If we found that the median annual incomes (adjusted for inflation) of the samples were $4,800, $4,950, and $5,200, we could say that from 1955 to 1965 the median income of 65-year-olds increased by $400.

The period of historical time also influences the nature of age change. If we compare Sample C with Sample F; Sample E with Sample H; and Sample G with Sample I, we would have measures of changes from age 65 to age 70 for three points in historical time. The average of the three measures would be the *average age change*. The advantage of this type of study is that the results are not unique to any one birth cohort or any one period of historical time.

These are the main ways that age can be used as a variable for analysis in social gerontology.[4] In evaluating research results, two crucial questions will always be,

---

[4]For a more advanced treatment of the complexities of developmental research design, see Friedrich (1972).

"Which effect is being examined: age difference, age change, or period effect?" and "Do the data collected provide the information necessary to answer the question?" For a concrete example, see Research Illustration 2 in Chapter 3.

## THE STAGES OF LATER LIFE

Defining the term *older person* is no easy task, for a number of reasons. First, aging begins very early in life. Biologists agree that almost as soon as the organism stops growing it begins the process of growing old. Second, it is possible to measure age in two quite different ways. **Chronological age** is calendar age. The **life course** measures a person's age in relation to an idealized sequence of events that begins with birth and ends with death. In between these two points, there are many stages, events, and phases. The terms *childhood*, *adolescence*, *adulthood*, *middle age*, *later maturity*, and *old age* refer to some of these phases. The chronological age of an individual is important in understanding aging only because it provides clues as to the current phase of the individual's life course.

In the search for a definition of *older person*, childhood and adolescence can be ruled out. Both of these terms obviously refer to periods in the life cycle when the organism is still growing. Young adulthood can also be ruled out because, although the aging process has technically started, none of the manifestations of aging have yet appeared.

Aging is a gradual process with relatively few abrupt changes. It varies, sometimes greatly, from individual to individual.

> It has been customary to assume that old age sets in somewhere during the seventh decade of life, and, until recently, much of the research and the majority of action programs have focused on the period beginning at or near age 65. It is now recognized, however, that the real turning point comes much earlier. On the basis of present knowledge, it seems possible to identify three stages of advanced adulthood: middle age, later maturity and old age (Tibbitts, 1960:9).

A crucial point is that the stages of later life are scientifically defined in terms of certain biological and social *symptoms* and not merely in terms of chronological age. People first become aware of the fact that they are growing older in **middle age**. Although the correlation is not perfect, this phase of the life course usually occurs during the forties and fifties. At this time individuals become aware that they have less energy than they used to, and they often begin to look for intellectual activities to replace more physical pursuits as sources of satisfaction.

Chronic illness becomes more prevalent. In the fifties, vision and hearing begin to fail. The work career often reaches a plateau, and the children have left home by the time most couples reach their early fifties. Some women go back to work; others sit around the house wondering what to do with themselves. This period can be frustrating for both men and women because it marks the close of childrearing and sometimes work careers and an end to the satisfaction such occupations brought. Yet middle age can also mark a new beginning for a marriage or a new occupation, and so provide new sources of satisfaction.

Finally, middle age is the time when many people come to grips with the fact that death is real, and not just something that happens to someone else.

The period of **later maturity** is marked by an even greater awareness of aging and by difficulty in orienting oneself toward the future. Chronologically, later maturity often corresponds to the sixties and seventies. There is a drastic reduction in available energy during this period, and people become very aware of failing sight and hearing.

Long-term chronic health problems begin to limit activity during this period. Retirement and the accompanying reduction of income sometimes combine with poor health to reduce personal contacts. Deaths of relatives and friends and movement of children may also reduce the size of the social environment. Many women are widows by the time they reach their middle sixties.

However, later maturity can be a pleasant period. Most people retain a fair measure of physical vigor, which, coupled with freedom from responsibilities, makes later maturity one of the most open and free periods in the life cycle for those prepared to take advantage of it.

The period of **old age** is the beginning of the end. It is characterized by extreme frailty, disability, or invalidism. Mental processes slow down. People think a lot about themselves and their pasts, and try to find some meaning in life. At this point, the individual knows the end is very near. Activity is greatly restricted. Loneliness and boredom are common. This period is not apt to be very pleasant.

The onset of old age often does not occur until the late seventies, *and many people in their eighties show no symptoms of old age*.

The effects of aging are present in all three phases. Nevertheless, when we talk about older people we will be talking about the last two phases in combination. Chronologically, this ideally would mean those in their very late fifties and older. However, as a practical matter, most studies designate 65 as the earliest chronological age at which people are defined as older. Therefore, unless otherwise specified, throughout this book the term *older* refers to persons who are 65 or older.

It is important to emphasize, first, that the stages of later life are based on sets of characteristics that seem to be related in many cases. Seldom will a particular individual show each and every symptom typical of a given phase, but most older people show the symptoms of one of these phases. A second important point is that these categories are based on characteristics *other than* chronological age. Chronological age is related usually, but not necessarily, to phases of the life cycle. A person may have the characteristics of old age at a number of chronological ages. One person could be in old age at 55 and another could be in later maturity at 85. Finally, it is worth remembering that retirement generally takes place in later maturity and not in old age. As we shall see later, much of the apprehension people feel about changes in later life stems from inaccurately equating retirement with old age.

## WHAT MAKES AGING AN IMPORTANT AREA FOR STUDY?

In American society, interest in the problems of older people is currently high. The federal government has created a special department within the National Institutes of Health called the National Institute on Aging, and all states now have an administrative body devoted to the problems of aging. The reason behind this concern with older people is that their situation has come to be defined as a social problem. A social problem exists when a group or category in society has a difficulty that stems at least in part from the structure, organization, or functioning of society; that threatens the balance of society; and that requires society to change. We generally believe that the more we know about a problem, the easier it is to solve. The sheer press of practical problems can thus force the development of science, and in the area of social gerontology there is a conspicuous overabundance of problems in search of solutions.

There is yet another significant motive for the study of social gerontology. The quest for knowledge for its own sake has always played a part in science, and many scientists agree that, no matter how noble the cause, it is very difficult to stay with a task that does not possess some degree of intrinsic fascination. For some people, observing the intricacy of social relationships is like watching a campfire—it never becomes tiresome or boring. For these people, the study of gerontology can become an end in itself.

## THE RISE OF AGING AS A SOCIAL PROBLEM

But why is aging a social problem? Surely the fact that large numbers of people now live to reach old age is one of modern society's greatest achievements. Yet most people look forward to old age with fear and apprehension.

The roots of the problem are complex. Modern science and technology have created a world in which most people will live their allotted threescore and ten. But society has not been prepared to receive this large new group of older members.

Three major trends have brought about the current situation. The first is related to the way the population has grown; the second is related to increased urbanization and industrialization; and the last is related to the increased pace of social change.

### Population Growth

If we use the widely accepted criterion of age 65 or over to define *older people* operationally, then what changes have taken place in this category since the beginning of the century?

The most obvious change has been the dramatic increase in the *numbers* of older people. In 1900 there were slightly more than three million older people in the United States and in 1970 there were over 20 million—a sixfold increase, nearly double the increase for the general population. Neugarten (1975) projects that by the year 2000, there could be over 35 million older Americans.

This increase resulted from several factors. First, the number of births has increased steadily over the past 100 years. Second, a larger proportion of those born are now surviving to age 65 than was formerly the case. Third, the large numbers of people who migrated to the United States in the late nineteenth and early twentieth centuries are becoming older (Sheldon, 1960).

In addition to increasing numbers, there has also been a steady rise in the *proportion* of older people in the U.S. population since 1900 (see Table 1-2).

**TABLE 1-2**
**Percent of Total Population**
**Age 65 and Over: United States, for Selected Years**

|                        | 1900 | 1930 | 1940 | 1950 | 1960 | 1970 | 2000 (projected) |
|------------------------|------|------|------|------|------|------|------------------|
| Percent Age 65 & Over  | 4.0  | 5.4  | 6.8  | 8.1  | 9.2  | 9.9  | 11.2             |

Obviously, the same factors that influence the numbers of older people also influence their percentage of the total. In this case, however, the percentage of older people rose slowly because all of the factors that increased the older population did so only slightly faster than births increased the younger population. This balance kept the percentage of older people relatively stable in spite of large increases in numbers.

The number of older people will probably continue to increase rapidly over the next few decades. And the proportion of the population 65 and over may actually increase more than projected in Table 1-2 if the birth rate decline that began in 1958 continues. The U.S. Bureau of the Census (1972) projects that if the United States achieves zero population growth, the proportion of older people in the population will reach 16 percent, an increase of 60 percent over the proportion in 1970.

**Life expectancy** is the average number of years persons born in a given year can be expected to live under the conditions prevailing in that year. For example, life expectancy in the United States was just over 49 years at the beginning of the century. Thus, people born in 1900 could be expected to live an average of 49 years under the conditions of 1900. By 1970, life expectancy in the United States had risen to 71 years. This is certainly a significant increase in the average length of life, and it helps explain why so many people are surviving to become older people. The fall in infant mortality is primarily responsible for the dramatic increase in life expectancy.

One important aspect of the increase in life expectancy is that women have experienced a greater increase as compared to men. In 1900, the life expectancy for women in the United States was just under 51 years, and for men it was not quite 48 years, a difference of about 3 years longer for women. In 1970, however, women had a life expectancy at birth of almost 75 years as compared with just over 67 for men, a difference of about 8 years. Thus, women have increased their advantage with regard to life expectancy. Some population experts have estimated that if this trend continues, older women will outnumber older men by two to one by the year 2000.

## Urbanization

In 1900, only about 40 percent of the U.S. population lived in cities. By 1970, this figure had risen to 73 percent, and by the year 2000 we can expect somewhere in the neighborhood of 90 percent of our population to be living in metropolitan areas. What about older people? Are they as "urbanized" as the general population? In 1970,

73 percent of the population 65 years of age and older was urban, exactly the same as the urban percentage of the general population.

Among urban areas of different size, however, older people do appear to differ slightly from the general population. Table 1-3 shows that older people tend to be overrepresented in all types of cities and in small towns, while they tend to be underrepresented in the urban fringe, the area where most of the "bedroom" suburbs are. By and large, however, older people do not seem to be located in disproportionate numbers in communities of any given size.

**TABLE 1-3**
**Percent of the Total Population Age 65**
**and Over, by Size of Place: United States, 1970**

| Size of Place | Percent Age 65 and over |
|---|---|
| Total Population | 9.9 |
| Urban | 9.8 |
| Urbanized Areas | 9.4 |
| Central Cities | 10.7 |
| Urban Fringe | 7.8 |
| Other Urban | 11.4 |
| Places of 10,000 to 50,000 | 10.8 |
| Places of 2,500 to 10,000 | 12.2 |
| Rural | 10.1 |
| Places of 1,000 to 2,500 | 13.6 |
| Other Rural | 9.6 |

*Source:* U.S. Bureau of the Census (1973c).

Nevertheless, there are geographic areas of the country where older people do live in disproportionate numbers. Everyone knows that older people congregate in Florida. Older people are also quite heavily represented in several other states. Nationwide, older people constitute 9.9 percent of the total population, yet they constitute more than 17 percent in sizable areas of Kansas, Nebraska, Iowa, Missouri, Oklahoma, and Texas. As Table 1-4 shows, among the top ten states in terms of the percent of the state population that is 65 and over, the majority are midwestern states. California and Arizona, commonly considered "retirement states," actually are far down the list, with less than the national average proportion of older people. Florida gained older people through migration, but in the middle and southwestern states the exodus of young people left older people overrepresented in many areas. Thus, most of the overrepresentation of older people has resulted from urbanization of the young rather than from movement by the old.

**TABLE 1-4**
**Ranked Order of States by Percent of the**
**Population Age 65 and Over: United States, 1970**

| Rank | State | Percent 65 and Over | Rank | State | Percent 65 and Over |
|------|-------|---------------------|------|-------|---------------------|
| 1 | Florida | 14.6 | 26 | New Jersey | 9.7 |
| 2 | Iowa | 12.4 | 27 | Idaho | 9.5 |
| 3 | Nebraska | 12.4 | 28 | Indiana | 9.5 |
| 4 | Arkansas | 12.4 | 29 | Alabama | 9.5 |
| 5 | South Dakota | 12.1 | 30 | Washington | 9.4 |
| 6 | Missouri | 12.0 | 31 | Ohio | 9.4 |
| 7 | Kansas | 11.8 | 32 | Arizona | 9.1 |
| 8 | Oklahoma | 11.7 | 33 | Wyoming | 9.1 |
| 9 | Maine | 11.6 | 34 | California | 9.0 |
| 10 | Massachusetts | 11.2 | 35 | Texas | 8.9 |
| 11 | West Virginia | 11.1 | 36 | Michigan | 8.5 |
| 12 | Rhode Island | 11.0 | 37 | Colorado | 8.5 |
| 13 | Oregon | 10.8 | 38 | Louisiana | 8.4 |
| 14 | Pennsylvania | 10.8 | 39 | North Carolina | 8.1 |
| 15 | New York | 10.8 | 40 | Georgia | 8.0 |
| 16 | North Dakota | 10.7 | 41 | Delaware | 8.0 |
| 17 | Minnesota | 10.7 | 42 | Virginia | 7.9 |
| 18 | Wisconsin | 10.7 | 43 | Maryland | 7.6 |
| 19 | Vermont | 10.7 | 44 | Connecticut | 7.6 |
| 20 | New Hampshire | 10.6 | 45 | South Carolina | 7.4 |
| 21 | Kentucky | 10.5 | 46 | Utah | 7.3 |
| 22 | Mississippi | 10.0 | 47 | New Mexico | 6.9 |
| 23 | Montana | 9.9 | 48 | Nevada | 6.3 |
| 24 | Illinois | 9.8 | 49 | Hawaii | 5.7 |
| 25 | Tennessee | 9.8 | 50 | Alaska | 2.3 |

Total United States: 9.9 percent 65 and over

*Source:* U.S. Bureau of the Census (1973c).

The issue of numbers is separate from the issue of the proportion of older people. As Table 1-5 shows, the states with the greatest number of older Americans are not necessarily those with a high proportion of older people in their population. It is also important to note that 56 percent of the older population of the United States lives in just ten states—those listed in Table 1-5.

Another important result of our rapid urbanization has been change within the cities themselves, particularly the change in stability of neighborhoods. In the early part of this century, rapid urbanization was already under way. Cities were being fed population from the rural areas and from European immigration. Population growth in the cities far outstripped the nation's ability to construct new housing, and it was not unusual to find three and four generations in a single household. We have idealized this

**TABLE 1-5**
**The Top Ten States in Number of**
**Persons Age 65 and Over: United States, 1970**

| Rank | State | Population 65 and over | Percent of Population 65 and over |
|------|-------|------------------------|-----------------------------------|
| 1 | New York | 1,960,752 | 10.8 |
| 2 | California | 1,800,977 | 9.0 |
| 3 | Pennsylvania | 1,272,126 | 10.8 |
| 4 | Illinois | 1,093,654 | 9.8 |
| 5 | Ohio | 997,694 | 9.4 |
| 6 | Texas | 992,059 | 8.9 |
| 7 | Florida | 989,366 | 14.6 |
| 8 | Michigan | 752,955 | 8.5 |
| 9 | New Jersey | 696,989 | 9.7 |
| 10 | Massachusetts | 636,185 | 11.2 |

*Source:* U.S. Bureau of the Census (1973c).

pattern over the years, but it is highly likely that these three- and four-generation households resulted less from choice than from the fact that there was no other housing available.

Neighborhoods in cities tended to remain stable for several reasons: once lodging was found it was not likely to be given up; adult children were forced to remain in their parents' household; and once jobs were found, they were kept. These factors produced neighborhoods with many long-term residents. Older people in this type of neighborhood often enjoyed the prestige of being such old-timers. They were regular gold mines of information about everything and everybody in the neighborhood. Often they were family patriarchs or matriarchs of considerable influence.

Today's big-city neighborhood is a much different place. The housing squeeze is gone for the majority of our population. When children grow up, they move out into their own households. With the availability of newer housing, older people themselves are also moving in increasing numbers. The result is a constant state of flux in the urban neighborhood and a sizable annual turnover of population. In this kind of situation, the position of older people is very much altered. Long-term residency loses prestige, and family members have scattered to the suburbs, thus destroying some of the older person's potential activity as head of the family.

In short, the changes in the urban neighborhood have created a situation in which older people have become detached from the neighborhood. It should be noted that older people are not alone in this respect. The closest thing to neighborhood in most of our cities are groups of several couples and their children who get together twice a year for a "neighborhood" picnic. Sustained, regular interaction with neighbors is fast being replaced by interaction with people met through work or other activities, particularly for the middle class.

Along with changes in the neighborhood, important and fundamental changes have occurred in the family as urbanization has increased. It is doubtful if three- or four-generation families were ever typical in this country except perhaps among European immigrants and long-time city dwellers. In frontier days, the trek across the country by wagon would have been too much for older people. The answer is, of course, that in those days there were very few older people and they were usually left behind with children who did not choose to migrate. Those people who did live to become older people became part of three- or four-generation households, but there were so few of them that such households made up a very small proportion of the total.

With the gradual increase in both the numbers and proportion of older people in the population, the small family has gradually become typical. The average family in the United States today consists of a husband and wife and their children living together in a single dwelling unit. Older people expect and are expected to maintain a household separate from their married children.

At one time, older people usually owned the family property, and they therefore had economic power. Nowadays, very few people make their living from property, and very few own any property other than the lot on which they live. Most people get money by trading for it in the job market. Therefore the economic power of older people is diminished. Furthermore, the information explosion has occurred so rapidly in recent years that the historical perspective of older people is judged, sometimes too hastily, as being of little value. Even babysitting is not really needed, since the trend toward early childbearing patterns and small families means that grandchildren are often grown by the time the grandparents reach retirement age.

Nothing can be gained by pining for the "good old days." As a matter of fact, the old days may not have been quite so good as we would like to believe they were. Family relationships were often based on tyranny rather than affection, and the power and influence of older people were not always cheerfully accepted by adult children. The point is not whether the older person's position has been downgraded, but rather that there has been a change. And older people's problems are caused at least partly by the difficulties associated with adjusting to this change.

## Industrialization

Industrial societies are characterized by their great per capita productivity and their tendency to use machine labor to replace human labor. One of the greatest challenges in a capitalist society is to sustain a rate of growth that will keep everybody working who wants to or needs to work and at the same time to maintain a reasonably stable wage–price structure. One way of stabilizing wages, or at least of preventing them from falling, is to reduce the size of the work force. This reduction keeps the supply of labor from exceeding the demand. In recent years, two factors have tended to reduce the work force. First, retirement policies have been introduced into almost every realm of labor, and second, the period of preparation (schooling) required to get the average job has been prolonged. Both of these trends have reduced competition for available jobs and have kept worker incomes at unprecedentedly high levels.

Retirement trends are of great interest to gerontologists. The national interest may require retirement at age 65 or 70, but the costs of such a policy are in many cases paid by the older person alone. Therefore, retirement will be examined in detail in later chapters.

## The Stigma

From a purely practical point of view, old age is in itself a stigma. This stigma is often the unjust and unearned result of false stereotypes, but it may also be the result of an adequate and necessary evaluation of actual capabilities. Regardless of source, however, the stigma of being old is important because it influences the way older people live. It influences what they expect of themselves, and it influences what others think about them. Understanding older people entails understanding this stigma, its roots in fact, its effects, and remedies for its unwanted effects. We will be examining this topic throughout this book.

By far the most important aspect of the stigma of old age is its negative, disqualifying character. On the basis of their age, older people are often relegated to a position in society in which they are no longer judged to be of any use or importance. Unless they have special talents or skills, or can afford to support themselves well in retirement, older people often find that the stigma of old age limits their opportunities. Like most other "expendable" elements in society, many older people are subjected to poverty, illness, and social isolation.

Part of the stigma attached to old age may result from the fact that in modern industrial societies death comes primarily in later life (Kalish, 1976). In other societies, where death rates are high, people die at all ages, and death is thus considered something separate from old age. But in societies with low death rates most people survive into later life and death thus becomes associated with later life. Because of this association, young people may shun older people, who remind them of their own mortality.

Another aspect of the stigma stems from the educational system. In modern societies, knowledge changes rapidly. Because we concentrate formal education, especially job preparation, at the beginning of the life course, with each year that passes after graduation our knowledge bases become more and more out-of-date. Yet there is no mechanism for periodically updating knowledge systematically. Adults must rely on newspapers and television as major sources of new knowledge *unless* continued growth is built into their jobs. The result of this haphazard system is built-in obsolescence. People whose education and job skills have grown obsolete are treated exactly like those who have never gained an education or job skills and are not encouraged or given the opportunity to begin anew.

Another aspect of the stigma relates to ability to perform. Because a few older people are unable to perform in normal adult roles, society has been quick to jump to the conclusion that aging is the cause of their inability. Norms have developed that generally exclude older people from employment. We have excluded them partly because we can afford to do so. Our industrial potential allows us the luxury of not having to use all of our work force potential. But this situation may change. For example, during World War II, the United States Government was quite successful in putting older workers back to work in defense plants. It appears, therefore, that whether we define older workers as capable or not depends to a great extent on whether their labor is needed.

It is well to remember that the stigma of old age is based on social definitions that can change. Retirement does not mean the same thing today that it did in 1950. Likewise, being an older person could lose some of its negative, disqualifying character in the future.

## The Pace of Social Change

When the pace of change in a society is slow, most people are able to keep abreast of what is expected of them. For the most part, the norms they learned early in life remain appropriate, and the few unprecedented situations do not cause major problems.

In a rapidly changing society, however, many people often find themselves in unprecedented positions for which norms are not yet specified. These people face the dilemma of having to play a role for which the dialogue and action are either missing or only partly established.

When changes are few and far between, the various parts of society can adjust easily because it is usually necessary to accommodate only a few changes at a time. Rapid change alters this strategy because many changes must be accommodated simultaneously.

Furthermore, the various parts of society do not change at the same rate. Any single change is like a rock thrown into a pond—the spot where the rock hits is changed very quickly, but the ripples reach the bank only gradually. Social change usually starts by affecting a subgroup within the whole, and slowly the other parts of society adapt until eventually the entire society feels the effects of the change. A particularly difficult period occurs just after the change begins, when the rest of society has not yet recognized or accepted a change within a subgroup. For example, older people often experience problems because other parts of society have not yet recognized or accepted the fact that chronological age is not a reliable indicator of an individual's capabilities. Compounding this problem even further is the fact that a rapidly changing society is rather like a pond with a hundred rocks being thrown into it at the same time.

Hence, the impact of population growth, urbanization, and industrialization on the lives of older people has been heightened by the fact that these changes are occurring rapidly. For example, norms for the **retired person** are still evolving, and this situation creates difficulties for older people both in the way they see themselves and in the ability of others to respond to them. Retired people are not always sure what they should expect of themselves, and other people may avoid them simply because they are not sure how to behave toward retired people. In addition, some people do not yet recognize retirement as legitimate, and a retired person may have difficulty relating to such people. Finally, attempts to mount a concerted societal effort to meet the needs of retired people are hindered by the fact that retired people are not by any means the only group whose problems have been increased by rapid population growth, urban-

## RESEARCH ILLUSTRATION 1

AGEISM COMPARED TO RACISM AND SEXISM[5]

Erdman B. Palmore and Kenneth Manton

**Ageism** is prejudice and discrimination leveled by one age group against another (Butler, 1969). As such, it is similar in impact to more familiar forms of bigotry—racism and sexism. Using data from the U.S. Bureau of the Census for the national population, Palmore and Manton examined the amount of inequality associated with ageism, racism, and sexism. Because these various forms of bigotry become institutionalized, they tend to produce observable inequalities. Palmore and Manton concentrated on inequalities in income, employment, and education by means of an *equality index.*

The equality index measures the degree of overlap in the percentage distributions of two groups on a particular trait. This overlap is easily computed by summing the lowest percentages in each category in each group. For example, if the U.S. Bureau of Labor Statistics' definition of a modest but adequate income is used to define income adequacy, 60 percent of older people have inadequate incomes, compared to 35 percent of Americans aged 45 to 54.

|              | *Percent* | |
| Age Group    | *Adequate Income* | *Inadequate Income* |
| --- | --- | --- |
|              | *(1)* | *(2)* |
| 45 to 54     | 65 | 35 |
| 65 and over  | 40 | 60 |

For these data, the equality index (EI) between the two age categories would be 75—40 percent from column (1) added to 35 percent from column (2).[6] The equality index can be used with categorical data and allows comparisons between variables.

Palmore and Manton addressed themselves to three important questions: How do ageism, racism, and sexism compare in terms of observable inequality? Are their effects cumulative? How have these various types of inequality changed in recent years?

In terms of the relative power of the various types of inequality, Table 1-6 shows that there are substantial inequalities of all three types in terms of income, occupational distribution, and education. Income and occupational inequalities are greatest with regard to sex, and educational inequality is greatest with regard to age. Palmore and Manton also report that, in terms of weeks worked, aged inequality is highest. No one form of inequality is consistently greatest on all dimensions.

Table 1-7 shows that age inequality in income is much greater among men than among women and is somewhat greater among nonwhites than among whites. It is particularly noteworthy that the

---

[5]Adapted from Palmore and Manton (1973).

[6]This illustration was not taken from Palmore and Manton. It is included here in order to clarify the meaning of the equality index.

**TABLE 1-6**
**Income, Occupation, and Education Equality**
**Indices by Race, Sex, and Age: United States, 1970**

| Comparison | Income EI | Occupation EI | Education EI |
|---|---|---|---|
| Nonwhite/White | 83 | 71 | 76 |
| Female/Male | 45 | 56 | 91 |
| 65 and over/25–64 | 65 | 79 | 63 |

*Source:* Adapted from Palmore and Manton (1973).

income equality index between older black women and younger white men is only 13! This index shows the reality of triple jeopardy.

**TABLE 1-7**
**Income Equality Index Between Older and Younger**
**Age Categories, by Sex and Race: United States, 1970**

| | White | Nonwhite | Total |
|---|---|---|---|
| Males | 44 | 45 | 45 |
| Females | 82 | 62 | 82 |
| Total | 65 | 57 | 65 |

*Source:* Adapted from Palmore and Manton (1973).

Table 1-8 shows that from 1950 to 1970, racial inequality decreased, sexual inequality remained about the same, and age inequality increased, substantially.

Palmore and Manton conclude that most of the age inequality in education and occupation is caused by cohort differences rather than by an absolute loss of educational or occupational level. The aged have simply been left behind as the educational and occupational levels of younger cohorts have risen. On the other hand, income inequality is caused by a combination of cohort differences and age discrimination in employment.

**TABLE 1-8**
**Changes in Income, Occupation, and Education**
**Equality Indices, by Race, Sex, and Age: United States, 1950 to 1970**

| Comparison | Income EI | Occupation EI | Education EI |
|---|---|---|---|
| Nonwhite/White | +3.5 | +11.7 | +13.2 |
| Female/Male | +1.1 | − 1.8 | − 3.5 |
| 65 and over/25–64 | −7.5 | − 0.6 | −16.6 |

*Source:* Adapted from Palmore and Manton (1973).

ization, and industrialization. The poor, blacks, and women all have recently claimed first priority in terms of the need for social adjustments.

At the risk of considerable oversimplification, the social problems of aging can be perhaps best seen in terms of changes in what happens to individuals as they go through the life course. In the early part of this century, American society was almost completely oriented toward bringing people into the system and keeping them there. Childhood was a period of preparation for the tasks of adulthood. Family, church, and school all combined to instill the skills, competitive spirit, and achievement motivation that are prime requisites of our economic and social system. Adulthood was a period characterized by increasing involvement in the system. Most young people began their occupational careers, as they do today, in positions with minimal responsibility, and gradually they were incorporated fully into the economic system. Promotions came slowly for most people, and, in general, the older the person was, the more responsible and secure his or her position. Keep in mind that age 50 in 1900 was about the equivalent of age 70 today in terms of distance from the end of the life course. Accordingly, the latter part of the life cycle was expected to be more or less a continuation of the middle years.

Since World War II, we have seen a significant change in the social definition of the life course. As society became more complex, the period of preparation for adulthood increased. Whereas 50 percent of young men were in the labor force by age 15 in 1910, a negligible percentage was in the labor force by that age in 1970.

For reasons mentioned earlier, policies have developed that arbitrarily disqualify people from economic participation once they reach a given retirement age. While most other institutions in society do not phase out older people in quite such a rigid fashion, certain norms nevertheless devalue the older person's contribution to family, church, neighborhood, and voluntary associations. Only in politics and government, and in the arts and certain professions like medicine and law, have older people been able to keep positions earned earlier in life more less intact.

Thus, since World War II there has been a significant change in society's response to the later stages of the life course. Young people are still courted eagerly by the system, and adults still become increasingly involved in society as they get older. But toward the end of the life cycle society gradually turns away from older people. Their participation is no longer sought or even desired, and they are left to their own devices for getting satisfaction from life. Their meaningful contacts are increasingly restricted to people their own age, and their power in the social system is limited.

In large measure, the problems of aging relate to the fact that the preparation for young adulthood, particularly for work and childrearing, is an institutionalized part of the system, while the preparation for later adulthood is left to the individual, and as a result is haphazard and often incomplete. Add the problems associated with any rapidly changing situation, and it becomes a wonder that older people are able to cope with aging at all. As we shall see, however, most of them do, and many cope quite well. The ones who do not are understandably a source of concern, and it is primarily they who have created the heightened interest in aging as a social problem.

However, this book is not about social problems. Problems of aging will be considered only as a part of the overall picture of aging in urban, industrial societies. What we will attempt to do is to present as much knowledge as possible about older people, in the hope that this knowledge will lead to a better understanding of the normal, as well as those aspects that make aging a social problem.

## APPROACHES TO THE STUDY OF AGING

Preceding sections have provided overviews of social gerontology as a discipline, the stages of later life, and the rise of aging as a social problem. This section briefly describes various approaches to the study of social gerontology. It will enable the reader to identify, as they appear in the text, some of the major conceptual frameworks currently in use and, more importantly, to relate the various frameworks to one another.

Social gerontologists can study society's system for defining people as "old" and treating them differently from people defined as "not old." They can also study how older people both individually and collectively cope with being defined and treated as "old."

### Aging and the Social System

There are several important questions dealing with society's system in relation to older members: In what ways are older people treated differently from other adults? Why are older people treated differently? and, How has society's system for dealing with older people changed?

When societies treat different age categories unequally, they use a system of **age grading**[7] to assign people to various age categories, or strata. The life course is an idealized timetable people are expected to follow from birth through infancy, childhood, adolescence, young adulthood, adulthood, middle age, later maturity, and old age. The life course roughly specifies the opportunities and responsibilities people have during these various phases of life.

The **age stratification** theory developed by Riley and her associates (Riley et al., 1972; Riley, 1971) holds that age grading and the life course combine to produce recognizable **age strata** or **generations**[8] and that people of different generations deal with each other not primarily as individuals but as members of different generations. Thus, if two men encounter one another on a park bench—one obviously old, the other middle-aged—their interaction will be greatly influenced by what they consider proper etiquette between members of different generations.

To those who use the perspective of age stratification, age groups are not merely statistical categories. Because of age grading, *birth cohorts*—people born during the same interval in history—tend to develop a subculture of their own. They tend to become *cohort-centric*—they tend to select friends and marriage partners from among

---

[7]The concepts introduced here will be developed more fully later in the text.

[8]The term *generation* is more familiar to most readers, but the term *age strata* avoids the connotation of reproductive generation.

age mates and collectively to interpret the various stages of life from the standpoint of the historical era in which they experienced it. For example, age cohorts do not have a generalized view of adolescence. They have a view of what adolescence was like when they went through it. The fact that each cohort going through adolescence faces a different set of problems leads to "the generation gap." The age stratification approach is thus primarily concerned with the processes that underlie the development of distinct age strata. This approach is a useful tool for conceptualizing relations between generations, but as a tool for empirical research its value is limited by practical problems of defining age strata operationally.

Closely related to the age stratification approach is the view of *older people as a subculture* (Rose, 1965a). This approach holds that by virtue of their shared characteristic of old age and of society's categorical negative response to anyone old, older people are forced to interact with each other. This forced interaction is seen as a forerunner of the development of a genuine group. Perhaps the critical flaw in this theory is that it has yet to be demonstrated that any significant interaction among older people is occurring across social class lines. Social class is still apparently a force strong enough to prevent the development of an old-age subculture.

Neither of the preceding approaches to the social system address the *content* of the system. Cowgill (1972; 1974a; 1974b) has developed a theory that holds that *as societies increase their level of modernization, the social status[9] of older people declines*. According to this theory, the social status of the aged is undercut by several processes that also produce highly developed societies.

Figure 1-1 shows how the status of the aged can be affected in the evolution of highly developed societies. A higher proportion of older people combines with a lower demand for workers to put older people and younger people in direct competition for jobs. To reduce unemployment, the institution of retirement was developed. But to the extent that the worth of people is defined by their function in society, leaving a job can lower status for the retired person or the retired household.

Economic development also produces new occupations, which normally are filled by newly educated younger adults. These new occupations often bring higher pay than an equivalent established occupation. They also often make the job skills of older people obsolete. Employers tend to encourage retirement rather than retraining. The result can be lowered status of older people. A fast pace of social change and an educational system that focuses almost exclusively on the young combine to make the general knowledge of older people obsolete and to create a situation in which young people may have a more adequate base of information about society as a whole than do older people. Both of these factors may reduce the social status of older people. Finally, urbanization produces residential age segregation, and therefore older people often live in deteriorated neighborhoods, which can in turn lead to a lowered status. Thus the lowered social status of older people can stem from several causes, not just one. Note that this evolutionary approach deals with the relative social status of older people *as a category* (there are many individual exceptions to the pattern described

---

[9]The term *social status* refers primarily to the prestige afforded to people, but it also has implications for economic resources and political power.

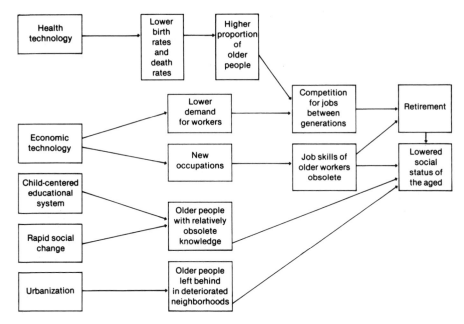

**Figure 1-1**   Causes of lowered social status of the aged.

above). A growing volume of research uses this evolutionary perspective (Palmore and Manton, 1974; Palmore and Whittington, 1971; Bengtson et al., 1975).

It is also possible to view *older people as a minority group* (Streib, 1965a). Viewed in this way, older people, like black people, are discriminated against because they share a common biological characteristic. Like racial discrimination, age discrimination depends on the visibility of the undesired trait. Older people who "do not look their age" escape the effects of age discrimination. This theory has much truth in it. The negative evaluation of, and prejudice against, old age is used as a criterion for discrimination. There certainly are parallels between the situations of many older people and those of various minority groups: low income, low status, self-hatred, and unequal opportunity. Yet there are also large numbers of older people for whom these parallels do not apply. For example, why do older people face job discrimination everywhere except in politics? Thus, the major task of this approach is to identify to whom the minority group designation applies.

The well-known disengagement theory (Cumming and Henry, 1961) also seeks to explain *why* older members of society are treated as they are. The fundamental basis for the theory of **societal disengagement** is mortality. All people must eventually die, and in order for society to outlive its individual members, some means must be found to carry out an orderly transition of power from older members to younger. This need is satisfied by the disengagement process. As one grows older, the probability that death will occur increases, and at some point it no longer pays society to rely on the services of those who are about to die. For this reason, it is profitable for society to phase out those members whose possible contributions are outweighed by the possible

*you can't die in the paddle any more*

disruption their deaths would cause to the smooth operation of society if the deaths occurred while the people were still functioning members.

When it becomes possible to categorize the people to be disengaged as old, disabled, and so on, the process becomes *institutionalized*. A set of norms is generated to provide criteria for selecting those to be disengaged and to provide individuals with guidelines for behavior during the disengagement process. Thus, we have rules that demand retirement at a particular age, and we have rudimentary rites of passage, such as retirement ceremonies, to indicate the transition from employment to retirement.

Disengagement is not a single event, but a gradual process that involves separation of the individual from a great many of his positions and roles. For each group role in which separation occurs regularly, a set of institutionalized norms might be expected to appear.

The theory of societal disengagement is functionalist. It assumes that society must constantly seek equilibrium, and that to maintain such an equilibrium, a set of absolute needs for survival must be met. To meet these functional requirements, the society must have people in key positions who will be able to carry out their jobs without interruption. It is therefore a functional requirement that society restrict eligibility for key positions to those who have a high probability of being able to carry through. This requirement leads to the institutionalization of disengagement, a mechanism whereby those who are incapable of filling key positions, either because of inability or because of a high probability of death, are shifted out of such positions and into less important ones.

A serious difficulty arises when we examine the political institution in the United States. If societal disengagement were a functional necessity, then we would expect it to apply to the political institution perhaps more than to any other. Yet when we examine the key positions in American politics we are forced to conclude that the norms of societal disengagement are clearly inoperative. The average age of senators, for example, is around 58, and many are over 70.

Obviously, societal disengagement is not a functional necessity, since politics is quite able to survive without it. Perhaps it would be more accurate to say that societal disengagement is a tendency more *possible* to realize in some institutions than in others. Thus, the theory of societal disengagement is better at explaining some aspects of society than others. It would appear that societal disengagement is more limited in its possible applications than its original formulation indicates.

### Aging and the Individual

There are also many ways to conceptualize the adjustment of individuals to their own aging. Probably the most well-known approach is **individual disengagement** (Henry, 1964). This approach is discussed in detail in Chapter 12. In short, individual disengagement holds that, as a result of aging, people inevitably and voluntarily seek to withdraw from society in order to conserve energy and have time for introspection. In general, research results have not supported this aspect of disengagement theory.

The *activity* approach to adjustment holds that maintaining the activity level of middle age is the best way to cope with aging. Since this criterion would lead most

*5. Cite two examples of gaps in knowledge of later life. What factors contribute to this situation?*

Chapter 1                                    The Scope of Social Gerontology     **27**

older people to define themselves as failures, it is not very realistic. However, some older adults accept the moral validity of the activity approach and thus may experience unnecessary feelings of worthlessness and uselessness.

The *continuity* approach to individual aging assumes that, in the process of becoming adults, individuals develop habits, commitments, preferences, and a host of other dispositions that become a part of their personalities. As the individuals grow older, they are predisposed toward maintaining continuity in habits, associations, preferences, and so on. Unlike the activity theory, the continuity theory does *not* assume that lost roles need be replaced.

In this context, *continuity* means that the individual's reaction to aging can be explained by examining the complex interrelationships among biological and psychological changes; the person's habits, preferences, and associations; situational opportunities for continuity; and actual experience. The lifelong experience thus creates certain predispositions that individuals will maintain if at all possible. These predispositions include such things as brushing one's teeth right-handed, shopping at a particular department store, living in a certain neighborhood, having certain friends, and working at a particular job. At all phases of the life course, these predispositions constantly evolve from interactions among personal preferences, biological and psychological capabilities, situational opportunities, and experience. Change is thus an adaptive process involving interaction among all of these elements.

These are some of the prominent ways people conceive of aging as a social process. Others will be brought in with respect to specific issues. It should be clear that no one perspective can explain all of the social aspects of aging. It should also be clear that, given a description of theory as a logically connected set of perspectives and assumptions, social gerontology offers a rich variety of theories. However, given a description of theory as an empirically established set of concrete and interconnected predictive propositions, social gerontology is not very well developed. This situation will no doubt improve as the number of trained researchers in social gerontology increases.

## Some Important Gaps in Knowledge

While most aspects of later life have been researched far more than one might expect, there are nevertheless two very important gaps in our present knowledge: the lack of cross-national data, and the lack of data on older minority group members. Both of these gaps stem at least in part from the research priorities in the United States, where a significant proportion of the research in social gerontology is carried on. Since research funds for social gerontology have never been generous, investigators have usually chosen to study white, middle- or working-class older Americans rather than attempt the more difficult task of drawing cross-national samples or samples from minority groups.

There is a great need for more cross-national data in social gerontology. Since aging becomes a visible social problem primarily in industrial societies, there is pitifully little research data on social gerontology in the nonindustrial nations of the world. In addition, the data for industrial nations are quite variable, with the United

States being by far the most widely researched. Thus, the body of knowledge we call *social gerontology* is heavily biased in terms of the American situation, and this book of necessity reflects this bias. However, the work of Shanas and her associates (1968) has shown that the situations of older people are remarkably similar in the United States, Great Britain, and Denmark. Therefore, biased as it is at this point, the knowledge we have of social gerontology is probably reasonably representative of industrial societies.

Moreover, despite the fact that older Americans have been researched far more than any other older population in the world, very little is known about significant subgroups of older Americans. Not only are there individual differences that produce heterogeneity in the older population, but there also are subgroup differences in culture and behavior that create diversity among older people. Sixty-five-year-old Americans cannot be understood apart from their earlier lives, and if they are minority group members, their experience has probably been quite different from that of most of their fellow older Americans. Thus, older people who also happen to be black, poor, Appalachian, foreign-born, or members of an ethnic minority probably face an old age different from the majority of the older population. But as yet we are in an incredibly poor position to say exactly how minority group elders differ from the majority (Suzuki, 1975). This significant research need is only beginning to be met, and as a result of this gap in our knowledge, most of what we have to say about older people in this book will not necessarily apply to older members of minority groups.

## SUMMARY

Gerontology is a complex field that is comprised of the efforts of all areas of study as they apply to describing and understanding older humans. Social gerontology is a subfield of gerontology that deals primarily with the nonphysical aspects of aging.

Social gerontology deals with scientific information, impressionistic information, and social criticism, all of which are important in the quest for understanding aging both in an individual and in a societal context.

In evaluating research and knowledge in social gerontology, it is essential to distinguish among age differences, age changes, and period effects. Each type of effect requires a different method of study.

Our definition of "older person" is based on the life cycle more than on chronological age. The criteria that define entry into the category of "older people" include a greater awareness of aging, drastic reductions in available energy, and awareness of failing senses and declining biological and psychological resiliency. Social changes such as retirement and widowhood may also occur at the onset of this period.

Ideally, people would be categorized as "older" only if they exhibited these symptoms, but since it is difficult to measure such symptoms we rely on the fact that there is a rough correlation between aging and chronological age, particularly during the period of old age. Because the Social Security Administration initially chose 65 as the minimum age for retirement, in American society the term *older* usually applies to those 65 and older. Therefore, this term applies to people *in general*, but it may not apply very well at all to a *particular* person, whatever his or her age.

Aging has emerged as an important area of study because it has come to be viewed as a social problem as well as because it is interesting. It is seen as a social problem because older people have become more visible as their numbers increased; because urbanization and industrialization have produced changes that undercut the traditional position of the older person in society; and because the fast pace of change in urban, industrial societies has created obstacles to social adjustment in terms of accommodating an increased number and proportion of older people.

Since World War II, society has increasingly withdrawn from its older members. The labor of older people is neither sought nor desired. They are left primarily on their own, particularly in terms of social contacts and life satisfactions. Preparation for the "freedom" of later life is largely left up to the individual and as a result is often inadequate.

There are many useful approaches for studying and understanding how societies develop their systems for dealing with older adults and how older adults cope with society's system.

The emphasis in this book will be on overall patterns of aging in modern societies. Its aim is to provide perspectives on *all* aspects of aging, including both normal and problem situations.

## SUGGESTIONS FOR FURTHER READING

Arth, Malcom. "Aging: A Cross-Cultural Perspective." In D. P. Kent, R. Kastenbaum, and S. Sherwood (eds.), *Research Planning and Action for the Elderly: The Power and Potential of Social Science*. New York: Behavioral Publications, 1972, pp. 352–364.

Bengtson, Vern L., James J. Dowd, David H. Smith, and Alex Inkeles. "Modernization, Modernity, and Perceptions of Aging: A Cross-Cultural Study." *Journal of Gerontology 30* (1975): 688–695.

Cowgill, Donald O. "Aging and Modernization: A Revision of the Theory." In J. F. Gubrium (ed.), *Late Life: Communities and Environmental Policy*. Springfield, Ill.: Charles C. Thomas, pp. 123–146.

Friedrich, Douglas. *A Primer for Developmental Methodology*. Minneapolis: Burgess, 1972.

Maddox, George L. "Growing Old: Getting Beyond the Stereotypes." In Rosamond R. Boyd and C. G. Oakes (eds.), *Foundations of Practical Gerontology*. Columbia, S. C.: University of South Carolina Press, 1969, pp. 5–16.

Nesselroade, John R., and H. W. Reese (eds.). *Life-Span Developmental Psychology: Methodological Issues*. New York: Academic Press, 1973.

Neugarten, Bernice L., and Joan W. Moore. "The Changing Age-Status System." In Bernice L. Neugarten (ed.), *Middle Age and Aging*. Chicago: University of Chicago Press, 1968, pp. 5–21.

Palmore, Erdman, and K. Manton. "Modernization and Status of the Aged: International Correlations." *Journal of Gerontology 29* (1974): 205–210.

Press, I., and M. McKool, Jr. "Social Structure and Status of the Aged: Toward Some Valid Cross-Cultural Generalizations." *Aging and Human Development 3* (1972): 297–306.

Riley, Matilda W. "Aging and Cohort Succession: Interpretations and Misinterpretations." *Public Opinion Quarterly 37* (1973): 35–49.

Schaie, K. Warner. "Age Changes and Age Differences." *Gerontologist 7* (1967): 128–132.

Shanas, Ethel, Peter Townsend, Dorothy Wedderburn, Henning Friis, Poul Milhøj, and Jan Stehouwer. *Older People in Three Industrial Societies*. New York: Atherton, 1968.

# Part Two
# The Aging Individual

Beliefs about the presumed biological and psychological changes that aging brings are used to formulate and justify the social behavior of the aged themselves and of others toward them. Throughout this book we will be constantly seeking to determine whether various social patterns exist because of the *actual* limitations imposed by aging, or because of *presumed* limitations that have no basis in fact. To do so, we must have "the facts" about the actual physical limits caused by aging. The chapters on the biology and psychology of aging help to provide some of these facts. While every effort has been made to make these chapters as accurate as possible, they are limited, nevertheless, by the scarcity of scientific studies on many aspects of aging. These chapters are intended only as background for a detailed examination of the social aspects of aging, and those who are strongly interested in the physical aspects of aging should certainly consult more complete sources.

The chapter on the social psychology of the aging individual deals with the psychological processes and factors that mediate between the outside world and what goes on inside the individual.

# 2
# Biological Aging

Sooner or later we must all face the progressive loss of our energies and our ability to resist disease. Eventually, no matter how well we look after ourselves, this loss will become so great that we will die. For most of us it is decidedly unpleasant to discover that we must decline in this way, that even if we escape wars, accidents, and diseases we will still die from old age. Most people tend to ignore these unpleasant facts until they are forced to face them, and even then they tend to search for fountains of youth. But aging and eventual death are facts of life that have haunted poets and philosophers since the beginning of human history.

390

Biologists call biological aging **senescence**. It has been described as

> a deteriorative process. What is being measured, when we measure it, is a decrease in viability and an increase in vulnerability. . . . Senescence shows itself as an increasing probability of death with increasing chronological age: the study of senescence is the study of the *group* of processes, different in different organisms, which lead to this increase in vulnerability (Comfort, 1964b:22).

Do not confuse the terms *senescence* and **senility.** Senility is an archaic, general term that was used in the past to refer to mental infirmities thought to be the result of aging. We now know that the symptoms formerly associated with aging, and called *senility*, are in fact symptoms of specific, and often treatable, diseases.

Senescence appears to be characteristic, not of an entire species, but rather of individual members of all species. There is no known animal species whose individual members do not at some time grow old and die. However, except for controlled inbred strains of certain laboratory animals, such as mice, the rates of senescence for most species vary greatly from individual to individual. Moreover, many investigators

**33**

(Heron and Chown, 1967; Strehler, 1962; Shock, 1966;) have shown that various functions decline at varying rates, even within the same individual. Heron and Chown (1967) contend that summary measures of aging are not feasible even when symptomatic measures are used. They found that general statements about senescence glossed over the fact that, with regard to various functions, variations among individuals increase with chronological age. They conclude that chronological age is a useless indicator of senescence and that, since senescence is a group of processes, measures need to be developed for *each* dimension of senescence.

One of the startling facts about senescence is that, although it is a phenomenon that will occur in each of us, we know very little about it. This is not to say that no research has been done on senescence. Over half a dozen different major theories of senescence are currently being pursued in biology; yet none of them seems to have produced firm results.

While the causes of senescence have so far eluded us, Strehler (1962) has pinpointed some criteria that he feels are useful in differentiating senescence from other biological processes. To begin with, for a process to be considered part of senescence, it must be *universal*; that is, it must eventually occur in *all* people. Thus, the fact that older people show a higher prevalence of some condition does not necessarily make that condition part of senescence. For example, more older people than young ones get lung cancer; but for this process to be accepted as part of senescence, *all* older people would have to get lung cancer. An example of a universal process is the decline with age in the effectiveness of the body's immune system. One of the body's primary defenses, the immune system is geared to recognize and destroy substances from both inside and outside the body that are not part of the "normal" self. Thus, immune cells attack foreign objects, viruses, germs, and even cancer cells, to keep them from interfering with the body's functioning. The immune system matures in early childhood; remains on an extended plateau in early adulthood; and begins to decline in effectiveness as chronological age increases. Part of the increase in vulnerability associated with age results from this decline in the immune system. But while some decline in the immune system is universal, the time of onset and the rate of the decline varies considerably from one individual to another.

Second, the changes that constitute senescence come primarily from *within the organism*. Thus, cosmic radiation would not be a part of senescence, since it is a part of the outside environment and can be modified. Third, the processes associated with senescence *occur gradually* rather than suddenly. This description rules out accidental changes. Finally, the processes of senescence contribute to the decline in function and consequent increased mortality that we observe as the organism ages. The changes that mark senescence thus have a *deleterious* effect on the organism (Strehler, 1962).

One point stands out here: Senescence is not one process, but many. This multiplicity may account for the large number of theories of biological aging. A cataloging of the theories of senescence will give some idea of the range of these processes.[1]

The "wear-and-tear" theory is based on a mechanical analogy. This theory suggests that the body is like a machine—eventually its parts wear out and the machine

---

[1]For more details, see Shock, 1966; Bjorksten, 1969.

breaks down. This theory seems logical, since we have so many organs performing highly specific functions in our bodies. And, in a limited sense, this theory proves true. For example, the valves of the heart perform a mechanical function, and some forms of heart disease result from calcification of these valves. However, it is difficult to show that any specific organ or system consistently goes bad or wears out in all older people. Also, the body can usually repair itself, even in advanced old age.

Another popular theory is that we all have a certain fixed amount of life to live, and the faster we use it up, the faster it is gone. This "rate-of-living" theory suggests that those who lead vigorous lives should die young. Unfortunately for the theory, but fortunately for active people, the evidence seems to indicate that a lifetime pattern of high exercise prolongs life. This evidence would seem to dispose of the "rate-of-living" theory.

The "waste-product" theory suggests that accumulated waste products in the body play a key role in the process of senescence. While it is true that various chemical wastes do collect in some tissues, no evidence has been found that these wastes interfere with cell functioning in any important way.

More promising is the "collagen" theory. Collagen is a substance associated with connective tissue. It is present in most organs, tendons, skin, blood vessels, and so on. Collagen stiffens with age and, as a result, the tissues containing collagen lose elasticity. This increased stiffness is caused by change over time in the cross-linkages between the strands of the collagen molecules (Curtis, 1966:19). Curtis says, "It seems quite likely that this will cause a deterioration of function in the organs affected and may well lead to some signs and symptoms of aging." Excess collagen in tissues is associated with aging, but apparently is not a basic cause of senescence.

The "autoimmunity" theory, stated as simply as possible, holds that as age increases, mutations cause some of the cells of the body to produce proteins that are not recognizable as part of "self" and are thus responded to as if they were foreign substances. When foreign substances appear in the body, the body produces antibodies that attempt to neutralize the effect of the foreign substance. This response to invasion is called an *immune reaction*. When antibodies respond to mutations within the body, their response is called an *autoimmune reaction*. Evidence for the autoimmunity theory comes from diverse sources. For example, McCay (1956) and his associates severely underfed rats during the first third to half of their lives, and found that this treatment greatly increased their ultimate longevity. The organs that showed the greatest weight loss were precisely those that produce antibodies. The results of McCay's experiment can thus be interpreted as showing that increased longevity is associated with slowed development of the ability to produce immune reaction (Walford, 1964). Several diseases common among older people, such as rheumatoid arthritis, are known to be caused by autoimmune reactions. Autoimmunity is therefore a promising theory.

The "mutation" theory relates to the fact that the functioning of the cells in our bodies is controlled by the genetic material (DNA), which can be found within each of them. Once mutations in DNA occur, subsequent cell divisions will perpetuate them. As more and more cells develop mutations, an appreciable fraction of the cells of any given organ may become mutated. Since most mutations are deleterious, mutated cells function less efficiently, and organs made up of these cells become inefficient and senescent. Rates of genetic mutation have been shown to increase steadily with age. When genetic material is artificially damaged by radiation, it shortens the life span of the organ in direct proportion to the amount of genetic damage that has been produced. Animals with shorter life spans have a less stable genetic structure than animals with longer life spans. In addition, the autoimmune reaction discussed earlier has been shown to be associated with genetic mutation. Even so, geneticists are reluctant to accept the mutation theory wholeheartedly because it still contains significant gaps. For example, genetic mutations can increase many times over, with only a small reduction in life expectancy in some cases. Evidently, some mediating factor minimizes the effects of genetic mutations in these cases. Because this and many other questions remain unanswered, the mutation theory of aging remains promising but nevertheless tentative.

A more complex variant of mutation theory is the "error" theory. Whereas the mutation theory concentrates on the cumulative effects of mutations in DNA, the error theory broadens this concern to include the cumulative influence of "mistakes" in RNA synthesis, protein synthesis, enzymic reactions, and so on. Because error is such a broad concept, there are literally scores of causes that may produce molecular and genetic errors. As a result, while this is a promising theory, research evidence on error theory is sparse.

In short, we have a number of promising notions concerning *why* human cells age, but much work remains to be done before we will have a well-developed answer. It is clear that so far none of the current theories has produced a body of concepts that fits the criteria of senescence mentioned earlier.

Apart from the question of why people age, there is the question of why people become more susceptible to illness and disease as they grow older. Our best guess at this point centers around declines in the effectiveness of the *immune system*—the body's defense system against disease. Human beings are born with a certain number of immune cells that must tide them over until their immune systems develop to the point where they can *produce* immune cells. However, at about age 40, on the average, the effectiveness of the immune system begins a decline that speeds up as age increases. The decline in the average ability to produce immune cells corresponds quite closely to the rise with age in mortality rates.

Biologists researching immune systems suggest that the decline may be primarily caused by lack of a necessary chemical "trigger." Some feel that if such a substance could be isolated and manufactured, then it could be used to alter the mortality curve. They do not suggest that we would achieve immortality, but they are suggesting the possibility that larger numbers of people might be able to live the entire theoretical life-span—about 120 years. If true, this substance would certainly have a profound impact on society's ways of dealing with aging.

One of the biggest stumbling blocks for biological theories of aging is the fact that aging is extremely variable among human beings. The quest for universal factors associated with senescence is very much complicated by the fact that even if they exist, they will probably not show up in all people at the same chronological age, or even within a 10-year range of chronological age. For this reason, biological researchers often concentrate on aging processes in genetically and environmentally controlled laboratory animals.

The variability of human aging may be partly caused by *heredity*. It is an inescapable fact that each of us is born with a slightly different program for development, which we inherit from our parents and the generations before them. It is highly probable that heredity is a significant determinant of the aging process. There is moderate correlation between the longevity of parents and that of their children. Among twins, even those who have been separated and thus exposed to environmental differences show marked similarities in longevity and bodily characteristics. Identical twins show more similarities than fraternal twins. These facts point to the conclusion that aging is definitely influenced by heredity. If research were done on people of similar heredity, some of the foregoing theories might fare better, because research would thus have controlled an important variable.

## RESULTS OF SENESCENCE

Although we may not know precisely *why* the body ages, we cannot very well escape the fact that it does. We will now consider some of the important bodily changes that occur as chronological age increases. These changes are important for social gerontology because they represent the concrete physiological limits around which social arrangements would ideally be built.

The easiest way to identify an older person is by the appearance of his or her skin. It tends to be wrinkled and rough, and spots of dark pigment can usually be observed. It is more vulnerable than the skin of younger people to malignancies, bruises, loss of hair, and dryness. Because it symbolizes many other biological changes, which are generally defined in negative terms, the skin of an older person is considered a badge of inferiority.

With age, the older person's joints tend to stiffen, particularly the hips and knees. Compressed spinal discs produce the shorter, bent posture that characterizes many older people.

Loss of muscular strength is a characteristic of aging. Shock and Norris (1970) found that static muscular strength in the arm and shoulder remained reasonably constant in men up until age 70 and only then did it begin to decline. However, the maximum power output in a manual cranking task declined steadily after age 40. They concluded that reduced coordination was the most likely cause of the deficit in power output relative to static strength in their older participants.

The cessation of menstruation in women is called *menopause*. While it usually occurs in middle age (often between 45 and 50), menopause is sometimes associated with later life in the minds of younger women. Menopause gradually alters the hormone balance of the body, particularly with regard to estrogen. The "hot flashes" and other physical symptoms thought to be common in menopause are usually receptive to estrogen therapy. As for the psychological impact of menopause, Neugarten et al. (1963) found that most women find the menopause at worst an unpleasant brief transition that has a beneficial outcome. The majority of postmenopausal women reported feeling better after menopause than they had in years. They also reported feeling calmer and happier.

Two important changes occur in the nervous system as age increases. Hardening of blood vessels may create circulatory problems in the brain, and aging reduces the speed of impulses traveling through nerve tissues. An adequate blood supply is crucial to an efficiently functioning brain, but fortunately most people are not bothered by this problem until well past age 75. Declines in the speed of nerve impulses, however, are a more widespread problem even at the beginning of later life. Most people begin to notice lagging reflexes and reaction time in their late forties. Changes in the nervous system also influence most psychological processes, and these will be dealt with in succeeding chapters.

Failure of the circulatory system is the most common cause of death for people over 40. Heart disease or interrupted blood flow to the brain or heart are prevalent among older people as a result of reduced cardiac output, reduced elasticity of the large arteries, and general deterioration of blood vessels. At age 75, the probability of death from cardiovascular disease is 150 times higher than at age 35. Of the major systems in the body, the kidneys show the greatest decline in function with increasing age (Heron and Chown, 1967). The kidneys of people over 80 perform only half as well as those of people in their twenties. The respiratory, digestive, reproductive, and temperature control systems all decline with age, but while these are among the most common and major effects of aging, only rarely do these systems decline enough to produce disability in older people.

Nutrition has an important influence on biological aging. Daily food intake must be enough to supply the needed proteins, minerals, vitamins, and energy, but because they engage in less vigorous activity, most older people must gradually reduce their calorie intake or get fat. Unfortunately, too many older people are like the elderly grandmother who said, "I watch everything I eat very carefully—then I eat it."

Older people need a greater *proportion* of protein in their diets, even if their overall intake is reduced. Otherwise, fatigue, swelling, or lowered resistance to infection may result. The need for protein makes adequate nutrition slightly more expensive for older people than for others.

The importance of good nutrition to the maintenance of the biological systems of older people cannot be overstressed. Unfortunately, as we shall see later, the incomes of most older people are such that malnutrition is rampant among this group. And under these circumstances it is often difficult to tell exactly what part of an individual's biological decline with age is inevitable, and what part is simply caused by poor nutrition.

## SUMMARY

In summary, the aging of the human body manifests itself in three ways, only two of which are probably based on things that happen within the body. Perhaps most important is the deterioration of the irreplaceable organs and systems of the body. The heart, lungs, nervous system, liver, kidneys, and digestive system all show a loss of function as the organism ages. This factor is very much related to a second, the loss of the ability to withstand disease. A strong, efficiently functioning human body has an amazing capacity to ward off disease. With advancing age, however, the body becomes less efficient and less capable of resisting disease. These two factors in combination make up what we have called *senescence*. It should be emphasized that it is not merely the failure of major systems that produces aging. Even one-celled organisms grow old and die. The problem is rather that the cells making up these major systems undergo the processes of aging. There seem to be no exceptions to this rule.

As yet, biologists do not know why or exactly how senescence occurs. Numerous theories of biological aging have been expounded and several have been tested, but none has proved an effective explanation of the various aging processes. Age changes in the immune system, the role of collagen, and age changes in DNA and RNA synthesis are three areas that are being very actively researched.

It is very important to remember that these biological aspects of aging do not take place in a vacuum. Major social factors operate alongside the process of senescence to produce the results we see in the older person. It should not be assumed that human aging is purely a biological problem.

It is also important to remember that biological aging occurs at different rates in different people. The result is an older population that is very heterogeneous as regards symptoms of senescence. This variability is an important reason why a symptomatic definition of aging is preferable to a purely chronological one.

## SUGGESTIONS FOR FURTHER READING

Bakerman, Seymour (ed.). *Aging Life Processes*. Springfield, Ill.: Charles C. Thomas, 1969.

Comfort, Alex. *Ageing: The Biology of Senescence*. New York: Holt, Rinehart, and Winston, 1964.

Curtis, Howard J. *Biological Mechanisms of Aging*. Springfield, Ill.: Charles C. Thomas, 1966.

Rockstein, Morris. "The Biological Aspects of Aging." *Gerontologist 8* (1968): 124–125.

Shock, Nathan (ed.). *Perspectives in Experimental Gerontology*. Springfield, Ill.: Charles C. Thomas, 1966.

# 3

# The Psychology of Aging

The psychology of aging is a wide realm that encompasses the sensory and psycho-motor processes, perception, mental ability, drives, motives, and emotions. While the various aspects of psychology may be dealt with separately, it must be remembered that the human mind as a whole is more than just the sum of its various functions. The importance of age-related psychological changes to social gerontology lies in the impacts these changes have on the *social functioning* of the individual, not on the drama these changes may introduce to an age graph of a particular psychological function.

## SENSORY PROCESSES

The senses are the means through which the human mind experiences the world both outside and inside the body. In order to adapt to and interact with their environments, individuals must be able to find out something about their environments. They depend on their senses to gather such information.

The sensory process is not particularly complex. Sensory organs pick up information about changes in the internal or external environment and pass this information on to the brain. All of the input from the sensory organs is collected and organized in the brain. The subjective result is called *sensory experience*.

The minimum amount of stimulation a sensory organ must experience before sensory information is passed to the brain is called a *threshold*. All individuals have their own thresholds for each sense. The higher the threshold, the more stimulus there must be to get information to the brain. For example, some people require very little noise before they begin to hear, while others require a considerable amount. In studying the operation of the sensory processes as a function of age, we will be concerned both with changes in threshold that occur with increasing age and with the complete failure of a particular sensory process.[1]

## Vision

Vision is particularly adaptable. It can record experience over a wide range of color, intensity, distance, and width of field. The eye has an iris, which controls the amount of light that can get to the optic nerve through the retina, and a lens, which bends the light pattern entering the pupil (the opening surrounded by the iris) so as to focus the pattern of light on the retina.

The lens must change shape in order to be able to focus on both near and distant objects. As age increases, the ability of the eye to change shape and therefore to focus on very near objects decreases. Hence many older people find glasses necessary for reading, if for nothing else. The tendency toward farsightedness increases about tenfold between age 10 and age 60, but does not appear to increase much more thereafter.

The size of the opening (pupil) of the eye is also influenced by age. The size of the pupil is important because it controls the amount of light that gets into the eye. In one study, 37 percent of those over 65 showed no change in pupil size in response to changes in light intensity. And 56 percent showed no change in pupil size in response to changes in lens shape (Howell, 1949). These two factors are important because proper focusing of an image on the retina requires both the proper quality of light (controlled by the lens) and the proper quantity of light (controlled by the iris). Since both the lens and the iris show a decline in function with increasing age, sight as a whole gets poorer.

The average diameter of the pupil also declines with age. This reduction in diameter greatly influences the amount of light entering the eye. The eye of the average 60-year-old admits only about one third as much light as the eye of the average 20-year-old.

In general, the visual acuity of young children starts off relatively poor and increases in quality, hitting its peak at about age 20. Thereafter, it remains relatively constant for most people until somewhere in the early forties, when a slow decline begins. Changes in the eye as a result of senescence do not occur until around age 70, and until then there is relatively little deterioration in visual acuity. However, there are many exceptions to this general trend, because visual acuity is one of the most variable of human senses. Figure 3-1 shows the changes in the percent of the population with normal vision as age increases.

Adaptation to dark involves both the speed and the adequacy of adaptation. Older people adapt about as fast as the young, but their adaptation is not nearly as good (Botwinick, 1973:122). They also find it more difficult to distinguish between levels

---

[1]For a more detailed discussion of aging and sensory processes, see Birren (1964b) and Botwinick (1973).

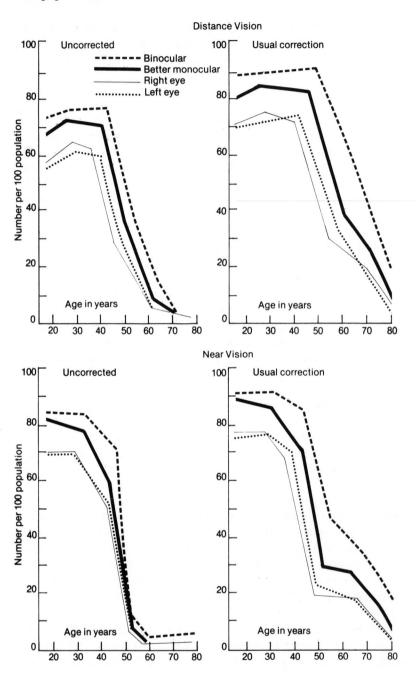

**Figure 3-1** Proportion of American adults with monocular and binocular visual acuity of 20/20 or better at distance and 14/14 or better at near: United States, 1961–1962. *Source:* National Center for Health Statistics, *Vital and Health Statistics*, Series 11, No. 30 (April, 1968), p. 3.

of brightness. In addition, the threshold of the optic nerve increases. Color vision also changes as the individual grows older. The lens gradually yellows and filters out the violet, blue, and green colors toward the dark end of the spectrum. The threshold for these colors increases significantly as people grow older; and for this reason it is much easier for older people to see yellow, orange, and red than to see the darker colors.

Accordingly, older people need either glasses or large-print books for reading, and close work of all kinds becomes more difficult. General levels of illumination must be significantly higher for older people to get the same visual result as young people. Poor adaptation to darkness means that older people have difficulty driving at night. This fact does not mean that older people should not drive, merely that they must exercise extra care when driving at night. Finally, changes in color vision mean that for older people to get the same satisfaction from looking at colors in their surroundings that young people get, their environment must present more yellow, orange, and red, and less violet, blue, and green.

Only a small percentage of older people are blind. Only 2.6 percent of Americans age 65 to 74 are blind, as compared to 8.3 percent of those age 75 or over (National Center for Health Statistics, 1959:9). Yet these people constitute a large proportion of the blind population. One California study found that 55 percent of the blindness in that state occurred after age 65, and 85 percent occurred after age 45 (Birren, 1964b:84). Thus, while the number of blind people is relatively small, blindness definitely appears to be related to age.

## Hearing

Hearing is the second major sense. Hearing is made up of many kinds of reactions, but the most essential ones are the detecting of the frequency (pitch) of a sound, its intensity, and the time interval over which it occurs.

As people grow older, their reactions to frequency and intensity change, but there is no evidence to indicate that ability to distinguish time intervals changes significantly with age. Why these changes occur is not clear (Weiss, 1959).

Hearing loss begins about age 20. Very gradually, as they get older, people lose their ability to hear certain frequencies. This type of hearing loss is very slight for low-pitched sounds, but the loss for high-pitched sounds tends to be considerable. Thus, as age increases, sounds in the higher range become relatively harder to hear.

Intensity threshold also changes with advancing age. There are some frequencies that older people cannot hear no matter how loud, but even within the range of pitch that they can hear, the intensity level necessary to produce hearing is greater among the old, particularly for higher pitches (Botwinick, 1973:123).

Botwinick (1973:123) cites some methodological problems that may lead to overestimation of hearing loss. Apparently, older people are more cautious and tend to report hearing things only when they are fairly sure that they have heard them. Older people also have more difficulty concentrating on hearing. Both of these factors may lead to an overestimation of hearing loss among older adults.

Older people are also more susceptible to ear damage than the young. For example, industrial noise produces a greater hearing loss among older workers than among younger ones. Older people, even those with relatively little hearing loss, have greater difficulty in making the fine distinctions required to hear speech than do younger people. After about age 55, a consistent sex difference appears in hearing ability. Up to that point, the prevalence of hearing loss is about equal for men and women, but after age 55 men show considerably greater incidence of hearing loss than do women. Botwinick (1973) suggests that greater exposure to noise pollution on the job may be the cause of this differential.

In summary, as people grow older it becomes more difficult for them to hear high-pitched sounds and sounds of low intensity. Older men have greater hearing difficulty than do older women. As a result, older people enjoy music with more low-pitched sounds and with uniform intensity. Organ music is popular among older people because of the richness of its lower tones. Older people must play radios and televisions louder in order to hear them, and many older wives can be irritated by the fact that their husbands play everything so loud.

Hearing loss is not as easy to measure as visual acuity, and for this reason it makes more sense to talk in terms of *impaired hearing* rather than "normal hearing." Impaired hearing is a hearing loss of sufficient magnitude to reduce the individual's capacity for interacting successfully with his or her environment. Impaired hearing does not always result when the sense of hearing declines. For example, if the individual still has good eyesight, he or she may be able to compensate for hearing loss by reading lips. As we noted earlier, however, eyesight too begins to decline in the early forties. The incidence of impaired hearing therefore increases sharply after age 45.

A decline of either sight or hearing can be partly compensated by the other, but when both decline simultaneously, as is so often the case among older people, a serious problem of adaptation to the environment occurs. Not only is the ability of these people to earn a living adversely affected, but those who deal with such people on a personal basis must learn to take these new limitations into account in order to help them make maximum use of their capabilities and opportunities.

## Other Senses

The inner ear consists of tiny hairlike projections suspended in a fluid environment inside a structure that looks like a horn of plenty. These hairlike projections are sensory receptors that pick up and pass on to the brain information about changes in the body position and orientation in space that constitute our sense of *balance*. The inner ear is very important in maintaining an upright posture. Its action is not usually a conscious process; balance is normally maintained by unconscious reflex movements.

The efficiency of the sense of balance is difficult to measure. One way is to spin a person around several times and then observe how long it takes the person to re-establish orientation in space. Maximum sensitivity of the sense of balance appears to occur between ages 40 and 50, later than most other senses; nevertheless, older people take longer to reorient themselves than do younger people.

It has not been established that aging causes a decline in the tissues of the inner ear, yet older people characteristically tend to fall more often. The difficulties in maintaining balance experienced by older people may result more from a failing blood supply than from a failing inner ear. Part of the problem may also be that the central nervous system's ability to coordinate the balance reflexes declines with age, particularly in terms of the speed with which corrections are applied. Whatever the cause, older people have difficulty in maintaining their balance. They tend to fall more than young people, and falls can be more serious for them.

As a sense, *taste* has less importance for indivudual's survival, but it certainly can have a good deal to do with satisfaction. The evidence indicates that all four taste qualities—sweet, salt, bitter, and sour—show an increase in threshold after age 50. Women remain more sensitive to taste than men. (Botwinick [1973:126] suggests that smoking may be a factor in this differential.) Not only do individual taste buds become less sensitive with aging, but also the number of taste buds declines. It is estimated that a man in his seventies has only about one sixth the number of taste buds that a young man in his twenties has. Nevertheless, it is unlikely that *large* changes in taste sensitivity occur before age 70.

People in old age are apt to require more highly seasoned food to receive the same taste satisfactions they received when they were 20. They also seem to prefer tart tastes and to show less interest in sweets.

We do not know how or even whether the sense of *smell* changes with age (Botwinick, 1973:126). From the lack of research in these areas, it appears that taste and smell are the "poor relations" of the senses. This situation is unfortunate, because these two senses are capable of giving great satisfaction, and compensation for declines in taste and smell could be very important to the individual.

The so-called general body sensations include touch, pain, muscle movement, and vibration. Sensitivity to touch appears to increase from birth to about age 45. From that point on, the threshold increases sharply. Pain is an important sense that alerts the body to a state of emergency, some state either within or outside the body that threatens its well-being. Older people appear not to feel pain as much as young people do. But pain is difficult to measure because both the feeling and reporting of pain are conditioned by cultural and personality factors. Laboratory data are few, and they often show no age change in pain sensation (Botwinick, 1973:126).

As people grow older, they increasingly make errors in estimating the direction of muscle motion. The ability to detect vibrations (**rinethesis**) appears to decline with age only for the lower extremities of the body.

## THE PERCEPTUAL PROCESS

The senses provide the means for assembling and classifying information, but not for evaluating it. The process of evaluating the information gathered by the senses and giving it meaning is called *perception.* Not all sensory input is perceived, for perception is a conscious process and some senses, such as the sense of balance, may be mainly unconscious. But for every sense in which there is consciousness of the stimulus received, there is an evaluative perception. In perception, not all of the information collected may be given equal weight. In visual perception, for example, shape appears to be a more important characteristic than color in evaluating an object.

Older people tend to underestimate the passage of time much more than younger people do. Thus, they are very likely to let time "slip by." They are also less capable of judging the speed of a moving object than are younger people.

Closure is the ability to come to a decision concerning the evaluation of a stimulus. People are thought to become more cautious and less capable of closure as they grow older. This tendency may partly account for the apparent indecisiveness of some older people. Moreover, people seem to suffer a decline with age in the general speed with which they can organize and evaluate stimuli.

For many of the sensory and perceptual processes, it would appear that declines in function do not often seriously hamper behavior until after age 70. "Until that time, disease and other unique circumstances would appear to be more relevant than an intrinsic age-related change would be" (Birren, 1964b:107). A word of warning is appropriate here, however. The available evidence concerning perceptual processes is far less conclusive than that concerning sensory processes.

## PSYCHOMOTOR PERFORMANCE

The term *psychomotor performance* refers to a complex chain of activity beginning with a sensory mechanism and ending with some sort of reaction, usually through a muscle. When a muscle acts as a part of the stimulus–response chain of events, it is called an *effector*. Between the sense organs and the effectors lies a chain of brain mechanisms that are called *central processes*. Ideally, psychomotor performance involves taking sensory input; attaching meaning to input through perception; incorporating the perceived information into the mind alongside other ideas (integration); making a decision concerning the action, if any, required by this new information; sending instructions to the appropriate effector; and activating the effector's response. This process is indeed much more complex than simple sensation or perception.

Psychomotor performance[2] is limited in its abilities by the capacities of the various parts of the system. In most cases, the sensory and effector mechanisms are more than capable of handling the task to be done. Hence, the limits on performance are usually set by "the central mechanisms dealing with perception, with translation from perception to action, and with the detailed control of action" (Welford, 1959:563).

Performance capacity is a function not only of the available pathways in the brain, but also of the strength of the sensory "signal" and its relative strength compared with other signals entering the brain at the same time. A decline in absolute or relative signal strength can be partially offset by taking more time to integrate incoming data. Such compensation may explain much of the slowness of performance associated with aging. Errors are likely to result if the older individual cannot take the extra time needed to process all the data. The errors result from the fact that too little information

---

[2]This discussion is based largely on Welford (1959).

can be processed between the time the sensory input is received and the time action must be taken.

> Adequate functioning of peripheral organs is a prerequisite for adequate performance, but the subtleties of timing, grading, and patterning included in the term "skill" are obviously dependent upon central factors. All we can ask is what function in any given circumstances *sets limits* to the performance. Any link in the chain from receptor to effector and any mechanism concerned in the serial characteristics of performance may in certain circumstances limit the level of achievement (Welford, 1959:564).

The most serious sensory limitation on psychomotor performance is the general rise in sensory threshold. Once sensory response is triggered, however, the senses do not pose much problem. Research findings suggest that changes in performance would remain, even if there were some way to eliminate sensory decline completely (Botwinick, 1973). There is also only a negligible decline in the speed of nerve conduction as age increases.

The effectors can be a prime weakness in the psychomotor chain. Maximum strength declines sharply in the later years. From the forties to the seventies, there is about a 45 percent decline in muscular output. A similar decline is observed in the endurance of the muscular structure. Nevertheless, recovery time from exertion and the mechanical efficiency of muscles are not the only factors influencing effectors. In fact, poor muscular performance in old age may be caused more by poor coordination than by decline in muscular strength or endurance (Shock and Norris, 1970). Since coordination is the result of control by the central processes, the inefficiency of effectors in old age could be considered a result rather than a source of poor psychomotor performance.

The important limitations on psychomotor performance, then, would appear to come from the central processes. But regardless of where the limitations come from, there are definite changes in observed psychomotor performance as the individual ages. The most important differences from the point of view of social functioning are in reaction time, speed and accuracy of response, and inability to make complex responses.

## Reaction Time

Reaction time is usually defined as the period that elapses between the presentation of the stimulus and the beginning of the response to that stimulus. Reaction time traditionally has been considered a measure of the time used by the central processes.

Reaction time increases with age. This increase is very slight for simple tasks, but it becomes greater as the tasks get more complex. The more choices that are involved in the task, the longer it takes people to react. When the duration of the stimulus is brief, the difference in reaction time between old and young people is negligible. However, when stimulus duration is long, older people react disproportionately slower. Waugh and his associates (1973) concluded that inefficiency in initiating responses, rather than problems in selecting responses, was the cause of this differential. Botwinick (1973:177) suggests that cautiousness may play a big part, since older people are perceptibly slower only when they have time to be cautious. When the magnitude of the stimulus is at or near the sensory threshold, the marginal signal also creates many obstacles to psychomotor reaction time.

The slowing of reactions in older people may result mainly from a tendency toward care and accuracy that seems to characterize this group. They tend to spend more than the average amount of time checking their results; therefore, part of their slowness may be the difference between the time required for *accuracy* and the time required for *certainty*. Moreover, older subjects may not be motivated to perform well in a laboratory situation.

The slowing of reaction time appears mainly to involve the central processes. Neither the speed of input nor the speed of output is responsible, and, as mentioned, slowing results partly from a desire for certainty rather than a physical inability to act quickly. Botwinick (1973:177) points out, however, that response time does not have a clear influence on higher processes such as cognition. In addition, he points out that exercise, increased motivation, and practice can reduce the effects of a slowing in reaction time. Extended practice may eliminate slowing completely. Finally, individual differences in reaction time are so great that, even with age changes, very many older people are quicker in responding than many young adults.

## Speed and Accuracy

Speed of movement also tends to decline with increasing age. Again the evidence seems to point to the central processes as the source of slowing rather than to any loss of ability to move quickly. In fact, when older people try to hurry, their control capabilities are often so poor that their movements appear jerky in comparison with the more fluid motions of younger people. Another factor pointing to the central processes as the source of slowing is that for simple movements the slowing with age is very slight, whereas for complex movements, in which the same muscles must be more controlled, the slowing with age is more marked.

These same observations apply to *accuracy*. Accuracy of movement declines as the individual grows older unless more time is taken to compensate for the greater difficulty in controlling the response (Welford, 1959:584–99).

## Complex Performance

Complex performance involves a series of actions in response to a complex stimulus. It has been found that the brain operates serially on data—that is, it deals with stimuli as they arrive—and if the "old" response is not completed when the "new" stimulus arrives, then the new stimulus must wait its turn. Processing may take older people longer. Certainly the research data point in this direction. If this hypothesis is true, it would explain why response time increases with age.

Another factor that seems important in producing age differences in complex response is the strategy used to organize a complex problem for solution. It appears that young people, knowing that they are capable of quick response, use the trial-and-error method extensively when trying to solve a complex problem. On the other hand, older people, knowing that they cannot respond quickly, tend to think the problem through and try to solve it in the fewest tries possible. The result is that when unlimited time is available, older people do about as well as their younger counterparts in solving complex problems. When time is limited, however, and reflection on the problem is not feasible, older people do much worse because they are forced to use the trial-and-error method. Trial-and-error methodology is only fruitful if a large number of trials can be made. The slowness of the older person makes such a task very difficult (Welford, 1959:600–02).

In summary, it would appear that the psychomotor performance of older people is limited more by the central processes than by any other factor. These central processes appear to have definite limits in terms of the amount they can do in a given time. A loss in capacity can be offset by taking longer, but when this is not possible, a much larger percentage of errors will be observed among older people than among the young. The more complex the integrating and controlling functions must be, the more aging slows down performance. Older people thus shift their emphasis from speed to accuracy.

The implications of these factors in psychomotor performance are important. First, factors other than changes in the central processes have relatively little influence on psychomotor response. Also, the central processes are very difficult to offset mechanically, the way glasses or hearing aids can offset poor sensory processes. Reaction time, speed and accuracy of movement, and organization of complex performance all suffer as a result of the decline in integrating and controlling ability that occurs in the central processes in the later years.

## MENTAL FUNCTIONING

Sensation, perception, and psychomotor performance are all very important for the functioning of the individual, yet in human beings as in no other animal these processes must take a back seat to what we will call mental functioning. The general term *mental functioning* refers to a large group of complex processes, subdivided for convenience into intelligence, learning, memory, thinking, problem solving, and creativity.

### Intelligence

When we think of intelligence, we usually imply both a *potential* and an *actual* ability. In practice, however, we always deal with *measured* ability. Measured intelligence is actual mental ability defined in terms of responses to items on a test. Yet no matter how extensive or well-prepared a test is, there is always a margin of error in its measurement of actual mental ability.

Perhaps the most frequently used test in studies of adult intelligence and age-related changes is the Wechsler Adult Intelligence Scale (WAIS). Intelligence quotient (IQ) is a number established by test performance which is taken as a point of comparison with the "normal" or average score of 100. When the WAIS is used for adults aged 20 to 75 and over, *there is an age factor built into the determination of what is normal*. In Figure 3-2 the heavy black line indicates the mean raw scores on the WAIS by age. Note that measured performance peaks about age 25 and declines thereafter, particularly after age 65. The shaded area on Figure 3-2 represents the handicap or advantage that is built into the WAIS IQ score to control for age. There could be a 40-point difference between the score at age 25 and the score at age 75, and yet the IQ score would be the same. The importance of this feature is that the most frequently used test of mental ability assumes that a 40-point drop in score from age 25 to age 75 is normal.

Because the WAIS is widely used and because cross-sectional data consistently has shown a decline in score with increasing age, it has been widely assumed that aging causes a decline in intelligence. There are several problems with this interpretation, however. To begin with, the prime use of intelligence tests is to aid in placing young people in appropriate academic and/or economic careers. As a result,

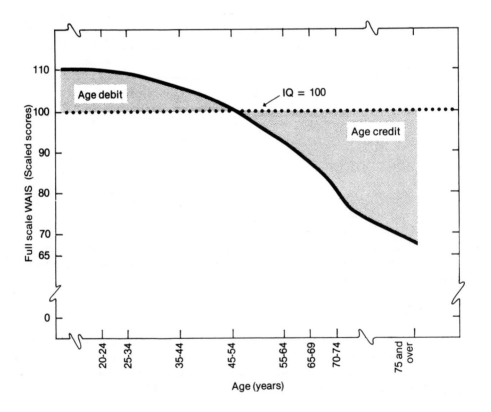

**Figure 3-2**   Full scale WAIS scores as a function of age. *Source:* Jack Botwinick, *Cognitive Processes in Maturity and Old Age* (New York: Springer, 1967), p. 3. Reprinted by permission.

most intelligence tests measure achievement in terms of skills currently being emphasized by the educational system, not skills that may have been emphasized in earlier eras. This bias puts older people at a disadvantage. Adults vary a great deal in terms of psychological states, educational backgrounds, career histories, health, and environmental factors. All of these have been shown to influence intelligence test scores. In addition, intelligence is a complex of abilities, not merely a single factor. Baltes and Labouvie (1973), for example, report various studies that considered as many as twenty primary mental abilities. Test scores by age vary depending on which abilities are emphasized. Heron and Chown (1967) question whether composite or overall scores have much validity. Another factor that clouds the issue concerns the effect of mortality. On the one hand, the possibility that people of lower intelligence die off sooner leads to an underestimate of the average drop in intelligence. On the other hand, intelligence test scores have been shown to drop significantly just before death (Jarvik and Blum, 1971), and this tendency would lead to an overestimation of the drop. Finally, quite different results are obtained from cross-sectional and longitudinal studies. Cross-sectional studies generally report significant age decrements in intelligence scores, while longitudinal studies tend to show stability or increase in measured intelligence (Baltes and Labouvie, 1973:168). Disentangling all of these various interconnected factors in order to define age changes in mental functioning is difficult indeed.

Baltes and Labouvie (1973:205–06) made an impressive review of the literature and concluded that individual differences are great enough to badly erode the predictive value of age and that, in addition, age has a differential impact for various ability dimensions. In general, age changes were "surprisingly small" in comparison to the effect of either generational (cohort) differences or the "terminal drop" just before death. In addition, studies of intervention suggest that age changes can be altered, even in old age. They also conclude that although biological aging undoubtedly influences intellectual functioning, there has been a tendency to underestimate or ignore the impact of environments for older people that are not conducive to "intellectual acquisition and maintenance."

## Learning

Learning is the acquisition of information or skills and is usually measured by improvements in task performance. When someone improves performance at a given intellectual or physical task, we say he or she has *learned*. All studies of performance indicate a decline with age.

Clearly, however, there are a number of factors other than learning ability that affect performance. These factors include motivation, speed, indigence, ill health, and physiological states. In practice, it is extremely difficult to separate the components of performance in order to examine the influence of learning ability, although a number of studies have attempted to do so. Because research to date has not been able to isolate learning ability from other causes of performance and because very little longitudinal research has been done on learning, we are in a poor position to say what effect age has on learning ability.

---

## RESEARCH ILLUSTRATION 2

## AGE CHANGES IN INTELLIGENCE[3]

### John R. Nesselroade, K. Warner Schaie, and Paul B. Baltes

Using a sample of 301 respondents ranging in age from 21 to 71 who were tested both in 1956 and again in 1963, Nesselroade, Schaie, and Baltes were able to assess the impact of both cohort differences and age changes in mental functioning.

The measures of mental functioning consisted of thirteen variables taken from the Primary Mental Abilities Test (Thurstone and Thurstone, 1949) and from the Test of Behavioral Rigidity (Schaie, 1960). Responses to these subtests were factor analyzed separately for both the 1956 and the 1963 data to yield four factors that were stable over the 7-year interval: crystallized intelligence, cognitive flexibility, visuo-motor flexibility, and visualization.

Crystallized intelligence was of particular interest since it was related to a theory of the development of intelligence (Horn, 1966). According to the theory, crystallized intelligence results directly from experience, while fluid intelligence is more biologically limited. As measured by Nesselroade, Schaie, and Baltes, crystallized intelligence was a composite of scores on tests of verbal meaning, reasoning, numbers, word fluency, capitals, and social responsibility.

Figure 3-3 shows the results of their data analysis. The solid lines reflect cross-sectional data, while the broken lines reflect the 7-year longitudinal data. These data show that, in general, the variations between generations (between groups in the cross-sectional data) tended to be much greater than the variations within specific cohorts (the dotted lines) and the 7-year study period. In fact, cognitive flexibility and visualization showed a persistent cohort difference, but no age change at all.

The two age changes that did occur went in opposite directions. Visuo-motor flexibility showed a decline with age. This decline was to be expected, given the data on psychomotor performance. Crystallized intelligence showed an increase in performance during the 7 years for all cohorts, but the older cohorts showed the largest increases. In other words, the generation gap in crystallized intelligence narrowed during the 7-year study period.

These findings led the investigators to conclude that for the cohorts they studied, the generational component was more important than the age component in explaining performance differentials on the dimensions they studied. They also concluded that historical change factors influence some cohorts and some ability dimensions more than others.

This study is an interesting example of what can be done to evaluate the impact of various causes of change. A word of caution is in order, however. The restudy involved only 301 of 500 original 1956 respondents. The 301 respondents who were restudied were higher on all ability dimensions than those who were not restudied, but there was no age difference in this bias. This situation illustrates the vulnerability of longitudinal research to the availability of study participants for retest.

---

From a practical point of view, it seems that learning performance tends to decline as age increases, although the declines are not noticeable until past middle age. All age groups *can* learn. Older people can usually learn anything other people can if given a bit more time. Tasks that involve manipulation of distinct objects or symbols, distinct and unambiguous responses, and low interference from prior learning are particularly conducive to good performance by older people.

---

[3]Adapted from Nesselroade, Schaie, and Baltes (1972).

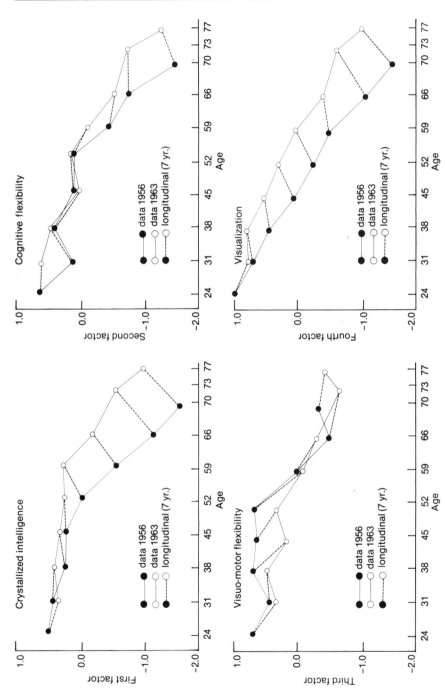

**Figure 3-3** Differential age functions for four second-order factors of intelligence based on two cross-sectional (1956, 1963) and eight seven-year (1956–63) longitudinal studies. (Reprinted by permission of the publisher, the Gerontological Society from J. R. Nesselroade, K. W. Schaie, & P. B. Baltes, "Ontogenetic and Generational Components of Structural and Quantitative Change in Adult Cognitive Behavior," *Journal of Gerontology, 27*, 1972. 222–228.)

## Memory

Memory is intimately related to both intelligence and learning, since remembering is a part of the evidence of learning and learning is a part of the measurement of intelligence. For example, if a person does not learn, he or she has nothing to remember. Conversely, if a person cannot remember, there is no sign of having learned.

There are essentially four types of memory. *Short-term* or immediate memory involves recall after very little delay, from as little as 5 seconds up to 30 seconds. *Recent* memory involves recall after a brief period, from 1 hour to several days. *Remote* memory refers to recall of events that took place a long time in the past, but that have been referred to frequently throughout the course of a lifetime. *Old* memory refers to recall of events that occurred a long time in the past and that have not been thought of or rehearsed since.

Regardless of type, there are three *stages* of memory. *Registration* refers to the "recording" of learning or perceptions. In concept, registration is analogous to the recording of sound on a tape recorder. *Retention* refers to the ability to sustain registration over time. *Recall* is retrieval of material that has been registered and retained. Obviously, in any type of memory, a failure at any of these stages will result in no *measurable* memory.

It is commonly believed that all kinds of memory show a decline with advancing age. However, studies do not overwhelmingly support this idea. While it is true that there is an age deficit in recall of various types, it is not clear whether this deficit results from declining memory or from declining ability to learn in the first place.

> Nevertheless, if we take the position of being interested only in whether or not there is a decline with age in the ability to reproduce previously exposed material, regardless of what the basis for the decline may be, the evidence seems to point to an age deficit in the performance of both immediate and delayed recall (Botwinick, 1967:116).

There appears to be a greater loss with age in short-term and recent memory than in remote or old memory, and the decline with age in memory function is less for rote memory than for logical memory. As age increases, the retention of things heard becomes increasingly superior to the retention of things seen, and use of both gives better results than the use of either separately.

Bright people are less susceptible to memory loss with increasing age than are their less intelligent counterparts, and some older people escape memory loss altogether. People who exercise their memories tend to maintain both remote and recent memory well into old age.

Any attempt to reverse or compensate for a decline in memory functions must obviously depend on some notion of why people forget. There are a number of theories of forgetting, and each has implications for various treatment solutions.

One theory holds that forgetting results from faulty initial registration. Studies supporting this theory have shown that when older people are not hurried in their learning or perception, recall is improved. It has also been held that retention declines with age, and there is some support for this idea. But perhaps the most widely supported theory of forgetting suggests that new material learned interferes with the recall of old material. Numerous studies have supported this idea, although the results to date are far from clear (Botwinick, 1967:199–200).

If the interference theory is true, then about all that could be done to ward off memory decline would be periodic rehearsal, a highly impractical method. Faulty registration could be at least partly countered by allowing an optimum pace for learning and/or perception to take place. Not much could be done about a decline in ability to retain material that has been registered.

## Thinking

Via intelligence, learning, and memory, human beings have at their disposal a great many separate mental images. Thinking, problem solving, and creativity are all terms that apply to the manipulation of ideas and symbols.

Thinking can be defined as the process of developing new ideas. It helps bring order to the chaos of data brought into the mind by learning and perception by *differentiating* and *categorizing* these data into constructs that psychologists call *concepts* (Botwinick, 1967:156). Thus, thinking is the process we use to form concepts.

Differentiation occurs at two separate levels. The first is the level of sensation, perception, or learning. Obviously, declines in these functions with age would serve as effective barriers to concept formation. A second level of differentiation involves a process psychologists call *stimulus generalization*. Stimulus generalization makes different stimuli functionally equivalent, and the more similar the stimuli, the more nearly equal the responses. For example, most oranges are unique. They vary according to weight, thickness of skin, number of seeds, number of bumps on their skins, and enough other characteristics to give an almost infinite set of possible combinations. Yet we have the mental capacity to treat all oranges alike. This capacity is stimulus generalization, and it is an essential prerequisite for the process of categorization.

It is thought that the ability to perform stimulus generalization declines as age increases, and early experiments have tended to confirm this supposition. When declines in speed were accounted for, it was found that most older people produce more accurate and specific differentiations and thus have less ability for stimulus generalization than their younger counterparts. Thus, when not given enough time, older people tend to be confused by tasks that require stimulus generalization. Botwinick (1967:158) advances this differentiation ability as a valid reason for the cautiousness older people seem to value.

Once mental data have been differentiated, they must be categorized. Categorization allows data to be dealt with in general terms, which is much easier than trying to deal with everything in specifics. Thus, when we encounter a stop sign we can deal with it as a member of a class of objects rather than trying to figure out why it is there, who put it there, and so on. The assumptions we make when we encounter a stop sign are the result of stimulus generalization and categorization.

Older people seem to be particularly poor at forming concepts. In fact, the age curve for conceptualization ability is very nearly the same as the one shown earlier for the WAIS (Figure 3-3). Concept formation often involves making logical inferences and generalizations. Older people have been found to resist forming a higher-order generalization and to refuse choosing one when given the opportunity. All studies seem to agree that as age increases, ability at concept formation and its components declines.

Yet common sense tells us that older people form concepts and that some do it exceedingly well. What does it mean, then, when we say that older people consistently show a decline in performance on tests of differentiation and categorization? At this point, it appears that at least part of this result may be attributed to the characteristics of the tests used. Two types of items are generally used: abstract and concrete. When an item requires generalization from a single case and inference beyond the specific details of that case, the item is said to be *abstract*. When the specific case need not be put into a broader framework and not much more than literal recognition is involved, then the item is said to be *concrete*. The idea has been advanced that the past training and experience of older people leaves them ill prepared to deal with the high proportion of abstract items found on most tests of thinking. Today's schools encourage generalization and inference, but the schools of 50 years ago are said not to have emphasized these skills (Botwinick, 1967:168).

Longitudinal data could give some key answers to these questions, but unfortunately very little is available. Data from studies where education level was controlled suggest that both level and type of education may modify, but not eliminate, the relationship between age and measured thinking ability (Botwinick, 1967:164).

Likewise, studies that have held IQ constant have shown a reduction in the age–thinking association, but not completely. Studies have also shown that declines in memory function do not account for the age decline in ability to form concepts. Other studies suggest that those who retain the greatest degree of verbal facility in old age are also those who retain the greatest amount of skill in concept formation.

In their entirety, these data suggest that concept formation is not completely independent of other skills such as learning and intelligence, but at the same time is not completely dependent on them either. A substantial part of the decline with age in measured ability to form concepts appears to be genuine, and not caused by artifacts of the measurement process or by the influence of intervening variables. The cohort effect has not been adequately evaluated, however, with respect to concept formation.

### Problem Solving

Problem solving is the development of decisions out of the processes of reason, logic, and thinking. Whereas thinking involves the differentiation and categorization of mental data, problem solving involves making logical deductions about these categories, their properties, and differences among them. Problem solving differs from learning in that learning is the *acquisition* of skills and perceptions, while problem solving is *using* these skills and perceptions to make choices.

In solving problems, older people are at a disadvantage if many items of information must be dealt with simultaneously. They have more difficulty giving meaning to stimuli presented and have more trouble remembering this information later when it must be used to derive a solution. The number of errors in solving problems rises steadily with age.

Older people take a long time to recognize the explicit goal of a particular problem. Their search for information is thus characterized by haphazard questioning rather than by concentration on a single path to the goal. They attain information randomly, have trouble separating the relevant from the irrelevant, and thus tend to be overwhelmed by a multitude of irrelevant facts. They also tend toward repetitive behavior, a tendency that can be disruptive in situations where the nature of problems and their solutions is constantly and rapidly changing. Repetition can be an advantage, however, in situations that are changing slowly or not at all (Botwinick, 1967:172–74).

In general, the same trend of decline is observed with regard to problem solving that was observed in the other mental processes. However, Arenberg (1968) has shown that when abstract reasoning is required in relation to concrete tasks, older people are in fact able to think at abstract levels. In addition, some of the data on the role of education indicate that older people whose jobs had trained them to perform deductions (for example, physicians) showed deductive ability comparable to younger colleagues (Cijfer, 1966). This finding suggests that there may indeed be sizeable cultural and social (cohort) factors operating in the cross-sectional data that have been the mainstay of our knowledge of the relationship between age and problem solving.

## Creativity

Creativity is unique, original, and inventive problem solving. The biggest problem is deciding whom to study—how to define creative people. Colleague ratings and psychological test scores have been used, but the most frequently used method is to count the number of publications. Lehman (1953) used historical accounts of major developments in various academic fields to pinpoint the age at which "major" contributions were made. Most of the studies have shown a decline in both the quantity and the quality of creative output with age, but Dennis (1966) presented data showing that in some academic fields the average output declined scarcely at all through age 70. Clemente and Hendricks (1973) found no correlation between age at receipt of doctorates and six operational indices of publication output. Certainly individual exceptions are prevalent enough in every field and declines are gradual enough that no one should assume that older people automatically reach an end of their creativity, particularly at a given chronological age. A crucial issue revolves around social supports of creative effort. Zuckerman and Merton (1972) point out that in science the political cards within the academic disciplines are stacked in favor of the older members of the discipline. Older scholars are overrepresented in committee posts, on proposal review committees, among journal referees, and so on. On the other side, however, is the pressure placed on established scholars to move into supervisory and leadership positions, which often takes them away from their own individual work. In addition, seldom does an individual get to be "established" just by virtue of growing old. Crane (1965) suggests that motivation and selection of research topics are both very important. In academic competition, people fall by the wayside and fade into obscurity, but it is difficult to experience falling into obscurity unless you live long enough. All these issues suggest that all sorts of social factors mediate whatever age changes may occur in raw creativity.

### Rigidity

Rigidity has commonly been thought to influence mental functioning by causing people to persist in habitual ways long after the weight of the evidence indicates that persistence is unprofitable (Botwinick, 1973:70). Rigidity has traditionally been treated as a general mental trait. However, recent research (Chown, 1961; Schaie, 1958; Brinley, 1965) has shown that rigidity is made up of many specific components, some of which appear to change with age and some of which do not.

After reviewing the literature on simple and multidimensional rigidity, Botwinick (1973:92) concludes that the data do in fact show that older adults have been generally more rigid in comparison with young adults, but that this rigidity results at least partly, perhaps totally, from cultural and experiential factors, quite independent of age itself. He also suggests that because of this cultural influence, when today's young adults grow old, they may not be as rigid as today's older people.

### Expectancies

Expectancies are mental sets. They can also be anticipations that predispose the individual to respond in a particular way. Mental sets are a very important aspect of human behavior. Without them, we would have to relearn almost everything we do every time we wanted to do it. Yet a very important element of mental flexibility seems to be the ability to inhibit, to ignore, or to modify our mental sets in situations where they are not appropriate. This ability appears to decline with increasing age, and this decline is an important factor determining the nature of response in older people (Botwinick, 1959).

## DRIVES

Drives are unlearned bodily states, frequently experienced as feelings of tension or restlessness, that make people want to act. When a person is hungry, for example, feelings of tension and restlessness do not have to be learned, they just appear. The primary drives that have been studied from the point of view of age changes include hunger, sex, and activity.

### Hunger

There has been little systematic study of age changes in hunger in humans, but data from animal studies indicate that older animals are less driven by food deprivation and can withstand greater food deprivation than younger animals. However, the literature on the food habits of older people does not exactly fit this picture. Some older people appear to have less appetite than their younger counterparts, but many older people also enjoy eating and do not reduce their food intake appreciably with age.

This seeming enigma raises an interesting point. Past learning associated with the satiation or reduction of drives is frequently overlooked as a factor influencing responses to drives. Certain drives appear regularly, and human culture contains patterns for satisfying them. These cultural patterns become ingrained in the individual as habits. Habits have a way of acting like drives, and a reduction in the physiological state (drive) need not necessarily lead to a change in behavior. Hence, eating habits may persist even though the physiological basis for eating has diminished. If food consumption remains constant or increases as age increases, then the source of this behavior is probably a result more of culture than of the hunger drive.

Another facet of this same question concerns the fact that behavior can serve more than one function. In measuring the hunger drive, we observe behavior toward food. However, this behavior can result from habit, from a desire for taste sensation, or from a desire to socialize at mealtime, as well as from hunger. These dilemmas are present in the study of human drives, regardless of which one we study.

## Sex

Next to hunger, the *sex drive* is perhaps the most important drive in humans. While sexual behavior declines with age, it does not disappear—all jokes to the contrary notwithstanding. Continued sexual activity in later life is associated with the capacity for orgasm, the age of the partner, and health. Once they have discovered their capacity for sexual response, women are apt to seek sexual gratification after the death of their spouse, and the same is true of men; but for men the problem is less acute because at later ages there are many more single women than there are single men.

In their pioneering study of human sexual response, Masters and Johnson (1966) studied the sexual activities of a limited number of older people in great detail. They found that in aging women steroid starvation and hormone imbalance following menopause often lead to changes in the sex organs that result in painful coition and orgasm. Masters and Johnson consider pain a primary cause of reduced sexual activity in the older woman; and they contend that hormone therapy in women is effective in increasing sexual capacity primarily because it eliminates pain rather than because it stimulates the sex drive, as had been widely thought. Even in spite of steroid and hormone problems, most older women who maintain a regular outlet for their sexual drives are able to retain a much higher capacity for sexual performance than their counterparts who do not have a regular outlet.

Masters and Johnson (1966) conclude that the sexual responsiveness of the male wanes as he ages. This decline appears to be true no matter what measure of response is used. After about age 60, sexual tension and reactive intensity during sexual expression are reduced. Masters and Johnson's data sustain the common notion that the sexual performance of the male declines with age. However, except in cases of drastic physical infirmity, they contend that the greatest causative factor in this change is sociopsychological rather than biological in nature. Boredom with one's partner, preoccupation with career or economic pursuits, mental or physical fatigue, overindulgence in food or drink, physical and mental infirmities, and particularly fear of failure are all held to be more important in the sexual performance decline in the older male than aging in itself. Masters and Johnson found that, as in the case of older women, one of the biggest factors associated with maintenance of effective sexuality in the older male was a continuing regular outlet for active sexual expression.

## Activity

Most animals appear to have a drive toward undirected, spontaneous activity (sometimes called *curiosity*). Animal studies have found that this drive first increases with age and then decreases. In rats, for example, spontaneous activity increases from birth to puberty, and declines from then on. This drive has not been studied in humans, but at least part of the lethargy to be found in some older people probably results from a decline in the drive toward activity. Nevertheless, the decline in available energy is probably more important than any decline in drive in reducing the spontaneous activity of older people.

In summary, it appears that drives do wane as age increases, but because a good many factors intervene between drives and overt behavior, drives play a relatively small part in explaining behavior changes in aging.

## MOTIVES

Motives are closely related to drives. Drives are very generalized dispositions toward action. Superimposed on these generalized states are patterns of learned behavior that give specific direction to these general tendencies to act. Motives are thus specific, goal-directed, and learned.

Motives intervene between biological drives and human behavior.

> Virtually all behavior that is distinctively human has little in the way of simple one-to-one connections with . . . primary drives. The same drive may be involved, for example, in many different motives. Although the hunger drive usually leads directly to food-getting behavior, it may also instigate behavior directed toward injuring others (aggressiveness), toward hoarding (acquisitiveness), or toward competing or cooperating with others (Newcomb et al., 1965:25).

Obviously, motives are an important aspect of human behavior, but we know very little about them. What evidence there is indicates that age changes in capacity for motivation are very slight. Botwinick (1959) suggests that the role of motivation in the behavior of older people cannot be understood outside the specific situation in which it occurs.

Since motives are learned, even relatively satiated human desires can be aroused, given a sufficient amount of stimulus, and motives can disappear if there is little opportunity to satisfy or reinforce them. As Kuhlen (1964a:210–11) has stated,

> A society or culture decrees in many subtle ways, and in some not so subtle, that certain types of stimulation will be brought to bear on certain age groups and largely withheld

from those of other ages. . . . Moreover, since the motivational tendencies of people are very largely learned as a result of the reward and punishment systems to which they are exposed during the course of early development, it is reasonable to expect that motives may be *changed* during adulthood if the individual is exposed to a new set of punishment and reward patterns.

Kuhlen has also advanced the notion that growth-expansion motives dominate the early adult years, while anxiety and threat represent primary motivators in the later years. Needs for achievement, power, creativity, self-actualization, and affiliation are said to give rise in early adulthood to growth-expansion motives, with behavior resulting from such motivation centering around family and work. As the person moves into later adulthood, however, Kuhlen sees work and family as becoming less and less capable of providing continued satisfaction, whereupon interests shift to other kinds of activity. Studies indicate that this process of forced reorientation in major goals is likely to result in considerable stress. This stress is most often felt as a general sensation of anxiety or threat.

This anxiety may not only generate constructive efforts to reduce it, sometimes through education or therapy, but is especially important as a generator of defensive and handicapping behavior patterns. . . . Various personality changes, such as conservatism, intolerance of ambiguity, and rigidity are construed as ego defenses, or maneuvers utilized to control the anxiety. . . . (Kuhlen, 1964a:224–25).

## EMOTIONS

Emotions are strong mental states, often of an agitated nature, that are frequently accompanied by physiological changes in the gastrointestinal system or in the vasomotor system. They include such things as fear, anger, anxiety, disgust, grief, joy, or surprise, and are usually a response to an external situation. Emotions often lead to observable behavior, but not necessarily. There is, however, always an internal state that arises as part of the emotional response.

Studies have shown that as people move into old age they show a decline in their ability to show emotional response (Dean, 1962). For example, the ability to experience irritation and anger has been shown to decline with increasing age. Yet older people are also under a great deal of social pressure against showing emotions such as anger, and at least part of the observed decline with age in emotionality may be caused by changing social demands rather than by changing capacity to feel emotion.

## PRACTICAL IMPLICATIONS

There are two points at which the implications of this chapter are of interest: general social functioning and job performance. In terms of general social functioning, it is unlikely that age-related decrements affect a sizeable proportion of the population prior to age 75. To begin with, continuity of life-style and habits means that most people

## RESEARCH ILLUSTRATION 3

## MOTIVATION OF AGED PERSONS[4]

Richard N. Filer and Desmond O. O'Connell

Working under the assumption that motivation for improvement is a big factor in any rehabilitation program, Filer and O'Connell investigated two methods of influencing the attainment of rehabilitative goals by older patients in a Veterans Administration home.

Attention was directed toward the following goals: (1) self-management of medication; (2) dependability in keeping appointments; (3) participation in some productive, constructive work; (4) housekeeping maintenance of their own living area; (5) personal appearance and hygiene; (6) responsibility for maintenance of their clothing; (7) management of their own finances; and (8) not being a disciplinary problem.

Based on interviews with patients, five rewards were selected that were important to them: (1) more privacy and a more attractive ward environment; (2) monetary pay for work in adapted workshops; (3) membership in a club, limited to members who maintained a high level of behavior; (4) increased privileges; and (5) eligibility to participate in ward self-government.

Two matching groups of 44 elderly male patients each (average age over 70) were then formed, using degree of disability (severe, moderately severe, and moderate) as the criterion for matching. Group A was to receive immediate and definite reinforcement and Group B was to receive no differential reinforcement. Both groups were then told about the behavior standards and informed that they would be evaluated every two weeks and that they would receive "report cards" telling them whether or not they had succeeded in meeting the standards.

continue to practice existing skills rather than to learn new ones. In addition, freedom from demands of a job for many means that learning, problem solving, and creative activity can be paced to suit the individual. There is no reason to believe that aging (as opposed to chronic disease or disability or generational differences) produces any significant limitations on social functioning. Even among older people who are residents of institutions, a large proportion exceed the minimum functional capacity necessary for adequate social functioning (Lawton, 1972a).

Concerning job performance, Fozard and Carr (1972) point to the need for functional measures and to the inadequacy of chronological age as an index of potential job performance. Not all pertinent job skills are influenced by age, and in those that are, the range of individual differences is too great to give much predictive power to age alone. E. Belbin and R. Belbin (1969) found that trainability tests consisting of small work samples, were more effective in measuring job potential than were general tests of aptitude or ability. Fozard and Carr (1972) report that both older workers and their employers consistently tend to overestimate the functional demands of jobs. At the present time, many older workers are being arbitrarily denied jobs on the assumption that beyond a certain chronological age, people cannot perform adequately. The use of job-specific testing could result in better job performance at all ages, but such testing is unlikely to be used so long as there is a labor surplus (McFarland, 1973).

[4]Adapted from Filer and O'Connell (1964).

Group B was not told what would happen should its members meet or fail to meet the standards. The implication was that they would continue to be treated like any other patients. They were given no indication that they would be rewarded for satisfactory performance.

On the other hand, Group A was carefully informed of the five rewards for which its members would be eligible if they performed satisfactorily on all eight behavior categories for two successive rating periods.

As expected, Group A's performance was much superior to Group B's, particularly with regard to keeping appointments, personal appearance, and work participation. Both groups improved during the study, and Filer and O'Connell attribute the improvement in Group B to the opportunity for participation, the clearly defined staff expectations, the knowledge of staff approval or disapproval, and the increased attention from the staff. Although both groups improved, the group that received the multiple rewards (Group A) attained satisfactory levels more often and more quickly, and maintained them longer than did the control group. One important implication of this study is that motivation depends highly on specific goals, and that the more explicit the goal and its reward, the greater the motivation.

Filer and O'Connell conclude that their results may apply to many institutional settings, including those where efforts to control a large mass of residents by focusing on preventing "bad" behavior have failed or have produced only token compliance. They observe that

> . . . some of the deterioration of behavior observed in aging, institutionalized persons seems to be fostered by the institutional climate and is not merely the result of the aging process. Elderly, disabled persons in such a setting may be functioning far below their capacity. When exposed to greater opportunity and increased expectancy for performance and increased attention and knowledge of approval or disapproval from the staff, functional levels rise. When additional incentives are consistently offered for specific behavior performances, further significant improvement of performance may be made (Filer and O'Connell, 1964:21).

## SUMMARY

Aging produces increases in sensory thresholds and declines in sensory acuity. However, there is a great deal of individual variability in the extent of decline and few people experience sensory limits on activity prior to age 75.

The evidence with respect to perception is less clear, but there appears to be some decline with age in various perceptual functions. Age changes in the central processes also seem to limit psychomotor responses, reaction time, and complex performance. However, important social factors may influence these psychological functions.

The evidence on mental functioning is even more confused. Cross-sectional studies tend to show a drop with age in measured intelligence, while longitudinal studies tend to report stability over time. An important study by Nesselroade, Schaie, and Baltes (1972) illustrated that intelligence is made up of several dimensions, some of which do not change with age, some of which improve, and some of which decline. In general, age changes in intelligence are minimal in comparison with generational differences or with the decline in intelligence associated with impending death. The evidence on learning is difficult to interpret, but there is no doubt that most older people can learn effectively. Memory declines with age. The prime problem appears to be in the retrieval function. Aging also seems to reduce ability to categorize and make logical inferences, although these trends may be partly social in origin.

The evidence with respect to creativity also suggests that social factors are at least

---

## RESEARCH ILLUSTRATION 4

## AGING AND THE DECLINE OF EMOTIONAL RESPONSE[5]

Lois R. Dean

Dean dealt with four specific emotions: anger, irritation, boredom, and loneliness. Her research was designed to answer two questions: (1) As people move from middle to old age do they report a higher or a lower incidence of these four emotions? and (2) As people grow older, do they attribute any different meanings to these four emotions?

The subjects were 200 men and women who were periodically interviewed over a 6-year period as a part of the Kansas City Study of Adult Life. Table 3-1 shows a summary of the results.

The results for intensity of emotions were as follows:

☐ There was a steady decline in felt irritation with each decade from the fifties through the eighties.

☐ There was also a decline in felt anger, but in this case the decline was very abrupt and occurred in the sixties.

☐ There was a slight decline in felt boredom as age increased (a result opposite that predicted by Dean).

☐ There was an increase in felt loneliness over the age range from the fifties to the eighties.

Anger dropped very abruptly in the sixties, and Dean found this drop to be closely related to absence of a work situation. The only group in which those not working showed more anger than those who were consisted of respondents in their seventies. Dean hypothesized that this rise resulted from the fact that inactivity leads indirectly to frustration and, in turn, to anger. This hypothesis would mean changing the definition of anger, for in middle age anger resulted from resistance to domination by others or from blocked instrumentality, while in old age anger resulted from the frustrations and inactivity.

Boredom defied Dean's predictions. It had been expected that boredom would be a passive emotion that would increase as the more active emotions of anger and irritation declined. But Dean found that boredom declined right along with anger and irritation. On closer examination it turned out that most people in all age groups defined boredom not as lethargy or ennui, but rather as an irritation at having to accommodate others by putting up with them. The following question was asked: "What is the most boring thing that happens to you, would you say?" A typical reply was: "To

---

as relevant as psychobiological age changes in the creative performance of older people. Rigidity, perhaps the opposite of creativity, seems to increase with age, but, again, social factors are thought to be very important in producing this result.

Drives appear to wane as age increases, but because many factors intervene between drives and behavior, declining drives apparently produce less behavior change with age than might be expected. Motives guide and direct action toward specific goals. There is some indication that as people grow older they become less motivated toward growth and expansion goals and more motivated toward reducing anxiety and perceived threat. However, motives can be changed, even in older people.

The ability to feel emotions apparently also declines with age, and in addition, the meanings and environmental sources of various emotions also change. However,

[5]Adapted from Dean (1962).

be with people who talk about themselves and the wonderful things they've done. Maybe I'd rather talk about myself!"

Invasion of privacy by others and interference by others with self-expression or self-assertion are the main sources of the irritation most people call *boredom*. Since boredom turned out in fact to be an active emotion, it is not surprising that it should show a decline with age. Loneliness conformed to Dean's expectations in that it increased with age, but it also changed meaning with increasing age. To the middle-aged, loneliness meant an absence of *interaction*, while among the old loneliness meant an absence of *activity*. Interestingly, Dean's findings lead to the hypothesis that anger, irritation, boredom, and loneliness among the old would all be reduced by an environment that emphasized activity and *deemphasized* interaction with others.

**TABLE 3-1**
**Age and Reported Incidence of Affective States**

|  |  | Age | | | | |
|---|---|---|---|---|---|---|
|  |  | *50–59* | *60–69* | *70–79* | *80 plus* | *Total* |
| How often do you find yourself feeling | | | | | | |
| Irritated | Never, hardly ever | 34% | 42% | 54% | 66% | 57% |
|  | Sometimes or oftener | 66% | 58% | 46% | 34% | 43% |
|  | N | (64) | (48) | (67) | (29) | (208) |
| Angry | Never, hardly ever | 46% | 78% | 78% | 69% | 66% |
|  | Sometimes or oftener | 54% | 22% | 22% | 31% | 34% |
|  | N | (63) | (49) | (66) | (29) | (207) |
| Bored | Never, hardly ever | 61% | 64% | 63% | 63% | 65% |
|  | Sometimes or oftener | 39% | 36% | 37% | 37% | 35% |
|  | N | (61) | (50) | (66) | (29) | (206) |
| Lonely | Never, hardly ever | 74% | 65% | 71% | 47% | 68% |
|  | Sometimes or oftener | 26% | 35% | 29% | 53% | 32% |
|  | N | (60) | (52) | (66) | (30) | (208) |

*Source:* Lois R. Dean, "Aging and the Decline of Affect," *Journal of Gerontology*, 17:441 (October, 1962). Reprinted by permission.

particular emotions such as loneliness show an increase with age. Again, social factors may influence emotionality in older people.

Many psychologists tend to look at the processes covered in this chapter as essentially psychobiological in nature. This tendency was particularly true of earlier work on aging. In recent years, however, there has been a growing recognition of the important role social factors play with regard to basic psychological functions. Throughout this chapter we have repeatedly seen instances where social factors, particularly historical and generational factors, were more important than age changes in producing the cross-sectional age data on various psychological functions. Thus, the psychology of aging is moving from an era in which age differences were assumed to be caused by psychobiological aging processes unless proved otherwise to an era in which there is a tendency to assume that social factors are at least as important as physical aging unless proved otherwise. This shift should lead to more complex and exciting research in the next decade.

## SUGGESTIONS FOR FURTHER READING

Bayley, Nancy. "Cognition and Aging." In Klaus W. Schaie (ed.), *Theory and Methods of Research on Aging*. Morgantown, W.V.: West Virginia University, 1968, pp. 97–119.

Birren, James E. (ed.). *Handbook of Aging and the Individual*. Chicago: University of Chicago Press, 1959.

———. *The Psychology of Aging*. Englewood Cliffs, N.J.: Prentice-Hall, 1964.

Botwinick, Jack. *Cognitive Processes in Maturity and Old Age*. New York: Springer, 1967.

———. *Aging and Behavior*. New York: Springer, 1973.

Bromley, Dennis B. *The Psychology of Human Ageing*. Baltimore: Penguin Books, 1974.

Chown, Sheila, and Klaus F. Reigel (eds.). *Psychological Functioning in the Normal Aging and Senile Aged*. New York: Karger, 1968.

Eisdorfer, Carl, and M. Powell Lawton (eds.). *The Psychology of Adult Development and Aging*. Washington, D.C.: American Psychological Association, 1973.

Heron, Alastair, and Sheila Chown. *Age and Function*. Boston: Little, Brown, 1967.

Koyl, Leon F., and Pamela Marsters Hanson. *Age, Physical Ability, and Work Potential*. New York: National Council on the Aging, 1969.

Talland, George A. (ed.). *Human Aging and Behavior*. New York: Academic Press, 1968.

Welford, Alan T. *Ageing and Human Skill*. London: Oxford University Press, 1958.

———. "Psychomotor Performance." In James E. Birren (ed.), *Handbook of Aging and the Individual*. Chicago: University of Chicago Press, 1959, pp. 562–613.

———, and James E. Birren (eds.). *Behavior, Aging and the Nervous System*. Springfield, Ill.: Charles C. Thomas, 1965.

———, and ———. (eds.). *Decision Making and Age*. Basel, Switzerland: Karger, 1969.

# 4

# The Social Psychology of the Aging Individual

In the previous chapter we saw that society probably influences even the most basic psychological processes through various patterns of social reinforcement. In the realm of social psychology, the influence of society is more obvious. It is impossible to consider the results of aging on the social psychology of the individual without directly taking into account the products of human interaction.

To examine the social psychology of aging, we will be concerned with (1) socialization—the processes through which society and culture take on meaning for the individual; (2) culture—the various kinds of symbols people learn; (3) personality—how those symbols combine with individual traits to form a reasonably consistent posture in relation to the physical and social environment; (4) the individual's conception of self; and (5) how these various sociopsychological aspects of the individual change with age.

This is no mean task, for when the focus of inquiry is the interaction that occurs *within* the individual, the empirical rules of science become difficult to satisfy and the results become more difficult to interpret. Motor coordination can be studied more or less directly, but a person's values can only be inferred from specific behavior. As a result, there is more room for controversy in the social psychological realm than there is in the "purely" psychological. Accordingly, the findings presented in this chapter should be taken as more tentative and speculative than the material in the preceding chapter.

## SOCIALIZATION

The term *socialization* encompasses the group of processes that result in the development of the individual into a social being capable of participating in society. Socialization is learning that either directly or indirectly affects the individual's ability to function socially. As a group of learning processes, socialization is never complete. A person can never learn all there is to know, particularly in a complex and fast-changing society.

It is possible to approach socialization from the viewpoint of both the individual and the society. To the individual, socialization is an important prerequisite for getting whatever the society has to offer. To the extent that people know and understand the social system, they can potentially put the system to use. But to the extent that they do not understand the system, their lives can be confusing and unpredictable. Individuals are said to be "socialized" to the extent that they have learned their culture and have accepted it as their own, particularly its language, social roles, and moral norms (Clausen, 1968). But simply gaining acceptance is usually not enough; it must also be maintained. In a changing society, therefore, people must continue to learn about the social system throughout their lifetimes.

For society, socialization produces a measure of continuity from one generation or cohort to another. After all, society needs new participants, and socialization is a major process through which society attracts, facilitates, and maintains participation. The efforts of the group to help individuals learn the system range from formal, structured programs in which the group is responsible for the outcome to unstructured, informal processes in which the individual is responsible for the outcome. For example, families are expected to teach children to speak, and schools are expected to teach children to read and write. On the other hand, adults must generally find out about the latest clothing styles on their own.

Age affects what the individual is expected to know and what he or she needs to know in order to be an effective participant in society. Early in life, the emphasis in socialization is on learning language and customs; then it shifts to preparing for adult social roles. In adulthood, expectations gradually shift toward self-initiated socialization; that is, adults often recognize their need for knowledge and skills and go after them without waiting to be told (Brim, 1968). At the same time, there are fewer publicly supported, formal opportunities for socialization in adulthood as compared to the opportunities that exist for young people.

Most societies pay little attention to the needs of their adult members for maintenance or renewal of their knowledge or skills. As we shall see later, this pattern seriously hampers the ability of some older members of society to remain integrated in the society. To the extent that older people have needs for information and skills that are necessary for participation in society but that cannot be secured by older people themselves, the socialization processes in the society are not adequate.

Much of what adults achieve in the way of socialization comes out of experience. For example, Kohlberg (1973a) points out that the moral development of young people is mainly cognitive and symbolic. But in order for the person to develop what Kohlberg calls *principled thinking*—"a postulation of principles to which the society and the self *ought to be committed*" (1973a:194)—it is not enough merely to "see" the principles. The person must also experience sustained responsibility for the welfare of others and experience having to make irreversible moral choices. A similar process occurs in other areas of life, such as mate selection, career choice, choice of residence, and so on. The adult develops life principles—a philosophy of life—in a dialectic process between what is known, what is experienced, and his or her personality. And, theoretically at least, the longer one lives, the greater the opportunity for this dialectic to produce refinements in one's approach to living.

The concept of *social roles* is important in understanding socialization because much of what we seek to learn is aimed at making us more effective role players. Every individual occupies many positions—slots in the organization of society. Some of these positions are general. For example, the position *male* implies no particular group memberships. Others are both general and specific. For example, the position *mother* implies a position both in an abstract type of group (the family) and in a specific family. Still other positions are specific and unique to a particular group. An example would be positions in emergent friendship groups, which cannot be discussed in much detail apart from the context of the specific groups.

Each position an individual occupies has norms attached to it that specify, sometimes in detail and sometimes vaguely, what is expected of the person in that position *and* what a person in that position is entitled to expect from others. These norms represent an important aspect of the social role.[1] The more general the position, the more likely it is that the role will be widely known and that there will be at least a nucleus of more or less formalized norms about the role.

As people grow older, they often experience role changes, and the trend of these changes is from roles that are mainly general to roles that are mainly specific. For example, people may leave a job role through retirement and cope with this change by increasing the time they spend in specific friendship relationships. This process has an important impact on socialization.

The process of *anticipatory socialization* involves learning the rights, obligations, resources, and outlook of a position one will occupy in the *future*. To the extent that the future position is a general one, it need not represent an unknown. Through fantasies it is possible to anticipate what the future will hold, identify potential problems, and to prepare in advance (Atchley, 1976b). The role changes common to later life can often be anticipated, thus smoothing the process of transition.

However, many roles we take up in later life have a degree of vagueness to them that allows a certain amount of flexibility in playing them but at the same time makes anticipatory socialization difficult. Such roles are not prepackaged in the way that the roles young people play are. For example, the role of high school student is much more clearly defined than the role of retired person. As a result, older people must often *negotiate* the rights and duties of their positions with significant other people in their environment. Thus, in late adulthood, socialization—learning or relearning how to function in one's social milieu—depends heavily on the characteristics of others with whom the older person must negotiate. The attitudes of others concerning what the aging person is becoming are probably crucial to the content of socialization in later life. As images of aging become less stereotyped in American culture, the outcome of these negotiations can be expected to become more positive.

[1]See Chapter 5 for a more detailed discussion of social roles.

Rosow (1974) argues that because norms for the aged do not exist or are weak and tenuous, there is nothing to socialize the aged *to*. The result is depression, anxiety, and anomie for the older person. Rosow's view of socialization demands a clearly defined set of societal norms to which people are tied through the socialization process. While Rosow's argument may be quite accurate at the societal level, it has questionable applicability at the level at which older people live their everyday lives. Older people often live in a *particularistic* social world, especially in terms of their *significant* interactions. They often have few required contacts with the general community. The bulk of their associations are with people they know and who know them. In addition, most older people continue to function mainly in roles they have occupied for many years. The point is that most of the roles older people play are roles they have been socialized to for a long time. Aging often results primarily in adjusting the nuances of role playing rather than its basic structure. In addition, the roles older people take up, such as the role of retired person, are not as vague as Rosow would have us believe (Atchley, 1976b). The research evidence clearly shows that older people are no more anomic than the general population. They exhibit none of the symptoms of psychological distress predicted by Rosow's posited void in socialization. The reason they do not is attributable to the part that socialization to particularistic roles plays in the lives of older adults.

## Results of Socialization

So far the discussion has centered on socialization as a *process*. However, the *results* of socialization—particularly with respect to attitudes, values, beliefs, and age norms—are also of interest.

The term *attitude* refers to a positive or negative orientation toward some object or idea. Attitudes may also represent predispositions to become motivated in relation to some object or idea. Attitudes can include evaluations on both cognitive and emotional levels. Attitudes are learned.

The relationship between age and attitudes is not a clear one. Part of the problem is the lack of longitudinal and cross-sequential studies that allow effects caused by aging to be separated from cohort effects.[2] We are left with information concerning how the attitudes of today's older people differ from those of today's younger people. *Why* these differences exist is up for grabs. Yet, from a practical point of view it may be instructive to review these differences briefly.

Older people in the United States tend to hold negative attitudes toward aging and toward life in general (Bennett and Eckman, 1973), but it is not clear if this tendency is markedly different from the views of older people themselves at an earlier point in life. Some of the negativeness of older people appears to stem more from isolation, inactivity, ill health, and institutionalization than from aging in itself (Bennett and Eckman, 1973:592; Youmans, 1974).

In terms of more specific attitudes, compared with the young, today's older people tend to have negative attitudes toward the medical care system, including hospitals, doctors, mental hospitals, psychiatrists, and nursing homes. Riley and

---

[2]See Chapter 1 for a discussion of the importance of this issue.

Foner (1968:585) suggest that negative attitudes toward institutions may be a result of (1) desire to stay in the family and (2) the outdated image of the poor farm. Older people currently have generally negative attitudes toward both physical and financial dependency. They are generally favorable toward family contacts, but less so if the contact involves receiving physical aid and even less so if the contact involves receiving financial aid (Streib, 1958).

Fear of crime is a common fear among Americans, including older people. About 20 percent of older middle-class people see crime as a very serious problem, compared to 10 percent of their younger social class peers. Among older blacks, 40 percent see crime as a very serious problem (Harris et al., 1975).

Today's older people generally favor retirement, particularly the younger cohorts within the older population (Streib and Schneider, 1971). Surprisingly, Streib and Schneider (1971:55) found that older women were less positive toward retirement than were older men. This difference was very much related to marital status. The same proportion of women who had never married had a positive attitude toward retirement that the men did, but less than half as many widows had a positive attitude. Atchley (1975b) found that this attitude was primarily caused by the greater incidence of poverty among retired widows. Thus, there appears to be a strong situational element in attitudes.

Attitudes toward death among today's older people are both positive and negative. While older people tend more than the young to see death as a blessing and not as a tragic thing, they also tend to see death as always coming too soon (Riley and Foner, 1968:334). Negative attitudes toward death are strongly related to educational attainment. Riley found that negative attitudes toward death were relatively uncommon among college-educated people and that in this category there were virtually no age differences in the prevalence of negative attitudes toward death (Riley and Foner, 1968:335).

Today's older people defy easy labeling as either conservative or liberal. Attitude depends on the issue. They tend to be negatively oriented toward nonconformists, minorities, and handicapped people (Gozali, 1971; Ross et al., 1973; Thune et al., 1971; Cutler, 1975b). On the other hand, older people accept the foibles of youth more than do the middle aged (Cryns and Monk, 1973). Also, older people tend to be politically liberal in regard to government programs for older people (Campbell, 1971).

The term *values* refers to ideas concerning the relative desirability of various goals. Values are arranged in a hierarchy of priority both by individuals and by groups. Not much is known about the relationship between age and values. Youmans (1973) compared young and older respondents in terms of several value orientations. He found that older people tended to be oriented, to a greater extent than were young people, toward a stable social order, interdependence within the family, "getting ahead," and religion. However, Youmans concluded that cohort differences probably had more to do with these differences than did age, since in an earlier longitudinal study he found a great deal of consistency over time in "outlook on life" among healthy aged men (Youmans and Yarrow, 1971).

To a great extent, what people value is what they have *learned* to want. To some extent this is what they are *told* to want. It seems reasonable to expect that what people are supposed to want might vary throughout the life cycle. We often evaluate maturity or immaturity in terms of the age appropriateness of an individual's goals. Buhler and Massarik (1968) emphasize the importance of changes in goals to understanding the aging individual.

Research on age changes in values is greatly needed. We know neither what values are expected of older people nor what values grow out of the experiences of growing old. Future studies may do well to consider both the hierarchy of values and various types of values. Atchley (1975a) has suggested that values can be classified as being related to material achievement, roles, or personal qualities and that the mix of these various types in an individual's hierarchy of personal goals could be expected to change over the life course.

The term *beliefs* refers to ideas concerning what is true. They are derived from culture and experience and often accepted without proof and acted on *as if* they were proved. Some beliefs, such as belief in the existence of God, may not be capable of being proved. Our ideas about the nature of human beings and the world have an important bearing on how we deal with them. For example, a large percentage of older Americans have endorsed, at one time or another, the following beliefs:

- ☐ Older people have to expect a lot of aches and pains (Riley and Foner, 1968:318).
- ☐ No matter how careful people are they have to expect a good deal of illness in their lifetimes (Riley and Foner, 1968:318).
- ☐ A person understands his or her own health better than most doctors do (Riley and Foner, 1968:319).
- ☐ Cancer is not curable (Back and Gergen, 1966b).
- ☐ Death is like a long sleep (Riley and Foner, 1968:334).

Obviously, people who endorse these beliefs present the medical care system with different problems than do people who reject these beliefs. Yet we know very little about how age affects beliefs or for that matter what many of the beliefs of the aged are. This aspect of aging offers another promising area for research.

The term *stereotype* refers to collections of beliefs about the nature of a particular category of people. Stereotypes may be correct or they may be overly negative or they may be overly positive. The stereotype associated with old age in American society is overly negative and biased and this bias certainly affects how older people are treated by others. For this chapter, the crucial question is whether age has any impact on the extent to which people accept the negative stereotype as being valid.

Old people are seen by society in general as:

- ☐ Valuing companionship more than sex.
- ☐ Being old-fashioned.
- ☐ Not caring much about their appearance.
- ☐ Being neglected.
- ☐ Being in only "fair" health.
- ☐ Being narrow-minded.

To a large extent, older people themselves also hold these stereotypes (Harris et al., 1975). Whether aging influences acceptance of these stereotypes is not known, however.

To sum up, the impact of aging on the socialization process or on the products of socialization is unclear. It seems reasonable to assume that aging does have an impact, at least in that age changes occur in the social groups within which socialization takes place. What is needed is more systematic descriptive research.

## PERSONALITY

Personality is a complex and interdependent system of mental faculties[3] and behavior patterns characteristic of a person, and recognized as such by self and others. The term *individual* implies discreteness. This discreteness results from the fact that personality is so complex and is shaped by so many different forces that it is unique for each human being. Yet, because people share a similar biological and social heritage, a great many aspects of personality are shared by large groups of people; thus one can make some generalizations about age-related changes in personality.

Personality arises out of the need to relate what goes on inside our minds to what goes on outside. Birren (1964b:223–24) distinguishes between the two as follows:

> There are two broad categories of responses that the individual makes, an inner, or covert, response and an outer, or overt, response. Inner responses consist of the ways in which we see ourselves, other people, and events; our thoughts and associations about them; and the meanings we read into them. We also respond in terms of moods. Our perceptions and motivations may lead to actions controlled in a way typical of us. Our overt actions involve other people; e.g., whether we characteristically move toward or away from others. Among other traits, whether we are friendly and interested in other persons or are suspicious and withdrawing, whether we are disposed to action or passivity, characterize our styles of responding and acting and are elements of our personality.

So many approaches have been used to study the human personality that it is difficult to present a unified picture of our knowledge in this area. Because personality is a complex phenomenon and because a large part of personality is not directly observable, there is room for considerable controversy about the nature of personality.

The term *ego psychology* refers, in a general way, to an approach to personality that assumes that the individual ego represents an ongoing synthesis of internal and external aspects of personality. It is often assumed that the capacity for synthesis is inborn and that development proceeds in more or less discrete stages. Because of its close ties to biological maturation (with little attention to possible declines), ego psychology was slow to confront the question of ego functioning in old age, but in recent years, Erikson (1963), and Loevinger (1969) have made noteworthy contributions. Perhaps one reason that the ego psychology of aging has not progressed very far

---

[3]Mental faculties include such things as drives, motives, emotions, expectancies, attitudes, knowledge, psychomotor performance, perception, intelligence, sensation, memory, learning, creativity, and the like.

## RESEARCH ILLUSTRATION 5

## THE IMAGE OF MOST PEOPLE OVER 65[4]

### Louis Harris and Associates

In cooperation with a panel of distinguished gerontologists, Louis Harris and his associates developed an in-depth survey of a wide variety of attitudes and beliefs about aging and the aged. The survey was conducted on a stratified random sample of the U.S. population. Responses were obtained from 1,457 people age 18 to 64 and 2,797 people age 65 or over. Two objectives of the survey were to see how the general public saw older people and to see how older people viewed themselves. Two kinds of questions were asked about "most people over 65": What personal qualities do they tend to have? and What kinds of things do they do?

**TABLE 4-1**
**Personal Qualities of Older People**

| Personal Quality | "Most People Over 65" as seen by Public 18 to 64 (Percent) | "Most People Over 65" as seen by Public 65 and Over (Percent) | Self-Image of Public 18 to 64 (Percent) | Self-Image of Public 65 and Over (Percent) |
|---|---|---|---|---|
| Very friendly and warm | 82 | 25 | 63 | 72 |
| Very wise from experience | 66 | 56 | 54 | 69 |
| Very bright and alert | 29 | 33 | 73 | 68 |
| Very open-minded and adaptable | 19 | 34 | 67 | 63 |
| Very good at getting things done | 35 | 38 | 60 | 55 |
| Very physically active | 41 | 43 | 65 | 48 |
| Very sexually active | 5 | 6 | 47 | 11 |

*Source:* Adapted from Harris et al. (1975).

With regard to personal qualities, Table 4-1 shows the beliefs of people under 65 about older people in general and about themselves in particular and the beliefs of older people about older people in general and about themselves in particular. These data lead to some interesting conclusions.

In terms of stereotypes, both young and old tended to agree that "most people over 65" are not very bright and alert, not very good at getting things done, not very physically active, and not very sexually active. Compared to older people, people under 65 were much more likely to see older people in general as very warm and friendly and somewhat more likely to see them as being very wise from experience. But older people were more likely to see the average older person as being very open-minded and adaptable. On balance, people under 65 had a slightly more positive view of "most people over 65" than older people did.

In terms of self-image, most of the older respondents saw themselves as having all of the personal qualities on the list except a very active sex life. Interestingly, this quality was the only one also seen as lacking in themselves by most of the younger people. Compared to people under 65,

[4]Adapted from Harris et al. (1975).

the older respondents more often saw themselves as very warm and very wise and less often saw themselves as sexually active. Otherwise the prevalence of various personal qualities was very similar.

**TABLE 4-2**
**Activities of Older People**

| Activity | Percent Seeing "Most People Over 65" as Spending "A Lot of Time" Doing Various Activities | | Percent Who Spend a Lot of Time Personally Doing Various Activities | |
|---|---|---|---|---|
|  | 18 to 64 | 65 and Over | 18 to 64 | 65 and Over |
| Socializing with friends | 53 | 42 | 55 | 47 |
| Gardening or raising plants | 47 | 34 | 34 | 39 |
| Reading | 45 | 33 | 38 | 36 |
| Watching television | 68 | 64 | 23 | 36 |
| Sitting and thinking | 66 | 42 | 37 | 31 |
| Caring for younger or older members of the family | 24 | 21 | 53 | 27 |
| Participating in various hobbies and recreational activities | 28 | 24 | 34 | 26 |
| Going for walks | 35 | 24 | 22 | 25 |
| Participating in organizations or clubs | 26 | 22 | 13 | 17 |
| Sleeping | 42 | 25 | 15 | 16 |
| Just doing nothing | 37 | 27 | 9 | 15 |
| Working part-time or full-time | 5 | 6 | 51 | 10 |
| Doing volunteer work | 15 | 10 | 8 | 8 |
| Participating in political activities | 9 | 10 | 13 | 17 |
| Participating in sports like golf, tennis, or swimming | 5 | 5 | 22 | 3 |

*Source:* Adapted from Harris et al. (1975).

With respect to activities, Table 4-2 shows that "most people over 65" were seen by both age groups as spending a great deal of time in sedentary activities such as watching television, sitting and thinking, and sleeping. Respondents who were 65 or over were only slightly less likely to see most older people as sedentary. The actual activities of the older respondents repudiated this stereotype. The older respondents were much less likely to be involved in sedentary activities than predicted by the stereotype. In fact, while the younger respondents were understandably more likely to spend a lot of time caring for family, working, and participating in sports, the activity profiles of the younger and older respondents were quite similar.

The survey thus showed that negative stereotypes about older people are shared by young and old alike but that much of this negativism is unwarranted both with regard to personal qualities and activity patterns.

is methodological. Ego psychology is a wholistic approach to personality that has traditionally developed out of clinical experience. This approach may be the only way to explore the uniqueness of a given patient, but it may not be the most effective way to explore the similarities among people in the response of personality to normal aging.

At the other extreme, *social learning theories* have stressed social determinism. For example, the social structure theorists argue that personality is situationally sensitive and is nothing more than the sum total of the person's social experiences and social roles (Brim, 1968; Becker, 1964). From a behaviorist point of view, social learning results from the patterns of reinforcement in the environment (Ahammer, 1973). From these perspectives, the individual is a blank page on which society writes a personality either through social roles or patterns of reinforcement. These approaches are weakened by their lack of concern for the *interaction* between internal and external aspects of personality.

An alternative approach has been employed by Neugarten and her colleagues (1964). While Neugarten is careful to point out that no theory of personality is yet adequate to explain the impact of age on personality, there has been a reasonable accumulation of findings on Neugarten's approach.

Neugarten sees personality not as a rigid or fixed entity but rather as an ongoing system that is continuously changing in response to events both internal and external to the individual. In this view, changes in personality related to chronological age would be expected.

Neugarten and her associates undertook a comprehensive series of longitudinal studies of adult personality, with particular emphasis on the effects of age. She reports that in those cases where the investigator was concerned with *intrapsychic processes*, or more exclusively internal processes, significant and consistent age changes emerged. For example,

> Forty-year-olds see the environment as one that rewards boldness and risk-taking and see themselves possessing energy congruent with the opportunities presented in the outer world. Sixty-year-olds seem to see the environment as complex and dangerous, no longer to be reformed in line with one's own wishes, and to see the self as conforming and accommodating to outer-world demands (Neugarten et al., 1964:189).

This change is generally described as a change from an active to a passive orientation in terms of mastery of the environment.

As age increases, preoccupation with the inner life becomes greater; ability to relate emotionally to people or objects declines; readiness to perceive people as active and as experiencing emotions is reduced; and a movement away from outer-world toward inner-world orientations develops. Gutman (1969) found that, compared to younger men, older men were less active in orientation in several nonliterate Indian cultures as well as in a Kansas City sample.

The ability to integrate a wide range of stimuli becomes constricted, and, simultaneously, an unwillingness to deal with complicated and challenging situations develops. Older people "tend less often to perceive affect (the subjective experiencing of emotions) as an important part of life; and tend toward inactivity or passivity rather than toward more active, assertive forms of behavior'' (Neugarten et al., 1964:99). Neugarten interprets her data as supporting the notion that, as age increases,

> there is less energy available . . . for responding to, or maintaining former levels of [psychological] involvement in, the outside world. The implication is that the older person tends to respond to inner rather than outer stimuli, to withdraw emotional investments, to give up self-assertiveness, and to avoid rather than embrace challenge (Neugarten et al., 1968:99).

Sex differences were found with regard to the influence of age on the intrapsychic processes. Older men were more willing to accept their impulses to like and be with other people, to help others, and to gratify their senses than were younger men. Older women were more willing to accept their aggressive and egocentric impulses than were younger women.

On the other hand, adaptational patterns showed no significant changes as age increased. The adaptive, goal-directed, and purposive qualities of personality, areas in which control of the self and of the life situation are conspicuous elements, seem to be relatively unaffected by age. Neugarten and her colleagues draw the implication from various studies, as well as from their own, that factors such as work status, health, financial resources, and marital status are more important than chronological age in influencing the *social* adaptation of people over 50.

Neugarten found that with age the inner life of the individual became more salient and that the efficiency of certain cognitive processes decreased. In fact, many older people who were given psychological tests showed what would be defined in younger persons as ''pathological'' patterns of thought and affect—for example, extreme paranoia. This is a finding frequently encountered by other investigators not only in tests but through other techniques as well. At the same time, Neugarten found no relationship between social adaptation and age. The same people who showed ''pathological'' affect and thought patterns showed no changes in the competence of their social role performance or in interpersonal skills. This seeming contradiction led Neugarten to ask:

> How is it that individuals, as they age, continue to function effectively in their social environments despite not only increased interiority but also decreased efficiency in certain cognitive processes? How do those men and women who give evidence of ineffective thought processes continue to appear integrated? (Neugarten et al., 1964:197).

Neugarten concluded that the answer lies in the stability of patterns for coping with the external environment. This stability develops over a period of time.

> In a sense, the self becomes institutionalized with the passage of time. Not only do certain personality processes become stabilized and provide continuity, but the individual builds around him a network of social relationships which he comes to depend on for emotional support and responsiveness and which maintain him in many subtle ways. It is from this point of view that the typical aging person may be said to become, with the passage of years, a socio-emotional institution with an individuated structure of supports and

interactional channels and with patterns which transcend many of the intrapsychic changes and losses that appear.

Along with increased interiority there seems to go a certain reduction of the complexity of the personality. With the shrinkage in psychological life space and with decreased ego energy, an increasing dedication to a central core of values and to a set of habit patterns and a sloughing off of earlier [likes or dislikes] which lose saliency for the individual seem to occur.

The direction of personality change, then, from middle to old age, seems to be one of increased inner orientation; increased separation from the environment; a certain centripetal movement which leads to increased consistency and decreased complexity and in which the synthesizing and executive qualities, in maintaining their centrality, maintain also the continuity of the personality (Neugarten et al., 1964:198–99).

Other investigators have also encountered a long-range continuity and consistency in personality. For example, Smith and Hall (1964) found that the unconscious remains relatively stable throughout life. Dennis (1960) found that verbal communications, a measure of thought structure, remained remarkably consistent over a period of six decades. Thaler (1956) observed that the cognitive rigidity so often found among older people results at least in part from an extremely consistent way of looking at things.

Neugarten's findings would seem to indicate that there are three sets of variables in the aging personality that merit study: the intrapsychic structure, the cognitive structure, and the interpersonal structure. We have already documented the changes with age in cognitive functioning in Chapter 3. Just as older people compensate for losses in hearing and so forth, they also compensate for losses in cognitive functions. For example, many older people compensate for a declining memory by keeping notes. The overall decline with age in cognitive functioning must change in either the intrapsychic or interpersonal structures, but it will not be considered in detail here. Discussion will center on the intrapsychic structure (the self) and on the interpersonal structure (social roles and social interaction).

## The Self — the "intrapsychic structure"

Human beings are unique in their ability to think about themselves. The ability of humans to use language and to form abstract ideas allows them to think about their own bodies, their own behavior, their own minds, and their own appearance to other people. The *interpretation* of perceived feedback from within ourselves and from others defines the self. As a result of interactions with the environment, individuals gradually differentiate a *part* of their total body of ideas as pertaining to *self*. The self is characterized as being organized but flexible. People strive to integrate all of their experiences, perceptions, and ideas into the structural system of their self-concepts (Riegel, 1959). Thus, the self is an intrapsychic system that depends in part on feedback from others, but that also feeds back upon *itself*.

The self consists of both cognitive and emotional elements. The cognitive element is called the *self-concept*. The self-concept is the individual's description *to himself or herself* of who he or she is and what he or she is like. The emotional element of the self is called *self-esteem*. Self-esteem is how the individual feels about the self-concept in comparison with some ideal—whether he or she likes or dislikes the self-concept, is proud or ashamed of it, and so on. Both self-concept and self-esteem represent a synthesis of data about the self that derives from both inside and outside the individual.

## Self and Roles  – the "interpersonal structure"

A key social factor related to the development of the self is the complement of social roles the person plays. Each social position has attached to it personal qualities and behavior that others *expect* of a person filling that position, and that any person filling that position can *claim*. Together with the position's title (if any), these expectations provide the person filling the position with a *self-concept* and with a basis for imagining the concept others will have of him.

> It is important to note that in performing a role the individual must see to it that the impressions that are conveyed in the situation are compatible with role-appropriate personal qualities effectively imputed to him: a judge is supposed to be deliberate and sober; a pilot, in a cockpit, to be cool; a bookkeeper to be accurate and neat in doing his work. These personal qualities . . . provide a basis of (self) for the incumbent and a basis for the image . . . others will have of him. A self, then, virtually awaits the individual entering a position; he need only conform to the pressures on him. . . . (Goffman, 1961:87).

However, the impact of roles on the self may not be uniform throughout the life course. When a person takes up a new role, including roles associated with later life, the stereotyped behavior associated with the role may be very much in evidence and have an influence on the self. But later on, the person begins to mold the role to fit his or her own personal qualities. Almost all roles are somewhat flexible. Also, the person must negotiate many details of role playing with other people, a process that allows further fitting of the role to the person. Role playing can be viewed as a dialectic process of interchange between social structure and the individual. It is probably erroneous to assume that the individual is very tightly tied, either by himself or by others, to formal role demands. In addition, taking up new roles is concentrated in the earlier phases of life. As a result, older people usually play a set of roles with which they are familiar and they play these roles with a set of familiar people.

## Age Changes in Self-Concept

Neugarten's findings, cited earlier, suggest that as people move into later life, the self-concept becomes dependent less on external factors than on an inner orientation that stresses consistency in self-concept. Atchley's research supports this idea in that a sizeable proportion of retired women in one sample appeared to have self-concepts that depended very little on feedback from other people (Atchley, 1969).

Role changes play a part in developing the self, and many role changes accompany later life. Widowhood, disability, retirement, dependency, and sickness all involve changes in position and role that are associated with age. Yet these changes bring about less change in self-concept than we would expect, because older persons tend to retain roles they formerly played as part of their self-concepts. For example, the retired railroader may still see himself as a railroader, and the older widow may still see herself as the wife of so-and-so. In doing research on aging, one is struck by the number of widows who still have telephones listed in their late husbands' names after many years of widowhood. Thus, our concepts of who we are, being based primarily on the social roles we play, often remain reasonably stable in later life because roles we no longer play can still be drawn on as sources for identity. This stability may not always be helpful, however, since roles such as mental patient or sick person may also become a durable part of the self-concept.

Social interaction is the major external source of information about individual characteristics and qualities. We find out whether we are perceived as smart or stupid, kind or cruel, from observing the ways others behave toward us. The impact of aging on this process depends largely on the style we develop in making use of such information. Some people develop a concept of their personal characteristics and qualities early in adulthood. They say to themselves, "So that's the way I am and will always be, and that's that." Once he or she reaches closure, this type of person is not as likely to be influenced by interaction at any stage of adulthood. And the orientation to the inner world that is brought on by aging would seem to reduce the likelihood of influence still further.

Other people never quite reach closure concerning their personal qualities. These people constantly seek more information about themselves, and they are likely to seek interaction actively throughout their lives. They may even seek interaction and at the same time want very much to turn their attention inward. What prevents them from turning inward is insecurity. In fact, a good definition of insecurity might be the inability to come to closure concerning one's self-concept.

## Age Changes in Self-Esteem

When people compare what they are like and who they are (self-concept) with what they seriously wish they were like and who they could be (self-ideal), the feelings they get as a result constitute their *self-esteem*. Inner feelings, social roles, and social interaction function in developing self-esteem much as they do in developing the self-concept. Yet there are some important differences. For one thing, self-esteem is much more volatile than self-concept. Since it is emotional in content, it can be more responsive to moods and bodily states, while our knowledge of ourselves (self-concept) tends to be more consistent and stable.

As individuals grow older, they tend to shift from seeing themselves as the captains of their fates to seeing themselves as primarily responsive to other people's demands. How they react to this shift depends on their vision of the ideal. If they idealize the rugged individualist, then the result of this shift on their self-esteem will probably be negative. If, on the other hand, they idealize accepting one's roles in life and playing them to the hilt, then the result could be positive.

Role performance is important to self-esteem because the prescriptions and proscriptions that make up social roles serve as a major source of self-ideal. People who perceive themselves as having done well in the past are also more likely to perceive themselves as doing well in old age than are people who come to old age feeling that they have not done well in the past (Reichard et al., 1962). Thus, the key to positive self-esteem in old age may in some cases reside in the past.

The various role changes encountered by older people tend to introduce a certain amount of fluidity in self-esteem. It is mainly the current roles one plays that generate the external information used to establish self-esteem. As older people pick up new roles, such as great-grandparent, widow, or sick person, they must rely on others, at least at first, to establish entitlement to self-esteem. For example, Anderson's (1967a) research showed that high self-esteem among newly admitted nursing home patients was directly related to a high frequency of social interaction. But Davis (1963) found that the influence of interaction on self-concept depended on the nature of the interaction. Those reacted to favorably by their peers had favorable self-concepts, while those not reacted to favorably had less favorable self-concepts.

Yet research results show less instability in self-esteem than might be expected. Secord and Backman (1964) have presented a theory of self that helps explain this seeming paradox. According to this theory, individuals may be pressured by circumstances to change, but they will *actively* attempt to maintain stability of self and behavior. They will not sit idly by and permit negative reactions from others to destroy their stable concept of themselves. In this theory, self-stability relies on congruency among three components: (1) a given aspect of the individuals' selves; (2) the individuals' perception of their behavior relative to that aspect; and (3) their beliefs about how other people behave toward them and feel toward them with regard to that aspect. Faced with a changing situation, the individual "actively uses techniques or mechanisms for maintaining his interpersonal environment so as to maximize congruency" (Secord and Backman, 1964:584). Such mechanisms include refusal to perceive negative feedback, avoidance of people apt to give negative feedback, devaluation of people apt to give negative feedback, and downgrading that particular aspect of the self. In one study, for example, a majority of people over 70 were found to identify with the description "middle-aged" rather than with "old" (Kuhlen, 1964a).

This theory is important for social gerontology because, if accurate, it would help explain how some older people can undergo significant reductions in their field of potential roles, and dramatic changes in their life situations—often changes most of us would label "bad"—and still retain a positive opinion of themselves. It would help also to explain some of the long-term consistency of personality mentioned earlier.

Rosow (1973) takes a somewhat different position. He assumes that without actual role playing there can be no social self or social identity. Rosow defines the self as a set of roles rather than as a set of ideas. He is not so much concerned with the internal aspects of personality as with the external system that controls the roles an individual can actually, physically lay claim to. Rosow assumes that role losses exclude older people from social participation and deprive them of social worth; that all older people experience such role losses and declines in prestige; that older people are unprepared for this sort of change; and that there are no roles to replace the ones lost. He attaches no social significance to any sort of *position* as a "former player of a given role." Rosow claims that this panorama represents "the social context of the aging self."

Other researchers have not found that very many older people are oriented toward what "people in general" think about them (Atchley, 1967; Cottrell and Atchley, 1969). On the contrary, even in the face of role loss, the individual usually retains enough familiar interpersonal pathways to his or her past to be able to demand and get prestige and respect for past role performance. And this ability is not merely a vagary of individual adjustment. It is a widespread aspect of the social structure in which older people live. Older people are generally not residentially mobile. They do not live in an anonymous mass society but rather in a specific community that they know well and in which they are known. Thus, in my opinion, the abstract processes Rosow describes, while logically sound, are not applicable to the social system of most older people. Rosow's analysis probably applies mainly to those older people who have encountered such extreme role loss that they have no primary group contacts left.

## SUMMARY

Social psychology concerns the interplay between the individual and his or her social environment. This chapter has dealt with the influence of age on the processes of socialization, the results of socialization, personality, and the self.

Socialization is a process that develops the individual socially so that he or she may participate in society. Because both society and the individual are constantly changing, socialization is a dialectic process that can never be completed. In later life, the individual is generally responsible for identifying his or her own needs for new information or skills and for initiating action to satisfy these needs. To the extent that older people have difficulty in getting what they need, this system is inadequate. Anticipatory socialization is a specific process aimed at preparation for a particular role. Many of the difficulties that might arise from role change in later life are minimized through informal anticipatory socialization. In addition, older adults are usually quite aware of how to negotiate or renegotiate ground rules in order to personalize the demands of social roles.

Socialization results in attitudes, values, and beliefs, among other things. We do not know how these results change with age, however; we can only say how the old differ from the young. Older people are neither consistently more positive nor consistently more negative than the young in terms of attitudes. Attitudes depend on the topic. Labels such as "conservative" or "liberal" are too inclusive to be very helpful in describing age differences in attitudes. The values of today's older people tend to emphasize social stability and achievement. The stereotypes concerning old age are generally negative and are believed by old and young alike.

Personality is a complex organization of mental capacities and tendencies that can be roughly subdivided into intrapsychic, cognitive, and interpersonal aspects. Personality is a complex mental system through which people are identified as individuals and through which they respond to the world around them. While certain elements of personality are unique to the individual, other elements of personality are common to large numbers of people. Social gerontology is concerned with the impact of aging on the common elements of personality.

Using the developmental approach, Neugarten found that the inner life of individuals became more important to them with age; that cognitive processes declined with age; and that competence in role performance and interpersonal skills showed little or no change with age. As people grew older, they displayed an increasing separation from the environment, and an increasing continuity, consistency, and simplicity of the personality.

The self is the intrapsychic aspect of personality that comprises the individual's thoughts and emotions about himself or herself. The self has two elements: (1) the *self-concept*, which relates to knowledge about oneself; and (2) *self-esteem*, which relates to feelings about oneself. *Social roles* are the expectations associated with a position in society, such as judge or mother. These expectations often become a part of the self-concept of the role player.

The self-concept tends to remain stable in later life. This stability is caused by the inward orientation the personality typically takes and by the fact that former roles can still be used as part of the self-concept.

Although role changes in later life force older people to rely on social interaction to establish self-esteem, any negative impact this reliance might have is probably largely offset by the defense mechanisms, such as selective perception, that older people use to protect their vulnerable self-esteem. Since self-esteem is the product of a comparison between self-concept and self-ideal, the older person can manipulate it by controlling the extent to which social interaction is allowed to influence self-concept.

Thus, while there are changes in self and personality in later life, they tend to be of consequence mainly for the person's inner orientations and tend to have little influence on his or her social functioning.

Given the conclusions of the various chapters in Part Two, it seems apparent that while older people do undergo certain significant physical and psychological changes with age, most older people find these changes more an inconvenience than a true handicap. These observations, of course, represent the "typical" case, and chronologically old people vary widely in terms of the symptoms of psychological aging. In terms of adequate social functioning, most people do not find themselves physically or psychologically disabled until the late seventies. Because it is socially rather than individually determined, social disability is an entirely different matter, however, and is the subject of the remainder of this book.

## SUGGESTIONS FOR FURTHER READING

Back, Kurt W. "Transition to Aging and the Self-Image." *Aging and Human Development* 2(1971):296–304.

Brim, Orville, and Stanton Wheeler. *Socialization After Childhood*. New York: Wiley, 1966.

Butler, Robert N. "The Life Review: An Interpretation of Reminiscence in the Aged." *Psychiatry 26*(1963):65–76.

Clark, Margaret. "The Anthropology of Aging, a New Area for Studies of Culture and Personality." *Gerontologist 7*(1967):55–64.

Dean, Lois R. "Aging and the Decline of Affect." *Journal of Gerontology 17*(1962):440–446.

Kalish, Richard A. *Late Adulthood: Perspectives of Human Development*. Monterey, Calif.: Brooks/Cole Publishing Company, 1975.

Kimmel, D. C. *Adulthood and Aging: An Interdisciplinary, Developmental View*. New York: Wiley, 1974.

Kohlberg, L. "Stages and Aging in Moral Development—Some Speculations." *Gerontologist 13*(1973):497–502.

Maas, H. S., and J. A. Kuypers. *From Thirty to Seventy*. San Francisco: Jossey-Bass, 1974.

Neugarten, Bernice L. "Personality and the Aging Process." *Gerontologist 12*(1972):9–15.

Riegel, Klaus F. "Personality Theory and Aging." In James E. Birren (ed.), *Handbook of Aging and the Individual*. Chicago: University of Chicago Press, 1959, pp. 797–851.

# Part Three
# Age Changes in Situational Context

The important psychological and biological changes that accompany old age are translated into an immediate reality in the various ongoing situations in which older people find themselves. The social situation is the total configuration of social factors influencing an individual's behavior or experience at a given point in time. A person's social situation determines how that individual fits into society. The social situation *is* society, from the individual's point of view, and research is greatly complicated by the fact that most people move in and among several different social situations.

Our concern is with situational changes that come with growing old. Chapter 5 presents an overview of situational changes that often occur in later life. Subsequent chapters deal more specifically with changes in health; financial status; occupational roles; death, dying, and widowhood; recreation and leisure; and personal independence and dependency. The final chapter in Part Three deals with personal adjustment to these changes.

# 5

# The Changing Social Context of Later Life

Writings about later life often give the impression that the individual is firmly in the grips of inexorable physical, psychological, and social processes and is allowed little room for individual or group initiative or maneuvering. It is easy to lose sight of the fact that while our abstractions concerning these processes are built up from individual or group experience, the categories we use are often intellectual conveniences or necessities and are not concrete elements of the social world. Thus, we read that having a certain social role does this or that to a person. Of course, what is meant is that certain concrete behavior or concrete ideas are more likely to occur in the lives of people who play a given social role. The term *social role* is merely a convenient shorthand that implies a certain pattern of behavior or a particular situation.

The earlier edition of this book stressed role change as the central element of situational change in the later phases of life. Certainly role changes are important and deserve a good bit of attention. However, roles are not the only elements of social structure that can change in later life. Moreover, the process of role change itself is governed by various definitions of the life course and by the age norms associated with it.

The term *social situation* is a general one that has been used by sociologists to emphasize that, for the individual, roles, groups, and norms have little meaning apart from the particular time and place in which the individual encounters them. The immediate social environment is very important in translating an abstract social order into concrete reality for the individual.

This chapter presents an overview of how the various elements of the social situation may change in later life. The life course, age norms, social roles, groups, and physical space are all important aspects of the social situation related to aging.


## THE LIFE COURSE

Social structure is age-differentiated. That is, assignment or access to various roles or groups is partly determined by age (Riley et al., 1972). The **life course** is an idealized and age-related progression or sequence of roles and group memberships that individuals are expected to follow as they mature and move through life. Thus, there is an age to go to school, an age to marry, an age to "settle down," and so forth. For example, Neugarten, Moore, and Lowe (1965) found considerable consensus among adults that people should marry in their early twenties and that men should be settled in a career by the time they are 24 to 26.

But the life course in reality is neither simple nor rigidly prescribed. For one thing, various subcultures (whether based on sex, social class, ethnicity, race, or region of the country) tend to develop somewhat unique ideals concerning the timing of the life course. For example, male auto workers tend to favor retirement in the mid-fifties, while college professors tend to prefer the late sixties as the age for retirement. In addition, even within subcultures, there are often several alternatives. For example, having made a decision to attend college, a young person often has a wide selection of institutions from which to choose. Thus, like a road map, the abstract concept of the life course in reality is composed of a great many alternative routes to alternative destinations.

Just as birth cohorts become successively more differentiated psychologically as they age, the life course represents an increasingly more complex maze of age-linked alternatives. Although later in life the options may diminish somewhat because of social and physical aging, the older population is considerably more differentiated than the young. Ten-year-olds are a much more socially homogeneous category than 70-year-olds are.

Yet even with the increased complexity of the life course with age, certain generally accepted standards serve as a sort of master timetable for the entire population. Even though there are many exceptions and variations, most Americans start school, finish school, get married, have children, experience the "empty nest," and retire, each within a span surrounding a particular chronological age, the age at which these events are *supposed* to happen. Most of us spend our lives reasonably on schedule, and when we get off schedule we are motivated to get back on again (Neugarten and Datan, 1973).

The various stages of the life course are brought to life for the individual in three ways. First, they are related to more specific patterns such as the occupational career or family development. Second, specific age norms also accompany various phases of the life course. And finally, people are forced to make particular types of choices during given phases of the life course.

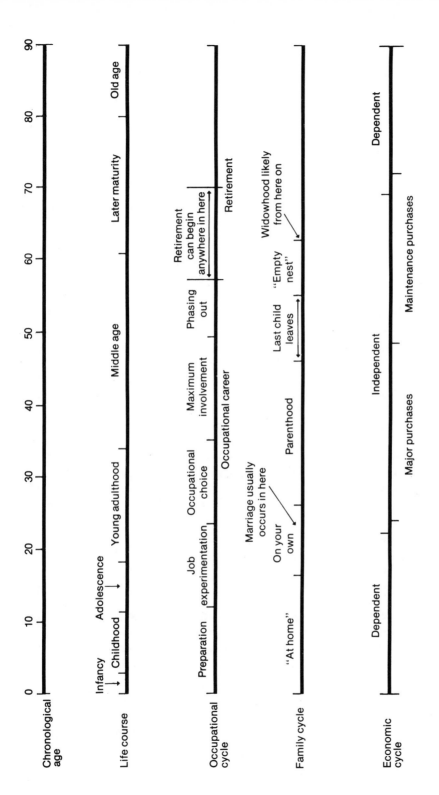

**Figure 5-1** Relationships among age, life cycle, occupational cycle, and family cycle. (These relationships fluctuate widely for specific individuals and for various social categories such as ethnic groups or social classes.) *Source:* Atchley (1975c).

Figure 5-1 shows, very roughly, how the life course is related to chronological age, occupations, the family, and the economy. More dimensions could be added, but the important point is that various social institutions tend to prescribe their own career cycles and that these cycles are related to the abstract conception of the life course.

## Age Norms

**Age norms** are tied to the life course and as such constitute the social *role* of the person in a given life stage. Age norms tell people what people in a given life stage are allowed to do and to be and what they are required to do and to be. Many age norms come down to us through tradition. On the other hand, legal age norms are often the result of compromise and negotiation. A series of assumptions underlie age norms. These assumptions, often uninformed, concern what people in a given life stage are capable of—not just what they *ought* to do, but what they *can* do. Thus, both children and older people experience limited opportunities because it is *assumed* that they are not strong enough, not experienced or educated enough, or not capable of adequately mature adult judgments.

Yet many age norms make useful and valid distinctions. It is probably true that the overwhelming majority of 10-year-olds are not mature enough to hold political office. And few of us would want to drive automobiles if 6-year-olds were allowed to take to the roads. Thus, physical and social maturation represent real limits on what people are capable of. In childhood, these standards can be applied with only a minimum of injustice. But beginning with adolescence it becomes increasingly difficult to justify the essentially arbitrary nature of many age norms. And the greater the gap between the actual level of individual functioning and the level implied by the age norm, the higher the likelihood that age norms will be seen as unjust. Because so many older people function at an adequate adult level, feelings of injustice at disqualifying age norms are probably as common among older people as among adolescents, although research is needed to examine this question.

Age norms are generally tied to stages of the life course. Individuals are tied to phases of the life course by chronological age, seniority, physical appearance, or level of physical and social functioning. A combination of these characteristics often is used to assign life stages. However, chronological age is a dominant force throughout the life span.

Age norms can tell a person what to do, what not to do, or what is allowable (but not necessary) to do. Age norms sometimes operate very generally to specify dress, personal appearance, or demeanor in a wide variety of cases. Other age norms govern approach, entry, incumbency, or exit from social roles, groups, or social situations (Atchley, 1975c).

Various mechanisms secure conformity to age norms. Socialization teaches people how to apply age norms to themselves. If they do not conform, friends, neighbors, and associates can be counted on to apply informal pressures. In the formal realm, regulations bring bureaucratic authority to bear. And finally, laws put the full power of the state behind age norms. For example, the idea of retiring at some point in the sixties is supported at every level along this continuum.

## Decision Demands

The sometimes chaotic nature of the alternatives presented by various life courses has been mentioned earlier. This chaos is minimized to some degree by sex, social class, ethnicity, and so forth. Age norms serve effectively to locate people in life stages. But how do people get into *specific* situations? It is impossible to assign people to each and every niche in complex, rapidly changing societies. In American society, one type of norm—the decision demand—forces the individual to participate in the job of matching people with slots in the organization of society.

Decision demands require that selections be made from an age-linked field of possibilities.[1] For example, after completing preparatory education, young adults usually enter a period of job experimentation. The field of possibilities expands dramatically immediately after graduation (certification) and continues to expand while the individual gains job experience. But there is an increasing expectation that people will find positions of employment into which they will settle; and during this period the field of jobs for which they are eligible may slowly contract. Contraction also occurs as jobs are selected by others in the age cohort. For many jobs, career[2] tracks are difficult to begin after 45. For others, it is difficult to break in after age 35.

Decision demands tend to be concentrated in the first half of the life course. That is, individuals are *required* to make choices and select their "career tracks" in all sorts of areas—education, employment, family, community, voluntary associations, and so on. Life-styles developed before or during middle age tend to persist as long as health and money hold out. Thus, older people who want to switch tracks or get involved in new areas are often confronted with the fact that the available slots were taken earlier by their age peers. We will discuss more examples of this problem in Part Four.

## SOCIAL ROLES

Social roles are very important, for *individuals* often define themselves in terms of these roles, and their places in society are determined by them. Roles are the means through which social structure is recreated in individuals and through which individuals function in society.

The term *positions* refers to slots in the organization of society that are based on common attributes, as in the case of black people or youngsters, or on similarities in behavior, as in the case of judges. The position of *older person* is based on a common attribute, age. By contrast, the position *computer operator* is based on behavior that computer operators have in common.

[1]For a more detailed discussion of decision demands, see Atchley (1975c).
[2]The term *career* as used here refers to experience in any particular role attached to an ongoing group.

---

## RESEARCH ILLUSTRATION 6

## THE ROLE COUNT[3]

### Elaine Cumming and William E. Henry

As a part of the Kansas City Study of Adult Life, Cumming and Henry reported age differences in the number of active roles played. Their subjects consisted of a random sample of 104 Kansas City men and women aged 50 or over and a sample of 107 men and women aged 70 and over. Interviews were used to establish the number of active roles for each subject. Each respondent got one score each for being a household member (if he or she did not live alone), kin (one score for each category of kin interacted with regularly), friend, neighbor, worker, churchgoer, or organization or club meeting attender, or for being a specific role player such as shopper or customer. The scores ranged from 1 to 9, and were distributed as follows:

| Number of Roles | Number of Respondents | Percent |
|---|---|---|
| 1–2 | 8 | 3.8 |
| 3–4 | 60 | 28.4 |
| 5–6 | 93 | 44.1 |
| 7–8 | 46 | 21.8 |
| 9 | 4 | 1.9 |
| Total | 211 | 100.0 |

Table 5-1 shows the percentages by age and sex for those who scored 6 or more on the role count. The pattern for the total is quite stable until age 65, when a sharp and significant decline in role count begins, and this general pattern holds for both men and women.

**TABLE 5-1**
**Percent with a Large Number of Roles, by Age and Sex**

| Age | Total N | Total Percent with a Large Number of Roles | Males N | Males Percent with a Large Number of Roles | Females N | Females Percent with a Large Number of Roles |
|---|---|---|---|---|---|---|
| 50–54 | 36 | 61.1 | 19 | 68.4 | 17 | 52.9 |
| 55–59 | 34 | 61.8 | 18 | 61.1 | 16 | 62.5 |
| 60–64 | 34 | 58.8 | 19 | 47.4 | 15 | 73.3 |
| 65–69 | 31 | 38.7 | 12 | 50.0 | 19 | 31.6 |
| 70–74 | 50 | 22.0 | 25 | 20.0 | 25 | 24.0 |
| 75 and over | 26 | 7.7 | 14 | 7.1 | 12 | 8.3 |
| Total | 211 | 41.7 | 107 | 42.0 | 104 | 41.2 |

[3] Adapted from Cumming and Henry (1961):38–45, 248–50.

Table 5-2 shows percentage of those interviewed who hold various types of roles, classified by age and sex.

As expected, roles became fewer with age for both men and women. For men, loss of formal roles such as worker or organization member accounted for most of the reduction. Women tended to lose these roles *plus* their roles as spouse and household member. From these data, it appears that women compensated for widowhood by increasing their contact with friends, while men compensated by remarrying. Older women were much more likely to live alone than older men.

**TABLE 5-2**
**Percent with Various Active Roles, by Age and Sex**

| Age and Sex | N | Roles | | | | | | |
|---|---|---|---|---|---|---|---|---|
| | | Spouse | Household | Kin | Friend | Neighbor | Worker | Organization |
| Males | 107 | | | | | | | |
| 50–54 | 19 | 89.5 | 100.0 | 68.4 | 73.7 | 68.4 | 94.7 | 36.8 |
| 55–59 | 18 | 88.9 | 94.4 | 61.1 | 50.0 | 66.7 | 100.0 | 55.6 |
| 60–64 | 19 | 84.2 | 84.2 | 63.2 | 73.7 | 47.4 | 78.9 | 21.1 |
| 65–69 | 12 | 91.7 | 100.0 | 83.3 | 83.3 | 66.7 | 33.3 | 33.3 |
| 70–74 | 25 | 64.0 | 76.0 | 76.0 | 72.0 | 48.0 | 24.0 | 20.0 |
| 75 and over | 14 | 78.6 | 85.7 | 71.4 | 71.4 | 35.7 | 21.4 | 7.1 |
| Females | 104 | | | | | | | |
| 50–54 | 17 | 82.4 | 82.4 | 64.7 | 70.6 | 58.8 | 82.4 | 35.3 |
| 55–59 | 16 | 62.5 | 87.5 | 87.5 | 75.0 | 75.0 | 31.3 | 43.8 |
| 60–64 | 15 | 60.0 | 86.7 | 80.0 | 66.7 | 73.3 | 53.6 | 53.3 |
| 65–69 | 19 | 36.8 | 57.9 | 52.6 | 63.2 | 57.9 | 26.3 | 36.8 |
| 70–74 | 25 | 28.0 | 52.0 | 56.0 | 60.0 | 52.0 | 16.0 | 32.0 |
| 75 and over | 12 | 16.7 | 50.0 | 50.0 | 83.3 | 50.0 | 16.7 | 25.0 |

A *social role* can mean any one of three things: (1) what is *expected* of a person in a given position; (2) what *most* people *do* in a given position; or (3) what a *particular* person does in a given position. For any given position, these three aspects of the social role may coincide or differ, depending on hundreds of factors. The first meaning is by far the most frequently used, but the gap between ideal (first meaning) and actual behavior (second and third meanings) is usually great enough to be significant. The reason most discussion of roles centers around expectations is that expectations are more general and therefore easier to discuss than is actual role behavior.

Roles are attached to positions. What is expected of us depends in large part on the *positions* we occupy (everyone occupies many positions, often simultaneously). Thus, we often need not know much about individuals to be able to predict their behavior; we need only know their position. For example, you do not need to be a psychoanalyst to predict at least 80 percent of the on-the-job behavior of a baseball umpire. Not many positions must be adhered to *that* rigidly; nevertheless, the fact that we all play our roles within certain bounds gives a comfortable predictability to human behavior.

The importance of any position and its role is reflected by the prestige, the wealth, or the influence attached to the position. Most positions have some degree of at least one of these elements; and some positions have a great deal of all three. Positions such as physician, state governor, or U.S. Supreme Court Justice tend to possess all three elements to a high degree, while positions such as sharecropper, window washer, or bartender tend to possess these elements to a very slight degree, if at all.[4]

In American society, the positions of older person, older man, or older woman do not in themselves enjoy much prestige, status, wealth, or influence. This is not to say that no older people have these characteristics; it merely means that if an older person has wealth or prestige or influence it is because he or she simultaneously occupies *some other position* to which these benefits are attached. Former President Eisenhower enjoyed a great deal of prestige and influence in his old age, but these qualities adhered to him not because he was old, but because he was a former president and a revered military chief.

To put the position of older person into proper perspective, one need only ask: Do people get wealthy, revered, or influential simply by growing old? The answer must be a resounding no. As a matter of fact, if anything happens to people as a result of getting old, it will probably be that the wealth, influence, or prestige of their other positions will *decrease*. Being defined as old may even cause them to be *removed* from some of their other positions. In America today, older people generally occupy a position of lower prestige than the middle aged; for example, they possess less economic and political power.

The position of old people in America has often been compared unfavorably with that of old people in other societies. In imperial Chinese society, for example, as individuals aged, they were said to have been given more and more respect and deference. There is reason to doubt, however, that in earlier times the aged of any society were uniformly valued as a category. Their status has probably always had both positive and negative elements, as shown in a study that analyzed the position of the aged of three traditional villages in India with regard to prestige, authority, power, and security (Neugarten, 1966:173). A wide gap was found to exist between the ideal norms and actual practices. Older people lost status with the death of a spouse; many felt neglected; and only a very few older people of the upper class played leadership roles in the village. After middle age, control of family affairs and participation in community affairs was generally relinquished. This picture is not unlike descriptions of the status of the aged in contemporary western societies.

Most people consider the twenties and thirties to be "the best years" of their lives, and both old and young people attach a negative value to the concept of "old age," although the old themselves are not quite so negative as the young. The older person thus occupies a position that tends to be downgraded by everyone.

The influence of the relatively low status of older people may be felt and dealt with in several ways. The individual's opinion of himself or herself may be lowered —however, many older people avoid this possibility by not seeing themselves as old. Also, the people with whom individuals interact may react to them differently once the

---

[4]For a more detailed discussion of role theory, see Biddle and Thomas (1966).

individuals become old—but older people who do not consider themselves old usually do not see others perceiving them as old. Thus, selective perception tends to minimize some of the impact of the status loss associated with moving from middle age to later maturity.

But older people cannot very easily misperceive the fact that *being old may make them ineligible to occupy positions they value.* Age is important in role behavior because age acts as one of the primary rules of eligibility for various positions. Whether we are merely *assigned* to the positions we occupy or whether we must have the opportunity to *achieve* them, we do not simply occupy or take over positions. They are usually opened to us as a result of our having met certain entry criteria. In most societies, particular positions, rights, duties, privileges, and obligations are set aside for children, adolescents, young adults, the middle-aged, and the old. Certain behavior is regarded as appropriate for each age group. In our culture, the primary entry criteria are health, age, sex, color, experience, and educational achievement. Entry criteria may be gradually modified, but in everyday life, most people abide by the rules.

Thus, as we pass through the life course, the field of positions for which we are eligible keeps changing. Young boys can *legitimately* be members of the neighborhood gang, pupils, and unemployed—all things they cannot be as adults. As young men they can be auto drivers, barflies, and voters—all things they cannot be as children. As older adults they can be retired, be great-grandfathers, or pretend to be deaf—all things they cannot do as young adults. Of course, age also works negatively. For example, older people are often prevented from holding a job, even if they want to.

In addition to governing eligibility for positions, age is important as a position in itself, and certain expectations are associated with it. Thus, an "older person" is expected to behave differently from a "younger person." For example, an older woman who attempted the latest teen-age dance at a party of youngsters she was chaperoning would be regarded with dismay, primarily because she would have behaved contrary to the expectations of "dignity and refinement" we hold for older women. Thus, aging changes not only the roles we are expected to play, but also the *manner* in which we are expected to play them.

## Retirement

Most people experience a number of role changes as they pass middle age. Perhaps the first, and for some the most important, change occurs at retirement. **Retirement** is the institutionalized separation of individuals from their occupational positions with a continuation of income based on prior years of service. Age is usually the prime consideration in such separation, although health may also be a big factor. Usually a certain latitude is given to allow the individual to choose the point at which he or she retires, sometimes as early as 50 and often as late as 70. Over age 65, about 70 percent of men and about 90 percent of women do not have an occupational position.

When people leave their occupations, many changes occur in their lives regardless of whether they retired voluntarily or were forced to retire. But, as we shall see in Chapter 9, retirement not only means giving up a role but also taking up a new one. Many people see retirement as a period devoid of challenge. However, the self-sufficiency required of retired people is certainly a challenge to many, if not most, retired people.

Retirement also influences the other roles an individual plays, but the direction of his influence is unpredictable. For example, some marriages are enhanced by retirement, while others are subverted. Some organizations shun retired members, while others rely heavily on them.

To some people, retirement represents a crisis, a world turned upside down. To others, retirement is merely the carrying out of a long-awaited and well-planned change. At this point it appears that two-thirds of those who retire do so with no great difficulty either in giving up their job roles or in taking up the retirement role (Atchley, 1976b).

## Widowhood

Widowhood is another role change that is commonplace among older people. In 1970, more than half the women and 17 percent of the men over 65 were widows or widowers. Unlike marriage, widowhood is a position that allows no fulfillment of sexual needs, an important item to many older people. It also diminishes the possibility of gaining identity through the accomplishments or positions of the spouse. Widowhood also marks the loss of an important type of intimate interaction based on mutual interests. For example, the widow often replaces one intimate, extensive, and interdependent relationship with her husband by adding several transitory and independent relationships with other widows. The case of Mrs. Willoughby is reasonably typical.

> Mrs. Willoughby is having problems adjusting to widowhood and compensating for restrictions in her social, as well as physical, life space after three decades of marriage and joint employment with her husband. Together, they managed an apartment building. She has no children. Today, her most regular contacts are with a younger sister, but there is little comfort in the relationship, for the sister is condescending toward Mrs. Willoughby and her abilities. Mrs. Willoughby feels she thinks too much about herself: "I just think about sitting here and vegetating. I didn't used to have time to think of myself before. I had my husband and we were busy taking care of the apartment house we managed." With the loss of her husband, Mrs. Willoughby's financial situation as well as her health began to deteriorate. She could not continue to manage the apartment building without her husband, and so she is now living on her savings and some Social Security benefits. She would like to work and try to find companionship, perhaps with a man, but her sister has persuaded her she could probably not succeed at either endeavor. She does have misgivings about her sister's wisdom in these things, but not enough self-confidence to act on her own initiative, for she is used to depending on the judgments of others: "I had to do everything my husband said because he was the boss, although I did resent it deeply." In near desperation, she seems to feel there *must* be a way for her to get some of the most pressing needs met; that somewhere, close at hand, there must be a new way of life—if only she could discover it. She would like to make a grasp at it: "I want to do something, but I don't know just what it is or how to go about it." She constantly chides

herself for minutes spent in late-morning sleep when she could be doing other things, but she admits frankly she does not know what those things might be (Clark and Anderson, 1967:408).

The role changes that occur with retirement and widowhood are not necessarily unwelcome to the individual. Often people give up the responsibilities of work happily and view retirement as a period of increased fulfillment. Likewise, after the initial shock of grief wears off, many widows enjoy the sense of freedom and relief from responsibility that comes with widowhood. For many, widowhood means a reunion with friends who have been widowed for some time. In fact, a frequent complaint of married older women is that their family obligations shut them out of many of the activities their widowed friends enjoy. Blau (1961) found that this is particularly likely to happen to widows over 70. Nevertheless, these changes still require that the individual adjust.

Perhaps the most significant factor influencing the adjustment of widows relates to the number of other roles available to widows in a given society. Lopata (1972) found that the more densely settled and the more urbanized the area of residence, the larger the field of available women's roles and the more freedom widows had in choosing among them.

### Dependency

Perhaps one of the most dreaded role changes accompanying old age involves **dependency**, the shift from the role of independent adult to that of dependent adult.[5] Older people, both in the community and in institutions, fear becoming dependent, whether physically or financially—either way, it is a difficult position for most adults to accept. This fear is easy to understand. We are taught from birth that becoming independent and self-sufficient is a primary goal. This is a deeply ingrained value for most people, and it is not surprising that they are hostile to the idea of giving up their autonomy and becoming dependent on others.

Dependency is all the more difficult to accept because of the changes it brings in other roles. For example, older people are sometimes forced by necessity to fall back on their children. This need strains the parent–child relationship for a number of reasons. Parents sometimes resist and often resent having to depend on their children. They may become angry and frustrated by the changes in interaction brought on by the reversal of positions. They may feel guilty because they feel that they should not be dependent. Their children, now adults, may also resent having to provide for both their own children and their parents, yet they may feel guilty for having this resentment. And finally, the spouses of the children may not willingly accept the diversion of family resources to aged parents.

What makes the position of ''dependent'' especially difficult is the set of expectations attached to it. Dependent people in our society are supposed to defer to

[5]While psychologists use *dependency* to refer to a psychological state, the usage here refers to a position and role characterized by the necessity to rely on others either physically or financially.

their benefactors, to be eternally grateful for what they receive, and to give up their rights to lead their own lives. We demand this behavior of our children, the poor, or any other dependent group. Is it any wonder, then, that older people, often having spent as many as 50 years as independent adults, rebel at the idea of assuming a dependent position? Interestingly, while many older Americans find themselves having to ask their children for some kind of help at one point or another, Shanas (1962) found that on balance older people tend to *give* more help than they receive.

## Disability and Sickness

Disability is another new role that older people are likely to experience. There are varying degrees of disability, and when disability becomes extreme, it usually turns into dependency. But even for the many older people whose disabilities have not reached that stage, disability restricts the number of roles one can play and changes other people's reactions. Over a third of the older population of the United States has some disability serious enough to limit their ability to work, keep house, or engage in other major activities (Wilder, 1973).

Sickness is similar to disability in that its influence is felt mainly through a limitation of role playing. Good health, or absence of sickness or disability, operates alongside age and sex as a major criterion for eligibility for various positions. Most positions outside one's circle of family and friends require activity that is impossible for severely sick or disabled people.

It has long been recognized in our society that sick people occupy a unique position. They are not expected to hold jobs, go to school, or otherwise meet the obligations of other positions, and they are often dependent on others for care. If they play the sick role long enough, they may be permanently excluded from some of their other positions, such as their jobs, offices in voluntary associations, or positions as family breadwinners. Sick people are usually exempt from social responsibilities, are not expected to care for themselves, and are expected to need medical help. The more serious the prognosis, the more likely they are to find themselves being treated as dependents.

Whether people are defined as sick partly depends on the seriousness and certainty of the prognosis. Even if they have a functional or physical impairment, individuals are less likely to be allowed to play the sick role if the prognosis is known not to be serious. Yet sick people are often expected to want to get well, and actually to do so, regardless of the prognosis (Gordon, 1966).

The importance of aging to sickness and disability is of course the fact that as age increases, the probability of disease, illness, or disability becomes greater. For example, as Table 5-3 shows, people aged 65 and over are much more likely to suffer limitations of activity due to chronic conditions.

## The Role of the Institutional Resident

When illness and disability become a serious handicap, many older people take up residence in nursing homes and homes for the aged. While only about 4 percent of the older population lives in institutional facilities at any one time, those who do enter an institution usually encounter important role changes. In the institutional setting, opportunities for useful activity, leisure activities, contacts with the outside world, and privacy are all less frequent than they are outside. Coupled with the extremely negative attitude of most older people toward living in an institution, these changes create significant obstacles to continuity of role playing.

**TABLE 5-3**
**Percent Distribution**
**of Persons by Activity Limitation Status**
**Due to Chronic Conditions by Age: United States, 1969–1970**

| Age | Total | No Activity Limitation | With Limitations, but Not in Major Activity | With Limitation in Amount or Kind of Major Activity | Unable to Carry on Major Activity |
|-----|-------|------------------------|---------------------------------------------|-----------------------------------------------------|-----------------------------------|
| All ages | 100.0 | 88.3 | 2.6 | 6.2 | 2.9 |
| Under 17 | 100.0 | 97.3 | 1.2 | 1.3 | 0.2 |
| 17–44 | 100.0 | 92.4 | 2.6 | 4.1 | 0.9 |
| 45–64 | 100.0 | 80.5 | 3.8 | 11.2 | 4.4 |
| 64 and over | 100.0 | 57.7 | 5.2 | 20.7 | 16.4 |

*Source:* Adapted from Wilder, 1973:17.

## Other Important Role Changes

There are also changes with age in roles that continue into later life. For example religious participation declines. Overall participation in voluntary associations also declines in terms of both the number of memberships held *and* the number of meetings attended. Contacts with friends appear to be maintained until about age 75, but after that there is a decline.

Thus far, the changes in position and role that we have found to be associated with aging would be defined by most people as changes for the worse. They represent a constriction of the individual's life space, a diminution of the number of positions such as breadwinner, husband, or employee to negatively valued positions such as widow, dependent, or sick person. While these changes are not without their positive aspects, they still appear generally negative overall to most people.

Are there no positive changes in position as one grows older? The answer is, yes, there are a few. For one thing, people appear to take a stronger interest in politics in their later years. Voting percentages peak at about age 62, and people over 70 as a group turn out over 75 percent to vote in presidential elections, as compared with about 60 percent for those aged 25. This same pattern exists with regard to party identification, or interest in political affairs. Older people have substantially higher representation among public officials in the United States (both elected and appointed) than among most other occupations. Thus, while only a small fraction of the population engages actively in politics, opportunities for increased participation seem to be present *for a few* older people in this area.

Older people may join special clubs such as Golden Age Clubs or Senior Centers. Yet seldom more than 3 to 5 percent of the older people in a given community join such organizations. There appears to be a widespread reluctance on the part of older people to identify themselves as old. One 70-year-old, when asked if she belonged to the local Senior Center, told me, "Who wants to be with those old fogies all the time?" This reluctance is likely to hamper attempts to form any kind of organization that is widely regarded as being for older people. Thus, while membership in such clubs is a position that opens up to people as they grow older, it is also a position that most older people tend to reject.

In their later years, people have much more time to devote to leisure roles. Most older people spend more time in leisure activity than on daily maintenance activities such as grooming, housekeeping, and cooking. Specific leisure activities that increase as age increases are watching television, visiting, reading, and gardening. Television watching occupies more of the older person's time than any other single activity, and particularly for those who live alone. Older people spend about 2 hours a day visiting, either inside or outside their own household. Time spent with friends tends to decline from the teens through the fifties, but tends to rise again after age 60. Reading is a more important activity to the old than to the young. As an activity, gardening tends to increase from the teens through the sixties. Generally speaking, then, the increase in time available for leisure practically forces a role change in this area.

## Groups

Much will be said in Part Four of this book about how older people relate to various types of groups. For now, our interest will center on how groups influence the individual's social situation.

Obviously, when people lose jobs through retirement or lose spouses through death, their changes in roles parallel changes in groups. However, certain changes do not correspond to gross role changes. To begin with, individuals may gain or lose power in a group, even though their role nominally may remain the same. Thus, an older member of a board of directors may experience a change in influence, and a retired executive may find it difficult to maintain roles in community organizations, having lost an economic power base in the community. Such changes are often subtle, but their impact on the social situation of an individual may be dramatic. Group memberships sometimes interlock in such a way that a status change in one group changes the individual's relationship to other groups. For example, Atchley (1976b) found that retirement reduced contacts with friends among retired telephone company men because interaction was tied to the work place, but increased contacts with friends among retired men teachers because it was not.

Another important situational issue concerns the fact that some groups have life spans and grow old along with their members. For example, in a small midwestern town that I studied, the American Legion Auxiliary was made up of women whose husbands had been in World War I. In 1971 the organization had five members, all widows ranging in age from 78 to 84. The group met frequently and considered each other as close friends. They relied on each other heavily for companionship and exchange of small services. In 1972, two of the group members died, one of whom had been a dominant influence in the group. The remaining group members found it difficult to carry on community service functions. But more important, they found it more difficult to fill their needs for stimulation and companionship within the group. Because new members are not being recruited, this group will eventually disappear.

In groups that recruit new members from upcoming age cohorts, change brings another sort of situational change. Older members of voluntary associations sometimes complain that the goals of the organization have changed or that the type of person being recruited is "not my kind of people." In such cases, nominal continuity of role playing masks some important changes in social situation.

## Environments

People play social roles in particular places, and part of how they feel about their role performance is influenced by the appropriateness of the environment. Aging can potentially bring three types of environmental change: work place, housing, and community. How people cope with the loss of contact with a familiar environment is a neglected aspect of gerontology research. However, it is safe to say that some people develop strong feelings about places and the things in them, and environmental change is an important type of situational change for these people.

Retired people often express the feeling of missing a familiar work place. Even if the work environment was not pleasant, at least in most cases it was mastered, and this feeling of mastery is important to many people. Also, social scientists tend to neglect the fact that people often personify machines and develop relationships with them. A ship or even a cantankerous furnace may seem like an old friend. In addition, skills associated with work may not be easily exercised in other settings. A retired salesman can use his verbal skills anywhere, but a retired printer cannot easily transfer his skills into other settings.

Few older people change housing in later life, and even fewer change communities. Those who do may experience dramatic situational change. People become attached to various aspects of their dwellings—the door that has to be opened just right, the pencil marks on the closet door that mark a child's growth, the stain on the carpet from a wedding reception. When a person lives in the same place for a long time, the environment grows rich in cues to the past. Of course, feelings about this past may as easily be negative as positive. In addition, the routines of role playing to some extent also depend on the environment. Being a wife in a high-rise apartment building may be different from being a wife in a single-family home.

It takes time to get to know a new community—how to get around, what facilities are there, who the influential people are, and so on. Older people who change communities often must disconnect themselves from a myriad of long-standing role relationships, and reestablishing oneself in a new community is always difficult and sometimes impossible. More than anything else, the potential negative impact of migration on the individual's social situation and integration into the community serves to keep older people from changing residence even in the face of strong pressures to do so (Goldscheider, 1971).

Movement to an institution is sometimes a necessary response to the symptoms of physical aging, and as such it is an age-related change in environment, probably the first that comes to mind. However, at most about 20 percent of older people ever experience such moves.

## SUMMARY

This chapter explored how the immediate social context or environment of the individual changes with age. The social situation of the older person is structured by the life course, age norms, past career decisions, role changes, changes in the individual's relationship to various groups, and changes in the physical environment. Each of these elements changes with age.

The life course is an age-related, ideal progression of slots in society's organization that people are expected to follow as they move through their biological life spans. There are many such ideal progressions based on subcultural differences and on the large number of equivalent choices usually available in the early adult stages of the life course. Most people conform to the schedule mandated by their particular subcultures, and when people get off schedule, they usually try to get back on.

Age norms constitute the social role of people in various life stages. They tell individuals in a given life stage what they are required to do, what they must not do, and what they are allowed to do. Age norms come down mainly through culture and are often based on inaccurate assumptions about human capabilities. People are assigned to phases of life by chronological age, seniority, physical appearance, or level of physical or social functioning, but chronological age is usually dominant. Various mechanisms of social control insure conformity to age norms.

People are forced to participate in the process of matching themselves to slots in society by the decision demand, a type of age norm that sets a time interval within which career choices must be made and after which opportunities become progressively more limited. Decision demands tend to be concentrated in the first half of the life course; older people have fewer opportunities to switch tracks or begin new careers.

In general, social roles are composed of the rights and duties of persons who occupy a given position. The role specifies not only what is expected of the role player, but also what he or she can expect in return.

The position of older person in urban–industrial societies is a negatively valued one. That is, no highly desirable rewards are gained by occupying the position. Yet it is impossible to live a long life without eventually becoming an "older person."

Age is a prime criterion of eligibility for entry into and maintenance of most desirable positions in urban–industrial societies. This norm is the strongest single link between aging and an individual's social roles. In addition, as individuals enter the latter part of the life course, they find that they are expected to change the manner in which they play even the most familiar roles.

Retirement, widowhood, dependency, disability, sickness, and institutionaliza-tion are some major role changes that accompany later life. Each of these, as well as many other role changes, will be discussed in more detail in the remainder of Part Three. Taken together, they represent very significant changes in the situation that individuals confront as they grow old.

Role change can affect group membership and vice versa. In addition, subtle changes can occur in an individual's relationship to groups even though his or her role may remain essentially the same. The individual's influence may either grow or decline with age, depending on the group. Lost group memberships may influence relations with other groups. Sometimes groups grow old and die along with the membership. In other cases, orientation to the group shifts as the composition of the membership changes.

Finally, environment is an important, but neglected, aspect of the social situation. Roles are played in specific places, and people can become quite attached to places and the things in them. Retirement usually brings a loss of relationship to the work place. Residential mobility creates a new housing situation and sometimes a new community situation as well. Institutionalization is without doubt potentially the most dramatic environmental change that older people experience in later life.

Thus, the elements of the individual's social situation are interconnected. Change in any one of them requires some degree of adjustment by the individual.

## SUGGESTIONS FOR FURTHER READING

Atchley, Robert C. "The Life Course, Age Grading, and Age-Linked Demands for Decision Making." In Nancy Datan and Leon H. Ginsberg (eds.), *Life-Span Developmental Psychology: Normative Life Crises*. New York: Academic Press, 1975, pp. 261–278.
———. *The Social Forces in Later Life*. (2nd ed.) Belmont, Calif.: Wadsworth, 1976.
Bengtson, Vern L., M. J. Furlong, and R. S. Laufer. "Time, Aging, and the Continuity of Social Structure: Themes and Issues in Generational Analysis." *Journal of Social Issues 30* (1974): 1–30.
Neugarten, Bernice L., and Nancy Datan. "Sociological Perspectives on the Life Cycle." In Paul B. Baltes and K. Warner Schaie (eds.), *Life-Span Developmental Psychology: Personality and Socialization*. New York: Academic Press, 1973, pp. 53–69.
———, and Joan W. Moore. "The Changing Age-Status System." In Bernice L. Neugarten (ed.), *Middle Age and Aging*. Chicago: University of Chicago Press, 1968, pp. 5–21.
Riley, Matilda W. "Social Gerontology and the Age Stratification of Society." *Gerontologist 11* (1971): 79–87.
Williams, Richard H. "Changing Status, Roles and Relationships." In Clark Tibbitts (ed.), *Handbook of Social Gerontology*. Chicago: University of Chicago Press, 1960, pp. 261–297.
Wood, V. "Age-Appropriate Behavior for Older People." *Gerontologist 11* (1971): 74–78.

# 6
# Health

Health is a central factor in everyone's life. Most people are fortunate enough to be able to take good health for granted. However, health affects life satisfaction, participation in most social roles, and the way we are treated by others. It would be difficult to overstate the importance of good health for a successful and satisfying life.

In later life, declining health cuts across all social, political, and economic lines. Health becomes a major influence on participation in the family, the job, the community, and in leisure pursuits, and health needs absorb a larger amount *and* proportion of older people's incomes as they grow older. In fact, a large proportion of the medical industry's facilities and services are geared toward meeting the needs of people with diseases and infirmities that are most common in old age.

Health is obviously a major influence on the older person's situation. Social gerontology is therefore concerned with the continuum of health all the way from good to bad, with programs for health improvement and rehabilitation, and with the importance of health to the life situations of older people.

The term *health* is complex and difficult to define. It refers not merely to the absence of disease or disability, but also to more positive things, such as mental, physical, and social well-being. It is most useful to look at health as a continuum. At the one end is complete social, physical, and mental well-being and at the other end is death. Figure 6-1 shows several stages along the health continuum.

Ideally, good health would be measured in terms of social, physical and mental well-being, but since these conditions are very difficult to measure, good health is operationally defined as the absence of disease or infirmity. This operational definition is placed just short of the good health pole of the continuum in Figure 6-1 to indicate that it falls short of being a true indicator of good health.

A *condition* is defined as a departure from physical or mental well-being. It has its onset when the condition is first noticed either by the individual or by a physician. Conditions obviously vary in many important ways. The term *chronic conditions*

| Good health | | | | | | | Poor health |
|---|---|---|---|---|---|---|---|
| Absence of disease or impairment | Presence of a condition | Seeks treatment | Restricted activity | Restricted in major activity | Unable to engage in major activity | Institution-alized | Illness, Death |

**Figure 6-1** Stages of the health continuum.

refers to long-term conditions that are permanent, leave residual disability, require special training for rehabilitation, or may be expected to require a long period of supervision, observation, or care. Chronic conditions include diseases such as asthma, high blood pressure, diabetes, heart trouble, or arthritis, and impairments such as deafness, paralysis, or permanent stiffness in joints. Conditions that are *acute* are expected to be temporary and may be as mild as a bruised foot or as serious as pneumonia. The third and final major category of conditions is the category of *injuries*. Within these categories, conditions can be discussed in terms of *incidence* (number of new cases per year), or of *prevalence* (average number of existing cases per year).

Once a condition becomes known, it may simply be ignored. Or the person may seek either self-treatment or professional treatment. The next phase of illness is the *restriction of activity*. The restriction in this phase, however, does not prevent individuals from carrying out their major activities. A *restriction of major activity* is more serious. Such restriction means that individuals are unable to carry out their most necessary activities, such as work or housework. This phase is commonly called *partial disability*. People who are unable to engage in major activities approach *total disability*. When a condition becomes medically demanding or very serious, or when disability reaches the point at which individuals cannot care for themselves, the phase of *institutionalization* usually begins. It should be recognized that these phases of illness are very arbitrary and merely provide a number of useful reference points along the health continuum that can be used to compare the health of older people with that of younger ones.

On the average, older people are comparatively less often afflicted than the young with conditions classified as *acute* (such as infectious diseases or common colds). They are more often afflicted with *chronic* conditions (such as heart trouble or deafness) and are more likely to suffer *disability* restrictions on their activity.

The extreme variability in the health status of older people definitely shows that poor health is by no means necessarily associated with old age. But *as a group*, older people do suffer disproportionately from chronic conditions.

## Acute Conditions

Acute conditions are illnesses or injuries that are temporary or short-term. The incidence of acute conditions decreases with age. From July, 1971 to June, 1972, Americans under 6 years of age had an average of 3.6 acute conditions per year, and the incidence decreased with increasing age to a rate of 1.1 acute conditions per year for those age 65 and over. While all types of acute conditions decrease with age, the decrease for influenza and accidental injuries is not as pronounced as the decrease for "childhood" diseases, such as mumps or measles, and for common colds (C. Wilder, 1974). However, when older people do experience acute conditions, they experience more days of bed disability or restricted activity (see Table 6-1).

**TABLE 6-1**
**Incidence of Acute Conditions per Person per Year**
**and Average Duration in Days of Restricted Activity and Bed**
**Disability per Condition, by Age: United States, July 1971 to June 1972**

|  |  | Average Duration of Disability | |
| --- | --- | --- | --- |
| Age | Incidence of Acute Conditions Per Person Per Year | Restricted Activity | Bed Disability |
| Under 6 years | 3.6 | 3.1 | 1.3 |
| 6–16 years | 2.8 | 3.0 | 1.4 |
| 17–44 years | 2.2 | 4.1 | 1.8 |
| 45–64 years | 1.4 | 6.4 | 2.5 |
| 65 years and over | 1.1 | 10.0 | 4.3 |

*Source:* Adapted from Wilder, 1974:4.

There is a substantial sex difference with regard to the incidence and duration of acute conditions. Compared to males, females at all adult ages show higher incidence of acute conditions and longer duration of disability periods. However, there does not appear to be an increase in this gap in the older age categories (C. Wilder, 1973:21).

## Chronic Conditions

Chronic conditions are illnesses or impairments of long-term or permanent nature. As Table 6-2 shows, the proportion of the population with one chronic condition or more increases steadily with age, from just over 20 percent for those under 17 to about 85 percent for the older population. Loss of teeth, for example, is an important chronic condition that increases with age but that is seldom disabling. The percentage of people without teeth climbs steadily with age to about 60 percent of those age 75 and over. In 1971, there were about 2.5 million older Americans without teeth who either did not have false teeth or never used them (Burnham, 1974). If we restrict our definition of chronic conditions to include only those that impose some limitation on the person having them, then 53 percent of older men and 41 percent of older women are limited in activity to some extent because of chronic conditions.

**TABLE 6-2**
**Percent Distribution of Persons**
**by Chronic Condition and Activity Limitation Status,**
**According to Sex and Age: United States, July 1965–June 1967**

| | | | Persons with 1 Chronic Condition or More | | | | | |
|---|---|---|---|---|---|---|---|---|
| Sex and Age | Total Population | Persons with No Chronic Conditions | Total | With No Limitation of Activity | With Limitation But Not in Major Activity[a] | With Limitation in Amount or Kind of Major Activity[a] | Unable to Carry on Major Activity[a] | Total with Some Limitation |
| *Both Sexes* | | | | | | | | |
| All ages | 100.0 | 50.5 | 49.5 | 38.0 | 2.9 | 6.4 | 2.1 | 11.4 |
| Under 17 years | 100.0 | 77.2 | 22.8 | 20.9 | 1.0 | 0.7 | 0.2 | 1.9 |
| 17–44 years | 100.0 | 45.9 | 54.1 | 46.7 | 2.7 | 4.1 | 0.6 | 7.4 |
| 45–64 years | 100.0 | 28.9 | 71.1 | 51.8 | 5.1 | 11.4 | 2.8 | 19.3 |
| 65 years & over | 100.0 | 14.4 | 85.6 | 39.6 | 6.5 | 25.7 | 13.8 | 46.0 |
| *Male* | | | | | | | | |
| All ages | 100.0 | 51.8 | 48.2 | 36.1 | 2.5 | 6.5 | 3.1 | 12.1 |
| Under 17 years | 100.0 | 75.8 | 24.2 | 22.1 | 1.1 | 0.8 | 0.2 | 2.1 |
| 17–44 years | 100.0 | 47.4 | 52.6 | 44.7 | 2.5 | 4.6 | 0.9 | 8.0 |
| 45–64 years | 100.0 | 30.5 | 69.5 | 48.7 | 4.4 | 11.9 | 4.5 | 20.8 |
| 65 years & over | 100.0 | 15.6 | 84.4 | 31.4 | 4.6 | 26.8 | 21.6 | 53.0 |
| *Female* | | | | | | | | |
| All ages | 100.0 | 49.3 | 50.7 | 39.9 | 3.3 | 6.3 | 1.2 | 10.8 |
| Under 17 years | 100.0 | 78.6 | 21.4 | 19.5 | 1.0 | 0.7 | 0.1 | 1.8 |
| 17–44 years | 100.0 | 44.7 | 55.3 | 48.5 | 2.9 | 3.6 | 0.4 | 6.9 |
| 45–64 years | 100.0 | 27.5 | 72.5 | 54.7 | 5.7 | 10.9 | 1.2 | 17.8 |
| 65 years & over | 100.0 | 13.5 | 86.5 | 45.9 | 8.0 | 24.9 | 7.7 | 40.6 |

[a]Major activity refers to ability to work, keep house, or engage in school or preschool activities.
*Source:* Adapted from C. Wilder (1971:19).

In young people, asthma and hay fever are by far the leading chronic conditions causing activity limitation, but after age 45 heart conditions and arthritis or rheumatism are the most prevalent (see Table 6-3). The rise in prevalence of chronic conditions in the older age categories stems mainly from increases in the prevalence of these two conditions as well as of visual impairments (C. Wilder, 1971).

If we define disability as inability to carry on one's major activity, then some interesting differentials occur within the older population. Among older people with one or more chronic conditions, males are three times more likely than females to be unable to carry on their major activity. As Table 6-4 shows, high prevalence of disability is also associated with receiving a low income, being nonwhite, and having very little education. Rural people not living on farms are also particularly prone to disability.

### TABLE 6-3
### Leading Causes of Activity Limitations, by Age: United States, July 1965–June 1967

| Age and Cause of Activity Limitation | Percent |
|---|---|
| **Under 17 years** | |
| Asthma–hay fever | 20.0 |
| Impairments of lower extremities and hips | 8.3 |
| Paralysis, complete or partial | 7.4 |
| Chronic bronchitis or sinusitis | 5.5 |
| Mental and nervous conditions | 3.8 |
| Heart conditions | 3.7 |
| **17–44 years** | |
| Impairments of back or spine | 15.1 |
| Mental and nervous conditions | 10.6 |
| Impairments of lower extremities and hips | 7.3 |
| Heart conditions | 6.6 |
| Arthritis and Rheumatism | 6.3 |
| Asthma–hay fever | 5.7 |
| Other diseases of muscles, bones and joints | 5.6 |
| **45–64 years** | |
| Heart conditions | 19.0 |
| Arthritis and rheumatism | 16.9 |
| Impairments of back or spine | 9.1 |
| Mental and nervous conditions | 8.8 |
| Hypertension without heart involvement | 6.5 |
| Impairments of lower extremities and hips | 5.8 |
| **65 years & over** | |
| Heart conditions | 21.9 |
| Arthritis and rheumatism | 20.2 |
| Visual impairments | 9.1 |
| Hypertension without heart involvement | 7.0 |
| Mental and nervous conditions | 5.8 |
| Impairments of lower extremities and hips | 5.4 |

*Source:* Adapted from C. Wilder, 1971:9.

**TABLE 6-4**
**Percent of the Population 65 and Over with**
**Chronic Conditions and Who Are Unable to Carry on**
**Major Activity by Selected Characteristics: United States, 1969–1970**

| | |
|---|---|
| *Sex* | |
| Male | 26.8 |
| Female | 8.5 |
| *Income* | |
| Less than $3,000 | 19.0 |
| $3,000–$4,999 | 16.0 |
| $5,000–$6,999 | 14.9 |
| $7,000–$9,999 | 14.7 |
| $10,000–$14,999 | 13.9 |
| $15,000 or more | 13.8 |
| *Color* | |
| White | 15.5 |
| All other | 25.8 |
| *Education* | |
| Less than 5 years | 28.2 |
| 5–8 years | 17.5 |
| 9–11 years | 11.2 |
| 12 years | 10.5 |
| 13–15 years | 9.0 |

*Source:* Adapted from C. Wilder, 1973:10.

Yet despite the high prevalence of chronic conditions among older people, only a small proportion are severely handicapped. While nearly 86 percent of the older population has one or more chronic conditions, 54 percent are not limited in any way by chronic conditions, and only about 14 percent are severely limited by them (see Table 6-2). Thus, while the expected increase in chronic conditions among older people does occur, the proportion who escape serious limitation by these factors is surprisingly large. Even among those who are disabled by illness or injury, most are not permanently bedridden. This is not to say that chronic conditions are not serious problems for older people. Clearly, they are. The point is that for many people old age is not accompanied by serious illness or disability. For example, in 1967 there were over 10 million older Americans who reported no serious limitations in activity caused by health problems (C. Wilder, 1971:19).

## Mental Illness

The line between mental health and mental illness is difficult to identify. Behavior that may be tolerated in one situation may be defined as "sick" in another. The term *mental illness* implies a loss of mental functioning in some way. In practice, people are identified as mentally ill if they show progressive or sudden negative

## RESEARCH ILLUSTRATION 7

## SOCIAL ISOLATION AND MENTAL ILLNESS IN OLD AGE[1]

Marjorie Fiske Lowenthal

As a part of an overall study of social isolation and mental illness, Lowenthal examined the relationship between age-linked isolation and mental illness. Her subjects were 534 persons age 60 or over admitted to the psychiatric screening wards of the San Francisco General Hospital and 600 community residents in the same age category drawn on a stratified random basis from 18 San Francisco census tracts. The base year was 1959.

With regard to social isolation, the subjects were separated into *pure isolates*—people who had no friends or relatives involved in the decision to enter the hospital and for whom no friends or relatives could be located after hospitalization, and community people who had had no contacts with friends or relatives within the past 3 years; *semi-isolates*—hospitalized people who resembled pure isolates except for having a few casual and infrequent social contacts prior to admission; *social interactors*—people in both samples who had attended a social function or visited friends within the 2-week period prior to the interview; and a *remainder* category that fell somewhere between the isolates and semi-isolates on the one hand, and the interactors on the other.

The following is a breakdown of the samples by type of social isolation.

| Hospital Sample | N |
|---|---|
| "Pure" isolates | 52 |
| Semi-isolates | 56 |
| Interactors | 39 |
| Remainder | 387 |

| Community Sample | N |
|---|---|
| Isolates | 30 |
| Interactors | 417 |
| Remainder | 144 |
| Unclassifiable | 9 |

Isolates were also differentiated into lifelong isolates and those whose isolation had developed relatively late in life.

Mental illness was defined in terms of a psychiatrist's rating of the subject as showing a high

changes in mental functions such as memory, cognition, decision making, perception, or emotional responses. Obviously, mental illness can range from mild to severe, but in this section we will be concerned only with mental illness that impairs the individual's ability to function socially. Riley and Foner (1968:363) conclude from their review of the literature that somewhere under 10 percent of the older population suffers from disabling mental illness, including 3 percent who are in institutions of various kinds.

One reason why mental illness is difficult to define is that it comes in many guises. Butler and Lewis (1973) list 131 diagnostic categories of mental illness, and theirs is only a partial listing! Yet it is reasonably feasible and convenient to classify

[1]Adapted from Lowenthal (1964b:54–70).

degree of psychiatric impairment, and was differentiated into psychogenic disorders, alcoholism, and organic disorders. The distribution of the 525 impaired subjects was as follows:

| Diagnosis | "Pure" Isolates % | Semi- isolates % | Inter- actors % | Remainder % |
|---|---|---|---|---|
| Psychogenic alone or in com- bination with organic | 22 | 25 | 44 | 23 |
| Alcoholism alone or in combination with organic | 20 | 21 | 15 | 15 |
| Organic alone | 58 | 54 | 41 | 62 |
| Total | 100 | 100 | 100 | 100 |
| N | (50) | (52) | (39) | (384) |

The psychiatrist also rated the subjects as to their physical health at the time of the interview.

Lowenthal found that organic disorders were more common among late isolates, and that psychogenic disorders were twice as prevalent among interactors as among isolates. Yet those with organic disorders showed no more social changes, such as death of a spouse or relative, change in living arrangements, or retirement, than did those with psychogenic disorders. As Lowenthal remarked,

> This leaves us with the rather obvious conclusion that the interactors' superior physical condition and lack of intellectual deterioration permit them to maintain their comparatively high degree of interaction, and that the generally poor physical condition and greater intellectual deterioration of the organics . . . has resulted in their greater isolation. *Relative isolation, then, may be more a consequence than a cause of mental illness in old age, and the consequences for psychogenics may be less severe than for organics because of their generally superior physical condition* (1964b:70; emphasis added).

In short, Lowenthal concluded that social isolation in old age results from mental illness, and that since organic mental illness is related to poor physical health, social isolation should be more prevalent among organics than among psychogenics.

---

mental illnesses common to later life into three primary categories: mental disorders with no apparent organic cause (usually called *functional disorders*), **reversible organic mental disorders**, and **chronic organic mental disorders.** Having reviewed the literature, Butler and Lewis (1973:50) conclude that older people with disabling mental illness are about evenly distributed among these three primary types.

Mental disorders that are classified as *functional* consist of psychoses and neuroses. Psychoses involve a severe loss of contact with reality. Delusions, hallucinations, strange behavior, and weak impulse control are key symptoms. The main types of psychoses are schizophrenia, affective psychoses, depression, and paranoia. Neuroses are thought to be reactions to acute anxiety and can take many forms, including anxiety states, hysteria, obsessive-compulsive behavior, phobias, hypochondria, or depression (without loss of reality contact). Whether neurotic or psychotic, depression is the functional disorder both most prevalent and most likely to begin in later life (Butler and Lewis, 1973).

Older people with functional mental disorders include both those who first became mentally ill early in life and remained so into later life as well as those who first became mentally ill in later life. Those for whom the onset of functional disorder occurs in later life are primarily people who are depressed by losses, which are as apt to be social as physical. Both Busse and Pfeiffer (1969) and Maas and Kuypers (1974) conclude that the people who are most likely to develop functional disorders in response to the stresses of aging are people who have had difficulty coping with changes earlier in life.

**Organic mental disorders** are typified by mental confusion—loss of memory, incoherent speech, and poor orientation to the environment. They are often accompanied by psychomotor problems as well. Organic mental disorders can be either *reversible* or *chronic*. Because symptoms of both types are similar, diagnosis depends heavily on knowledge of prior health events. For example, if a doctor sees a patient with symptoms of organic brain disorder, before settling on a diagnosis he or she may check for malnutrition, find out what drugs the patient has been taking, and check for infections or diseases such as diabetes or hyperthyroidism. Any of these factors can cause reversible organic brain disorders. Reversible brain disorders can also accompany congestive heart failure, alcoholism, or stroke. If none of the possible causes of reversible organic brain disorders is present, then it is usually assumed that the patient has a chronic brain disorder.

Chronic brain disorders fall into two categories: those caused by a deterioration of brain tissue and those caused by cerebral arteriosclerosis, which cuts off the blood supply to the brain. All chronic brain disorders involve a gradual deterioration of mental functions, but sometimes they also bring agitated behavior, depression, or delirium.

The prevalence of both types of organic brain disorders increases with age. In addition, organic brain disorders are related to functional depression. No doubt some reversible brain disorders are brought on by environmental factors indirectly through strokes, heart attacks, or alcoholism. However, no data on indirect causes of organic brain syndromes are available. Research is needed in this area.

Busse and Pfeiffer (1969) conclude that there is little increase with age in the proportion of people with mental disorders. However, there is an increase with age in the proportion with *disabling* mental illness. This increase is primarily caused by an increase in the prevalence of serious organic mental disorders rather than by any appreciable increase in functional disorders.

## TREATMENT

There are no available data on self-treatment, but if television commercials are any indication, the older population is *seen* by society as doing a lot of self-medicating. Certainly some chronic conditions such as arthritis or rheumatism are widely treated with readily available nonprescription medicines, and sales of nonprescription tranquilizers are brisk. About 40 percent of acute conditions are self-treated.

In 1969, people aged 17 to 44 averaged 4.2 physician visits, compared to 6.1 visits among people 65 and over. Older people with annual family incomes over $10,000 averaged 7.5 physician visits. From 1963 to 1969, the average number of physician visits dropped for all age categories, but the drop was greatest in the older population. House calls accounted for about 10 percent of the physician visits of older Americans in 1969, a sharp decrease from 23 percent in 1959. In 1969, about 70 percent of the older population saw a doctor at least once (Namey and Wilson, 1972).

As Table 6-5 shows, a sizable number of older Americans receive **home care** of various types. The bulk of the home care provided is personal care, such as help in moving about, dressing, or bathing, rather than medical care. About 80 percent of the home care is provided by relatives living in the household. The prevalence of home care increases sharply with age, from 2.1 percent at age 55 to 64, to 12.5 percent at age 75 and over. In terms of duration, 75 percent of the home care has been being provided for longer than 1 year, and 30 percent is constant care (M. Wilder, 1972).

### TABLE 6-5
### Number of Persons 55 Years and Over Receiving Care
### at Home and Percent of Total by Age and Sex, According
### to Specific Care Provided: United States, July 1966–June 1968

| Specific Care Provided | Total Persons Receiving Care | Age | | | Sex | |
|---|---|---|---|---|---|---|
| | | 55–64 years | 65–74 years | 75 years and over | Male | Female |
| | | Number in thousands | | | | |
| All care provided | 1,747 | 363 | 499 | 886 | 694 | 1,053 |
| | | Percent of total | | | | |
| Moving about | 44.8 | 41.0 | 41.1 | 48.5 | 36.7 | 50.1 |
| Dressing | 53.5 | 56.2 | 53.3 | 52.5 | 61.2 | 48.4 |
| Bathing | 60.7 | 52.1 | 55.1 | 67.3 | 67.9 | 56.0 |
| Eating | 18.8 | 15.2 | 16.8 | 21.3 | 18.0 | 19.2 |
| Changing bandages | 6.6 | * | 7.0 | 6.5 | 8.1 | 5.7 |
| Injections | 14.1 | 16.0 | 17.4 | 11.5 | 12.7 | 15.1 |
| Other medical treatment | 10.4 | 8.8 | 11.6 | 10.4 | 11.0 | 10.1 |
| Changing bed position | 13.2 | 11.3 | 14.2 | 13.5 | 12.8 | 13.5 |
| Physical therapy | 10.5 | 11.0 | 12.2 | 9.3 | 10.7 | 10.4 |
| Cutting toenails | 59.3 | 50.4 | 56.3 | 64.4 | 61.2 | 58.0 |
| All other care | 9.4 | 9.1 | 9.8 | 9.3 | 8.8 | 9.8 |

*Less than .1 percent.
Note: The sum of percent of persons receiving care may be greater than 100 percent since a person may have received more than one type of care. Care received from a physician is excluded.

Source: Adapted from C. Wilder (1972:7).

Older people are more likely than the young to go to a short-stay hospital, and, once there, are more likely to stay longer (see Table 6-6). Compared to people under 17, older people have more than three times as many hospitalizations per 1,000 persons and have about three times as long an average duration of stay. However, from July 1965 to June 1966, *87 percent of the 17.5 million older people in the United States had no hospital episodes.* This figure is not significantly different from the 90 percent figure for the total population.

**TABLE 6-6**
**Rates of Discharge from Short-Stay Hospitals and**
**Average Duration of Stay, by Age and Sex: United States, 1968–1969**

|  | Age | | | |
|---|---|---|---|---|
|  | *Under 17* | *17–44* | *45–64* . | *65 and over* |
| Discharge rates (per 1,000 persons) Total | 62.6 | 147.4 | 143.1 | 232.6 |
| Male | 68.4 | 86.8 | 140.3 | 242.6 |
| Female | 56.6 | 201.5 | 145.6 | 225.0 |
| Duration of stay (in days) Total | 5.6 | 6.8 | 11.3 | 15.3 |
| Male | 5.5 | 9.5 | 12.4 | 15.4 |
| Female | 5.7 | 5.7 | 10.3 | 15.2 |

*Source:* Adapted from Namey and Wilson (1972:6).

## Financing Medical Care

Cooper and Piro (1974) indicate that in 1972 the average medical bill for an aged individual 65 or over was $1,052. For a person aged 19 to 64 the bill was $384 per year and for those under 19 years of age it was $167 per year. Of these bills, 70 percent were paid by a third party, that is, private health insurance or government programs. In 1972, slightly less than 42 percent of the health bills of people 65 and over were paid by Medicare.

**Medicare** is a program of health insurance for older Americans administered by the Social Security Administration. It consists of two parts: hospital insurance and medical insurance. Nearly all older Americans are eligible for hospital coverage. It pays most of the costs of inpatient care for up to 90 days for any spell of illness. In addition, there is a "lifetime reserve" of 60 days that can be used if more than 90 days of hospitalization is required. Hospital insurance also covers up to 100 days in an approved **extended-care facility.** Hospital insurance is financed through payroll deductions and employer contributions to a Medicare trust fund.

Supplementary medical insurance is a voluntary program that requires a monthly premium from the older person. The premium is matched by the federal government out of general tax revenues. Medical insurance pays costs of doctors' services and outpatient physical therapy beyond an annual deductible amount. It does not pay for medical checkups, prescription drugs, eyeglasses, dentures, or hearing aids.[2]

West (1971) concluded that Medicare has covered almost all persons age 65 and over since July 1, 1966. Initially the in-hospital services rose, along with all supporting medical services, with the introduction of the program, and continued to increase, but at a declining rate. However, the average length of each hospital stay has actually dropped slightly. The use of the ambulatory physician services has remained fairly stable throughout the period since 1966, and there has been very little use of the post-hospital alternatives—extended care facilities and home health services. Per capita expenditures under Medicare have more than doubled since the program began, owing mainly to increases in charges to the program for covered services. A large proportion of the funds are spent on the behalf of a relatively small number of people with serious illnesses. About 20 percent of the insured population uses no covered service in a given year. Another 20 percent is hospitalized. Among the 20 percent that is hospitalized, a fourth are hospitalized more than once in the year, and the bulk of the physician costs arise from hospitalized illness. In 1967, reimbursement for the total covered costs of illness for hospitalized persons accounted for 86 percent of the program funds.

K. Davis (1973) concluded that the increase in medical costs after Medicare were simply a continuation of a trend that existed prior to Medicare. Capital expenses accounted for most of the increase and basic room and board accounts for less of the total increase. Her findings tend to support the demand theory of hospital inflation and she concluded that costs per patient day would have risen at 6 percent per year even if wages had remained constant. Medicare affected hospital costs in the same way that growth of private insurance did in an earlier period, primarily by increasing the demand for hospital services.

Palmore and Jeffers (1971), on the other hand, concluded that before and after Medicare there were no significant changes in the demand for physicians in terms of overall increases in physician's visits or hospitalization, but they did find a significant change in the method of paying for medical care.

**Medicaid** is a comprehensive health care program designed to provide health care to the poor, regardless of age. It is administered by local welfare departments using federal funds. Medicaid pays for everything that Medicare does, as well as many other services, including drugs, eyeglasses, and long-term care in licensed nursing homes.

About 55 percent of older Americans carry private health insurance to fill the major gaps in Medicare coverage. However, at present none of the available policies provide complete medical care coverage. Thus, out-of-pocket expenses for medical services remain a major expense item for older Americans.

[2]Because Medicare regulations are constantly changing, it is not possible to include much detail about the program. This situation represents a minor headache to authors writing books in gerontology and a major headache to older persons who are never quite sure what is covered or for how long.

## INSTITUTIONALIZATION

Less than 4 percent of all people 65 or over live in **long-term institutions**, but as age increases after 65, so does the percentage. For example, 17 percent of those age 85 or over are institutionalized. Of those who are institutionalized, most are in nursing and personal care homes. Kastenbaum and Candy (1973) found that 20 percent of the deaths of older people in Detroit in a given year occurred in nursing or personal care homes. This figure implies that while only 4 percent of older people are in institutions at any one time, the percentage that will *eventually* experience life in a nursing home is much larger. Table 6-7 shows the rates of residency in various types of institutions by age, sex, and color. Between 1964 and 1969, the number of residents living in nursing or personal care homes increased by 47 percent, but the increase in the number at 85 or over was 72 percent (Mathis, 1973).

Various studies have shown that while many older people in institutions are mentally and physically impaired, impairment is not necessarily related to institutionalization. Thus, the rates of institutionalization present an inaccurate picture of the health of the older population because they include people who live in homes for the aged but who are not impaired, disabled, or ill. In nursing homes, about half the older patients are ambulatory and continent; while in mental hospitals the proportion of such older patients reaches 80 percent.

A key factor in institutionalization appears to be the residential setting and family system. Older people in nursing and personal care homes tend not to have a spouse or children. They also tend to have lived alone. Indications are that many older people are able to avoid institutionalization if they have relatives to help care for them and adequate financial resources. In fact, breakdowns in this support system appear to be the primary cause of institutionalization among older people. Another important factor is loss of residence. Many moves to homes for the aged are precipitated by urban renewal, changes in apartment ownership, and so on.

Older people do not end up in institutions overnight. Usually a series of attempts to solve the person's problems precede institutionalization. The nursing home is often viewed as a last resort. The fact that admission to a nursing home so often comes at the end of a long string of disappointments is bound to affect patients and their families.

Most older people look on nursing homes in a very negative way. These views result partly from a desire to remain in familiar surroundings and near relatives, but they are also partly influenced by the concept of the poorhouse that has survived from another era. In fact, the nursing home is about the *last* place most older people would prefer to go, although many of them recognize that this living arrangement may be the best for people who can no longer take care of themselves. Most of the fear that leads older people to reject the idea of living in a nursing home is related to a perceived loss of independence, a perception that the nursing home represents formal proof that death is near, and a fear of rejection by their children. Older people who live with their spouses, with their children, or in an owned home are the most resistant to the idea of living in a Home.[3] But these negative attitudes do not prevent older people from moving into nursing homes.

[3]In this section Home is capitalized to differentiate the nursing or personal care facility from an independent household.

TABLE 6-7
**Rates of Residency in Institutions of Various Types by Age, Sex, and Color: United States, 1963 (per 1,000)**

| Age | Total | | | White | | | Nonwhite | | |
|---|---|---|---|---|---|---|---|---|---|
| | Total | Male | Female | Total | Male | Female | Total | Male | Female |
| **(1) Nursing and personal care homes** | | | | | | | | | |
| All ages, 20+ | 4.5 | 3.2 | 5.6 | 4.8 | 3.4 | 6.0 | 1.7 | 1.8 | 1.7 |
| 20–64 | 0.6 | 0.7 | 0.6 | 0.6 | 0.7 | 0.6 | 0.6 | 0.7 | 0.5 |
| 65–74 | 7.9 | 6.8 | 8.8 | 8.1 | 6.9 | 9.1 | 5.9 | 6.2 | 5.6 |
| 75–84 | 39.6 | 29.1 | 47.5 | 41.7 | 30.5 | 49.9 | 13.8 | 12.4 | 15.0 |
| 85+ | 148.4 | 105.6 | 175.1 | 157.7 | 111.9 | 185.8 | 41.8 | 40.4 | 42.9 |
| **(2) Geriatric and chronic disease "hospitals"[a]** | | | | | | | | | |
| All ages, 20+ | 0.7 | 0.8 | 0.6 | 0.7 | 0.8 | 0.6 | 0.6 | 0.8 | 0.5 |
| 20–64 | 0.2 | 0.3 | 0.1 | 0.2 | 0.3 | 0.1 | 0.3 | 0.4 | 0.2 |
| 65–74 | 1.7 | 2.5 | 1.1 | 1.6 | 2.4 | 1.0 | 2.3 | 3.3 | 1.5 |
| 75–84 | 4.4 | 4.5 | 4.4 | 4.5 | 4.5 | 4.5 | 3.5 | 4.6 | 2.6 |
| 85+ | 13.6 | 12.4 | 14.3 | 14.2 | 13.2 | 14.8 | 6.7 | 4.7 | 8.2 |
| **(3) Long-stay mental hospitals** | | | | | | | | | |
| All ages | 4.4 | 4.9 | 3.9 | 4.1 | 4.4 | 3.7 | 7.0 | 8.9 | 5.3 |
| 15–44 | 2.4 | 3.1 | 1.8 | 2.1 | 2.6 | 1.6 | 4.9 | 6.8 | 3.2 |
| 45–54 | 5.0 | 5.6 | 4.6 | 4.6 | 5.0 | 4.3 | 8.8 | 11.0 | 6.9 |
| 55–64 | 6.7 | 7.0 | 6.3 | 6.3 | 6.5 | 6.0 | 10.7 | 12.1 | 9.4 |
| 65–74 | 8.8 | 9.7 | 8.0 | 8.4 | 9.3 | 7.7 | 12.7 | 14.6 | 11.1 |
| 75+ | 10.8 | 10.2 | 11.3 | 10.5 | 9.7 | 11.1 | 14.8 | 16.1 | 13.7 |

[a] "Hospitals" include only geriatric and chronic disease hospitals and chronic disease wards and nursing home units of general hospitals.

*Source:* Adapted from Wunderlich (1965:4) and Taube (1965:5).

The facts of life in long-term care facilities often justify the negative view most older people have of them. Many Homes lack adequate physical facilities, staff, and provision for activities. Seldom is any effort made to prepare either the patient or his family for life in the Home. Many Homes have overly restrictive institutional rules, and often do not offer any useful occupations and leisure activities. Most nursing homes also tend to be completely cut off from the community and make little or no use of community resources for the benefit of their patients. Finally, there is far less privacy in most nursing homes than the patients would like.

Older people fear nursing homes largely because they fear the influence of the Home on their chance for survival—and, it appears, with good reason. Mortality rates for older people in institutions are higher than for those outside, particularly during the first year. This situation, of course, exists partly because sickness often prompts the move to a nursing home in the first place.

Living in a nursing home does not appear to have any direct influence on life satisfaction or self-image, but no doubt it has indirect effects via family and other relationships. The Home's overall rating in the community is a key factor determining satisfaction with it. Regardless of the objective facts, Homes that are more positively viewed in the community produce more satisfaction in their patients.

New residents in the Home often face several simultaneous changes that can make it hard for them to adjust to their new circumstances. Illness, dependency, widowhood, and loneliness are the changes most frequently encountered.

Illness can bring important changes for two reasons. First, illness *forces* the individual to become dependent. Second, it creates internal states within the individual that make it difficult to maintain a reasonable perspective on the outside world. When people are in pain, or under medication, or just plain fatigued from fighting illness, they find it much easier to allow themselves to become irritable and depressed. For some people, a long-term illness can produce profound personality changes.

In addition to the unfamiliar surroundings, the shock of moving, and often the depressing influence of illness, patients also find that they have lost their independence. They have lost personal control over many of the simplest everyday functions. When to get up, when to go to sleep, when and what to eat, whom to associate with, whether the television will be on or off, whether the windows will be open or closed, whether to use a heavy or a light blanket—these and a host of other *seemingly* trivial decisions are often now out of patients' hands. They also lose their ability to manipulate the images others have of them.

Widowhood often precipitates a move into an extended-care facility. The newly widowed person faces a great many problems: grief, homesickness, loss of outside contacts, financial insecurity, and a feeling of uselessness. It is hard to overestimate the impact of moving into a Home on a woman who has been a housewife for most of her adult life. She has lost her husband, who was more than likely the most important person in the world to her. She has lost her function of keeping a house, and what is more, she misses her familiar physical surroundings.

Thus, new Home residents often face difficult changes in addition to their institutionalization. But the nursing home can seldom help them deal with these very personal concerns. Most extended-care facilities are not oriented toward the *patients*; instead, the organization revolves around instrumental tasks such as making beds or giving medication. It is not that these tasks are unimportant, it is just that they often seem to be the staff's reason for being—to the exclusion of contact with the patient as a person.

The following incidents reported by J. Henry (1963) illustrate this emphasis on the mechanistic to the total exclusion of the human element.

☐ Patients' being bathed in assembly-line fashion in order to get the task done quickly with no thought to the patient's privacy or modesty

☐ Inability to call patients by name who have been in the facility several months

☐ Patients not spoken to except to issue directions such as "turn over," "sit down," and so on

☐ Complete and continuous disregard of patients' requests to contact relatives to bring them things

☐ Several patients being bathed in the same water

☐ Patients who cause trouble being tied to the bed

A final example:

> (Nurse) Beck came into the room and went over to one of the beds and turned the patient on her side without saying anything. . . . She pulled up the gown exposing the patient's buttocks and gave her an injection. I glanced back at the patient as Beck left the room and saw that the patient was still on her side, buttocks exposed, blood oozing from the injection site (Henry, 1963:395).

The dehumanization of the patient is usually excused on the grounds of administrative and medical necessity. However, it is important to note that patients judge the adequacy of the care they receive *as much* in terms of its humanitarian effectiveness as of its medical effectiveness. Bureaucratic structure is a system of organization that supposedly uses institutional rules to enhance the operating efficiency of the organization. Too often, however, people working in bureaucratic organizations lose sight of the goals beyond the rules and set the rules up as ends in themselves. The result is a stifling and dehumanizing rigidity that prevents the institution from being able to deal with each individual as a unique person with a unique set of problems.

Kahana (1973) found that humane treatment was not necessarily related to the degree of professionalism of the Home staff or to having modern facilities. Humane treatment seemed to be more related to the value attached to showing respect for the *person* of the aged resident. In most cases, we tolerate the depersonalization of bureaucracy because it does not intrude into our primary relationships. In the case of the Home resident, however, the Home *is* the setting for his or her most important relationships and associations. Its bureaucratic rules need to be flexible enough so as not to interfere with the resident's relationships.

One of the biggest problems patients have is that they cannot find anyone who will tell them honestly what is the matter with them. This problem is particularly acute among the victims of cancer or heart disease. Even the physician often has a difficult time being honest with seriously ill patients, simply because it is sometimes very hard to admit that the field of medicine has its limits. Another factor that compounds the problem is the increasing depersonalization of medicine. With the rise of the specialist and the demise of the family GP, there is a tendency for doctors to look at a patient as a collection of physical symptoms and to know very little of his or her personal history. This tendency also makes it easier for the physician to kid the patient along. Finally, some patients want to know what is wrong with them and some do not. The end result is that very often the physician simply cannot be relied on to discuss patients' diagnoses with them, to lay out their options, and to answer their questions.

Nor are relatives very good at talking honestly with patients about such taboo topics as terminal cancer or impending death. They, more than anyone else, often attempt to keep up a sham that everything will turn out all right, that the patients may get well and come home again, or that the situation will improve to the point where Home residents can once again be self-sufficient. Usually the patients know that this optimism is mostly sham, and it puts a strain on them to have to keep up the farce for the benefit of their relatives. Many patients express relief at finding someone they can talk to without having to keep up a front.

From the standpoint of communication, terminal patients are the biggest problem. At the point where cases become absolutely hopeless, we tend to write off patients and to begin to treat them as if they were objects. Usually the surest way for patients to know when the end is near is to observe how other people behave toward them. When the staff starts talking openly about their cases in the patients' presence—with each other, as if the patients were not there—it is usually a sure sign that they think death is just around the corner.

Given the shortage of staff in most facilities, the temptation to concentrate efforts on the "salvageable" cases is understandable. Then, too, many terminal patients, particularly cancer victims, are so preoccupied with the pain they are experiencing that they are oblivious of anything else. Yet are these reasons good enough to excuse treating people as objects, no matter how hopeless their cases?

Kleemeier (1961) proposed three dimensions along which institutions differ and that could be expected to influence the response of the older person to the institution: degree of segregation of the patients from the outside world, congregate as opposed to individual orientation, and the degree to which the institution controls the daily life of the individual. Kahana (1973) cites research showing that the more segregated the patients are from the outside world, the greater the depersonalizing effects of the institution. The staff of institutions for the aged often develop an informal staff subculture that emphasizes congregate orientations and high institutional control as the easiest and most effective way to "master" the patients. Yet the morale and well-being of patients depends on the congruence between their perceived needs and the orientation of the institution. Flexible procedures would allow patients to choose the degree of segregation, of congregate programs, and of structured control over daily life that will be imposed on them. Kahana (1973) sees this flexibility as the keystone of humane treatment in institutions.

About 1 percent of the older population resides in long-stay mental hospitals. On top of inadequacies in personal or medical care, older people in mental hospitals also confront an institutional attitude to the effect that mental patients do not need and cannot use activities or enriched environments. However, research has shown that when environments are changed, the behavior of patients changes too.

Gottesman (1973) reports the results of a milieu therapy project that replaced a sex-segregated, factorylike ward, in which the patients were given nothing to do, with a more homelike atmosphere, in which patients were given personal space, responsibility for taking care of it, responsibility for personal care, and a wider range of activities, including employment in a sheltered workshop. Compared to an unchanged control ward, people on the experimental ward improved measurably with respect to self-care, money management, and activity. Patients on the experimental ward knew each other better and had more friendships than those on the control ward. There was also a reduction of clinical symptoms such as hallucinations, delusions, and intellectual impairment on the experimental ward, but not on the control ward. About 75 percent of the hospital patients over 55 were judged capable of participating in milieu therapy.

The feasibility of programs like milieu therapy depends on money and staff attitudes. Gottesman (1973) points out that 65 percent of the funds used to operate the institutions that house the aged come from the public. If social programs were a prerequisite for receiving public funds, there would be more social programs. The attitude problem is more complex. Most mental patients have been marginal members of society—poorly educated people with low occupational status and unsuccessful marriages. It is hard for staff members to offer, or for these patients to accept, normal life roles. In addition, mental patients behave in ways that are upsetting and that encourage staff members to minimize contact with them. However, Gottesman (1973) reports that group sessions and positive responses by patients to new programs can sucessfully produce new staff attitudes concerning the capabilities of mental patients.

## THE CONTINUUM OF HEALTH CARE

S. Brody (1973) has pointed out that when health is viewed as a positive good to be pursued rather than merely as an affliction to be eliminated, the range of services required for adequate health care expands. He argues strongly against viewing personal services such as bathing and dressing, support services such as recreational therapy, maintenance services such as housekeeping, and coordinative services such as counseling or referral as "ancillary" services—somehow not quite as essential as direct medical care to the maintenance of good health. Brody further points out the uneven availability of nonmedical health services. For example, Medicare and third-party medical insurance will pay for such services in a short-stay hospital or extended-care facility, but not in the patient's home. Although home health service is technically available under Medicare, it is seldom used because the patient must be virtually housebound but still able to make do with only intermittent care—a condition Brody calls a latter-day Catch-22.

Brody's criticisms seem well-founded. Our system for meeting the health needs of older people does overemphasize remedial treatment at the expense of *preventive* health care. Several measures could improve the overall health system available to older people.

☐ *Periodic health examination.* Early detection is often valuable for the treatment of chronic diseases.

☐ *Accident prevention.* Programs to design safer housing for older people and to alert them to potential hazards in the home can prevent many of the accidents that so often lead to more serious complications.

☐ *Nutrition.* Common causes of poor nutrition among the elderly include inadequate income, living alone (fixing meals for one is too much trouble), loss of teeth, difficulty in food shopping, and long-standing poor eating habits. Meals-on-Wheels is a good example of a public program designed to provide better nutrition for older people by serving home-delivered meals.

☐ *Exercise.* Exercise is particularly important in warding off cardiovascular diseases. Even diabetes is helped by exercise.

☐ *Rehabilitation.* A major aspect of health care, rehabilitation is geared toward relieving or controlling clinical symptoms, strengthening and retraining the capacities remaining, creating motivation, or giving self-care training. Only a small proportion of mental health care facilities now in existence use rehabilitation programs as part of their care for older people. However, studies have shown that such programs can be extremely successful in making older people self-sufficent, and much more effort along the lines of rehabilitation is needed.

Our health system is also spotty with respect to the continuum of mental health care. As age increases, utilization of outpatient mental health services drops, and by age 65 the use of outpatient services is very low. Butler and Lewis (1973) point out that while an estimated 15 percent of the older population need mental health services, they represent only 2 percent of psychiatric clinic patients, 4 percent of patients in community mental health centers, and 2 percent of the patients of private practitioners. And this finding suggests that the trend toward moving older mental patients out of mental hospitals and into "the community" may be ill-advised since most communities provide little in the way of out-patient mental health care.

Since 1960, the trend has been toward the wholesale transfer of "geriatric" mental patients out of mental hospitals. This trend is partly responsible for the dramatic rise in nursing home residents cited earlier. Such policies may look good on paper, but in actuality patients are being sent out into a community environment that is totally unprepared to monitor their progress. In many cases there is not even a provision for necessary drug therapy (Butler and Lewis, 1973). Home mental health care is even less available than home physical care.

## SUMMARY

Conditions of ill health can be chronic or acute, depending on the duration of the condition. Older people show an increased prevalence of chronic conditions and a decreased prevalence of acute conditions in comparison with the young. However, when acute conditions do strike older people, they tend to linger twice as long as among middle-aged people. Arthritis, rheumatism, and heart conditions are the chronic conditions producing the most disability among older people. But although 85 percent of the older population has at least one chronic condition, only about 14 percent is seriously limited by them.

The prevalence of disabling mental illness also increases with age. There is some increase in disabling depression, but the bulk of the increase results from organic brain disorders, half of which are at least partially reversible.

The health of the age group 65 to 74 differs significantly from that of the 75-and-over group. In general, health declines do not become precipitous until after age 75. This profile is no doubt related to the fact that biological declines in function do not become marked until after age 75. Most older people consider themselves to be in reasonably good health, and most are not limited in their activities by illness or injury.

Older people generally make more use of medical facilities and services than do younger people, but only about 4 percent reside in long-term institutions. However, as much as a quarter of the population age 85 or over resides in such institutions.

Older people with spouses or living children and adequate financial resources can usually delay or avoid entering a nursing or personal care facility. Loss of residence and widowhood are two events that often precipitate a move into an institution. Most older people view nursing homes negatively, but enter them if necessary. The inability of our system to develop a way to finance genuinely adequate long-term health care means that most nursing homes are lacking in staff and facilities. It also results in an organizational structure that must stress efficiency and that often neglects the socioemotional needs of the residents.

Adjustment to nursing homes is made difficult by the negative stereotype most people hold, the isolation of the Home from the community, the weakened condition of the residents, loss of independence, and often widowhood. In addition, many institutions have policies that unnecessarily segregate their residents from the outside world, stress congregate solutions to individual needs, and seek to control even the most minute aspects of the patient's life. Programs such as milieu therapy illustrate that humane treatment can be successfully incorporated into institutions.

Current health programs stress eliminating negatives rather than accentuating positives. Many essential support services are unavailable outside hospitals. Preventive health care is rarely stressed. Mental health services are also lacking outside institutions. Periodic examination, accident prevention efforts, better nutrition, and more exercise are all important ways to promote better health among older people.

## SUGGESTIONS FOR FURTHER READING

American Association of Homes for the Aged. *The Social Components of Care.* New York: The Association, 1966.

Brody, Stanley J. "Comprehensive Health Care for the Elderly: An Analysis. The Continuum of Medical, Health, and Social Services for the Aged." *Gerontologist 13* (1973):412–418.

Butler, Robert N., and M. I. Lewis. *Aging and Mental Health.* St. Louis, Mo.: C. V. Mosby, 1973.

Coe, Rodney M., and Elizabeth Barnhill. "Social Participation and Health of the Aged." In

Arnold M. Rose and Warren A. Peterson (eds.), *Older People and Their Social World.* Philadelphia: F. A. Davis, 1965, pp. 211–223.

Gottesman, Leonard E. "Milieu Treatment of the Aged in Institutions." *Gerontologist 13* (1973):23–26.

Kahana, Eva. "The Humane Treatment of Old People in Institutions." *Gerontologist 13* (1973):282–289.

Lawton, M. Powell, and Fay G. Lawton (eds.), *Mental Impairment in the Aged.* Philadelphia: Philadelphia Geriatrics Center, 1965.

Mendelson, Mary A., and David Hapgood. "The Political Economy of Nursing Homes." In Frederick R. Eisele (ed.), *Political Consequences of Aging.* Philadelphia: American Academy of Political and Social Sciences, 1974, pp. 95–105.

Wilder, Charles S. "Chronic conditions and limitations of activity and mobility: United States, July 1965 to June 1967." *Vital and Health Statistics*, Series 10, No. 61., 1971.

———. "Limitation of Activity due to Chronic Conditions: United States, 1969 and 1970." *Vital and Health Statistics*, Series 10, No. 80., 1973.

# 7
# Finances

Financial security largely determines the range of alternatives people have in adjusting to aging. Older people with adequate financial resources can afford to travel, to go shopping, to entertain friends, to seek the best in health care, and to keep a presentable wardrobe and household. Older people without money can do none of these things, and herein lies perhaps the single most demoralizing fact of life for most older people, for most older people are relatively poor.

In 1973, American families with annual incomes of less than $6,000 or individuals with incomes under $3,000 were in the bottom fifth of the U.S. population and therefore relatively poor. As Table 7-1 shows, the median incomes for nearly all categories of older people were well below the national averages. Even among the relatively advantaged white couples, more than half were relatively poor. Among older black females in families, 96 percent had incomes that would classify them as poor. In all, *six out of every ten older Americans are poor.*

This chapter details the financial aspects of growing old, first by defining a minimum financial *need*, and then by examining the financial resources of older people in relation to this need. We will also consider changes in level of living that occur as one grows old and the prospects for the future financial security of older people.

## THE FINANCIAL NEED

It is difficult to determine the financial needs of older people in general because the older population varies so. Some older people own their homes, have their own cars, or have financial assets to supplement their retirement incomes. Others have neither assets nor income. Certainly no single "financial requirement" could fit the needs of both groups. Also, the situation of couples is markedly different from that of single individuals.

**TABLE 7-1**
**Median Incomes for Couples**
**and Unrelated Individuals Age 65**
**and Over, by Age and Race, United States: 1973**

|  | Age | |
|---|---|---|
|  | *65 to 72* | *73 and over* |
| *Couples* | | |
| White | $6,873 | $5,304 |
| Black | 4,538 | 3,190 |
| *Single Individuals* | | |
| White | | |
| In families | | |
| Male | 3,302 | 2,800 |
| Female | 2,421 | 1,895 |
| Not in families | | |
| Male | 3,882 | 3,037 |
| Female | 3,024 | 2,516 |
| Black | | |
| In families | | |
| Male | — | — |
| Female | 1,489 | 1,322 |
| Not in families | | |
| Male | 2,029 | 1,890 |
| Female | 2,127 | 1,775 |

*Source:* U.S. Bureau of the Census (1975:114–15).

A common method of estimating income needs is the absolute approach, in which income need is tied to a dollar amount necessary to provide a bare minimum healthful level of living. Using this approach, the annual need for older Americans in 1973 was as follows:

**TABLE 7-2**
**Annual Financial Requirements,**
**Couples and Single Individuals**
**Age 65 and Over: United States, 1973**

|  | *Couples* | *Individuals* |
|---|---|---|
| Own home | | |
| free and clear | $3,250 | $2,440 |
| Do not own home | 3,770 | 2,730 |

By these standards, over 20 percent of older couples and nearly 70 percent of older individuals have financial resources below the bare minimum.

All estimates of this variety tend to fall short of the actual requirements because they do not include any slack for "contingencies." For example, slightly more than one out of every ten older people will end up in a hospital this year and the average stay will be *12 days*. The cost will run about $1,000 for the hospital alone. It is not difficult to see what such an expenditure would do to an annual budget of $3,000. Even if the individual has hospitalization insurance (and only about half of the older population does), and Medicare pays part of the cost, the individual will still have to cover about a third of the cost of the health care (Cooper and Piro, 1974). Thus, the figures given in Table 7-2 can be considered conservative.

The absolute approach to determining income requirements has several other flaws, perhaps the most serious of which is its inability to take past income history into account. Henle (1972) estimates that in order to maintain the same level of living following retirement, older couples with no children at home must have a retirement income that replaces about 75 percent of their preretirement income. About 80 percent of older Americans have *no* source of income other than Social Security, and Social Security replaces, on the average, only about 45 percent of preretirement income for older couples and only about 30 percent for older individuals. Even those lucky few who have both Social Security and another pension seldom reach the 75 percent replacement level. Thus, nearly all retired older Americans experience a decline in real income. For some, the decline in level of living can be as high as 60 to 70 percent.

Regardless of how income adequacy is measured, a substantial portion of the older population has inadequate incomes. Why this situation exists and what might be done about it requires a detailed analysis of the part various income sources play in producing the total income picture for older Americans.

## DIRECT INCOME SOURCES

Older Americans have several sources of direct income. A few have earnings. Most have a retirement pension of one kind or another. Many receive welfare payments. Very few receive income from assets or cash contributions from relatives. Each of these sources of direct income will be considered in detail.

### Earnings

Only about one sixth of the older people in the United States are employed, and earnings have a drastic impact on income. For example, in 1967 those married couples who were eligible for Social Security but who were not drawing it averaged annual incomes of $6,470, compared to only $3,480 for couples who were drawing Social Security benefits. About half of the older people who report earnings are also drawing Social Security benefits, and the benefit amount for those who are still employed tends to be low in comparison with those who are fully retired. This fact suggests that about half of the older people who are still employed need earnings to supplement an inadequate Social Security pension.

### Retirement Pensions

There are two basic types of **retirement pensions**: **general public pensions** available to every jobholder and administered by the national government, and **job-specific pensions** available only through a specific position of employment and administered by a work organization, union, or private insurance company. Job-specific pensions can be further subdivided into public employee pensions and private pensions.

**Social Security** is a colloquial term that refers to a general, public retirement pension administered by the federal government. To qualify for Social Security, an individual must have worked on a covered job for a specified minimum period of time (usually 10 years) and have reached at least age 62. Social Security pensions also carry a spouse benefit that provides retired couples with 150 percent of the pension entitlement of the covered individual. By 1968, virtually all jobs in the United States, including self-employment, were covered by Social Security. The only exclusion from Social Security is for people with jobs that are covered by some public employee pensions or by Railroad Retirement. Nine out of ten older Americans draw retirement benefits from Social Security. For 80 percent of retired Americans, Social Security is the *sole* source of income. In 1972, the average annual Social Security pension was $3,270 for married couples, $2,124 for single men, and $1,682 for single women.[1] These pension levels are clearly below the level necessary to provide an adequate income by most standards.

**TABLE 7-3**
**Retired Worker Benefits Under Social Security**
**Monthly Average: United States, 1950–1972**

| Year | Men Actual Amount[a] | Men Constant 1967 Dollars | Women Actual Amount | Women Constant 1967 Dollars | Couples Actual Amount | Couples Constant 1967 Dollars |
|---|---|---|---|---|---|---|
| 1950 | $ 44.60 | $ 61.86 | $ 34.80 | $ 48.27 | $ 71.70 | $ 99.45 |
| 1955 | 64.60 | 80.56 | 49.80 | 62.10 | 103.50 | 129.06 |
| 1960 | 79.90 | 90.05 | 59.60 | 67.17 | 123.90 | 139.64 |
| 1965 | 90.50 | 95.75 | 70.00 | 74.06 | 141.50 | 149.71 |
| 1968 | 107.10 | 102.82 | 84.20 | 80.83 | 166.30 | 159.65 |
| 1970 | 128.70 | 110.68 | 101.60 | 87.38 | 198.60 | 170.80 |
| 1971 | 143.70 | 120.71 | 113.30 | 95.17 | 222.30 | 186.73 |
| 1972 | 177.00 | 140.36 | 140.20 | 111.18 | 272.50 | 216.09 |

[a]Social Security Administration (1972).

[1]Data on income for older Americans are available from two primary sources, the Social Security Administration and the Bureau of the Census. Unfortunately, the base year of the latest detailed information varies and this variation introduces some problems in integrating the materials that must be kept in mind.

In recent years, Social Security pensions have increased substantially, as Table 7-3 shows. However, in terms of purchasing power, the increases have been less substantial. In addition, while average benefit levels have risen, major segments of the older population still receive woefully inadequate Social Security benefits. For example, about 15 percent of those who draw Social Security receive the minimum— $1,125.60 per year in 1975. Of those who receive the minimum, *half* are retired single women, a quarter are widows or single men, and a quarter are married couples. Drawing the minimum benefit is associated with having had very low earnings, irregular employment, a short period of employment, or a combination of those characteristics. The factors that cause people to draw the minimum pensions also prevent them from accumulating other kinds of resources that could be used to provide retirement income (Lauriat, 1970; Reno and Zuckert, 1971).

Single women do not fare very well as Social Security pensioners. Because women are concentrated in jobs with low earnings, because their work careers are often interrupted for childrearing, and because widows do not qualify for the full value of their deceased husband's pensions, single women dominate the group receiving pensions far below the poverty line. Only women with professional or technical occupations escape high proportions receiving the minimum pension.

In general, widows who draw survivor's benefits are better off than are single women who draw pensions based on their own earnings. Only 11 percent of the widows draw the minimum pension, while 28 percent of retired women workers draw the minimum. However, hidden in these statistics is a sizable group of widows who draw pensions based on their own earnings because their survivor's benefits would have been even lower than the minimum pension.

The Social Security pensions of black workers also reflect the effects of past job discrimination. A quarter of the men and a fifth of the women who draw the minimum benefit are black. In 1970, black workers, both men and women, received pensions averaging $250 per year below the average for whites. For all categories of pension recipients, blacks receive pensions that are consistently about $20 per month lower than the pensions for whites in the same category. Other minority groups are similarly disadvantaged, but exact data on the magnitude of the disadvantage are hard to find.

In general, the older the individual, the lower the Social Security pension. This situation results from the fact that while cost-of-living increases have been applied to ease the impact of inflation, little has been done to adjust for the overall increases in real income since 1935. Admittedly, cost-of-living increases partially take care of this problem, but even so, the average pension of new beneficiaries at age 65 was $1,771.92 in 1970 as compared with $1,073.40 during the same year for those age 95 or over. And this problem is compounded because extreme old age drastically increases the need to buy services (Atchley, 1976b).

## Private Pensions

Since most private pensions came along after the Social Security Act became law, it is not too surprising that private pensions are designed primarily as supplements to Social Security pensions. Private pensions currently provide meager supplementary income because those who are drawing the benefits generally had only a few years of coverage prior to retirement. However, as private pension systems begin to mature, the level of benefits they provide should improve. Kolodrubetz (1970:19) reports that from 1962 to 1967 the median private pension income for couples rose from $790 per year to $970.

Schulz (1970) concludes that private pensions grew primarily out of a need for additional retirement income to supplement Social Security. A dramatic increase in new private pension plans covering large numbers of workers took place shortly after the 1947 Supreme Court ruling that pensions were a proper issue for collective bargaining. Feelings of social obligation on the part of industry, wage stabilization policies associated with the Korean War, favorable tax treatment for industries setting up pensions, and the development and expansion of negotiated multiemployer pension plans combined to open up coverage to millions of workers. However, a slowdown in rates of growth in private pension coverage since 1960 indicates that those segments of the labor force still not covered by private pensions are having trouble securing coverage. The most accessible groups are already covered, and the next likely target, small business, will probably remain an area of the economy with relatively poor access to private pensions.

Even for those covered by private pensions there are problems. For example, employees of Studebaker had what they thought was an excellent pension plan; but the company went out of business before the pension fund was filled. The result was that those employees over 65 received a reduced pension, and those not yet 65 lost the money they had paid in.

Another problem is nontransferability. In most private plans, retirement credits cannot be transferred to another plan. This restriction means that if workers change jobs, they stand to lose all of their retirement credits because they can never accumulate enough to entitle them to pensions.

These and similar problems led one U.S. Labor Department official to state

> In all too many cases the pension promise shrinks to this: "If you remain in good health and stay with the same company until you are sixty-five years old, and if the company is still in business, and if your department has not been abolished, and if you haven't been laid off for too long a period, and if there is enough money in the fund, and if that money has been prudently managed, you will get a pension" (Schulz, 1970:39).

The major virtue of private pension plans is held to be their flexibility, their ability to deal with the unique situation of the particular worker and his or her particular company. This ability is an especially attractive feature for managers who use pension plans as a tool in meeting labor problems. Yet private pensions also serve the public interest by providing income maintenance for older people.

Schulz concludes that the advantages of flexibility must be weighed against what it does to the interests of the employee and of the general public.

> For example, is it in the employee's and public interest that a large proportion of workers who build up credits under private pension plans never qualify for an eventual pension

because of insufficient periods of service with any one company? Is it in the employee's and public interest that the final pensions earned by short-term workers are so much less than those earned by career employees because there are few provisions for transferring and accumulating pension credits from a host of jobs? Is it in the employee's and public interest that private funds be permitted to promise the payment of future benefits without providing sufficient guarantee that the money will be there when needed? In short, to what extent can it be assumed that pension plan provisions geared to meet the special problems of individual firms are also of maximum benefit to the worker, the public, and the economy? (Schulz, 1970:49).

In 1974, Congress passed the Employee Retirement Income Security Act, which is aimed at solving some of these problems. This law seeks to protect workers from losing their pension rights by placing federal controls over vesting and financing of private pensions. An employee is "vested" at the point he or she is guaranteed a share of the employer's private pension fund. A vested individual is entitled to some benefits even if he or she leaves the organization prior to retirement age. The new law offers employers three options for vesting the pension rights of their employees:

*Option 1:* Employees' accumulated benefits are 25 percent vested after 5 years, gradually increasing to 100 percent vested at the end of 15 years.

*Option 2:* After 10 years, 100 percent vesting of accumulated benefits; nothing before 10 years.

*Option 3:* When age and length of service combined equal 45, 50 percent vesting; the remaining 50 percent vested within 5 years.

The new law also creates a Pension Benefit Guarantee Corporation under the Labor Department to protect workers covered by pension plans that fold. In addition, standards are established for financing and administering pension plans. If these standards are adhered to, then private pension funds should be more solvent in the future than in the past (Atchley, 1976b).

While the Employee Retirement Income Security Act was landmark legislation, it is clearly a compromise that leaves several issues unresolved. First, there is no requirement that employers provide private pensions. Second, there are no provisions to guarantee portability of pension rights—the ability to take pension rights from one employer to another. Finally, the machinery for enforcing violations of the act has yet to be tested.

## Public Pensions

Three fifths of those who receive public pensions but not Social Security are drawing pensions from Railroad Retirement. The rest are drawing some other form of government or military retirement. Public pensions of this type are considerably higher than either private pensions or Social Security pensions. In 1967, the median pension income for those receiving public pensions alone was $2,720 for couples, $1,995 for single men, and $1,090 for single women (Kolodrubetz, 1970:9). This median is substantially higher than the Social Security pension medians for couples and single men, but the figure for single women is about the same (Kolodrubetz, 1970:8).

For the 7 percent who receive a public pension *and* Social Security, the picture is even better. In this category, couples average public pensions of $1,800; single men $1,394; and single women $1,005, all receiving this money in addition to their Social Security pensions (Kolodrubetz, 1970:9).

Public retirement programs tend to relate pensions to peak earnings and to contain automatic provisions for cost-of-living increases. Also, public employees in general have more orderly work histories, which in turn entitles them to higher benefits. A third factor is the maturity of public pension plans in relation to private pensions. Public pension programs also typically involve high levels of employee contributions. All of these factors combine to make public pensions generally more adequate than private pensions.

Within the public sector, however, there are some wide variations, just as there are in the private sector. In Ohio in 1969, for example, the average pension for retired school employees was $1,188 per year, as compared to an average of $4,152 for retired highway patrolmen (Atchley et al., 1972:20).

### Dual Pensions

In 1967, 20 percent of the retired households in the United States were receiving two pensions, a Social Security pension plus either a private group pension or a public pension. These people enjoyed retired incomes well above the level required to meet minimum needs. The average was more than $4,300 for couples in this category, over $2,700 for single men, and over $2,300 for single women. The only category of single women with an average pension even at the bare minimum was single women with dual pensions.

Dual pensions serve to widen the gap between the haves and have-nots in terms of pension incomes because second pensions are concentrated among well-paying employers and occupations. The higher earnings, which make a second pension possible, also result in high Social Security pensions. Persons with private pensions are particularly likely to have high Social Security pensions. Dual pensioners thus average combined pensions twice as high as the average for persons with Social Security pensions alone (Atchley, 1976b).

### Assets

Many would argue that income need not support older people because they have other financial assets that can be used for this purpose. The rationale here is that older people should gradually liquidate their personal assets to supplement their money incomes.

Financial assets are things like automobiles, homes, insurance policies (only the kind with cash value), stocks, bonds, and cash savings. Such assets can provide housing and directly contribute to income via rents, interest, and dividends. Perhaps the most important points about older people's assets are the following:

On the average, older people, with their years of asset accumulation behind them, tend to own more and owe less than younger people (under fifty-five). Yet assets tend to be correlated with income, so that those families with the highest incomes are most likely to have substantial assets; whereas those with the lowest incomes are least likely to have any assets (Riley and Foner, 1968:85).

Saving money for one's old age is a time-honored tradition. Yet few people live up to the ideal in any substantial way. About half of the retired population has income from assets, but the level of asset income is generally low. In fact, most retired people have liquid assets of $2,000 or less. Depending on the form of investment, $2,000 will yield no more than around $160 per year, hardly a substantial supplement to pension income. Those with enough liquid assets to provide substantial incomes tend to be the same people who enjoy substantial pensions (J. Murray, 1972). Only a tiny proportion have incomes from private annuities.

About 60 percent of retired couples own their homes free and clear, as compared with only about 30 percent of retired single people. Homes are the most common financial asset of retired people, and it is widely thought that home ownership drastically cuts income requirements. But home ownership is worth less than $500 per year in terms of reducing income requirements. In addition, home ownership is worth very little as a contingency reserve.

## Cash Gifts

Cash gifts from family or friends not in the household were reported by only 3 percent of the retired, but among unmarried women the figure was 5 percent (Bixby, 1970:13). In terms of aggregate income, contributions from outside the household accounted for less than 1 percent of the income of retired people.

## Supplemental Security Income

In January 1974, an important change took place in the Social Security system. At that time, a special **Supplemental Security Income** payment (**SSI**) went into effect that guaranteed every older American $146 per month from Social Security regardless of prior work history ($239 to older couples). Obviously, this provision departs from the old concept of pensions based on prior service. For example, if an individual received a Social Security retirement pension of $110 per month as the only income under the old system, that individual now can exclude $20 of his or her pension income, giving an effective pension income of $90 per month. This income level would entitle the individual to an additional $56 per month in supplemental benefits, and thus the total benefit amount would be $166 per month. Therefore, for those receiving Social Security retirement pensions, the guarantee is actually $166 per month, and only those who did not qualify for any job-based pension would receive the $146 per month minimum (Atchley, 1976b).

Despite the fact that the supplemental payment is available to everyone, regardless of prior work history, Social Security will probably continue to be regarded generally as a legitimate income source. However, should the supplemental provisions come to be viewed as welfare, then Social Security retirement pensions may decline in terms of social acceptability. This area of public opinion is an excellent subject for research, for the new provisions have put more people on an equal income level than ever before.

The SSI program replaced Aid for the Aged, a federal-state public assistance program administered by local welfare departments. The need for SSI is indicated by the fact that in its first month of operation average payments of around $70 per month were going to nearly 2 million older Americans (Callison, 1974).

## INDIRECT INCOME SOURCES

Many public and private programs directly serve older people and also indirectly help to supplement inadequate incomes. Federal programs that indirectly give financial aid to older people include the low-rent public housing program, Medicare, Medicaid, the food stamp program, and the nutrition program for the elderly. Many states give property tax exemptions to persons over 65. In addition, local meals programs, senior centers, and transportation programs often provide services at reduced prices.

In 1972, Medicare expended 8.4 billion on health care for older Americans, including payments made under supplementary insurance. Medicaid paid another 2.7 billion dollars. Between 1966 (before Medicare) and 1972, the share of the health bills of older Americans being paid by government programs rose from 30 percent to 66 percent, while the share being paid directly by the patient declined from 53 percent to 28 percent. Yet the proportion of the health bills of older Americans being paid by Medicare declined between 1969 and 1972, primarily because restrictions were tightened.

Housing may also be subsidized for the aged. As of 1971, there were 22 federal housing programs either directly aimed at the older Americans or available to them. About half of these programs provide housing to older people below the cost for a similar housing unit on the open housing market (Robbins, 1971).

Thus, it is clear that indirect income sources increase the real incomes of older Americans, but research into the magnitude of this factor has not yet been done, partly because of the difficulties involved in getting comparable information on various sources of indirect income. It is probably safe to say that most indirect income sources help the poor more than they do the middle class.

## LEVEL OF LIVING

At this point an examination of spending patterns may help illustrate the practical impact of income on level of living. Table 7-4 shows the expenditures for various items at various age and income intervals.

First let us compare people aged 45 to 54 having $5,000 per year income with those 75 or over having $1,000 per year. This comparison comes closest to the facts of life, since well over half of those in the first age group have incomes of $5,000 or more, and well over half of those in the second have incomes of around $1,000.

**TABLE 7-4**
**Consumer Expenditures for Households**
**by Age and Annual Income of Head: United States, 1960**

| Item | Income of $1,000 | | Income of $5,000 | |
|---|---|---|---|---|
| | Age 45–54 | Age 75 plus | Age 45–54 | Age 75 plus |
| Food | 311 | 389 | 1460 | 1615 |
| Housing | 224 | 316 | 755 | 750 |
| Household operations | 43 | 54 | 215 | 235 |
| Furnishings | 46 | 26 | 340 | 295 |
| Clothing | 81 | 41 | 615 | 560 |
| Transportation | 89 | 38 | 665 | 565 |
| Medical care | 73 | 73 | 245 | 370 |
| Personal care | 20 | 17 | 115 | 100 |
| Recreation | 27 | 21 | 280 | 290 |
| Miscellaneous | 85 | 25 | 310 | 220 |

Source: Adapted from Goldstein (1960:118).

The difference in terms of food is staggering. The younger household with the larger income spends nearly four times as much on food as the older household with the lower income. This difference cannot be attributed to a larger household at a younger age, either, since the older household with the higher income spends *over* four times as much on food as its poorer counterpart. For a lot of people, this difference means a dramatic decline in the level of nutrition between age 50 and age 75. This fact is particularly relevant for the health of older people, since malnutrition is a significant contributing factor in disease. With an average of $32.42 per month to spend on food, the older poor household is bound to concentrate on foods with more starch and less protein or vitamins than it would buy if $121.66 per month were available for food.

Going down the line, the average older household has half as much for housing, one quarter as much for household operations, one thirteenth as much for furnishings and recreation, one fifteenth as much for clothing, one seventeenth as much for transportation, one third as much for medical care, and one seventh as much for personal care as has the average younger household. These figures are among the most important "facts of life" that confront many older people.

Other comparisons are also instructive. For example, expenditures within income groups are more consistent than are expenditures within age groups. While expenditures do change with age, these changes are relatively minor. Changes in income obviously have more important results.

Medical care is a good case in point. In the $1,000-income group, the health expenditure is a consistent $72 across the age groups, while in the higher-income group the figure increases from $245 to $370 with increasing age. This difference is a good example of the type of constraint low income places on the alternatives people have in adjusting to aging. Although all people suffer some decline in health as they get older, those with low incomes are unable to increase the level of medical attention to compensate for the decline, while those with higher incomes can. In practical terms, those with money can afford the option of better health, while those without money cannot, particularly since neither Medicare nor Medicaid will pay for preventive health care.

In summary, then, we find that lowered income produces critical deficiencies in level of living, particularly with regard to food and medical care. All of the basic needs—food, clothing, and shelter—tend to become more difficult to meet with increasing age. At a time in life when expenditures for recreation naturally tend to go up, low-income older people are forced to reduce expenditures for recreation. What kind of recreation can be bought for $21 *per year*? This sum hardly allows for maintaining a television set, much less for buying one. Particularly serious is the negative impact of poverty on transportation and the resulting social isolation. In addition, most older people have no other assets to fall back on. The result is a level of financial support that barely meets physical needs and leaves psychological needs almost totally neglected.

Obviously, many older people experience poverty for the first time as a result of retirement, widowhood, or divorce. Tissue (1970) studied 256 Old Age Assistance (welfare) recipients in Sacramento County, California. He used education and former occupation (for married women, husband's occupation) to divide the sample into 127 people who had been middle class and 129 who had been working class. Conceptually, Tissue treated the former middle-class welfare recipients as downwardly mobile and the former working-class welfare recipients as having remained stable.

Tissue found that compared to the stable poor, the downwardly mobile older people were much more solitary. They simply did not see as many friends, neighbors or relatives. And this lack of contact was caused by role loss. More than half of the downwardly mobile older people had lost four or more significant social roles. They were also more isolated from children.

However, despite their solitude, the downwardly mobile older people generally had a high capacity to enjoy solitary leisure, a capacity that is at least one benefit of having been middle class. In addition, their situation does not lead the majority of downwardly mobile older people to see themselves as unhappy or dissatisfied with their lives. They do resent specific elements such as retirement and often the housing into which their incomes have pushed them. But they have not become alienated or anomic, and nine out of ten still believe that hard work is the best route to success. It would seem that downward mobility has a great impact on the older person's social environment but little impact on the internal, psychological life of the person.

## THE FUTURE

The prospects for the future are not encouraging. The incomes of older people have increased over time, but little or no progress has been made in bringing retirement incomes more closely into line with preretirement levels.

In the future, we can expect to see a continuation of the trend toward early retirement. We can expect that earnings will occupy a progressively less important place as a source of income for older people.

Social Security, on the other hand, stands to become even more important as a source of income in the later years. As coverage becomes more complete, Social Security plus Medicare will no doubt become the leading financial resource for older people. In practical terms, these programs offer the greatest promise of an adequate income, particularly if the level of minimum benefits can be raised above the bare subsistence level, and if cost-of-living increases can be made automatic.

Private pension plans will become increasingly important as a source of supplementary income in retirement. Estimates indicate that by 1980, 25 to 30 percent of older people will be receiving payments from this source. In addition, over the years the paid-in shares of private pension holders will probably result in a significantly higher average benefit than is the case now.

As Social Security and Medicare assume an increasingly larger share of the public benefits, Supplemental Security Income can be expected to decline accordingly, even though many older people's incomes will still fall far short of their needs.

Compounding the problem is the fact that many older people will be relying on fixed or semifixed sources. For these people, inflation has been disastrous. An individual can currently expect to live about 20 years after retirement. In that length of time, inflation can significantly reduce the purchasing power of a dollar. For example, a couple with an income of $2,400 per year could buy more than twice as much in 1940 as they could in 1960. Only income from interest, rents, and dividends can be expected to increase, but the proportion of older people getting more than a token payment from these sources is apt to remain quite small.

## SUMMARY

As people grow old, their incomes drop. Even before retirement, many older people need some sort of supplementary income. At retirement, income usually drops by 50 percent or more, and during the years that follow, it drops even further.

Income for older people comes primarily from earnings, assets, and Social Security. Only one sixth of the older population has earnings, and only a very small proportion has any appreciable income from assets. Social Security provides the only income of any consequence to the vast majority of older people. As a result, over 60 percent of the older people in the United States are relatively poor.

Possible strategies for attacking this problem include opening up more employment opportunities for older people, encouraging people to save more, expanding private pension coverage, and expanding Social Security. While all of these strategies can be used to some extent, it is probably fair to say that the one that holds genuine promise for the vast majority of older people is the development of more adequate Social Security benefits.

The primary importance of financial resources to older people lies in the influence of money on the range of alternatives an individual has in attempting to adjust to aging. For most older people, finances sharply limit the available options even in such basic areas as food and medical care. For most older people, poverty is like a vise—it holds them down and leaves them no room to maneuver. In this regard, freedom from work and family is more than offset by the constraints of poverty. The end result is often a hopeless, stifling existence in place of what might be the most satisfying period of human life.

## SUGGESTIONS FOR FURTHER READING

Beresford, John C., and Alice M. Rivlin. "Privacy, Poverty, and Old Age." *Demography 3* (1966):247–258.

Bixby, Lenore E. "Income of People Aged 65 and Over: An Overview from the 1968 Survey of the Aged." *Social Security Bulletin 33* (1970):3–34.

Cohen, Wilbur J. "Social Security–The First Thirty-Five Years." In *Occasional Papers in Gerontology*, No. 7. Ann Arbor, Mich.: University of Michigan, Wayne State University Institute of Gerontology, 1970, pp. 1970.

Kreps, Juanita M. "Employment Policy and Income Maintenance for the Aged." In John C. McKinney and Frank T. de Vyver (eds.), *Aging and Social Policy*. New York: Appleton-Century-Crofts, 1966, pp. 136–157.

Peterson, D. A. "Financial Adequacy in Retirement: Perceptions of Older Americans." *Gerontologist 12* (1972):379–383.

Polinsky, Ella J. "The Position of Women in the Social Security System." *Social Security Bulletin 32* (1969):3–19.

Reno, Virginia P., and Carol Zuckert. "Benefit Levels of Newly Retired Workers." *Social Security Bulletin 34* (1971):3–31.

Schulz, James H. *The Economics of Aging*. Belmont, Calif.: Wadsworth, 1976.

Shulman, Harry. "Beneficiaries with Minimum Benefits: Their Characteristics in 1967." *Social Security Bulletin 32* (1969):3–20.

Thompson, Gayle B. "Work Experience and Income of the Population Aged 60 and Older, 1971." *Social Security Bulletin 37* (1974):3–20.

United States Bureau of the Census. "Money Income in 1973 of Families and Persons in the United States." *Current Population Reports*, Series P-60, No. 97. Washington, D.C.: United States Bureau of the Census, 1975.

West, Howard. "Five Years of Medicare—A Statistical Review." *Social Security Bulletin 34* (1971):17–27.

# 8
# Retirement

The process of retirement involves the separation of an individual from a job role—a role performed for pay[1]—and the acquisition of the role of retired person. While people can indeed give up such nonpaying positions as scoutmaster, church deacon, or volunteer worker, the term **retirement** is generally reserved for separation from those positions that bring monetary rewards.

Operational definitions seek to define an abstract conception such as retirement in terms of simple, observable procedures. At various times, **retired person** has been operationally defined as:

- ☐ Any person who performs no gainful employment during a given year
- ☐ Any person who is receiving a retirement pension benefit
- ☐ Any person not employed full-time, year-round

Palmore (1967) found that in 1963 among men 65 and over, 64 percent had *no* work experience in the previous year, 80 percent received some kind of retirement benefit, and 87 percent worked less than year-round, full-time. Thus, the way *retired person* is operationally defined makes quite a difference in who can be included and in the number of people defined as retired, but the definitions usually emphasize separation from the job rather than acquisition of the role of retired person.

For our purposes, an individual is retired if he or she is employed at a paying job less than full-time, year-round (whatever that may mean in a particular job) *and* if his

---

[1]Note that retirement relates to *jobs* rather than *work*. In general terms, one never stops working. A person's job, however, refers to his position of employment, and it is from a job that an individual retires.

or her income comes at least in part from a retirement pension earned through prior years of employment. Both of these conditions must be met for an individual to be retired. For example, many former military personnel draw retirement pensions but are employed full-time, year-round. Widowed housewives often are not employed, but neither are they eligible for a retirement pension.

Sometimes couples as well as individuals may be considered retired. A couple is retired if neither person is employed full-time, year-round and if most of the couple's income is from one or more retirement pensions. The extent of retirement can be measured by the number of weeks *not* employed (over and above usual vacation periods) for individuals who are drawing retirement pensions (Palmore, 1971a). These definitions are arbitrary to some extent, but they illustrate some important dimensions of retirement; namely, that retirement is an *earned* right and that its main effects concern separation from a job and a shift in the source, and usually the amount, of individual or family income.

There is increasing recognition that housewives make an enormous contribution to society through maintaining households and rearing children. Perhaps one day this recognition will be appropriately translated into the right to a general public retirement pension but it does not appear that this will happen in the near future.

Retirement marks the end of what is generally thought to be a close relationship between the kind of job an individual holds and the kind of life-style and livelihood he or she enjoys. This relationship results, of course, from the fact that for most people in American society, the only fully acceptable way of getting money is through a job. Americans tend to identify a job with a style of life, and this way of assessing a person's status is usually correct, for job usually determines income and income sets limits on life-style.

Another factor in the relationship between people and their jobs is the idea that careers can be pursued as ends in themselves, purely for the satisfaction of doing a fine job. This idea springs from the notion that job careers can give people their greatest opportunities for creation, and in this way can become their entire life. Mills incorporates these ideas into his concept of craftsmanship:

> Craftsmanship as a fully idealized model of work gratification involves six major features: There is no ulterior motive in work other than the product being made and the processes of its creation. The details of daily work are meaningful because they are not detached in the worker's mind from the product of the work. The worker is free to control his own working action. The craftsman is thus able to learn from his work; and to use and develop his capacities and skills in its prosecution. There is no split of work and play, or work and culture. The craftsman's way of livelihood determines and infuses his entire mode of living (1956:220).

Mills also says,

> Work may be a mere source of livelihood, or the most significant part of one's inner life; it may be experienced as expiation or as exuberant expression of self; as bounded duty, or as the development of man's universal nature. Neither love nor hatred of work is inherent in man, or inherent in any given line of work. For work has no intrinsic meaning (1956:215). *(of itself)*

## THE LINK BETWEEN PEOPLE AND THEIR JOBS

Understanding retirement thus involves understanding the nature of the links between people and their jobs. It can be said with some certainty that this relationship has changed over the years. In the days of medieval guilds, the idea of a vocation as a way of life was generally accepted. Not many people lived to become old in those days, but those who did continued to be employed until they grew too feeble or died. Since one's vocation was a major satisfaction in life, people worked as long as possible. Then, too, there were no provisions for gaining income in any other way. The industrial revolution, assembly line production, and automation have made some important changes in this picture.

To begin with, our system has become increasingly productive; today, fewer and fewer people are needed to produce the nation's greater and greater output. This increase in productivity was made possible largely by the switch from low-energy power converters such as animals, wind, and water to high-energy converters such as steam and electricity (Cottrell, 1955). Also, the demographic revolution reduced death rates, particularly in infancy, and prolonged life. The eventual result was a significant proportion of older people in the population. Declining birth rates meant a smaller proportion of young dependents to support, and this decline meant that it was possible to support more older dependents.

The rise of industrial production systems increased the need for planning and coordination within the economic system. Mechanisms such as the corporation and the bureaucracy were introduced into the economic system and gradually spread throughout society. Government bureaucracy grew to become the political counterpart of the economic corporation. Once the state became a large-scale organization, it was capable of pooling the nation's resources and allowing a segment of society to be supported in retirement. It was thus no accident that the first retirement program, inaugurated in 1810, consisted of pensions for civil service workers in England. America's failure to introduce civil service pensions until 1920 can be partly explained by the slow development of our national government.

The rise of industrialism brought with it urbanization and extensive physical mobility. These two factors combined to change the traditional ties to family and local community that had been the source of a great many different kinds of services. These trends resulted in a redefinition of the relationship between the individual and the government. At the same time, the wage system was putting an end to the traditional economic functions of the family. All of these trends combined to give individualism more weight in the relationship between the person and society.

## THE EVOLUTION AND INSTITUTIONALIZATION
## OF RETIREMENT

Accordingly, the link between people and jobs came to be separated from political and family life. One important result was to reduce the amount of cohesion that people could gain in their lives through their jobs. Another result was that the new relation between the individual and the state set the stage for establishing an institutionalized *right* to support in one's old age. Thus Social Security was established, and with its introduction the institution of retirement came of age in the United States. As it has continued to mature, the concept of retirement has come to embody the idea that by virtue of a long-term contribution to the growth and prosperity of society, its individual members earn the *right* to a share of the nation's prosperity in their later years without having to hold a job. For example, Ash (1966) found that between 1951 and 1960, steelworkers shifted substantially in terms of how they justified retirement. In 1951, the majority said that retirement was justified only if the individual was physically unable to continue. By 1960, the majority of steelworkers felt that retirement was justified by years of prior service on the job. The idea that the right must be earned is related to the fact that retirement is reserved only for those who have served the required minimum time on one or more jobs.

Industrialization and the rise of the corporation developed the concept of jobs, as opposed to crafts, and generated a large economic surplus that could be used to support adults who were not jobholders. The rise of strong national government created the political machinery that could then divert part of the economic surplus to support retired people. The depression provided strong incentive to cut down on the number of older workers competing for scarce jobs. Because industrial jobs are often boring and meaningless to the people who do them, the promise of retirement also served as an incentive for people to endure a growing number of repetitious industrial jobs. And gradually the average jobholder has come to accept the idea that people can legitimately live in dignity as adults without holding jobs, provided they have earned the right to do so. All of these conditions helped to pave the way for the development of retirement as an institution in American society.

Among industrial nations, only Japan has a high proportion of its older population in the labor force—55 percent in 1965. Palmore (1975) found that almost twice as many aged men continue employment in Japan as compared to other industrial countries. The reasons for this divergence include a national system of retirement pensions that only very recently allowed people to develop entitlement to a pension that would provide enough to live on; higher-than-average proportions of people employed in small business and farming—areas of the economy in which partial retirement is common in the United States as well as Japan; and chronic labor shortages, which, combined with low pension levels, created incentives to use older workers as a labor reserve. But this unusual situation does not necessarily mean that the lot of older Japanese is easier or that they enjoy higher status as compared to older workers in other countries. Japanese typically retire at age 55, and at that point they may receive a meager pension. They lose their seniority, and most must leave the job they held prior to retirement. They become part of what the Japanese government euphemistically calls "the mobile labor reserve," which means in reality that older employees are temporary employees who get shuffled from one job to another.

Thus retirement does not automatically emerge as a result of industrialization. In order for it to do so, there must be a mechanism to generate adequate retirement income; there must be incentives to allow older people to leave the labor force; and older people must be able to accept life in retirement as good and proper.

The factors mentioned above constitute the social evolution and justification for retirement. There is, however, also a further rationale for retirement that assumes that older workers are no longer capable of doing their jobs. It is this indefensible rationale that forms the basis for compulsory retirement policies.

## THE RETIREMENT PROCESS

Retirement is a *process* that involves withdrawing from a job and taking up the role of retired person. In studying retirement, we are interested in retirement policy, in the preparations people make both for withdrawing from the job and for taking up the retirement role, in the decision to retire, in the retirement event, and in the dimensions of retirement as a social role. We are also interested in the consequences of retirement both for the individual and for the society and in how individuals adjust to the changes retirement brings. Retirement is a complex social institution that is intertwined with the economy, the family, and the life course of individuals. Therefore, several different approaches are required for a balanced understanding of how retirement operates in society and in the lives of individuals.

### Attitudes toward Retirement

The retirement process begins when individuals recognize that some day they will retire. How younger people view the prospect of retirement has a bearing on how they assess their retired friends and, more importantly, perhaps, on how they themselves fare when retirement comes. In a real sense, one's attitudes about retirement can become a self-fulfilling prophecy; that is, the older person who looks forward to enjoying retirement is much more likely to enjoy it than someone who dreads it.

In general, people's ideas about retirement seem to be favorable. In a study of adults ranging in age from 45 on up, Atchley (1974a) found that the concept of retirement had four separate dimensions—activity, physical potency, emotional evaluation, and moral evaluation. On all four dimensions, the concept of retirement was very positive, regardless of the age or sex of the respondent. The only variation from this very positive view of retirement occurred among retired people who would have liked to have continued on the job. These people felt that retirement was unfair and bad. Most adults expect to retire (less than 10 percent do not), and most of them expect to retire *before* age 60 (Harris, 1965a). Only a very few say they dread retirement (Katona, 1965). Generally, the individual's attitude toward retirement is closely allied to his or her financial situation. The higher the expected retirement income, the more favorable the attitude. About two-thirds of employed adults envision no financial troubles in retirement, although most expect retirement to reduce their incomes by 50 percent from their preretirement levels.

The relationship between income, education, and occupation on the one hand and attitudes toward retirement on the other is complex. People with high incomes realistically expect to be financially secure in retirement, although they tend to estimate their income requirements at a level substantially below their present incomes. People with college education are more likely than others to plan an early retirement (Morgan, 1962), and those at higher occupation levels, with the exception of professionals, executives, and government officials, tend to see retirement more favorably than do people in lower occupational groups (W. Thompson, 1956). Workers at the higher occupation and education levels not only have higher earnings and more favorable attitudes toward retirement, but they also find their jobs more interesting and in actual practice are less prone to retire (Riley and Foner, 1968:445). People who feel they have achieved what they wanted in life are very likely to favor retirement, but people who still feel *committed* to their work seldom seek retirement, although they may not be antagonistic toward it (Atchley, 1971c).

People at lower occupational levels have less income and anticipate more financial insecurity in retirement. These people favor retirement, but dread poverty. Here, the question is money. Apparently, few people at the lower occupational levels continue to work because they love their jobs. At the middle occupational level, positive orientation toward retirement is at its peak. These people anticipate sufficient retirement income and at the same time have no lasting commitment toward the job.

At the upper occupational level, the picture is mixed. Income is less problem. The primary factor that produces attitudes against retirement appears to be commitment to work. In terms of proportions, the evidence indicates that more than half of the people who occupy upper-level occupations have a high work commitment, but also look forward to retirement (Atchley, 1971b).

Age may also be related to attitudes toward retirement. Early studies found that the older a person gets, the more likely he or she is to dread retirement (Katona, 1965). This correlation may be caused by the fact that with increasing age the proportion of workers that anticipate financial difficulties in retirement increases. It is also possible, however, that younger cohorts are more accepting of retirement. Ash's (1966) data, coupled with those of Streib and Schneider (1971), suggest that retirement is becoming more accepted over time *within* various age cohorts and that younger cohorts are more accepting of retirement than are older cohorts. That finances are important in the relationship between age and attitude toward retirement is illustrated by the fact that if adequate income could be assured, the proportion who would retire increases steadily with age from 21 to 64 years of age (Riley and Foner, 1968:445).

## Retirement Preparation

Since almost everyone expects to retire, it is useful to examine the planning and preparation that precede retirement. Very few people make plans for retirement, and very few are exposed to retirement preparation programs. Yet favorable attitudes toward retirement are associated with planning for retirement activities, company counseling, personal discussions of retirement and exposure to news media presentations about retirement (Greene et al., 1969). It would appear, then, that some type of anticipatory program helps people adjust to retirement.

That retirement involves a change in position, and that one element of this change is socialization concerning what to expect, has already been established. Learning the prerequisites for a future position is at least as important as learning specific skills or knowledge. Thus, retirement preparation programs need to alert people to the financial, physical, and psychological prerequisites of the retirement role. More will be said later concerning the retirement role, but it is important here to recognize that retired people are expected to be financially, physically, and socially self-sufficient. Retirement preparation involves seeking information, evaluating it, and making decisions. Ideally, the individual has learned these skills early in life, but in reality many people never develop them while their lives are structured by jobs and child-rearing. Thus, retirement preparation programs often need to devote attention to remedial education about decision making as well as to providing specific information or counseling.

Perhaps the most important facet of any retirement preparation program should be a very early exposure to the facts of life concerning retirement income. Some employers or unions will be able to point with pride to programs providing a retirement income high enough to meet the individual's needs. Others will have to spell out the shortcomings of their programs and the steps individual employees can take to guarantee their own financial security in retirement. Professional associations should also make it a point to provide realistic retirement information to their members, particularly to those just entering the profession. It is imperative for the individual to know as soon as possible precisely where he or she stands with regard to retirement income. For example, many younger workers will receive only Social Security on retirement. They do not know specifically what benefits they will receive; they only feel vaguely that Social Security will somehow take care of them. A direct comparison between the average salary of a mature worker in a given occupation and the Social Security benefits he or she would receive is probably the quickest way to illustrate the need for additional individual financial planning. And this education should be offered before it is too late for the individual to do anything about planning. The income picture may improve in the future. But at present the most important element of retirement preparation certainly is teaching people how to assure their own financial security, if indeed it is possible to do so.

Retirement preparation can have other desirable features. Learning how to take care of one's health in the later years and developing interests outside work are two important aspects of successful adjustment to retirement. The retiring person needs to be taught that continued activity is an effective way to retain the capacity for activity. Gradually increasing the time spent in roles other than work and gradually decreasing the time spent working can be particularly useful. This tapering off has been accomplished by gradually increasing the length of the annual vacation, but perhaps a method more in tune with the physical decline in energy is gradually reducing the length of the work day. This proposal would only apply if the transition were to be begun after age 60. Before that, the declines in energy are probably not great enough to matter.

Right now, most people retire suddenly, usually because of health, or because their jobs disappear because of a company transfer, a business failure, reductions in personnel, and so on. About a third of the work force is forced to retire because of reaching a mandatory retirement age. In the future, however, more and more people can be expected to benefit from a gradual transition and from early retirement provisions.

Education, above all, determines the need for retirement preparation. Generally, the higher the level of formal education, the less retirement preparation is needed. However, the high correlation among income, education, and occupation means that those people who need retirement preparation most are at income and occupational levels at which they are least likely to get it.

Retirement preparation programs are on the increase. Almost all are offered by companies whose workers are covered by a private pension and by government agencies. These retirement preparation programs fall into two categories. The *limited* programs do little more than explain the pension plan, the retirement timing options, and the level of benefits under various options. The *comprehensive* programs attempt to go beyond financial planning and deal with such topics as physical and mental health, housing, leisure activities, and legal aspects of retirement. Research indicates that only 20 to 30 percent of retirement preparation programs are comprehensive (Greene et al., 1969).

Yet these programs seem to pay off. People exposed to retirement preparation programs do more planning for retirement and have higher retirement incomes, more activities after retirement, and less belief in the stereotypes concerning retirement, in comparison with peers who have not had retirement preparation. Surprisingly, exposure to these programs produces results even if the participants see the program as not being very helpful (Greene et al., 1969). Thus, whether they know it or not, heightened sensitivity to their needs in retirement probably has beneficial long-range results for individuals exposed to retirement preparation programs (Hunter, 1968).

However, retirement preparation programs cover, at most, only about 10 percent of the labor force (Schulz, 1973). In addition, most programs should begin sooner, especially if they are to succeed in encouraging development of activities and interests and adequate financial planning. Thus far, the need for retirement preparation is not being met for the vast majority of people. In addition, more adequate evaluation of retirement preparation programs needs to be done (Kasschau, 1974).

## The Retirement Decision

Both attitudes toward retirement and planning or preparation for it have an impact on the decision to retire. Other important factors include the hiring and retirement policies of employers and the health of the individual.

First, an individual may decide to retire because he or she cannot find a job. Hiring policies, particularly in manufacturing, tend to discriminate against hiring older workers. Almost the only jobs that grow no harder to find as one grows older are jobs that pay badly, or jobs for which there is a chronic labor shortage.

When asked to defend their hiring policies, employers usually say that older people cannot meet the physical or skill requirements of the jobs. There is apparently no foundation for these allegations; nevertheless, they are acted on as if they were true.

A case illustration may make clear just how this kind of hiring discrimination can influence decisions to retire. In December of 1956, a large printing company that published several widely-circulated magazines ceased operations and closed down its nine-story plant. Over 2,500 workers were left jobless.

Among those affected was John Hilary, age 59, who was a master printer with 42 years of experience. Hilary was put in a real bind by the shutdown. He could have secured employment elsewhere, but it would have meant a move of over 1,000 miles for himself and his family. Hilary was reluctant to leave his home town. He had been born there and many of his relatives and all of his friends were there. He was active in his church and in local politics. In short, his ties to the community were too strong to make it worth his while to uproot himself completely in order to continue his chosen trade.

Instead, Hilary tried to find employment outside his profession. His age prevented him from being hired by any of the many local manufacturing concerns, even though his skills were easily adaptable to any situation requiring skill in running or repairing machinery. Even though he was willing to work for less than he had made as a printer, he was unable to get a job. He finally decided to retire from the labor force.

Now 73, Hilary supplements his union and Social Security retirement incomes by doing carpentry work for relatives and neighbors. He says bluntly that he is not really sorry he was forced to retire, but that if he could have found a job he would have continued to work for another 10 years. He is bitter that in order to get any kind of job that would allow him to maintain his self-respect, he would have had to leave everything else that had any meaning to him. Hilary's decision to retire clearly was precipitated prematurely by the fact that employer hiring policies prevented him from gaining employment.

On the other side of the coin are employer policies that allow employees to generate entitlement to early retirement. Early retirement plans usually allow employees to retire before they become eligible for a Social Security retirement pension by providing supplemental pension payments to keep pensions at an adequate level until the retired person becomes eligible to collect Social Security. For example, in 1970 the United Auto Workers negotiated a contract with General Motors that allows employees with 30 years service to retire at 56 on a pension of $500 per month. At age 65, the private pension drops to cover the difference between the employee's Social Security retirement pension and $500 per month.

Early retirement is being promoted by dissatisfied factory workers who want to retire as soon as it is economically feasible (Barfield and Morgan, 1969), and by employers who see early retirement as an effective way to deal with technological change, mergers, plant closings, and production cutbacks.

A third factor involved in the retirement decision is mandatory retirement policies. Only a small proportion of workers is forced to retire by mandatory retirement policies, but this proportion is increasing (Schulz, 1974). Many firms have such policies, and mandatory retirement is universal within the realm of government employment. While seniority usually protects the worker until the mandatory retirement age, the fact that the mandatory policy *is there* probably has an influence on the extent of voluntary retirement prior to the mandatory age.[2] The age specified for retirement can range from 55 to 70; but retirement before 65 usually means taking reduced benefits.

Mandatory retirement policies are often rationalized on the grounds of needing to phase older workers out of a complex production process in an orderly fashion. However, it is by no means clear that mandatory retirement policies are the best means of accomplishing this task.

Mandatory retirement is most often rationalized by contending that it is simple and easy to administer; that retirement "for cause" would require complicated measures; that mandatory retirement eliminates bias or discrimination in the phase-out process; and that it opens channels of promotion for younger workers (Palmore, 1972). None of these arguments is very persuasive. Since many, if not most, people retire before the mandatory retirement age, especially in more recent years, an unpredictable point of retirement is obviously quite possible to administer. If incompetence is not obvious, and therefore, not easy to measure, then one can question how serious a problem incompetence really is. Employers consistently exercise bias in the face of mandatory retirement policies by keeping people on after the mandatory retirement age if it suits their purposes. Thus, mandatory retirement policies are not a fool-proof way to eliminate discrimination. The most persuasive argument concerns making room for younger workers. This is the argument older workers are most sensitive to. *Given that there are more people than jobs, a good case might be made for the idea that an individual is entitled to hold a job only so long.* But note that here seniority, not age, is the criterion.

No one today can seriously argue that at age 65 or 70, people in general are so decrepit that they should be excluded wholesale from the labor force. It is even questionable whether this argument was true 40 years ago, when many mandatory retirement policies were being formulated. The mandatory retirement age by definition discriminates against an age category, and thus violates the principle of equal employment opportunity. Since chronological age alone is a poor predictor of ability to perform on the job, it is seen by many older workers as an inappropriate criterion for use in implementing a mandatory retirement policy. Mandatory retirement policies also waste talent and productive potential (Palmore, 1972). In addition, mandatory retirement often forces poverty on the retired person.

Harris and his associates (1975) found that 86 percent of both the general public and the older population felt that nobody should be forced to retire because of age if he or she wanted to continue and were still able to do a good job. Thus, mandatory retirement is not a general social policy. It is an employment policy imposed on the public by economic decision makers. On the other hand, nearly 70 percent of the

---

[2]Streib and Schneider (1971) suggest that many employees eagerly await the date when they "have to quit," and that in many cases it is erroneous to infer that someone who waits until the mandatory retirement date is retiring involuntarily.

American population feel that most people retire of their own choice. Accordingly, offering the opportunity to retire seems to be a policy that the public does support.

The arguments against mandatory retirement ages are for the most part soundly based. While the overwhelming majority of people retire because they want and can afford to, there is a small but important minority who either do not want to retire or cannot afford to, and mandatory retirement certainly unjustly discriminates against these people. The use of age as the sole criterion cannot be defended on rational grounds. Mandatory retirement certainly robs individuals of the opportunity to exercise talents and skills and society is deprived of their product. Mandatory retirement ages are almost always accompanied by private pensions. Therefore, the idea that mandatory retirement forces poverty is true mainly for those not so covered or for those whose irregular work histories deprive them of adequate pensions. There are indeed thousands of older people working at jobs that have fine pension plans but who will reach the mandatory retirement age without working long enough at the same job to be entitled to a pension. Many mandatory retirement age policies are based on an erroneous assumption that retirement will not hurt the older worker financially (Atchley, 1976b).

Actually, when the individual approaches retirement age, the course of action he or she takes is not entirely predetermined. Compulsory retirement policies, hiring discrimination, anticipated income, and health do impose certain limitations, but within these boundaries, most older people still have some leeway.

Undoubtedly an individual's decision to retire is also influenced by the informal norms of the work situation. For example, most professionals are probably discouraged from retiring by the attitudes of their colleagues. Since retirement tends to be viewed negatively among professionals, to retire is to buck the system. On the other hand, assembly-line workers are generally favorable toward retirement and indeed show a growing tendency toward early retirement (Barfield and Morgan, 1969). It would be absurd to assume that two individuals anxious to retire face the same decision in these two quite different occupational areas.

Attitudes of friends and family also probably play an important role in the retirement decision. One man's children may want him to retire, another's may not. One woman's husband may want her to retire, another's may not. One man lives in a neighborhood where retirement is sneered at, another lives in a leisure community where retirement is the rule rather than the exception. If we retire, then the characteristics our friends and family impute to retired people will be imputed to us. All of these factors may encourage or discourage retirement (Atchley, 1976b).

About two thirds of the wage and salary workers who retired between 1958 and 1963 did so voluntarily, and this proportion is increasing. Among those who retire voluntarily, however, poor health has been by far the major reason given historically (see Table 8-1). This factor can be mitigated somewhat by a less physically demanding occupation. Despite its importance in the past, however, health seems to be declining as a factor influencing the decision to retired.

**TABLE 8-1**
**Reasons for Retirement[a]**
**Given by Men Aged 65 and Over: United States, 1963**

| Reason for Retirement | Total | OASDI[b] Beneficiaries | Non- Beneficiaries |
|---|---|---|---|
| Number (in thousands) | | | |
| Not employed full time, 1962 | 6,009 | 4,707 | 1,303 |
| Reporting on retirement | 5,329 | 4,302 | 1,029 |
| Retired in 1957 or earlier[c] | 3,362 | 2,561 | 802 |
| Retired since 1957 | 1,967 | 1,741 | 227 |
| Wage and salary workers retired since 1957 | | | |
| Number (in thousands) | 1,509 | 1,332 | 178 |
| Total percent | 100 | 100 | 100 |
| Own decision | 63 | 62 | 65 |
| Poor health | 35 | 35 | 36 |
| Preferred leisure | 19 | 19 | 22 |
| Other reasons | 9 | 9 | 7 |
| Employer's decision | 37 | 38 | 35 |
| Compulsory retirement age | 19 | 20 | 17 |
| Poor health | 6 | 5 | 6 |
| Laid off or job discontinued | 8 | 8 | 8 |
| Other reasons | 4 | 4 | 4 |
| Self-employed retired since 1957 | | | |
| Number (in thousands) | 441 | 394 | 47 |
| Total percent | 100 | 100 | —d |
| Poor health | 53 | 53 | —d |
| Preferred leisure | 29 | 31 | —d |
| Business went bad | 5 | 4 | —d |
| Other reasons | 13 | 12 | —d |

[a]"Retirement" is defined here to mean not working at a regular, full-time job (35 hours or more a week for 6 months or more).
[b]Old Age, Survivors, and Disability Insurance.
[c]Includes a few who never held regular, full-time jobs.
[d]Percentage not shown where base is less than 50,000.

*Source:* Adapted from Palmore (1964b:3–10).

People who voluntarily retire tend to be dissatisfied with their jobs and less likely to view work as an end in itself. More and more people are citing a preference for leisure as their reason for retirement. Most people who would rather work than retire give financial reasons, and the higher the individual's earnings, particularly in relation to expected retirement income, the less likely he or she is to retire.

This general analysis of decisions to retire is based primarily on research from the United States. Shanas and her associates found that Americans were more likely to retire voluntarily than either Danes or Britons (Shanas et al., 1968).

## Retirement As Event

Retirement as an event takes on the characteristics of a rite of passage. That is, the event of retirement marks the end of employment and the beginning of life without a job (at least a full-time job). It marks the passage from one role to another. Retirement rites are largely informal; in fact, except in the case of some VIP's, the event is usually approached as if it were one that people would like to forget rather than remember.

Retirement as an event is a poorly developed rite of passage. The ceremony usually stresses past success and seldom deals with future life in terms of separation from work or the obligations of retirement. Retirement is not made visible by a rite of passage—partly, at least, because it is a status change that our society teaches people to keep quiet about.

## Retirement As a Role[3]

After the event, be it formalized or not, the individual is expected to assume the role of "retired person." Gerontologists have had a lengthy debate over the nature of the retirement role; and, in fact, over whether such a role even exists. Most people agree that there is a position, *retired person*, that individuals enter when they retire. The disagreement comes when an attempt is made to specify the *role* associated with that position. The term *role* can refer either to the culturally transmitted, general norms governing the rights and duties associated with a position in society or to a relationship between holders of complementary positions.

The rights of a retired person include the right to economic support without holding a job (but at the same time without the stigma of being regarded as dependent on society, as in the case of the unemployed); autonomy concerning the management of time and other resources; and often more specific rights associated with the former job, such as the right to retain library privileges.

The retirement role also involves duties. Jobs are almost always more than merely instrumental tasks. They also include mannerisms, ways of thinking, and generalized skills that the individual incorporates as part of the self. The person is expected to remain the same *type* of person after retirement as before.

In addition, retired people are expected to assume responsibility for managing their own lives. For a great many people, retirement means a great deal of added decision-making responsibility. This responsibility, added to the responsibilities of parenthood, friendship, and so forth that continue after retirement, means that by no

---

[3]For an extended discussion of the material presented in this section, see Atchley (1976b).

---

### RESEARCH ILLUSTRATION 8

### HEALTH AS AN EARLY RETIREMENT FACTOR[4]

A. William Pollman

Retirement research in the 1950s established that poor health was the most prevalent reason for early voluntary retirements. Most investigators agreed that the low level of benefits at that time produced pressure against early retirement that only very poor health could overcome.

Pollman sought to examine the relationship between health and early retirement when a reasonable retirement income was assured. To do this he took a sample of 725 male auto workers who, in 1965, retired early from the Chrysler Corporation with incomes of around $400 per month. Using a mail questionnaire, Pollman asked the subjects to rank job satisfaction, fellow workers, supervision, retirement benefits, health, and desire for free time in terms of their influence on their retirement decisions. Questionnaires were returned from 60 percent, about average for research on older people.

**TABLE 8-2**
**Primary Reason for Early Retirement**

| Reason for Retirement | Percent of Subjects Citing as Primary Reason |
|---|---|
| Adequate retirement income | 47.34 |
| Poor health | 24.49 |
| Wanted more free time | 19.49 |
| Dissatisfied with Job | 5.52 |
| Didn't like the boss or people on the job | 3.16 |

Table 8-2 shows the percentage of respondents citing various factors as the *primary* reason they retired early. Only a quarter of these early retirees cited poor health as their primary reason, and nearly 70 percent retired early either because they felt they could afford it or because they wanted more free time. Thus, when retirement income was perceived as adequate, poor health assumed a relatively minor role in the decision to retire voluntarily. If adequate retirement benefits become the rule rather than the exception, then health will probably assume a minor role in voluntary decisions to retire among the older population in general.

---

means all of the time of the retired person is available for leisure.

Retired people are also expected to manage to live within their incomes. Certainly many people cannot live up to this expectation, usually through no fault of their own, but the expectation is there, nevertheless. Retired people are expected to avoid becoming dependent either on their families or on the community (Atchley, 1976b).

As a *relationship*, the retirement role connects retired people to those who are still employed, either in a particular profession or in a particular organization. The crux of the relationship is the fact that both the retired person and the person still on the job

[4]Adapted from Pollman (1971a:41–45).

tend to identify themselves in terms of the same occupation or work organization. In this sense the position of retired person is similar to the position of alumnus or alumna.

While retirement *does* represent a role, this role is usually defined in flexible, qualitative terms rather than in concrete, instrumental terms.[5] It was probably the absence of the instrumental element found in job roles that led many investigators to view retirement as a "roleless role" and therefore as an inevitable problem for the retired person. These people felt that retirement created a gap that only a new instrumental or "functional" role could fill. Much of the retirement literature still contains discussions of possible functional alternatives to work (S. Miller, 1965).

However, other work (Schneider, 1964; Streib and Schneider, 1971) indicates that instrumental norms may never need to develop around retirement. Schneider makes the point well:

> A clearly-defined role facilitates activity and gives a sense of security to a person involved in a network of impersonal universalistically-oriented judgements and evaluations. This may not be the kind of world in which many older people live. In the later years of life, the *important* persons in one's life—friends and relatives—know who the older person is and, therefore, he moves in a world that is familiar to him, and with which he is familiar. He may not need a sharply defined extra-familial "role" to give him an identity or to facilitate his own activity in his everyday world. We suggest, therefore, that so far as the older person himself is concerned, his willingness to leave the work force and perhaps his satisfaction with other aspects of life are not dependent upon whether he has a clearly defined alternative role or not (1964:56).

Following this rationale, the retirement role, by its very vagueness, allows the individual a certain amount of flexibility in adjusting to his or her less consistent physical capabilities.

### Phases of Retirement

It is useful also to consider the various phases through which the retirement role is approached, taken, and relinquished. These phases are charted in Figure 8-1.

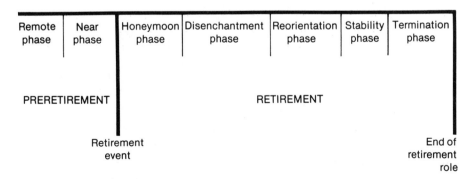

**Figure 8-1**   Phases of retirement. *Source:* Atchley (1976b).

[5]Jobs also have important qualitative aspects, but these are seldom emphasized in "job descriptions" or in discussion about jobs, and this is perhaps a major oversight.

**Preretirement**   The preretirement period includes a *remote* phase, in which retirement is seen by the individual as a vaguely positive something that will happen someday, and a *near* phase, in which individuals orient themselves toward a specific retirement date.

Two important things often happen during the near phase of preretirement. First, people begin to gear themselves for separation from their jobs and the social situations within which they carried out those jobs. They may adopt a "short-timer's attitude." They may begin to notice subtle differences in how they are viewed by others. Second, people often develop fairly detailed fantasies of what they think their retirement will be like. These fantasies may be quite accurate pictures of the future or they may be totally unrealistic. If the fantasies are realistic, they can serve as a "dry run" that may smooth the transition into retirement by identifying issues that require advanced decision making. But if the fantasies are unrealistic, they may thwart a smooth transition into retirement by setting up detailed but unrealistic expectations.

**Honeymoon**   The retirement event is often followed by a rather euphoric period in which the individual tries to "do all of the things I never had time for before." A typical person going through this phase says: "What do I do with my time? Why, I've never been so busy!" Some people do not go through a honeymoon phase. For one thing, honeymoons require a positive orientation. They also require money, a scarce commodity for some older people. The honeymoon period of retirement may be quite short or may extend for years, depending on the resources available and the individual's imaginativeness in using them. However, most people cannot keep up the hectic pace of the honeymoon period indefinitely, and they then settle into a retirement routine.

The nature of the retirement routine is important. If the individual is able to settle into a routine that provides a satisfying life, then that routine will probably stabilize. People whose off-the-job lives were full prior to retirement are often able to settle into a retirement routine fairly easily. These people made choices among activities and groups earlier in life. All that remains for them to do is to realign time in relation to those choices.

**Disenchantment**   However, some people do not find it so easy to adjust to retirement. After the honeymoon is over and life begins to slow down, many people experience a period of letdown, disenchantment, or even depression. During the honeymoon period the retired person lives out the preretirement fantasy. The more unrealistic the preretirement fantasy turns out to have been, the more likely the individual is to experience a feeling of emptiness and disenchantment. The failure of the fantasy actually represents the collapse of a structure of choices, and what is depressing is that the individual must start over again to restructure life in retirement.

**Reorientation**   A reorientation often occurs among retired people who are disenchanted with retirement. During reorientation, depressed individuals "take stock" and "pull themselves together." This process involves using their experiences as retired people to develop a more realistic view of alternatives given a particular set of resources. Reorientation also involves exploring new avenues of involvement. Very few people elect to become hermits in retirement. Most want to remain involved with the world around them.

*If plans were unrealistic*

Groups in the community sometimes help people reorient themselves toward retirement. For example, many people become involved in Senior Center activities for the first time during this phase. But for the most part, people are on their own during the reorientation phase, and they seek help most often from family and close friends. The goal of this reorientation process is a set of *realistic* choices that can be used to establish a structure and a routine for life in retirement that will provide at least a modest amount of satisfaction.

**Stability**    The stability phase of retirement occurs when people have developed a set of criteria for dealing routinely with change. People with stable retirement life-styles have well-developed sets of criteria for making choices, and these criteria allow these people to deal with life in a reasonably comfortable, routine fashion. Life may be busy, and certainly it may have exciting moments, but for the most part it is predictable and satisfying. Many people pass into this phase directly from the honeymoon phase; others reach it only after a painful reassessment of personal goals; others never reach it. In the stability phase of retirement, people have mastered the retirement role. They know what is expected of them and they know what they have to work with—what their capabilities and limitations are. They are self-sufficient adults, going their own way, managing their own affairs, bothering no one. Being retired is for them a serious responsibility, seriously carried out.

**Termination**    Some people reach a point where the retirement role is not very relevant to their lives. Some return to a job, but most often the retirement role is canceled out by illness and disability. When an individual is no longer capable of engaging in major activities such as housework, self-care, and the like, the retirement role is displaced by the sick and disabled role as a primary organizing factor in the individual's life. This change is based on the loss of able-bodied status and the loss of independence, both of which are necessary for adequate playing of the retirement role. Another way that a person may lose his or her retired status is to lose financial support. At that point, the person ceases to be retired and becomes dependent.

The increasing dependence forced by old age usually comes gradually enough that the retirement role is given up in stages. Only on institutionalization do independent choices begin to become so limited that the dignity adhering to the retirement role is totally lost.

**Timing of Phases**    Because there is no universal point of retirement, there is no way to tie the phases of retirement to a chronological age or to a period of time. These phases refer rather to a progression of processes involved in approaching, playing, and giving up the retirement role. They represent an ideal type, an illustrative device that hopefully makes it easier to view retirement as a process.

## THE CONSEQUENCES OF RETIREMENT

In addition to affecting the individual's other roles, retirement and the loss of a job have various effects on the individual and his or her situation. Retirement is widely thought to have an adverse effect on health. Everyone seems to know people who carefully planned for retirement only to get sick and die shortly after leaving their jobs.

However, the crucial question is whether people retire because they are sick or whether they are sick because they retire. If people retire because they are sick, then it should not be surprising that some of them die. The decisive test of the impact of retirement on health is the state of health following retirement, as compared to just preceding retirement. Using their data from a large longitudinal study of people both before and after retirement, Streib and Schneider (1971), concluded that health declines are associated with age, *but not with retirement*. That is, retired people are no more likely to be sick than people of the same age who are still on the job. In fact, unskilled workers showed a slight *improvement* in health following retirement.

A good deal of research has been devoted to the impact of retirement on mental disorders, but no definite impact has yet been found (Nadelson, 1969). Lowenthal (1964b) found that mental illness tended to cause social isolation, not the reverse. Likewise, it is quite probable that mental illness causes retirement, rather than the other way around. It is true that several studies point to a higher incidence of mental impairment among retired people (Nadelson, 1969:10). However, Lowenthal and Berkman (1967:76) found that the association between retirement and mental illness was mainly a function of poor health, low social activity, and unsatisfactory living arrangements rather than of retirement in itself.

Much of the research on the personal consequences of retirement concerns the impact of retirement on social adjustment. The broad category of social adjustment includes such factors as acceptance of retirement, life satisfaction, morale, self-esteem, age identification, and job deprivation. It has been generally assumed that retirement has a negative impact on social adjustment, but research disproves this assumption.

Morale and life satisfaction are two concepts that have been used to assess overall emotional reaction to one's life at a given point in time. For example, Simpson, Back, and McKinney (1966c) found that morale was generally unconnected to work or retirement. They concluded that morale is influenced as much or more by health, family situations, and other personal factors as by work or retirement. Using the same data, Kerckhoff (1966a:192) found that high morale was associated with independence between generations in the family and with a functional, home-based pattern of activities within the older couple. The only work-related factor associated with morale was the tendency for those with orderly work histories to have high morale in retirement (Simpson et al., 1966c:67). Streib and Schneider (1971) found that retirement produced no significant change in life satisfaction. Nearly half of their respondents did not expect retirement to reduce life satisfaction, but even so a sizable proportion overestimated the adverse effect of retirement on life satisfaction.

Cottrell and Atchley (1969) found that depression was uncommon among retired teachers and telephone company employees. No category showed as much as 10 percent with a high degree of depression. However, women were significantly less likely to show a low degree of depression (72 percent), as compared to men (80 percent), particularly among the teachers. In all categories, however, over 70 percent showed a low degree of depression.

Apparently, no matter how the subjective reactions to the retirement life situation are measured, retirement makes little difference. The proportion with a high degree of satisfaction depends more on factors such as family situation, job history, and other personal factors than on retirement itself.

Another area of interest concerns the *self*. Several aspects of the impact of retirement on self have been studied. Back and Guptill (1966) used a semantic differential to study the self concept among preretirees and retirees. They identified three dimensions: involvement, optimism, and autonomy. They found that the involvement scores for retired people were considerably lower than for people in preretirement, regardless of socioeconomic characteristics. However, retirement had very little effect on the optimism or autonomy dimensions. Back and Guptill conclude that the decline in perception of self as involved results almost entirely from loss of job. Their findings indicate that an individual who was healthy, had a middle- or upper-stratum occupation, and had a high number of personal interests, would feel a minimal loss of a sense of involvement brought on by retirement. Nevertheless, they also conclude that even these people did not successfully fill the gap left by the loss of their jobs.

Cottrell and Atchley (1969) studied the impact of retirement on the self-esteem of older adults. Using M. Rosenberg's (1964) scale of self-esteem, they found that self-esteem in retirement tends to be quite high, much higher than among the high school students studied by Rosenberg. They also found that retirement produced no differences in self-esteem scores.

The construct of *job deprivation* refers to the extent to which an individual misses his or her job. Simpson, McKinney, and Back (1966a) found that low job deprivation in retirement was related to (1) having looked forward to retirement;[6] (2) having achieved most of one's job-related ambitions; and (3) having an adequate retirement income. From these findings, it appears that job deprivation in retirement depends on how retirement compares with life on the job. If retirement is anticipated as a negative thing; if the individual feels that job goals remain unmet; if retirement income is inadequate; and if health is poor in retirement—then it should not be too surprising that the retired individual misses the "good old days" on the job. Given the low levels of retirement income, it is surprising that high job deprivation is not more prevalent than it is.

Feelings of usefulness represent another area of the self related to the job. Streib and Schneider (1971) found that the percentage of persons who "often" or "sometimes" felt useless averaged around 12 percent before and 27 percent after retirement. They report a consistent and marked increase in the percentage feeling useless following retirement, but at no point does the proportion feeling useless go much over a quarter. Putting it another way, over 70 percent of their respondents seldom or never felt useless in retirement.

Another area in which retirement is widely thought to have a negative effect is *social participation*. Social participation is assumed to be tied to support from a job role; loss of the job role presumably hinders participation. Only in a relatively small

---

[6]This finding matches Thompson (1958) and Streib and Schneider (1971).

minority of cases does retirement produce a decrease in participation and consequent loneliness and isolation. And if the effects of widowhood are controlled, the proportion in this category is substantially reduced. G. Rosenberg's (1970) data suggest, however, that retirement is more likely to produce social isolation among the working class.

Bengtson (1969) examined the level of role activity among retired teachers and factory workers in six national samples.[7] He found three basic patterns of activity in relation to roles in (1) families, (2) organizational settings, and (3) informal settings. The most prevalent pattern was typified by a high level of family activity, intermediate activity in informal settings, and low activity in organizational settings. This pattern was present among the Polish and Italian samples and among factory workers in the United States, West Germany, and Austria. Teachers in the United States and West Germany had a pattern in which activity was moderate to high and showed relatively little difference in activity level among the three areas (family, formal settings, and informal settings). Finally, the Dutch showed a pattern in which family activity was very high, activity in formal settings was considerably lower, and activity in informal settings was lowest. However, within the Dutch sample, the teachers showed much higher levels of activity in nonfamily settings than did the factory workers. Bengtson's data indicate that there are indeed national differences in terms of what kinds of activities occupy people in retirement. The Dutch, especially, show a unique lack of involvement with friends and neighbors in retirement. Yet certain trends reflected occupational rather than national differences. For example, a low degree of involvement in organized settings was typical of retired factory workers in all six national samples.

Simpson, Back, and McKinney (1966a) found that many patterns of involvement supported by jobs persist into retirement. They found that having a higher status occupation and an orderly work career were as crucial for involvement in retirement as at earlier ages. They also found that if social involvement is not developed prior to retirement, it is unlikely to be initiated after retirement. Finally, they found that retirement itself is not responsible for the lack of involvement among semiskilled retired people and some middle-status workers, but rather *work histories* that had not allowed these people to become integrated into society. Simpson and her coworkers particularly stress the role of financial security in providing support for participation in society.

Most people continue to do in retirement the same *kinds* of things they did when they were working. About a third increase their level of nonjob-related role activities to fill the gap left by retirement. About a fifth of the retired population experiences a decrease in activities. However, gains or losses in activity are a relative matter. For someone who was uninvolved prior to retirement, leaving the job can result in an increase in activities and still leave gaps of unfilled, unsatisfying time. On the other hand, for an overinvolved professional, retirement may reduce the net amount of

[7]Austria, West Germany, the Netherlands, Italy, Poland, and the United States.

activity, but at the same time bring the level down to a point more suitable to the person's capabilities and desires.

A great deal of attention has been paid to the impact of retirement on *leisure participation*. According to one school of thought, leisure cannot legitimately be engaged in full-time by adults in western societies without resulting in an identity crisis for the individual and a social stigma of implied inability to perform (S. Miller, 1965). At one time, and in some cultures more than others, this set of assumptions may have been widely applicable. In fact, much of the retirement research done in the United States in the early fifties supports such a view. However, there is growing evidence that in recent years the leisure of retirement (to the extent that retirement brings leisure rather than a new set of obligations) is viewed both by retired people and by society at large as an earned privilege and opportunity (Atchley, 1971c; G. Thompson, 1973). The "embarrassment" that has been cited as an obstacle to leisure participation among retired people is probably more a function of the poverty retirement often brings than a function of embarrassment caused by feelings of worthlessness brought on by leaving the job.[8]

Another source of embarrassment concerns the social context in which leisure skills must be learned by older adults. If leisure skills can be learned in an environment structured around the needs and abilities of older people, then embarrassment can be minimized. However, all too often older adults must learn in an environment developed to teach children—an embarassing situation. Of course, another point is that taking the first few inept steps toward learning a new skill is always embarrassing, regardless of the age of the person trying to learn or his or her social position.

## Situational Consequences

Much of the preceding discussion reflects individual response to changes in situation. We will now discuss three important situational changes related to retirement that deserve special attention: income changes, changes in residence, and changing family structure.

Chapter 7 dealt with *income* sources and strategies in detail. In the present context, our concern is with the social impact of the income changes that accompany retirement. Retirement generally diminishes economic security. Income in retirement is usually about half what it was prior to retirement. And not only is income reduced, but *feelings* of economic deprivation increase (Riley and Foner, 1968:455). However, feelings of economic deprivation tend to decrease in prevalence as the number of years retired increase. Clark and Anderson (1967) found that reduced income had a significant impact on self-image, especially for people at the bottom of the socioeconomic scale. However, they concluded that lifelong poverty has more impact on self-esteem than does a deteriorating standard of living.

A change in situation that is closely associated with retirement in the minds of not

---

[8]For a more thorough discussion of this issue see Chapter 9.

## RESEARCH ILLUSTRATION 9

## THE EFFECT OF RETIREMENT ON PERSONAL ADJUSTMENT[9]

Wayne E. Thompson, Gordon F. Streib, and John Kosa

Thompson, Streib, and Kosa examined the influence of retirement on the personal adjustment of older men. They began with a group of 1,559 men, all gainfully employed, who were between 65 and 68 in 1952. By 1954, 477 of these men had retired. While the sample overrepresented large, affluent, and progressive organizations and prosperous and well-educated individuals, it did represent most major industries, all walks of life, and all parts of the country.

The study was designed to answer the question: Given a certain personal adjustment score in 1952, when all of the subjects were still on the job, were there differential changes in personal adjustment score among those who subsequently retired as compared with those who continued on the job? Personal adjustment was measured by three indices that ranged from "satisfaction with life" through "dejection" to "hopelessness" in terms of decreasing adjustment. Table 8-3 shows the impact of retirement on personal adjustment. In general, the view that retirement has negative effects on personal adjustment was not supported by these findings. In fact, Table 8-3 shows that those who retired were consistently more likely to show *gains* in personal adjustment.

Thompson, Streib, and Kosa also classified their subjects as "willing" and "reluctant" based on their preretirement attitudes toward retirement. "Reluctants" were those who viewed retirement as mostly bad for people, who disliked the idea of retirement, and who, if given a choice, would have continued on the job.

Reluctant retired men were more likely to become dissatisfied and dejected, while those who were willing were no more likely to become dissatisfied than those who stayed on the job and were the *least* likely to become dejected. There were no differences in terms of hopelessness.

Thompson, Streib, and Kosa (1960:169) state,

> In all it would appear that the negative effects of retirement have largely been overestimated. Changes in the direction of maladjustment occur only when the retirees hold an unfavorable preretirement attitude toward retirement and then only as indexed by the two less extreme indices of personal adjustment.

In further analysis, they found that this pattern held even among those who were not economically deprived, who were in good health, and who did not have trouble keeping occupied. In other words, even when the effects of other major causes of maladjustment were controlled, there was still this slight tendency toward maladjustment among those retired men who were reluctant.

only laymen, but of professionals as well, is *change of residence*. For example, Arnold Rose (1965a) considered the movement of older people to retirement communities as a major impetus for the development of an old-age subculture. However, because of their very high densities of older people, retirement communities such as Sun City, Arizona, and St. Petersburg, Florida, have perhaps commanded more attention than they deserve, given the fact that only a tiny proportion of the older population moves to such communities.

The fact of the matter is that, while older people do move, only about 10 percent ever moves across county lines, and only about 2 percent ever moves across state lines.

[9]Adapted from W. Thompson et al. (1960:165–69).

From their findings, Thompson, Streib, and Kosa conclude that

> In all, retirement appears to have a negative effect upon personal adjustment only insofar as it has an effect upon economical wherewithal . . . and upon difficulty in keeping occupied. Also, as indexed by the least extreme of the indices. . . . reluctance to retire evidently plays an independent part in changes in personal adjustment. However, there is no evidence that extreme maladjustment is a typical result of retirement, even among those who are economically deprived, are in poor health, or are finding it difficult to keep occupied (1960:169).

**TABLE 8-3**
**Changes in Personal Adjustment between 1952 and 1954**
**among Those Who Stayed on the Job and Those Who Retired**

|  | Stayed on the Job Throughout (N equals 1,082) | Retired between 1952 and 1954 (N equals 477) |
|---|---|---|
| Satisfaction with Life | | |
| Satisfied in 1952 who became dissatisfied | 34%   (550)[a] | 44% (238) |
| Dissatisfied in 1952 who became satisfied | 22%   (532) | 26% (239) |
| Dejection | | |
| Not dejected in 1952 who became dejected | 14%   (810) | 19% (349) |
| Dejected in 1952 who ceased being dejected | 49%   (272) | 51% (128) |
| Hopelessness | | |
| Hopeful in 1952 who lost hope | 10% (1,003) | 12% (416) |
| Without hope in 1952 who became hopeful | 62%   (79) | 77%   (61) |

[a] The number in parentheses is the percentage base. The percentages represent "changers." For example, the top left-hand cell shows that of the 550 persons on the job throughout who were satisfied with their life in 1952, 187 or 34 percent became dissatisfied between 1952 and 1954.

*Source:* Adapted from W. Thompson, et al. (1967:167).

In addition, movers are not randomly distributed throughout the older population, but instead are concentrated among those who are widowed, disabled, retired, well-educated, or living in households other than their own. When the effects of retirement alone are examined, it becomes clear that retirement has little impact on migration. The percentage who move is slightly higher among retired people age 65 or over, as compared to those who are still on the job at that age, but the difference is significant only for men who move across county lines. Retirement has very little impact on the movement of people who move within the same county (Riley and Foner, 1968).

The overwhelming majority of those who retire stay put. Those who do move do so for reasons other than a search for "retirement living." The most influential impact of retirement is the economic incentive to find less expensive housing, but such moves are usually accomplished within the same general vicinity. The common notion that retirement brings on massive migrations is a myth. However, in the future, as younger, better-educated cohorts become old, the tendency to move at retirement may increase somewhat, but probably will never become a prevalent trend.

Retirement can also be expected to affect *family structure.* Most retired people are married and living with a spouse. Retirement could be expected to affect the relationships within couples. Kerckhoff (1966b) found that retiring husbands look forward more to retirement, experience more satisfaction in retirement, and are more involved in the retirement process than their wives.[10] Compared to couples with a higher-level occupational background, couples in which the husband was retiring or had retired from a semiskilled, unskilled, or service job were more passive in their anticipation of retirement. They also regarded retirement as an unpleasant experience, and they tended to view retirement much more negatively.

Kerckhoff attributes this difference to the impact on the couple of greater involvement on the part of the husband in household tasks following retirement. Among all occupational levels, retired men took a greater part in household tasks after retirement. The difference was in how this increased household involvement was viewed by their wives. In the middle and upper strata, the increase was welcomed by the wives and seen as desirable by both husbands and wives. The picture was different in the lower stratum. Working-class marriages were less companionate and more authoritarian. In addition, working-class wives expected more exclusive control over the household. Thus, after retirement in the working class, *both* husbands and wives tended to see increased involvement of the husband as undesirable. But the husbands increased their involvement despite themselves, which led to conflict based on the guilt of the husbands and on the irritation of the wives at having had their exclusive domain invaded.

Heyman and Jeffers (1968) also studied the impact of retirement on couples. They found that more than half of the wives were sorry that their husbands had retired. These wives tended to be working class, had husbands who were in poor health, and had had unhappy marriages before retirement.

## Personal Adjustment to Retirement

In a sample of retired teachers and telephone company employees, Cottrell and Atchley (1969:20) found that nearly 30 percent felt they would never get used to retirement. This percentage was higher among retired teachers. Streib and Schneider (1971) classified about 70 percent of their sample as being not completely satisfied with retirement.

Some people avoid the problems of adjustment to retirement by going back to a paying job. In their longitudinal study of retirement, Streib and Schneider (1971:145–58) observed a number of people (about 10 percent) who returned to jobs after having retired. Those who return are characterized by having had a negative attitude toward retirement, by attaching a positive value to the satisfactions of work, by having been

[10]Kerckhoff did not ascertain whether the wives themselves were also engaged in retirement from jobs of their own.

forced to retire, and by having a high degree of *felt* economic deprivation. Of these factors, low income provides the greatest incentive to reject retirement and seek a job. Factors that *allow* people to return to a job are good health and an upper-status occupation.

On the other hand, Cottrell and Atchley found that 49 percent of their sample had adjusted to retirement in 3 months or less. Surprisingly, women consistently showed more difficulty adjusting to retirement quickly than did men (Cottrell and Atchley, 1969; Streib and Schneider, 1971). Quick adjustment to retirement was related to having an adequate income and having had a semiskilled job.

Heidbreder (1972a) examined white-collar and blue-collar differences in adjustment to early retirement. While she found that an overwhelming majority of people were satisfied with retirement, she also found that adjustment problems were concentrated among former blue-collar workers who had low incomes, poor health, and little education.

About a third of the retired population encounters difficulty in adjusting to retirement. A Harris Poll (1965a) found that adjusting to reduced income was by far the most frequently encountered difficulty (40 percent) *among those who have difficulty* adjusting. Missing one's job accounted for about 22 percent of the adjustment difficulties. The remaining 38 percent was accounted for by factors such as death of spouse or declining health, factors that are directly related to retirement adjustment only in that they influence the situation in which retirement adjustment must be carried out. This last finding suggests that there may be certain situational prerequisites for a good adjustment.

Adjustment to retirement is greatly enhanced by sufficient income, the ability to give up one's job gracefully, and good health. In addition, adjustment seems to be smoothest when situational changes other than loss of job are at a minimum. In other words, assuming that one's fantasy concerning the retirement role is based on reality, factors that upset the ability of retired people to live out their retirement ambitions hinder their ability to adjust to retirement smoothly.

People who have difficulty adjusting to retirement tend to be those who are either very inflexible in the face of change or faced with substantial change or both. The prime aspects of retirement that require adjustment are loss of income and loss of job. Very little research has been done on how people adjust to loss of income.

Atchley (1975a) developed an approach to retirement adjustment based on the impact of retirement on the individual's hierarchy of personal goals. If a job is high in that hierarchy and yet is an unachieved goal, then the individual can be expected to seek another job. If a substitute job cannot be found, then the hierarchy of personal goals must be reorganized. If the individual is engaged in a wide variety of roles, then reorganization can take place by simple consolidation. If the individual has only a few roles other than a job, then he or she must seek an alternative role. If an alternative is not available, the individual must disengage. Of course, if the job is not high on the individual's list of priorities to begin with, then no serious change in personal goals is occasioned by retirement.

Any type of role behavior is at least partly the result of negotiations between the role player and the other role players to whom his or her behavior relates. Thus retirement also changes the set of people with whom one negotiates. At work one negotiates behavior in the work role with one's peers, superiors, subordinates, and audiences. One's family and friends are involved only on the extreme periphery of work role negotiations. In retirement, the people associated with one's former work drop out of the picture almost entirely (except for friends who also were work associates); and one negotiates primarily with family and friends in order to translate the general demands of retirement into particular behavior.

Most people seem able to make these transitions reasonably smoothly. A major influence on this transition is the generally held stereotype of the retired person. The fact that both the retired person and the people with whom he or she interacts share at least to some extent a common idea of the nature of the retirement role gives everyone a place to begin the interaction. Very quickly, however, the individual retired person learns how to personalize this interaction. Thus, the vagueness of the retirement role and stereotype allows retired individuals to negotiate definitions of the retirement role that fit their particular situations and that are consistent with their own personal goals.

## THE FUTURE OF RETIREMENT

The future of retirement as an institution seems assured. Increasingly larger proportions of our labor force can be expected to retire and to do so at increasingly earlier ages. The commitment to a vocation as an end in itself will probably continue to decline. There is no indication at present that the nature of jobs in American society will change in any way that would reverse this trend.

Compulsory retirement policies will also probably be extended to a larger segment of the labor force, but an ever-decreasing proportion of the labor force will remain in it long enough to be pushed out. Thus, mandatory retirement will become increasingly prevalent and increasingly irrelevant.

The retirement income picture should improve somewhat, but it is unlikely that Social Security will rise above the bare subsistence level in the near future. The prospects for individual planning to bridge the gap left by inadequate Social Security payments are poor because information programs tend to be too little and too late and because the people who need self-planning the most are the least likely to grasp its importance on their own. Thus, during the next two decades inadequate income is likely to remain the major problem associated with retirement.

## SUMMARY

The term *retirement* refers to a situation in which an individual is employed less than full-time or year-round *and* in which he or she receives a retirement pension. Households are considered retired if retirement pensions represent their major source of income.

Economic and social change has changed the linkage between people and jobs. In industrial societies today, jobs are not necessarily the prime determinant in the structure of people's lives. Many jobs are boring and meaningless to the people doing them. The right to economic support in retirement is widely considered an incentive for people to put up with rotten jobs.

A mature retirement system in society requires an economic system productive enough to be able to support people without jobs, a political system strong enough to divert some of that surplus to support people in retirement, and acceptance by the people that retirement is a legitimate adult role.

Retirement can be viewed as a process in which the retirement role is approached, taken up, and eventually, if the person lives long enough, given up. The process begins with people's attitudes toward retirement, which are generally favorable. Dread of retirement is closely related to anticipated financial insecurity. Acceptance of retirement is closely related to having achieved one's job-related goals. Acceptance of retirement increases with age within age cohorts, but at the same time younger cohorts are more accepting of retirement than older ones are.

Preparation for retirement should alert people to the financial, physical, and psychological prerequisites of retirement, and should do so early enough to be effective. Retirement preparation involves informing people about decisions that they need to make and helping them get the information and learn the skills necessary to ensure that their decisions will be good ones. Education is more effective than counseling as an approach to retirement preparation.

Individuals often have a period within which they *can* retire and a final date at which they *must* retire. Most people retire before the date that they must retire, and even among those who wait for the mandatory date there is a sizable proportion who look upon that date as permission to retire and eagerly await it. Thus, most people are not negatively affected by mandatory retirement rules.

However, for a small proportion of older workers, mandatory retirement means denial of their right to hold a job and/or means forced poverty. The use of age as the sole criterion for mandatory retirement cannot be defended on rational grounds. It is primarily a political expedient to keep down unemployment. The retired poor are not counted as unemployed.

The decision about the if and when of retirement is also influenced by occupational norms and by family and friends.

The retirement event is a poorly developed rite of passage that seldom deals with the opportunities and obligations of the retirement role. Yet retirement does represent a definable role that offers people freedom of time and space and that requires physical, social, and financial independence. The retirement role also demands a certain amount of continuity in areas of life not related to the job. As a relationship, the role of retired person is similar to that of alumnus or alumna.

However, the freedom given to the retired person makes the retired person responsible for defining his or her own life-style. As such, the retirement role is flexible. Some gerontologists have argued that such a role has negative consequences for self-esteem, but the research results do not support this argument. It appears that poverty, not the vagueness of the retirement role, is primarily responsible for self-esteem problems in later life.

The retirement process has identifiable phases. In the *preretirement* period, people develop fantasies about what their lives in retirement will be like and make some decisions in advance. When retirement actually occurs, most people enter a *honeymoon* period in which they attempt to live out their retirement fantasies. If retirement fantasies are based on realistic ideas and information, they have a good chance of success. If the projected retirement life-style is successful, the person will move into a period of *stability* characterized by a firm set of criteria for making day-to-day decisions and a routine for daily life. If the retirement is unsuccessful, the person must start over again to develop a new concept of life in retirement. The person becomes *disenchanted* with the original retirement fantasy and must *reorient* himself or herself to develop more realistic criteria for making decisions. This reorientation is necessary in order to achieve a manageable retirement routine. Finally, if a retired person loses physical or financial independence, the retirement role recedes and is replaced by the sick role, the role of dependent person, or perhaps the role of institutional resident.

Despite the popular myth, there is no evidence that retirement has a significant impact on either the physical or the mental health of the vast majority of people who retire. Health declines can be traced to aging but not to retirement.

In terms of social adjustment, retirement has been found to have no effect on morale, life satisfaction, depression, or self-esteem. Activity patterns tend to be carried over into retirement. Retirement does produce a *slight* increase in the proportion of people who feel less involved and who feel "useless," but the proportion with such feelings in retirement is still only about 25 percent.

Retirement increases the prevalence of felt economic deprivation. Only a tiny proportion of people change residence as a result of retirement and those who do often do so to be nearer their children. Retirement tends to be good for middle-class marriages and to put a strain on working-class ones.

About 10 percent of those who retire at age 65 eventually get another job. The prime reason is money. However, most people get used to retirement within 3 months or less. Adjustment to retirement requires sufficient income, willingness to give up one's job gracefully, and good health. Adjustment to loss of job at retirement depends largely on whether job-related goals have been achieved and on whether the individual has developed interests and skills apart from those centered around the job. Sometimes retirement requires negotiating a new social identity with others in the social environment.

In the future, retirement will probably become an even more well-entrenched institution. However, a relative shortage of labor caused by present declines in the birth rate may result in more flexible retirement policies, including more options for those who prefer partial retirement. Retirement incomes should improve as more retired people are covered by better private and public pensions over and above their Social Security. However, income will probably remain the primary retirement problem for the forseeable future.

## SUGGESTIONS FOR FURTHER READING

Atchley, Robert C. *The Sociology of Retirement*. Cambridge, Mass.: Schenkman, 1976.
Barfield, Richard E., and James Morgan. *Early Retirement: The Decision and the Experience*. Ann Arbor, Mich.: University of Michigan, Institute of Social Research, 1970.

Eisdorfer, Carl. "Adaptation to Loss of Work." In Frances M. Carp (ed.), *Retirement*. New York: Behavioral Publications, 1972, pp. 245–266.

Fillenbaum, Gerda G. "Retirement Planning Programs—At What Age, and for Whom?" *Gerontologist 11* (1971):33–36.

Friedmann, Eugene A., and Robert J. Havighurst (eds.). *The Meaning of Work and Retirement*. Chicago: University of Chicago Press, 1954.

Friedmann, Eugene A., and Harold L. Orbach. "Adjustment to Retirement." In Silvano Arieti (ed.), *American Handbook of Psychiatry*. New York: Basic Books, 1974, pp. 609–645.

Harris, Louis and Associates, Inc. *The Myth and Reality of Aging in America*. Washington, D.C.: National Council on the Aging, 1975.

Kasschau, Patricia. "Reevaluating the Need for Retirement Preparation Programs." *Industrial Gerontology 1* (1974):42–59.

Kelleher, C. H., and D. A. Quirk. "Preparation for Retirement. An Annotated Bibliography of Literature 1965–1974." *Industrial Gerontology 1* (1974):49–73.

Kreps, Juanita M. (ed.). *Employment, Income, and Retirement Problems of the Aged*. Durham, N. C.: Duke University Press, 1963.

Lozier, J., and R. Althouse. "Retirement to the Porch in Rural Appalachia." *International Journal of Aging and Human Development 6* (1975):7–15.

Mitchell, William L. *Preparation for Retirement*. Washington, D.C.: American Association of Retired Persons, 1968.

Palmore, Erdman. "Why Do People Retire?" *Aging and Human Development 2* (1971):269–283.

Pollman, A. William. "Early Retirement: A Comparison of Poor Health to Other Retirement Factors." *Journal of Gerontology 26* (1971):41–45.

Reno, Virginia P. "Compulsory Retirement Among Newly Entitled Workers: Survey of New Beneficiaries." *Social Security Bulletin 35* (1972):3–15.

Shanas, Ethel. "Adjustment to Retirement: Substitution or Accommodation?" In Frances M. Carp (ed.), *Retirement*. New York: Behavioral Publications, 1972, pp. 219–244.

Simpson, Ida H., and John C. McKinney (eds.), *Social Aspects of Aging*. Durham, N.C.: Duke University Press, 1966.

Streib, Gordon F., and Clement J. Schneider. *Retirement in American Society*. Ithaca, N.Y.: Cornell University Press, 1971.

Thompson, Gayle B. "Work Versus Leisure Roles: An Investigation of Morale Among Employed and Retired Men." *Journal of Gerontology 28* (1973):339–344.

# 9
# Leisure

Roles that are not obligatory in the formal sense that job and family roles often are can be defined as **leisure roles**. Subjectively, leisure roles are seen as discretionary—the individual has a great deal of leeway concerning when, where, how much, and even if these roles will be played. M. Kaplan (1961) isolated several important elements of the concept of leisure roles. The individual expects to and is expected to perform leisure roles without pay or economic gain, to derive pleasant experiences and recollections from them, and to feel psychologically free while playing them. There is often, but not always, an element of play in leisure roles. In addition, leisure roles are seen as a legitimate means of pursuing important cultural values such as self-expression or autonomy.

Havighurst (1972) found that leisure has the same potential meaning for people that jobs do. Except for the economic meaning, which attaches only to a job, both jobs and leisure are potential sources for individual self-worth or self-respect, loci for social participation (a place to make friends), sources of status or prestige, sources of new experience, opportunities to be of service to others, and ways to make time pass.

Information about patterns of leisure among older people is essential in examining the nature of growing old. People gradually expand the time they spend in leisure roles as they get older (Riley and Foner, 1968:513). After retirement, leisure pursuits occupy a great deal of the individual's time, but leisure roles may not fill the void left by relinquishing the job. Leisure can certainly fill the *time* formerly occupied by the job, but may not give the individual the kind of *self-respect* and identity that he or she got from the job.

## IDENTITY CRISIS AND LEISURE PARTICIPATION

Perhaps the most articulate and repeatedly quoted spokesman on the negative side is S. Miller (1965), who has taken the following positions:[1]

1. Retirement is basically degrading because, although by implication retirement is a right that is earned through lifelong labor, there is also a tacit understanding that this reward is being given primarily to coax the individual from a role he or she is no longer able to play.
2. Occupational identity invades all of the other areas of the person's life. Accordingly, the father or mother and head-of-household roles, the friend role, and even leisure roles are mediated by the individual's occupational identity.
3. Of all roles that could be used as a source of identity, people are taught to prefer jobs.
4. Leisure roles cannot replace job roles as a source of self-respect and identity because they are not supported by norms that would make this replacement legitimate. That is, the retired person does not *feel justified* in deriving self-respect from leisure because leisure is not defined as a legitimate source of self-respect by the general population.
5. Beyond the simple need to be doing something, most people feel a need to do something defined as utilitarian or gainful. Thus, the stamp collector emphasizes the financial rewards of the hobby, artists offer paintings for sale, and woodworkers confine their craft to immediately "useful" projects. In short, the only kind of leisure that can provide identity is the work substitute.
6. A stigma of "implied inability to perform" is associated with retirement and is carried over into all of the individual's remaining roles, resulting in an identity breakdown.
7. Identity breakdown is a process whereby the individual's former claims to prestige or status are invalidated by the implied inability to perform. This invalidation embarrasses the stigmatized person (Miller calls this result "the portent of embarrassment").
8. Embarrassment leads the individual to withdraw from situations or prevents him or her from participating to begin with.
9. The answer lies not in inventing new roles for the aging, but rather in "determining what roles presently exist in the social system . . . , offering vicarious satisfactions that can reduce the socially debilitating loss accompanying occupational retirement" (1965:90).
10. Creating an ethic that would make full-time leisure an acceptable activity for a worthwhile person is a possible way to resolve the dilemma of the retired leisure participant.

[1]The analysis of Miller's theory that occupies the next several pages is a revised version of a paper that appeared earlier (Atchley, 1971a).

Miller's analysis of the situation contains many insights. Nevertheless, it rests on the assumption that prior to retirement the individual derived his or her identity primarily from a job. Miller's identity crisis theory also implies that most people want to stay on the job, since the job is their main identity, and that therefore most retirement is involuntary. This assumption no doubt arises because Miller does not discuss those who retired voluntarily. Miller also implies that he subscribes to the activity theory of adjustment in aging, since he assumes that lost roles need to be replaced (Havighurst, 1963).

Several questions emerge from an examination of Miller's identity crisis theory. First, is his portrayal of the relationship between involuntary retirement and leisure an accurate one? Second, is the pattern, even if accurate, typical of most older leisure participants? Third, what is the pattern among those who are voluntarily retired? Data from recent studies of retired people can shed some light on these questions.

## IDENTITY CONTINUITY AND LEISURE PARTICIPATION

Some of these data will be drawn from the Scripps Foundation studies in retirement, a series that has produced several published reports and that is still continuing.[2] These studies suggest that:

1. Retirement has been found to result in a loss of a sense of involvement, *but this loss was unrelated to other self-concept variables of optimism and autonomy* (Back and Gupti, 1966).

    Disengagement theory tells us to expect some withdrawal from involvement, and this loss of involvement does not appear to have adverse results for other aspects of the self-concept. This fact makes one skeptical about Miller's "portent of embarrassment."

2. A strong orientation toward work *is* frequently found among retired people, but is *not* accompanied by anxiety, depression, dislike of retirement, or withdrawal from activity (Cottrell and Atchley, 1969; Atchley, 1976b).

    Cottrell and Atchley's (1969:48) findings indicate that a strong positive orientation toward work "*exists* apart from the job itself but . . . has no *import for the individual* apart from the job." In terms of adjustment, carrying a positive orientation toward work into retirement apparently had *no* negative result.

3. When men retired from upper-white-collar, middle-status, and semiskilled jobs were compared, it was found that the upper-white-collar people had internalized occupationally oriented norms. Middle-status workers were oriented toward specific tasks and situations, often giving them skills that were transferable to leisure situations. Semiskilled workers were engaged mainly in activities oriented toward *things* (Simpson et al., 1966a).

[2]See Atchley (1969); Atchley (1971b); Atchley (1971c); Atchley and George (1973; Atchley (1974c; 1975a, b, and c); Cottrell and Atchley (1969).

Of these occupational strata, the upper-white-collar stratum comes closest to Miller's model of the retired person, producing work-oriented people. However, neither of the other two strata fits the work-oriented model. Middle-status people develop skills on the job that carry over into their leisure roles. Semiskilled people are oriented around the job, but not necessarily because they have any deep, abiding commitment to it. They may simply not have been trained for anything else.

4. The *style* of work activities tends to remain dominant in retirement.

Simpson, Back, and McKinney (1966a) found that upper-white-collar jobs were oriented around *symbols*; middle-status jobs were oriented around *people*; and semiskilled jobs were oriented around *things*. The middle-status people showed the greatest continuity in style from pre- to postretirement. This correlation suggests that retirement, and leisure roles in particular, offer greater opportunities for practicing interpersonal skills than for practicing skills oriented around symbols or things.

The implication of this finding is that it is not so much the *ethic* learned on the job that interferes with successful pursuit of leisure in retirement as it is the *skills*. Those who learn job skills that cannot be readily used in leisure pursuits have a hard time adjusting to an increase in leisure unless they have had the opportunity to learn these skills elsewhere. This notion is reinforced by the finding that middle-status people who had thing-oriented jobs resembled the semiskilled more than they did their middle-status peers in terms of retirement activities.

5. In addition, data from retired railroaders indicates continuities in the situations people face minimize the impact of retirement (Cottrell, 1970). Family, friends, church, and other roles continue despite retirement. Cottrell's data suggest that embarrassment and loss of identity are minimized by the tendency to select friends on the job from among those of one's own age. The end result of this process is to create *retirement cohorts* of people who have known each other on the job and who retire together. In the Scripps Foundation studies of retirement, this phenomenon has been observed in retirement from occupations as diverse as teacher, railroader, and telephone operator. It results in a group of retired friends who have known each other for years and whose concepts of each other involve a great deal more than the mere playing of an occupational role. This group is also capable of sustaining the prestige gained on the job because they know how this prestige was generated.

Geographically mobile older people may lose these continuities, but most retired people, particularly the semiskilled or unskilled, do not move away from their places of long-term residence.

6. Cottrell's (1970) data also indicate that as the concept of retirement is incorporated into the culture, the tendency to look on work as a temporary part of life increases.

The implication here is that if work is not viewed as a permanent part of life, one puts greater emphasis on other parts of life that are more permanent. For example, if a man knows the day he begins on the job that he will work 25 years and then retire, he is very likely to avoid letting work become an all-consuming part of his life.

7. In terms of ethic, it is not at all clear whether most people regard work as a necessary prerequisite for making leisure legitimate, or simply as a necessary economic function that interferes with the pursuit of leisure. It *is* quite clear that our heritage has always included those who did not work because they could afford not to. Accordingly, legitimacy of leisure may rest not so much on job holding as on the idea that the money used to sustain leisure came from a legitimate source; that is, it was either earned on a job or inherited. In the Scripps Foundation studies of retirement, many middle-income retired people have shown not the slightest reluctance to embrace the leisure role, provided their income was secure (Cottrell and Atchley, 1969). Perhaps if most retired people were not pauperized by retirement, the "portent of embarrassment" mentioned by Miller as an obstacle to increasing acceptance of leisure activity would fade away.

8. Nearly two thirds of retired men retired as a result of their own decision. Less than *one in five* was retired involuntarily as a result of reaching retirement age (Palmore, 1964b:5). By leaving out those in poor health and those who voluntarily retired, Miller effectively limited the group he was talking about to less than a third of the retired men and an even smaller percentage of the retired women.

9. *Acceptance of leisure roles is high among middle-aged and older people.* Pfeiffer and Davis (1971) interviewed 502 people aged 46 to 71 and found that, in all age groups, between 80 to 90 percent of their respondents were satisfied with the amount of free time they had or wished they had more. Unfortunately, Pfeiffer and Davis did not examine the relation between retirement and leisure acceptance.

We may seem to have dwelt too long and too deeply on the relationship between leisure and retirement. Nevertheless, if we are to understand the nature of leisure roles among older people, these roles must be put in their proper context. Miller's position is a very common one, and it is constantly being used as a basis for decisions that influence older people's lives. Our detailed examination has shown this approach to be at least questionable.

To begin with, the Scripps Foundation studies and other sources offer evidence that the adjustment problems sometimes associated with retirement are *not* the result of loss of the job and the identity it provides. In fact, a highly positive orientation toward work had little influence on retirement adjustment. There is no indication that highly work-oriented people are unable to take up leisure roles; in fact, just the opposite is true. There is no concrete evidence that retirement in and of itself necessarily influences the *quality* of one's family life, friendships, or associations in any negative way.

Accordingly, an alternative to Miller's identity crisis theory of the relationship between retirement and leisure might contain the following points.

Many people are never highly oriented toward work and thus may very well provide a model to show others what it would be like to derive self-satisfaction from leisure. The ethic of the system allows such satisfaction as long as the money used to lead a life of leisure is legitimately earned.

Self-respect *can* be gained from leisure pursuits in retirement if the individuals have enough money, and if they have a cohort of retired friends who accept full-time leisure as legitimate and who help negate the stigma of implied inability to perform. As retirement becomes a more and more accepted part of the life cycle, this orientation should spread beyond the cohort of friends. In any event, retired individuals will continue to *see themselves* as railroaders, teachers, and so forth, even though they no longer play the role. Thus, the crux of this alternative approach is *identity continuity*.

Recent research by Oliver (1971) shows that there is indeed a corresponding continuity in leisure pursuits, even among those who migrate to new communities after retirement. In fact, Oliver's analysis indicates that people who move out of central cities after retirement are people who are already oriented toward leisure and who relocate in areas that offer opportunities for more efficient continued pursuit of long-standing leisure roles.

There are many people for whom interpersonal interaction *was* their occupational skill, and who derive pleasure from exercising this skill, rather than striving toward a goal. Leisure can thus act as a work substitute when it uses work-derived skills.

Very few people rest their entire identity on a single role. If they did, there would surely be far more suicides than there are now. The only thing that makes failure bearable is that we seldom fail in all of our roles at once. Each person generally stakes his or her identity on several roles. Work may be at or near the top, but not necessarily. There simply is no homogeneous consensus that job holding should be the top value for everyone. In fact, the many systems of competing values in a complex society *ensure* a wide variety of self-values. Thus, the probability that retirement will lead to a complete identity breakdown is slight, and just as many people may rely on leisure pursuits for self-respect as rely on work, particularly among those with unsatisfying jobs.

Some decline of involvement may be natural as the individual adjusts to declining energy, but most people expand the time they spend playing leisure roles when they retire. Nevertheless, most retired people do not regard this change negatively. In fact, most people retire voluntarily, and many of these volunteers cite a preference for leisure as their reason for retiring.

No doubt for some people Miller's identity crisis pattern is a grim reality, but it does not appear to be typical even among the minority of older people who are forced to retire. Among those who retire voluntarily, a third retire to devote more time to leisure. The ethical issue may be difficult for some to resolve, but not for the majority, even among highly work-oriented people.

The identity continuity theory and the data that give rise to it suggest that leisure can have a great deal of positive value in retirement, and that this value will increase in the future. Between them, the continuity and identity crisis theories probably account for the majority of cases. Nevertheless, to determine what proportion of retired people fits each model, studies are needed that are broader in scope and wider in range than any thus far brought to bear on the question. One of the intriguing but often frustrating aspects of studying aging in the United States is the sometimes overpowering geographic, social, and psychological diversity of the older population. Perhaps further probing will uncover still other patterns of relationship between retirement and leisure participation.

## LEISURE COMPETENCE

Yet apart from the question of acceptability, there is also the question of the older person's competence to take advantage of leisure roles. Older people enjoy a wide variety of leisure pursuits, but the data suggest that older people—particularly the less well-educated—are reluctant to engage in autonomous leisure activities such as reading, listening to music, painting, sculpting, or writing. This reluctance is at least partly caused by the older person's feeling of incompetence in such activities.

Critics of American education have attacked this apparent deficiency in our orientation toward education. Contemporary education, it is said, devotes anywhere from 80 to 90 percent of the students' time for 12 to 19 years to teaching them how to fill jobs, but makes little effort to prepare them for life outside the job. As Norman Cousins (1968:20) puts it, "I contend that science tends to lengthen life, and education tends to shorten it; that science has the effect of freeing man for leisure, and that education has the effect of deflecting him from the enjoyment of living." The point is that to open up the full range of leisure possibilities requires some training.

Recent research on exposure to "high culture" in American society has shown that the college-educated person is no more likely to enjoy a wide range of leisure pursuits than is the semiskilled worker (Wilensky, 1964). Television, which often requires little competence, is the major leisure pursuit among all people in American society. One can conclude that our education and communication systems do little to develop the potential for the creative use of leisure.

There is some evidence that the learning necessary for a full-blown leisure style must begin early. Many gerontologists are pessimistic about the possibility of completely resocializing older people into a life of leisure. This pessimism is mainly based on the decline in learning speed that occurs with age, the reluctance most older people show toward attempting anything entirely new, and the extreme stability that activity patterns show. The findings lead to the conclusion that leisure competence created early in life can be maintained into later life. Oliver (1971) found little change with age in the types of leisure roles played among his healthy, financially solvent respondents. But if leisure competence is not learned by middle age, it may never be. Lambing (1972a) found, for example, that lack of leisure skills and literacy seriously limited the leisure roles available to older lower-class blacks in Florida, a situation that Lambing's respondents recognized and wished to correct. The individual should probably begin to develop leisure competence as soon as possible. An active and creative use of leisure in one's youth is the surest way to guarantee a similar pattern in old age, since older people tend to retain patterns and preferences developed in the past.

There is also a physical element in leisure competence, but between age 40 and 75 the physical mobility limits on leisure options often change very little, although overall energy may decline. Only very active sports show drastic declines with age. Less strenuous sports such as bowling and golf can be maintained much longer.

## VARIETY IN LEISURE ROLES

Activities differ on several dimensions: expensive–inexpensive; at home–away-from-home; spectator–participant; solitary–group; physical–no-physical-exertion; intellectual–manual–social; or family–outside-family. Zborowski (1962) found considerable stability between activities at age 40 and activities in later maturity. The stability of activity was slightly higher for men than for women. Men showed significant increases in the spectator–home dimensions as well as in the solitary-intellectual–outside-home dimensions. Both groups showed significant declines in activities involving physical exertion, group-manual activities, and group-intellectual–outside-home types of activities.

Havighurst (1973a) reported significant sex and social-class differences in the mix of leisure roles played. Voluntary associations, sports, reading, and gardening were favored by the upper middle class, while those of middle socioeconomic status tended to favor manipulative activities, reading, and television. Lower-class people were especially fond of "visiting" with neighbors or kin. Lambing (1972a) reported similar variations among older blacks, except that former professional blacks were not interested in sports and were more interested in "visiting" than were upper-middle-class whites. Part of this differential, however, may be caused by differences between small town and urban people, since Lambing studied a small town in Florida and Havighurst's data were from Kansas City. More research is needed on variations in leisure patterns in various regions and for various ethnic groups.

Leisure roles are extremely diverse, yet seldom will an older individual be able to select from the *entire* range of possibilities. To begin with, physical limitations rule out some alternatives. But perhaps the most important limitation on older people's leisure options is their lack of money. Pursuits such as travel, entertaining, or going to a movie, concert, or play require money. Finally, older people's activities are severely limited by deficiencies in transportation. Obviously, if you cannot get there, you cannot participate. Club and church socials or activities, outings, shopping, eating out, and visiting are all examples of leisure pursuits that can be greatly hampered by a lack of transportation.

People faced with retirement are offered three general alternatives: finding a work substitute, engaging in leisure activities, or doing nothing. Idleness is literally deadly for older people, just as it would be for anyone else, and as a result not very many people select this alternative. The other two types of activity are difficult to separate because they may differ only with respect to motivation.

People expand their leisure activities following retirement, but not drastically. Patterns of leisure vary from weekdays to weekends. On weekdays the most frequent activity for both men and women is watching television. On weekends the main activity is visiting and entertaining, followed by watching television. The bulk (35 percent) of the older American's leisure is spent at home, most of it in activity that can be done alone. After television, the next most prevalent activities are visiting, reading, gardening, going for walks, and handiwork. Older people do devote a conspicuous amount of time to just sitting, looking out a window, or napping. Idleness does not become an important part of life, however, until the very advanced ages.

There are strikingly few differences between young and old with regard to leisure patterns, but some of these differences are important. Older people read fewer books and magazines, but about the same number of newspapers. Older people rate newspapers as more important than television (even though they spend more time with television). Movie-going falls off rapidly after age 50. Older people attend the theater, concerts, or sports events less frequently. Older people tend to prefer *serious* content. Their favorite television programs center around public affairs, news, and information. Also, older people tend to devote more attention to the "local news" section of newspapers (Riley and Foner, 1968:518–26).

Only a small proportion of older people occupy themselves with crafts, hobbies, or intellectual and artistic activities. The only outdoor activities that increase with age are gardening and walking.

Travel may be a more prevalent leisure role among older people than might be expected, given the low incomes of most retired people. Carp (1972c) and Friedsam and Martin (1973), reporting on two Texas communities, found that more than half of the older people surveyed had taken at least one long trip, usually with spouse and by car, in the previous year. Such trips often combined sightseeing with visits to kin. Older black people traveled about as much as whites, but not as far and usually more often by bus (Friedsam and Martin, 1973:207). Use of travel as leisure was related to income. In Friedsam and Martin's sample, a third of those with annual incomes of $2,000 reported a trip, as compared to two thirds among those with incomes above $4,000.

A note of caution. Research data on leisure differences by age come primarily from cross-sectional sources. Therefore, the age differences observed may be the result of changes in childrearing, education, or social fads rather than age changes in leisure preferences. Much more longitudinal and cohort research is needed in this area. Another problem that has plagued research on leisure concerns how to gather data. Getting accurate information on just how people perceive leisure roles and use them is a difficult task. Time budgets, diaries, activity check lists, and most of the other methods used to study leisure are very vulnerable to respondent error, and as a result we are in a poor position even to describe the mix of leisure roles played and how it is affected by age, much less to explain it. We find ourselves on the frontier, with only the crudest conceptual and empirical maps for finding our way around.

## SUMMARY

Leisure participation in the later years is individualized, in the sense that each person is free to choose from a wide variety of possibilities. Yet this variety is limited by physical, financial, and transportation factors. A few older people are hamstrung by an ethic that does not allow play without work. Personality, family, and social class values narrow the field of choice still more. Lack of facilities can also limit the options. If the older person is to be able to enjoy creative, self-enhancing leisure in retirement, options must be as wide open as possible.

Studies of leisure among older people who live in their own homes show that autonomous and spectator leisure play a major role, even though many older people prefer participant activities. Perhaps one of the few remaining independent decisions an institutionalized older person can make concerns leisure activities. Therefore, the activity schedules of many retirement homes may be a mistake. A television set, frequent opportunities to shoot the breeze, and a good light to read by may well be all the older person wants.

About all that can be said of the pursuit of leisure in retirement is that most people seem to be able to cope with it successfully. Those who have good health and money do quite well, but the poorer and sicker people get, the harder it is to accept constraints on their life of leisure.

Given the nature of the leisure activities older people prefer, few *facilities* are required. In order to maximize opportunities, the key requirements seem to be (1) having enough personal income, (2) being in close proximity to friends and relatives, and (3) having transportation to take advantage of existing community facilities. Mental declines hamper leisure pursuits for only a tiny minority.

Leisure roles are an integral part of life in American society. Because leisure choices are so often individual decisions, leisure *can be* one of the greatest sources of continuity for the individual across the life-span. To make it so, however, one must realize early in life that leisure activities are an important part of life. This realization is particularly important for young adults who expend a great deal of energy on the job and rely mainly on television for their leisure.

## SUGGESTIONS FOR FURTHER READING

Christ, Edwin A. "The 'Retired' Stamp Collector: Economic and Other Functions of a Systematized Leisure Activity." In Arnold M. Rose and Warren A. Peterson (eds.), *Older People and Their Social World*. Philadelphia: F. A. Davis, 1965, pp. 93–112.

Cowgill, Donald O., and Norma Baulch. "The Use of Leisure Time by Older People," *Gerontologist* 2(1962):47–50.

Durkee, Stephen. "Artistic Expression in Later Life." In Robert Kastenbaum (ed.), *New Thoughts on Old Age*. New York: Springer, 1964, pp. 305–315.

Havighurst, Robert J., and Kenneth Feigenbaum. "Leisure and Life-Style." In Bernice L. Neugarten (ed.), *Middle Age and Aging*. Chicago: University of Chicago Press, 1968, pp. 347–353.

Havighurst, Robert J. "Life Style and Leisure Patterns: Their Evolution Through the Life Cycle." In *Leisure in the 3rd Age*. Paris: International Center for Social Gerontology, 1972, pp. 35–48.

Kaplan, Max. "Implications for Gerontology from a General Theory of Leisure." In *Leisure in the 3rd Age*. Paris: International Center for Social Gerontology, 1972, pp. 49–64.

Kleemeier, Robert W., ed. *Aging and Leisure*. New York: Columbia University Press, 1961.

Kreps, Juanita M. *Lifelong Allocation of Work and Leisure*. Washington, D.C.: Social Security Administration, 1968.

Martin, Alexander, R. *Leisure Time–A Creative Force*. New York: National Council on Aging, 1963.

Miller, Stephen J. "The Social Dilemma of the Aging Leisure Participant." In Arnold M. Rose and Warren A. Peterson (eds.), *Older People and Their Social World*. Philadelphia: F. A. Davis, 1965, pp. 77–92.

Rosow, Irving. "Retirement, Leisure, and Social Status." In Frances C. Jeffers (ed.), *Duke University Council on Aging and Human Development: Proceedings of Seminars 1965–1969*. Durham, N.C.: Duke University Center for the Study of Aging and Human Development, 1969, pp. 249–257.

Whiskin, Frederick E. "On the Meaning and Function of Reading in Later Life." In Robert Kastenbaum (ed.), *New Thoughts on Old Age*. New York: Springer, 1964, pp. 300–304.

# 10

# Death, Dying, Bereavement, and Widowhood

In the nineteenth century, everyone was familiar with death. Infant mortality was high, and many families had to face the deaths of young children. In twentieth-century industrial societies, however, it is primarily older people who must deal with change brought on by death. And each new generation of older people has had less and less experience in dealing with death during their childhood and early adult lives. Thus, today's older people must face their own deaths and the deaths of others in their generation with scant preparation.

We will start our discussion of mortality by defining some terms and by presenting the demography of death. The meaning of death will then be considered, followed by issues involved in the dying process. We will then move on to bereavement and conclude the chapter with a discussion of widowhood.

## DEFINING DEATH

Death can be defined as a process of transition that starts with *dying* and ends with *being dead* (Kalish, 1976).[1] For practical purposes, a dying person is a person identified as having a condition from which no recovery can be expected. Dying is thus the period during which the organism loses its viability. The term **dying trajectory** refers to the speed with which a person dies, the rate of decline in functioning. The word *death* can also be defined as the point at which a person *becomes physically dead*. Often when we say that someone died yesterday we are not referring to the entire dying

[1] I owe a tremendous debt to Richard Kalish for allowing me to draw from an advance copy of his synthesis of the literature on death and dying (Kalish, 1976).

process but instead to its final product. The moment in time when a person becomes dead was once considered an easy practical issue to resolve. Recently, however, it has become possible to stimulate artificially both breathing and heartbeat. As a result, there is currently a huge legal tangle over the issue of when a person is physically dead.

Death can also be a social process (Kastenbaum, 1969). People are socially dead when we no longer treat them as people but as unthinking, unfeeling objects. Social death has occurred when people talk *about* the dying person rather than *to* the dying person even when the dying person is capable of hearing and understanding what is being said. Thus, social death sometimes occurs *before* physical death does.

## THE DEMOGRAPHY OF DEATH

Every year, about 6 percent of the total population of older people in the United States can be expected to die. It is obvious that older people die at a much greater rate than young ones, but the *causes* of death at various ages differ in important ways. For example, older people most frequently die from heart disease, cancer, strokes, influenza, and pneumonia. In contrast, people between 25 and 44 most frequently die from accidents, heart disease, cancer, suicide, and cirrhosis of the liver. For all ages, infectious diseases have declined in importance in recent years, while chronic diseases have taken over as the leading causes of death.

In 1900, the list of leading causes of death among older people was exactly the same as it is today. The main difference now is that more people live to reach the ages at which these diseases become prevalent. Since 1960, death rates have fallen rapidly for people 85 and over (from 198.6 in 1960 to 163.4 in 1970). For the future this decline means an increasing rate of survival not only *to* very old ages but *at* very old ages (see Table 10-1).

**TABLE 10-1**
**Death Rates by Age, Color, and Sex: United States, 1970**

|  | Under 1 | 1–4 | 5–14 | 15–24 | 25–34 | 35–44 | 45–54 | 55–64 | 65–74 | 75–84 | 85 & Over |
|---|---|---|---|---|---|---|---|---|---|---|---|
| Total | 21.4 | 0.8 | 0.4 | 1.3 | 1.6 | 3.1 | 7.3 | 16.6 | 35.8 | 80.0 | 163.4 |
| Male |  |  |  |  |  |  |  |  |  |  |  |
| Total | 24.1 | 0.9 | 0.5 | 1.9 | 2.2 | 4.0 | 9.6 | 22.8 | 48.7 | 100.1 | 178.2 |
| White | 21.1 | 0.8 | 0.5 | 1.7 | 1.8 | 3.4 | 8.8 | 22.0 | 48.1 | 101.0 | 185.5 |
| Other | 40.2 | 1.4 | 0.7 | 3.0 | 5.0 | 8.7 | 16.5 | 30.5 | 54.7 | 89.8 | 114.1 |
| Female |  |  |  |  |  |  |  |  |  |  |  |
| Total | 18.6 | 0.8 | 0.3 | 0.7 | 1.0 | 2.3 | 5.2 | 11.0 | 25.8 | 66.8 | 155.2 |
| White | 16.1 | 0.7 | 0.3 | 0.6 | 0.8 | 1.9 | 4.6 | 10.1 | 24.7 | 67.0 | 159.8 |
| Other | 31.7 | 1.2 | 0.4 | 1.1 | 2.2 | 4.9 | 9.8 | 18.9 | 36.8 | 63.9 | 102.9 |

*Source:* National Center for Health Statistics (1974).

### Variations

Older women differ significantly from older men in terms of death rates. Males die at a higher rate than females at *all* ages, even in the fetal period. Among all causes of death common to both sexes, men have higher rates than women. As age of the cohort increases, the size of the differential in death rates between men and women also increases until about age 75, after which it decreases.

In terms of trends in mortality, the outlook for the future is for a further decline in death rates for older women and stable or increasing death rates for older men. The principal cause of this trend is a growing differential in deaths from heart and kidney ailments, influenza and pneumonia, and diabetes. Death rates from all of these causes are declining for older women, but are stable or increasing among older men (Moriyama, 1964). In terms of social impact, these data suggest that the proportion of single women in the older population is likely to continue to increase for the forseeable future.

The black population in the United States has always experienced higher mortality rates than the white population, but in recent years these differences have been declining. After age 75, mortality rates are considerably lower for blacks than for whites, for both sexes. Death rates among older blacks for such diseases as cancer and diabetes are increasing rapidly, while the rates for whites are stable or declining. As a result of the generally higher rates, sex differences in mortality are less significant among older blacks than among older whites.

For the immediate future, relatively high mortality rates for blacks can be expected, mainly because of their comparatively low socioeconomic position. The long-term prospects are better. As the economic position of the older black population improves, gradual declines in differential mortality between white and black older people will probably occur.

Married people have lower death rates than do single people, and the differential is greater among the old than among the young. Single older people tend to be malnourished more often and to be without the necessary emotional support—both important elements in recovery from disease.

Death rates for older persons of lower economic status are considerably higher than for the economically advantaged groups. Unfortunately, most older people fall into the lower economic category.

One of the most common stereotypes about aging is that after retirement many older people become sick and die. This stereotype is untrue. There is no evidence that retirement has *any* deleterious effects on health. If anything, people show a tendency toward *improved* health upon retirement.

## THE MEANING OF DEATH

How people approach their own deaths and the deaths of others depends to some extent on what death means to them—and death can have many meanings. Back (1971a) examined the meaning of death through ratings of various metaphors about what death is like. He found little age variation in the meaning of death among respondents who were over 45. Kalish (1976) suggests that death is more salient for older adults than for younger ones because they see themselves as having less time remaining in their life spans and because their own physical condition and the deaths of others in their age group serve as constant reminders of their proximity to death.

Back (1971) did find a significant sex difference in the meaning of death. Women tended to be accepting of death, to see it as a peaceful thing. Women tended to see death as most like a compassionate mother and as an understanding doctor. Men tended to see death as an antagonist, as a grinning butcher, or as a hangman with bloody hands.

The two most common reactions to the idea of death are *fear* and *denial*. Whether fear of death is inevitable or a learned response is an unresolved issue. But whatever their cause, death fears exist. Older people do not appear to be extremely afraid of death, and older people express fewer death fears than younger people do (Kastenbaum, 1969; Kalish, 1976). There also appears to be no tendency for death fears to increase among older people with terminal conditions (Kastenbaum, 1969). Among the young, however, terminal illness increases the prevalence of death fears (Feifel and Jones, 1968).

Kalish (1976) attributes the lower prevalence of death fears in the face of a higher prevalence of death to several factors: (1) older people see their lives as having less prospects for the future and less value; (2) older people who live past what they expected have a sense of living on "borrowed time"; and (3) dealing with the deaths of friends can help socialize older people toward acceptance of their own death.

Fear of death also depends to some extent on religiosity. Kalish (1976) reports that the most consistent finding is that people who are strongly religious show few death fears, as do affirmed atheists. Uncertain and sporadically religious people show the most death fears.

Garfield (1974) reports that people who use psychedelic drugs or who practice meditation have lower death anxiety compared to others. Kalish (1976) suggests that because "altered mind states" tend to blur ego boundaries, death of the self is less threatening to people familiar with such mental states. Peck (1968) found that blurring boundaries of ego in old age served as a mechanism for transcending pain, and Kalish feels that this blurring may be related to the lower prevalence of death fears among older people.

To *deny* death is to believe that people continue to be able to *experience* after their physical death. Physical death is undeniable. It is mental death that is deniable. Belief in an afterlife, belief in the existence of ghosts, spirits, angels or demons, and belief in reincarnation are all ways of denying the death of the ability to experience. Denial can also mean the repression of the knowledge that one's physical death is imminent. Kalish (1976) reports that physicians often tell patients directly and clearly that they are going to die only to find out at a later meeting that their message was not heard.

Death seems to be accepted with only a modicum of fear by older people, presumably because older people have more experience with death, regard it as fair, and are less integrated into society. However, it seems reasonable to assume that some identifiable categories of older persons would not react to death in this way. Less acceptance and more fear of death might be expected among older people who have dependent children, disabled spouses, career goals still to be achieved, and socially crucial positions. We know, for example, that legislators are often old. How does the prevalence of death fears among older legislators compare with that of the general older population? This and other questions along these lines need to be researched.

## Dealing with Dying

For some people, dying is quick; for others, it is lingering. When a person is diagnosed as terminal, that person is assigned the *social role* of *dying person*. The content of the role depends a great deal on the *age* of the dying person and his or her *dying trajectory*. People with short dying trajectories do not spend much time in the role of dying person, regardless of age. However, age heavily determines whether or not a person is defined as terminal. Sudnow (1967) found that older people were more likely than the young to be routinely defined as dead in hospital emergency rooms, with no attempt made to revive them. Among those with long trajectories, however, age is an important element in determining what is expected of dying persons. Young persons are expected to fight death, to try to finish business, to cram as much experience as possible into their time remaining. In short, we expect young people to be active and antagonistic about dying. Older persons who are dying are expected to show more passive acceptance. Older people in the role of dying person are less likely than the young to see a need to change their life-style or day-to-day goals (Kalish, 1976). Older people are also less apt to be concerned about caring for dependents or about causing grief to others (Kalish, 1976). Older people are more apt than the young to find that the role of dying person also means having less control over their own lives. All dying people find that family members and medical personnel, usually with good intentions, take away their free choices. This interference is particularly true for older patients. Finally, all people in the role of dying persons are expected to cope with their impending death, but older people are allowed less leeway than the young in expressing anger and frustration about their death.

A great deal has been written about the stages people pass through in the process of dying. Kubler-Ross (1969) proposed five stages in the dying process: (1) denial and isolation, (2) anger and resentment, (3) bargaining and attempt to postpone, (4) depression and sense of loss, and (5) acceptance. How universally applicable Kubler-Ross's model has not been determined. Kalish (1976) suggests that while denial is probably more common in the early stages of dying and acceptance is more common later on, there is considerable movement back and forth; and it is doubtful that Kubler-Ross's stages represent a regular progression. People may also show the characteristics of several stages simultaneously. Kalish (1976) reports that many people have mistakenly treated Kubler-Ross's stages of dying as an inevitable progression. As a result, people have been chided for not progressing through their own dying on schedule, and dying persons have felt guilty for not having accomplished the various tasks.

Weisman (1972) has called attention to the fact that acceptance of death as an outcome does not necessarily translate into capitulation during the dying process. Certainly, accepting death is not the same as wanting to die.

For people approaching death, the where and when of death can also be important (Kalish, 1976). Most people die in health care institutions, but most people *prefer* to die at home. Death at home imposes a heavier burden on the family, but most family members are glad when death at home is possible (Cartwright et al., 1971).

As for when death occurs, the prime issue is when a person should be permitted to die. There is no clear consensus among older people about whether "heroic" measures should be used to keep them alive or whether death should be speeded in hopeless cases involving great pain. However, many older people are very aware of the burden their medical care may place on their families and may prefer to die rather than incur the expense required to keep them alive a little longer.

Kalish (1976) reports that "living wills" are being used as one means of giving patients' wishes more weight. Living wills specify the conditions under which people prefer not to be subjected to extraordinary measures to keep them alive. Kalish (1976) points out that although living wills are not now legally binding, some state legislatures are drafting laws to make them so. He goes on to say that

> One drawback, of course, is that the person facing imminent death may feel quite differently about his desires for heroic methods than he had anticipated when his death appeared much further removed in time, yet his condition may well preclude any opportunity to alter his living will (Kalish, 1976).

In caring for the dying, it is important to remember that most dying persons fear being abandoned, humiliated, and lonely at the end of their lives (Weisman, 1972). Thus, encouraging the maintenance of intimate personal relationships with others is an important aspect of the social care of dying persons. Deciding who should be told about the terminal diagnosis has a significant impact on intimate relationships. Kalish (1976) concludes that it is difficult for the patient to maintain such relationships unless the topic of death can be openly discussed. Thus, when the dying people are kept in the dark about the nature of their condition, they are denied an opportunity to resolve the question of death in the company of those they love, for by the time the prognosis becomes obvious their condition may prevent any meaningful discussion. In evaluating the question of who should know, Weisman suggests that "To be informed about a diagnosis, especially a serious diagnosis, is to be fortified, not undermined" (1972:17). Yet some people do not want to be told that they are dying (Kalish, 1976). In addition, some dying people keep their own prognoses secret.

A lengthy dying trajectory not only allows the dying person to resolve the issue of dying but also allows the survivors to resolve many grief reactions in advance. In some cases, the dying process is slow enough that the final event brings more relief than grief (Kalish, 1976). This relief does not mean that the survivors are calloused people who have no regard for the person who died. It merely means that it is possible to grieve *in advance* of a person's death. To assess a person's grief reaction to another's death requires knowledge of the reaction during the entire dying process, not just at the funeral.

## Bereavement

**Bereavement** is the process of getting over another person's death. The process may be finished quickly or it may never be finished. In Lopata's (1973) study of widows, 48 percent said they were over their husbands' deaths within a year, while 20 percent said they had never gotten over it and did not expect to. Individual bereavement takes three forms: physical, emotional, and intellectual. Some common physical reactions to grief include shortness of breath, frequent sighing, tightness in the chest, feelings of emptiness in the abdomen, loss of energy, lack of muscular strength, and stomach upset (Kalish, 1976). These reactions are particularly common in the period immediately following the death and generally diminish with time. The mortality rates of widowed people are slightly higher than for the married.

Emotional reactions to bereavement include anger, guilt, depression, anxiety, and preoccupation with thoughts of the deceased (Parkes, 1972). These responses also diminish with time. A longitudinal study of widows and widowers found that those who reacted to bereavement by becoming depressed were more likely than others to report a disproportionately higher level of poor health a year later (Bornstein et al., 1973).

The intellectual aspect of bereavement consists of what Lopata (1973) calls the "purification" of the memory of the deceased. In this process, the negative characteristics of the person who died are stripped away, leaving only a positive, idealized memory. Somehow we think it wrong to speak ill of the dead. Lopata (1973) reports that even women who hated their husband thought that the statement, "My husband was an unusually good man," was true. The content of obituaries and memorial services also attest to the results of this process. The idealization of the dead has positive value in that it satisfies the survivors' need to believe that the dead person's life had meaning. But it can have serious negative consequences for the future of the bereaved widow or widower because it can interfere with the formation of new intimate relationships (Lopata, 1973).

Glick, Weiss, and Parkes (1974) found that men and women react somewhat differently to bereavement. In terms of reaction to loss of a person loved, men more often respond in terms of having lost part of themselves, while women respond in terms of having been deserted, abandoned, and left to fend for themselves. Men find it more difficult and less desirable to express grief and they accept the reality of death somewhat more quickly than women do. On the other hand, men find it more difficult to work during bereavement than women do.

People usually do not have to go through bereavement alone. There are various ways in which others help the individual through bereavement. At the beginning, bereaved people are exempted from certain responsibilities. They are not expected to go to their jobs. Family and friends help with cooking and caring for dependents. Older women often find their decisions being made for them by their adult children.

But social supports to the bereaved person are temporary. People are expected to reengage the social world within a few weeks at most.

## LOSING A SPOUSE

We often think of widowhood as something that happens primarily to women. Yet in 1970 about a third of the male population over 75 were widowed. It is reasonable to assume that losing a spouse has different effects on women than on men; therefore, we will examine the role of widow first, then look at the role of widower. We will then discuss the controversy over whether losing a spouse is harder for women or for men.

### Being a Widow

The role of widow in American society is a long-term role primarily for older women. Young widows can play the widow role for only a short time and then they are considered single rather than widowed (Lopata, 1973). Because they are so much in the minority, younger widows feel stigmatized by widowhood, but older widows see widowhood as more normal because even as young as 65, 36 percent of women are widows. The prevalence of widowhood in later life combines with low rates of remarriage to produce for women a more definite social position for the older widow.

Yet the role of older widow is a vague one. Ties with the husband's family are usually drastically reduced by widowhood. The position of older widow serves primarily to label a woman as a member of a social category with certain salient characteristics. Older widows are supposed to be interested in keeping the memory of their husbands alive. They are not supposed to be interested in men. They are supposed to do things with other widows or with their children. Thus, being an older widow says more about the appropriate social environment for activity rather than the activity itself.

Being a widow changes the basis of self-identity for many women. For traditionally-oriented women, the role of wife is central to their lives. It structures their lives not only in their households but also on the job. In answering the question, "Who am I?" these women often put "wife of" at the top of their list. In addition to loss of a central role, widowhood often also causes the loss of the person best able to support the woman's concept of herself in terms of her personal qualities. If a woman's husband knows her better than anyone else and is her best friend and confidant, his opinions may be very important in supporting her view of herself as a good person. I have encountered older widows who after more than 10 years of widowhood still "consulted" their dead husbands about whether they were "doing the right thing," by referring to the husband's values.

How these women cope with the identity crisis that widowhood brings depends to a large extent on whether they base their identity on roles, personal qualities, or on possessions. Role-oriented women often take a job or increase their investment in a job they already have. They may also become more involved in various organizations. Those who need confirmation of their personal qualities may become more involved with friends and family. Those who are primarily acquirers base their identity on things rather than on people. For such women, an adjustment in self-concept is required only if widowhood brings a substantial change in acquisition power. Unfortunately, many widows find that their level of living changes markedly. Of course, all of these orientations may be present in the same person.

Widowhood obviously carries great potential for creating an identity crisis. However, that potential remains unrealized far more than might be imagined. The ability of older women to maintain their conceptions of self as Mrs. John Doe means that their memories can preserve a continued identity. Other widows help legitimatize this continuity. Children are also important reinforcers of a continued identity.

However, women vary a great deal in the extent to which the role of wife is central to their identity. For many women, the role of mother supersedes the role of wife and after the children grow up and leave, the role of wife is an empty prospect. Other women have resented the traditional role of wife because of its subordinate status. Others have never developed a close, intimate relationship with their husbands. For any one or all of these reasons, some widows do not wish to preserve their identities as wives. These widows must then negotiate with family and friends to gain acceptance in their own right rather than as someone's wife. This renegotiation of social identity is a particularly necessary prelude to remarriage. Thus, for some widows, the identity problems brought on by widowhood are more external and social than they are internal and psychological.

Loneliness is a particularly prevalent problem among widows. Widows most often miss their husbands as persons and as partners in activities (Lopata, 1973). While no doubt much of the loneliness is caused by the absence of a long-standing and important relationship, some of it results from economic factors. Widowhood means poverty for most working-class women, and this poverty is translated into lower social participation outside the home (Atchley, 1975b). The influence of economic factors on loneliness in widowhood deserves more research attention than it has received thus far.

However, it would be a mistake to equate aloneness with loneliness. Many widows quickly grow accustomed to living alone, and more than half continue to live alone. And as they become more involved with friendship groups of older widows, they tend to miss a partner in activities less. In residential areas with a high concentration of older widows, loneliness is much less prevalent.

The social disruption caused by widowhood depends largely on the number of role relationships affected by the spouse's death. Middle-class women are particularly likely to have seen themselves as part of a team and to see their involvement in a wide variety of roles as having been impaired by widowhood. Such feelings are particularly common in cases where the couple operated a family-owned farm or business.

Widowhood has the most immediate impact on family roles. When older women become widows, they usually lose their contacts with their in-laws, especially if their children are grown. Contacts with children usually increase for a time, but those widows who move in with their children do so as a last resort (Lopata, 1973). There are two basic reasons why widows seem to prefer "intimacy at a distance." First, they do not wish to become embroiled in conflict over managing the flow of household activity, and after being in charge it is hard for widows to accept a subordinate position in another woman's house, especially a daughter-in-law's. Second, they do not want to be involved in the dilemmas of rearing children. They feel that they have done their work, raised their children, and deserve a rest (Lopata, 1973).

Patterns of mutual aid between children and parents are altered by widowhood. Older widows often grow closer to their daughters through patterns of mutual assistance (Adams, 1968a). Widows usually grow more distant from their sons. Because adult sons often feel responsible for their mothers' welfare and because older widows often want to be responsible for themselves, there is great potential for conflict and guilt in the older widow-son relationship. However, widows over 75 who live with children are more likely to be parents rather than parents-in-law of the household head (see Table 10-4). This finding suggests that widows are slightly more likely to move in with sons than with daughters.

Relationships with the extended family (brothers, sisters, aunts, uncles, cousins, and so on) increase immediately following the spouse's death. But within a short time, widows generally retain only sparse contact with extended kin (Lopata, 1973). This decrease is partly caused by the fact that married women tend to focus on wife and mother roles and spend little time maintaining close relationships with other kin.

The impact of widowhood on friendship largely depends on the proportion of the widow's friends who are also widows. If she is one of the first in her group of friends to become widowed, she may find that her friends feel awkward talking about death and grief—they do not want to face what in all likelihood is their own future. If friendship groups consisted mainly of couples, then the widow may be included for a time, but she will probably feel out of place. The widow may also encounter jealousy on the part of still-married friends.

On the other hand, if the widow is one of the last to become widowed in a group of friends, then she may find great comfort among friends who identify very well with the problems of grief and widowhood. As a group of women friends grows older, those who are still married sometimes feel somewhat "left out" because their friends do many things as a group that they do not feel free to leave their husbands in order to do. For these people, widowhood brings the compensation of being among old friends again.

In the community, churches and voluntary associations offer avenues for increased contact with people. Church groups often present opportunities for increased involvement that do not hinge on having a spouse. The same is true of voluntary associations oriented around interests (as opposed to purely social clubs). However, in heterosexual groups, widows are apt to encounter the stigma of the lone woman. It is no accident that many widows are drawn more to women's groups than to heterosexual groups. Again, the age at which widowhood occurs is important in determining the impact on community involvement.

Throughout the discussion of the impact of widowhood, the importance of age has cropped up again and again. The younger the widow, the more problems she faces; the older the widow, the more "normal" widowhood is considered to be and the more supports are available from the family, friends, and the community to help women cope with widowhood. Older widows appear to adjust better than younger widows (Blau, 1961).

The impact of widowhood also varies considerably, depending on the social class of the widow. Middle-class women tend to have balanced their roles between being a wife and companion to their husbands and being mothers. The loss of this comradeship triggers considerable trauma at the spouse's death. As a result, middle-class women tend to have difficulty dealing with grief. However, middle-class women also tend to be broadly engaged. They have a number of friends and belong to various organizations. They have many personal resources for dealing with life as widows. They usually have a secure income, they are well educated, and they often have job skills and careers. On the other hand, working-class women tend to emphasize the mother role more than the wife role. Consequently, they experience less trauma associated with grief. But working-class women have fewer friends, fewer associations, less money, and fewer of the personal resources that make for an adequate long-term adjustment to widowhood. Working-class widows are thus much more likely to be isolated and lonely than are middle-class widows.

Class differences are particularly large among blacks. Working-class black women tend to become widowed at much earlier ages than working-class whites. Overt hostility between the sexes is more prevalent among blacks, and therefore widows sanctify the husband's memory less. As a result, widowhood results in even less emotional trauma among working-class blacks than among whites (Lopata, 1973).

There are also considerable ethnic differences in the impact of widowhood. Foreign-born widows are much more likely than others to have had a traditional marriage, which, as we saw earlier, can entail greater identity problems with widowhood. In addition, the impact of widowhood on family relations has more potential for conflict among the foreign-born. Many foreign-born older women were reared in cultural traditions that offer widows a greater degree of involvement with extended kin. To the extent that the extended kin do not share this orientation, there is room for a greater gap between what the older foreign-born widow expects from her family and what she gets. A similar pattern prevails among older widows reared in an Appalachian tradition.

## Being a Widower

The impact of widowhood on older men has received little attention. The literature on this subject is long on speculation and short on systematic research. Nevertheless, it is important to outline both what we do know and what we need to know about being a widower, as a stimulus for further research.

The role of widower is probably even vaguer than that of widow. Because widowers are not very common in the community until after age 75, the status of widower does not solidify groups of older men as it does groups of older women. But older widowers are expected to preserve the memories of their wives, and they are not expected to show an interest in women. Indications are that many widowers adhere to the former and ignore the latter.

Because the male role traditionally emphasizes other roles in addition to the role of husband, widowers are probably not as apt as widows to encounter an identity crisis caused by loss of the husband *role*. But men are more likely than women to see their spouse as an important part of *themselves* (Glick et al., 1974). In addition, older men are less likely than women to have a confidant other than their spouse (Powers et al., 1975). Thus both sexes are likely to have problems with the loss of a significant other.

How older men cope with widowhood's impact on their identity also probably depends, as older women's reactions do, on how the lost relationships fit into the men's personal goal structures. Despite current stereotypes concerning men's overinvolvement with their jobs, there is little evidence that widowhood is any less devastating for men than for women. In fact, widowhood is very likely to wreck a man's concept of life in retirement completely. Likewise, there is little basis for assuming that marriage is less important to older men than it is to older women.

There is no apparent difference in the extent to which older widows and widowers experience loneliness (Atchley, 1975b). However, this finding may be caused by the higher average age of widowers. When the factor of age is controlled in research, older widowers may be less lonely than older widows.

Thus far, there has been little study of the impact of widowhood on men's roles outside the household. Widowers do have more difficulty with work during the grief period (Glick et al., 1974). It also appears that widowers are more cut off from their families than widows are (Troll, 1971). Widowhood tends to increase contacts with friends among middle-class widowers and decrease them among lower-class widowers (Atchley, 1975d). It is quite likely that the large surplus of widows inhibits widowers in developing new roles in terms of community participation. Particularly at Senior Centers, widowers tend to be embarrassed by the competition among the widows for their attention. They also feel pressured by widows who constantly try to "do" for them.

Very little has been written about age, social class, racial, or ethnic variations in the impact of widowhood on older men. However, some of the variations noted for widows no doubt apply to men as well. This area is greatly in need of research.

## Which Is More Difficult?

There is currently a controversy over whether widowhood is more difficult for older women or more difficult for older men. Age is an important compounding factor in comparing being a widow with being a widower. Widowhood occurs in old age for most men, while it occurs in middle age or later maturity for most women. It is important therefore to compare widowers with widows *of a similar age* in order to cancel out the impact of age. Much of the research that has been done to date has not thus controlled for age.

Berardo (1968;1970) is the leading proponent of the idea that older men find widowhood more difficult than older women do. He suggests that men are ill-prepared to fend for themselves—to cook their own meals, keep house, and so on—and therefore end up having to give up their independent households. Berardo also feels that men have more difficulty finding a substitute source of intimacy. He says that courtship opportunities are limited for widowers and that friends and children see them as being too old for "that sort of thing." Widowers also find it more difficult to move into their children's homes and find a useful place there. In addition, widowhood combines with retirement to give the widower severe identity problems. The retired widower has no job to use as an alternate source of identity and norms for behavior. On the other hand, Berardo feels that widows have the advantage of the continuation of the role of housewife, a meaningful activity that provides continuing standards for behavior. He sees widows as being much more able to maintain an independent residence and at the same time more able to gain acceptance in the households of their children should the need arise.

On the other side, R. Bell (1971:509) concludes that widowhood is harder on older women than on older men because: (1) being a wife is a more important role for women than for men; (2) widows are given less encouragement to remarry; (3) widows face a bleaker financial future with fewer financial skills; (4) widows are more isolated because women are expected not to be socially aggressive; and (5) the lack of prospects makes remarriage difficult for all but a few older widows.

Atchley (1975b) compared various dimensions of widowhood among 72 widowers and 233 widows, all 70 to 79 years old. Widows were significantly higher than widowers in prevalence of high anxiety, but even the widows had only 15 percent with high anxiety. Widowers were more likely to have a high level of anomie, but even the widowers had only 20 percent with a high level of anomie. Widowers were more likely to increase participation in organizations and increase contacts with friends than were widows. Sex differences in response to widowhood were greater among working-class respondents. Here the widows were more likely than widowers to be isolated and to have inadequate incomes.

Atchley concluded that working-class widows were considerably worse off than middle-class widows and widowers in both social classes. The key seemed to be their inadequate incomes. Income inadequacy in turn produced lowered social participation and loneliness.

These separate and diverse accounts raise several issues in comparing widowers with widows. It might be well, therefore, to examine each of them in more detail.

**Ability to Live Alone**    Many widowers may well have to learn to care for themselves, but there is little evidence that they cannot do it. Berardo's research is inconclusive in this respect because his study sample consisted primarily of very old, rural widowers—a population in which health and disability cloud the issue of ability to care for oneself. Table 10-2 indicates that from age 65 to 74, widowers are slightly more likely than widows to live in group quarters rather than independent households, but that after age 75 there is little difference. Table 10-3 shows that widowers living in households are slightly *more* likely to live alone than widows are. Thus, those men who remain widowers are not significantly less likely than widows to live alone.

TABLE 10-2
Living Arrangements of Widowed
Men and Women, by Age: United States, 1970

|  | Widowers | Widows |
|---|---|---|
| Age 65 to 74 (N) | (594,514) | (2,946,251) |
| Total | 100.0% | 100.0% |
| In households | 94.0 | 96.8 |
| In group quarters | 6.0 | 3.2 |
| Age 75 and Over (N) | (847,435) | (3,141,386) |
| Total | 100.0% | 100.0% |
| In households | 86.5 | 86.8 |
| In group quarters | 13.5 | 13.2 |

Source: U.S. Bureau of the Census (1973c).

TABLE 10-3
Living Arrangements of Widowed Men and Women
Living in Households, by Age: United States, 1970

|  | Widowers | Widows |
|---|---|---|
| Age 65 to 74 |  |  |
| In families | 32.0% | 35.8% |
| Living alone | 63.5 | 62.4 |
| Living with nonrelatives | 4.5 | 1.8 |
| Age 75 and Over |  |  |
| In families | 42.6% | 46.0% |
| Living alone | 54.0 | 52.2 |
| Living with nonrelatives | 3.4 | 1.8 |

Source: U.S. Bureau of the Census (1973c).

**Living with Children**   Table 10-4 shows that widowers are less likely than widows to be living with children, but the differences are not impressive. Interestingly, both widows and widowers are about as likely to be parents-in-law of the household head as they are to be parents of the head. It is only among widows over age 75 that we find a significantly greater likelihood of being a parent rather than a parent-in-law of the household head. When widowers live in multiperson households, they are much more likely than widows to be considered the household head rather than a subordinate member of the household.

**Problems with Retirement**   Berardo makes the usual assumptions that jobs are more important to men than to women and that retirement is an identity crisis primarily for men. He sees widowhood as a cumulative loss only for men.

Atchley (1976b) presents somewhat different analysis. Since he found little evidence that leaving the job at retirement represented an identity crisis for large

**TABLE 10-4**
**Family Position of Widowed Men and Women**
**Living in Families, by Age: United States, 1970**

|                             | Widowers | Widows |
|-----------------------------|----------|--------|
| Age 65 to 74                |          |        |
| Head                        | 53.0%    | 44.9%  |
| Parent of head              | 16.3     | 22.7   |
| Parent-in-law of head       | 16.8     | 20.9   |
| Sibling of head             | 5.9      | 6.1    |
| Sibling-in-law of head      | 2.7      | 1.9    |
| Other relative of head      | 5.3      | 3.5    |
| Age 75 and Over             |          |        |
| Head                        | 36.5%    | 28.7%  |
| Parent of head              | 27.5     | 33.1   |
| Parent-in-law of head       | 26.8     | 28.5   |
| Sibling of head             | 3.0      | 4.2    |
| Sibling-in-law-of head      | 1.3      | 1.0    |
| Other relative of head      | 4.9      | 4.5    |

Source: U.S. Bureau of the Census (1973c).

proportions of either men or women, he concluded that job loss is not a significant source of distress even in widowhood. He suggested that widowhood interacts with retirement to the extent that widowhood wrecks plans for a retirement life-style built around being a member of a couple. And this type of interaction between retirement and widowhood is probably as applicable to widows as to widowers.

From the point of view of cumulative role loss, it seems plausible that some widows actually have more problems than widowers do with the interaction of retirement and widowhood. When the empty nest occurs, many women respond by taking jobs or becoming more involved with jobs and this change is not usually negatively defined. Widows who are widowed early also tend to compensate by increasing their investment in their jobs. But when the woman is older, widowhood often comes on top of both retirement and the empty nest. Thus, widows may encounter more role loss than widowers do.

But what about the housewife role? Berardo feels that the continuity of the housewife role is an advantage for widows. However, what is retained is the role of house*keeper*, not house*wife*. The widow loses the housewife role because widowhood and the empty nest take away her clients (Lopata, 1973). The satisfaction of doing for oneself is often much less than the satisfaction of doing for others.

In sum, then, an effective case can be made for the idea that retirement and widowhood interact just as much for older women as for older men. However, more research is needed to put this discussion on sounder footing.

**Alternate Sources of Intimacy**  Berardo feels that widowers have more difficulty than widows with finding alternate sources of intimacy because of social norms against courtship and remarriage for older men. However, the statistics of the matter indicate that if such norms exist, older widowers do not heed them. Every year nearly 30,000 older widowers remarry, compared to about 15,000 older widows who remarry. Moreover, older widows outnumber older widowers four to one. Not only do older widows have to fight the scarcity of older widowers, but *half* of those older widowers who do remarry choose wives that are under 65. Thus, older widowers have a much greater chance than older widows do of finding new intimacy through remarriage.

Widowers are much less likely than widows to have had a confidant—a very close friend—other than their wives. Therefore, widowers *need* remarriage more than widows do, in order to find a new confidant. As far as the social discouragement of remarriage, McKain (1969) reports no sex differences in the extent to which children oppose remarriage. However, he does report that children's opposition to remarriage is a significant obstacle to remarriage.

**Financial Resources and Skills**   There can be little doubt that widows are far worse off financially than widowers, especially in the working class. In traditional marriages, the wife is usually ignorant of the family finances and has no training in how to manage money (Lopata, 1973). In addition, the incomes of widows average considerably less than the incomes of widowers. And Atchley's (1975b) research suggests that this poverty is a critical factor for working-class widows.

**Isolation and Loneliness**   Atchley (1975) found that widowed older people were significantly more often lonely than married older people, and that working-class widowed older people were more often lonely than those in the middle class. Atchley found no significant sex differences in the prevalence of loneliness among the widowed. However, widowers were much more likely than widows to increase participation in organizations and contact with friends.

Thus, no aspect of widowhood appears demonstrably more difficult for older widowers than for older widows. On the other hand, widows are worse off than widowers in terms of finances and prospects for remarriage.

## SUMMARY

Death touches the lives of older people more often than it does other age categories. The process of dying, the meaning of death, bereavement, and widowhood are all more salient to older people than to younger people, at least in industrial societies.

Death is both an end state and a physical and social process. In a given year, about 6 percent of the older population will die. Yet more and more people are not only surviving *to* old age but *in* old age as well. Variations in death rates for categories within society mean that women outnumber men a great deal and that a smaller proportion of black people survive to become old. Married people have higher rates of survival compared to others. Poor people die at faster rates than others. Retirement has no demonstrable effect on the probability of dying.

Death seems to be more salient to older adults than to others. Men tend to see death as an antagonist while women tend to see death as merciful. In general, older people fear death less than do other age categories. However, more research is needed on death fears among specific categories of older people who are still highly integrated into society.

For older adults, the role of dying person demands passive acceptance of death. Older people are less apt than the young to change their life-style when they learn that they are dying. Older people are also apt to find that being a dying person means having less independent control over one's life.

People go through various stages in dying, but there is no set sequence or necessary progression. Denial and isolation, anger and resentment, bargaining and attempt to postpone, depression and sense of loss, and acceptance are all common reactions to dying—and dying persons often experience more than one of these characteristics at the same time. Acceptance of death does not mean a wish to die. It is merely an acknowledgment of an inevitability.

Where and when a person dies is a matter of values. Most people prefer to die at home. However, just when in the process a person should be allowed to die is still a subject of controversy.

Two crucial aspects of care for the dying are maintaining personal relationships and reassuring the dying person that he or she will not be abandoned or humiliated.

A lengthy dying trajectory allows the survivors to grieve in advance and often softens the final blow. Bereavement is the process of dealing with someone's death. It usually encompasses symptoms of physical, psychological, and emotional stress. In addition, bereavement usually results in a sanctification of the memory of the person who died. People usually receive social support during bereavement, but only for a short time.

Being a widow is a long-term role primarily for older women. The prevalence of widowhood in later life combines with low prospects for remarriage to create a "community of widows." For women with traditional marriages, widowhood creates identity problems. It removes a valued role that is hard to regain, and it takes away the person who was most able to confirm the older woman's conception of herself. Some of the potential for crisis is softened by the fact that society allows older widows to maintain an identity based on being someone's wife in the past.

However, not all women have a high investment in the role of wife. For these people, the impact of widowhood on identity may be minimal.

Loneliness is the greatest problem for widows, especially in terms of having someone around the house and someone to go places with. However, aloneness does not necessarily mean loneliness. Many widows adjust quickly to living alone.

The impact of widowhood on family relations is ambiguous. Children respond to widows' needs in times of illness, but the widow enters the household of a married child only as a last resort. "Intimacy at a distance" is the preferred pattern. Extended kin are not usually important sources of interaction for widows.

If the woman is one of the first of a group of friends to become widowed, she tends to be cut off from friends. But if she is one of the last, widowed friends can be an important source of support and interaction. Generally, the younger the widow the more problems she faces, and the older the widow, the more "normal" widowhood is considered to be.

Social class is also important. On the average, working-class widows adjust better during bereavement but later have economic problems that make widowhood difficult. On the other hand, middle-class widows encounter more problems with bereavement, but because of their greater personal and economic resources they make a better long-term adjustment to widowhood. Class differences are especially great among widows who are black. Owing to their traditional values, foreign-born widows also have more difficulty.

Widowers have many of the same problems that widows face—vague role definition, identity problems, and loneliness. Widowers seem to be able to take care of a household. They are only slightly less likely than widows to live with children.

Both widows and widowers are likely to see their retirement plans wrecked by widowhood, and this problem is perhaps worse for some older women than for the average older man. The housewife role is lost without clients to serve.

Widowers are more likely than widows to remarry, but widowers are less likely to have a confidant other than their wife. Both may have trouble replacing the intimacy lost through widowhood.

Widows are far worse off than widowers economically, including both income and financial management skills.

Widowhood can be a difficult role for persons of either sex. In the last analysis, however, widowers have better economic resources and a better chance for remarriage. This would seem to put them at a distinct advantage.

## SUGGESTIONS FOR FURTHER READING

Atchley, Robert C. "Dimensions of Widowhood in Later Life." *Gerontologist 15* (1975):176–178.

Averille, J. R. "Grief: Its Nature and Significance." *Psychological Bulletin 6* (1968):721–748.

Blau, Zena S. "Structural Constraints on Friendship in Old Age." *American Sociological Review 26*(1961):429–439.

Farberow, Norman L., and Sharon Y. Moriwaki. "Self-Destructive Crises in the Older Person." *Gerontologist 15* (1975):333–337.

Glick, Ira O., Robert S. Weiss, and C. Murray Parkes. *The First Year of Bereavement.* New York: Wiley, 1974.

Kalish, Richard A. "Death and Dying in a Social Context." In Robert Binstock and Ethel Shanas (eds.), *Handbook of Aging and Social Sciences.* New York: Van Nostrand Reinhold, 1976.

Kastenbaum, Robert J. "Death and Bereavement in Later Life." In A. H. Kutscher (ed.), *Death and Bereavement.* Springfield, Ill.: Charles C. Thomas, 1969, pp. 28–54.

Lopata, Helena Z. *Widowhood in an American City.* Cambridge, Mass.: Schenkman, 1973.

Parkes, C. M. *Bereavement.* New York: International Universities Press, 1972.

Troll, Lillian E. "The Family of Later Life: A Decade Review." *Journal of Marriage and the Family 33* (1971):263–290.

Weisman, Avery D. *On Dying and Denying.* New York: Behavioral Publications, 1972.

# 11
# Independence
# and Dependency

To be independent is to be self-reliant; to be dependent is to be in the position of having to rely on other people. This chapter focuses on two social positions—independent adult and dependent adult—and the ramifications of change from one to the other. Our concern is with what is expected from and allowed to people in these very different positions, particularly as these factors are affected by age.

Self-sufficiency is a matter of degree, and for each stage in adult life and for each sex there is a socially defined threshold of self-sufficiency that an individual must attain in order to be accepted as a full-fledged, independent adult. If self-sufficiency drops below the threshold, or never gets there to begin with, then the individual is assigned to the role of dependent adult. There are four basic dimensions to our concept of adult independence: economic, physical, mental, and social.[1] Economic self-reliance means that the individual has the wherewithal to provide himself or herself with food, clothing, and shelter. Physical self-reliance means the ability to move about freely and the ability to take care of one's physical needs. Mental self-reliance means having an alert mind that can exercise knowledge, experience, and skills to solve problems posed by the social and physical environment. Social self-reliance means having the social power to demand various rights without having to rely entirely on the goodwill of other people.

Kalish offers two sketches that show how differently dependency may be viewed:

An elderly American woman . . . sits in her hospital bed and talks to her roommate. "Well, now, I've always believed that old folks shouldn't be a burden to young people,

[1]Psychological dependency was discussed in Chapter 5.

because young people need their happiness and independence. I don't know what I'll do when I get out of here—maybe I'll try to get into a nursing home. I want my independence too."

An elderly Japanese woman . . . says to her roommate, "When I leave here, I will live with my eldest son and his wife. My daughter-in-law is not happy about this, but her happiness is not so important just now" (Kalish, 1967:65).

The contrast between these two vignettes illustrates the following points: (1) our ideas about being independent or dependent can vary, depending on how we are brought up; (2) being independent and being dependent are related, but not mutually exclusive; and (3) our ideas about being dependent and being independent can have a strong influence on the choices we make.

## LEARNING TO BE INDEPENDENT

A great deal of the socialization American children experience is aimed at making them independent adults, self-sufficient on all four necessary dimensions. It is important to note, before going further, that the concept of adult independence does not imply isolation from other people. To be independent simply frees adults to develop genuinely reciprocal relationships based on mutual respect, responsibility, and trust. Becoming a self-reliant adult is a prime goal for members of American society, old and young alike. But as people grow older, they experience changes that influence their ability to continue to be self-reliant. To know how older people cope with this kind of change, it is necessary to know something about the origins and development of ideas about being self-reliant, about changes with age in the meaning of self-reliance, about reactions to losses of self-reliance that sometimes come with old age, and about various possibilities for preserving self-reliance.

Babies are notoriously self-centered, but at the same time they are the most helpless and therefore most dependent creatures on earth. The child's inability to do things obliges him or her to depend on others, to lean on them for physical security, support, sustenance, protection, and assistance. Early in the individual's life, this need to be dependent is fully accepted. At the same time, in American society the child is gradually expected to develop his or her own talents and resources, to make decisions, and to learn to solve problems.

The child thus learns that there are times to be dependent and times to be independent. The child also learns how much independence and dependence is appropriate for people of various ages. He or she learns that a small child can run to mother with a skinned knee, and that parents are to decide about clothes, friends, bedtime, and television-watching habits. At the same time, the child is rewarded for learning to go to the toilet unassisted, to put away toys without being asked, to dress unassisted, and so on.

Gradually, as the child grows older, approval for independent behavior increases and approval for dependent behavior diminishes. Refusing to leave home for school, seeking adult support in arguments with other children, continuous requests for reassurance from parents, and other such dependent acts meet with increasing disapproval from both family and peers. Teasing, humiliation, and ostracism are strong forces that teach the child that dependency is to be avoided as one gets older.

The child also must learn to distinguish between the ability to be socially independent and the ability to develop lasting reciprocal relationships with other people. The child must learn that to rely on others, to trust them, and to get emotional support from them and vice versa is not a lack of independence but instead a manifestation of independence.

Children are increasingly rewarded for showing initiative in becoming an independent individual. In fact, a key element involved in creating the achievement motivation that Americans so highly prize appears to be the rewards for doing *new* things independently. As an indicator of independence, mastery of care-taking tasks is much inferior to moving out on one's own, acquiring new skills, and exploring new possibilities. Apparently, the dependent child never quite develops the confidence required to compete with others for achievement (Brown, 1965:445–50).

As the child approaches adulthood, he or she is rewarded by both parents and peers for assuming the adult role and for doing more and more things without supervision. In addition, the independent adolescent is rewarded by the intrinsic satisfaction that comes from being in control of one's environment. The expectations concerning independence are so strong that we suspect something wrong when an adolescent does *not* rebel against parental authority. We expect children to gradually assume control over their own decisions, and in fact, it is this very process that separates child from adult.

This pattern of socialization teaches people particular ideas about being independent. Gradually, the individual learns to hate the idea of being dependent. The terms we use to describe dependents reveal our orientation toward the state of dependency itself. For example, *moocher*, *sponge*, *leech*, *lazy good-for-nothing*, and *bum* are all terms we frequently apply to people who cannot take care of themselves financially. We learn very early in life that anyone of adult age who has to rely on others for support is inferior, relegated to a subordinate, subservient position in relation to others of the same age and expected to give up many rights of self-determination in exchange for support. Usually the support required is financial, but our hatred of dependency extends to most other kinds of support as well. To the average, well-reared, adult American, the role of dependent is appropriate only for kids and misfits.

On the other hand, we gradually learn to prize being independent very highly. We regard it as a state to be striven for and, once gained, to be jealously guarded. Our heritage of self-reliance and individual autonomy goes back to the dawn of European civilization and even before. It is such an integral part of our culture that most Americans think of it as a basic aspect of human nature, even though it is not.

Our emphasis on self-reliance and autonomy is translated into norms that permeate our lives. We are expected to be self-sufficient in terms of our financial security, to operate an autonomous household, to get around by ourselves, and to manage our own affairs. The very fact that we are free to make our own decisions serves to expand the alternatives we have for solving the problems we face.

But at the same time we also expect these same things of ourselves. When individuals who have been rewarded for acts of independence by their parents, who have been approved of by peers, who have received the satisfaction of manipulating and controlling their environments, and who have probably experienced the mixed pleasures of having others depend on them realize that they are losing their ability to function independently, they must cope not only with society's disapproval of dependence, but also with their own fear and disapproval of the dependent role (Kalish, 1967).

The only respite from this anxiety and fear exists for those segments of the population who are allowed a little dependency. For example, housewives are allowed to depend financially on their husbands. Sick people are allowed to be more physically dependent than are healthy people. Very old people are allowed more physical dependency than are middle-aged people. Bereaved people are often encouraged to be dependent for a short time. These exceptions notwithstanding, anxiety and fear are the usual reactions of older adults who face dependency.

Becoming independent is a task that occupies most of childhood, adolescence, and young adulthood. Conversely, many people believe that learning to accept dependency is a major task of old age, when old age is defined in symptomatic terms.

The concept of independence has a great many aspects, because it refers to *how* we play our various roles, as well as to the roles we play. For this reason, the role of independent adult influences almost every aspect of American life that requires individual participation: family, friendships, community, the job, politics, the church, recreation and leisure, and many others. Independence is perhaps *most influenced by finances, housing, and mobility.*

## TYPES OF INDEPENDENCE

Financial independence is a necessary condition for maximizing older people's options and opportunities. This necessity has been well documented throughout this book. Lack of financial resources is the most frequent reason that older people cite for having to rely on others—for becoming dependent.

Housing is another important aspect of independence. One of the norms of adult independence requires maintaining one's own household. This norm is reflected in older people's attitudes toward their living arrangements, since only 8 percent of people 65 and over say that they would rather live with a child or other relative than in their own homes (Shanas, 1962). The norm of household independence is also reflected in the fact that 90 percent of American older people were living in their own households in 1970.

Housing is crucial to independence. In an individual's household, he or she has much more privacy and freedom of choice than when it is necessary to accommodate to the desires of others. When an older person lives with an adult child, for example, the child often makes the decisions in the household. For an adult who is accustomed to making decisions not only for himself or herself but for others, deferring to a child can represent a significant reduction in independence. However, it should not be assumed that every older person who lives in a household with his or her adult children is dependent. Many older people are heads of households in which their adult children are the dependents. In still other cases, neither generation is dependent.

Mobility is also a vital aspect of independence, particularly in the United States with its sprawling cities. It is quite literally impossible to live an independent life in many American cities without an automobile. The shopping facilities, service facilities such as barber shops, beauty shops, shoe repair shops, and even churches are often located far from the city's residential areas. Our middle-sized cities—those with populations ranging from 50,000 to 200,000—are encountering a steady decline in public transportation.

The older person who can no longer afford to maintain an automobile, or who is physically unable to operate one can seldom avoid depending on friends and relatives for transportation. The fact that less than half of the older population owns an automobile suggests how prevalent this kind of limitation on independence is. More research is greatly needed in this area. There are very few data on the extent to which independence in the later years is hampered by inadequacies in transportation.

Most older people retain mental self-sufficiency. Lowenthal and Berkman (1967) report that although reports of failing memory increase with age (after 60), only one in five of their community respondents reported problems such as losing or misplacing things. Kay and his associates (1964) report results from several European and American communities that show that no more than 5 percent of the older population can be expected to experience chronic brain syndrome or senile brain disease.

Often the changes that occur in physical and social life as people grow older leave them with virtually no alternatives. When these changes happen, the individual is almost bound to sense a loss of independence. For example, role loss can deprive older people of friends, kin, leisure pursuits, and sources of social status. Older people who experience such losses often find themselves in the position of having to ask for help from people they do not know, from agents of bureaucratic organizations who are not interested in what the older person may have to *give* in order to preserve self-respect. The significant question is just how much independence older people have, and how much they are forced to give up.

Only about 40 percent of older people in the United States have incomes at or above the modest-but-adequate level. About four fifths have independent housing and around half have the use of an automobile. From these data, it appears that older people tend to lose their financial independence first, their independence of movement second, and their independence of household last.

A certain level of health is necessary for independence, but the necessary level is not very high. As one older person put it, "I'm not looking to be a spring chicken, I just don't want to be an invalid." In fact, twice as many disabled older people live in private homes as in institutions. No doubt this situation is partly the result of financial problems, but there is a strong possibility that a feared loss of independence may keep many people from entering Homes even when entry would be to their advantage.

A definite problem with the sociological concept of social independence at this point is the paucity of data. The only research that has dealt extensively with social dependency and its relationship to aging is that done by Clark and Anderson (1967).

Their study of aging in San Francisco hit on the idea of dependency almost by accident. They set out to study the cultural aspects of aging, placing particular emphasis on the relationship between culture and personality. The social institutions they devoted the most attention to were the family, friends and neighbors, organizations, work, retirement, and religion. They attempted to relate the older person's social situation to personal characteristics such as morale, isolation, and loneliness. At the conclusion of their study, Clark and Anderson state:

> The most unequivocal finding to come out of our social analysis of this sample is the singularity of the subjects in it. This singularity is interpreted by these subjects in many ways: it is proud independence; it is autonomy prized as befitting "a good, upstanding American"; or it is shrinking from others for fear of rejection, or an invasion into sacred privacy for purposes of manipulation or the offering of unwanted "charity" (1967:425).

Much of what Clark and Anderson present must be confirmed by additional research, yet something may be gained by considering the implications of their findings, tentative as they may be.

Apparently, the meaning of independence changes with increasing age. To the young adult, independence means a newly found freedom; to the middle-aged adult it means the normal way of living—as continuing proof of adulthood and self-worth; and to the adult in later maturity or old age it means the same thing as in middle-age, with the added feeling that independence is something to be protected. In old age, the need to maintain independence sometimes approaches desperation because of the physical problems involved, but for the majority of older adults the expectation of continued independence, particularly with regard to staying in one's own household, is realistic. Typically, when job and adequate income are both long gone, remaining an independent adult is an important source of self-esteem.

## MAINTAINING INDEPENDENCE

Clark and Anderson (1967) observed that two quite different sets of reasons were offered for wanting to remain independent in one's later years. One set of reasons is basically adaptive for the individual; it includes pride in autonomy and concern for the freedom of others. The pride that comes from making decisions and doing things for oneself is a major source of self-esteem in a society that values independence as highly as ours does. The desire to remain independent in order to preserve one's pride is basically an adaptive motive, because pride is akin to self-esteem, a personality trait most people seek to attain or maintain.

It is likewise adaptive to respect the independence of others. The aged parent who goes out of his way to avoid imposing on his children has a greater chance of having his children respect his own independence. Many older people in America say they wish to avoid being a burden on their families, and this desire provides strong motivation for remaining independent as long as possible. The negative evaluation of dependency also provides motivation. Being dependent not only inconveniences the person being depended on, but also lowers the dependent's status. Thus we would expect that the stronger the desire for respect from one's children, the greater the motivation to remain independent.

The maladaptive reasons for wanting to remain independent include fear and mistrust of others and the need for psychological defenses. Older people often seek to remain independent because they are afraid that others will attempt to use them, to manipulate them, and thus to impose an unacceptable situation on them. They may also feel that once others get into one's life, it is not so easy to get them out. Old people also mistrust motives others may have for helping them, the rationale being that the only reason a person would seek out an older person in our society would be for personal gain.

A second maladaptive reason for preserving independence is the use of isolation as a defense mechanism. A study of people who refused a personal interview concluded that a sizable number of older women held very unrealistic concepts of themselves and sought to restrict their interaction with others in order to avoid a negative reaction to the unrealistic self they presented (Atchley, 1969). Independence may thus be used as a tool for preserving a vulnerable self-concept. An independent person is more capable of controlling whom he or she sees and in what situations.

Both of these reasons are maladaptive simply because they lead to isolation. It is very clear from the research findings that isolation can be deadly for the older person. Isolation has some important side effects. It increases privacy, but in older people it also increases vulnerability to illness, accidents, malnutrition, and loneliness. In addition, isolation greatly increases the social distance between the generations. If the motives just mentioned became the main reason for seeking independence, they can gradually lead to complete withdrawal, whereas adaptive motives for retaining independence are positive, in the sense that they specify conditions to be sought rather than avoided and are attainable without resorting to isolation.

## DEPENDENCY

It would be very difficult for an adult American to avoid valuing independence, given the value placed on it. There is, therefore, probably a very strong relationship between the value people put on independence for themselves and their reaction to both the possibility and the fact of dependency.

Older people's attitudes toward dependency tend to be very negative, a fact no doubt related to the generally high degree of motivation among older people to remain independent. The positive value of independence, as well as the negative value of not encroaching on the independence of others, result in strongly negative attitudes toward the mere idea of dependency.

Apparently the negative attitudes toward dependency and the strong positive valuation of independence combine to make the dependent older person miserable. In their intensive sample, Clark and Anderson (1967:222) found that the primary cause of low morale among older people was dependency, either financial or physical.

Older people usually first attempt to solve the problem of remaining independent themselves. They cut down on how much they spend, to preserve financial self-reliance. They cut down on how much they do, to conserve physical energy and independence. They compensate for failing memory by keeping notes. They avoid social dependency by disengaging from contacts in which they have no power. For most, personal solutions succeed. For some, however, losses become too great for personal solutions and outside help must be sought.

The first place older people usually go for help is to their kin. If the older person is dependent on children, a great strain is usually put on their relationship—another factor that contributes to a negative attitude toward dependency. If the older person can remain autonomous, or if there is mutual dependence, then the relationship can remain a good one, but apparently there cannot be a happy reversal of roles between parent and child. Many psychologists have remarked about the crisis of authority that most children encounter. This crisis may be a mere shadow in comparison to the authority crisis older people go through if they must become dependent on their children. Both the parent and the child resent the change; both feel guilt as a result of their resentment; and both tend to become hostile toward the source of their guilt. This kind of relationship is a vicious circle of resentment, guilt, and hostility that tends to grow increasingly worse—often to the point of a breakdown in the relationship between parent and child.[2]

The dread with which most older people regard dependency is thus very realistic. Yet as age increases, so does their need for outside help. Illness, poverty, disability, declining energy, failing hearing or sight—all of these roads lead to dependency. Older people avoid seeking help from community agencies because there is no way to preserve even a semblance of reciprocity in dealing with bureaucratic organizations. The rules and regulations, the forms, the prying into the personal life of the client that often typify social service agencies are indication enough that the older person has been assigned to the dependent role. Often, services in the older person's own home might well allow him or her to retain a measure of autonomy, and in some cases such services are being provided. Visiting nurses, homemaker services, and Meals-on-Wheels are examples of community services that are available in some areas. Unfortunately, most older people do not have access to these services, and even those who do either do not know about them or find them inadequate.

There is a shortage of medical and service personnel in the United States, especially in rural areas, and providing specialized home service for older people is regarded as expensive and inefficient. Instead, efforts are focused on institutions—nursing homes and homes for the aged. Here the needed supports can be provided, but here also even the illusion of self-help or self-determination all too often disappears.

Clark and Anderson found that:

> Some of the aged in our sample feel that, if help can be obtained only at the expense of institutionalization, if the small sphere of respectable autonomy that constitutes the aged

---

[2]For an additional discussion of intergenerational relations, see Chapter 18.

person's shrunken life-space can be punctured like a child's balloon—then it may be best to gamble on one's own with survival. Such people will draw their curtains to avoid critical appraisals of their helplessness; they will not get enough to eat; they will stay away from the doctor and forego even vital drugs; they will shiver with cold; they will live in filth and squalor—but pride they will relinquish only as a last resort (1967:391).

Not all older people react in this extreme fashion, but there is some evidence that older people who do enter institutions are reluctant to do so because they fear loss of independence. More research is needed on the relationship between individual social independence within the institutional setting and adjustment to institutional life. The most reasonable hypothesis would appear to be that the more choices the individual is given in the institutional setting, the better he or she will like living in the institution and the better adjustment will be. This hypothesis implies that the decisions left to the individual must be as important as possible.

## SUMMARY

Americans prize their independence highly. From infancy, Americans are taught to go it alone, to do things for themselves. Adulthood is related to physical, financial, and social independence. Dependency is deplored, and dependents are relegated to inferior positions.

Objectively, social independence means having enough money to get by on, having a household of one's own possessions, social graces, and enough health to be able to get around. Independence is a very relative concept. We almost always have some degree of independence, even if it consists of refusing to eat tomato soup. Having money and health are the primary keys to independence in American society, and accordingly there are identifiable phases in the loss of independence. Money is generally lost first, often as a result of retirement. Health is lost second, partly as a result of loss in income, and with it often goes a large measure of the individual's ability to get around. Finally, when health declines to the point of incapacity, the individual enters an institution.

A strong desire for independence has been found to be typical of older people. Sometimes this motivation comes from the pride of being self-sufficient, sometimes from a desire to avoid burdening others, sometimes from a fear and mistrust of others, and sometimes from a desire to defend an unrealistic concept of oneself. The latter two types of motivation are often maladaptive because they tend to increase isolation and vulnerability.

As a result of the high value placed on independence, most older people hold extremely negative attitudes toward dependency. The reaction to dependency is thus highly predictable. It makes older people despise themselves and their situation. Compounding the problem is the fact that older people often must depend on their children—a situation that degrades older people and puts a strain on relationships with their children.

It should not be surprising, then, that some older people would literally prefer to die rather than become dependent. This situation is aggravated by the fact that our community supports are inadequate, and many of our medical services are organized in such a way as to deprive the individual of independence.

## SUGGESTIONS FOR FURTHER READING

Blenkner, Margaret. "The Normal Dependencies of Older People." In Richard A. Kalish (ed.), *The Dependencies of Old People*. Ann Arbor, Mich.: University of Michigan, Wayne State University Institute of Gerontology, 1969, pp. 27–37.

Clark, Margaret. "Cultural Values and Dependency in Later Life." In Richard A. Kalish (ed.), *The Dependencies of Old People*. Ann Arbor, Mich.: University of Michigan, Wayne State University Institute of Gerontology, 1969, pp. 59–72.

Kalish, Richard A., "Of Children and Grandfathers. A Speculative Essay on Dependency." *Gerontologist 7* (1967):65–69.

# 12
# Personal Adaptation to Aging

The physical, mental, and social changes that accompany aging eventually become so serious that they cannot be ignored. For some, declining energy begins to require adaptation as early as age 30, and aging requires small adjustments in activities and life-style throughout adulthood. However, the pace and magnitude of change picks up dramatically for many people who reach their sixties or beyond. And the process of adapting to change is accordingly both more complex and more obvious.

Examining how people respond to age changes in themselves and in the social situations that confront them is difficult, for several reasons. First, changes associated with aging do not occur all at once for any given individual. Hearing may decline before vision does; personality changes may occur before any of the biological changes. Second, no two individuals are apt to confront *exactly* the same changes at exactly the same stage of their lives. Third, the manner in which different people respond to the same change varies greatly. Nevertheless, there are typical changes that occur in later life and there are typical ways of adapting to those changes. The following list of changes is neither a comprehensive catalog nor a rigid sequence, but all become more likely with advancing age:

- ☐ Energy decline
- ☐ "Empty nest"
- ☐ Retirement
- ☐ Income decline
- ☐ Sensory loss
- ☐ Declining health

☐ Widowhood
☐ Poverty
☐ Disability
☐ Institutionalization

In terms of adjustment to energy decline, the principle of conservation of energy seems to apply. The relatively inefficient operation of their bodies reduces the energy available to older people and restricts the number and kinds of things they can do and how they can do them. Confronted with too many activities for the amount of energy available, older people are most likely to drop those activities they consider marginal to their lives. Only after a considerable limitation in energy are they apt to drop or restrict activities they consider essential. Increased susceptibility to disease also restricts activity. Physical impairment and sickness are in some ways more difficult to adjust to than the decline in energy, because physical impairment often dictates the activities that must be dropped. Retirement and widowhood are also major exceptions to the pattern of voluntary choice. Certainly this process involves compromises, but little research has been done to determine how people arrive at them.

Initially, it was thought that when the last adult child left the household, the mother was confronted with a stressful adjustment to an "empty nest." In recent years, however, investigators have begun to agree that adjustment to the empty nest is not particularly stressful for women (Lowenthal and Chiriboga, 1973). The typical adaptive strategy on the part of mothers is to begin a job career or increase involvement in an existing job career. Interestingly, we know little about the father's reaction to the empty nest. The assumption that fathering is not a major element in men's lives seems dubious, and would be an excellent topic for research.

As we saw in Chapter 8, adaptation to the loss of job at retirement can take several forms, depending on the position the job occupied in the individual's hierarchy of personal goals. Some people find another job, some find new activities, some become more involved in old activities, and some withdraw. An individual's adaptation depends on opportunities in society, the person's resources, and the person's goals.

As yet we know little about how people cope with the income decline that often accompanies retirement. Again, it would seem that compromises are involved, but we do not know how these compromises are reached, especially among those with incomes well above the poverty level. Certainly, the average income drop of 50 percent will require adaptation at any income level.

Many older people suffer a steady erosion of the purchasing power of their pensions, and among the oldest retired people the incidence of poverty is quite high. When they are faced with fixed costs of housing, Oliver (1975) reports, many older poor people cut their expenditures for food below the level necessary for good health or nutrition.

Deterioration of vision and hearing also restricts older people's activities. Fortunately, most older people can wear corrective glasses or hearing aids and thus maintain adequate social functioning. Only a very small proportion of older people must make a greater adjustment, when their vision or hearing losses cannot be corrected.

Adaptation to widowhood is seldom an easy task. In fact, Holmes and Masuda (1974), who reported the degree of stress associated with various life events, ranked death of a spouse at the top. Moreover, the social system provides support for the adaptation of widows and widowers for only a brief period after the event occurs.

Disability and institutionalization seem to be universally dreaded and resisted. Yet many people manage successfully to adapt to physical changes that many of us would consider intolerable. And many people find that they are reasonably happy in long-term care institutions. Two key prerequisites for these successful adaptations appear to be personal resilience on the part of the older individual and a humane environment.

This brief review of various changes and some of the ways people adapt to them is not intended to be complete, comprehensive, or detailed. The details are provided in earlier chapters. The intent here is to reinforce the notion that adaptation to aging is not a generalized phenomenon. Instead, it is a series of perhaps cumulative adaptations to *specific* changes. And each of these specific changes is not only objectively real, but also relates to the person's past. For example, reactions to retirement are impossible to predict without knowledge of both the person's past and the person's present.

It may therefore be a mistake to assume, as some gerontologists have, that adjustment to aging is a global phenomenon that can be summed up in terms such as *disengagement*. Instead, it may be more useful to think of the literature on adaptation to aging as a *loosely organized set of suggested assumptions about the process of adjustment—assumptions that must be tested with respect to each specific type of change*. What follows are some of the more prominent approaches that have been used to explore the adaptive process in later life.

## DISENGAGEMENT

Neugarten (1964) has noted the increasingly inward orientation of older people. Cumming and Henry (1961) applied the term **disengagement** to refer to a process whereby the individual responds to aging by gradually and inevitably withdrawing from the various roles he or she occupied in middle age toward ever-increasing concern with self and decreasing involvement with others. Fifteen years of research later, it seems clear that disengagement is neither a universal nor an inevitable response to aging, although *some* people undeniably do show such a response.

**Individual disengagement** is usually selective; that is, the individual withdraws from some roles but not from others (Streib and Schneider, 1971). With each withdrawal from a role, the individual becomes increasingly preoccupied with himself or herself. Gradually, the individual equilibrium achieved in middle age and oriented toward society is replaced through the process of disengagement by a new equilibrium centered around the individual's inner life in old age.

Disengagement is a mutual withdrawal of individual and society from one another, resulting in *decreased interaction* between the aging person and others in the social system to which he or she belongs. The process may be initiated by the individual or by others in the situation. Older people may withdraw more markedly from some classes of people, while remaining relatively close to others. Their withdrawal may be accompanied from the outset by an increased preoccupation with themselves; certain retirement and health care institutions in society may make this withdrawal easy. When the disengagement process is complete, the equilibrium that existed in middle life between the individual and society has given way to a new equilibrium characterized by a greater distance and an altered type of relationship (Cumming and Henry, 1961: 14–15).

The reduced frequency of interaction supposedly weakens the hold of norms over the individual. Freed from social pressures, disengaged individuals with their declining physical energy are content to live with memories from the past. If roles are available to allow them to live in their own self-centered worlds, their morale will remain high; but if they cannot find such roles, their morale will probably decline with increasing disengagement.

People are said to be ready for disengagement when they become aware of the short amount of life remaining to them, when they perceive their life-span and their ego energy as shrinking. The disengagement process is molded by the same character traits that influence the individual's behavior at other points in the life cycle.

**Engagement** is the degree to which the individuals are involved with the world around them. They may be *broadly* engaged in a number of roles, *deeply* engaged in a few roles, or *symbolically* engaged as one who stands for something, as an elder statesman does (Cumming, 1964). Obviously, engagement involves not only roles, but a psychological *commitment* on the part of the individual. For example, an older person who is very active, in the sense of interacting frequently with people, may simply be a disengaged person searching for a new identity. Accordingly, in order to measure disengagement, the investigator must study changes over time in the individual's commitments to roles, and in the types of roles to which the individual is committed. The disengaged person is thus one who has a low commitment to various roles normally thought of as important.

Disengagement is thus *one* possible response to shrinking life space and reduced energy. Individuals who are disengaging are withdrawing from the world rather than adjusting to it. At some point, the paths of society and of the individual cross with respect to disengagement. At this point, the societal and individual mechanisms of disengagement interact—the most obvious example is in initiating disengagement. In an industrial society with a growing population, success depends on knowledge and skill, which are thought to decline with age. Therefore, disengagement is initiated by older individuals because they recognize their lack of knowledge and skill, by society because it recognizes their lack, or by both simultaneously. In the last instance, *mutually satisfactory* disengagement occurs. If, however, the individual desires disengagement and society does not, *forced engagement* will result. And if society desires disengagement and the individual does not, the result is *forced disengagement*.

Only in the first case can the individual be satisfied with the outcome, while in either of the latter cases his or her morale will be seriously lowered.

Society and the individual are both responsible for disengagement. Society creates the situation in which disengagement takes place, and the individual attitude toward disengagement can determine the form the process will take. We will have more to say about society's role in this process in Chapter 13.

The individual disengagement theory of adjustment does not adequately explain the effect of norms on individual behavior. The theory assumes that the withdrawal of reinforcement for an internalized norm will result in the withering away of that norm as far as the individual is concerned. This assumption is not supported by the evidence. For example, people retired for more than 20 years have been found to retain very positive attitudes toward the norm of getting intrinsic satisfaction from work (Atchley, 1967). Once a norm has been internalized, something more than an absence of interaction seems to be required to eliminate that norm.

Another difficulty with the individual disengagement approach is its assumption that desire for disengagement encounters no competition from desires that would dispose the individual toward continued engagement. For example, it has been found that among people in attractive occupations such as teaching, a high potential for disengagement can be overcome by an even higher predisposition to continue receiving the satisfactions that come from continued engagement. Cottrell and Atchley (1969) and Streib and Schneider (1971) found that following retirement, people are as apt to increase engagement as they are to decrease it.

There are further difficulties with the individual disengagement theory. The first is its simplicity. The study of social psychology requires models even more complex than those required to study society alone. The compound influences of biology, sociology, and psychology that produce individual disengagement will eventually require a much more sophisticated theory than has been presented to date. Hochschild (1973) notes two other defects with the theory as it now stands. One is that the various formulations have provided so many escape clauses that no amount of evidence would prove it false. Second, the theory also assumes that role loss *means* the same thing to everyone who encounters it.

Adequate testing of the individual disengagement hypothesis has been hampered by severe difficulties in identifying operationally the people in whom individual disengagement could be expected to occur. Most often, chronological age has been used to indicate the aging process, producing contradictory results. Adequate testing of the disengagement hypothesis must involve *specific* hypotheses concerning the conditions under which individual disengagement occurs.

Yet there can be little doubt that some people do withdraw from the world rather than go through the process of adjusting to change. Whether this withdrawal is seen as desirable by them is questionable. Indications are that withdrawal is an outcome primarily associated with lack of *opportunities* for continued involvement (Rose, 1964; Atchley, 1971b; Roman and Taietz, 1967; Carp, 1968b). In addition, withdrawal is far from being a typical outcome.

## SUBSTITUTION

When people lose certain roles or the capacity to perform certain activities, an obvious way to adapt is to find a substitute (Friedmann and Havighurst, 1954; Havighurst, 1963). How available this avenue is depends on a number of factors. First, substitutes must be available. Second, the person must have the physical and mental capacity to perform a substitute role or activity effectively. Finally, the person must *want* a substitute.

Substitutes are often not readily available. Retired people often cannot easily find new jobs. Widows cannot easily find new mates. If roles or activities are lost through income decline or physical decline, then substitution is not a very available strategy. And to the extent that the person is overextended in terms of activities, he or she may not want to look for a replacement for lost activity. Thus, while substitution may be a feasible and attractive way to cope with loss early in life, with age it becomes increasingly more difficult to put into practice.

## CONSOLIDATION

Consolidation of commitments and redistribution of available energy is another way to cope with lost roles, activities, or capacities. People who are involved in several roles and a variety of activities may not need to find a substitute for lost roles. It may be easier simply to redistribute their time and energies among their remaining roles and activities. The general level of activity that results from this redistribution may be on a par with the preloss level or there may be some reduction.

The **consolidation approach** is available to most people. However, some people have so few roles or activities that when they lose roles or activities, the ones remaining are not able to absorb the energies freed by the loss. Unless they can find a substitute, these people are forced to disengage. Consolidation may also not be a satisfactory solution if the lost activity was extremely important to the person's life and the remaining activities, though perhaps plentiful, are not able to serve as the basis for a meaningful life.

## LIFE-STYLE SOLUTIONS

Williams and Wirths (1965) have advanced the notion that the adjustment an individual makes to aging is very much related to the main focus of his or her style of life. This approach is individualistic, because it contends that the individual's reaction to aging springs from a particular style of life. Williams and Wirths identified six styles of life among the older people they studied.

### World of Work

People who adhere to this life-style focus their attention on work to give meaning to their lives. This focus is narrower than is characteristic of the other life-styles, and accordingly, this life-style allows little leeway for attempting adjustment. The person with a World of Work style is apt to resist retirement as long as possible, and attempts to replace work as quickly as possible with volunteer jobs or other work substitutes. However, people do develop secondary life-styles, and some World of Work people successfully shift to make their secondary style their primary style. When work is the *only* life-style the individual has ever attempted, then all alternative styles are closed, and adjustment is usually difficult.

## Familism

The focus for people who use this style is their family. Their major decisions are made in relation to the family, their values center around the family, and family is the most important area of their lives. This style is more affective (emotional) than instrumental (as in the World of Work style) and thus encompasses a much wider range of activities. Individuals with this life-style usually have a considerable range of possible reactions to aging.

## Living Alone

People using this life-style are social isolates. Aloneness here does not necessarily refer to living arrangements, but rather to the central focus of the individual's style of coping with the world. When this style is developed in the later years, it is equivalent to total disengagement. It is prevalent among inner-directed people, particularly among those who *like* being loners.

## Couplehood

The focus of this style is the significant paired relationship. It can be related to familism, but need not be. For example, two elderly women may live together and focus their lives on the bond between them. Like familism this style has a wide range and is typified by affective rather than instrumental emphasis. It may also be precarious, because something could happen to either person in the couple.

### Easing Through Life with Minimal Involvement

People using this style have only a minimal commitment to most of the roles they play, including work, marriage, and family roles. This style is difficult to achieve, primarily because there are many informal sanctions against it. Social pressures to become involved are always present. If this style persists throughout life, the person never really becomes engaged in the social world, but if it is adopted later in life, it represents a type of disengagement.

### Living Fully

People using this style do not focus their energies on any specific part of life; instead they spread themselves rather broadly. Yet their involvement in most aspects of living is more than minimal, and they tend to be engaged. Even when disengagement is forced on them, they deal with it effectively.

Living Fully, as a style, expresses one facet of the Christian ethic, "I am come that you might have life and that you might have it more abundantly." It is a socially approved style, and many popular programs of living arrangements and recreation for the aged are based on the assumption that this is a greatly preferred style of life (Williams and Wirths, 1965:155).

Williams and Wirths caution that each of these life-styles may involve varying degrees of commitment to the style, of satisfaction derived from the style, and of energy utilization. In addition, no single style was found more likely to yield a "successful" adaptation.

## ADAPTIVE TASKS

Erikson (1963) separates personality development into eight stages: early infancy, later infancy, early childhood, middle childhood, adolescence, early adulthood, middle adulthood, and late adulthood. Late adulthood is characterized by the need to accept one's life as having been inevitable, appropriate, and meaningful. This need, or task, requires certain adjustments.

Borrowing elements from various developmental theories, Clark and Anderson (1967) have suggested that there is a set of *adaptive* tasks, as they call them, that most aging people will eventually face if they live long enough. Clark and Anderson differentiate *development*, which is learning to live with oneself as one changes, from *adaptation*, which is learning to live in a particular way according to a particular set of values as one changes or as one's culture changes. These researchers depart from what is essentially a personality theory by bringing social pressures into the act, because they feel that adaptation requires not only internal accommodation to one's personal system of needs but also conformity to the demands of society. The five adaptive tasks that Clark and Anderson associate with later adulthood and aging are:

1. Recognition of aging and definition of instrumental limitations
2. Redefinition of physical and social life space
3. Substitution of alternate sources of need satisfaction
4. Reassessment of criteria for evaluation of the self
5. Reintegration of values and life goals

The first task, *recognition of aging and definition of instrumental limitations*, "requires an awareness and an acceptance of changes in one's own physical and/or mental capabilities, with acknowledgement that certain activities can no longer be pursued as successfully as they were in one's earlier life" (Clark and Anderson, 1967:402). Better adapted older people conserve their health and energies, and they can come to terms with the limitations society puts on the roles they can play.

There must be an awareness of social pressures to relinquish the roles and activities of middle-life and a realistic assessment of what those pressures mean in terms of available supports. . . . The important point in this task is that, although an individual need not *like* his own personal or social circumstances as he grows old, he must not deny the reality of certain limitations, if they exist for him (Clark and Anderson, 1967:402–03).

The second task, *redefinition of physical and social life space*, involves redefining the boundaries of one's life space. Individuals must manipulate their situations to achieve an ideal level of control over their personal action systems. As age increases, individuals may no longer be able to control as large a segment of the environment as they did when they were younger. "In social terms, this means that certain roles and activities must be relinquished, and there must follow a reconstitution of one's network of social relationships" (Clark and Anderson, 1967:404). Often this reconstruction of social relationships is also a constriction of them.

Clark and Anderson offer this example of what can happen when this task is not accomplished:

At sixty-six, Mr. Butler can best be described as a man with a very diffuse life. He is simultaneously headed in several major directions; first, he is trying to finish his term of teaching in order to receive his full pension. His goal in teaching has been to become an administrator: "The reason why I wanted to be an administrator—well, they make much more money. And it gives you the importance and responsibility you seek." Now, he is finding it difficult even to manage his classes. He speaks of difficulties in maintaining discipline in his classroom, in handling "behavior problems," and recently he received a reprimand from his school principal for losing his temper with a student and giving the boy a severe shaking. He admits that, with age, he has become more irritable and less able to cope with the demands of public school teaching. In spite of this fact, however, Mr. Butler is still trying simultaneously to fill his teaching position, study for a state license as a real estate salesman, arrange for the purchase and management of a large apartment building, plan business and stock investments, stabilize a precarious relationship with his wife, support a daughter in Switzerland, and maintain active contacts with a wide circle of friends.

Mr. Butler insists on keeping many irons in the fire. Yet, with the loss of energy due to advancing age, he is finding it increasingly difficult to be successful in this. He admits to making several errors of judgement in business within recent years; we have already pointed to his irritability and impatience with the students; also he admits to some chronic marital difficulties, in part because he is drinking so much more now than he used to (he admits that drinking has become a problem for him); and he is even concerned about maintaining friendships because he fears being "found out a phony."

Interestingly enough, Mr. Butler gave us the following formula for successful aging: "Well, keep your expectations within limits so that you can achieve your goals." Certainly, he himself has not been able to accomplish this, and his control over his environment is being eroded day after day. His horizons, once so far and wide, now seem to be receding beyond his failing grasp. Mr. Butler is a very unhappy man (1967:405–06, reprinted by permission).

The third task, *substitution of alternative sources of need satisfaction*, requires that aging individuals substitute feasible interests, activities, and relationships for those they can no longer pursue successfully, thus providing alternative sources of need satisfaction. Adaptation requires a willingness and an ability to identify and engage in new, feasible pursuits. Socially, the individual must have access to possible alternatives within the environment. People who cannot live without work or who cannot cope with widowhood or dependency are failing at this task. For Clark and Anderson, substitution not only involves new activities related to old values, but also the development of new values in response to a new life situation.

The fourth task, *reassessment of criteria for evaluation of self*, means that individuals must modify the ideas they use as the basis for their self-concepts. For example, it is not adaptive for older people to continue to derive their self-concepts from their performance in the work role. Likewise, society must provide criteria other than work for determining a person's worth. In order to maintain self-esteem, older people must establish their identity on roles other than those of worker, builder, manager, or leader. Without self-approval, of course, the individual is apt to feel utterly useless. As one man put it,

> Now? Now I don't care. You have to be realistic about this. I feel I have lived my life. There is none of me left. . . . What am I good for? I just keep on living. Oh, I'm not a morose man—it isn't a question of that. I have enough money to live decently. My wife is alive and the children come from time to time. I find things to do around the house to keep me busy. But it's not enough. Somehow, it's just not enough. I keep wishing I could do some good—be useful (Clark and Anderson, 1967:410–11).

The fifth and last task, *reintegration of values and life goals*, requires revising life goals and values to give coherence, integration, and social meaning to one's new style of life. The older person must not only preserve self-esteem, but must also find a new place for himself or herself in the broader scheme of things. This reintegration gives his or her life added meaning and purpose.

Using their adaptive tasks to define adaptation to aging, Clark and Anderson found that, in general, older people do adapt. Of their community sample (San Francisco), 61 percent was rated as adapted and 39 percent as maladapted.

In terms of specific tasks, Clark and Anderson (1967:427) found that the maladapted were distributed as follows:

| | |
|---|---|
| Acceptance of aging | 11% |
| Reorganization of life space | 14 |
| Substitute sources of need satisfaction | 54 |
| Revision of criteria for self-evaluation | 14 |
| Reintegration of values and life goals | 7 |

From these data, it appears that finding substitutes for the things that satisfy their needs is the skill most lacking among maladapted older people.

Clark and Anderson conclude:

> Those in our sample whom we found to be adapted in their old age have suggested the answer to this problem [of maladaptation and alienation in old age]. These are the elderly who have successfully developed personal codes of values which have eased their resolution of the adaptive tasks of aging. . . . These codes are not alien to American culture—they are the secondary values—and those who survive best in their later years

are simply those who have been able to drop their pursuits of primary values . . . and to go on to pick up, as workable substitutes, the alternative values which have been around all along; conservation instead of acquisition and exploitation; self-acceptance instead of continuous struggles for self-advancement; being rather than doing; congeniality, cooperation, love, and concern for others instead of control of others. These are the values the aged in our society have been forced to embrace (1967:429).

This model of adaptation is closely akin to the continuity approach mentioned earlier in connection with retirement and leisure participation. Those who were most able to pick up leisure in retirement were precisely those who had concentrated on "secondary" roles earlier in life.

## MAINTAINING COMPETENCE

Restoring the individual to his or her maximum feasible level of performance is an implied goal of all of the approaches to the study of adaptation considered thus far. Kuypers and Bengtson (1973) have suggested that perhaps a more crucial problem is to avoid slipping below the threshold of what society defines as the minimum acceptable level of adult performance.

People can be defined as *incompetent* in several ways. They can be thus labeled if the roles they play are not viewed as appropriate for the full-time energies of adults. At one time, for example, retirement to leisure was not justifiable for able-bodied adults. People can be judged incompetent if they do not display ability to cope with change. Gladwin (1967) suggests that coping skill involves knowing more than one way to achieve desired results, knowing how to use the system to good advantage, and being able to test reality effectively. People can also be considered incompetent if they do not show feelings of personal mastery or effectiveness in the world around them. Of course, these three aspects of competence are interrelated.

Individuals thus not only have the problem of adapting to their own aging, but they must also guard against being defined as incompetent by society in the process. In other words, the choices people have in adapting to aging are constrained by society's definition of competence.

## VARIETIES OF ESCAPE

The approaches mentioned all involve efforts to identify, confront, and solve the problem of adjusting to the changes that come in later life. Not all people choose to confront the adjustment problem directly. Instead, some seek to escape from it via alcoholism, drug abuse, or suicide.

### Alcoholism

At least 15 percent of the older population has serious alcohol problems, and in some urban neighborhoods the proportion is as high as 40 percent (Zimberg, 1974:222). On reviewing the literature on alcoholism in later life, Zimberg (1974) concludes that there are two types of older alcoholics—long-time alcoholics who have grown old and people who have become alcoholics in later life. People who become alcoholics in later life are generally responding to stresses of aging such as widowhood, loneliness, or depression (Butler and Lewis, 1973).

## Drug Abuse

Anxiety often accompanies the changes that aging brings. Physicians often prescribe tranquilizers to alleviate these anxieties, and tranquilizers sometimes become a permanent solution to the problem of coping with aging. In one study, tranquilizers accounted for 35 to 40 percent of the medication prescribed for older Medicaid patients in Illinois, Ohio, and New Jersey (Butler and Lewis, 1973:249). Twelve of the top 20 drugs commonly prescribed for older adults are tranquilizers. Tranquilizers such as Librium can become addictive, in that emotional dependence develops and physical withdrawal symptoms can occur if the drug is withheld. If used to excess, stronger tranquilizers such as Mellaril can reduce physical activity to the point at which muscle atrophy occurs (Butler and Lewis, 1973:249).

## Suicide

From early in life, suicide increases with age, for men, in all societies for which reliable statistics are available (Atchley, 1974). While suicide rates are sensitive to cultural and economic factors, the increase in suicide rates with age for males remains consistent over time for various cohorts (Atchley, 1974b). We do not know why suicide rates increase with age for men and not for women.

Bock (1972) reports that suicides of older people are associated with widowhood and social isolation. Failing health, depression, and sexual frustrations have also been linked to suicide among the elderly (Butler and Lewis, 1973:62; Farberow and Moriwaki, 1975). Since most of these factors are more common among older women than among older men, it is even more puzzling that suicide rates of older males are so much higher than those of older women.

In addition to overt suicides, some older people also die because they have given up. Failing to continue treatment for illnesses such as heart disease or diabetes, engaging in detrimental activities, or neglecting one's health are all indirect ways to kill oneself. No one knows how many older people die as a result of such actions.

## Why Escape?

A crucial question concerns why some people confront and resolve the problems of adjustment posed by aging and others choose various forms of escape. The various forms of escape cited above are often interrelated. Many older people use both tranquilizers and alcohol. Farberow and Moriwaki (1975) found that heavy alcohol use often precedes consideration of suicide. Use of tranquilizers sometimes causes older people to fear that they are failing faster than they really are (Butler and Lewis, 1973). This sort of fear is also related to consideration of suicide. Farberow and Moriwaki (1975) stress that suicide among older people is strongly related to *accumulated* losses.

Based on bits and pieces of data on various forms of escape, a picture of the process that leads people to seek escape begins to emerge. People who encounter a *multiplicity of losses* are prone to seek escape, even if briefly. Often, *social supports* from the community, family, and friends can lead the person out of escapism. However, some people perceive their losses as too great to be coped with. Others see the available "solutions" to their problems as involving intolerable compromises. For these people, escape is a preferred alternative. Some people are able to gain the escape they need with alcohol, tranquilizers, or both. For others, the pain is too great, and they eventually choose suicide.

## SUCCESSFUL AGING

But what of those people who do manage to cope with aging? Implied in the concept of successful aging is a value judgment to the effect that some adjustments are better (successful) than others (unsuccessful). Social gerontology contains many definitions of successful aging.

The *activity* approach to successful aging holds that to age successfully one must maintain into old age the activity patterns and values typical of middle age. These values stress maintaining a large number of roles and being very active in them. To age successfully, the individual should avoid shrinkage of the life space and find substitute activities when necessary. Evidence indicates that for most older people, the level of activity they have developed over a lifetime tends to persist into their later years (Riley and Foner, 1968:418).

Yet activity theory is idealistic, for it sets up the expectation that older people will be carbon copies of middle-aged people, with no patterns of behavior peculiar to themselves. This expectation is unrealistic for all but a small minority of older people, in view of the limitations imposed by biological changes alone.

The *disengagement* approach to successful aging sees old age as a potential developmental stage in its own right, with features very different from those of middle age. Old age is seen as a period during which the individual gradually and voluntarily disengages from his or her various positions and roles. Activity reduction in old age is thus welcomed by the individual and should be considered normal. Successful aging, in these terms, would mean successfully coping with disengagement; people who tried to maintain a large array of activities in their old age would be deemed unsuccessful. Thus, the activity and disengagement theories provide diametrically opposed definitions of successful aging.

In terms of *personality*, people are said to have aged successfully if they maintain a mature and integrated personality while going through the aging process. As people age they must be able to make their past experiences and their current experiences live well with each other.

The *life satisfaction* approach holds that people have aged successfully if they feel happy and satisfied with their present and past lives. This basically subjective approach defines success in terms of inner satisfaction rather than of external adjustment. Havighurst, Neugarten, and Tobin isolated what they feel to be five components of positive life satisfaction: (1) zest—showing zest in several areas of life, liking to do things, being enthusiastic; (2) resolution and fortitude—not giving up, taking good with bad and making the most of it, accepting responsibility for one's own personal life; (3) agreement between desired and achieved goals—feeling of having accomplished what one wanted to; (4) positive self-concept—thinking of oneself as a person of worth; and (5) mood tone—showing happiness, optimism, and pleasure with life (Havighurst et al., 1963).

Williams and Wirths (1965) have developed a definition of successful aging based on the individual's *personal action system*. The personal action system is defined as follows:

> The social system of an individual actor is a system of action, that is, behavior which is meaningful. Meaningful means oriented toward ends, goals and values which, in turn, can be communicated to and usually shared in by others. Thus, it is composed of all the transactions of an individual in his social life space. . . . A given actor . . . can be taken as the focal point and questions about the dimensions and structure of his social life space, modes of interaction in it, attitudinal set toward it, satisfaction or dissatisfaction he derives from it, and degree of its stability over time (1965:5).

The elements of the personal action system that are said to be pertinent to success in aging are *autonomy* and *persistence*. Autonomy involves the exchange of energy between the actor and the rest of his or her action system. If the actor puts about as much energy into the action system as is taken from it, the actor is said to be *autonomous*. If the actor takes more from others than he or she gives to them, the actor is said to be *dependent*.

The element of *persistence* involves the stability of the personal action system. A persistent action system is one that is apt to remain stable for some time. Conversely, a *precarious* system may collapse or change its characteristics significantly at any time.

Successful aging is defined in terms of both autonomy and persistence. If the overall relation of the individual to the social system is both autonomous and persistent, the person is aging successfully. If it is autonomous but precarious, the person is aging less successfully. If it is dependent and persistent in dependency, the person is aging still less successfully; and if it is dependent and precarious, the person is least successful (Williams and Wirths, 1965:10). In their Kansas City sample, Williams and Wirths found that 64 percent of those questioned fell into the autonomous-persistent category and were therefore rated as being successful agers.

## A Case of Successful Aging

Clark and Anderson (1967) cite the following interesting case history of a person who had aged successfully:

> To complete this discussion, we will describe one additional case, that of Mr. Ed Hart, a man who has skillfully adapted—both personally and socially—to all five tasks. We first saw Mr. Hart when he was ninety years old. He was born in 1870, the only child of middle-aged parents. He started working and contributing significantly to the household

budget at a very early age; while still in his teens, he turned over his considerable savings to his parents, enabling them to purchase a home. Still in his youth, he assumed a "parental" role toward his parents, being obliged to do so because much of his father's time was spent in taking care of the then invalid mother. Mr. Hart attended school, learned cabinet-making from his father, and devoted himself to caring for his parents.

Mr. Hart idolized his father throughout his life. Cabinetwork was always dear to him because it had been taught him by his father. He regarded his father's guidance as invaluable: it was he who kept his son away from the alcohol which he dearly loved, and it was also from his father that he acquired a sincere love for people. The relationship was a very harmonious one, each gladly accommodating himself to the wishes of the other. Although Mr. Hart married at the age of twenty-four, he and his wife continued to live with his parents until their death in 1912. Mr. Hart was closely attached to his wife, but his father had always remained the most important figure in his life.

He was content with cabinetwork until the age of thirty-five, at which time he bought a ranch, deciding to become a financial success for the sake of his children. He describes himself during this period as over-ambitious and given to excessive chronic worry. His preoccupation with making a fortune from this ranching endeavor led to a nervous breakdown and confinement in a sanitarium for two months. This experience, when he was about forty, proved to be the turning point of his life. He emerged with a highly integrated personality and a satisfying personal philosophy. He had formerly been a zealous member of the Methodist Church, but following this hospitalization, he eschewed all organized religions, feeling he needed no one to dictate to him how he should serve God. Nonetheless, Mr. Hart expresses a profound belief in divinity, a love of his fellow man, a full acceptance of everything life has to offer, and an adamant refusal to be unhappy.

Following his hospitalization, Mr. Hart sold his ranch and worked as a vocational teacher for the following six years. Again, he found deep satisfaction in his work and was loved by students and fellow teachers alike. He showed great understanding and evidently displayed remarkable skill in nurturing the talents of his students, adapting his teaching to the individual child's potential. His dislike for the regimentation practiced in the school led him to resign and to return to his former vocation of cabinetmaking, work he pursued up to the age of fifty-five. An injury to his arm, however, finally made him give up this successful occupation (some of his work had been exhibited at the 1939 San Francisco International Exposition). For the next twenty years, he was employed in the hotel business, work that he found congenial because of his interest in people. Retirement did not find him idle. Up to the age of ninety, he did cabinetwork as a hobby, manufacturing various items to present to his numerous friends.

Mr. Hart looks back on sixty-four years of harmonious and contented married life. His first wife died suddenly after twenty-five years of marriage when he was forty-nine years old. After living alone with his children for two years, he remarried at the age of fifty-one. Thirty years later, he lost his second wife, and it was upon her "last request" that he again remarried. His third wife had been a widowed friend they had both known for almost thirty years. This final marriage lasted for nine years. During the last two years of her life, the third wife was severely ill, and Mr. Hart nursed her through to the end. She died in 1960. Even during his last wife's terminal illness, Mr. Hart showed the same serenity and the same positive acceptance of life he expressed in all of our interviews with him. He does not differentiate among his wives: he describes them all as "dear, loyal women."

Mr. Hart finds it somewhat "humiliating" that he has outlived three wives and both of his sons. He took pains to raise his children as best he could and was anxious to let them develop their own individual ways. Rather than seeing himself as the provider of an estate, a role he had once thought so important, he finally perceived his parental role as that of the provider of good examples and wise guidance. His close relationship with his sons changed when they married, and Mr. Hart believes that it is only right that this should be so: "With marriage the offspring form independent units of their own, and parents should release their hold upon them." Mr. Hart was never possessive in his life. The persons closest to him at present are his daughter and step-daughter, who are equally dear. He mentions with pride that both have invited him to come and live with them, but he will not take this step until it is absolutely necessary. He does not wish to inconvenience them, but unlike many other of our subjects, he does not harp on the prospect of "becoming a burden" to somebody else.

From his middle years onward, Mr. Hart suffered a number of major illnesses: in 1926 he was operated on for a bilateral hernia; and in 1949, for a perforated ulcer; finally, a prostatectomy and colostomy in 1953 (he was eighty-three years old at the time) resulted in a complete loss of control over his bladder, requiring him to wear a urinal twenty-four hours a day. When he was ninety, his physical condition no longer permitted him to indulge in his hobby of woodworking, and, at ninety-three his failing eyesight ruled out television and limited his reading to one hour a day. Yet he takes his declining physical functions in stride, not finding it irksome to make necessary adjustments. His mental faculties have remained remarkably intact. He is keenly aware that few men his age are as mentally alert as he is, or have aged as gracefully. He is proud of this fact and attributes it to the philosophical orientation he has worked out for himself and incorporated into his life.

Although Mr. Hart has been obliged to curtail many of his social activities, he still corresponds with numerous friends and receives almost daily visits from solicitous neighbors. He gives much of himself and is warmly appreciated by others; he appears to bring out the best in others, which may be one of the reasons he claims he has never been disappointed by a friend. Mr. Hart has led a full, creative, and serene existence. It is perhaps because his life has been one of fulfillment that he is ready to surrender it at any moment; he still finds life quite enjoyable, but he is as willing to die as he is to continue living.

This man made a profound impression on all our interviewers. They found him alert, intelligent, serene, and wise. His self-acceptance is complete. He found it difficult to answer our self-image questions or to describe himself in terms of the list of various personality traits we submitted to him; he simply stated, more appropriately, "I'm Ed Hart and I don't want to be anyone else—I will be the same ten years from now, if I'm alive."

According to American middle-class standards, Mr. Hart has not been a particularly successful man. Looking at his life in one way, he has no particular reason not to be disappointed with his past and depressed with his present. He failed in his one great effort to become wealthy. After a nervous breakdown, he gave up on this venture altogether. He quit a second time when he dropped out of the teaching profession because he disagreed with established policy. One might expect him to be bitter about this, or terribly lonely, since he has outlived nearly all his friends and relatives—but he is neither. Crippled with disease, forced to wear a urinal at all times, and nearly blind, Mr. Hart gave one of our interviewers his philosophy of life: "I have an original motto which I follow: 'All things respond to the call of rejoicing; all things gather where life is a song.' "

It is clear that Mr. Hart has adapted to aging. He has admitted to and accepted physical limitations, first giving up the demanding manual labor of cabinetmaking, and later retiring without regret from hotel work.

Mr. Hart has no problems in controlling his life space—he does not over-extend himself: "As long as I don't strain myself, I'm okay. I take it easy. The other day I declined an invitation to go on board a ship, since I knew there would be stairs there."

All of his life, Mr. Hart has successfully practiced substitution, so this adaptation has been natural for him. He enjoyed married life and never remained a widower for long. He was capable of substituting one vocation for another, as necessity required, developing a deep interest and satisfaction in each. Even after his retirement from hotel work, his last job, he continued to be interested and active in union affairs. "That's my pork chop, so to speak," he says.

In personal philosophy, Mr. Hart has no problems at all. His standards for self-evaluation are not predicated on mutable factors such as productivity, wealth, or social status. He is first, last, and always himself: "I'm Ed Hart and I don't want to be anyone else." This is a standard not likely to totter with age.

However, his discovery of adaptive values and life goals was hard-won: at forty, he early found himself unable to cope with the instrumental and achievement-oriented values of his society. He suffered a severe emotional upheaval at that time, was hospitalized for a period, and emerged with a warm, humanistic philosophy which has carried him not only through middle age, but through old age as well (Clark and Anderson, 1967: 415–19, reprinted by permission).

## SUMMARY

Aging brings a wide variety of changes that require some sort of adjustment or adaptation on the part of the aging individual. Adaptation to aging is not a generalized phenomenon. Instead, it is a set of specific adjustments to specific changes such as retirement, widowhood, income decline, or physical decline.

There are several strategies through which people adjust to aging. Disengagement is gradual withdrawal from involvement with the outside world. Sometimes older people cut down their involvements voluntarily, but more often disengagement is thrust on older people by circumstance or by the norms of society. Whether disengagement is seen as desirable by older people who disengage is still a controversial issue in social gerontology. People can sometimes cope with role loss by substituting a new role for a lost one. However, this strategy has limited applicability, because appropriate substitutes are scarce. People can also cope with role loss by realigning their energies and commitments among the roles that remain. This strategy is most feasible for people who already play a wide variety of roles.

Adaptation to aging takes place in the context of an individual's life-style. Williams and Wirths (1965) point out that successful adjustment to aging is possible in any life-style, but that it is often more difficult for people whose life-styles revolved around either their jobs or their spouses to the exclusion of other commitments. Adaptation also requires certain skills. Being able to admit one's aging and the physical and social limits it imposes, being able to redefine one's place in the social world, being able to accept new definitions of oneself, and being able to take up new values are all important skills that help in the adjustment process. In addition, the aging individual must be skilled at presenting changes to others in such a way that these others continue to define the aging person as a competent adult.

Not everyone grapples with the effects of aging. Some people choose to run away from it. Evidence for this escapism can be found in the statistics on alcoholism, drug abuse, and suicide. Indications are that *cumulative* and serious change is most often what causes aging individuals to attempt escape rather than to attempt adjustment.

Regardless of the strategy used to cope with aging, adjustment can be called successful if the person remains at least as autonomous and mentally stable as he or she was earlier in adulthood. There are many definitions of success and they vary widely from person to person, as do the means used to pursue success.

## SUGGESTIONS FOR FURTHER READING

Bennett, Ruth, and Lucille Nahemow. "Socialization and Social Adjustment in Five Residential Settings for the Aged." In D. P. Kent, R. Kastenbaum, and S. Sherwood (eds.), *Research Planning and Action for the Elderly: The Power and Potential of Social Science*. New York: Behavioral Publications, 1972, pp. 514–524.

Butler, Robert N. "Successful Aging and the Role of the Life Review." *Journal of American Geriatric Society 22* (1974):529–535.

Cumming, Elaine. "New Thoughts on the Theory of Disengagement." In Robert Kastenbaum (ed.), *New Thoughts on Old Age*. New York: Springer, 1964, pp. 3–18.

———, and William E. Henry. *Growing Old: The Process of Disengagement*. New York: Basic Books, 1961.

Dowd, J. J. "Aging as Exchange: A Preface to Theory." *Journal of Gerontology 30* (1975): 584–593.

Edwards, John N., and David L. Klemmack. "Correlates of Life Satisfaction: A Reexamination." *Journal of Gerontology 28* (1973):497–502.

Henry, William E. "The Theory of Intrinsic Disengagement." In P. From Hansen (ed.), *Age with a Future*. Copenhagen: Munksgaard, 1964, pp. 415–418.

Lowenthal, Marjorie F. "Intentionality: Toward a Framework for the Study of Adaptation in Adulthood." *Aging and Human Development 2* (1971):79–95.

Solomon, Barbara. "Social Functioning of Economically Dependent Aged." *Gerontologist 7* (1967):213–217.

Williams, Richard H., and Claudine Wirths. *Lives Through the Years*. New York: Atherton, 1965.

Zimberg, Sheldon. "The Elderly Alcoholic." *Gerontologist 14* (1974):221–224.

# Part Four
# Societal Response to Older People

Thus far, aging has been viewed in terms of its importance for the individual. Yet much of the social situation confronting the older person is the product of the way older people are viewed by their society, and of the roles society expects them to play. Accordingly, the remainder of this book is devoted to examining general responses of society to the fact that it has older members and to examining the roles older people play in the economy, politics and government, the community, religion, voluntary associations, and the family. In addition, the roles of friend and neighbor are also examined in relation to aging.

# 13

# Societal Disengagement

Society's reactions to the fact that many of its members are old is a very important aspect of aging. Thus far we have considered the biological and psychological aspects of aging, and situational elements as they affect aging. But apart from a specific situation, it is important to know *in general* how older people are expected to fit into the family, the peer group, the economic realm, the community, government, politics, voluntary associations, and religion.

Part of the problem arises from the fact that social institutions outlive the people who comprise them, and thus most institutions are constantly phasing young people in and old people out. This pattern is as true of the family as it is of a factory or a state. The process whereby society withdraws from or no longer seeks the individual's efforts is called **societal disengagement**.

As part of an overall theory of disengagement, Newell (1961) suggested that societal disengagement is half of the inevitable withdrawal of older people and society from each other. Societal disengagement is characterized by a "thinning out of the number of members in the social structure surrounding the individual, a diminishing of interactions with these members, and a restructuring of the goals of the system" (Newell, 1961:37). It has already been established that individual disengagement reduces the number of interactions for the individual. From the societal point of view, older people may no longer be sought out for leadership in organizations, their labor may no longer be desired by their employers, their children may no longer want them to become involved in their decisions, their unions may no longer be interested in their financial problems, and their government may no longer be responsive to their needs. These are the realities of societal disengagement. More often than not, societal

**227**

disengagement is unintended and sometimes even unrecognized by society, but is nonetheless a reality for older people. Cowgill and Holmes (1972) conclude that societal disengagement results from the depreciated status of older people in modern societies (see Chapter 1).

## ROLE LOSS

To measure societal disengagement, Newell and his associates first took a *role count*, an inventory of the number of separate *active* relationships the individual had. Then they used an *interaction index* to measure the amount of interaction with others each day. Newell (1961:39) found that role count "is quite stable between the ages of fifty and sixty-four; about 60 percent of this younger group act in six or more roles, but by age sixty-five only 39 percent do, and the proportion decreases steadily until at age seventy-five and over, only 8 percent act in more than five roles." Fewer work and family roles account for most of the age difference for both older men and older women. Thus, in older cohorts the variety of roles people play is lower than in younger cohorts.

The interaction index was concerned with the density of interaction, and again Newell found a decrease with age. However, here there are marked declines after age 65. Table 13-1 shows that interaction declines steadily from age 50 onward, the average decline between 5-year age groups being just over 11 percent.

**TABLE 13-1**
**Rates of Interaction by Age**

| Age | Percent with High Daily Interaction |
|---|---|
| 50–54 | 72.2 |
| 55–59 | 58.8 |
| 60–64 | 58.8 |
| 65–69 | 45.2 |
| 70–74 | 34.0 |
| 75 and over | 15.4 |

*Source:* Cumming and Henry (1961:40).

The Cumming and Henry theory of disengagement, to which Newell contributed, has been criticized on the ground that some people may be relatively nonengaged throughout their entire lives. For example, one study showed that 90 percent of *both* engaged and disengaged people over 65 were in the same categories, respectively, 5 years earlier (Rose and Peterson, 1965:362), and another found a high potential for disengagement for professors of all ages (Atchley, 1971b). The theory has also been criticized for its assumption that disengagement was associated with low morale and was apparently not as functional as the theory indicates it should be (Lipman and Smith, 1968). These criticisms relate mainly to the individual aspects of disengagement.

## ATROPHY OF OPPORTUNITY

For those who use society as a point of departure, the major criticism is that the theory of disengagement does not give enough weight to the role of the socially determined situation in the genesis or processes of disengagement (Roman and Taietz, 1967). The crux of the matter is whether the pattern observed by Newell and others[1] is the result of individual disengagement or societal disengagement or both.

One important aspect of the problem has been dealt with by Frances Carp (1968d), who set out to study the effect of moving from "substandard housing and socially isolating or interpersonally stressful situations to a new apartment house" having within it a senior center. Prior to the move, the 204 subjects were assessed in terms of their engagement in three separate roles: paid work, volunteer work, and leisure pastimes. Opportunities for all three were very limited in the premove situations of the study sample. "Special effort was necessary in order to participate in any of the three. Expenditure of this effort was assumed to express a strong need for involvement" (Carp, 1968d:185).

Following the move, opportunities for volunteer work and leisure pastimes were expanded, but opportunities for paid work remained about the same. Carp predicted that those who had expended the effort on leisure or volunteer in the antagonistic premove setting would be happier and better adjusted in an environment that facilitated continued engagement. She also predicted that those who had worked for pay in the premove setting would be no different in terms of satisfaction or adjustment after the move. Her results fully supported her predictions. People who had been involved in leisure pursuits or volunteer work prior to entering the apartment building tended to be happier, more popular, and better adjusted than the other tenants. On the other hand, those who had worked were not significantly different from the other tenants.

Carp interpreted her findings as supporting the idea that the greater the congruence between the person's desires for continued engagement and the opportunities for such engagement offered by the situation, the higher the degree of adjustment and satisfaction. She concludes:

> The results suggest that involvement is reactive to person-situation congruence, and that engagement-disengagement is not a general trait but one which is specific to various domains of involvement. . . . They suggest also that services for the elderly might profit from prior awareness of prospective clients' engagement in various behavioral domains. . . . (Carp, 1968d:187).

---

[1]For example, Havighurst et al., 1963; Williams and Wirths, 1965.

Implicit in these conclusions is the idea that many people want to remain engaged, and that one of the main obstacles preventing them from doing so is societal disengagement, which creates a situation in which continued engagement is difficult.

In order to assess the impact of societal disengagement directly, Roman and Taietz (1967) undertook the study of an occupational role in which continued engagement after retirement is allowed—the role of the "emeritus professor." Unlike most organizations, American colleges and universities, instead of removing retired faculty from the organization, make available a formalized, postretirement position with a flexible role, whose definition is a function of the individual's preretirement position, as well as of his or her own choice of postretirement activity. The important point here is that this system allows the *opportunity* for role continuity between full-time employment and retirement.

The amount of continuity possible varied. The research professors had the most, since they could generally continue to get research grants through the university. Those involved in teaching, public service, or administration still had opportunities for involvement, but their emeritus role was quite different from their preretirement role. They often ended up writing books, consulting, or becoming administrators. In no case, however, was the continuity complete. The emeritus professor always gave up a measure of involvement (Roman and Taietz, 1967). This situation was perfect for studying psychological disengagement, since the societal disengagement is very low.

Disengagement theory would lead us to believe that since the individual naturally wants to disengage, he or she would do so in this situation. Roman and Taietz assumed that disengagement was the product of *particular* social systems, not of systems in general, and that opportunity structures would greatly influence the individual's "readiness to disengage." Cumming and Henry (1961) had viewed readiness to disengage as a result of aging, regardless of the social system. Given their own assumptions about opportunity structures, Roman and Taietz (1967:149) predicted "that a significant proportion of emeritus professors would remain engaged, and that those allowed role continuity would exhibit a higher degree of continued engagement than those required to adopt new roles." They found that 41 percent of the emeritus professors were still engaged within the same university, 13 percent had taken employment in their profession elsewhere, 24 percent were in bad health, and 22 percent were disengaged from both the university and their profession. If these percentages are recomputed, leaving out the group in bad health, for whom no determination of voluntary disengagement is possible, and combining both categories of those still engaged, the pattern shows 71 percent still engaged and 29 percent disengaged. In addition, they found that those emeritus professors who had had a research role were still engaged significantly more often than the others. Thus, all of Roman and Taietz's predictions were supported by their findings.

These data suggest that the frequency of disengagement is very much a product of the opportunity for continued engagement. The fact that the organization provided a continuing role after retirement allowed 71 percent of the healthy people to remain engaged, whereas in many occupations the percent allowed to remain engaged would have been near zero. This finding is all the more revealing given the fact that almost half of Roman and Taietz's sample was over 75 years old.

It is entirely possible that most voluntary individual disengagement has resulted from the fact that people see disengagement as inevitable *by the rules of the institutions they participate in*. That is, voluntary disengagement is really the result of societal disengagement.

A study that supports this idea was done by Carp (1968b). She found that disengagement from the family role was negatively associated with disengagement from other roles. This finding suggests that when people give up a particular role, their resistance to giving up their other roles increases. Again, the study implies that the social situation is an important factor influencing disengagement, and that the individual is more reluctant to disengage than the disengagement theory would indicate.

Tallmer and Kutner (1969) have attempted to assess the impact of "stress-inducing environmental and circumstantial disturbances" in producing consequences similar to those generally attributed to disengagement. The stress factors they used included illness, widowhood, retirement, receiving welfare, and living alone. One of the fundamental tenets of the Cumming and Henry disengagement theory is that growing old causes, or is at least associated with, disengagement. *Tallmer and Kutner found that practically all of the relationship between age and engagement was accounted for by the relationship between age and the various stress situations.* They concluded:

> There appears to be substantial evidence for our hypothesis that disengagement among the aged can be predicted to occur as a concomitant of physical or social stresses which profoundly affect the manner in which the life pattern of the person is redirected. Because they have ignored the apparently definitive effect of such factors on disengagement, Cumming and Henry were led to the conclusion that advancing age was a sufficient explanation of the facts obtained in their study. It is not age which produces disengagement in our investigation but the impact of physical and social stress which may be expected to increase with age. It is tempting to hypothesize that as one enters into later decades, disengagement is bound to grow, and indeed it does. The real difficulty lies in the fact that it is the correlates of old age, i.e., failing health, loss of peers, death of relatives, and the general shrinking of the social world due to factors related to aging, that appear to produce the social withdrawal known as disengagement (Tallmer and Kutner, 1969:74).

The point is that the external aspects of aging and the socially structured situation can have a far greater influence than personal desires on the social withdrawal of older people. A recurrent theme throughout our examination of how older people fit into a modern industrial society will be that the difficulties many older people face are brought on less by withdrawal on their own part than by decisions, often consciously made, on the part of others to exclude them from the mainstream of society. Illness, loss of peers and relatives through death, and the shrinking pool of alternatives the older person faces are often unnecessarily stressful simply because, in a social system built around production, rationality, and efficiency, it is often more expedient to write off older people than to expend the energy required to create a "citizen emeritus" role.

Disengagement theory is comforting in a way, particularly for the young, because it seems to justify the way older people are treated: After all, being cut off from everything is just what they want. Nevertheless, the research evidence shows that disengagement is *not* what most older people want. It is, however, what older people get.

The confusion concerning the desire to disengage probably results from the failure of most investigators to recognize the possibility that ambivalence can arise from competing values. For example, professors are high in potential for disengagement at all ages, yet most "retired" professors still work. This seeming contradiction is apparently accounted for by the fact that professors are also usually highly committed to a relatively attractive job. This fact suggests that people in high-status, attractive jobs tend to preserve continuity and remain on the job as long as they can, despite a high potential for disengagement. It is simply a case of competing positive incentives. The corollary is, of course, that people in low-status, unattractive jobs would disengage when given the opportunity, even if they also had the continued opportunity to work. The data on early retirement (Barfield and Morgan, 1969) would seem to bear this prediction out.

## SUMMARY

Society disengages from older individuals by isolating them and no longer seeking their efforts. Yet each institution in society accomplishes disengagement in a slightly different way and at a different stage of later life. For example, while retirement is a formalized pattern that occurs for most people between ages 65 and 70, the family often does not withdraw from older individuals until they lose their mental faculties.

Societal disengagement is manifested as a decrease in the number of active roles played and in the density of interaction. Research evidence indicates that the relationship between individual desires for disengagement and societal disengagement is very complex. However, it appears certain that much of the "inevitability" of disengagement springs from the roles of society rather than from the motives of the individual. Even in an occupation with high potential for disengagement, continued engagement was the norm when the opportunity existed. Also, people who must disengage from one role tend to resist disengagement from their remaining roles more strongly. Apparently, much of what has been called individual disengagement is a result of various stresses such as retirement and widowhood rather than of aging itself.

The separation of older people from society is a fact of modern life. But it is a pattern that has resulted from people's decisions, not from some immutable social force. There can be little doubt at this point that much of the social rejection that older people experience stems from the fact that the societies they live in are more interested in production, rationality, and efficiency than in maintaining a spot for the "citizen emeritus."

Societal disengagement is no more uniform than individual disengagement. Many social institutions allow older people to keep up their ties, while many others cut older people off from participation almost completely. Beginning with the economic institution, the remainder of this book will examine the opportunities for participation that various social institutions afford to older people.

## SUGGESTIONS FOR FURTHER READING

Atchley, Robert C. "Disengagement Among Professors." *Journal of Gerontology 26* (1971): 476–480.

Carp, Frances M. "Some Components of Disengagement." *Journal of Gerontology 23* (1968): 382–386.

———. "Person-Situation Congruence in Engagement." *Gerontologist 8* (1968):184–188.

Newell, David S. "Social Structural Evidence for Disengagement." In Elaine Cumming and W. E. Henry (eds.), *Growing Old.* New York: Basic Books, 1961, pp. 37–74.

Roman, Paul, and Philip Taietz. "Organizational Structure and Disengagement: The Emeritus Professor." *Gerontologist 7* (1967):147–152.

Rose, Arnold M. "A Current Issue in Social Gerontology." *Gerontologist 4* (1964):45–50.

Seltzer, Mildred M., and Robert C. Atchley. "The Impact of Structural Integration into the Profession on Work Commitment, Potential for Disengagement, and Leisure Preferences Among Social Workers." *Sociological Focus 5* (1971):9–17.

Streib, Gordon F. "Disengagement Theory in Sociocultural Perspective." *International Journal of Psychiatry 6* (1968):69–76.

Tallmer, Margot, and Bernard Kutner. "Disengagement and the Stresses of Aging." *Journal of Gerontology 24* (1969):70–75.

# 14
# The Economy

This chapter concerns the parts older people play as jobholders and as consumers in the economy.[1] Perhaps the best way to begin is by examining the economic roles held by older people in the past. Some care must be exercised here, however, because there is often a tendency to equate older with elderly. As Cottrell (1960b) has pointed out, in a low-energy society people do not live very long. Nevertheless, the head of the family is most often the oldest surviving member. Those older people who survive without becoming severely decrepit can thus expect to assume control over the family decisions. This pattern is important for understanding the economic roles of older people, because in a rural, agricultural society the family is the basic unit of economic production and distribution. The major economic decisions in such a society are largely a matter of day-to-day operations, and there is often very little conscious effort to coordinate the work of the various producing units. Hence, not only does the patriarch (or matriarch, in some cases) make the decisions, but he or she is relatively free of external social pressures. Naturally, physical factors limit the range of alternatives, but there are no fair-trade prices or tariffs and few other governmental controls to take into account.

The older person in such a society enjoys considerable power over economic production and distribution, almost purely as a result of his or her position in the family. As industrialization has progressed in modern societies, the family has lost most of its production and distribution functions and is now mainly a consuming unit. With this change, the family head has lost many economic roles.

Modern society is compartmentalized. Whereas the family once encompassed practically all the institutionalized patterns people needed in order to achieve their goals, we now have a great many relatively autonomous institutions. One's positions in one institution are no longer *necessarily* related to one's positions in other institutions (although they still *tend* to be). This trend means that being the head of a large family no longer carries with it a large measure of economic power in the local

[1]For a more detailed exploration of this topic see Schulz (1976).

community. Elders rarely have significant influence on economic decisions and policy. And when they do, the influence is not a function of being old but is instead a function of valuable experience.

## OLDER PEOPLE AS JOBHOLDERS

Beyond age 40, the older a person is, the less likely he or she is to be employed, particularly in industrial societies (see Figure 14-1). In 1975, the *Manpower Report of the President* (U.S. Department of Labor, 1975) gave the following portrait of labor force participation[2] for older Americans from 1947 to 1974:

☐ Participation of older men dropped from 48 percent to 22 percent.
☐ Participation of older women remained constant, at around 10 percent.
☐ Among males, older whites have higher participation rates than do older men of black and other races. The opposite is true for older females.
☐ Unemployment rates for older people tend to be lower than for 25- to 34-year-olds.
☐ Older workers were consistently more prevalent among the long-term unemployed than among the total unemployed. For example, in 1974 men 65 and over constituted 1.2 percent of the total unemployment, but 3.5 percent of those unemployed for 27 weeks or more.
☐ Participation of older people drops sharply after age 70 (see Table 14-1).

The U.S. Department of Labor (1975:309) estimates that by 1990 participation of older people in the labor force will probably decline to somewhere around 19 percent for men and 8 percent for women (see Table 14-1). These projections reflect a

### TABLE 14-1
### Actual and Projected Annual Average Labor Force
### Participation Rates of Older Americans by Age and Sex: 1960 to 1990

|      | Total Age 65 and over | Age 65 to 69 | Age 70 and over |
|------|------|------|------|
| *Males* | | | |
| 1990 | 19.3 | 33.6 | 11.0 |
| 1980 | 21.2 | 35.5 | 12.7 |
| 1970 | 25.8 | 40.7 | 16.9 |
| 1960 | 32.2 | 45.8 | 23.5 |
| *Females* | | | |
| 1990 | 8.3 | 16.4 | 4.6 |
| 1980 | 8.6 | 16.5 | 4.9 |
| 1970 | 9.2 | 16.4 | 5.0 |
| 1960 | 10.5 | 17.0 | 5.4 |

*Source:* U.S. Department of Labor (1975:309).

[2]Labor force participation includes both people who are employed and those who are seeking employment.

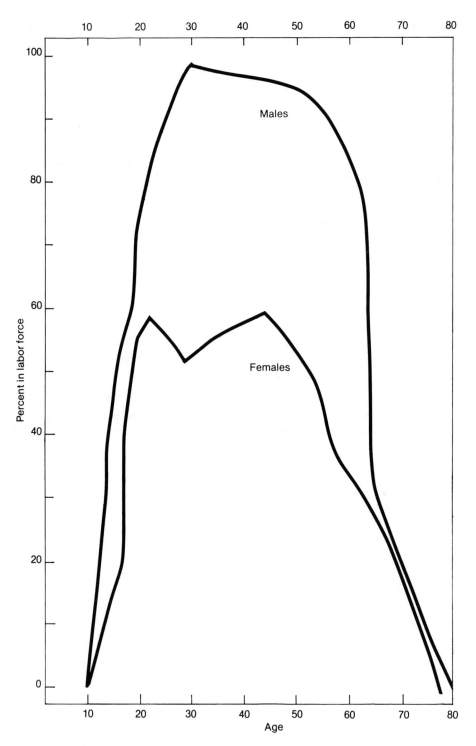

**Figure 14-1**  Labor force participation rates by age: United States, 1970.
*Source:* U.S. Bureau of the Census, 1973b:31–32.

slowdown in the rate of decline in the labor force participation of older Americans.

In the United States, women are less likely than men to be employed. And women who are employed are less likely to be employed full-time or year-round. However, the gap between males and females in terms of percent with full-time employment narrows slightly after age 55, primarily because full-time employment rates drop faster for men than for women. The sex differential is much lower after 65 because, compared to employed women, a greater percentage of employed men retire (see Tables 14-2 and 14-3).

Older people who do remain in the labor force quite often work only part-time or only part of the year. For example, in 1969, 85 percent of employed men age 30 to 35 work 35 or more hours per week, but by age 65 and over the proportion drops to

**TABLE 14-2**
**Weeks Worked by Employed Males**
**Age 14 and Over: United States, 1969**

| Age | Percent Employed | Percent Distribution of Weeks Worked | | |
| --- | --- | --- | --- | --- |
| | | 50–52 Weeks | 27–49 Weeks | 26 Weeks or Less |
| 14 and over | 79.4 | 66.2 | 19.8 | 14.1 |
| 14–19 | 50.6 | 16.2 | 21.5 | 62.3 |
| 20–24 | 91.4 | 49.7 | 26.9 | 23.5 |
| 25–34 | 96.2 | 76.9 | 18.8 | 4.3 |
| 35–54 | 95.4 | 80.1 | 16.7 | 3.1 |
| 55–64 | 86.0 | 73.3 | 19.9 | 6.8 |
| 65 and over | 35.2 | 45.6 | 24.4 | 30.0 |

*Source:* U.S. Bureau of the Census (1973b).

**TABLE 14-3**
**Weeks Worked by Employed Females**
**Age 14 and Over: United States, 1969**

| Age | Percent Employed | Percent Distribution of Weeks Worked | | |
| --- | --- | --- | --- | --- |
| | | 50–52 Weeks | 27–49 Weeks | 26 Weeks or Less |
| 14 and over | 47.6 | 43.1 | 27.8 | 29.1 |
| 14–19 | 36.5 | 12.0 | 20.6 | 67.4 |
| 20–24 | 72.6 | 35.7 | 29.9 | 34.4 |
| 25–34 | 54.5 | 41.9 | 29.4 | 28.6 |
| 35–44 | 56.3 | 49.8 | 28.3 | 21.9 |
| 45–54 | 57.6 | 56.0 | 27.7 | 16.3 |
| 55–64 | 47.9 | 55.3 | 28.3 | 16.4 |
| 65 and over | 14.0 | 38.6 | 28.0 | 33.4 |

*Source:* U.S. Bureau of the Census (1973b).

around 55 percent. In addition, older people constitute less than 4 percent of the American labor force. Similar trends were found in 20 other industrial nations (United Nations, 1973).

The job is thus an economic role that less than a fifth of the older population plays, and over half of those who do work do so only part-time or part of the year. Older workers tend to be relatively powerless. Because of their seniority they are not likely to become unemployed, but if they do lose their jobs, age discrimination makes it difficult for them to find new ones. The Hilary case cited in Chapter 8 is probably typical of what happens to displaced older workers. Sheppard (1970) reports that over half of the companies involved in a mass layoff of over 190,000 workers from 1963 to 1965 went out of business or moved their business elsewhere. Seniority is little protection from this type of economic change.

It is illegal in the United States to deny an individual aged 45 to 64 a job because of his age, but such laws have no impact unless businesses voluntarily comply, and they have not. In addition, the Age Discrimination in Employment Act of 1967 does not protect workers over 65. Employment studies show that older workers have superior attendance records, that they are less likely to change jobs, and that their output is equal to that of younger workers. While it is true that some older workers are slow to learn, the range of individual differences is quite large, and many older people are still quite capable of learning new skills. Age discrimination in employment thus deprives the economy of human resources and creates hardships for older workers. The small number of older workers in job retraining programs probably reflects cynicism about finding a job rather than an unwillingness to be retrained.

Industrial health counseling can help minimize problems of using older workers. In one study, an Industrial Health Counseling Service was set up in Portland, Maine. The program used a system developed by Kaye (1973) to diagnose workers' capacities in seven functional areas—general physique, upper extremities, lower extremities, hearing, eyesight, intelligence, and personality. Jobs were also rated on the same criteria. Individuals were then matched with jobs whose functional profiles matched theirs. As a result, 51 percent of the 2,400 job applicants examined by the program were placed in jobs, and half of these workers were over 40. Over 100 firms participated in the program. While the program was not a panacea, it was a major step toward demonstrating the feasibility of using functional criteria in hiring in place of arbitrary age criteria (Quirk and Skinner, 1973).

Ironically, retirement pension plans represent one of the important forces operating against older workers. Taggart (1973) reviewed the evidence on the labor market impact of private pension plans and concluded that the existence of retirement plans has lowered the normal retirement age and increased the number of firms using mandatory retirement ages. In addition, firms that pride themselves on providing adequate pensions may be reluctant to hire workers in their fifties or sixties because they would not have long enough to work prior to the mandatory retirement age to qualify for an adequate pension. It is also more costly to provide a given benefit for a new older employee because employer contributions are spread over a shorter period. Pension plans also increase pressure to retire early. These pressures come from both management and labor. Management uses early retirement provisions to cope with periods of economic decline. Taggart (1973:95) found that in some cases the number of people retiring increased most rapidly during periods when employment was stagnant or declining. In addition, Jaffe (1972) found that workers between 45 and 54 years of age tended to pressure older workers to retire earlier in order to create opportunities for promotion. Taggart (1973) concludes that while the magnitude of these factors has thus far not been great, they will probably become more important in the future.

## OLDER PEOPLE AS CONSUMERS

The largest single economic function remaining for the family is that of consumer. Older people's ability to participate as consumers is determined first, and perhaps mostly, by income. Most older people are living on inadequate incomes, and obviously they cannot buy things when they have no money. On the average, older people spend far less for goods and services than younger people do, and are less likely to spend beyond their incomes. A major factor that influences older people's spending is the relatively small size of their families.

Very little attention has been paid to the older person as a consumer (McConnell, 1960). Ad agencies have not yet come to view older people as a significant market. Aside from aspirin, laxative, denture adhesive, and iron tonic commercials, few appeals are aimed directly at older people. One obvious reason may be that older people buy the same kinds of things most other adults do. Older people tend to retain most of their living habits, and therefore one might expect that their buying patterns would reflect this consistency in ethnic, class, and individual preferences.

Nevertheless, older people have a significant amount of purchasing power. For example, in 1973 older Americans received 61 *billion* dollars from the Social Security system alone. And very little of the incomes of older people go into savings. On the contrary, *spending savings* is the rule in later life. But buying power is passive; it is reactive power. People seldom boycott in an attempt to influence the type of goods produced. The fact that older people buy very few items that are not bought by everyone else makes them a relatively stable and reliable market, although their purchases tend to be more concentrated in the areas of medical care, food, and personal care. And since much advertising is aimed at encouraging impulse buying of nonessential items, and since most older people cannot afford these items, it is little wonder that business feels no need to court the market older people represent.

Unfortunately, there are some exceptions to this rule. These are mainly the clandestine operators and fringe businesses that deal in fraud, deception, fad, and quackery. While older people are not the sole victims of many of these schemes, they are often the most vulnerable.

To begin with, older people on fixed incomes and with barely enough to live on are very susceptible to any kind of "sure fire" scheme that will yield them more money or a supplementary income. Also, loneliness and isolation often make older people susceptible to deception by a friendly, outgoing person who takes an apparent interest in them. Finally, hopeless illness is more frequent among older people, and many unscrupulous people have exploited the desperation that it can evoke. A few examples should illustrate the point.

Perhaps the most vicious of the "get more money for your money" swindles was the Maryland savings and loan scandal of 1961. From 1958 to 1961, many state-chartered savings and loan associations operating in Maryland were not federally insured. These companies advertised nationally that savings invested with them would yield as high as 8 percent, twice the interest rate of most legitimate, federally insured institutions. The appeal of increasing yields was particularly attractive to older people who were trying to make the most of a fixed amount of savings that provided them with their living. For people in this situation, such a promise was like saying, "Double your income in one easy step." Hundreds of older people transferred their life's savings into these companies from all over the country.

At best these companies were ill conceived. They were able to pay such high rates of interest only by investing heavily in second, third, and even fourth mortgages; a very lucrative but also a very risky business. Following a wide-scale investigation, many of the officers of these companies were indicted on charges of fraud and embezzlement. Most of the companies went bankrupt, and hundreds of people lost their entire life's savings.

Another example is the "investment property" business. Generally, a promoter buys a large tract of cheap land, often swampy land in Florida or desert in Arizona. Then he carves the property up into the smallest parcels allowable. Then he prints beautiful brochures and advertises in newspapers, magazines, and so on. Stress is put on holding the land as an investment for resale later at a profit, or as a place for a retirement home. In the words of a Florida realtor,

> Lots are usually sold on installment contracts, and no deed is recorded until the contract is paid off. Most contracts stipulate that the property reverts to the seller if the buyer misses one or two payments, and the seller is not required to notify the buyer that he is delinquent.
>
> Many, but not all, contracts carry interest on the unpaid balance, usually 5 or 6 percent. Many of these lots are sold over and over again, year after year, as buyers stop their monthly payments for any number of reasons—they die, come upon hard times, come down and see the land, *et cetera*.
>
> Several years ago I spent almost two days, using a slow plane and a four-wheel drive, radio-equipped jeep, trying to locate a certain parcel (a Florida development) located approximately ten miles west of Daytona Beach in a dismal swamp.
>
> After two days of some of the roughest riding, we had to give up, as it was impossible to penetrate deep enough into the swamp to the point we had spotted from the air.
>
> Incidentally, this parcel was sold to a woman from Syracuse, N.Y., who had intended to use it as a homesite for a trailer house (U.S. Senate Special Committee on Aging, 1965:34).

Many other examples could be given of "make money" or "save money" schemes that have bilked older people out of what little they have. Confidence persons have preyed on older people in numerous ways. One of the more frequent has been the "bank examiner" gambit. A person posing as a bank examiner calls on the intended victim. He or she explains that one of the employees of the bank is suspected of embezzlement, but unfortunately the bank officials have been unable to catch the employee in the act. The "examiner" then attempts to elicit the cooperation of the intended victim. The "examiner" explains that if the victim will go to the bank and withdraw all of his or her savings, this move will force the suspect in the bank to alter account books, and the bank will then "have the goods on the employee." If the intended victim takes the bait, and the savings are withdrawn, the "examiner" telephones, says that they have caught the suspect, thanks the victim, and then offers to send a "bank messenger" to pick up the money—"to save you the trouble of having to come all the way down here, since you have been so kind as to cooperate with us." The "messenger" then appears, takes the money, gives the victim an official-looking deposit slip, and that is usually the last the victim ever sees of his or her money. The number of unfortunate people who have fallen for this ruse is surprising. Older people are particularly susceptible because many of them are flattered to feel needed, and in addition, many of them are reluctant to seek advice in such cases.

Many of the practices found in the "preneed" funeral business are also fraudulent. People have been sold "complete burial service" for a thousand dollars or more and all the survivors received, if they were lucky, was a hundred-dollar casket. People have been sold crypts in mausoleums that do not exist. One ad read:

> Do you qualify for these U.S. Government death benefits? U.S. Social Security, maximum $255, United Memorial's answer to the ever-increasing cost of funeral services, the United plan. The preneed plan that costs $10.

For ten dollars, the customers got a "guarantee" from United Memorial that they could have their burial service performed by whatever mortuary they chose. When the customer died, however, the relatives found that most of the mortuaries "endorsed" by United Memorial had no contract with them and refused to perform the service for anything even approaching a Social Security benefit price.

It has been estimated that in Colorado alone the annual sales of preneed burial service total eight to ten million dollars (U.S. Senate Special Committee on Aging, 1965). This business thrives on the deep-seated desire of many older people to take care of burial arrangements ahead of time in order to "avoid being a burden" on their relatives. Even for the reputable business people, it may be unethical to take money from older people for prearranged funerals since, as business people, they fully realize the problems of prearranging funeral services in a society where people travel as much as they do in ours. If the person dies far from the city in which the prearrangements were made, the relatives either lose the money spent for the prearranged funeral or must pay to have the remains shipped back for burial. By encouraging prepayment, the funeral director is merely relieving the older person of his or her savings, often without paying interest on the money held.

The most frequent hazard to older people is medical swindlers and quackery. Arthritis is a good case in point. The United States Senate Special Committee on Aging found that:

> Arthritis offers special opportunities to the unscrupulous. Twelve million Americans have some form of arthritis; and, as one witness testified: "If we fall for the phoney, and sooner or later most of us do, it is because the pains of arthritis are something that you just can't describe because nobody knows why it comes or how or when it goes." . . . Mrs. Bramer also made a comment often expressed by arthritis victims: "There must be an

exchange list of arthritic victims because if you get on one list you receive material advertising all manner of devices, items such as vibrators, whirlpool baths, salves, uranium mits, and things of that sort" (1965:7).

The committee commented on various aspects of fraud:

☐ *Worthless devices*

These devices are often used by phoney practitioners to impress victims with "up-to-date" methods or "secret" treatments. One highly mobile pitchman, using and selling a machine that did little more than give colonic enemas to victims of major diseases, made an estimated $2½ million before conviction on a mail fraud charge (1965:3).

☐ *Misleading claims*

People will buy almost anything that purports to cure whatever real or imaginary ailments they have. The enforcement of fraud laws is a constant word game between those who are trying to protect the public and those who are trying to swindle it. Thus, "cures" is replaced by "aids in curing" is replaced by "is thought to aid in curing" (1965:8).

☐ *The victims*

The actual extent of frauds is unknown because many victims either never suspect that they have been taken, or more likely, they are afraid to report it for fear of appearing the fool (1965:8).

☐ *Complex technology*

This gives the quack the capability of sowing the seed of doubt about the validity of accepted medical methods because most people are not able to evaluate his claims (1965:8).

The cost of quackery has been estimated as follows:

| | |
|---|---|
| Vitamin and health food quackery | $500 million |
| Arthritis quackery | $250 million |
| Ineffective drugs and devices for reducing | $100 million |

And this review probably only scratches the surface. The true cost of fraud and quackery was summed up well by Senator Harrison Williams:

It seems to me that there are losses that go far beyond the original purchase price for the phoney treatment, the useless gadget, the inappropriate drug or pill. How can you measure the cost in terms of suffering, disappointment, and final despair (1965:10)?

One of the heaviest of these costs is surely the attitudes such practices create among older people. They become suspicious and reluctant to get involved with strangers. And unfortunately, it is too often true that only the confident person feels he or she has anything to gain from seeking out older people.

It is encouraging, however, that hearings have been held and legislative proposals have been made that would in some ways ease the situation. Moreover, the Administration on Aging, a part of the U.S. Department of Health, Education, and Welfare, has instituted a program aimed at collecting consumer data on older people; at preparing information for use by both professional and lay leaders who intend to conduct educational programs for older people and older people themselves; and at supporting demonstration projects concerning

☐ Sound nutrition
☐ Economy food purchasing
☐ The careful purchase of credit
☐ Avoidance of quackery
☐ Avoidance of fraudulent products and practices
☐ Safe and effective use of drugs
☐ Management of retirement income
☐ Medicare and supplementary health insurance
☐ Care of clothing and household equipment

The Administration on Aging has also indicated an interest in exploring the possibilities for consumer cooperatives among older people.

While these attempts are encouraging, little is still known about older people as consumers and about the influence various types of fraud and deception have on their lives. For all we know now, the sad tales just depicted may be relatively rare. They are, at the least, illustrations of *potential* dangers to be guarded against.

The fact that some theater owners, transit companies, and druggists, to name a few, have offered substantial discounts to older people indicates that the business community can recognize older people as a potential market and that they also recognize that price is a prime motivating factor for many older people. Unfortunately, this rationale has not been transferred to the essential areas of food, clothing, shelter, or medical care.

## OTHER ECONOMIC ROLES

Hypothetically, older people may also participate in the economy as dependents or as members of unions. Participation as a dependent is largely passive, although it does sometimes create jobs in state administrations on aging, in Social Security offices, in welfare departments, and the like. Certainly the older person's power is no greater in this role than in the consumer role.

Studies have shown that, in general, union contracts do not favor or even take into account the needs of retired union members (McConnell, 1960). However the rail unions have included in their wage contracts a 2 percent increase to be used to pay supplementary benefits to retired railway employees (Cottrell, 1970). In this case, however, it was not the retired railway employees who applied the pressure, but those who were still working. Likewise, early retirement provisions of recent United Auto Workers' contracts have broad support among the rank and file.

## SUMMARY

In the economic institution as a whole, a sizable number of older people still hold jobs, but generally on terms that give them little choice about transferring, quitting, and so forth. Older people consume their share of the goods and services bought, yet are victimized by fraud and quackery on a scale that more powerful members of society would find intolerable. Older people, once they become public dependents, have their decisions on how they spend their money made for them by an agency bureaucrat. The person who is no longer on the job—whether he or she is old or not—is left completely out of the economic decision-making process.

## SUGGESTIONS FOR FURTHER READING

Belbin, R. M., and S. Clarke. "International Trends in Employment Among Men over 65." *Industrial Gerontology 9* (1971):18–23.

Chown, Sheila M. "The Effect of Flexibility-Rigidity and Age on Adaptability in Job Performance." *Industrial Gerontology 13* (1972):105–121.

Clague, Evan. "Work and Leisure for Older Workers." *Gerontologist 11* (1971, 1, part 2): 9–20.

Feldman, L. "Employment Problems of Older Workers: A Review by the International Labor Organization Advisory Committee." *Industrial Gerontology 2* (1975):69–71.

Fillenbaum, Gerda G. "A Consideration of Some Factors Related to Work After Retirement." *Gerontologist 11* (1971:18–23.

Fisher, Paul. "Labor Force Participation of the Aged and the Social Security System in Nine Countries." *Industrial Gerontology 2* (1975):1–13.

Goldstein, Sidney. "Negro-White Differentials in Consumer Patterns of the Aged, 1960–1961." *Gerontologist 11* (1971):242–249.

Kreps, Juanita M. "Economic Policy and the Nation's Aged." *Gerontologist 8* (1968, 2, part 2):37–43.

Schulz, James H. *The Economics of Aging.* Belmont, Calif.: Wadsworth, 1976.

Sheppard, Harold L. *Industrial Gerontology.* Cambridge, Mass.: Schenkman, 1970.

Smith, John M. "Age and Occupation: A Review of the Use of Occupational Age Structures in Industrial Gerontology." *Industrial Gerontology 1* (1974, 2):42–58.

Stagner, R. "Boredom on the Assembly Line: Age and Personality Variables." *Industrial Gerontology 2* (1975):23–44.

Thompson, Gayle B. "Work Experience and Income of the Population Aged 60 and Older, 1971." *Social Security Bulletin 37* (1974):3–20.

United States Department of Health, Education, and Welfare, Office of Consumer Affairs. *An Approach to Consumer Education for Adults.* Washington, D.C.: Office of Consumer Affairs, 1973.

United States Senate Special Committee on Aging, "Frauds and Deceptions Affecting the Elderly," Washington, D.C.: U.S. Government Printing Office, 1965.

# 15
# Politics and Government

Power, the ability to realize one's own goals even against opposition, is the central core of politics, and people engage in politics as a way of securing power. Practically all large-scale institutions have their power and political aspects, but we generally reserve the label of *politics* for the relationships that surround the struggle for power over the machinery of the state. In examining the relationship between aging and politics, we will concentrate on three fundamental issues: the political *participation* of older people, the political *power* of older people, and finally older people as the *object* of governmental programs and policies.

## POLITICAL PARTICIPATION

Political participation takes many forms in American society. It involves expressing political opinions, voting, participation in voluntary associations centered around politics, or holding political offices. Forming political opinions requires the least involvement on the part of the individual. Several researchers have found that the proportion of people who answer "no opinion" to political poll questions increase with age, and this finding has been taken as an indication of the relatively disengaged status of older people in American society (Turk et al., 1966; Gergen and Back, 1966). However, Glenn (1969) has found that if the effect of *education* is controlled, there is no evidence that older people become less interested in political affairs or less likely to form political opinions. In fact, he found that when education was precisely controlled, older people were slightly *more* likely to hold opinions than were younger people. Also, Turk and his coworkers (1966) found that people who were committed to the community and anchored to the community through social ties tended to increase opinionation with age. While the tendency to form political opinions, by itself, may possibly decline with age, education and involvement in the community are strong forces that more than counteract this trend for many people.

It is commonly thought that people become more politically conservative as they grow older. However, the available evidence does not support this notion. Glenn (1974) concluded that in recent years people who have passed middle age have become *more* liberal in many respects. But political liberalism has grown more slowly in older cohorts than in younger, which means that older cohorts have become *relatively* more conservative while *absolutely* they have grown more liberal. Thus, though there is evidence to suggest that attitudes become somewhat less susceptible to change as people age, there is no evidence that their attitudes become more conservative (Glenn, 1974; Foner, 1974; Lipsett and Ladd, 1972; Agnello, 1973).

In an ambitious cohort analysis of political opinion data from 1940 to 1970, Douglass, Cleveland, and Maddox (1974) assessed the separate effects of *time*, *cohort*, and *age*.[1] They found that, in general, political opinions are more sensitive to time effects than to age or cohort effects. That is, the time period when the opinion was asked was more important than the age of the respondents or the era in which the respondents were reared. Age was usually a secondary effect and then only if the opinion concerned family issues. They also found that which effect (time, cohort, or age) is significant varies with the specific political attitude. For example, *none* of the effects was significant in determining which respondents saw economic issues as the foremost national problem. On the other hand, *time* was the only significant factor in determining who saw foreign policy as the prime national problem.

Similarly, Cutler and Bengtson (1974) found that political alienation was more closely related to the historical time of measurement than to either age or cohort effects. In their analysis, the impact of educational differences between cohorts was controlled.

Opinion formation is no doubt related to information seeking, and research results indicate that older people try hard to remain informed about political affairs. In comparison with the young, older people give greater attention to political campaigns and are more likely to follow public affairs in the newspapers and on television (Riley and Foner, 1968:468). In addition, older people are more apt to seek practical knowledge, such as the name of their own congressional representative, than academic knowledge, such as the makeup of the electoral college (Erskine, 1963). This finding leads one to suspect, without necessarily being able to prove, that older people recognize that they have an interest in politics, and that they are at least predisposed toward political action. Glenn and Grimes (1968) found, for example, that those showing the highest interest in politics were consistently those aged 60 or over.

Voting behavior ranks just above opinion formation as a relatively mild form of involvement in politics. Voting behavior shows a pattern of change with age that is as complex as it is interesting. In general, it appears that voting participation is lowest at age 18; it builds to a plateau in the fifties, and then begins a gradual decline after age 65. Voters in their eighties still vote more than voters in their early twenties. Men and

---

[1]See Chapter 1 for a more detailed discussion of time, cohort, and age effects.

women show approximately the same curve of voter participation, although the overall participation of women is lower for all ages. Hence, a substantial part of the apparent decline in voter participation among older people results from sex differences in voter participation and from the high mortality rates among older men.

**TABLE 15-1**
**Voter Participation**
**by Age and Education: United States, November 1964**

| | *Percent Voting* | | | | | | | |
| | *Years of Education* | | | | | | | |
| | *Elementary* | | *High School* | | *College* | | | |
| *Age* | *0–7 years* | *8 years* | *1–3 years* | *4 years* | *1–3 years* | *4 years or more* | *Total* | *"Effect" of education (high–low education)* |
|---|---|---|---|---|---|---|---|---|
| Males | | | | | | | | |
| 21–24 | 14 | 30 | 34 | 56 | 70 | 80 | 53 | +66 |
| 25–44 | 43 | 58 | 65 | 76 | 82 | 87 | 71 | +44 |
| 45–64 | 63 | 79 | 81 | 88 | 88 | 93 | 79 | +30 |
| 65+ | 66 | 79 | 80 | 88 | 91 | 88 | 74 | +22 |
| Total 21+ | 58 | 73 | 69 | 80 | 82 | 88 | 73 | +30 |
| "Effect" of age (old—young) | +52 | +49 | +46 | +32 | +21 | + 8 | +21 | |
| Females | | | | | | | | |
| 21–24 | 22 | 21 | 33 | 55 | 69 | 78 | 52 | +56 |
| 25–44 | 34 | 52 | 53 | 76 | 85 | 87 | 68 | +53 |
| 45–64 | 52 | 69 | 75 | 84 | 87 | 92 | 74 | +40 |
| 65+ | 46 | 63 | 72 | 76 | 82 | 93 | 61 | +47 |
| Total 21+ | 45 | 63 | 63 | 76 | 83 | 89 | 68 | +44 |
| "Effect" of age (old—young) | +24 | +42 | +39 | +21 | +13 | +15 | + 9 | |

*Source:* U.S. Bureau of the Census (1965:16–19).

Table 15-1 leads us to conclude that education had a significant impact on the age pattern of voting in the 1964 November election. Among men, there was very little difference between the voting patterns of those aged 65 or over and those aged 45 to 64, if comparisons are restricted to those with similar education (read down the columns in the table). Among women, age made more difference, but there was still more similarity of voter participation within education categories than within age categories. Among those people with some college education, the difference between older men and older women in terms of voter participation was quite small, whereas it was greatest among those who did not complete elementary school. Increased education thus decreased the influence of both age and sex on voter participation in the United States. Unfortunately, the information is not available to perform this same type of analysis for the 1968 or 1972 elections.

In an interesting analysis of aging, voting, and political interest, Glenn and Grimes (1968) found that there was scarcely any change in voting turnout when the same age cohort was examined over the course of six presidential elections (20 years). This analysis suggests that people develop a style of participation as a result of their own unique political socialization and then stick to it. The importance of this finding is its implication that as the general level of education in our population increases, we should expect the age curve of voter participation to rise faster, peak higher, remain at the high plateau longer, and decline even more slowly than the cross-sectional data given in Figure 15-1 indicate. It also implies a generational change in the direction of greater voter participation on the part of older people. For example, between 1964 and 1972, there was a general decline in the percent voting. This decline was the smallest in the age groups over 65.

In fact, Glenn and Grimes (1968:570) carry their analysis even further to hypothesize that "only widespread disability and lack of transportation keep the voter turnout of the elderly down near that of the middle-aged persons with the same amount of education." Otherwise, older people would vote in *higher* proportions than middle-aged persons with the same education and sex. In support of this idea, Turk and his associates (1966) found an increase with age in the proportion voting among people who were involved in the community. In addition, Gubrium (1972a) found that widowhood and divorce tended to reduce the proportion of older people who vote.

Party affiliation is another significant role in the political institution. The proportion who identify strongly with a political party increases gradually with age, but unlike voting behavior, party identification does not decline in the later years. The strength of a person's party attachment appears to be a function less of age than of the duration of that particular bond. Age provides the opportunity for the long-term identification that appears to be necessary for a strong bond, but among those with the same duration of affiliation age is *negatively* associated with the strength of the bond. The end result, however, is that people in their twenties are only half as likely as people over 65 to identify themselves with a major party.

Consistent with this high level of party identification is the fact that among people who are involved in their communities there is an increase with age in political activities (working for the party in a local vote, signing petitions, belonging to political groups [Turk et al., 1966]).

Among older people, there are about equal proportions of Republicans and Democrats. This finding implies a substantial change with age, since at the younger ages there are many more Democrats than Republicans. Here again, however, we run into the difficulty of trying to infer changes through time from data collected at one point in time. A closer examination of the longitudinal data suggests that when those who entered politics during and after the New Deal become a majority among older people, a preponderance of Democrats may emerge (Glenn and Hefner, 1972). There is no evidence that people are more likely to become Republican as they grow older.

Older people seem to be amply represented in party organizations. What evidence

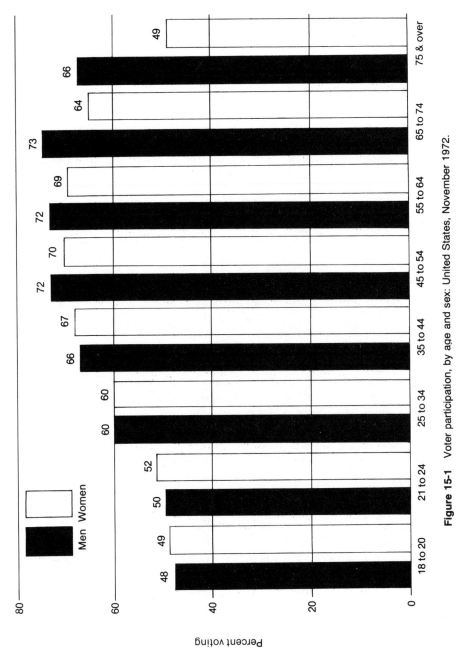

**Figure 15-1** Voter participation, by age and sex: United States, November 1972.
*Source:* U.S. Bureau of the Census (1973a:22).

**249**

there is indicates that older people represent about the same percentage of the party organization that they represent of the total population. In addition, one study has shown that older people have a disproportionately greater influence in the nominating conventions (Kapnick et al., 1968). Thus it appears that older members of the party organizations have a great deal of influence over the selection of party candidates for political office.

Indeed, older people are also overrepresented in various political offices. Leadership in all areas related to public affairs seems to be amply accessible to older political leaders. Presidents, cabinet ministers, and ambassadors usually acquire their positions in their late fifties, and often retain them well beyond age 60. Supreme Court justices are also most likely to be appointed in their late fifties, and most continue to serve well beyond age 65, since retirement usually depends on their own personal desire. In the Ninety-third Congress (1973) there were 35 Senators and 102 Representatives aged 60 or over. In both houses combined there were 34 members over age 70 (U.S. Bureau of the Census, 1974:433). Proportions of older people in state and local offices (whether elected or appointed) are substantially higher than among the rank and file of other occupations.

One reason why older members of political organizations are influential is the weight that tenure alone carries in politics. In politics, perhaps more than in any other institution, the older person is still able to play the role of sage. In fact the word *politic* means "wise" or "shrewd." This situation probably exists partly because political processes have felt the impact of industrialization and rationalization to a lesser degree than has the economic institution or even the family. The professionalization of politics is much less complete than that of education or the economy. As a result, political prowess is still felt to be largely something one learns from experience rather than out of a book or in a professional school. There seems to be public appreciation of this factor. Turner and Kahn (1974) found that age of the candidate was an insignificant issue among voters of all ages.

Thus, older people do not seem to be at any great disadvantage in terms of access to political roles. Yet what does this accessibility mean to the older person?

Glenn and Grimes (1968) feel that people turn increasingly *toward* political activity as they age simply because they have no other absorbing interests or activities. They further suggest that as one grows older, politics tends to be viewed more as a means of personal fulfillment and less as a means to some instrumental end. This rationale gains support from studies showing that as they grow older people maintain and perhaps even increase an interest in politics, while simultaneously feeling that their individual political action neither does nor can have an impact on the political process (Schmidhauser, 1968). In short, older people appear to enjoy political participation but at the same time to be cynical about its concrete effects.

## POLITICAL POWER

There are many approaches to the study of older people's political power. Some say that older people serve primarily as a pressure group that attempts to coerce politicians into either enacting legislation beneficial to them or opposing legislation harmful to them. Others see the problems of aging as the central focus for the formation of a social movement that involves not only older people but people of all ages in an attempt to solve these problems. Still others view older people as a category that, because of the discriminatory and categorical treatment it receives at the hands of society at large, is rapidly developing a subculture of its own in much the same way that Oscar Lewis (1961) depicts the development of a "culture of poverty." Still others view politics as being run by a gerontocratic power elite who make many policy decisions without having to account to anyone for their actions.

Political success for political groups formed around older people's interests has been more often a hope than a reality. As Carlie (1969:259–63) concludes:

> We have indicated [previously] that the old age political organization left a great deal to be desired as pertains to such matters [as] organization (a failure to develop strong secondary leadership), pressure (if there were not too few members then they were regionally segregated), votes (the aspiring representatives of old age political programs failed to secure enough votes to place them in pivotal political positions), and money. . . .
>
> It seems as though one of the necessary conditions for the formulation and maintenance of interest groups is a homogeneity of characteristics among the membership. An effective interest group, then, should have more in common than just age. Other important shared characteristics may be ethnicity, nativity, educational background, occupational status, race, and rural-urban residency. Lacking similarity beyond age (and perhaps the state of retirement), the old age political movements were handicapped from their very inception.

Effective political pressure groups have to be able to deliver votes in a bloc. The leadership must be able to guarantee the vote in return for favorable political action. There has never been an instance in the history of the United States in which the leadership of an old-age interest group could deliver what would even approach "the old folks' vote." Thus, the view that older people comprise a unified interest group that can mobilize political pressure by bloc voting is an illusion, and is quite likely to remain so (Binstock, 1972).

Arnold Rose (1965a) has been perhaps the strongest proponent of the idea that patterns of aging in American society are producing a subculture of the aging. According to Rose, a subculture will develop whenever people in a given category interact with each other more than they interact with people in other categories. The subculture grows as a result of the positive affinity that draws like people together and the discrimination that excludes these same people from interacting with other groups. Rose cites the growing numbers of older people with common problems—usually related to health—living out their retirement in self-segregated retirement communities where a relatively high standard of living makes possible the development of a unique life-style. And he contends that older people are rapidly shifting from the status of a category to that of a group. He further states that, in addition to pure self-interest, there is also an interactional basis for the development of an age-conscious group. This interaction results from our society's policy of phasing older people out of almost every other kind of group, thus forcing them to seek each other out. Rose feels that this trend cuts across the subcultures based on occupation, sex, religion, and ethnic identification that typify the middle-aged population. It is this type of old age group identification, rather than any specific organization of older people, that leads Rose to conclude that "the elderly seem to be on their way to becoming a voting bloc with a leadership that acts as a political pressure group" (1965a:14).

This type of analysis is intuitively attractive to many because it postulates the existence of the old-age pressure group without necessarily requiring that this group manifest itself in an overt form of organization. The "leaders" speak for a kind of silent group—a group that recognizes itself and is capable of the bloc voting required to achieve political influence. Again, however, history deserts us when we attempt to find evidence for the trends that Rose predicts.

To begin with, most older people interact more *across* generational lines than within them, simply because their most frequent source of interaction is their children. Neighbors and friends come far behind in terms of both frequency and duration of interaction. Second, the stereotype that older people are flocking in masses to retirement communities is largely a myth. The data on migration show that over a 5-year period less than 10 percent of older people moved across county lines. In fact, most older people have lived in the same residence for a long time. As a result, older people tend to be interspersed among the general population, even though they rarely live in newer apartment complexes because of the high rents. Third, while there may be a rising number of older people who can afford a unique leisure life-style, our examination of the economics of aging must lead us to conclude that life-styles vary widely among older people. Thus, several of the key conditions on which Rose based his case for the subculture approach turn out to be nonexistent. There are still no adequate grounds for assuming that older people have the kind of political power that comes from bloc voting.

The view that political action favoring older people stems from a social movement involving not only the aged but others as well is the view most often expressed by the political scientists (Cottrell, 1960a). According to this approach, older people have a great deal of *potential* power by virtue of the fact that in the more rural areas they constitute a larger proportion of the population, and that these rural areas are overrepresented in both the state legislatures and the U.S. Senate. The presumed reason that this potential has never been realized, however, is that the older population is divided among a great many interest groups, most of which do not make the welfare of the aged their primary goal. But if this reason is valid, we may ask, how did legislation in behalf of older people manage to get passed?

The answer is that old-age political organizations, while not effective as pressure groups, have been effective in making the older person's plight politically visible. As a result, the "cause" of the elderly has been picked up by groups not based on age, such as unions and political parties. The readiness of various groups interested in the general welfare to commit themselves to programs for the aged was caused largely by the existence, at almost every level of organization, of large numbers of adult children who were anxious to shift the growing burden of financial support for older people off themselves and onto the government. It is for this reason, as well as the votes the elderly themselves command, that no major political party, trade union, or other large-scale organization dares oppose the income provisions of Social Security. This view of older people's power fits the facts better than any other so far. It describes relatively accurately the political processes that brought passage of Social Security and Medicare, the two most sweeping legislative proposals affecting older people.

In addition to persistently keeping problems of the aged in the public eye, organizations such as the National Council of Senior Citizens (NCSC—3,000,000 members) and The National Retired Teachers Association–American Association of Retired Persons (NRTA–AARP—6,000,000 members) have been reasonably effective in gaining a larger share for older people from existing federal programs (Binstock, 1972; Pratt, 1974).

In a very lucid article, Pratt (1974) attributes the increased effectiveness of current voluntary associations for older people, compared with the old age interest groups of the 1930s, to three factors: (1) sources of funds in addition to member dues; (2) reliance on bureaucratic performance rather than charisma as a criterion for selecting leaders; and (3) a sympathetic political climate for lobbying activities. The NCSC derives nearly half its financial support from the large labor unions, while NRTA–AARP gets most of its income from insurance programs it offers to its membership (Pratt, 1974). While both organizations are headed by persons over 65, in both cases they are people of proven administrative capability. Political sensitivity to the concerns of old-age interest groups was readily apparent in the concessions extracted from the Nixon administration through a threatened boycott of the 1971 White House Conference on Aging.

In addition to the organizations discussed above, several other organizations promote political attention on behalf of older people. The National Council on Aging (NCOA) is a federation of over a thousand agencies that deal with older people. The National Caucus on the Black Aged is a group of professionals seeking to emphasize the unique problems of black older people. The Gray Panthers, currently under Margaret Kuhn, is a coalition of young- and old-age groups to publicize and promote alternative life-styles for older people.

Thus, while interest groups of older people have not been, and are not likely to be, very effective in bringing about a drastic move toward equality for older people, they have been effective in improving results of current programs for older people.

The view that older people form a large part of the power elite that can act in favor of older people is questionable on the same grounds as the view that "old folks' power" is the power of an interest group or subculture. Age simply does not appear to be a variable that unites people regardless of their differences. Even if there is such a thing as a power elite—and it is by no means clear that there is—political, financial, and business interests would take a much higher priority than the mere age of the decision maker as a factor influencing the directions decisions might take. Decision makers tend to be older than the rank-and-file, but they retain their positions only so long as their decisions adequately represent the rank-and-file. Therefore, older decision makers may support programs for older people only to the extent that the organizations they represent favor such programs.

The view we emerge with is that older people themselves have relatively little power *as older people*. Some powerful people are old, but they are not powerful *because* they are old. Most of political power behind programs for older people is generated by others on behalf of older people rather than by older people themselves. There are good reasons to expect that this situation will continue to exist.

First, the sense of group identity that has created large ethnic voting blocs such as among blacks, Catholics, or Italians is not now present among older people, and it is unlikely that such an identity will develop, for the reasons stated earlier. Second, older people are dispersed throughout the population both socially and geographically. This dispersal creates even less possibility of concentrating their votes, because it involves a dispersal of interests. Third, older people are among the least likely to desert a long-term party affiliation to vote on a specific issue. Thus, the organizational leader cannot guarantee the votes of older people because these votes are largely already committed, and furthermore, most politicians know that they can usually count on the votes of the older members of their party without giving in to pressure group demands. This reliability is particularly true at the state and national levels. Finally, older people represent a vote almost evenly divided between parties. As a result, what power they might have is cut in half.

The role older people are left to play in politics is generally confined to the local area, unless they have been involved in politics steadily throughout their lives. At the local level, older people may indeed be influential, particularly in close elections on nonpartisan issues, but nationwide politics offers older people as such very little in terms of either power or participation. Therefore, while politics is relatively unique in not *demanding* disengagement from its older participants, it does not very often offer older people the opportunity to *increase* their active participation, even though they might like to. Older people can increase their efforts to form strong opinions in political affairs, and they can increase their involvement in voting; but unless they have "paid their dues" in the form of earlier participation in politics, they are not apt to gain access to positions within party organization or government itself.

## GOVERNMENT AND OLDER PEOPLE

It is well known that the United States government operates Social Security and Medicare primarily for the benefit of older people. The goals of these programs are to shift the financial burden of income and health maintenance for older people onto the federal government. Older people have other needs, however, that many people feel could best be served by government. Consider the following list:

☐ Vocational rehabilitation　　☐ Nursing home financing
☐ Housing　　　　　　　　　　☐ Design factors (in buildings,
☐ Transportation　　　　　　　　　furniture, clothing, and so forth)
☐ Taxes　　　　　　　　　　　☐ Inflation
☐ Recreation　　　　　　　　　☐ Homemaker services
☐ Mental health　　　　　　　　☐ Retirement
☐ Consumer protection　　　　　☐ Protective services
☐ Suicide prevention　　　　　　☐ Alcoholism
☐ Referral services　　　　　　　☐ Blindness and deafness
☐ Independence　　　　　　　　☐ Education

☐ Poverty                              ☐ Mass media coverage
☐ Activity                             ☐ Isolation
☐ Long-term care                       ☐ Dental care

How likely is the government to respond to these needs? To satisfy them first requires a commitment to spend government money on the aged and then some consensus concerning priorities. The first requirement brings us to perhaps the most fundamental problem that politicians face—the problem of choosing the things that are possible from among the many things that people want, given the fact that government can almost never command enough resources to satisfy everybody. And as Cottrell (1966:96) has pointed out:

> They [the politicians] know that to gain anything people must sacrifice something else they might have had. They try to judge the worth of an objective in terms of what the voter is willing to sacrifice to achieve it. If they judge correctly, they can continue to make policy; but if they err too greatly, policy will be made by others who have organized a more effective coalition in support of [other] policies.

To build the power necessary to design, develop, and implement governmental programs for older people, the politician must find out in which areas older people's interests coincide enough with those of other groups to form an effective voting coalition—since we have already seen that older people do not by themselves have the necessary power. He or she must also stay out of areas, however strong the need may be, that most people consider none of the government's business. As we shall see, some sizable obstacles block governmental programs intended only for the aged.

The first of these obstacles is conflicts of interest. Meeting the needs of older people often conflicts with meeting the needs of the young, and often the choice that must be made resembles the choice between aid to schools and aid to nursing homes. Most of the time the needs of youth are placed first. The same can be said of other categories and programs such as Aid to Dependent Children, the Economic Opportunity Act, the 1965 Voting Rights Act, and so on.

Vested interests also play their part. The American Medical Association's (AMA) opposition to Medicare is a good example. The physicians did not oppose the idea of better medical care for older people. They opposed the idea of government involvement in programs that have traditionally been dominated by doctors. It was to protect this vested interest that the AMA opposed Medicare. This intent is quite evident from the fact that within 6 weeks after Medicare was put into operation, over 80 percent of doctors expressed approval. By this time it had become obvious to most of them that the government had no intention of becoming involved in their everyday decisions. The fact that the AMA's fears for their vested interest were unfounded is unimportant. But the fact that they *felt* that the threat was real was enough to block the passage of Medicare for quite some time.

Another factor that inhibits programs for older people is the inertia of bureaucratic organizations. One of the factors that worked against the Social Security legislation was the fact that at the time the legislation was being considered there was no recognized bureaucratic structure in the government around which those interested in supporting income programs for the aged could rally. At that time, the Townsend Movement and Eliminate Poverty in California under Upton Sinclair were both going strong, but there was no office in Washington through which their support could be funneled. At the time Medicare was being considered, there was an Office of Aging under the Department of Health, Education, and Welfare (HEW) and the Special Committee on Aging in the U.S. Senate. These mechanisms made gaining support for programs for older people easier in the sense that there was an office staff paid by the government to keep tabs on the interests of the aged.

The Senate Special Committee on Aging was created in 1961 as a temporary study group (as opposed to a committee with the authority to report legislation to the full Senate). It has survived its 1-year mandate many times over to become a *de facto* standing committee of the Senate with 21 members. In an analysis of the committee's role, Vinyard (1972) concludes that it serves several important functions. First, the committee serves as a watchdog to see that the interests of older Americans do not get lost or ignored in broad-ranging government programs. The committee also serves as a legislative catalyst, supporting legislation and lobbying for the aged within Congress. The committee also serves as a rallying point for senators who wish to demonstrate their interest and support to the public. It is often a legislative ally of old-age interest groups. Finally, the committee is a symbol of the concern of Congress for the interests of older Americans.

Going back to the list of needs presented earlier, probably not a single one would receive enough general support in competition with other programs to make possible a self-contained legislative proposal. This situation prompts a fundamental question: Is it better to have low priority in a system having great power (that is, a large coalition), or to have high priority in a system competing for and receiving much less (that is, the National Council on Aging)? Everything we have discovered thus far indicates that if success is the measure of good, then low priority in a large coalition is the only hope older people have. Their needs must be incorporated into general programs to enjoy any real possibility of success. For example, combining the transportation needs of older people with those of the poor could result in gains for both. This type of combination is the essence of political coalitions. Many political scientists are convinced that since Social Security and Medicare have both been enacted, there will never again be an issue relating primarily to older people that will mobilize the support of the young. Accordingly, the only hope that older people seeking government action on their problems have is to attach their requirements to broader proposals. Over the past several years, the track record of lobbyists using this strategy has been encouraging. From 1967 to 1972, the share of all federal money that went to people over 65 rose from 15.8 percent to 20.2 percent (Administration on Aging, 1971).

This train of argument brings us to the political role of the "expert." Trained or experienced gerontologists have the greatest potential impact in terms of formulating policies related to older people. They have access to more information about older people than perhaps anyone else, and, as a society, we are accustomed to letting the experts handle our problems. Governmont experts in gerontology can influence programs that are being developed in various agencies.

The only difficulty with this system is the fact that in gerontology the "experts" are in fact much less expert than the experts in, let us say, the Agriculture Department. There is simply not enough evidence yet for gerontologists to make policy recommendations with full confidence that they know what is best or what most older people want. This uncertainty arises largely because we do not know enough yet about the changes with age that occur in people's values.

Fortunately the Senate Special Committee on Aging serves a very useful function here by allowing input from interested citizens concerning older people's problems. By holding hearings throughout the country, the committee attempts to give as many older people as want it a chance to be heard. Of course, a great many older people are never heard from, but the access is there should they need it.

With regard to governmental programs, then, we can expect to see the needs of the aged being combined with broader programs. We should not expect to see old-age programs emerge as a separate issue. We should expect to see the influence of gerontological "experts" on old age programs increase, although their knowledge of older people's needs is far from perfect.

Aside from the issue of how programs for older people can win political support, there is the equally important issue of how these programs should be organized and coordinated. The federal government can do a reasonable job of providing direct support to older people through programs such as Social Security. However, solutions to a great many of the problems older people face must be based on personal considerations and the *local* situation. In cases where personalized service is necessary, the local community is the only governmental agency capable of doing the job.

Cottrell (1971a:1–2) has outlined several important questions concerning the nature of governmental programs:

☐ What should be the functions of a central agency on aging and what are the relationships between it and other departments and agencies within the federal government?

☐ What should be the functions of official state agencies on aging? Where should they be located, and what should be their relationships with other units of state government?

☐ What type of agency is needed at the community level to serve as a focal point for broad action in aging? What should its functions be? From whence should it derive its authority and financial support?

☐ What is the most desirable method of integrating or interrelating the activities of overall agencies in aging at federal, state, and community levels?

☐ How can government at each level best maintain working relationships with voluntary organizations and with the private sector of the economy?

☐ What should be the division of responsibility among public and private agencies and organizations?

☐ Should government take initiative in stimulating roles in aging on the part of organizations? If so, what types of organizations?

Another issue concerns the variety of different chronological ages used in the law to differentiate older people from the general public. Cain (1974) reports that legal definitions of "old" begin as early as 45 and as late as 72. This sort of confusion creates problems for people who find that they are not uniformly eligible for services under government programs for the elderly.

The existing intergovernmental division of labor with respect to programs for older people has resulted from variations in the ability of various agencies to muster the political clout necessary to enact legislation. The record at the national level is familiar. Social Security, Medicare, and agencies on aging in various federal departments attest to a small but sometimes effective political power base at the federal level.

At the state and local levels, however, the picture has changed considerably since 1973. Prior to that time, most state programs for older people were very limited, and the average state agency for aging consisted of three people. Various governors' conferences on aging, forums, and so on brought home to state politicians the fact that there is an interest group to be served, but state involvement in programs for older people was hindered primarily by the fact that the four major programs—Social Security, Medicare, Aid for the Aged, and Federal Housing—all bypassed state government on their way to the people.

At the local level, the only governmental agency serving older people was usually the welfare department. Given the connotations attached to welfare programs by the public and by older people themselves, this situation was very unsatisfactory. Only in very large cities had the concentration of older people at the local level been great enough to produce a separate office to respond to their needs. Multipurpose senior centers were also sometimes an effective community agency for translating public programs for older people into action.

Since 1972, the situation has changed considerably. The 1973 Comprehensive Service Amendments to the Older Americans Act required that in order to receive federal funds, each state must set up a network of Area Agencies on Aging. The nutrition program funneled large amounts of federal funds through state agencies. In addition, a great deal of the responsibility for planning and for administering training and demonstration programs was delegated to the states. This reorganization had sweeping effects. For the first time, state agencies on aging had administrative control over a sizable budget. Accordingly, state agencies have grown considerably in size and power since 1973. Also, the need for Area Agencies on Aging (AAA's) required that local areas designate a single agency to serve as local coordinator for both state and federal programs, thus improving coordination at the local level. This reorganization has created effective advocates for older people in many areas of the country where previously they had none.

## SUMMARY

Politics is the route to political power, and political power means control over the machinery of government. Older people are concerned with politics and government because they participate in politics through voting, working in political organizations, and holding office. They are also the object of governmental programs.

Older people seek to remain informed about and interested in politics, particularly if they are well-educated or involved in local affairs. Older people vote in about the same proportions as they did when they were middle aged. Each age cohort apparently develops its own level of participation, which stays relatively stable throughout life. But differential mortality and the tendency for women to vote less reduce the actual proportion voting.

Older people have stronger party identification than the young only if they have been associated with the party over many years. It is years of affiliation, not age in itself, that produces a strong party identification. Older people are evenly split between the Republican and Democratic parties. Since they are overrepresented among people who have served long apprenticeships in politics, older people are also overrepresented at nominating conventions and public offices. However, there is no evidence that this overrepresentation is the result of deference to age. In politics, youth apparently still bows to experience, and experience rather than age is the crucial variable. Older people have equal opportunity in politics, but only if they have been lifelong participants. There is little room for the retired grocer who suddenly decides to get into politics.

In terms of political power, pressure groups of older people have seldom counted for much. Lack of leadership, regional segregation, heterogeneity of interests among older people, and lack of funds have all proved too much for those who would create an "old folks' power" bloc. These same factors have prevented older people from developing into a subculture or a genuine minority group.

Action in behalf of older people has almost always depended on the political support of organizations not based on age, such as unions or political parties. The role of old-age interest groups is to make the need for action highly visible and to lobby for the interests of older people within existing programs. In recent years, older Americans have gradually increased their share of benefits from general government programs.

Governmental programs for older people seek to shift the responsibility for meeting some of their needs from the family to the various levels of government. The federal government operates programs in income and health maintenance. But many other needs require involvement on the part of state and local governments. The 1973 reorganization, which gave states and local areas both authority, funds, and responsibility was a large step toward creating needed local advocates for older Americans.

The biggest problems in creating governmental programs for older people are convincing the public at large that older people deserve a higher priority than other needy groups, setting priorities among older people themselves, and deciding how these programs should be organized and coordinated, particularly in terms of inter-governmental relations.

In terms of realistic prospects, the best bet for older people is probably to settle for being one of many claimants on broad programs. They have found it extremely difficult to get action based on their needs alone. Older people tend to agree that income, housing, and transportation deserve top priority. In terms of organization, the best system for governmental programs seems to be a strong federal agency capable of gathering support for national fund-raising legislation, and strong state agencies on aging to administer federally funded programs through local Area Agencies on Aging.

## SUGGESTIONS FOR FURTHER READING

Agnello, Thomas J., Jr. "Aging and the Sense of Political Powerlessness." *Public Opinion Quarterly 37* (1973):251–259.

Binstock, Robert H. "Interest-Group Liberalism and the Politics of Aging." *Gerontologist 12* (1972):265–280.

———. "Aging and the Future of American Politics." In Frederick R. Eisele (ed.), *Political Consequences of Aging*. Philadelphia: American Academy of Political and Social Sciences, 1974, pp. 199–212.

Cain, Leonard D., Jr. "The Growing Importance of Legal Age in Determining the Status of the Elderly." *Gerontologist 14* (1974):167–174.

Campbell, Angus. "Politics Through the Life Cycle." *Gerontologist 11* (1971, 2, part 1): 112–117.

Carlie, Michael K. "The Politics of Age: Interest Group or Social Movement?" *Gerontologist 9* (1969, 4, part 1):259–263.

Cottrell, Fred. "Aging and the Political System." In John C. McKinney and Frank T. de Vyver (eds.), *Aging and Social Policy*. New York: Appleton-Century-Crofts, 1966, pp. 77–113.

———. *Government and Non-Government Organization*. Washington, D.C.: White House Conference on Aging, 1971.

Douglass, Elizabeth B., William P. Cleveland, and George L. Maddox. "Political Attitudes, Age, and Aging: A Cohort Analysis of Archival Data." *Journal of Gerontology 29* (1974):666–675.

Foner, Anne. "Age Stratification and Age Conflict in Political Life." *American Sociological Review 39* (1974):187–196.

Glenn, Norval D. "Age and Conservatism." In Frederick R. Eisele (ed.), *Political Consequences of Aging*. Philadelphia: American Academy of Political and Social Science, 1974, pp. 176–186.

Jackson, Jacquelyne J. "NCBA, Black Aged and Politics." In Frederick R. Eisele (ed.), *Political Consequences of Aging*. Philadelphia: American Academy of Political and Social Sciences, 1974, pp. 138–159.

Pratt, Henry J. "Old Age Associations in National Politics." In Frederick R. Eisele (ed.), *Political Consequences of Aging*. Philadelphia: American Academy of Political and Social Sciences, 1974, pp. 106–119.

Turk, Herman, Joel Smith, and Howard P. Myers. "Understanding Local Political Behavior: The Role of the Older Citizen." In Ida H. Simpson and John C. McKinney (eds.), *Social Aspects of Aging*. Durham, N.C.: Duke University Press, 1966, pp. 254–276.

Turner, Barbara F., and Robert L. Kahn. "Age as a Political Issue." *Journal of Gerontology 29* (1974):572–580.

Vinyard, Dale. "The Senate Special Committee on Aging." *Gerontologist 12* (1972):298–303.

# 16
# Community

A *community* is a group of people who interact with one another frequently, who share their location in space, who depend on one another—even if indirectly—to fill their needs, and who share an identity with the place where they live. Members often share certain ideas that have grown from the unique social heritage of the community. The ideal community is a relatively autonomous locality with a population large enough to foster a full-fledged social system complete with social institutions but small enough to remain integrated. The larger the size and density of a locality, the harder it is to maintain the daily interaction, shared culture, economic and social interdependence, and sense of identity necessary to community. Most localities have some characteristics of a "pure" community but few meet the ideal.

Communities, or subcommunities in larger areas, are important focal points in the lives of most people. People are born, reared, educated, married, housed, fed, healed, mourned, and buried in a local community. The effort devoted to work, play, love, politics, fellowship, or self-discovery most often is expended in the context of a local community. Thus, the picture of society people gain is substantially influenced by the extent to which the cities or neighborhoods they live in are unified communities. Because older people are usually long-term community residents, they are especially likely to see the community as the locus of life's most salient moments.

Communities differ from each other in that each community has a somewhat individual culture. Therefore, local politics, groups, opinions about government spending, criteria for establishing social class membership, family attitudes and values, and many other features will differ slightly from one community to another. Thus moving from one community to another can be a difficult experience if the cultures in the two communities are quite different. Older people are particularly susceptible to difficulties of this kind because they tend to be more committed than younger people to the cultures of communities they have lived in for many years. This commitment accounts in part for the reluctance many older people show toward moving. They realize that a new community will mean many new ways of doing things. A move means cutting themselves off from their personal and family history. Of course, this cultural commitment also helps explain the attractiveness of communities housing like-minded older people.

As social systems that are tied to a relatively small geographic area, communities begin with people who have needs they would like to satisfy. The ideal community is one in which the interrelated social institutions function so smoothly that everyone who attempts to meet personal needs within the community context has at least one realistic and effective alternative. The effectiveness of any given community for its older citizens thus depends on the degree to which the community structure can be used effectively by older people to meet their own needs. Community structure has many dimensions, but for our purposes the most important are the *social structure* within the community, *community facilities*, and *community services*.

## SOCIAL STRUCTURE

For older people, the salient organizations in a community are those they belong to and those that serve them either directly or indirectly. Older people as voluntary association members are discussed in Chapter 17. Groups that serve older people directly are discussed later in this chapter under social services. This section addresses two remaining topics: interrelations among organizations and social enforcement of family care for older people.

The social structure of a community includes the interrelations among organizations that provide services. The recent 1971 White House Conference on Aging noted that lack of coordination among community organizations providing services for older Americans was a high-priority need. Yet, because local organizations tend to compete with one another rather than cooperate, calls for better coordination within communities were generally to no avail (Estes, 1973). In 1973, this situation changed.

The Older Americans Comprehensive Service Amendments of 1973 created a new community organization, the Area Agency on Aging (AAA). Along with significant increases in federal funds to local programs for older Americans, the Comprehensive Service Amendments, through the AAA's, brought new priorities on coordination of services and on *planning*. There are currently just under 400 AAA's, each of which is charged with developing plans for a comprehensive and coordinated network of services to older people and with offering facilitating services in the areas of information and referral, escort, transportation, and outreach. The concept of the Area Agency on Aging emphasizes flexibility in uniting particular sets of local organizations to meet the needs of local older people and thus allows for local and regional variations in resources and service needs. At the same time, the AAA concept seeks to make a minimum set of services available to all older people. The majority of

AAA's were created in 1974; therefore, it will be some time before the effectiveness of the community approach to federal programs can be assessed.

Community social structure also includes norms that affect the lives of older people. Whether older people are respected or rejected varies widely from community to community in American society. In large urban areas, older people are sometimes isolated outcasts preyed on by both businessmen and criminals. In some rural areas, they are simply forgotten. In a study of a small rural township, Cottrell (1971b) found more than 20 isolated older people whose existence was unknown to a single organization in the community. Yet in many other communities older people are important and valued citizens.

Lozier and Althouse (1974) suggest that whether older people have social status and security within a community depends primarily on the existence of a social system in which the way older people are treated has social significance and social consequences for younger people. If respect for elders is a community norm *and* if people who disregard this norm are visible *and* if those who disregard this norm are punished, then older people are respected. Unpleasantly Machiavellian as this view of people may be, it seems useful in explaining what happens to many older people in urban areas. While family members in urban areas tend to give respect and support to their elders, there is no punishment for those who disregard this norm in the anonymous world of secondary contacts. There is no punishment for the store clerk who brushes off an older customer to serve a more prosperous-looking middle-aged one. Visibility to *significant others* seems to be the key here. If the store clerk's own mother were watching, the behavior toward the older person might be quite different.

## COMMUNITY FACILITIES

Facilities in a community are organized service centers such as stores, banks, churches, doctors' offices, hospitals, schools, and so forth. There is usually a mixture of public and private facilities in any given American community.

Taietz (1975a) made an intensive study of community facilities in 144 New York communities. He found that specialized facilities tended to be present only in communities that had a high degree of complexity and specialization (see Table 16-1). Note that only the most rudimentary facilities were available in a majority of the 144 communities surveyed and that facilities are particularly lacking in the rural areas.

Generally, the bigger and the more complex the area, the greater the variety of facilities available. This correlation is not surprising. What *is* surprising is how the size of communities influences *knowledge* of facilities in the community. Taietz (1975b) found that because communication in rural areas tends to be by word-of-mouth, the larger the rural area the less the average older person knows about available facilities. In urban areas, the opposite was true. Because in cities mass communication is the prevalent mode of communication, the larger the urban area (and the larger the target population for facility use) the greater the average level of knowledge of facilities.

Because most Americans live in urban areas, it is easy to forget that the majority of America's communities are in rural areas. In 1974, 86 percent of the land area of the United States was rural, nonmetropolitan land. The impact of this fact on the prevalence of facilities is a topic very worthy of study.

**TABLE 16-1**
**Percentage Distribution of Facilities**
**in Rural and Urban Communities: New York State, 1967**

| Item | Rural | Urban | Total |
|------|-------|-------|-------|
| Senior citizens' club and/or center | 26.5% | 73.6% | 61.4% |
| Hospital with operating certificate only | 17.6 | 70.0 | 57.9 |
| Fully accredited hospital | 14.7 | 66.4 | 54.5 |
| Nursing home(s) | 17.6 | 56.4 | 47.6 |
| Psychiatric clinic | 5.9 | 43.6 | 35.2 |
| Home health agency | 20.6 | 38.2 | 34.5 |
| Department of Social Services | 17.6 | 39.1 | 34.5 |
| Homemaker service | 2.9 | 26.4 | 21.4 |
| Department of Health | 5.9 | 25.5 | 21.4 |
| Family service agency | 0.0 | 25.5 | 20.0 |
| Sheltered workshop | 0.0 | 15.5 | 12.4 |
| Free-standing clinic | 0.0 | 14.5 | 11.7 |
| Accredited hospital with medical specialty | 0.0 | 12.7 | 10.3 |
| Number of communities (N) | (34) | (110) | (144) |

Source: Taietz (1975b:18).

## SOCIAL SERVICES

Social services consist of a broad range of often unrelated programs that revolve around a general goal of helping people get the things they want. The range includes family service, senior centers, the foster grandparent program, talking books, meals programs, employment services, and protective services. Communities vary widely with regard to the number and range of such programs and program titles vary widely. Therefore, instead of trying to describe the typical community, it is probably more useful to examine general types of programs that are commonly found in communities.

Service programs can be divided into programs of service *to* older people and programs of service *by* older people. This section deals with specific programs; later sections deal with broader areas of service such as health services, transportation, and education.

### Services to Older People

Services that provide *meals* either take food to people or bring people to food. "Meals on Wheels" programs deliver hot meals to older people in their own homes. Congregate meals programs bring older people to a central site for meals. In recent years the congregate meals approach has been gaining favor because it provides fellowship as well as more opportunities to tie in with other social service programs at the congregate meals sites.

Services providing *information and referral* serve as a bridge between people with needs and appropriate service agencies. Area Agencies on Aging are responsible for these programs in most areas. Many areas have directories of services for older people.

Some programs offer *visitor* contact between older shut-ins and the outside world. Visitor programs often serve institutionalized older people as well as older people living in their own homes. These programs are usually staffed by volunteers, and older people often work as visitors.

Programs involving *outreach* services seek out older people in the community who need services. Older persons who need services often become known to the program via relatives or neighbors. Outreach workers contact the older person and refer him or her to the appropriate agency. Sometimes outreach workers make agency contacts on behalf of older people.

Programs offering *telephone reassurance* give isolated older people a point of contact and a sense of continuity. In the ideal reassurance program, the people working on the phones are well trained in referral and yet also know the older person through regular telephone visits. Regular calls from the program assure older people that someone cares about them and will be checking on their welfare regularly. Volunteers are often used for telephone reassurance.

Certain *employment* services seek to place older workers in jobs. Sometimes such services maintain a file of retired people from various occupations who are available for short-term or part-time employment.

Various *homemaker* services provide household support services to semi-independent older people living in their own homes. In addition to the usual housekeeping chores such as cleaning, shopping, and laundry, some programs also offer home maintenance and food preparation services. Berg, Atlas, and Zeigler (1974) stress the need for a continuum of service that can be suited to the older person's level of impairment. Highly impaired people need a variety of housekeeping services on a daily basis, while others may only need occasional specialized services.

Services that offer *income counseling* help people get maximum use of their income resources by making sure they are aware of all possible sources of income and by helping them make the transition from a pre- to a postretirement budget. Income counseling often includes such things as how to buy consumer goods at the lowest prices, how to take advantage of seasonal sales, the cost of credit buying, how to form consumer cooperatives, how to save on rent or get into low-rent public housing, ways to save on auto insurance, ways to save on building repairs, and so on. While this type of assistance is highly valued by older people, very few communities offer it.

Most larger communities have senior centers, which usually take the form of private nonprofit corporations, often underwritten with United Fund money. The several thousand senior centers in the United States often constitute the sole community attempt to offer recreational and educational programs for older people.

The small percentage of older people who use them (1 to 5 percent) would seem to indicate that senior centers do not constitute a focal point for recreation and education among the overwhelming majority of older people. Of course, many older people who might otherwise use a senior center's facilities are prevented from doing so by difficulties of access—poor transportation service, disability, health, and so on. Yet even in communities where concerted efforts have been made to give older people access to senior centers, only a small minority took advantage of them. For some older people, the senior center is a beacon in the night, a place for self-renewal. For others, it is a continued reminder that older people are treated like isolated outcasts. Perhaps the difficulty is that in any community older people's needs are too complex to be effectively satisfied by any single organization, particularly one that gets a very low-priority share of community funds.

The average multipurpose senior center tends to adopt a flexible program—one that involves informal companionship, community services, self-government within the center, and a wide variety of other possible features. Membership in senior centers tends to be drawn from a wide area rather than from a single neighborhood. Initial membership is often related to a major life change such as retirement or widowhood, and joiners tend to be healthy and able to get around. Members of senior centers do not seem to be very different from other older people. However, Tissue (1971c) indicates that centers cannot easily accommodate members from different social classes.

At this point we still do not know how widely accepted senior centers are as an institution in the American community, partly because many senior citizens' organizations are semiformal groups operating under the auspices of churches, unions, fraternal organizations, and the like. Much more research is needed before we will know very much about regional trends in the acceptance of senior centers, community attitudes toward senior centers, and the variety of services provided. However, the growing tendency for federal support of programs in local areas to be channeled through senior centers has provided considerable impetus for such research.

Some programs offer *protective services*, taking over the affairs of older people who are no longer capable of taking care of themselves. Everyone has heard of aging, confused hermits who have outlived their families and who are starving because they have hidden their Social Security checks and cannot recall where they put them. Ross (1968) provides a case illustration:

> For several years Mr. M. has been complaining to a variety of agencies about Mrs. S., an eighty-eight-year-old woman whose house is adjacent to his—and he finally reached Senior Information Center. Mrs. S. is a recluse who has harassed the M's by making loud noises in their bedroom window, banging her porch door, calling over vile and obscene things to their children playing in the yard. Her house is run down, weeds and bushes are overgrown, and neighbors photographed her feeding rats in her back yard. They described her as resembling the witch of fairy tales—with flowing grey hair and long dirty skirts, living in seclusion in a silent house. The only relative is a niece, who for the last several years has refused to be involved. Her income is only $72.00 a month from Social Security.
>
> A home call confirmed the grim picture. Mrs. S., suspicious at first, refused to let the caseworker into the house, but came out on the porch to talk. She tried to hide a dirty,

stained slip; and there was a strong odor of urine about her. She denied having any problems other than those caused by the "gangsters" next door, and there was a paranoid trend in her thinking. As she talked she became almost friendly, joked about getting a mini-skirt, and assured the caseworker that there was nothing to worry about in her situation.

Later, a city sanitation inspector went through the house, saw one rat and evidence of their presence throughout the house. He believes that she does actually feed rats. The odor of urine and feces was strong for Mrs. S. apparently does not bother to use the upstairs toilet or is incontinent. The inspector also found about fifty wine bottles, which adds to the frightening picture. Suppose she became intoxicated and a rat attacked her?

Another aspect was recently uncovered. Mr. M. in his anger over the continued harassment, nailed shut the back door to her house. Fortunately, another neighbor, realizing the danger in case of fire, removed the nails (1968:50).

Protective services are used by the community when it becomes clear from the behavior of older people that they are mentally incapable of caring for themselves and their interests. It is estimated that something on the order of one in every 20 older people needs some form of protective service. In addition, this proportion can be expected to increase as the proportion of older people over age 75 increases.

The typical response to someone like Mrs. S. is to put her away in a mental hospital, but this solution is coming under increased scrutiny. Many older people now in mental hospitals could easily be left at home with a minimum of help in securing the support services that are already available to them. Often, commitment to mental hospitals is done against the will of older people "for their own good," but a U.S. District Court of Appeals has ruled that a person cannot be involuntarily committed until it has been shown that all other alternatives for caring for him or her have been exhausted (Hall, 1966). In addition, mental hospitals are already too crowded to be able to care for incompetent older people.

The most difficult problem is often to find someone to initiate action. In many states, the law assumes the proceedings will be initiated by a relative. In the absence of a relative, no one is willing to take the responsibility. Laws need to be changed in such a way that responsibility is pinpointed.

Ultimately, protective services are casework, outreach services rather than deskbound ones. Legal intervention is usually a last resort, used only when all other alternatives have been exhausted. Agencies must often seek out people who may not want the service at all. It is obvious that protective services must be a part of any community service program for older people, but assigning responsibility for such services is a difficult task.

## Services by Older People

The *Foster Grandparent Program* uses the services of low-income older people to help provide personal, individual care to children who live in institutions. In a series of studies, the impact of the Foster Grandparent Program has been shown to be of great benefit to both the older people involved and the children they served. After exposure to the program, children have been observed to be more outgoing and to have improved relationships with both their peers and institutional authorities. Children have shown increased self-confidence, decreased insecurity and fear, and improved language skills.

Older people also receive a greal deal from the program. To begin with, older people are able to augment their incomes by $40 to $50 per week, and for most older people this addition is quite a help. Many older people who are involved have reported feelings of increased vigor and youthfulness, of an increased sense of personal worth, of a renewed sense of purpose and direction to life, and of pleasure in renewed personal growth and development.

Administrators have been pleased with the way older people seem to adapt to the various tasks—many of them involving new skills that the older people had to learn. Special assignments in day care, physical therapy, speech therapy, and as teacher's aides have been made possible by the willingness and ability some of the older people have shown. Several inferences can be drawn from the experience of the Foster Grandparent Program. For one thing, low-income older people will work for modest but reasonable pay if the job proves satisfying to them, and thus they offer a vast pool of relatively inexpensive labor that can be used to do needed work within the community. The role that older people might play in day care alone is enough to stagger one's imagination. It has also shown that older people are interested in continued participation in community affairs, particularly in useful and dignified participation.

The *Retired Senior Volunteer Program* (RSVP) offers people over 60 the opportunity of doing volunteer service to meet community needs. RSVP agencies place volunteers in schools, hospitals, libraries, courts, day care centers, nursing homes, and a host of other organizations. RSVP programs provide transportation to and from the place of service.

The *Service Corps of Retired Executives* (SCORE) offers retired businessmen and businesswomen an opportunity to help owners of small businesses and managers of community organizations who are having management problems. Since 1965, over 175,000 businesses have received help from SCORE. Volunteers receive no pay but are reimbursed for out-of-pocket expenses.

The *Senior Companion Program*, modeled after Foster Grandparents, offers a small stipend to older people who help adults with special needs, such as the handicapped and the disabled.

A program called *Green Thumb*, sponsored by the National Farmers Union in 24 states, provides part-time employment in conservation, beautification, and community improvement in rural areas or in existing community service agencies.

The U.S. Department of Labor has three programs that offer part-time employment to older people who serve as aides in a variety of community agencies including child care centers, vocational training programs, building security, clerical service, and homemaker services. The *Senior Aides* program is administered by the National Council of Senior Citizens; *Senior Community Service Aides* is sponsored by the National Council on Aging; and *Senior Community Aides* is sponsored by the National Retired Teachers Association/American Association of Retired Persons.

The success of these programs illustrates that older people can be quite effective in both volunteer and paid positions. For the time being, however, we can expect volunteer opportunities to outnumber opportunities for part-time employment. A major obstacle to the effective use of older volunteers has been an unwillingness to assign them to responsible, meaningful positions on an ongoing basis. The result is a vicious circle. Because volunteers are assigned to menial tasks, they get bored or frustrated and quit. Because they quit, administrators are reluctant to put volunteers in anything other than nonessential jobs.

Studies have shown that older volunteers can be counted on to perform well on an ongoing basis (Babic, 1972; Sainer and Zander, 1971), particularly if the agency placing volunteers adheres to the following guidelines. First, agencies must be flexible in matching the volunteer's background to assigned tasks. If the agency takes a broad perspective, useful work can be found for almost anyone. Second, *volunteers must be trained*. All too often agency personnel place unprepared volunteers in an unfamiliar setting. Then the volunteer's difficulty confirms the myth that you cannot expect good work from volunteers. Third, a variety of placement options should be offered to the volunteer. Some volunteers prefer to do familiar things; others want to do *anything but* familiar things. Fourth, training of volunteers should not make them feel that they are being tested. This point is particularly sensitive among working-class volunteers. Fifth, volunteers should get personal attention from the placement agency. There should be people (perhaps volunteers) who follow up on absences and who are willing to listen to the compliments, complaints, or experiences of the volunteers. Public recognition from the community is an important reward for voluntary service. Finally, transportation to and from the placement should be provided (Sainer and Zander, 1971).

## COORDINATION OF SERVICES

Coordination of services is an important determinant of the effectiveness of communities in serving the needs of older citizens. Bucks County, Pennsylvania, is a good example of a community with coordinated services. Designated as an Area Agency on Aging in 1974, the Bucks County Department of Adult Services has developed a complex of services that includes counseling and referral, protective services, foster home care, day care, nutrition programs, RSVP, and homemaker–home-health-aide services to a population of 8,000 older adults. In conjunction with the Bucks County Association for Retired and Senior Citizens, the department operates five Senior Centers throughout the county. The department also maintains a close relationship with Neshaminy Manor Home, a modern public nursing home. The department refers patients to the nursing home (77 admissions in 1974), and the nursing home refers patients to the department for foster home or day care. In addition, the nursing home provides services such as physical therapy to day care patients of the department and cooks the food for the nutrition program.

Here is how the services work. A call to the Counseling and Referral Service of the department gets an immediate response. If the problem is a complicated one, a caseworker visits the person who needs service. In 1974, caseworkers drove over 14,000 miles in processing over 2,000 requests for services. In addition, a caseworker visits each of the five senior centers once each week to provide information and referral. Caseworkers mobilize the resources of the county to help with many types of problems.

One caseworker works completely in the area of protective services. In 1974, there were 80 older people with an average age of 75 receiving protective services. Half of these were able to stay in their own homes as a result of the services, and the other half were placed in foster homes. Foster home placements are used for older persons who are too disabled to live independently but who do not need nursing care. There were 136 older persons in foster care homes at the end of 1974. Mental difficulty was the basis for 80 percent of the foster home placements. Most of the foster care is done in personal care homes rather than in the homes of families. The department also operates two day care centers to serve physically and/or mentally impaired older people. These persons are given physical therapy and occupational therapy. At the end of 1974, 30 older people were receiving this service. Transportation to the day care centers is provided by the department, which uses a van with a power lift. Thus, in 1974 over 200 disabled older people were involved in either protective services, foster care, or day care. In addition, the department employed 48 homemaker–home-health-aides to provide homemaker service to over 250 adults who need assistance with keeping house, cooking, laundry, or personal care. One overall result of these services was a reduction in the nursing home "high-priority" waiting list from 30 to 6 during the last half of 1974. The agency is a good illustration of the "continuum of care" concept—the idea that a variety of *levels* of assistance should be available.

The Bucks County Nutrition Program, operated by the department, provided nearly 300 older people with hot meals at three sites. In addition, meals are delivered to the home bound. Transportation is provided to and from the meals sites. Part-time site managers, who are also older people, coordinate volunteers who serve the meals, which are prepared at Neshaminy Manor Home. Recreational activities are planned around the meals, along with other services such as information and referral. Nutrition education mainly in the form of recipes, is provided by the Penn State Nutrition Aides.

The RSVP program had 212 older volunteers serving in 29 placement locations in 1974. These volunteers provided over 2,000 hours of service per month to the community.

The Bucks County program could not exist without staff personnel and funds. In 1974, the Bucks County Department of Adult Services employed a director, a planner, a bookkeeper, 5 secretaries, 5 field supervisors and program directors, 7 caseworkers, 2 case aides, 5 drivers, 4 nutrition site managers, and 48 homemaker–home-health-aides—a total of 79 people. The operations of the department cost $441,000, half provided from federal funds and half from the county commissioners.

## TRANSPORTATION

In this country we have been experiencing a long-term trend away from public transportation. Its use is declining in all but our largest cities. No longer a paying proposition, and usually requiring tax subsidy, public transportation is most used for travel to and from work. The needs of the elderly are not considered in most decisions about public transportation.

Older people fall into two categories with regard to transportation: those who can use present facilities and those who cannot. Those with no transportation problem tend to be the ones who can afford to own and operate their own cars, represented by about 46 percent of those 65 and older. For these people, public transportation is something to be used when it snows or when going on a long trip. The elderly with a trans- portation problem fall into three groups: (1) those who could use existing public transportation but cannot afford it; (2) those who for one reason or another need to be picked up and returned directly to their homes; and (3) those who live in areas where there is no public transportation.

Cost is an important factor. In this country we have roughly ten million older people who are hampered by the cost of transportation. Some of the limiting factors are: they cannot afford a car; bus fares of $.50 or higher are beyond their means; and they cannot pay cab fares of $1.25 or more. For these people, lack of adequate, inexpensive transportation is one of the most important limitations on their indepen- dence and activities.

Carp (1970) found that only about 15 percent of the older people in her study had unlimited access to automobiles. More than half walked wherever they went, but walking was not a preferred mode of transport. For those who used public transit, the more they used it the less they liked it. S. Cutler (1972b) found that mobility restrictions were translated into constricted life space and low levels of life satisfaction. Older people are not primarily sedentary by choice. They are more often forced into being sedentary by inadequate transportation.

Among older people with transportation problems, most are still able to get to the doctor, dentist, and grocery store. But many do not get out to see their friends and relatives or go to church or recreation facilities. Although they still manage to keep alive, they are unable to do the things that give meaning to life. And when they can get out, it is usually at someone else's convenience. Pride and a sense of dignity often prevent older people from relying on friends and relatives to transport them. What they need is a dependable transportation system at prices they can afford.

Solutions that have been tried in various communities include: (1) reduced fares for older people at specific hours; (2) public subsidy to improve bus schedules and routing; (3) use of volunteers in private automobiles; (4) nonprofit transportation services operated by senior centers; and (5) use of church buses.

The ideal transportation plan for older people would consist of: (1) fare reductions or discounts on all public transportation, including interstate transport; (2) public subsidies for adequate scheduling and routing of existing public transportation; (3) reduced taxi fares for the disabled or infirm; and (4) funds to be used by senior centers to purchase and equip vehicles to use in transporting older people, particularly in rural areas and in places with no public transportation. Increasingly, the federal government has been willing to provide funds for transportation as a necessary element of service delivery in programs for older people.

## HOUSING

Housing is a key feature in the relationship between older people and their community for several reasons. First of all, where a person lives largely determines his or her opportunities for contact with other people. It also affects access to various community services. The relationship between the housing preferences of older people and the availability of the preferred types of housing in a community are important factors in an older person's overall evaluation of the desirability of a particular community. Finally, one's home is where a large part of one's life is led, and it can either help or hinder the individual in his or her attempts to enjoy life.

Table 16-2 shows the continuum from independent to dependent housing. Older people prefer independent housing.

**TABLE 16-2**
**Levels of Housing by Degree of Independence**

| Housing Type | Significant Criteria |
|---|---|
| **Independent** | |
| Fully independent | Self-contained, self-sufficient household; residents do 90 percent or more of the cooking and household chores. |
| Semiindependent | Self-contained but not entirely self-sufficient; may require some assistance with cooking and household chores. Example would be independent household augmented by Meals-on-Wheels and/or homemaker services. |
| **Group Housing** | |
| Congregate housing | Can still be self-contained, but is less self-sufficient; cooking and household tasks are often incorporated into the housing unit. Most common type is the retirement hotel. |
| Personal care home | Neither self-contained nor self-sufficient; help given in getting about, personal care, grooming, and so forth, in addition to cooking and household tasks. Most common type is the retirement home. |
| Nursing home | Neither self-contained nor self-sufficient; total care, including health, personal, and household functions. |

As Table 16-3 shows, 95 percent of older Americans live in independent households. Only about 10 percent live in independent households headed by a person *under* 60. A majority of older Americans live in a husband-wife family with a head 60 years of age or older, and this majority is greater in rural areas as compared to urban.

Most older Americans live in single-family houses that they own. The homes older Americans live in tend to be older homes, to have relatively low value, and to be relatively more often dilapidated. A majority of older Americans have lived in their homes 20 years or longer.

**TABLE 16-3**
**Housing Characteristics**
**of Persons 60 Years Old and Over: United States, 1970**

|  | Urban | Rural Nonfarm | Rural Farm |
|---|---|---|---|
| Living alone | 23.5% | 21.5% | 10.3% |
| In husband-wife families with head 60 or over | 53.5 | 59.6 | 70.3 |
| In households with head under 60 | 10.0 | 7.3 | 8.3 |
| In single-unit housing | 67.0 | 89.2 | 97.9 |
| In mobile homes | 2.2 | 5.7 | 1.1 |
| In group quarters | 4.6 | 4.2 | 0.1 |
| In owner-occupied unit | 64.9 | 80.7 | 90.3 |
| In units with incomplete plumbing | 4.3 | 19.5 | 21.2 |
| Population, in millions (N) | (22.9) | (4.8) | (1.1) |

*Source:* Adapted from Atchley and Miller (1975).

One fifth of the housing of older rural Americans is lacking in complete plumbing facilities. The percentage of rural older people with low housing adequacy is greatest for older blacks living in the rural South (54 percent) (Atchley and Miller, 1975). Black-white differences in value of housing are notable. As Figure 16-1 shows, older black households are concentrated at the bottom of the housing value scale, as compared to older white households. The same trends appear in terms of monthly rent.

It is not clear just what percentage of these independent households are semi-independent. Some certainly are. Research on this subject is greatly needed. It would probably be a safe guess, however, that a great many so-called independent households desperately need the support services involved in semiindependence. But very few communities have the facilities to provide such services, and, as we saw earlier, many older people would prefer to suffer and perhaps even die rather than give up their independence. The chances are that the semiindependent type of housing would be popular not only with many older people now living in marginally independent households but also with some now living in less self-contained housing.

Only about 5 percent of the older people in the United States live in some type of group housing. Of these, about 1 percent live in congregate housing, and the remainder is split almost evenly between personal care and nursing homes. A small percentage of older people live with their children. This pattern will be discussed later, when we examine the family.

To a large extent, older people use their homes as the center for their social contacts. They entertain there, they have overnight guests there, they have people in

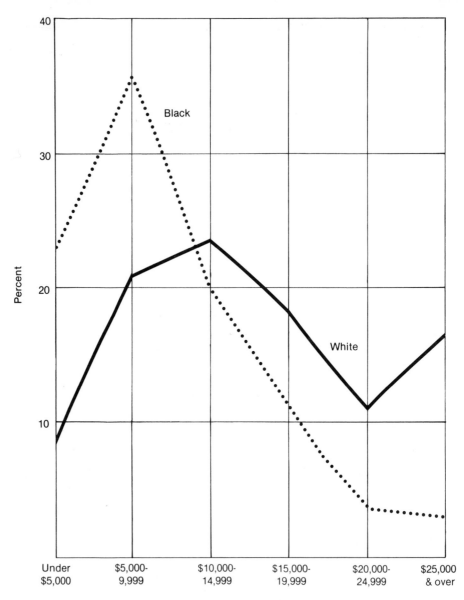

Value of owner-occupied housing units

**Figure 16-1**   Percent of husband-wife families with head 65 years and over, by race of head, by value of owner-occupied housing units: United States, 1970.

*Source:* U.S. Department of Housing and Urban Development, *Population, Housing and Income, and Federal Housing Programs* (Washington, D.C.: Government Printing Office, 1971), p. 22.

for meals. Home ownership also appears to encourage involvement in community affairs. It is therefore extremely significant for most communities that the overwhelming majority of older people have living arrangements that do not limit their community participation.

Finally, in planning housing especially for older people, there are many design features that can help the individual stay independent. Ramps to go up and steps to come down, wide doorways, large rooms with few hallways or corners, and sturdy hand-support fixtures in the bath are some of these. However, in the long run the social, rather than the physical, conditions appear to be most important.

## EDUCATION

In the field of education, we see perhaps the ultimate in the withdrawal of support from older people. Education systems in the United States are oriented toward youth and toward jobs. The purpose of school in America is primarily to prepare the student for a job. Even adult education tends to be oriented around the types of skills needed to secure a better job or a promotion. Only a very tiny portion of formal education, including adult education programs, is devoted to the skills involved in the enjoyment of living. It should not be too surprising, then, to find that education programs are one of the last things most older people consider in terms of community participation. There is some question how relevant education is for the young, but there can be no question that most formal educational programs have been irrelevant for older people.

There is some evidence, however, that this situation is changing. De Crow (1975) surveyed 3,500 learning programs for older Americans and came to the following conclusions:

☐ The "classroom" format was the most common.
☐ Support services were often lacking.
☐ Older people sought educational experiences *if* the program was suited to their style of life and especially if they had some opportunity to initiate and guide the experience.
☐ Topics covered a broad range including hobbies, consumer education, health, personal development, liberal arts, basic education (the three R's), regular university courses, and vocational training.
☐ Only about a third of the programs were offered by public school systems, community colleges, or universities. The remainder were given by senior centers, recreation departments, libraries, and cooperative extension services.
☐ About half of the programs were less than 1 year old.
☐ People over 75, older men, and minority groups were poorly served by existing programs.

Another bright light on the horizon is a growing trend for universities to offer tuition-free courses to older people. The prospects for more in the future seem good. The prime difficulty, however, is that the very people who need educational programs the most are often also the least able to take advantage of free college programs because their public school education has not prepared them to enjoy college-level courses of study. Another difficulty is that gradually the colleges have become more and more specialized, and the liberal arts—which include most of the courses that interest older people—are fast becoming the weakest part of public higher education.

Other educational programs of note include the Institute for Lifetime Learning in Washington, D.C., where members of the American Association of Retired Persons and National Retired Teachers Associations can go to learn such subjects as typing, sewing, painting, stamp collecting, or public speaking. Another significant educational program is the community education concept now in operation in Flint, Michigan. Through grants from the Mott Foundation, Flint has been engaged for over 20 years in creating a genuine cradle-to-grave educational system—a system that would meet the needs of community citizens, not just as children, but throughout their lives. Senior centers are operated as part of the public school program in Flint, and it is perhaps a commentary on the rigidity of our notions about education that this program seems unusual.

## PLANNED RETIREMENT COMMUNITIES

Among the large majority of older people who live in independent households is a small percentage that lives in planned retirement communities. Retirement communities tend to be homogeneous with respect to social class, racial, and ethnic backgrounds of the residents and there are retirement communities for people at most points on the social spectrum. However, the majority of retirement communities draw residents from the more affluent social classes (Bultena and Wood, 1969a).

People who move to retirement communities are more often childless than is the general older population. In addition, those who move to retirement communities often do so to be nearer to their children. Nevertheless, contacts with children are less prevalent among people in retirement communities than among the general older population.

Movement to retirement communities seems to self-select those older people who are amenable to life in age-homogeneous settings. As a result, morale in retirement communities is quite high. Conversely, there are indications that many older people who remain in age-integrated communities would not be at all happy in a retirement community (Bultena and Wood, 1969a).

The homogeneity of retirement communities fosters greater social interaction and formation of new friends. Because retirement communities draw heavily from former managers and professionals, their members are often quite accustomed to moving and have the skills needed for making new friends. For the vast majority of people in retirement communities, the move did not bring increased isolation from children. In addition, retirement communities provide normative support for those retired people who want to concentrate on leisure roles rather than to continue involvement in an age-integrated larger community. While living in planned retirement communities may not be for everyone, there is no evidence that it is detrimental for those who choose it.

The working-class equivalent to Sun City is the mobile home park for older adults. Basing her analysis on the situation in California in the mid-1960s, S. Johnson (1971) concluded that the mobile home park is a mixed blessing for retired residents. Most older people who live in mobile home parks want to live in a controlled environment without having to pay a high price for it.

> Slightly authoritarian in outlook, justifiably fearful of urban violence, and anxious to maintain all the visible outward signs appropriate to "decent people," the retired working-class mobile home resident wants to live in a park that is neat, attractive, quiet, safe, all-white, and friendly (S. Johnson, 1971:174).

These people are willing to pay a park owner to control the neighborhood, but they complain bitterly if these controls infringe too much on *them*. All too often, the cost of living in a mobile home park also includes considerable economic exploitation by park owners (S. Johnson, 1971). Nevertheless, the popularity of such parks in many areas of the country attests to the felt need for living areas that provide a safe, secure environment for a community made up largely of older adults.

## SUMMARY

For older people the community is important, particularly if they have lived there a long time. Nevertheless, older people are, in general, either expected to withdraw from participation or prevented from participating by the structure of the various public institutions in the community. Educational participation is largely done through senior centers and extension services. The schools and colleges are not very much involved. Economic participation is curtailed by retirement and low incomes. Housing of older people tends to be old and often dilapidated. There are too few support services, such as homemaker services, available to older people living in their own homes. In the areas of health and welfare a great deal is being done *for* older people, but very little of it is done *by* older people. In social services, there is often a mixture of uncoordinated programs; and older people are only just beginning to be relied on as a community resource. Protective services often tend to serve the public rather than older people. Transportation systems largely ignore the needs of older people, as do housing plans, particularly in the area of semiindependent housing.

The ideal community is one in which the interrelated social institutions function so smoothly that everyone who attempts to solve his or her personal problems within the community context is given at least one realistic and effective alternative. The concept of the Area Agency on Aging was created by the federal government to help make a minimum of planned and coordinated services available to all older Americans. The full impact of this effort will not be known for several years, but there can be no doubt that services to and by older Americans have improved in thousands of communities since 1973.

Planned retirement communities are available at all socioeconomic levels. However, most such communities are middle class. Retirement communities seem to be good for those who seek them out, and are especially likely to serve a felt need for safety and security.

## SUGGESTIONS FOR FURTHER READING

Atchley, Robert C., and Sheila J. Miller. "Housing of the Rural Aged." In Robert C. Atchley (ed.), *Environments and the Rural Aged*. Washington, D.C.: The Gerontological Society, 1975, pp. 95–143.

Bell, W. G., and W. T. Olsen. "An Overview of Public Transportation and the Elderly: New Directions and Social Policy." *Gerontologist 14* (1974):324–330.

Blenkner, Margaret, Edna Wasser, and Martin Bloom. *Protective Services for Older People: Progress Report for 1966–67*. Cleveland, Ohio: The Benjamin Rose Institute, 1967.

Bultena, Gordon L. "Structural Effects on the Morale of the Aged: A Comparison of Age-Segregated and Age-Integrated Communities." In J. F. Gubrium (ed.), *Late Life: Communities and Environmental Policy*. Springfield, Ill.: Charles C. Thomas, 1974, pp. 18–31.

———, and Vivian Wood. "The American Retirement Community: Bane or Blessing?" *Journal of Gerontology 24* (1969):209–217.

Carp, Frances M. "Retired People as Automobile Passengers." *Gerontologist 12* (1972):66–72.

De Crow, Roger. *New Learning for Older Americans: An Overview of National Effort*. Washington, D.C.: Adult Education Association, 1975.

Gubrium, Jaber F. "Victimization in Old Age: Available Evidence and Three Hypotheses." *Crime & Delinquency (July 1974)*:245–250.

Hall, Gertrude H., and Geneva Mathiasen (eds.). *Guide to Development of Protective Services for Older People*. Springfield, Ill.: Charles C. Thomas, 1973.

Hochschild, A. R. *The Unexpected Community*. Englewood Cliffs, N.J.: Prentice-Hall, 1973.

Johnson, S. K. *Idle Haven: Community Building Among the Working-Class Retired*. Berkeley, Calif.: University of California Press, 1971.

Korim, A. S. *Older Americans and Community Colleges: A Guide for Program Implementation*. Washington, D.C.: American Association of Community and Junior Colleges, 1974.

Lawton, M. Powell, and T. Byerts (eds.). *Community Planning for the Elderly*. Washington, D.C.: Gerontological Society, 1973.

Lopata, Helena A. "Support Systems of Elderly Urbanites: Chicago of the 1970's." *Gerontologist 15* (1975):35–41.

Lozier, J., and R. Althouse. "Special Enforcement of Behavior Toward Elders in an Appalachian Mountain Settlement." *Gerontologist 14* (1974):69–80.

Stephens, J. "Society of the Alone: Freedom, Privacy, and Utilitarianism as Dominant Norms in the SRO." *Journal of Gerontology 30* (1975):230–235.

Taietz, Philip. "Community Facilities and Social Services." In Robert C. Atchley (ed.), *Environments and the Rural Aged*. Washington, D.C.: The Gerontological Society, 1975, pp. 145–156.

Terris, Bruce J. *Legal Services for the Elderly*. Washington, D.C.: National Council on the Aging, 1972.

# 17

# Moorings in the Community: Religion and Voluntary Associations

For most older Americans, religion and voluntary associations are their most salient ties to the overall community. Hence, it is important for us to explore these two dimensions of community involvement in depth.

## RELIGION

Religion is as diverse as the population, and an individual's relation to it is as complex and dynamic as himself or herself. Consider the following list of topics:

- ☐ Religious identification
- ☐ Church attendance
- ☐ Religious associations
- ☐ Personal religious observances
- ☐ Participation in religious ritual
- ☐ Religious faith
- ☐ Religious "experience"
- ☐ Religious beliefs
- ☐ Personal importance of religion
- ☐ Religious morality

All these aspects of religious experience and activity can change as the individual grows older.

One of the things that makes religion an interesting and also frustrating area for study is the diversity of meanings that attach to the term. What does it mean to say that a person is "religious"? What do we mean when we talk about a religious faith?

Attempting to answer these questions is frustrating partly because many variables prevent religion from being a unified institution. For one thing, the range and variety of religious groups is considerable, all the way from the one-of-a-kind storefront church to the most stately denomination. Wide variety also exists even within or among congregations of the same denomination or sect. Within denominations, factions place differing emphases on various aspects of church doctrine. Religions also differ in terms of the amount of participation and interest demanded of their adherents, the degree of organization they possess, and the opportunities they offer for the individual to achieve his or her goals through the church. Consequently, we can make only limited, general statements about religion and aging. Caution should be used in drawing inferences from these generalizations.

Most people apparently identify with some religion. In a sample of 35,000 households, the U.S. Bureau of the Census found that in 1957 only 2 to 3 percent of those responding reported no religion. The older people in this sample were neither more nor less likely to report no religion. Proportionally, there are slightly more Protestants and slightly fewer Catholics among older people than among the general population, but the differences are very small and can be largely explained by changes in differential rates of immigration, fertility, and mortality (U.S. Bureau of the Census, 1958).

### Church

While most people identify with some religion, they do not necessarily attend church. About half of the general population attends church regularly (twice a month or more). Catholics are much more likely to attend regularly than Protestants or Jews, although this tendency is diminishing. A higher proportion of women than men attend frequently. Also, church attendance is positively related to income, education, and length of residence in the community. Age is thus only one among many factors that influence church attendance. Based on cross-sectional data, an analysis of age patterns in church attendance shows, in general, a steady increase from the late teens until it peaks in the late fifties to early sixties. After that, the curve shows a consistent but very slight decline, almost certainly the result of the increasing prevalence of ill health, disability, and transportation difficulties. The only significant trend appears to be the increase in percent never attending among older people. Only Jews do not show a discernible age pattern in church attendance. Orbach (1961) attempted to determine the influence of age on church attendance while holding other variables constant, and found no consistent age trends. Using retrospective accounts, Bahr (1970) found that older men tended to see their church attendance as having declined steadily since their early teens, regardless of social class. Wingrove and Alston (1971) analyzed cohort data for the period from 1939 to 1969 and found that each of the five white cohorts they studied showed a unique church attendance profile both in terms of absolute rates of attendance and in terms of variation in attendance by age. These researchers did, however, find some similarities among the various cohorts and at nearly all ages. All cohorts experienced their peak attendance during the 1950s, and all cohorts showed a decline in attendance after 1965, regardless of age. Wingrove and Alston concluded that effective research on church attendance and age must control at least for the effects of the general social climate, sex, and specific age cohort membership. Obviously, a good deal more work needs to be done before we will be in a good position to describe what the relationship between age and church attendance *is*, much less explain it. For example, some people increase their church attendance as they grow older; therefore, probably a larger proportion of people reduce their attendance than would appear from the composite data alone. At this point, we simply do not have enough longitudinal data to be able to tell what impact this factor has on overall attendance figures.

In their study of older people in San Francisco, Clark and Anderson (1967) found that only a minority of their subjects attended church services even as often as once a month. Interestingly, they found that "frequent church attendance is more characteristic of the mentally ill than of the mentally healthy subjects, in spite of the fact that more of the latter attend on special occasions from time to time" (1968:329). Of course, this finding does not mean that most older people who attend church are mentally ill; it simply means that the *proportion* who regularly attend church was significantly higher among mentally ill older people than among other older people in the sample studied by Clark and Anderson. Clark and Anderson's findings also may be somewhat confounded by the fact that their sample came from California, where people of all ages attend church less frequently than in other regions of the United States.

Their analysis is particularly enlightening in terms of the factors they discovered that tended to discourage church attendance. Most of the nonchurchgoers were people who had never developed an association with a church or had had some sort of antagonistic experience with church organizations early in life, usually in adolescence. For some, the demands of religious doctrine were too difficult to reconcile with the events of their lives. Still others based their antagonism on hostility toward a particular minister.

Clark and Anderson found two basic reasons why mentally ill older people were more preoccupied with religion. First, mentally ill people are anxious and fearful. They seek strength wherever they can—and sometimes they find it in religion. Second, mentally ill people can become obsessed with just about anything, including religion. The mentally ill people sought emotional support from religion, while the normal controls gave it more social value. Another factor is feelings about immortality and death. Compared with the controls, the mentally ill older people had less tolerance for ambiguity concerning death. They needed to *know* what was going to happen. The controls seemed more able to accept death as an inevitable fact of life. As one said: "Death? Well, darling, I know from nothing about death. But one thing I'm sure of— I'll look back on it as an experience" (1967:342).

## Religious Observances

The declines in church attendance, where they occur, are probably at least partially offset by increases in regular listening to church services and other religious broadcasts on radio and television and in Bible reading. In terms of personal observances, older people are more likely to read the Bible at home, to react favorably to the idea of religious meditation, to pray in private, and to describe Sunday as a day for religious observance rather than for relaxation. In one study, the aspects of religious involvement were identified as (1) *knowledge* of the Bible; (2) *activism*, including church attendance, financial support, organizational participation, and leadership; (3) *creed* or adherence to doctrine, and (4) *devotional observance*, including personal prayer and private ritual. The percent of people who were religiously oriented on each of these dimensions was then measured and classified by age of the respondent. All dimensions except the devotional showed a decline in the 70-or-over age group, but on this dimension there was a sizable increase over the group in their sixties. Devotional observance apparently does not become very important until the fifties, whereas the other dimensions of religious orientation reach peak levels much sooner (Fukuyama, 1961). It may also be that some fairly sizable changes have taken place in the devotional practices of later generations. As with so many other questions, reliance on cross-sectional data leaves us at a loss.

## Religious Beliefs

Although they are not very likely to participate in adult education generally, older people are more likely to study religion than most other subjects when they do decide to become students. It is for this reason that Maves (1960) emphasizes the importance of religious instruction in the formulation of church programs for older people. This preference indicates an interest on the part of older people in religious knowledge. On the other hand, the few studies that have been done are unclear as to the effect of age on religious knowledge. This area is greatly in need of research.

Regarding religious beliefs, there is some evidence that

> Belief in life after death may increase with age; at least a higher proportion of old people than of younger generations believe that there is a life after death. Older people also are more certain that there is a God and apparently are more inclined to hold to traditional and conservative beliefs of their religion (Moberg, 1965c:80).

But again we cannot tell whether the apparent differences are caused by age or by the fact that the early childhood experiences with religion took place in different historical eras for the different cohorts.

Older people are more likely to feel that religion is important to them than are their younger counterparts. This likelihood is indicated by the larger proportions of older people who say that religion is very important in their lives, that religion is important to them aside from church attendance, that they are religious, and that they have a strong interest in religion (Riley and Foner, 1968:495). In terms of life cycle changes, there is a wide variety of individual patterns. Some feel that the usefulness of religion declines, but more think that it increases. The saliency of religion to the individual's self-image seems to increase with age, as does the stability of self-image.

As age increases, the tendency to identify oneself as a religious person increases, and indecision about this aspect of the self declines (Moberg, 1965c).

## Results

Religion also tends to be related to life satisfaction. Compared with older people in general, those who are church members, who read the Bible or attend church frequently, who are church leaders rather than followers, or who frequently listen to religious broadcasts are more likely to be well adjusted in their old age (Riley and Foner, 1968:496). At this point, however, we cannot tell whether religious involvement aids adjustment or whether it is adjustment that leads to religious involvement. It would be possible to find out, but such research has not yet been done.

Contrary to popular belief, interest and participation in religious activities does not appear to protect people from loneliness or fear of death, nor do lonely people tend to turn to religion (O'Reilly, 1958). Only the most conservative of religious people show serenity and a decreasing fear of death (Moberg, 1965c). Kalish (1976) reports that older true believers (whether religious or atheist) have fewer death fears compared to older people who are uncertain. On other personal dimensions, such as self-esteem, identity, attitudes, values, beliefs, and norms, religion appears to increase in importance with age. Again, however, we do not know if this increase is a change with age or simply an intergenerational difference.

From what we have seen so far, it should be clear that a great many gaps still exist in our knowledge about the place of religion in the lives of older people. One reason is that research in this area has a very low priority. Rightly or wrongly, depending on one's point of view, the federal government has tended to avoid any connection with questions concerning religion and aging. Therefore, we cannot expect to see many of these gaps filled for some time.

## How the Church Deals with Older Adults

What about older people's place in the church? For one thing, Jewish programs for older people have tended to be more responsible, imaginative, and creative than either Protestant or Catholic programs (Maves, 1960). Protestants sometimes tend to view misfortunes such as the physical or financial dependency that often befall older people as somehow related to moral turpitude or a lack of responsibility. This individualistic approach has been somewhat mitigated by the tendency for Protestant groups to found church-related old-age homes. However, these homes tend to be only distantly related to the church and to be open to persons of all faiths. Therefore, the church membership usually considers them philanthropy rather than a support service for "their own." Catholics were forced to develop their own institutions by a strong sense of responsibility for members of the faith, and by the difficulty of providing the required religious care within public quasi-Protestant institutions. They have also developed a considerable array of health services open to older people of all faiths. The assimilation of Catholics into the mainstream of American life has meant less need for separate institutions, but those that already exist will probably continue to operate.

In all three major religious traditions in American life, there is a basic conflict between principles of individual responsibility ("I am not my brother's keeper"), respect for elders, and charity toward the unfortunate. Thus far, individual responsibility has won out in the form of a spotty record of support for social welfare legislation for the aged. Currently, however, some churches are becoming more vocal lobbyists for better programs for older Americans. It is probably safe to say that "progressive" and "conservative" congregations can be found at all levels of religious life in America, but that organized religion shows a trend toward increased respect for the needs of older people.

On the local level, most ministers, priests, or rabbis assume that worship services are as available to older people as they are to others. It is usually through contacts with shut-ins, hospitalized older people, and older people in nursing homes that local congregation pastors first confront the problems of older members of the congregation. Only gradually do they come to recognize that many of their ambulatory older members also have problems. Moreover, church leaders are not impervious to the irrational, and sometimes unconscious, fears of aging, felt by society as a whole, that so often lead to unjust discrimination against older people, in and out of church.

Older people can come to feel neglected by churches in a number of ways. Moberg (1972) notes that many churches tend to emphasize programs for adolescents and young families, lack outreach programs for older people, and tend to push older people out of positions of responsibility within the church. These tendencies are important mechanisms that encourage older adults to disengage from organized religion. In research on church attendance, for example, it would be useful to relate feelings of neglect by organized religion to church attendance by age. What many consider to be personal disengagement might turn out to be socially induced.

Some churches set up Golden Age clubs; others allow their facilities to be used by such groups. The churches are also becoming interested in housing programs, particularly retirement homes for middle-income older people. They are beginning to see housing programs as a legitimate service, and not merely as an act of charity. Since the proportion of older people in the average congregation is about the same as the proportion in the total population, it is not too surprising that the churches have begun to feel some pressure from their older members concerning housing problems.

At this point, however, church programs for older people are few and far between. While 80 percent of the Presbyterian churches, for example, report special social groups for older people (including age-segregated Sunday school classes), only two thirds report any type of educational program specifically for older people, and very few have employment, homemaker, or health services. Only about 13 percent have special budget items involving ministries to older people (Maves, 1960). There is some indication, however, that older black people participate in and receive more from their churches than do older whites (Kent, 1971a).

Thus, while it appears that most churches are quite willing to *passively accept* the participation of older people in church affairs, few are willing or able to *actively solicit* the participation of ill, handicapped, or isolated older people.

## VOLUNTARY ASSOCIATIONS

A voluntary association is a nonprofit group that develops around a collective desire to achieve some purpose or pursue some interest. It differs from other groups in that it is voluntary—the individual is not compelled by social pressure or necessity to join, but instead is free to weigh the advantages and disadvantages of group membership and to decide whether or not to join.

Many sociologists believe that voluntary associations have become as prevalent in American society as they are because they perform large-scale functions that were performed by the extended family in agrarian eras. No matter how we got that way, we are said to be the "joiningest" nation in the world. S. Cutler (1975b) found that nearly 60 percent of Americans surveyed belonged to at least one voluntary association excluding unions.

Using data from a number of recent nationwide surveys, Cutler (1975) found that when the effects of socioeconomic differences on participation are controlled, age bears little relationship to voluntary association participation in middle age or later life. He found that young adults have low membership levels, middle-aged people have higher levels, and older people are either at the middle-age level or still higher. Cutler also suggests that we look for a slight decrease in participation associated with entry into the labor force of women between 45 to 54 years old. There may also be a slight decrease associated with retirement for men, but Cutler feels that this decrease may be only temporary.

Maximum involvement in voluntary associations apparently is related to stable residence in, and involvement with a community over a number of years. Once established, the pattern of participation tends to remain stable unless influenced by situational changes such as residential mobility, widowhood, retirement, or declines in health or financial resources. The main exceptions occur in organizations such as Jaycees or Junior Leagues, where one is expected with experience to "outgrow" the organization.

Changes such as residential mobility, retirement, or widowhood have no predictable, consistent impact on participation in voluntary associations. For example, retirement has been found to increase, decrease, or produce no change in participation, depending on the situation (Cottrell and Atchley, 1969). However, poor health or dwindling financial resources—factors that are particularly prevalent among the working class—have a more predictable dampening effect on participation. The impact of declining health is direct and obvious. Eroded financial resources have a subtler impact. Because voluntary associations are almost always nonprofit, they must be subsidized, usually by member contributions. Also, the older person on a fixed income often finds himself or herself limited by finances in terms of the frequency he or she can afford to participate. Both Taietz and Larson (1955) and Bahr (1970) found that upper-class people were less likely than others to show age differences in voluntary association participation.

For those who do continue to participate, voluntary associations take up a great deal of time. Yet for many there is a decline with age in the satisfaction they report from participation as they see groups "letting in a different sort of people" or "having changed so much." Others are self-conscious of their age and would rather "leave it to the youngsters." Still others have done every job in the organization two or three times and see little opportunity for continued growth in further participation. Thus, voluntary associations often subtly "squeeze out" older members in many of the same ways that churches do.

Transportation is an important factor influencing the participation of older people in voluntary associations, particularly in small towns and rural areas that lack public transportation. Cutler (1974) found that older people who did not drive or who did not have a car had much lower levels of participation than did those who had access to a car. He also found that this effect increased with distance between residence and meeting sites, particularly with respect to frequency of attendance at meetings. Health certainly influences participation, for it determines both the energy available and the individual's ability to get around. Another factor that reduces participation is fear of going out at night.

Participation in voluntary associations is often assumed to have a positive influence on the personal adjustment of older people, and past research tended to support this assumption. However, recent work by S. Cutler (1973) and by Edwards and Klemmack (1973) has shown that when the effects of important other variables such as health and socioeconomic status are taken into account, the impact of voluntary association participation on the personal adjustment of older people is negligible.

Earlier we found that senior centers and special clubs for older people suffer from the dual handicap of serving a group with no money, and of often forcing older people to disrupt the continuity of their leisure styles if they are to participate. Under these conditions we should not be surprised that Golden Age clubs do not serve a large proportion of the older population. Such organizations are infinitely more viable in cases where the members have good retirement incomes, and where members carry over former work associations to provide the necessary continuity.

When we see in what types of organizations older people continue to participate, the continuity theory of aging takes on added credence. In the civic or service area, where participation is often linked to the occupational role, older people show a substantial decline in participation. In lodges, fraternal and patriotic organizations, and church organizations, there are no consistent declines in participation with increasing age. This finding indicates a great deal of continuity in group participation in *leisure*-oriented voluntary associations.

Religious groups (organized groups as opposed to congregations) are the most common voluntary associations for older people. Membership in these associations tends to be higher in the older cohorts, especially after 75. Leadership positions in these associations also tend to be concentrated among older people. Participation in religious organizations declines among older people at a much slower rate than participation in other types of organizations. In addition to church groups and fraternal organizations, older people also participate in union organizations. The United Auto Workers Union, for example, has set up centers open to all older people in order to provide a meeting place for retired members. Other unions have similar facilities, and many have local union halls that also serve as meeting places for retired union members and other older people.

At the national level, voluntary associations, such as the American Association of Retired Persons, offer "at large membership," send out monthly magazines, and often offer group activities at various localities. However, unless the association has an active local chapter, it does not function as a genuine association. Such organizations do, however, play an important political role at the national level (see Chapter 15).

Voluntary associations could perform many necessary functions for most older people—if they participated. To begin with, the association often enables its members to obtain certain services, such as credit, with a minimum of red tape. Voluntary associations also serve as a source of social contacts and of personal identification. They also serve as a means of keeping a routine in the individual's life-style, which is important for some people. Perhaps most important, associations give the individual a means of staying in the flow of things, of feeling worthwhile. For the community, voluntary associations often perform useful services without pay. For all of these reasons it is very fortunate that many older people can continue to be participating members of voluntary associations.[1]

## SUMMARY

Religion can mean various things to a person. It can represent either a personal resource, a group resource, or both. As they grow older, people in the United States seem to decrease their use of religion as a source of group support but to increase their use of religious faith and beliefs as a source of support from within themselves. At least part of the apparent decline with age in church attendance is probably caused by unconscious neglect of older people by many congregations.

Participation in voluntary associations is frequently mentioned as an option for older people seeking new roles. However, there is no consistent evidence that older people are taking this option in great numbers. In fact, health and financial problems consistently erode *ability* to participate in voluntary associations.

Older people appear to be motivated toward continued involvement, and when their situations allow, they can and do continue their involvement with churches and voluntary associations, provided the involvement begins in middle age. Age discrimination within churches and mixed-age voluntary associations often makes it difficult to begin involvement from scratch in later life.

---

[1]Some of these benefits of voluntary association membership go to all members, but most are reserved for participating members. For a humanistic portrait of what participation can mean to the older person, see Ailor (1969). For a cross-national picture of the place of voluntary associations in the lives of older people, see Havighurst (1960).

Once again, we are confronted with institutions that have much to offer older people, but that are not particularly oriented toward doing so. Religion and voluntary associations may occupy a big spot in the hearts of many older people, but unfortunately, these institutions less often reciprocate.

## SUGGESTIONS FOR FURTHER READING

Ailor, James W. "The Church Provides for the Elderly." In Rosamonde R. Boyd and C. G. Oakes (eds.), *Foundations of Practical Gerontology*. Columbia, S.C.: University of South Carolina Press, 1969, pp. 191–206.

Gray, Robert M., and David O. Moberg. *The Church and the Older Person*. Grand Rapids, Mich.: W. B. Eerdmans, 1962.

Havighurst, Robert J. "Life Beyond the Family and Work." In E. W. Burgess (ed.), *Aging in Western Societies*. Chicago: University of Chicago Press, 1960, pp. 299–353.

Maves, Paul G. "Aging, Religion and the Church." In Clark Tibbitts (ed.), *Handbook of Social Gerontology*. Chicago: University of Chicago Press, 1960, pp. 698–749.

Moberg, David O. "The Integration of Older Members in the Church Congregation." In Arnold M. Rose and Warren A. Peterson (eds.), *Older People and Their Social World*. Philadelphia: F. A. Davis, 1965, pp. 125–140.

———. "Religiosity in Old Age." *Gerontologist* 5 (1965):78–87.

———, and Marvin J. Taves. "Church Participation and Adjustment in Old Age." In Arnold M. Rose and Warren A. Peterson (eds.), *Older People and Their Social World*. Philadelphia: F. A. Davis, 1965, pp. 113–124.

Rose, Arnold M. "The Impact of Aging in Voluntary Associations." In Clark Tibbitts (ed.), *Handbook of Social Gerontology*. Chicago: University of Chicago Press, 1960, pp. 666–697.

Wilensky, Harold. "Life Cycle, Work Situation and Participation in Formal Associations." In Robert W. Kleemeier (ed.), *Aging and Leisure*. New York: Oxford University Press, 1961, pp. 213–242.

# 18

# Primary Relationships: Family, Friends, and Neighbors

Interpersonal relationships vary considerably in terms of the degree of intimacy involved. Highly intimate relationships are called *primary*, and relationships involving little intimacy are called *secondary*.

Most of the social relationships considered up until now have been secondary. As MacIver and Page (1949:221) put it:

> The relations within which people confront one another in such specialized group roles as buyers and sellers, voters and candidates, officials and citizens, teachers and students, practitioners and clients, are *secondary*, involving categoric or "rational" attitudes.

Secondary group contacts are rational in the sense that they do not involve emotional intimacy or sentiment and therefore are relatively impersonal. A great many of older people's relationships in politics, government, the community, the church, and the economy are of this type.

At the other end of the continuum is the primary relationship, one that is intimate, durable, and personal. Primary relationships are usually limited to certain types of social situations. A group is apt to develop primary relationships if the members are in frequent and enduring interaction, if they are close to each other in space, if the group membership remains small, if there is basic equality among the members, and if the membership remains relatively stable. Each of these preconditions limits the extent to which any given group could develop primary relationships, and cases in which such relationships develop without these preconditions are rare.

Primary relations are not unheard of in institutions such as politics, government, or the economy. In fact, they are quite common. The essential point is that although the close working relationship between coworkers may produce a primary relationship, the nature of the *essential* relationships in the economy does not *require* a primary bond, but only requires a secondary one.

Few institutions in American society are oriented primarily toward the development and nurturance of primary relations. The most obvious is the family, which meets all of the preconditions for primary group formation.

The family is perhaps the most basic of social institutions. Almost everyone is born into a family. Most people spend most of their lives residing in a family group. Most people play several family roles—for example, son, husband, father, grandfather, uncle—in the course of a lifetime. For many people, the family group is the center of their world, the highest priority in their system of values. Troll (1971) estimates that no more than 6 percent of the older population are without family.

There are a great many different types of family organizations throughout the world. We will concentrate on the American pattern. The family has a life cycle just as people do. It begins with marriage, the formation of a couple from two previously unrelated people. There are many ways that families may develop. Some develop intact, others split, and still others represent a uniting of parts from split families. What family sociologists call the *family life cycle* is an ideal type, an ideal representation of the stages in the life of a couple that marries, has children, and stays together until one spouse dies in old age.

Conceptions of the family life cycle vary from simple (Glick and Parke, 1965: Duvall, 1971; Rollins and Feldman, 1970) to complex (Hill and Rodgers, 1964). A relatively simple scheme is sufficient to illustrate the concept:[1]

1. Beginning families (couples married 0 to 10 years without children)
2. Early childbearing (oldest child under 3)
3. Families with preschool children (oldest child over 3 but under 6)
4. Families with schoolage children (oldest child over 5 and under 13)
5. Families with teenagers (oldest child over 12 and living at home)
6. Families as launching centers (oldest child gone to youngest's leaving home)
7. Families of middle years (empty nest to retirement)
8. Families in retirement (one spouse retired to onset of disability)
9. Families in old age (one spouse disabled to death of one spouse)

Of course, since the children and grandchildren usually begin their own family cycles, the chain seldom stops. As we shall see, increasingly it is only the last three phases of family cycle that occur in later maturity of old age.

The family that produces these relationships (spouse, parent, grandparent, great grandparent, widow) is called the *family of procreation* because it is the family within which a person's own procreative behavior occurs.

People also belong to a *family of orientation*, usually the family they are born or adopted into. Older people very often carry into their later years the roles from this family (son, daughter, brother, sister) as well as from the family of procreation.

---

[1]The model presented here is adapted from Rollins and Feldman (1970).

There are also family roles such as cousin, uncle, nephew, brother-in-law, and so on, that derive from an *extended family*, the complex network of kin that parallels both the family of procreation and the family of orientation, usually through the sibling relationship or the marital bond uniting two separate families of orientation.

Kinship is an extremely complex subject. We will not emphasize extended kinship, but will concentrate on roles in the family of procreation and in the family of orientation as they relate to the effects of aging. We will start with marital status, since it is the most obvious criterion for distinguishing older people who are in families from those who are not.

## THE OLDER COUPLE

Most older people are married and live with their spouses in separate households. It is becoming unusual for people to live through the entire life cycle without marrying, and in 1970 fewer than one in ten older people had never married. Among older people, however, there are some important age differences in marital status.

**TABLE 18-1**
**Marital Status by Age: United States, 1970**

| Marital Status | Age 65–69 | Age 70–74 | Age 75–79 | Age 80–84 | Age 85+ | Total Age 65+ |
|---|---|---|---|---|---|---|
| Males | | | | | | |
| Married | 76.8% | 72.1% | 64.5% | 52.9% | 37.7% | 72.4% |
| Widowed | 8.8 | 13.8 | 21.2 | 32.0 | 43.4 | 17.1 |
| Divorced | 3.5 | 3.1 | 2.7 | 2.4 | 2.4 | 3.0 |
| Single | 7.1 | 7.3 | 7.3 | 7.6 | 10.8 | 7.5 |
| Females | | | | | | |
| Married | 49.1 | 37.4 | 25.4 | 14.8 | 8.5 | 36.4 |
| Widowed | 36.5 | 49.0 | 61.1 | 71.9 | 76.9 | 52.2 |
| Divorced | 4.1 | 3.3 | 2.7 | 2.1 | 1.7 | 3.2 |
| Single | 7.4 | 7.8 | 8.4 | 8.8 | 10.7 | 8.1 |

*Source:* U.S. Bureau of the Census (1973c).

The proportion of single older people is about the same across the age categories. The proportion divorced shows a small but steady decline in cohorts at higher ages. This trend may be related to changes in the feelings of various generations about the acceptability of divorce, and may also reflect the higher death rate for divorced people. The major changes occur in the married and widowed categories. The proportion married is lower in each succeeding age group, but the drop starts sooner and is steeper for older women. At age 80 most men are married, while only 16 percent of women are. This trend reflects the fact that men tend to marry women younger than themselves, and also the fact that women currently live an average of 6 years longer than men.

Thus, couples are very prevalent among older people. Marriage tends to be the focal point in the lives of most older people who have a living spouse, especially when the departure of the children and retirement have limited other sources of primary relationships. As the average life expectancy increases and the age of childbearing decreases, the average number of years a couple lives together after the children leave home increases greatly. One consequence has been a greater sharing of activities between spouses. Sussman (1955) found that if the children had *all* left, the older couple was much more likely to do things together than if one or more children were still living at home.

What happens to marital satisfaction as the length of time married increases is still an open question. Cross-sectional studies of marital satisfaction that have included older respondents have tended to show a curvilinear pattern with marital satisfaction high among those recently married, somewhat lower among those in the child-rearing period, and higher again among those in the later stages of the family cycle (Rollins and Feldman, 1970; Gurin et al., 1960; Rollins and Cannon, 1974; Stinnett et al., 1972; Burr, 1970; Orthner, 1975). There are two reasons for caution in accepting these results as indicative of change over time, however. Some measures of marital satisfaction do not produce a curvilinear pattern (Rollins and Feldman, 1970). In addition, longitudinal data are necessary in order to rule out the possibility that the higher prevalence of happy marriages in later life is simply a result of attrition due to divorce among the unhappy marriages.

For the happily married older couple, marriage is a blessing. It is a source of great comfort and support as well as the focal point of everyday life, and happily married couples often experience an increasing closeness as the years go by. In addition, there is often a high degree of interdependence in these couples, particularly in terms of caring for each other in times of illness. The older husbands in this happily married category are particularly likely to view their wives as indispensable pillars of strength. For people in these happy marriages, widowhood is a dismal prospect indeed.

One key finding about these happy marriages is that they tend to be characterized by a much greater equality between the partners than is true of unhappy older couples. This equality is brought about especially by a gradual loss of boundaries between the sex roles and a decreasing sexual definition of the household division of labor (Clark and Anderson, 1967:237–41).

While most older couples fit more or less into the happy category, a few are filled with hostility. Some older people feel that their spouses are the cause of all their troubles, and they often wish that they could somehow terminate their marriages. Religious orthodoxy, such as the strong Catholic policy against divorce, has no doubt kept couples together who otherwise would have separated. The same could be said of social pressure in the community: The stigma of divorce has kept people together for years under a more or less armed truce. Many of these unhappy older people simply cannot cope with the increased demands that illness generates for the old (Clark and Anderson, 1967:237–41). Every year, nearly 10,000 older Americans are divorced.

One of the key elements in the married couple's adjustment to aging is the issue of retirement. Apparently, older couples in the various social classes differ widely in their response to retirement. Table 18-2 summarizes these differences. Men retired more than 5 years seemed to be slightly less favorable toward the retirement experience than those retired less than 5 years, and wives were apparently less involved and less affected by their husbands' retirement process than the husbands themselves were (Kerckhoff, 1964:516).

**TABLE 18-2**
**Pre- and Post-retirement**
**Experience of Married Couples**
**Concerning Retirement Experience**

| Occupational Status | Pre-retirement Attitude | Post-retirement Experience |
|---|---|---|
| Upper | Negative | Positive |
| Middle | Positive | Less positive |
| Lower | Passive | Negative |

Retirement contributes to the egalitarian nature of the happy older couple by promoting the sharing of household tasks and by emphasizing the expressive aspects of marriage, such as giving love, affection, and companionship. These trends also tend to reduce the differences between male and female roles, another characteristic of happy older marriages. The trend in successful older marriages thus appears to be moving away from social bonds based on the instrumental functions of marriage, such as providing money and status, to bonds based on a common identity that comes from sharing and cooperating in many of the same roles (Lipman, 1961).

No doubt all marriages have both instrumental and expressive aspects. Nevertheless, most marriages concentrate on one aspect or the other at any given point in time. Older couples who approach retirement life from a predominantly expressive perspective apparently have a better chance for a successful adjustment to retirement than those with an instrumental orientation. One study indicates that women who stress instrumental aspects such as housework rather than the expressive functions such as love or understanding have much lower morale than their counterparts (Lipman, 1962). Note that throughout this discussion we have emphasized the need not only of the individual but of the couple to adjust to retirement.

Not all older couples have to make the transition into retirement, however, since some of them are not formed until the partners are already retired. In 1970, over 45,000 older Americans got married. About 5 percent of these were first-time marriages; the rest were remarriages (National Center for Health Statistics, 1974). Three quarters of those who remarried were widows and widowers and a quarter were divorced at the time of remarriage. The factors that affect marrying in later life are numerous, but two of the most important are income and the sex ratio. Older people generally must have enough money between them to support the marriage. This is a limiting factor, particularly for the lower-income men, who find it difficult to find a marriage partner unless they can bring what they see as a man's share of financial support to the union. The other factor is the overabundance of older women. Because older men are vastly outnumbered by women of their own age, and because men tend to marry women younger than themselves, older men always have a much larger field of eligibles than older women. In 1970, older men marrying outnumbered the older women marrying two to one. There are about 75 men per hundred women in the age category 65 and over. In addition, only 29 percent of these men are unmarried as compared with 62 percent of the women. Thus, if everyone were matched evenly by age, more than half of the unmarried older women would still be left over. Of the 31,000 men 65 and over who married in 1970, 59 percent married women under 65 whereas only 15 percent of the 15,000 older women who married in 1970 married men under 65. The sexual imbalance in the prevalence of marriage in later life is dramatically reflected in the marriage rates: 15.6 per 1,000 per year for older men, and 2.4 per 1,000 per year for older women. These data help to explain the fact that no matter how much a happy marriage may ease the pain of adjustment to aging, this option simply will not be available to many older women.

In a study of 100 older couples who married in later maturity, McKain (1969) found that the desire for companionship was by far the most frequently given reason. Previous experience with marriage also predisposed older people to remarry. Few of the couples believed in romantic love, but they were interested in companionship, lasting affection, and regard. As McKain (1969:36) states,

> The role of sex in the lives of these older people extended far beyond love-making and coitus; a woman's gentle touch, the perfume on her hair, a word of endearment—all these and many more reminders that he is married help to satisfy a man's urge for the opposite sex. The same is true for the older wife.

A few older people remarried to allay their anxiety about poor health, and some remarried to avoid having to depend on their children.

Many older people tended to select mates who reminded them of a previous spouse. Also, older couples followed the same pattern of homogamy, the tendency for people of similar backgrounds to marry, that is found among younger couples.

Using such unobtrusive measures as displays of affection, respect and consideration, obvious enjoyment of each other's company, lack of complaints about each other, and pride in their marriage as indicators of successful marriage, McKain found that successful "retirement marriage" was related to several factors. Couples who had known each other well over a period of years before their marriage were likely to be successfully married. A surprisingly large number of couples McKain studied were related to each other through previous marriages. Probably the prime reason that long friendship was so strongly related to successful marriage in later life is that intimate knowledge of the other allowed better matching of interests and favorite activities. Marriages in which interests were not alike were less successful.

Approval of the marriage by children and friends is also important for the success of marriage in later life. Apparently, considerable social pressure is exerted against marriage in later life, probably growing partly out of a misguided notion that older people do not *need* to be married and partly out of concern over what will happen to their estates. Older people are very sensitive to this pressure, and encouragement from children and from friends is important in overcoming it. Also, a marriage that alienates older people from their families or friends is not likely to be successful.

People who experienced difficulty in adjusting to the reduced life space of the older person also had a difficult time adjusting to marriage in later life. An element of adaptability involved in adjustment to life changes in general apparently influences the ability to adjust to marriage in later life in particular. And unless both the bride and the groom were reasonably well-adjusted individuals, marriage in later life was not likely to be successful.

Financial factors were also related to successful marriage in later life. If both partners owned homes, success was more likely than if one or neither did. The importance of dual home ownership was probably symbolic, indicating that each partner brought something equally concrete to the marriage. If both partners had a sufficient income prior to marriage, they usually had a successful marriage. The arrangements for pooling property or giving it to children were important for predicting success of the marriage because they indicated the priority one partner held in the eyes of the other. It was important for the marriage partner to have first priority on resources, if the marriage was to be successful.

## WIDOWS AND WIDOWERS

Widowhood was discussed in detail in an earlier chapter. By age 70 a majority of older women are widows, but a majority of men are not widowers until after age 85. As we said earlier, this trend results from lower female mortality rates and the tendency for men to marry women younger than themselves. Most women have to adjust to widowhood sooner or later, but the trend is for widowhood to come increasingly later.

One objective consequence of widowhood appears to be a higher mortality rate. Suicide rates are also higher for widowed older people than for those who are still married. Divorced older people have the highest mortality and suicide rates, however.

Although most people are able to cope with widowhood, studies show that older widows and widowers are preoccupied with grief, show a greater tendency toward worry and unhappiness, and fear death more than those whose spouses are still with them. Morale appears to be particularly low among those widowed within the last 10 years (Gurin et al., 1960; Kutner, 1956). Widowhood is less traumatic for older people than it is for younger people because older widows have more widowed friends available to them (Troll, 1971; Blau, 1961).

Most older couples are not entirely unprepared for widowhood, because most of them have thought about the possibility of losing their spouses. These thoughts usually take the form of anxiety, and are often ambivalent. Many people genuinely do not care to survive their partners, but on the other hand, someone must go first and someone must be left a widow or widower.

The most common response to widowhood is to try to keep occupied, but often circumstances make this response difficult. For one thing, widowhood often comes at the end of a spouse's long, financially and physically taxing illness. The physical and financial resources available to keep "in the swing of things" are thus reduced.

Many widows seek a male companion in widowhood in order to feel needed by someone and to have someone to escort them to the places they want to go. More common, however, is the pattern in which a group of widows gets together to provide each other with companionship and someone to go places with.

Widowhood affects all family relationships. Shortly after the death of the spouse there is usually a flurry of support from family members, but this support is not very enduring. Within a few weeks, widowed persons usually find themselves on their own. Most widowed people live alone, and their major resource in coping with loneliness comes most often from friends rather than family.

Widowed parents must adjust to a new relationship with their children. Widows can usually grow closer to their daughters, but not very often to their sons (Lopata, 1973). There is no clear picture of how widowed fathers' relations with their children are altered, although we can be reasonably sure that they are altered.

Because of their lifetime commitment to marriage, most widowed people find that they have neglected their relationships with extended kin. As a result, extended kin often play only a minimal role in the lives of older widows and widowers.

## NEVER-MARRIED OLDER PEOPLE

In 1970, 8 percent of the older people in the United States had never married. On the surface, one would expect that as these people reach old age, they would have trouble getting along as single individuals living in an independent household. Clark and Anderson (1967:256) found, however, that apparently because they learn very early in life to cope with loneliness and the need to look after themselves, older single people living alone have developed the autonomy and self-reliance so often required of older people. In addition, the "loners" among single people living alone are often spared the grief that comes from watching one's friends and relatives die. Thus, while it is possible to argue that people who never marry and perhaps live solitary existences are missing a lot of the "good" parts of life, they also apparently miss some of the "bad" too (Gubrium, 1975).

Gubrium (1975) found that never-married older people tended to be lifelong isolates who were not especially lonely in old age. He suggests that isolation is viewed by these people as normal. They resent the assumption often presented to them by researchers that relative isolation is necessarily bad and leads to loneliness. This point is a good one for researchers to bear in mind.

Most men stay unmarried because they want personal freedom from involvement. The bachelor appears to be motivated by an intense desire to escape the kind of involvement present in his family of orientation. The never-married older woman, on the other hand, often appears to be motivated by her desire to stay close to her family of orientation and by her choice of career (this latter factor is becoming less important because today there are very few careers that require one to remain unmarried).

Older people who have never married might be expected to have more contacts with extended kin than those who married. However, Atchley, Pignatiello, and Shaw (1975) found that this contact depends a great deal on social class, at least for women. Never-married older women teachers interacted with extended kin significantly more than those who were married. But older telephone operators who had never married had much lower levels of interaction with extended family than did those who were married. In their total interaction patterns, teachers appeared to compensate for being single by a disproportionate involvement with relatives while telephone operators tended to compensate by having relatively more contacts with friends. Single older women teachers had about the same overall level of interaction as married older women teachers, but among older telephone operators, the overall interaction levels of single women were much lower than those of the married women.

## DIVORCED OLDER PEOPLE

In 1970, about 3 percent of the older population was divorced, and about 10,000 older Americans get divorces each year. Yet there has been very little research on the impact of divorce on older persons or on the impact that being divorced may have on an older person's life. For example, many women who are divorced are effectively deprived of income in later life. In many cases, they are not entitled to Social Security nor are they eligible for private pension benefits. If they are not entitled to retirement benefits in their own right, they are forced into financial dependency. In addition, divorce of older parents can be expected to have an impact on relations with adult children and other kin. This topic is one of the most neglected areas of research in social gerontology.

## TRENDS IN MARITAL STATUS

Even with recent declines in marriage rates, more people get married today than got married 50 years ago. If this trend continues, the percentage of older people who are married should continue to increase throughout the century. The increase in average length of life for the general population should result in a larger proportion of couples surviving into later maturity. This trend would also result in an increase in the proportion married. The widening differential in average length of life between men and women will tend to increase the proportion of widows among those over 70.

The overall impact of these trends should be to substantially increase the percent married between ages 65 to 75 during the next 20 years. But at the same time the percent widowed at age 75 or over should also increase during this same period.

## SEXUALITY IN OLDER PEOPLE

Earlier, we noted that older people who have some degree of continuity in their sex lives continue to enjoy sexual relationships throughout the entire life span. Sexual ability does appear to deteriorate in old age (late seventies to early eighties), particularly among the men. But evidence indicates that part of this problem is psychological rather than physical.

Sex is an integral part of the couple's relationship. In American society, the married couple is the only legitimate place where a sexual outlet is possible. In counseling older couples and older people in general, it is essential that the sexual component of human interaction be taken into account.

Masters and Johnson (1966) have done the most complete research on the sexual response of older people. For older females, they found that several major factors served to limit sexual response: (1) steroid starvation, which makes coitus painful; (2) lack of opportunity for a regular sexual outlet; (3) the lingering Victorian concept that women should have no innate interest in sexual activity; (4) physical infirmities of the desired partner; and (5) the fact that many women never learn to respond to sexual desire, and use menopause as an excuse for total abstinence. They also found, however, that with hormone therapy to eliminate the pain associated with coitus and with the uterine contractions that often accompany orgasm, there was no time limit drawn by the advancing years to female sexuality.

Among older men, there is little doubt that sexual performance wanes with age. Levels of sexual tension, ability to establish coital connection, ability to ejaculate, and masturbation or nocturnal emission all show declines as age increases. Yet for those older men who have established a high sexual output, by whatever means, in their middle years, there appears to be a much less significant decline.

Masters and Johnson tie the increase with age in sexual inadequacy to a number of factors, the least of which is physical. The Victorian myth that older men have no sexuality is identified by Masters and Johnson as being a major force leading to self-doubts and secondary impotence among older men. Research evidence indicates that a large proportion of the older men who suffer secondary impotence can be trained to overcome it by adequate counseling.

Masters and Johnson state that once a high sexual output is established in the middle years, it is usually possible to maintain it physically into the eighties, provided health is maintained. They go on to say that several factors reduce this possibility: (1) boredom with one's partner, (2) preoccupation with career or economic pursuits (this factor would affect only a tiny proportion of older men), (3) mental or physical fatigue, (4) overindulgence in food or drink, (5) physical and mental infirmities, and (6) fear of poor performance. They further state: "There is no way to overemphasize the importance that the factor 'fear of failure' plays in the aging male's withdrawal from sexual performance" (1966:269).

The available data indicate that wives very often lack insight into the "fear of failure" problem and as a result are very likely to feel personally rejected by their husbands' alienation from marital sexual activity. Thus, the older couple faces some serious sexual problems that do not usually confront younger couples. Very often the older couple is not aware of the exact nature of these problems. To solve them in a genuinely satisfactory fashion, the couple must understand what conditions are necessary to the maintenance of sexual functioning and what can be done to create these conditions.

## THE OLDER PARENT ROLE

The role of parent is without doubt one of the pivotal roles that Americans play in their middle years, and particularly for the housewife. Three out of four older people in the United States have at least one living child; and of those who have living children, four out of five have seen one of their children within the past week (Stehouwer, 1965:147). Over 60 percent reported seeing their child either that day or the day before. Most older people with children, then, play the older parent role quite frequently.

Even parents with adult children very far away manage to see their children on holidays and special occasions. Contacts with children seem to be maximized if the children live nearby and if there are only one or two children. Retirement seems, if anything, to increase contact with children (Stehouwer, 1965; Harris, 1965a).

As was true of the older married couple, there are significant differences in older-parent–adult-child relationships. Clark and Anderson found:

> A good relationship with children in old age depends, to large extent, on the graces and autonomy of the aged parent—in short, on his ability to manage gracefully by himself. It would appear that, in our culture, there simply cannot be any happy role reversals between the generations, neither an increasing dependency of parent upon child nor a continuing reliance of child upon parent. The mores do not sanction it and children and parents resent it. The parent must remain strong and independent. If his personal resources fail, the conflicts arise. The child, on the other hand, must not threaten the security of the parent with requests for monetary aid or other care when parental income has shrunk through retirement. The ideal situation is when both parent and child are functioning well. The parent does not depend on the child for nurturance or social interaction; these needs the parent can manage to fulfill by himself elsewhere. He does not limit the freedom of his child nor arouse the child's feelings of guilt. The child establishes an independent dwelling, sustains his own family, and achieves a measure of the hope the parent had entertained for him. Such an ideal situation, of course, is more likely to occur when the parent is still provided with a spouse and where a high socioeconomic status buttresses the parent and child (1967:275–76, reprinted by permission).

Most older parents, particularly the men, apparently dread the day when they may become dependent on their children. Part of this reluctance is based on the perceived differences in values between the generations. Differences in drinking practices, childbearing attitudes, manners and etiquette, and religious beliefs are all major obstacles to good communication between the generations. Another obstacle is the adult child's reluctance at times to accept advice from an older parent, often accompanied by a strong need on the part of the older parent to give advice. Finally, the strong paternalistic bent among foreign-born older parents sometimes produces difficulties in intergenerational relations.

Given all of these difficulties, one might expect to find a great deal of alienation among older parents, and this notion is indeed prevalent among those working with older people. Nevertheless, study after study has failed to support this view. As Blenkner (1965:48) says,

> The older person prefers to maintain his independence as long as he can, but . . . when he can no longer manage for himself, he expects his children to assume that responsibility; his children in turn expect to, and do, undertake it, particularly in terms of personal and protective services.

Sussman and Burchinal (1962a) found that illness of an older parent usually brought almost instantaneous response from children. Close ties with children are particularly prevalent among the very old. Shanas and her associates (1968) found that among older people with children, 98 percent of women and 72 percent of men who were over 80 either lived with a child or within 10 minutes travel time of one.

Perhaps the reasons for the myth are to be found in the attitudes of professional workers and childless older people. The childless older person is the one most likely to believe that children neglect their older parents, and while they may be very vocal about it, these childless people are in perhaps the worst position to judge the validity of this particular idea. The same criticism applies to the perceptions of professionals who work with older people. Their view of the situation is biased by the fact that, by definition, the older people they see are disproportionately alienated and neglected; otherwise there would be no occasion for them to seek professional help (Blenkner, 1965).

The evidence indicates that most parents understand and comply with the norms for older-parent–adult-child relationships (note that we do not refer here to simple parent-child relationships). The demands on the older parent are to recognize that the adult children have a right to lead their own lives, to not be too demanding and thus alienate oneself from one's adult children, and above all, to not interfere with their normal pursuits. At the same time, the adult child is expected to leave behind the rebellion and emancipation of adolescence and young adulthood, and to turn again to the parent, "no longer as a child, but as a mature adult with a new role and a different love, seeing him for the first time as an individual with his own rights, needs, limitations, and a life history that, to a large extent, made him the person he is long before his child existed" (Blenkner, 1965:58).

This type of relationship requires that both the older parent and the adult child be mature, secure persons, and it is for this reason that mental, physical, and financial resources on both sides improve the chances of developing a satisfactory relationship.

Before we leave this particular family role, it might be worthwhile to mention that a growing number of the children of older people are themselves older people. About one out of ten older people has a child who is over 65. In these cases, an even greater strain is usually put on both parties by the financial squeeze in which they find themselves and by the greater incidence of disabling illness among the very old.

## THE GRANDPARENT ROLE

Seventy percent of older people have living grandchildren, and about 5 percent of households headed by older people contain grandchildren. Yet the research evidence suggests that the grandparent role is not one that usually brings continuing interaction into the lives of the grandparents. If older people are separated from their children by the need for autonomy and independence, they are separated even farther from their grandchildren. Ideological differences between generations can become a chasm across three generations, and the strong peer orientation of adolescents in American society leaves little room in their lives for older people.

The satisfying period of grandparenthood is usually when the grandchildren are small, but with the trend toward early marriage and early parenthood, most people become grandparents in their mid or late forties. Few have very young grandchildren after age 65. Since teen-age grandchildren usually shy away from their grandparents, the grandparent role is basically an inactive one for most older people. As time goes on, the decline in marriage age since World War II should make this trend even more prevalent.

An interesting, but unanswered, question concerns whether grandparenting is more important or satisfying in the lives of widowed older people. Adams (1968a) found that widows more often than married mothers had patterns of mutual assistance with their daughters. It would not be surprising to learn that this increased involvement also brought increased saliency to the grandparent role.

Grandmothers appear to have a somewhat better chance of developing a relationship with their granddaughters than grandfathers have in developing one with their grandsons. The key to this trend is the relative stability of the housewife role in comparison with the occupational roles of men. It is simply a matter of the grandmothers' having more to offer their granddaughters that is pertinent to the lives they will lead. Sewing, cooking, and childbearing are but a few of the subjects that granddaughters often want to learn about. In contrast, the grandfathers very often find their skills to be unwanted, not only by industry but by their grandsons as well. As women's roles in society change, however, there is a good chance that the grandmothers' knowledge will be less pertinent to the aspirations of their granddaughters.

It also appears that visiting patterns are important in the middle and upper social classes in developing ties of affection between grandparents and grandchildren (Boyd, 1969b). Troll (1971) concludes that the "valued grandparent" is an achieved role that is based on the personal qualities of the grandparent and that it is not automatically ascribed to all grandparents.

## THE GREAT-GRANDPARENT ROLE

About 40 percent of the older people in the United States are great-grandparents, and this role, unlike the grandparent role, does involve older people with very young children. This relationship can create problems, because young children, particularly American children, are very active and are apt to irritate very old people with their impatience.

## RESEARCH ILLUSTRATION 10

## THE CHANGING AMERICAN GRANDPARENT[2]

Bernice L. Neugarten and Karol K. Weinstein

Noting that sociologists have tended to neglect grandparenthood as an aspect of the family life of older people, Neugarten and Weinstein sought to examine three dimensions of grandparenthood: the degree of comfort with the role (as expressed by the grandparent), the significance of the role as seen by the role player, and the style with which the role was enacted.

Through open-ended interviews with 70 sets of middle-class grandparents in the metropolitan Chicago area, Neugarten and Weinstein were able to secure data on how often and on what occasions the grandparents saw their grandchildren, and on the significance of grandparenthood in their lives and how it had affected them. Table 18-3 shows their results.

**TABLE 18-3**
**Ease of Role Performance, Significance of Role,**
**and Style of Grandparenting in 70 Pairs of Grandparents**

|  | Grandmothers (N = 70) | Grandfathers (N = 70) |
|---|---|---|
| Ease of role performance |  |  |
| Comfortable/pleasant | 59% | 61% |
| Difficulty/discomfort | 36 | 29 |
| Insufficient data | 5 | 10 |
| Significance of the grandparent role |  |  |
| Biological renewal and/or continuity | 42 | 23 |
| Emotional self-fulfillment | 19 | 27 |
| Resource person to child | 4 | 11 |
| Vicarious achievement through child | 4 | 4 |
| Remote; little effect on the self | 27 | 29 |
| Insufficient data | 4 | 6 |
| Style of grandparenting |  |  |
| Formal | 31 | 33 |
| Fun-seeking | 29 | 24 |
| Parent surrogate | 14 | 0 |
| Reservoir of family wisdom | 1 | 6 |
| Distant figure | 19 | 29 |
| Insufficient data | 6 | 8 |

*Source:* Neugarten and Weinstein (1964:202).

While a clear majority of the grandparents expressed comfort and pleasure in the role, nearly a third were uncomfortable enough to mention this discomfort to the interviewer. The sources of discomfort or disappointment included the strain associated with thinking of oneself as a grandparent, conflict with parents over the rearing of a grandchild, and self-chastisement about indifference toward taking care of or assuming responsibility for a grandchild.

While it was recognized that grandparenthood usually had multiple significance for grandparents, Neugarten and Weinstein nevertheless categorized all of the grandparents into one of five somewhat overlapping categories on the basis of their rating of the *primary* significance of

[2]Based on Neugarten and Weinstein (1964).

grandparenthood to the individual as expressed throughout the interview. As Table 18-3 shows, the prime significance of grandparenthood was in terms of biological renewal and/or continuity the grandparent sees himself or herself extended into the future. Neugarten and Weinstein caution that the difference between grandfathers and grandmothers in the significance of this factor may be because only one third of the grandparents studied were the parents of the young husband. They consider it likely that grandfathers are more inclined to trace their biological continuity through their sons than through their daughters. Neugarten and Weinstein could have explored this notion further by examining the percentages while holding sex of immediate offspring constant, but apparently they did not do so. For some, grandparenthood offers the opportunity to succeed in a new emotional role—to be a better grandparent than he or she was a parent.

The other large group comprised those who felt relatively remote from their grandchildren, and who acknowledged that grandparenthood had relatively little effect on their own lives. Most people in this category felt that this sentiment was unusual, and while a few expected that as their grandchildren grew older the relationship might develop more fully, most of them—men and women alike—perceived the role as basically empty of meaningful relationship.

As for *style* of grandparenting, Neugarten and Weinstein found that few of their respondents served primarily as reservoirs of family wisdom. Considering the rapidly changing nature of knowledge, this finding should not be surprising. And being a parent surrogate was apparently a style reserved for grandmothers, although few grandmothers served primarily as parent surrogates to their grandchildren.

The majority of grandparents exhibit a style that is either formal or distant. The formal style emphasizes the "proper" role of the grandparent. It leaves parental functions up to the parents, but there is constant interest in the grandchild. The "distant figure" style is similar except that contact is fleeting and infrequent—often reserved for holidays and special occasions such as Christmas or birthdays.

The fun-seeking style emphasizes informality and playfulness. Authority lines are considered irrelevant, and the emphasis is on making the relationship between grandparent and grandchild a mutually satisfying one. A quarter of the grandparents showed this style.

**TABLE 18-4**
**Age Differences in Styles of Grandparenting[a]**

|  | Under 65 (N = 81) | Over 65 (N = 81) |
|---|---|---|
| Formal | 31% | 59% |
| Fun-seeking | 37 | 21 |
| Distant figure | 32 | 21 |

[a]These age differences are significant at the .02 level.
*Source:* Adapted from Neugarten and Weinstein (1964).

Neugarten and Weinstein were also interested in the impact of age on the style of grandparenting. Table 18-4 shows that grandparents were more likely to be under 65, and that those who were under 65 were much more likely to adopt a fun-seeking or distant figure style; whereas better than half of those over 65 had adopted a formal style. They conclude that this pattern may be the result of the socialization processes in different eras (secular trends) or simply the influence of age on the role itself. Neugarten and Weinstein conclude that grandparenthood as a role is perhaps more salient in middle age than in later maturity or old age, particularly in terms of the assumption of new roles or adult socialization. Perhaps more importantly, Neugarten and Weinstein conclude that the younger grandparents are much less concerned with a style that revolves around an authority relation than are their older counterparts.

While there are many four-generation families, little attention has been paid to this phenomenon by gerontologists. We know something about mutual aid patterns in multigenerational families, but we know very little about the psychological and sociological consequences of having a four-generation family, particularly in terms of intergenerational relationships, although Bekker and Taylor (1966) found that young people with living grandparents and great-grandparents tended to be less prejudiced than others against older people.

## THE SIBLING ROLE

About 80 percent of older people have living brothers and/or sisters. Clark and Anderson (1967:294) found that the most common kinship role among their sample of older people was that of sibling.

With the advent of old age, many older people seek to pick up old family loyalties and renew old relationships. More effort is made to visit siblings, even at great distance, in old age than in middle age, and the narrower the older person's social world, the more likely he or she is spontaneously to mention a sibling as a source of aid in time of trouble or need. Next to adult children, siblings are the best prospects for providing older people with a permanent home. Except in those cases that involve long-term family feuds, siblings offer a logical source of primary relationships, particularly for older people whose primary bonds have been reduced by the death of a spouse of the marriages of children. Shanas and her associates (1968:166) report that siblings are particularly important in the lives of never married older persons. The death of a sibling, particularly when the relationship was a close one, may shock an older person more than the death of any other kin. Such a loss apparently brings home one's own mortality with greater immediacy.

In summary, then, having a spouse is one of the greatest possible assets in terms of a successful adjustment to aging. Unfortunately, it is very vulnerable to attrition, and widowhood often serves as an obstacle to adjustment in old age.

Rather than replacing lost spouses with new ones, most widowed older people substitute platonic relationships with men and women friends. Relationships between the generations are restricted by the norms that call for individual autonomy, and this restriction may be related to the strong trend toward seeking primary contacts among siblings.

Thus, for older people the deepest primary relationships come from kin, and sometimes from kin of the same generation. There is a great deal of interchange between generations, but some older people are reluctant to lean too heavily on their children for personal contacts for fear of disrupting their lives.

## FAMILY STRUCTURE

Thus far we have considered relationships within the family of procreation and the family of orientation separately. In order to get a good overall view of family structure, however, it is necessary to view the family as a collection of relationships, many of which might involve a single person. Thus, the family involves these roles: mother, daughter, grandmother, wife, and aunt (or father, son, grandfather, husband, uncle) —all of which might be held by a single person, although not usually at the same time and in the same situation.

A number of contemporary changes have influenced the constellation of roles within the family. To begin with, the decline in mortality rates since 1900 has had the result of adding a fourth generation to many families; thus the positions of great-grandparent, great-aunt, and so on have become a more evident part of the American family in the latter part of this century. Another important trend that also affects family structure is the family cycle. As the parent's age at birth of the last child declines, the result is a shorter period between generations. Hence, in 50 years the length of time between generations has declined from about 30 to about 20 years. This factor also promotes a greater number of generations in the family.

Finally, birth rates have a strong influence on the structure of the family. In 1910 the average completed family had produced 4.5 children, but by 1970 this number had declined to 2.6. This decline means that not only were there fewer children per completed family, but that there were fewer family roles *within* each generation. Since birth rates have fluctuated a good bit since 1900, we can expect those entering later life in the future to have widely varying average numbers of siblings, cousins, aunts, and uncles. For example, children of the 1930s will generally have smaller numbers of siblings than will children of the 1950s. Because of fluctuating birth rates and timing of births, the future structure of the family can be expected to fluctuate accordingly.

If American family structure is anything, it is diverse. Around 5 percent of older people have no spouse, children, or brothers and sisters. On the other hand, a majority of older people have at least two children, and they have grandchildren and great-grandchildren. In addition, most older people have surviving brothers and sisters. The older person may thus either have no kin at all or be incorporated into a very complex kinship network involving several generations.

Many studies have documented the fact that at least 40 percent of the older population have great-grandchildren and are thus members of a four-generation family. The question remains, however, how much older people are *involved* in these extended structures. Some researchers claim that the conjugal pair is the central focus of family life in American society, and that it makes little sense to examine relationships that are very far removed from the isolation of the family of procreation (Gibson, 1972). Others contend that extended family systems are the most typical and functional. These systems are seen as complicated networks of aid and service activities in which nuclear units are linked together both within and across generations. At this point, the evidence seems to weigh more heavily on the side of those who see the extended family system as typical (Sussman and Burchinal, 1962a; Hill, 1965; B. Adams, 1968a; Shanas, 1967).

## FAMILY VALUES

Obviously the trends presented thus far do not represent a unity. The different patterns in the family lives of older people result largely from differences in values. Kerckhoff (1966b) has done perhaps the most thorough study of this matter. He found three relatively clear norm value clusters, based mainly on the older person's conception of the norms in the parent-child relationship. In what Kerckhoff called the *extended family* cluster, both husband and wife expected to live near their children, to enjoy considerable mutual aid and affection with their children, and to divide the family tasks between husband and wife according to a definition of woman's work and man's work. These people did not attach much value to change, and they saw considerable conflict between self-improvement for the children and family values. At the other end of the continuum was the *nucleated family* cluster in which the older couple expected neither to live near their children nor to aid or be aided by them. They expected to share equally in the same tasks, they accepted change as a benefit, and they saw little conflict between family values and the children's attempts to improve on the social position given to them by their parents. A third cluster, called a *modified extended family*, accepted mutual aid and affection, rejected nearness as a requirement, and took an intermediate position on the other values. Members of this last category were genuine middle-of-the roaders.

Kerckhoff found that these norm value clusters were strongly related to social position. Families allied with the extended family cluster were very likely to have heads with blue-collar occupations and low levels of education, to have lived on a farm, to have not moved around much in their lives, and to have large families. In other words, the extended family cluster was associated with a complex of characteristics we normally link with the rural working class. Families allied with the nucleated family cluster tended to be just the opposite—to have a head with a white-collar occupation, to have high levels of education, to be city-reared, to have been geographically mobile, and to have relatively small families. Families allied with the modified extended family cluster were intermediate on all measures, but tended more toward the extended family pole. About 20 percent of the families fell into the extended family cluster and 20 percent into the nucleated family cluster, with the remaining 60 percent in the modified extended family cluster. It appears that most older people are getting about what they think they ought to have from the parent-child relationship. This finding is not surprising since Troll (1971) found several studies that show a large degree of similarity in values across generations.

In comparing the differences between the value norm clusters and actual family experiences, Kerckhoff brings up an interesting point. Since most of the experience falls into the modified extended family pattern, those who hold extended family values are very likely to be disappointed in their expectations, while those who hold the nucleated family view are apt to be pleasantly surprised by more mutual aid and affection than they expect. All of the data we have on changes in occupation, education, and urban-rural residence lead us to expect that the group identifying with the extended family cluster will decline in proportion in the future.

When we speak of socialization, we normally think of teaching the young, but, as Brim and Wheeler (1966) have pointed out, socialization is a lifelong process. Our earlier discussion should lead us to expect a minimal role for older people in the socialization of their young grandchildren or great-grandchildren—but what about a continued role in the socialization of their adult children? One of the primary ways we learn is by example, and one of the things older people offer their adult children, and the younger generations as well, is an illustration of how or how not to grow old gracefully. Whether the learning be positive or negative, the lives of older people serve as a resource that younger people can use in patterning their own lives when they reach their later years. Ways of handling retirement, grief, poverty, and illness are some of the lessons to be learned from watching older people.

## FAMILY DYNAMICS

Some very practical considerations that have a significant impact on the family relationships of older people include living arrangements, proximity to children, frequency of contacts, and exchange of family services.

**TABLE 18-5**
**Family Living Arrangements**
**of Older People: United States, 1962**

|  | People with Living Children | |
| --- | --- | --- |
|  | Married | Divorced, Widowed, Single |
| Total | 100.0% | 100.0% |
| Living alone | 0 | 46.5 |
| Living with: | | |
|    Spouse only | 77.9 | 0 |
|    Married daughter | 1.0 | 14.5 |
|    Married son | 1.1 | 4.1 |
|    Unmarried child | 14.6 | 24.1 |
|    Sibling | 1.3 | 2.5 |
|    Grandchild | 2.3 | 2.2 |
|    Other relative | .8 | 1.4 |
|    Nonrelative only | 1.0 | 4.6 |

*Source:* Stehouwer (1965:146).

Table 18-5 shows the living arrangements of older people in the United States, by marital category. The table shows, basically, what one would expect. Married older couples tend to live by themselves, and unattached older people tend to live alone. Widowed, divorced, or single older people are much more likely to live with an unmarried child, but both groups are more likely to live with an unmarried child than with anyone else, relative or nonrelative. Perhaps the most interesting statistic is the percentage living with married children. Less than 10 percent of the unattached older people live with married children. Perhaps there is no better indicator of the reluctance on both sides to enter into such an arrangement, and given our earlier discussion about the norms of autonomy between generations we should not be surprised. It would be useful to be able to examine the living arrangements of single, widowed, and divorced people separately, but Stehouwer's report (1965) does not allow this separation.

Living in a different household from children does not mean isolation from them. About 90 percent of the older people in the United States with living children live less than an hour's trip from at least one of their children. This proportion is even higher for unmarried older women (see Table 18-6).

**TABLE 18-6**
**Proximity of Older People**
**to Their Nearest Child (People with**
**Living Children): United States, 1962**

| Proximity | Percent |
|-----------|---------|
| Same household | 27.6 |
| 10 minutes' journey or less | 33.1 |
| 11–30 minutes | 15.7 |
| 31 minutes to 1 hour | 7.2 |
| Over 1 hour but less than 1 day | 11.2 |
| 1 day or more | 5.2 |

*Source:* Stehouwer (1965:147).

Concerning contacts with family, Riley and Foner (1968:544) found that,

> Altogether, most older people, with or without children, maintain contacts with relatives, though the frequency varies with the geographical (as well as the geneological) closeness of the older person's relatives, his ties to home and community and other factors.

Mutual aid includes exchange of both money (or goods) and services. It is commonly assumed that most aid flows *to* older people. However, research has uncovered a mixed pattern. Some investigators have found that the proportion of older people who give help to their children exceeds the proportion who receive help from their children (Streib, 1965b; Shanas, 1967). Hill (1965) concludes that grandparents generally give less often than they receive for most categories of mutual aid. The differences in these results may stem from social class differences in the samples used. In the middle class, considerable aid continues to flow from old parents to middle-aged children even into old age, but in the working class more help goes to old parents from middle-aged children (Schorr, 1960; Shanas et al., 1968; B. Adams, 1968a; Sussman and Burchinal, 1962a). A key factor in patterns of mutual aid appears to be the financial and physical capacities of older parents to offer aid. Troll (1971) concludes that most parents give to their children as much as they can for as long as they can.

Mutual aid patterns differ considerably by the type of aid being exchanged. Hill (1965) studied mutual aid patterns in over 100 three-generation families in Minneapolis. Hill's sample was biased toward the low income end of the spectrum for all three generations.

**TABLE 18-7**
**Comparison of Help Received and Help Given by**
**Generation for Chief Problem Areas: By Percent[a]**

| | Economic | | Emotional Gratification | | Household Management | | Child Care | | Illness | |
|---|---|---|---|---|---|---|---|---|---|---|
| | *Gave* | *Rec'd* | *Gave* | *Rec'd* | *Gave* | *Rec'd* | *Gave* | *Rec'd* | *Gave* | *Rec'd* |
| Total | 100 | 100 | 100 | 100 | 100 | 100 | 100 | 100 | 100 | 100 |
| Grandparents | 26 | 34 | 23 | 42 | 21 | 52 | 16 | 0 | 32 | 61 |
| Parents | 41 | 17 | 47 | 37 | 47 | 23 | 50 | 23 | 21 | 21 |
| Married children | 34 | 49 | 31 | 21 | 33 | 25 | 34 | 78 | 47 | 18 |

*Type of Crisis*

[a]Percents may not total 100 due to rounding.
*Source:* Hill (1965:125), reprinted by permission.

Table 18-7 reveals some interesting patterns. We are usually quite willing to assume that the differential between help given and help received would be greatest for older people in the economic sphere, particularly since so many older people are poor. Yet the differential in the economic sphere turned out, in fact, to be the smallest. In terms of emotional gratification, household management, and illness, grandparents received much more than they gave, but in the economic area, grandparents gave almost as much as they received. The middle generation was the one that apparently gave the most in terms of economic aid. Note, however, that Hill's conclusions are less applicable to upper middle-class families.

Another important point is the extent to which aid is exchanged. The picture is very balanced in terms of exchange of economic aid across generations. It is uneven with regard to child care, for obvious reasons, and it varies for the other kinds of aid. No one generation comes off clearly a giver or receiver when all types of aid are considered.

## FRIENDS AND NEIGHBORS

Friends and neighbors are important sources of primary relationships in later life. They also provide help and contact with the outside world, although they are less important in this regard than children or other relatives.

Friendships tend to be retained into later life from middle age, and the higher the socioeconomic status of the individual, the more likely this tendency is. Older people tend to pick their friends from among people with similar characteristics (including age). As a result, the longer the person lives in a given neighborhood, the more extensive his or her ties are apt to be (Riley and Foner, 1968:561).

Most people report a decline in friendships over the years, but a small minority of

---

**RESEARCH ILLUSTRATION 11**

**SOCIAL INTEGRATION OF THE AGED[3]**

Irving Rosow

Rosow studied the relationship between the residential density of older people and the integration of older people into friend and neighbor roles. The study was conducted in several hundred apartment buildings in Cleveland. These buildings were divided, in terms of the density of aged households, into *normal*, with 1–15 percent aged households; *concentrated*, with 33–49 percent aged households; and *dense*, with 50 percent or more aged households. (The category 16–32 percent was intentionally omitted to emphasize differences.)

The study included 1,200 people. The men had to be at least 65 and the women 62 to be included. A range of social classes was purposefully included in the sample by screening apartment buildings for occupation of head of household and by using public housing units. Interviews were conducted on three successive occasions, with a 25 percent dropout rate, about average for panel studies.

Rosow predicted that dense neighborhoods would produce more friendships among older people, and that the friends of older people would come disproportionately from among their old, as opposed to their younger, neighbors. He found that middle-class older people had significantly more friends than the working class, and that working-class older people depended more on the neighborhood for friendships than did those of the middle class. Middle-class older people formed slightly more new friendships than those in the working class. Also, those in the working class were "far more sensitive and vulnerable to variations in residential age composition in making and maintaining friendships" (Rosow, 1967:294).

The basic hypotheses of the study were borne out. Older people did have more friends when there were more older neighbors in the neighborhood, and these friends were drawn from among their age peers. The implication of this finding is that, for fighting social isolation among older people, it is apparently better to have a *dense* concentration of older people than a cross-section of the general population in the neighborhood.

In cases of high role loss, such as might occur through retirement or bereavement, a high residential density of older people afforded greater opportunities for replacing friends. Even though the middle-class older people did not usually base their friendships on locality, they could and would do so if the density was high. This pattern held particularly true for women. For working-class older people, of course, the pattern of finding one's friends locally is well established. Rosow noted that before the residential density would produce an increase in social ties, the proportion of aged households had to exceed half.

Nevertheless, Rosow cautioned that we should avoid looking on high residential density of older households as a panacea. In his study, there were many who simply did not care to associate with neighbors. Table 18-8 shows an array of categories that could be used to type people in terms of their contacts with neighbors and their desire for contacts with neighbors.

Rosow was interested in the effect of density on the relationship between neighboring and morale. He found that, as density increased, the morale of the isolates *declined*. They felt

---

older people report that they have *more* friends than ever before. Numerous friendships among older people are related to high socioeconomic status, good health, high density of older people in the neighborhood, long-term neighborhood residence, and residence in a small town rather than a large city (Riley and Foner, 1968:562–71).

[3]Based on Rosow (1967).

**TABLE 18-8**
**Functions of Neighboring**
**in Older People's Lives**

| Type | Contact with Neighbors | Desired Contacts with Neighbors |
|---|---|---|
| Cosmopolitan | Low | None |
| Apathetic (phlegmatic) | Low | None |
| Isolated | Low | More |
| Sociable | High | No more |
| Insatiable | High | More |

depressed, apparently, by their continued inability to make friends even in the face of improved opportunity. The morale of the sociables remained the same because they retained a relatively constant level of interaction, as they wished to. The morale of the insatiables *increased* because they increased their opportunities for new contacts. The cosmopolitan and apathetic did not figure in the analysis because neither type was socially motivated as far as the neighborhood was concerned; therefore, density had no bearing on morale.

Rosow's data indicate that at least half of the isolated group could not take advantage of a dense neighborhood without assistance. The cosmopolitans found their friends outside the neighborhood, and the apathetics were just that.

Rosow also examined the extent to which neighbors served as a reference group. He found that neighbors were almost never asked for financial help. In terms of identity, loyalty, and closeness, he found that older people attached a greater salience to current friends and neighbors than to those of the past, if the two did not coincide. Finally, in terms of help at times of illness, he found two patterns. For those older people who lived with someone, less than 10 percent got help from outside the family. For those who lived alone, however, there was quite a different pattern, particularly if they had no local family.

Living in dense areas was apparently the only way older people with no relatives and no money could cope with illness.

> These neighbors take care of more solitary people in longer illness than do friends, as many as relatives, and almost as many as children. This attention is not confined to brief sickness, but is sustained longer if necessary. For all their stoicism and self-reliance, solitary residents do use neighbors' help for longer illness when they can get it, but dense apartments are the only ones that can provide this to any significant element (Rosow, 1967:308).

The result is that tenants in dense housing learned to rely on their neighbors in a crisis, and thus reduced their apprehensions about living alone. The interesting point here is that older neighbors in dense apartments can be an effective reference group even for people who have never personally made use of them in this capacity.

Regardless of how many friends they have, there is evidence that older people are fairly restrictive in terms of *who* they will accept. To begin with, age peers seem to have priority as potential friends. Also, friends tend to be selected from among those of the same sex, marital status, and socioeconomic class (Riley and Foner, 1968:571–73).

On the surface it would seem that the role of friend is one that older people can hang onto indefinitely. Long after the roles of worker, organization member, or even spouse have been lost, the role of friend remains. The demands of the friend role are flexible and can be adjusted to fit the individual's capability in terms of health and energy. It is the greatest source of companionship next to that of spouse.

How do older people define *friendship*? Quite a variety of relationships are lumped together under this label. They range from close, intense, and continuous interaction marked by mutual understanding and concern all the way to cursory contacts over the years with people whose names one happens to know (Clark and Anderson, 1967:303–10). Probably the best way to divide them is to call the former *friends* and the latter *associates*.

Clark and Anderson (1967:305) observed that older women seemed to have an abundance of friends, while older men had an abundance of associates. In comparison to men, women appeared to speak more about their friendships and to place more value on them. They also tended to depend more on them. Men were much more passive about their friendships, and Clark and Anderson attribute this passivity to the fact that many more of the men were married and thus had less need for friends as a source of primary bonds. Yet men seemed to feel the implied stigma that being old and friendless brings. In addition, men were apparently less willing to continue friendships via correspondence or telephone, which may have shut them off from potential contacts.

Most older people recognize that the loss of friends is an inevitable accompaniment to growing older, and most also believe that replacing lost friends is a very difficult task. Older people cite difficulties in transportation, geographic moves, lowered economic status, and a life-style limited by illness or disability as significant obstacles to the replacement of lost friends.

Confidants are important, especially to older people, and confidants tend to be selected from among friends rather than siblings or children. Most older people can identify at least one confidant—a person with whom they have a close, intimate relationship (Powers et al., 1975; Cantor, 1975). Lowenthal and Havens (1968) found that presence of a confidant served as an important buffer against trauma in adjusting to reduced life space, widowhood, and retirement.

Friendships play an important role in the everyday lives of older people. Most older people have at least 15 friends (Powers et al., 1975), most want more interaction with friends than they have (Martel and Morris, 1960), and most feel no need to make new friends (Pihlblad and McNamara, 1965). These trends appear to be more pronounced in rural areas (Powers et al., 1975).

## SUMMARY

Unlike most other institutions, the family allows the older person to remain a full participant. In later life, the family is still the individual's main source of primary relationships, just as it is in middle age.

Most older people are married and living with their spouses, but as age increases, progressively more of them, particularly women, are widowed. Older couples are generally happy, particularly where there is equality in the relationship, and retirement can enhance the success of older couples by providing more opportunities for equality. Older people who concentrate on the expressive aspects of marriage instead of on the instrumental aspects tend to adjust better to retirement.

Those who marry in later life tend to seek companionship above all, and the success of such marriages depends on many of the same factors that influence the success of marriage among younger people. Knowing each other well, having approval of friends and family, being well-adjusted individuals, and having financial security were all important for the success of "retirement marriages."

Widowhood is difficult to cope with, but most older people succeed in doing so. Most respond to widowhood by increasing their involvement in various activities. Variations in urbanization and cultural norms can apparently produce a wide variety of responses to widowhood.

The proportion of older people under 75 who are married can be expected to increase in the future, while the proportion 75 or over who are widowed can also be expected to increase.

Sexual problems in later life very often stem from the influence of various myths about the effects of age on sexual capacity, cultural norms that lead people to avoid sex when they get older, and fear of failure among older men. Older people apparently need to understand more about their own sexuality than they do now.

Older parents with adult children tend to see their children often and to regard these as their most important relationships. The more autonomous the parent, the better the relationship, but when the time comes, most children take up the responsibility for their aged parents. There is little evidence that reluctance to accept such responsibility is widespread. The norms of the relationship tend to emphasize the independence and dignity of both older parent and adult child.

The grandparent role is one that most older people enjoy, but for most of them it is not a meaningful primary relationship. It tends to be pursued, if at all, out of interest in their grandchildren or out of a desire to have fun with them. There is some indication that grandparent roles are being viewed as more informal and that the salience of the role is higher in middle age than in later maturity or old age.

About a third of older people are great-grandparents, but this role probably has little interactive meaning for most of them.

The sibling role seems to be more important in later life than it is in middle age, particularly as a substitute for lost friends and spouses. Next to children, siblings are the most important source of primary relationships the older person has.

Changes in family structure caused by changes in birth rates mean fluctuating chances that kin can provide a substantial reservoir of potential relationships. Smaller families mean fewer aunts, uncles, cousins, siblings, children, and grandchildren and larger ones mean more. Nevertheless, extended kinship relations typify the family lives of most older people.

Older people who expect many extended family relationships are mainly concentrated in the working class, and they are very likely to be disappointed by the amount of mutual aid and affection they actually receive from their extended families. Those who expected little in the way of extended kin support were concentrated in the urban upper-middle class and were generally pleasantly surprised at the amount of mutual aid and affection they actually received from their families. Those in between expected a medium amount from the extended family and got about what they expected.

In terms of family dynamics, most older people live in their own household, but near at least one of their children. They are in frequent contact with their children. In terms of exchange of family services, no one generation clearly predominates as giver or receiver when all types of aid are considered.

In our examination of primary roles, we encounter a familiar pattern. If primary relationships are carried over from middle age, they tend to be maintained, but beginning new ones as an older person is a difficult task. Thus, the role of spouse can easily be carried over into old age, but to find a new spouse in old age is another matter, particularly for older women. Most other family roles, such as father, grandfather, uncle, and brother, once lost can never be replaced.

The role of friend or neighbor is also easy to carry over but difficult to replace, except in the relatively unusual case where 50 percent or more of the neighboring households are made up of older people. Having a confidant is especially important in staving off loneliness and isolation.

Family values and family dynamics all reflect some distance expected between the generations. On the other hand, as a practical matter it is obvious that there is a great deal of contact and mutual aid among the generations. Certainly, if there is disengagement by the family or by friends, it occurs on a much smaller scale than in the other areas of social life we have discussed.

## SUGGESTIONS FOR FURTHER READING

Ballweg, John A. "Resolution of Conjugal Role Adjustment after Retirement." *Journal of Marriage and the Family 29* (1967:277–281.

Blenkner, Margaret. "Social Work and Family Relationships in Later Life with Some Thoughts on Filial Maturity." In Ethel Shanas and Gordon F. Streib (eds.), *Social Structure and the Family*. Englewood Cliffs, N. J.: Prentice-Hall, 1965, pp. 46–59.

Boyd, Rosamonde R. "Emerging Roles of the Four-Generation Family." In Rosamonde R. Boyd and Charles G. Oakes (eds.), *Foundations of Practical Gerontology*. Columbia, S.C.: University of South Carolina Press, 1969, pp. 35–50.

———. "The Valued Grandparent: A Changing Social Role." In Wilma Donahue (ed.), *Living in the Multigenerational Family*. Ann Arbor, Mich.: University of Michigan: University of Michigan–Wayne State, Institute of Gerontology, 1969, pp. 90–102.

Bultena, Gordon L. "Rural-Urban Differences in Family Interaction of the Aged." *Rural Sociology 34* (1969):5–15.

Gibson, Geoffrey. "Kin Family Network: Overheralded Structure of Past Conceptualizations of Family Functioning." *Journal of Marriage and the Family 34* (1972):13–28.

Gubrium, Jaber F. "Being Single in Old Age." *International Journal of Aging and Human Development 6* (1975):29–41.

Hill, Reuben. "Decision Making and the Family Life Cycle." In Ethel Shanas and Gordon F. Streib (eds.), *Social Structure and the Family*. Englewood Cliffs, N. J.: Prentice-Hall, 1965, pp. 113–139.

Jackson, Jacquelyne J. "Sex and Social Class Variations in Black Aged Parent-Adult Child Relationships." *Aging and Human Development 2* (1971):96–107.

Kerckhoff, Alan C. "Norm-Value Clusters and the Strain Toward Consistency Among Older Married Couples." In Ida H. Simpson and John C. McKinney (eds.), *Social Aspects of Aging*. Durham, N. C.: Duke University Press, 1966, pp. 138–159.

Schorr, Alvin L. "Filial Responsibility and the Aging, or Beyond Pluck and Luck." *Social Security Bulletin 25* (1962):4–9.

Shanas, Ethel, and Gordon F. Streib (eds.). *Social Structure and the Family: Generational Relations*. Englewood Cliffs, N. J.: Prentice-Hall, 1965.

———, Peter Townsend, Dorothy Wedderburn, Henning Friis, Poul Milhøj, and Jan Stehower. *Older People in Three Industrial Societies*. New York: Atherton, 1968.

Sussman, Marvin B., and Lee Burchinal. "Kin Family Network: Unheralded Structure in Current Conceptualizations of Family Functioning." *Marriage and Family Living 24* (1962):231–240.

———. "Parental Aid to Married Children: Implications for Family Functioning." *Marriage and Family Living 24* (1962):320–332.

Troll, Lillian E. "The Family of Later Life: A Decade Review." *Journal of Marriage and the Family 33* (1971):263–290.

# 19

# Epilogue: What Does It All Mean?

Obviously, lots of work is needed in social gerontology. But where do we go from here? What are the implications of the facts, figures, and perspectives given in this book? It would require another book to answer these questions fully. Yet, as someone observed, a book should not "just end." Therefore this chapter attempts to outline some of the implications of this book for the field in general. Be forewarned that a generous helping of my own educated opinions is included.

## RESEARCH

*There is not a single area of social gerontology that does not need more answers to crucial questions.* In fact, the past decade of work in social gerontology has only just enabled us to begin to ask the right questions. Yet there are some areas where the research needs are particularly pressing. For example, we know very little about America's older minority group people. We still do not fully understand the retirement process. Very little is known about transportation as it relates to older people. We still do not understand why some people are devastated by old age and others are not. We do not fully understand the dynamics of the age differentiation process. The vast amount of aging research in the United States needs to be complemented by research in other areas of the world.

In addition to the many stones as yet unturned, there is a crying need for *replication*. Knowledge is built piece by piece, and it takes many repeated studies to establish a scientific proposition. Social gerontology is loaded with conflicting research evidence, and only more high-quality research can give us the tools to sort it out. Thankfully, since the first edition of this book, the quality of research reports in aging has risen steadily.

Because their focus is narrower than all of social reality, social gerontologists have many opportunities to do genuinely interdisciplinary research. The Kansas City Study of Adult Life and the Langley Porter Institute Studies in Aging were noteworthy in that their study designs brought together psychologists, social psychologists, sociologists, psychiatrists, and social anthropologists to do simultaneous longitudinal studies on the same samples of older people. In fact, the interplay of various traditions that goes on in social gerontology could be viewed as a step in the direction of needed theoretical integration in the social sciences. The literature of social gerontology is full of cases where supposedly general social theories failed the test when applied to older people, and of cases where insights gained from theories of personality or developmental psychology have helped to refine sociological theories that have been found wanting. And there are also many cases where the reverse is true.

In particular, detailed research on community systems holds great promise for understanding how the various social institutions and aging interact. Often institutions and organizations pick up each other's slack, and needs not being met by one will be met by another. This kind of give-and-take is most observable at the local level. Also, it is at the local level that the individual most often comes into direct contact with the economy, politics, religion, health and welfare institutions, and his or her family, friends, and neighbors. The impact of any given institution or organization thus occurs in the content of a locally based *system* of institutions and organizations. We are just beginning to sort out the various types of community systems.

To date, there have been all too few attempts to study the *interdependent situational context* in which the individual experiences later life. To my mind, more interdisciplinary, community-based research like the Kansas City Study of Adult Life and the Langley Porter Institute Studies in Aging is needed. Much was learned from those studies that could be used to do new and better community studies. The work of Clark and Anderson (1967) in particular shows that both the individual's personal system and his or her interaction with the social system can be studied successfully in a community context. More studies of this kind are especially needed to partially offset the tunnel vision one tends to get in large-scale survey research studies of specific topics such as retirement, widowhood, or voting behavior done by scholars in a single discipline.

Large-scale studies are also necessary in order to get a view of a particular phenomenon, such as retirement or income, that is *representative* of an entire nation or set of nations and not just of a particular community. To date, the large-scale studies that have been done have tended to suffer greatly from sampling problems. Hopefully, future survey research in aging can use better techniques, and thus give better, more representative answers.

An important key to the quality of research in social gerontology is the amount of research money available in the United States. When the Older Americans Act was passed in 1965, it established the U.S. Administration on Aging and included funds for research in social gerontology. For a while there was a flurry of research activity, but slowly the funds for aging research were diverted to other purposes, and by the time of the 1971 White House Conference on Aging there was only a trickle of research money available. There are signs that the level of research funding may increase somewhat, but the important question is whether or not this support will be *sustained*. Gerontology research centers cannot be established and maintained with only sporadic sources of funds. A persistent commitment is needed. The funding of research has always been a complicated matter, but with the rising cost of social research and the growing inability of state and local governments to increase public revenue, the federal government is the prime realistic source of research funds. And until there is greater federal support of research in social gerontology, closing the research gaps listed in this book will be a slow process.

The recently established National Institute on Aging (NIA) within the National Institutes of Health could provide the research leadership and financial support needed at the national level to develop a coherent effort toward narrowing the research gaps. Part of Congress's rationale in creating NIA was a recognition that research in aging has not received a level of support that anywhere near matched the effects of aging on the lives of the general population.

In beginning its effort, NIA commissioned three separate panels to develop research priorities for the remainder of the 1970s in (1) biomedical sciences, (2) behavioral and social sciences, and (3) services for older people. The final research priorities in social gerontology were not available as of this writing, but the following list of topics is probably representative of the kinds of research priorities to be stressed by NIA.

☐ Psychological research to differentiate age decrements caused by environmental and disease factors from those caused by aging and to identify decrements that will yield to intervention.

☐ Demographic projections and simulations aimed at constant reevaluation of retirement and income maintenance policies.

☐ Research to develop functional criteria of work competence to aid in placement of older people who wish to remain employed.

☐ Research on personality, social, and environmental factors affecting social competence and life satisfaction, particularly in terms of sex and ethnic differences.

☐ Research on the family as a support system for older people.

☐ Research on the relationships among psychological, social, and physical health.

☐ Research on the social consequences of the imbalanced sex ratio in later life.

☐ Research to evaluate "natural" social experiments such as gradual retirement, service networks, or specially designed housing.

☐ Research on the effects of government policy on the everyday lives of older Americans.

## TRAINING

Obviously, if there is to be an increased research effort in social gerontology, people must be trained to do it. There has been an encouraging increase in the number of institutions offering research training in social gerontology at both the graduate and undergraduate levels. A part of this increase was financed through federal programs. Hopefully, training will continue to be a high priority for NIA. Not only the actual research, but also the existence of trained people to do it, depends on a continuing federal commitment to research in social gerontology.

In addition to the need for research training, more training in social gerontology is needed for professionals working in fields that serve older people, and, in turn, there must be organizations to provide this training. Experience in recent years has shown that gerontology is an attractive area to students and that courses in aging can more than pull their weight in terms of student demand. Such courses are essential for students in the human services professions. All too often the practitioner is hampered by the same faulty stereotypes about older people that pervade industrial societies.

## POLICY AND PLANNING

The theme of the 1971 White House Conference on Aging was "Toward a National Policy on Aging." Just how far toward that goal the conference got is debatable, but the issues raised there show considerable consensus concerning needed changes in planning and policy that derive from the present status of older people in American society. It is impossible to present all of the issues or recommendations that came out of the conference, but here are a few that are particularly pertinent to this book.

### Education

1. Adult education should be expanded to include more of the specific concerns of the elderly.
2. Federal funds should be earmarked specifically for library services to older people.
3. Knowledge relative to aging should be part of educational curricula from preschool through higher education.
4. Preretirement education should be available to *everyone* and well in advance of retirement.

### Employment and Retirement

1. Employment and retirement policy should create a climate of free choice between continuing in employment as long as one wishes and is able, or retiring on adequate income with opportunities for meaningful activities.

2. More rigorous efforts are needed to eliminate age discrimination in employment.
3. Retirement ages should be more flexible.
4. More effort should be made to use the talents of older people in public service jobs.

*Physical and Mental Health*

1. Present health care delivery systems should be expanded to include preventive medicine, long-term health care, special needs such as eyeglasses and dental services, and rehabilitation services.
2. Adequate, appropriate alternatives to institutional care should be developed.

*Housing*

1. Housing programs should give special attention to the housing needs of older people who are poor, who live in rural areas, who are members of minority groups, who are disabled, or who are isolated.
2. The range of housing choice for older people should include long-term care facilities; facilities with limited medical, food, and homemaker services; congregate housing with food and personal services; and housing for independent living with recreational and activity programs.
3. Housing for older people should adopt architectural guidelines based on the needs of the elderly and the disabled.

*Income*

1. Older people (individuals as well as couples) should have a total cash income in accordance with the "American standard of living."
2. More earnings should be allowed without penalty under Social Security.
3. Private pension plans should be solvent and should provide for early vesting, portability, survivor benefits, and complete disclosure of provisions to those covered.
4. Tax relief should be given to older people.

*Nutrition*

1. Research should be conducted on the nutritional status of older Americans.
2. Nutrition should be emphasized in health care programs and in education for older people.
3. The equivalent of the national school lunch program should be developed for all older people, not just those with low incomes.

*Spiritual Well-Being*

1. Institutions for the aged should include chaplain services.
2. More religious programs should be available to older people in their own homes.
3. Religious bodies and the government should affirm the right to, and reverence for, life and recognize the individual's right to die with dignity.

*Transportation*

1. Increased transportation services should be provided to both rural and urban older people. Both system subsidies and payments to elderly individuals should be available, depending on the availability and usability of public and private transportation.
2. Individualized, flexible transportation should be part of social service programs.
3. Insurance companies should be prevented from raising premiums on, or canceling, auto insurance on the basis of age alone.
4. Special attention should be given to the transportation needs of the rural elderly.

*Facilities, Programs, and Services*

1. All older persons should have real choices as to how they shall spend their later years.
2. Older people should be enabled to maintain their independence and their usefulness at the highest possible levels.
3. Older people should have the opportunity for continued growth, development, and self-fulfillment and for expanded contributions to a variety of community activities.
4. An effective network of facilities, programs, and services should be readily available and accessible to permit older people to exercise a wide range of options, regardless of their individual circumstances or where they live.
5. Specific agencies at the local, state and federal levels should be assigned the responsibility for planning and coordinating services to older people.
6. Consumer protection of the elderly should be emphasized.
7. Protective services should be developed for those older persons in the community who are unable to manage their affairs because their mental and/or physical functioning is seriously impaired.

*Government and Nongovernment Organizations*

1. Planning and programing for the aged should coordinate the efforts of both private and public agencies at the local, state, and federal levels.
2. Government action on issues pertaining to older people must include a local-state-federal partnership.
3. Agencies responsible for programs in aging should be strong advocates for older people's interests.
4. Responsibility for planning and coordinating programs for older people should be consolidated under a single, high-level office of government, and this pattern of pinpointing responsibility should apply at all levels of government.

*Planning*

1. Comprehensive planning in aging should be done on both a state-wide basis and a local basis.

*Research and Demonstration*

1. Research aimed at understanding the basic processes of aging and alleviating the suffering of those who encounter difficulty in adapting to this phase of life should be accelerated.
2. Research on racial and ethnic minority groups should assume a proportional share of the total research effort.
3. A major increase in research and research training funds in aging should be appropriated and allocated.

*Training*

1. Additional federal funds should be provided for training professionals both in colleges and universities and on an in-service basis.
2. All service programs for older people should contain funds earmarked for the training of personnel.

This incomplete list of the concerns of the 1971 White House Conference on Aging shows that many of the problems highlighted in this book are receiving the attention of politicians and planners. However, implementing these policy recommendations is a political problem, and in order for the efforts of the conference to bear fruit, older people and their advocates must exert enough political pressure to make it costly for politicians to ignore their needs. Of the recommendations listed above, nutrition, planning, and pension reform have received widespread attention in the years since the White House Conference.

## THE FUTURE OF SOCIAL GERONTOLOGY

The United States Bureau of the Census estimates that by the year 2037, the year the United States would reach zero growth at today's fertility levels, the population of *older people* in the United States could reach nearly 60 million, over twice the number of older people in 1970 (U.S. Bureau of the Census, 1972). Twenty million of those would be over 75 (three times as many as in 1970). People over 60 would then represent about a *fifth* of the total population.

With the older population growing this fast, there is little chance that interest in aging will lessen. In fact, during the coming decades, services to older people may well represent one of the fastest-growing areas of employment in the western world. And the demand for knowledge in the field of social gerontology can be expected to grow accordingly. All of this implies a rosy future for social gerontology—and it's about time.

There are plentiful career opportunities in social gerontology. We are just beginning to grapple with the problems in many areas of research and practice. The "establishment" in the field is relatively small, and interest in research results and innovative programs is high. Funding levels for gerontology research and demonstration projects are increasing, and gerontology centers have been established in several universities. This situation offers people ready to embark on a new career an opportunity to "get in on the ground floor." I hope that this book will motivate some of its readers to join me in this fascinating field.

## SUGGESTIONS FOR FURTHER READING

Binstock, Robert H. "Planning for Tomorrow's Urban Aged: A Policy Analyst's Reaction." *Gerontologist 15* (1975):42.

Lowy, L. "The Role of Social Gerontology in the Development of Social Services for Older People." In D. P. Kent, R. Kastenbaum, and S. Sherwood (eds.), *Research Planning and Action for the Elderly*. New York: Behavioral Publications, 1972, pp. 20–36.

Neugarten, Bernice L. "The Future and the Young-Old." *Gerontologist 15* (1975, 1, part 2): 4–9.

Seltzer, Mildred M., and Robert C. Atchley. *Developing Educational Programs in the Field of Aging*. Oxford, Ohio: Scripps Foundation Gerontology Center, Miami University, 1974.

United States Bureau of the Census. "Projections of the Population of the United States, by Age and Sex (Interim Revisions): 1970 to 2020." *Current Population Reports*, Series P-25, No. 448. Washington, D.C.: United States Bureau of the Census, 1970.

# Appendix
# on Methodology

The term *methodology* refers to the *procedures* used to develop and maintain knowledge. It includes the analysis of the basic assumptions of science, the process of theory construction, the interrelationship of theory and research and the procedures of empirical investigation. Methodology is thus at the heart of any discipline. The scientific method of collecting knowledge is characterized by a preoccupation with the *design of research* and with the rigorous identification and control of *error*. Error can get into research results from a number of sources: (1) from the fact that observers are not conscious of everything that goes on around them and are thus apt to miss something; (2) from their not knowing where to look; (3) from their rationalizing or repressing what they see; (4) from their looking at a part of the social world that is unrepresentative; (5) from their asking the wrong questions; (6) from their asking questions in the wrong ways; and (7) from their using faulty measurement. Research design aims to identify and control these sources of error.

## METHODOLOGICAL PROBLEMS
## IN SOCIAL GERONTOLOGY

Hundreds of books have been written on social research and how such research should be done, and anyone who intends to do research in social gerontology must be thoroughly familiar with general research procedures.[1] However, there are also several methodological problems that are unique to the study of older people.

---

[1] Some good books on research methods are Babbie (1974); Kerlinger (1974); Rosenberg (1968).

### Defining *Older People*

A symptomatic approach to defining the term *older person* is preferable to a chronological approach. Yet we are forced to continue to use chronological age as the operational definition because no one has come up with a satisfactory way of identifying older people symptomatically. It is conceivable that a scale could be constructed that, in addition to chronological age, would take into account energy level, health, social roles, awareness of death, degree of orientation toward the future, mental slow-down, and activity restriction. Yet even should an operational definition by symptoms be possible, much of the available *data* on older people would still be accessible only in terms of chronological age.

### Heterogeneity of the Study Group

In the literature of social gerontology, one constantly finds the terms the *aged* or *older people* being used as if they identified a single, homogeneous category of people. In reality, however, the older population in many ways exhibits a greater variety of personalities, life-styles, and life chances than any other category in society. Race, religion, social class, education, occupation, and many other social characteristics often produce differences among people that can all but completely obscure the influence of aging. A crucial methodological issue is the problem of holding these factors constant so that the impact of aging can be observed.

In addition, the older population is a composite of many groups of people who were born and reared in quite different times. Thus, the characteristics people attribute to aging are often actually the result of differences in experience, and these differences produce heterogeneity in the older population. It is therefore important to recognize that the historical era in which one enters various phases of the life cycle may also obscure the influence of aging.

Nevertheless, while it is good to be aware that all older people are to some extent individual, recognizing heterogeneity in no way denies the fact that people have certain characteristics and situations in common as a result of being old. Our job is to identify this communality and at the same time to respect individual uniqueness.

### Sampling

A crucial problem in social gerontology involves *sampling*. Very seldom is it necessary to examine an entire population to answer a given research question. Instead, a representative sample can be examined and the results generalized to the entire population. But adequate sampling requires some sort of *concrete* representation of the population, such as a list of names and/or addresses. For the general population, addresses can be used, because the U.S. Bureau of the Census maintains a file of addresses for residences throughout the country. But for subgroups within that population the task is more difficult. How would you locate a list of all older people in Atlanta? Social Security is out because they are forbidden by law to release the names of their pensioners. Besides, many older people have never established entitlement to

Social Security. Internal Revenue and the Census Bureau are out for the same reasons. These lists are the most inclusive, but even less inclusive lists are hard to get because people do not like to have their names and addresses given out. The only surefire way to sample the older population of Atlanta would be to conduct your own census to locate and list all of the older people and then draw a sample from the list. This project is obviously an expensive one, and as a result such a census is almost never made.

Sampling difficulties have often obliged social gerontologists to settle for the samples they can get rather than the samples they need. For example, a researcher studying retirement needs a sample that represents all retired people, from former Pullman porters to former bank executives. Yet because there is no listing available, the typical retired sample is drawn from the retirement rolls of a particular company or union. Obviously, if investigators attempt to generalize about all retired people from a sample of this type, they will be on shaky ground indeed. It is precisely because of such problems that our knowledge of the effects of retirement is not very firm at this point, and the same can be said for many other aspects of social gerontology as well.

## Research Design

Most research on older people is cross-sectional. Therefore, the research is conducted in a short time, and inferences as to the effect of aging itself are made by comparing people of different ages at the time the research was conducted. For example, people 65 to 74 might be compared with those 75 and over, and the differences attributed to the influence of aging. This procedure is based on the assumption that observing different people at successive points in the life cycle produces the same result as observing a single group of people as they move through the life cycle.

While a great many of the generalizations in social gerontology are based on this assumption, it is very questionable. The most serious flaw in the cross-sectional approach is that people in different phases of the life cycle at the same point in calendar time differ in other ways than simply the impact of aging. For example, in a cross-sectional sample of retired women teachers, the older the women were, the higher they scored on a scale designed to measure the extent to which they thought work should be considered an end in itself rather than simply a means to an end. Using cross-sectional logic, it might be inferred that aging produced an increase in this kind of orientation toward work. The problem is that there is another possible explanation: namely, that women reared later were taught a different attitude toward work. With cross-sectional data it is literally impossible to tell which of these explanations is the correct one.

A good example of the power of cohort analysis occurred in the area of voting patterns. It had been widely assumed that as people grow older, their interest in voting declines, and most cross-sectional studies showed just such an age pattern. Yet when samples from the same cohorts were traced through the life cycle, it was found that people remain relatively constant over their adult lives in terms of interest in voting. Thus, what appeared to be the result of aging when only cross-sectional data were used turned out to be the result of differences between people who became politically active in different eras. (See Chapter 15 for a more detailed discussion of this research.)

Longitudinal research and cohort analysis are the only ways that ongoing events in the world can be held reasonably equal so that the impact of aging can be observed. But such research requires observing the same people over a period of years, and thus is expensive and difficult to conduct.

In addition, it is not enough to follow only one group through the life cycle. This longitudinal research must be done for several groups, so that we can see the changes, if any, that are occurring in the impact of aging.

Social gerontology is in its infancy in terms of developing and accumulating knowledge through longitudinal studies, and the difficulties of conducting research spanning a period of years, plus the research priorities of the agencies that pay for research, will probably retard its development.

## Measurement

Measurement involves translating observations into meaningful numbers. The adequacy of the procedures we use to measure social variables is judged by two important criteria, validity and reliability. The term *validity* refers to the correspondence between what the measurement process is supposed to measure and what it actually measures. The closer the correspondence, the more valid the measure. Validity is usually assessed by comparing the results of the measure in question with an accepted measure of the same characteristic. Most of the time, however, there is no other accepted measure, and the researcher has to guess what the validity of his or her measure is. Since validity often cannot be concretely established, the investigator must therefore be constantly on the alert for impressionistic data concerning validity.

The term *reliability* refers to the extent to which a given measure gives stable results over successive trials. For example, a test may be given to the same people more than once, and the results compared. This method is called the *test-retest* method of assessing reliability. A measure can be reliable without being valid, but it cannot be valid without being reliable.[2]

Problems of validity and reliability are important for gerontological research because the validity and reliability of many of the measures we want to use were established for young subjects but not for older ones. It is quite possible for a test to be valid and reliable for college students but not for retired professors. The investigator who wants to use an already established measure will ordinarily want to reestablish the validity and reliability of the measure when it is used with older people. Too little attention has been paid to this problem by gerontological researchers.

These and many other methodological issues related to the study of aging are covered in more detail by Riley, Johnson, and Foner (1972), Nelson and Starr (1972), and Nesselroade and Reese (1973).

---

[2]For a detailed discussion of problems of validity and reliability, see Selltiz et al., *Research Methods in Social Relations* (New York: Holt, Rinehart and Winston, 1959), Chapter 5.

# Glossary

Included in this glossary are only those words that are unique to gerontology. Common terms from the various social sciences are not included, nor are terms that are adequately defined in the various collegiate dictionaries. Numbers in parentheses following definitions indicate page on which terms are discussed.

**Age changes**  Changes in an individual as a result of the aging process. (See also *aging*; *age differences*.)  (8)

**Age, chronological**  Age measured by number of years lived.  (10)

**Age differences**  Differences among categories of people of different chronological age at a particular point in time. Such differences are only *partly* the result of the aging process.  (8)

**Age grading**  A social process whereby eligibility and responsibility for various positions in the group are primarily determined by chronological age.  (23)

**Age norms**  Norms tied to the life course that tell people of a given age what is allowed or not allowed for someone of that age.  (90)

**Age strata**  Categories used to classify persons into a given age interval. Used to compare age *differences* within a given population at a particular point in time.  (23)

**Age stratification**  Division of society into age groups or strata such that people are dealt with not primarily as individuals but as members of age strata.  (23)

**Ageism**  Prejudice and discrimination leveled by one age stratum against another.  (20)

**Aging**   A general term used for various biological, psychological, and social processes whereby an individual acquires the socially defined characteristics of old age. (See also *senescence*; *old age*.)   (5)

**Bereavement**   The process of getting over another person's death.   (185)

**Cohort**   All individuals of approximately the same age; for example, all persons born in the year 1900.   (8)

**Cohort analysis**   Studies that examine data from samples taken from the same cohort at different points in time.   (9)

**Cohort centrism**   Using one's age peers as one's preferred source of values, attitudes, knowledge, and social relationships.   (23)

**Consolidation approach**   An approach to adjustment to role or activity loss that emphasizes redistribution of efforts to remaining roles or activities.   (212)

**Cross-sectional studies**   Studies that examine people of different ages at the same point in time.   (8)

**Dependency**   A social state in which the individual must rely on others for financial or physical support.   (97)

**Disengagement, individual**   The process whereby the individual withdraws commitments to various social roles. May be manifested either by dropping various roles or by "going through the motions."   (26–27, 209)

**Disengagement, societal**   The process whereby society withdraws support from the individual and ceases to seek a commitment from him or her. May be active, such as in compulsory retirement, or passive, as in no encouragement of the older individual to stay on.   (25–26, 209–210, 227)

**Dying trajectory**   The length of time between a terminal diagnosis and death. The rate of terminal decline in functioning.   (179)

**Engagement**   A commitment on the part of the individual to a particular social role. Commitment can be to one role or to several, it may be deep or superficial, and it may be real or symbolic.   (210)

**Extended-care facility**   A long-term health care facility equipped to provide skilled nursing care around the clock. Is equipped for more medical services than a nursing home.   (115)

**Generation**   The average age of mothers at the birth of their first child. Can also be synonymous with *cohort* and *age stratum*.   (23)

**Gerontology**   Literally, the logic of aging. A field of investigation comprised of the results from various traditional disciplines and professions directed toward understanding the processes of aging and their consequences.   (4–5)

**Home care**   Personal care in an independent household.   (113)

**Institution**   A housing facility organized primarily to perform services such as personal care, housekeeping, mental health care, and/or medical care for its residents.   (116)

**Later maturity**  A life cycle stage socially defined or typified by energy decline; awareness of sensory loss; onset of chronic health problems; difficulty in remaining future-oriented; recognition that one's time is growing short; loss of social contacts through retirement; widowhood, and movement of children; and freedom from responsibilities such as work or child rearing.  (11)

**Leisure roles**  Roles that are not obligatory in the formal sense that job roles and family roles often are. Discretionary roles in which the person has a great deal of leeway about when, where, how much, and even if, the role will be played.  (168)

**Life course**  The life of an individual seen as a series of stages, such as infancy, childhood, adulthood, middle age, later maturity, and old age. The life history of an organism.  (10, 88)

**Life expectancy**  The *average* length of time a group of individuals of the same age will live, given current mortality rates. Life expectancy can be computed from any age, but is most often computed from birth.  (13)

**Longitudinal studies**  Studies conducted on the same people over time.  (9)

**Medicaid**  A federal program that provides reasonably complete medical care to welfare clients, regardless of age.  (115)

**Medicare**  A national health insurance program for older Americans. All persons 65 or over are eligible for hospital coverage without payment. Medical coverage requires payment of a monthly premium by the older person. *Complete* medical care coverage requires private health insurance coverage in addition to Medicare.  (114)

**Mental disorders, chronic organic**  Organic mental disorders caused by an irreversible loss of brain tissue or arteriosclerosis.  (112)

**Mental disorders, organic**  Disorders typified by confusion, loss of memory, incoherent speech, or poor orientation to the environment and caused by physical disease.  (112)

**Mental disorders, reversible organic**  Organic mental disorders caused by treatable disease or illness.  (112)

**Middle age**  A stage of the life cycle socially defined or typified by energy decline; shifting from physical to mental activities; feelings of having reached a goal or plateau in one's career; awareness that life is finite; shrinking of family as children leave home; entry of women into the labor force; employment troubles; and feelings of restlessness, of not getting anywhere. (See also *later maturity*; *old age*.)  (10–11)

**Old age**  A stage of the life cycle socially defined or typified by increasing frailty and disability; much introspection and concern over the meaning of life; distinct awareness of approaching death; financial and physical dependency; isolation, boredom, and loneliness. (See also *middle age*; *later maturity*.)  (11)

**Older person**  Conceptually, an individual in the later maturity or old age stages of the life cycle. Socially, people are usually classified as older if they are chronologically 65 or older. Legally, there are several chronological ages that are used to define people as *old*, beginning as early as 45. (See also *later maturity*; *old age*.)  (10–11, 258)

**Pension**   A periodic payment to a person or his or her family, given as a result of previous on-the-job service.   (128)

**Pension, general public**   Retirement pensions available to every job holder and administered by the national government.   (128)

**Pension, job-specific**   Retirement pensions available only through a specific position of employment and administered by a work organization, union, or private insurance company.   (128)

**Pension, retirement**   Income received by retired persons by virtue of having been employed at least a minimum number of years in the past on a job covered by a pension system. (See also *general public pension* and *job-specific pension*.)   (128)

**Period effect**   The extent to which the historical era in which measurements are made affects the results of those measurements.   (9)

**Retired household**   A household whose income comes primarily from retirement pensions.   (132)

**Retired person**   A person who is employed something less than full-time, year-round (whatever that may mean on a particular job) and whose income comes at least in part from a retirement pension.   (139)

**Retirement**   The period following a career of job holding, in which job responsibilities and often opportunities are minimized and in which economic support comes by virtue of having held a job for a minimum length of time in the past.   (95)

**Retirement cohort**   A group of coworkers who retire at the same time from the same place of employment or in the same neighborhood or community.   (171)

**Retirement processes**   The processes whereby the people prepare for, accomplish, adjust to, and live out their retirement. (See also *retirement*.)   (143)

**Senescence**   The group of biological processes whereby the organism becomes less viable and more vulnerable as chronological age increases. Manifests itself as an increased probability of disease, injury, and death.   (33)

**Senility**   An archaic term formerly used as a general term for mental infirmities thought to be the result of aging. (See also *organic mental disorder*.)   (33)

**Senior center**   A voluntary organization for older people that offers its members a range of services (recreation, nutrition, education, transportation, referral, and so on) and that has a specific facility for this purpose.   (265–266)

**Social gerontology**   A subfield of gerontology dealing with the developmental and group behavior of adults and with the causes and consequences of having older people in the population.   (5)

**Social security**   Generally used as a colloquial term referring to the general public retirement pension administered by the federal government. Technically, Social Security also provides a number of other types of benefits to survivors and disabled people. It also administers Medicare.   (128)

**Supplemental Security Income (SSI)**   A national income maintenance program for older Americans that guarantees a minimum income to older people with insufficient resources. Replaced the state-federal Aid for the Aged welfare program.   (133)

# References

| | |
|---|---|
| **7*** | Aaron, Henry<br>1967     "Social security: international comparisons." Pp. 13–48 in Otto Eckstein (ed.), Economics of Income Maintenance. Washington, D.C.: Brookings Institution. |
| **4** | Aaronson, Bernard S.<br>1966     "Personality stereotypes of aging." Journal of Gerontology 21:458–62. |
| **12, 16** | Abdo, E., J. Dills, H. Shectman and M. Yanish<br>1973     "Elderly women in institutions versus those in public housing; comparison of personal and social adjustments." Journal of American Geriatic Society 21: 81–87. |
| | Adams, Bert N. |
| **18** | 1964     "Structural factors affecting parental aid to kin." Journal of Marriage and the Family 26:327–31. |
| **10, 18** | 1968a     Kinship in an Urban Setting. Chicago: Markham. |
| **18** | 1968b     "The middle-class adult and his widowed or still-married mother." Social Problems 16:51–59. |
| **12** | Adams, David L.<br>1971     "Correlates of satisfaction among the elderly." Gerontologist 11 (4, part 2): 64–68. |
| **15** | Administration on Aging<br>1971     "Federal outlays in aging, fiscal years 1967–1972." Facts and Figures on Older Americans, No. 4. Washington, D.C.: U.S. Government Printing Office. |
| **14** | Agan, D.<br>1966     "The employment problems of people over forty." Journal of Employment Counseling 3:10–15. |
| **15** | Agnello, Thomas J., Jr.<br>1973     "Aging and the sense of political powerlessness." Public Opinion Quarterly 37:251–59. |
| **4** | Ahammer, I. M.<br>1973     "Social-learning theory as a framework for the study of adult personality development." Pp. 253–84 in Paul B. Baltes and K. Warner Schaie (eds.), Life-Span Developmental Psychology: Personality and Socialization. New York: Academic Press. |

*Relevant text chapters

**17**     Ailor, James W.
           1969    "The Church provides for the elderly." Pp. 191–206 in Rosamonde R. Boyd
                   and Charles G. Oakes (eds.), Foundations of Practical Gerontology. Columbia,
                   South Carolina: University of South Carolina Press.
**18**     Albrecht, Ruth
           1969    "The family and aging seen cross-culturally." Pp. 27–34 in Rosamonde R.
                   Boyd and Charles G. Oakes (eds.), Foundations of Practical Gerontology.
                   Columbia, South Carolina: University of South Carolina Press.
**18**     Aldous, Joan
           1965    "The consequences of inter-generational continuity." Journal of Marriage and
                   the Family 27:462–68.
**9**      Alford, Harold J.
           1968    Continuing Education in Action: Residential Centers for Lifelong Learning.
                   New York: Wiley.
           Allyn, M. V.
           1975    About Aging: A Catalogue of Films. Los Angeles: Ethel Percy Andrus Geron-
                   tological Center, University of Southern California.
**12**     Alston, J. P., and C. J. Dudley
           1973    "Age, occupation, and life satisfaction." Gerontologist 13:58–61.
**6**      American Association of Homes for the Aged
           1966    The Social Components of Care. New York: The Association.
**6, 16**  American Hospital Association
           1971    Winds of Change: Report of a Conference on Activity Programs in Long-Term
                   Care Institutions. Chicago: The Association.
**12**     Amster, L. E., and H. H. Krauss
           1974    "The relationship between life crises and mental deterioration in old age." Inter-
                   national Journal of Aging and Human Development 5:51–55.
**4, 10**  Anderson, Barbara G.
           1965    "Bereavement as a subject of cross-cultural inquiry: an American sample." An-
                   thropological Quarterly 38:181–200.
           Anderson, Nancy N.
**4**      1965    "Institutionalization, interaction, and self-conception in aging." Pp. 245–57 in
                   Arnold M. Rose and Warren A. Peterson (eds.), Older People and Their Social
                   World. Philadelphia: F. A. Davis.
**4**      1967a   "Effects of institutionalization on self-esteem." Journal of Gerontology 22:
                   313–17.
**1**      1967b   "The significance of age categories for older persons." Gerontologist 7:164–67.
**4**      Andrew, J. M.
           1973    "Coping style and declining verbal abilities." Journal of Gerontology 28:
                   179–83.
**16**     Andrews, R. B.
           1963a   "Housing for the elderly: aspects of its central problem." Gerontologist 3:
                   110–16.
**16**     1963b   "Housing for the elderly: state and city-county based market analysis, an outline
                   of method and administration." Gerontologist 3:148–51.
**14**     Angel, J. L.
           1969    Employment Opportunities for Men and Women after 60. New York: Regents.
**12**     Antonucci, T.
           1974    "On the relationship between values and adjustment in old men." International
                   Journal of Aging and Human Development 5:57–59.
**12**     Apfeldorf, M., P. J. Hunley and G. D. Cooper
           1972    "Disciplinary problems in a home for older veterans: some psychological as-
                   pects in relation to drinking behavior." Gerontologist 12:143–47.

**18**    Apple, Dorrian
          1956    "The social structure of grandparenthood." American Anthropologist 58:656–63.
          Arenberg, David
**3**     1968    "Concept problem solving in young and old adults." Journal of Gerontology 23:279–82.
**3**     1974    "A longitudinal study of problem solving in adults." Journal of Gerontology 29:650–58.
          Arth, Malcolm
          1968    "An interdisciplinary view of the aged in Ibo culture." Journal of Geriatric Psychiatry 2:33–39.
**1**     1972    "Aging: a cross-cultural perspective." Pp. 352–64 in D. P. Kent, R. Kastenbaum and S. Sherwood (eds.), Research Planning and Action for the Elderly: The Power and Potential of Social Science. New York: Behavioral Publications.
**8**     Ash, Phillip
          1966    "Pre-retirement counseling." Gerontologist 6:97–99; 127–28.
**16**    Ashford, N., and F. M. Holloway
          1972    "Transportation patterns of older people in six urban centers." Gerontologist 12:43–47.
          Atchley, Robert C.
**8**     1967    Retired Women: A Study of Self and Role. Unpublished doctoral dissertation. Ann Arbor, Michigan: University Microfilms.
**1, 11** 1969    "Respondents vs. refusers in an interview study of retired women." Journal of Gerontology 24:42–47.
**8**     1971a   "Retirement and leisure participation: continuity or crisis?" Gerontologist 11(1, part 1):13–17.
**13**    1971b   "Disengagement among professors." Journal of Gerontology 26:476–80.
**8**     1971c   "Retirement and work orientation." Gerontologist 11(1, part 1):29–32.
**8**     1974a   "The meaning of retirement." Journal of Communications 24:97–101.
**12**    1974b   "The Age Pattern in Suicides in the United States." Paper presented to the Annual Meeting of the Gerontological Society, Portland, Oregon, October 26.
          1974c   Empirical Studies in Social Gerontology. Oxford, Ohio: Scripps Foundation.
          1974d   "Social problems of the aged." Pp. 391–415 in Rodney Stark (ed.), Social Problems. New York: CRM Book/Random House.
**8, 12** 1975a   "Adjustment to loss of job at retirement." International Journal of Aging and Human Development 6:17–27.
**10**    1975b   "Dimensions of widowhood in later life." Gerontologist 15:176–78.
**5**     1975c   "The life course, age grading, and age-linked demands for decision making." Pp. 261–78 in Nancy Datan and Leon H. Ginsberg (eds.), Life-Span Developmental Psychology: Normative Life Crises. New York: Academic Press.
**5**     1975d   "Sex differences among middle class retired people." Pp. 22–31 in Robert C. Atchley, Research Studies in Social Gerontology. Oxford, Ohio: Scripps Foundation.
          1976a   "Orientation toward the job and retirement adjustment among women." In Jaber F. Gubrium (ed.), Time, Self, and Aging. New York: Behavioral Publications.
**7, 8**  1976b   The Sociology of Retirement. Cambridge, Massachusetts: Schenkman.
          1976c   The Social Forces in Later Life. Second edition. Belmont, California: Wadsworth.
          Atchley, Robert C., and W. Fred Cottrell
          1969    Retired Women: A Preliminary Report. Oxford, Ohio: Scripps Foundation.
**8**     Atchley, Robert C., and Linda K. George
          1973    "Symptomatic measurement of age." Gerontologist 13:136–41.

| | |
|---|---|
| 16 | Atchley, Robert C., and Sheila J. Miller |
| | 1975   "Housing of the rural aged." Pp. 95–143 in Robert C. Atchley (ed.), Environments and the Rural Aged. Washington, D.C.: The Gerontological Society. |
| | Atchley, Robert C., and Judith A. Seltzer |
| | 1975   "Prediction of age identification." Pp. 32–44 in Robert C. Atchley, Research Studies in Social Gerontology. Oxford, Ohio: Scripps Foundation. |
| | Atchley, Robert C., and Mildred M. Seltzer |
| | 1971a   "The impact of structural integration into the profession on work commitment, potential for disengagement, and leisure preferences among social workers." Sociological Focus 5:9–17. |
| | 1971b   "The concept of old: changing attitudes and stereotypes." Gerontologist 11:226–30. |
| | 1976   The Sociology of Aging: Selected Readings. Belmont, California: Wadsworth. |
| | Atchley, Robert C., and Ruth W. Smith |
| | 1975   Research Studies in Social Gerontology. Washington, D.C.: Administration on Aging. |
| **10, 18** | Atchley, Robert C., Linda Pignatiello and Ellen Shaw |
| | 1975   "The effect of marital status on social interaction patterns of older women." Oxford, Ohio: Scripps Foundation. |
| **7, 15,** | Atchley, Robert C., W. Fred Cottrell, Linda K. George and Ruth W. Smith |
| **19** | 1972   Ohio's Older People. Oxford, Ohio: Scripps Foundation. |
| **6, 16** | Atlas, L., and M. M. Morris |
| | 1971   "Resident government: an instrument for the change in a public institution for indigent elderly." Gerontologist 11:209–12. |
| **7** | Attkisson, C. C. |
| | 1970   "Suicide in San Francisco's skid row." Archives of General Psychiatry 23:149–57. |
| **8, 14** | August, R. L. |
| | 1974   "Age discrimination in employment: correcting a constitutionally infirm legislative judgment. Southern California Law Review 47:1311–52. |
| **10** | Averill, J. R. |
| | 1968   "Grief: its nature and significance." Psychological Bulletin 6:721–48. |
| **18** | Axelson, Leland L. |
| | 1960   "Personal adjustments in the postparental period." Marriage and Family Living 22:66–70. |
| | Babbie, Earl R. |
| | 1975   The Practice of Social Research. Belmont, California: Wadsworth. |
| **16** | Babic, Anna L. |
| | 1972   "The older volunteer: expectations and satisfactions." Gerontologist 12:87–89. |
| | Back, Kurt W. |
| **8** | 1969   "The ambiguity of retirement." Pp. 93–114 in Ewalde W. Busse and Eric Pfeiffer (eds.), Behavior and Adaptation in Late Life. Boston: Little, Brown. |
| **10** | 1971a   "Metaphors as a test of personal philosophy of aging." Sociological Focus 5:1–8. |
| **4** | 1971b   "Transition to aging and the self-image." Aging and Human Development 2:296–304. |
| | Back, Kurt W., and Kenneth J. Gergen |
| **1** | 1966a   "Cognitive and motivational factors in aging and disengagement." Pp. 289–95 in Ida H. Simpson and John C. McKinney (eds.), Social Aspects of Aging. Durham, North Carolina: Duke University Press. |
| **12** | 1966b   "Personal orientation and morale of the aged." Pp. 296–305 in Ida H. Simpson and John C. McKinney (eds.), Social Aspects of Aging. Durham, North Carolina: Duke University Press. |

8          Back, Kurt W., and Carleton S. Guptill
          1966    "Retirement and self-ratings." Pp. 120–29 in Ida H. Simpson and John C. McKinney (eds.), Social Aspects of Aging. Durham, North Carolina: Duke University Press.

17         Bahr, H. M.
          1970    "Aging and religious disaffiliation." Social Forces 49:59–71.

2          Bakerman, Seymour (ed.)
          1969    Aging Life Processes. Springfield, Illinois: Charles C. Thomas.

18         Ballweg, John A.
          1967    "Resolution of conjugal role adjustment after retirement." Journal of Marriage and the Family 29:277–81.

          Baltes, Paul B.

1, 19                1968    "Longitudinal and cross-sectional sequences in the study of age and generation effects." Human Development 11:145–71.

1                    1973    "Prototypical paradigms and questions in life-span research on development and aging." Gerontologist 13:458–67.

3          Baltes, Paul B., and Gisela V. Labouvie
          1973    "Adult development of intellectual performance: description, explanation, and modification." Pp. 157–219 in Carl Eisdorfer and M. Powell Lawton (eds.), The Psychology of Adult Development and Aging. Washington, D.C.: American Psychological Association.

          Baltes, Paul B., and K. Warner Schaie
          1973a   (eds.), Life-Span Developmental Psychology: Personality and Socialization. New York: Academic Press.

1                    1973b   "On life-span developmental research paradigms: retrospects and prospects." Pp. 365–95 in Paul B. Baltes and K. Warner Schaie (eds.), Life-Span Developmental Psychology: Personality and Socialization. New York: Academic Press.

3                    1974    "Aging and I.Q.: the myth of the twilight years." Psychology Today 7(10): 35–38, 40.

8          Barfield, Richard E.
          1970    The Automobile Worker and Retirement. Ann Arbor, Michigan: University of Michigan, Institute of Social Research.

8          Barfield, Richard E., and James Morgan
          1969    Early Retirement: The Decision and the Experience. Ann Arbor, Michigan: University of Michigan, Institute of Social Research.

8          Barresi, C. M.
          1974    "The meaning of work: a case study of elderly poor." Industrial Gerontology 1:24–34.

16         Barresi, C. M., and H. F. Coyle, Jr.
          1972    "Elderly services and industries: a pilot program of part-time employment for elderly poor." Gerontologist 12:371–74.

1          Barron, Milton L.
          1953    "Minority group characteristics of the aged in American society." Journal of Gerontology 8:477–82.

8, 14      Bauder, Ward W., and Jon A. Doerflinger
          1967    "Work roles among the rural aged." Pp. 22–43 in E. Grant Youmans (ed.), Older Rural Americans. Lexington, Kentucky: University of Kentucky Press.

6          Bauer, Mary Lou
          1972    "Health characteristics of low-income persons." Vital and Health Statistics, Series 10, No. 74.

3          Bayley, Nancy
          1968    "Cognition and aging." Pp. 97–119 in K. Warner Schaie (ed.), Theory and Methods of Research on Aging. Morgantown, West Virginia: West Virginia University.

3    Bayley, Nancy, and Melita Oden
    1955    "The maintenance of intellectual ability in gifted adults." Journal of Geron-
         tology 10:91–107.

16    Bayne, J. R. D.
    1971    "Environmental modification for the older person." Gerontologist 11:314–17.

1    Beale, Calvin L.
    1964    "Rural depopulation in the United States: some demographic consequences of
         agricultural adjustments." Demography 1:264–72.

16    Beattie, Walter M., Jr.
    1960    "The aging negro: some implications for social welfare services." Phylon 21:
         131–35.

    de Beauvoir, Simone
    1972    The Coming of Age. New York: G. P. Putnam's Sons.

4    Becker, Howard S., and Anselm Strauss
    1968    "Careers, personality, and adult socialization." Pp. 311–20 in Bernice L. Neu-
         garten (ed.), Middle Age and Aging. Chicago: University of Chicago Press.

4    Becker, W. C.
    1964    "Consequences of different kinds of parental discipline." Pp. 91–107 in M. L.
         Hoffman (ed.) Review of Child Development. Volume I. New York: Russell
         Sage Foundation.

18    Bekker, L. de Moyne, and Charles Taylor
    1966    "Attitudes toward aging in a multigenerational sample." Journal of Gerontology
         21:115–18.

3    Belbin, E., and R. Meredith Belbin
    1969    "Selecting and training adults for New York." Pp. 66–81 in A. T. Welford
         (ed.), Decision Making and Age. New York: S. Karger.

14    Belbin, R. M., and S. Clarke
    1971    "International trends in employment among men over 65." Industrial Geron-
         tology 9:18–23.

18    Belcher, John C.
    1967    "A consequence of the isolated nuclear family." Journal of Marriage and the
         Family 29:534–40.

12    Bell, B. D.
    1974    "Cognitive dissonance and the life satisfaction of older adults." Journal of Ger-
         ontology 29:564–71.

    Bell, B. D., and G. G. Stanfield
4    1973a    "Chronological age in relation to attitudinal judgments: an experimental anal-
         ysis." Journal of Gerontology 28:491–96.
1    1973b    "The aging stereotype in experimental perspective." Gerontologist 13:341–44.

10    Bell, Robert
    1971    Marriage and Family Interaction. Third edition. Homewood, Illinois: Dorsey
         Press.

6    Bell, Tony
    1967    "The relationship between social involvement and feeling old among residents
         in homes for the aged." Journal of Gerontology 22:17–22.

16    Bell, W. G., and W. T. Olsen
    1974    "An overview of public transportation and the elderly: new directions and social
         policy." Gerontologist 14:324–30.

18    Bellin, Seymour S., and Robert H. Hardt
    1958    "Marital status and mental disorders of the aged." American Sociological Re-
         view 23:155–62.

Bengtson, Vern L.

**8**  1969 "Differences between subsamples in level of present role activity." Pp. 35–49 in Robert J. Havighurst, J. M. Munnichs, B. Neugarten and H. Thomae (eds.), Adjustment to Retirement: A Cross-National Study. New York: Humanities Press.

**18**  1971 "Inter-age perceptions and the generation gap." Gerontologist 11(4, part 2): 85–89.

**11**  1973 "Self-determination: a social-psychologic perspective on helping the aged." Geriatrics 28:118–30.

**18**  Bengtson, Vern L., and Joseph A. Kuypers

1971 "Generational difference and the developmental stake." Aging and Human Development 2:249–60.

**4**  Bengtson, Vern L., and M. C. Lovejoy

1973 "Values, personality and social structure: an intergenerational analysis." American Behavioral Scientist 16:880–912.

**5, 12**  Bengtson, Vern L., M. J. Furlong and R. S. Laufer

1974 "Time, aging, and the continuity of social structure: themes and issues in generational analysis." Journal of Social Issues 30:1–30.

**1**  Bengtson, Vern L., James J. Dowd, David H. Smith and Alex Inkeles

1975 "Modernization, modernity, and perceptions of aging: a cross-cultural study." Journal of Gerontology 30:688–95.

Bennett, Ruth G.

**6**  1963 "The meaning of institutional life." Gerontologist 3:(3, part 3):117–25.

**19**  1970 "Social context—a neglected variable in research on aging." Aging and Human Development 1:97–116.

**16**  1973 "Living conditions and everyday needs of the elderly with particular reference to social isolation." International Journal of Aging and Human Development 4:179–98.

**8**  1974 "Retirement: the emerging social pattern." Pp. 119–33 in W. C. Bier (ed.), Aging: Its Challenge to the Individual and to Society. The Pastoral Psychology Series, No. 8. New York: Fordham University Press.

**1**  Bennett, Ruth G., and J. Eckman

1973 "Attitudes toward aging: a critical examination of recent literature and implications for future research." Pp. 575–97 in C. Eisdorfer and M. P. Lawton (eds.), The Psychology of Adult Development and Aging. Washington, D.C.: American Psychological Association.

Bennett, Ruth, and Lucille Nahemow

**6**  1965 "Institutional totality and criteria of social adjustment in residences for the aged." Journal of Social Issues 21(October):44–76.

**12**  1972 "Socialization and social adjustment in five residential settings for the aged." Pp. 514–24 in D. P. Kent, R. Kastenbaum and S. Sherwood (eds.), Research Planning and Action for the Elderly: The Power and Potential of Social Science. New York: Behavioral Publications.

**10**  Benson, R. A., and D. C. Brodie

1975 "Suicide by overdoses of medicine among the aged." Journal of American Geriatric Society 23:304–08.

Berardo, Felix M.

**10**  1968 "Widowhood status in the U.S.: perspectives on a neglected aspect of the family life cycle." The Family Coordinator 17:191–203.

**10**  1970 "Survivorship and social isolation: the case of the aged widower." The Family Coordinator 19:11–15.

| | |
|---|---|
| **7** | Beresford, John C., and Alice M. Rivlin<br>1966 "Privacy, poverty, and old age." Demography 3:247–58. |
| **4** | Berezin, Martin A.<br>1969 "Sex and old age: a review of the literature." Journal of Geriatric Psychiatry 2: 131–49. |
| **16** | Berg, W. B., L. Atlas and J. Zeiger<br>1974 "Integrated homemaking services for the aged in urban neighborhoods." Gerontologist 14:388–93. |
| **15** | Bernard, Jessie<br>1974 "Age, sex and feminism." Pp. 120–37 in Frederick R. Eisele (ed.), Political Consequences of Aging. Philadelphia: American Academy of Political and Social Sciences. |
| **7** | Bernstein, M. C.<br>1974 "Forecast of women's retirement income: cloudy and colder; 25 percent chance of poverty." Industrial Gerontologist 1(2):1–13. |
| **1, 19** | Berwick, Keith<br>1967 "The 'senior citizen' in America: a study in unplanned obsolescence." Gerontologist 7:257–60. |
| **18** | Bettelheim, Bruno<br>1962 "The problem of generations." Daedalus 91(1):68–96. |
| | Beyer, Glenn H. |
| **16** | 1962 "Living arrangements, attitudes, and preferences of older persons." Pp. 348–69 in Clark Tibbitts and Wilma Donahue (eds.), Social and Psychological Aspects of Aging. New York: Columbia University Press. |
| **16** | 1963 Economic Aspects of Housing for the Aged. Ithaca, New York: Cornell University Center for Housing and Environmental Studies. |
| **16** | 1965 Housing and Society. New York: Macmillan. |
| **16** | Beyer, Glenn, and F. H. J. Nierstrasz<br>1967 Housing the Aged in Western Countries: Programs, Dwellings, Homes, and Geriatric Facilities. New York: Elsevier. |
| **16** | Beyer, Glenn, and S. G. Wahl<br>1963 The Elderly and Their Housing. Ithaca, New York: Cornell University Center for Housing and Environmental Studies. |
| **17** | Beyer, Glenn H., and Margaret Woods<br>1963 Living and Activity Patterns of the Aged. Research Report No. 6. Ithaca, New York: Cornell University Center for Housing and Environmental Studies. |
| **5** | Biddle, Bruce J., and E. J. Thomas<br>1966 Role Theory: Concepts and Research. New York: Wiley. |
| **12** | Bigot, A.<br>1974 "The relevance of American Life Satisfaction Indices for research on British subjects before and after retirement." Age and Ageing 3:113–21. |
| | Binstock, Robert H. |
| **19** | 1969 "The Gerontological Society and public policy: a report." Gerontologist 9(1):69. |
| **15** | 1972 "Interest-group liberalism and the politics of aging." Gerontologist 12:265–80. |
| **15** | 1974 "Aging and the future of American politics." Pp. 199–212 in Frederick R. Eisele (ed.), Political Consequences of Aging. Philadelphia: American Academy of Political and Social Sciences. |
| **19** | 1975 "Planning for tomorrow's urban aged: a policy analyst's reaction." Gerontologist 15:42. |
| | Birren, James E. |
| **3, 4** | 1959 (ed.), Handbook of Aging and the Individual. Chicago: University of Chicago Press. |
| | 1964a Relations of Development and Aging. Springfield, Illinois: Charles C. Thomas. |

**3**        1964b    The Psychology of Aging. Englewood Cliffs, New Jersey: Prentice-Hall.
**1**        1969    "The aged in cities." Gerontologist 9(3, part 1):163–69.
**3**        1973    "A summary: prospects and problems of research on the longitudinal develop-
                    ments of man's intellectual capacities throughout life." Pp. 149–54 in L. F.
                    Jarvik, C. Eisdorfer and J. E. Blum (eds.), Intellectual Functioning in Adults:
                    Psychological and Biological Influences. New York: Springer.

**4**        Birren, James E., and D. S. Woodruff
            1973    "Human development over the life span through education." Pp. 305–37 in Paul
                    B. Baltes and K. Warner Schaie (eds.), Life-Span Developmental Psychology:
                    Personality and Socialization. New York: Academic Press.

**7**        Bixby, Lenore E.
            1970    "Income of people aged 65 and over: an overview from the 1968 survey of the
                    aged." Social Security Bulletin 33(4):3–34.

**8**        Bixby, Lenore E., and E. Eleanor Rings
            1969    "Work experience of men claiming retirement benefits, 1966." Social Security
                    Bulletin 32(8):3–14.

**7**        Bixby, Lenore, Wayne Finegar, Susan Grad, Walter Kolodrubetz, Patience Lauriat and
            Janet Murray
            1975    Demographic and Economic Characteristics of the Aged: 1968 Social Security
                    Survey. Washington, D.C.: United States Government Printing Office.

**2**        Bjorksten, Johan
            1969    "Theories." Pp. 147–79 in Seymour Bakerman (ed.), Aging Life Processes.
                    Springfield, Illinois: Charles C. Thomas.

**7**        Blackburn, John O.
            1963    "Pensions, the national income, and the national wealth." Pp. 178–98 in Juanita
                    M. Kreps (ed.), Employment, Income, and Retirement Problems of the Aged.
                    Durham, North Carolina: Duke University Press.

**1**        Blau, David, and Martin A. Berezin
            1968    "Some ethnic and cultural considerations in aging." Journal of Geriatric Psy-
                    chiatry 2:3–5.

**10, 18**   Blau, Zena S.
            1961    "Structural constraints on friendship in old age." American Sociological Re-
                    view 26:429–39.

**10**       Blauner, Robert
            1968    "Death and social structure." Psychiatry 29:378–94.

            Blenkner, Margaret
**18**       1965    "Social work and family relationships in later life with some thoughts on filial
                    maturity." Pp. 46–59 in Ethel Shanas and Gordon F. Streib (eds.), Social Struc-
                    ture and the Family. Englewood Cliffs, New Jersey: Prentice-Hall.
**16**       1967    "Environmental change and the aging individual." Gerontologist 7:101–05.

**16**       Blenkner, Margaret, Edna Wasser and Martin Bloom
            1967    Protective Services for Older People: Progress Report for 1966–67. Cleveland,
                    Ohio: The Benjamin Rose Institute.

**9**        Bley, N., M. Goodman, D. Dye and B. Harel
            1972    "Characteristics of aged participants and non-participants in age-segregated
                    leisure program." Gerontologist 12:368–70.

**16**       Blonsky, Lawrence E.
            1974    "Problems in development of a community action program for the elderly."
                    Gerontologist 14:394–401.

**4**        Bloom, Kenneth L.
            1961    "Age and self-concept." American Journal of Psychiatry 118:534–38.

Bloom, Martin

5      1964    "Life-span analysis: a theoretical framework for behaviorial science research." Journal of Human Relations 12:538–54.

16    1973    "Gerontological evaluation in the 21st century: a fable." Gerontologist 13: 318–21.

16    Bloom, Martin, and M. Nielsen

        1971    "The older person in need of protective services." Social Casework 52:500–09.

2     Blumenthal, H. T., and Aline W. Berns

        1964    "Autoimmunity and aging." Pp. 289–342 in Bernard L. Strehler (ed.), Advances in Gerontological Research. Volume 1. New York: Academic Press.

12    Bock, E. Wilbur

        1972    "Aging and suicide: the significance of marital, kinship, and alternative relations." Family Coordinator 21:71–80.

10    Bok, S.

        1973    "Euthanasia and the care of the dying." Bioscience 23:461–66.

10    Bornstein, P. E., and others

        1973    "The depression of widowhood after thirteen months." British Journal of Psychiatry 122:561–66.

4     Bortner, R. W., and D. F. Hultsch

        1974    "Patterns of subjective deprivation in adulthood." Developmental Psychology 10:534–45.

     Botwinick, Jack

3     1959    "Drives, expectancies, and emotions." Pp. 739–68 in James E. Birren (ed.), Handbook of Aging and the Individual. Chicago: University of Chicago Press.

3     1967    Cognitive Processes in Maturity and Old Age. New York: Springer.

3     1973    Aging and Behavior. New York: Springer.

     Botwinick, Jack, and M. Storandt

4     1974a   "Cardiovascular status, depressive affect, and other factors in reaction time." Journal of Gerontology 29:543–48.

3     1974b   Memory, Related Functions and Age. Springfield, Illinois: Charles C. Thomas.

1     Bouvier, Leon F.

        1974    "The demography of aging." Pp. 37–46 in W. C. Bier (ed.), Aging: Its Challenge to the Individual and to Society. New York: Fordham University Press.

     Boyd, Rosamonde R.

18    1969a   "Emerging roles of the four-generation family." Pp. 35–50 in Rosamonde R. Boyd and Charles G. Oakes (eds.), Foundations of Practical Gerontology. Columbia, South Carolina: University of South Carolina Press.

18    1969b   "The valued grandparent: a changing social role." Pp. 90–102 in Wilma Donahue (ed.), Living in the Multigenerational Family. Ann Arbor, Michigan: University of Michigan, Wayne State University Institute of Gerontology.

     Boyd, Rosamonde R., and Charles G. Oakes (eds.)

        1973    Foundations of Practical Gerontology. Second edition. Columbia, South Carolina: University of South Carolina Press.

7     Brady, Dorothy S.

        1965    Age and Income Distribution. Washington, D.C.: United States Government Printing Office.

12    Brand, Frederick N., and Richard T. Smith

        1974    "Life adjustment and relocation of the elderly." Journal of Gerontology 29: 336–40.

8     Breen, Leonard Z.

        1963    "Retirement—norms, behavior, and functional aspects of normative behavior." Pp. 381–88 in Richard H. Williams, Clark Tibbitts and Wilma Donahue (eds.), Processes of Aging. Volume 2. New York: Atherton Press.

7        Brennan, Michael J., Philip Taft and Mark Schupack
         1967    The Economics of Age. New York: W. W. Norton.
16       Breslau, Naomi, and Marie R. Haug
         1972    "The elderly aid the elderly: the Senior Friends Program." Social Security Bul-
                 letin 35(11):9–15.
4        Brim, Orville
         1968    "Adult socialization." Pp. 182–226 in John Clausen (ed.), Socialization in
                 Society. Boston: Little, Brown.
4, 18    Brim, Orville, and Stanton Wheeler
         1966    Socialization After Childhood. New York: Wiley.
7        Brinker, Paul A.
         1968    Economic Insecurity and Social Security. New York: Appleton-Century-Crofts.
3        Brinley, G. F.
         1965    "Cognitive sets and accuracy of performance in the elderly." Pp. 114–49 in
                 Alan T. Welford and James E. Birren (eds.), Behavior, Aging, and the Nervous
                 System. Springfield, Illinois: Charles C. Thomas.
         Britton, Joseph H.
16       1964    "Living in a rural Pennsylvania community in old age." Pp. 99–105 in Frances
                 M. Carp and W. M. Burnett (eds.), Patterns of Living and Housing of Middle-
                 Aged and Older People. Washington, D.C.: Public Health Service.
4        1972    Personality Changes in Aging. New York: Springer.
18       Britton, Joseph H., and Jean O. Britton
         1967    "The middle-aged and older rural person and his family." Pp. 44–74 in E. Grant
                 Youmans (ed.), Older Rural Americans. Lexington, Kentucky: University of
                 Kentucky.
16       Britton, Joseph H., William G. Mather and Alice Lansing
         1962    "Expectations for older persons in a rural community: community participa-
                 tion." Rural Sociology 27:387–95.
8        Brodsky, Carroll M.
         1971    "Compensation illness as a retirement channel." Journal of the American Geri-
                 atrics Society 19:51–60.
         Brody, Elaine M.
18       1963    "The transition from extended families to nuclear families." Pp. 77–82 in Rich-
                 ard H. Williams, Clark Tibbitts and Wilma Donahue (eds.), Processes of
                 Aging. Volume 2. New York: Atherton Press.
18       1966    "Aging as a family crisis: implications for research and planning." Pp. 49–52
                 in Proceedings of the Seventh International Congress of Gerontology. Volume
                 7. Vienna: Wiener Medizinischen Akademie.
6        1971    "Long-term care for the elderly: optimums, options and opportunities." Journal
                 of American Geriatric Society 19:482–94.
16       Brody, Elaine M., and C. Cole
         1971    " 'Deferred status' applicants to a voluntary home for aged." Gerontologist 11:
                 219–25.
6        Brody, Elaine M., and Geraldine M. Spark
         1966    "Institutionalization of the aged: a family crisis." Family Process 5:76–90.
6        Brody, Stanley J.
         1973    "Comprehensive health care for the elderly: an analysis. The continuum of med-
                 ical, health, and social services for the aged." Gerontologist 13:412–18.
3, 4     Bromley, D. B.
         1974    The Psychology of Human Ageing. Second edition. Baltimore: Penguin Books.
16       Bronson, E. P.
         1972    "An experiment in intermediate housing facilities for the elderly." Gerontol-
                 ogist 12:22–26.

Brown, A. S.

16     1972     Final Report on the Problems of Mobilizing the Elderly with a Special Transportation Project. Missoula, Montana: University of Montana, Institute of Social Science Research.

12     1974     "Satisfying relationships for the elderly and their patterns of disengagement." Gerontologist 14:258–62.

7     Brown, J. D.

    1972     An American Philosophy of Social Security: Evolution and Issues. Princeton, New Jersey: Princeton University Press.

11     Brown, Roger

    1965     Social Psychology. New York: Free Press.

5     Bruhn, J. G.

    1971     "An ecological perspective of aging." Gerontologist 11:318–21.

4     Buhler, Charlotte, and D. Massarik (eds.)

    1968     The Course of Human Life. New York: Springer.

17     Bull, C. N., and J. B. Aucoin

    1975     "Voluntary association participation and life satisfaction: a replication note." Journal of Gerontology 30:73–76.

Bultena, Gordon L.

8     1969a     "Health patterns of aged migrant retirees." Journal of the American Geriatrics Society 17:1127–31.

12     1969b     "Life continuity and morale in old age." Gerontologist 9(4, part 1):251–53.

18     1969c     "The relationship of occupational status to friendship ties in three planned retirement communities." Journal of Gerontology 24:461–64.

18     1969d     "Rural-urban differences in family interaction of the aged." Rural Sociology 34:5–15.

16     1974     "Structural effects on the morale of the aged: a comparison of age-segregated and age-integrated communities." Pp. 18–31 in Jaber F. Gubrium (ed.), Late Life. Communities and Environmental Policy. Springfield, Illinois: Charles C. Thomas.

6, 12     Bultena, Gordon L., and R. Oyler

    1971     "Effects of health on disengagement and morale." Aging and Human Development 2:142–48.

Bultena, Gordon L., and Vivian Wood

8, 16     1969a     "The American retirement community: bane or blessing?" Journal of Gerontology 24:209–17.

8     1969b     "Normative attitudes toward the aged role among migrant and nonmigrant retirees." Gerontologist 9(3, part 1):204–08.

6     Bultena, Gordon, Edward Powers, Peter Falkman and David Frederick

    1971     Life After 70 in Iowa. Sociology Report 95. Ames, Iowa: Iowa State University.

1     Bunzel, J. H.

    1972     "Note on the history of a concept—gerontophobia." Gerontologist 12:116, 203.

Burgess, Ernest W. (ed.)

    1960     Aging in Western Societies. Chicago: University of Chicago Press.

6     Burnham, Clinton E.

    1974     "Edentulous persons: United States—1971." Vital and Health Statistics, Series 10, No. 89.

Burnside, I. M. (ed.)

6     1971     "Long-term group work with hospitalized aged." Gerontologist 11:213–18.

3     1975     Sexuality and Aging. Los Angeles, California: Ethel Percy Andrus Gerontology Center, University of Southern California.

18     Burr, Wesley

    1970     "Satisfaction with various aspects of marriage over the life cycle: a random middle-class sample." Journal of Marriage and the Family 32:29–37.

**6**    Busse, Ewald W.
    1965    "The aging process and the health of the aged." Pp. 220–25 in Francis C.
            Jeffers (ed.), Duke University Council on Gerontology: Proceedings of Semi-
            nars, 1961–1965. Durham, North Carolina: Duke University Regional Center
            for the Study of Aging.
        Busse, Ewald W., and Eric Pfeiffer (eds.)
    1969    Behavior and Adaptation in Late Life. Boston: Little, Brown.
        Butler, Robert N.
**4, 12**  1963    "The life review: an interpretation of reminiscence in the aged." Psychiatry
            26:65–76.
**6**    1968    "Patterns of psychological health and psychiatric illness in retirement." Pp. 27–
            41 in Frances M. Carp (ed.), The Retirement Process. Washington, D.C.:
            United States Government Printing Office.
**1**    1969    "Age-ism: another form of bigotry." Gerontologist 9:243–46.
**7**    1973    "Public interest report No. 9. How to grow old and poor in an affluent society."
            International Journal of Aging and Human Development 4:277–79.
**12**   1974    "Successful aging and the role of the life review." Journal of American Geri-
            atric Society 22:529–35.
    1975    Why Survive? Being Old in America. New York: Harper & Row.
        Butler, Robert N., and M. I. Lewis
    1973    Aging and Mental Health. Saint Louis, Missouri: C. V. Mosby.
        Byerts, T. O. (ed.)
**16**   1973    Housing and Environment for the Elderly. San Juan Conference Summary.
            Washington, D.C.: Gerontological Society.
**16**   1974    Housing and Environment for the Elderly. Complete Proceedings of the Soci-
            ety's Working Conference on Behavioral Research Utilization and Environmen-
            tal Policy held in San Juan, Puerto Rico, December 16–20, 1971. Washington,
            D.C.: Gerontological Society.
**16**   Byerts, T., J. Gertman, A.-M. Guillemard, M. P. Lawton, M. Leeds, R. Rajic and F. M.
        Carp
    1972    "Transportation." Gerontologist 12(2, part 2):11–16.
        Cain, Leonard D., Jr.
**5**    1964    "Life course and social structure." Pp. 272–309 in Robert E. L. Faris (ed.),
            Handbook of Modern Sociology. Chicago: Rand McNally.
**5, 6**   1967    "Age status and generational phenomena: the new old people in contemporary
            America." Gerontologist 7:83–92.
    1968    "Aging and the character of our times." Gerontologist 8:250–58.
**15**   1974    "The growing importance of legal age in determining the status of the elderly."
            Gerontologist 14:167–74.
        Cain, L. S.
**6**    1969    "Determining the factors that affect rehabilitation." Journal of the American
            Geriatrics Society 17:595–604.
**16**   California Commission on Aging
    1970    Delivery and administration of services for the elderly. Based on series of train-
            ing institutes presented by Gerontology Center, University of Southern Cal-
            ifornia and California Commission on Aging, 1968–69. Sacramento, California:
            California Commission on Aging.
**7**    Callison, James C.
    1974    "Early experience under the supplemental security income program." Social
            Security Bulletin 37(6):3–11.
        Cameron, Paul
**12**   1967    "Ego strength and happiness of the aged." Journal of Gerontology 22:199–202.
**6**    1972a   "Pre-Medicare beliefs about the generations regarding medicine and health."
            Journal of Gerontology 27:536–39.

| | | |
|---|---|---|
| 12 | 1972b | "Stereotypes about generational fun and happiness versus self-appraised fun and happiness." Gerontologist 12:120–23, 190. |
| 3 | 1973 | "Which generation is believed to be intellectually superior and which generation believes itself to be intellectually superior." International Journal of Aging and Human Development 4:257–70. |
| 12 | 1975 | "Mood as an indicant of happiness: age, sex, social class, and situational differences." Journal of Gerontology 30:216–24. |

Cameron, Paul, and H. Biber
| | | |
|---|---|---|
| 3 | 1973 | "Sexual thought throughout the life-span." Gerontologist 13:144–47. |

Cameron, Paul, L. Stewart and H. Biber
| | | |
|---|---|---|
| 10 | 1973 | "Consciousness of death across the life-span." Journal of Gerontology 28: 92–95. |

Cameron, Paul, L. Stewart, L. Craig and L. J. Eppelman
| | | |
|---|---|---|
| 4 | 1973 | "Thing versus self versus other mental orientation across the life-span: a note." British Journal of Psychology 64:283–86. |

Campbell, Angus
| | | |
|---|---|---|
| 15 | 1971 | "Politics through the life cycle." Gerontologist 11(2, part 1):112–17. |

Campbell, M. E.
| | | |
|---|---|---|
| 6 | 1971 | "Study of the attitudes of nursing personnel toward the geriatric patient." Nursing Research 20:147–51. |

Cantelli, Edmund J., and June L. Shmelzer (eds.)
| | | |
|---|---|---|
| 16 | 1970 | Transportation and Aging: Selected Issues. Washington, D.C.: United States Government Printing Office. |

Cantor, Marjorie H.
| | | |
|---|---|---|
| 18 | 1975 | "Life space and the social support system of the inner city elderly of New York." Gerontologist 15:23–27. |

Carlie, Michael K.
| | | |
|---|---|---|
| 15 | 1969 | "The politics of age: interest group or social movement?" Gerontologist 9(4, part 1):259–63. |

Carp, Frances M.
| | | |
|---|---|---|
| 16 | 1966a | A Future for the Aged: Victoria Plaza and Its Residents. Austin, Texas: University of Texas Press. |
| 16 | 1966b | "Effects of improved housing on the lives of older people." Pp. 147–67 in Frances M. Carp and W. M. Burnett (eds.), Patterns of Living and Housing of Middle-Aged and Older People. Washington, D.C.: United States Public Health Service. |
| | 1967 | "Attitudes of old persons toward themselves and toward others." Journal of Gerontology 22:308–12. |
| 16 | 1968a | Factors in the Utilization of Services by the Mexican-American Elderly. Palo Alto, California: American Institute for Research. |
| 13 | 1968b | "Some components of disengagement." Journal of Gerontology 23:382–86. |
| 8 | 1968c | The Retirement Process. Washington, D.C.: United States Department of Health, Education and Welfare. |
| 15 | 1968d | "Differences among older workers, volunteers, and persons who are neither." Journal of Gerontology 23:497–501. |
| 12, 13 | 1968e | "Person-situation congruence in engagement." Gerontologist 8:184–88. |
| 4 | 1969a | "The psychology of aging." Pp. 100–16 in Rosamonde R. Boyd and C. G. Oakes (eds.), Foundations of Practical Gerontology. Second edition. Columbia, South Carolina: University of South Carolina Press. |
| 16 | 1969b | "Use of community services and social integration of the aged." Pp. 169–76 in Frances C. Jeffers (ed.), Duke University Council on Aging and Human Development: Proceedings of Seminars 1965–69. Durham, North Carolina: Duke University Center for the Study of Aging and Human Development. |
| | 1969c | "Compound criteria in gerontological research." Journal of Gerontology 24: 341–47. |

16     1969d    "Housing and minority-group elderly." Gerontologist 9:20–24.

16     1970     "The mobility of retired people." Pp. 23–41 in Edmund J. Cantelli and June L. Shmelzer (eds.), Transportation and Aging: Selected Issues. Washington, D.C.: United States Government Printing Office.

19     1971a    "Research goals and priorities in gerontology." Gerontologist 11(1, part 1):67.

18     1971b    (ed.), Retirement. New York: Behavioral Publications.

16     1972a    "Retired people as automobile passengers." Gerontologist 12:66–72.

16     1972b    "The mobility of older slum-dwellers." Gerontologist 12:57–65.

16     1972c    "Mobility among members of an established retirement community." Gerontologist 12:48–56.

4      1974     "Reactions to gifts as indicators of personality-behavior traits in the elderly." International Journal of Aging and Human Development 5:265–80.

16     1975a    "Long-range satisfaction with housing." Gerontologist 15:68–72.

16     1975b    "Life-style and location within the city." Gerontologist 15:27–34.

10     Cartwright, A., L. Hockey and J. L. Anderson

       1971     Life Before Death. London: Routledge & Kegan Paul.

16     Casey, G. M.

       1971     "Public library service to the aging." American Libraries 2:999–1004.

10     Cassell, E. J.

       1973     "Permission to die." Bioscience 23:475–78.

18     Cavan, Ruth S.

       1956     "Family tensions between the old and the middle-aged." Marriage and Family Living 18:323–27.

12     Cavan, Ruth S., and others

       1949     Personal Adjustment in Old Age. Chicago: Science Research Associates.

7      Chandler, Suzannah

       1968     Home Maintenance and Repair Program for the Older Poor. New York: National Council on the Aged.

       Charles, Don C.

8      1971     "Effect of participation in a preretirement program." Gerontologist 11(1, part 1):24–28.

3      1973     Explaining intelligence in adulthood: the role of life history. Gerontologist 13: 483–88.

16     Chase, John A.

       1969     "Better housing for senior citizens." Pp. 207–10 in Rosamonde R. Boyd and Charles G. Oakes (eds.), Foundations of Practical Gerontology. Second edition. Columbia, South Carolina: University of South Carolina Press.

       Chen, Yung-Ping

7      1966a    "Economic poverty: the special case of the aged." Gerontologist 6:39–45.

8      1966b    "Low income, early retirement and tax policy." Gerontologist 6:35–38.

10     Chevan, A., and J. H. Korson

       1972     "The widowed who live alone: an examination of social and demographic factors." Social Forces 51(September):45–53.

8      Chicago Department of Human Resources

       1971     Survey of Pre- and Post-Retirement Programs in Metropolitan Chicago. Chicago: Division for Senior Citizens.

16     Chinn, A. B. (ed.)

       1971     Working with Older People: A Guide to Practice. Volume 4. Clinical Aspects of Aging. PHS Publication No. 1459. Washington, D.C.: United States Government Printing Office.

       Chown, Sheila M.

3      1961     "Age and the rigidities." Journal of Gerontology 16:353–62.

14     1972     "The effect of flexibility-rigidity and age on adaptability in job performance." Industrial Gerontology 13:105–21.

3      Chown, Sheila, and Klaus F. Reigel (eds.)
         1968    Psychological Functioning in the Normal Aging and Senile Aged. New York: S. Karger.

9      Christ, Edwin A.
         1965    "The 'retired' stamp collector: economic and other functions of a systematized leisure activity." Pp. 93–112 in Arnold M. Rose and Warren A. Peterson (eds.), Older People and Their Social World. Philadelphia: F. A. Davis.

18      Christenson, Cornelia V., and John H. Gagnon
         1965    "Sexual behavior in a group of older women." Journal of Gerontology 20: 351–56.

4, 18      Christenson, Cornelia V., and A. B. Johnson
         1973    "Sexual patterns in a group of older never-married women." Journal of Geriatric Psychiatry 6:80–98.

3      Cijfer, E.
         1966    "An experiment on some differences in logical thinking between Dutch medical people, under and over the age of 35." Acta Psychologica 25:159–71.

14      Clague, Evan
         1971    "Work and leisure for older workers." Gerontologist 11(1, part 2):9–20.

14      Clague, Evan, B. Palli and L. Kramer
         1971    The Aging Worker and the Union: Employment and Retirement of Middle-Aged and Older Workers. New York: Praeger.

4      Clark, Margaret
         1967    "The anthropology of aging, a new area for studies of culture and personality." Gerontologist 7:55–64.

5, 11      Clark, Margaret, and Barbara Anderson
12          1967    Culture and Aging. Springfield, Illinois: Charles C. Thomas.

4      Clausen, John (ed.)
         1968    Socialization in Society. Boston: Little, Brown.

14      Clelland, P. G.
         1973    "Age discrimination law: rights and responsibilities of employers and individuals." Industrial Gerontology 18:53–64.

     Clemente, Frank
14          1973    "Age and academic mobility." Gerontologist 13:453–56.
15          1975    "Age and the perception of national priorities." Gerontologist 15:61–63.

3      Clemente, Frank, and Jon Hendricks
         1973    "A further look at the relationship between age and productivity." Gerontologist 13:106–10.

12      Clemente, Frank, and W. J. Sauer
         1974    "Race and morale of the urban aged." Gerontologist 14:342–44.

1      Clemente, Frank, and G. F. Summers
         1973    "Industrial development and the elderly: a longitudinal analysis." Journal of Gerontology 28:479–83.

16      Clifford, M. E.
         1972    "Learning ability and age: a bibliography for training programs." Industrial Gerontology 12:50–68.

4, 6      Coe, Rodney M.
         1965    "Self-conception and institutionalization." Pp. 225–43 in Arnold M. Rose and Warren A. Peterson (eds.), Older People and Their Social World. Philadelphia: F. A. Davis.

6      Coe, Rodney M., and Elizabeth Barnhill
         1965    "Social participation and health of the aged." Pp. 211–23 in Arnold M. Rose and Warren A. Peterson (eds.), Older People and Their Social World. Philadelphia: F. A. Davis.

4    Coet, L., and R. C. Tindall
     1974    "Definition of 'handicap' as a function of age and sex." Psychological Reports
             34:1197–98.

6    Cohen, Burton H.
     1964    "Family patterns of mortality and life span." Quarterly Review of Biology 39:
             130–81.

15   Cohen, Elias S.
     1974    "Legal research issues on aging." Gerontologist 14:263–67.

8    Cohen, Wilbur J.
     1970    "Social Security—the first thirty-five years." Pp. 1–32 in Occasional Papers in
             Gerontology, No. 7. Ann Arbor, Michigan: University of Michigan, Wayne
             State University Institute of Gerontology.

     Comfort, Alex
2    1964a   Ageing: The Biology of Senescence. New York: Holt, Rinehart, and Winston.
2    1964b   The Process of Aging. New York: New American Library.
4    Conte, H. R.
     1971    "Studies of body image: body worries and body discomforts." Pp. 595–96 in
             Proceedings of the 79th American Psychological Association Annual Conven-
             tion, 1971. Division 20: Maturity and Old Age. Washington, D.C.: American
             Psychological Association.

7    Cooper, Barbara S., and Mary F. McGee
     1971    "Medical care outlays for three age groups: young, intermediate, and aged."
             Social Security Bulletin 34(5):3–14.

7    Cooper, Barbara S., and Paula A. Piro
     1974    "Age differences in medical care spending, fiscal year 1973." Social Security
             Bulletin 37:3–14.

6    Corbin, Mildred, and Aaron Krute
     1975    "Some aspects of medicare experience with group-practice prepayment plans."
             Social Security Bulletin 38(3):3–11.

     Cottrell, Fred
8    1955    Energy and Society. New York: McGraw-Hill.
15   1960a   "Governmental functions and the politics of age." Pp. 624–65 in Clark Tibbitts
             (ed.), Handbook of Social Gerontology. Chicago: University of Chicago Press.
14   1960b   "The technological and societal basis of aging." Pp. 92–119 in Clark Tibbitts
             (ed.), Handbook of Social Gerontology. Chicago: University of Chicago Press.
15   1966    "Aging and the political system." Pp. 77–113 in John C. McKinney and Frank
             T. de Vyver (eds.), Aging and Social Policy. New York: Appleton-Century-
             Crofts.
15   1968    "Political deprivation and the aged." in Perspectives on Human Deprivation.
             Washington, D.C.: National Institute of Mental Health.
8, 14 1970   Technological Change and Labor in the Railroad Industry. Lexington, Massa-
             chusetts: D. C. Heath.
15   1971a   Government and Non-Government Organization. Washington, D.C.: White
             House Conference on Aging.
16   1971b   "Transportation of older people in a rural community." Sociological Focus 5:
             29–40.

8, 12, Cottrell, Fred, and Robert C. Atchley
17   1969    Women in Retirement: A Preliminary Report. Oxford, Ohio: Scripps Foundation.
9    Cousins, Norman
     1968    "Art, adrenalin, and the enjoyment of living." Saturday Review, April 20, pp.
             20–24.

Cowgill, Donald O.

**1**    1972    "A theory of aging in cross-cultural perspective." Pp. 1–14 in Donald O. Cowgill and Lowelyn Holmes (eds.), Aging and Modernization. New York: Appleton-Century-Crofts.

**15**    1974a    "The aging of populations and societies." Pp. 1–18 in Frederick R. Eisele (ed.), Political Consequences of Aging. Philadelphia: American Academy of Political and Social Sciences.

**1**    1974b    "Aging and modernization: a revision of the theory." Pp. 123–46 in Jaber F. Gubrium (ed.), Late Life. Communities and Environmental Policy. Springfield, Illinois: Charles C. Thomas.

**9**    Cowgill, Donald O., and Norma Baulch
        1962    "The use of leisure time by older people." Gerontologist 2:47–50.

**13**    Cowgill, Donald O., and Lewelyn Holmes
        1972    Aging and Modernization. New York: Appleton-Century-Crofts.

**5, 10**    Cox, Peter R., and J. R. Ford
        1964    "The mortality of widows shortly after widowhood." Lancet 1:163–64.

Crane, D.

**3**    1965    "Scientists at major and minor universities." American Sociological Review 30:699–714.

**10**    1973    "Physicians' attitudes toward the treatment of critically ill patients." Bioscience 23:471–74.

Cribier, F.

**8**    1970a    "Les migrations de retraite en France; matériaux pour une geographie du troisième âge." Bulletin, Association de Geographes Français (381):1–4.

        1970b    "La migration de retraite des fonctionnaires parisiens." Bulletin, Association Geographes Français (381):16–24.

Crittenden, John

**15**    1962    "Aging and party affiliation." Public Opinion Quarterly 26:648–57.
**15**    1963    "Aging and political participation." Western Political Quarterly 16:323–31.
**14**    Crockett, Jean A.
        1963    "Older people as consumers." Pp. 127–46 in Harold L. Orbach and Clark Tibbitts (eds.), Aging and the Economy. Ann Arbor, Michigan: University of Michigan Press.

**15**    Crouch, B. M.
        1972    "Age and institutional support: perceptions of older Mexican-Americans." Journal of Gerontology 27:524–29.

**12**    Crumbaugh, J. C.
        1972    "Aging and adjustment: the applicability of logotherapy and the Purpose-in-Life Test." Gerontologist 12:418–20.

Cryns, A. G., and A. Monk

**4**    1972    "Attitudes of the aged toward the young: a multivariate study of intergenerational perception." Journal of Gerontology 27:107–12.

        1973    "Attitudes toward youth as a function of adult age: a multivariate study of intergenerational dynamics." International Journal of Aging and Human Development 4:23–33.

**12**    Cumming, Elaine
        1964    "New thoughts on the theory of disengagement." Pp. 3–18 in Robert Kastenbaum (ed.), New Thoughts on Old Age. New York: Springer.

**5, 12,**    Cumming, Elaine, and William E. Henry
**13**        1961    Growing Old: The Process of Disengagement. New York: Basic Books.

**12**    Cumming, Elaine, Lois R. Dean, David S. Newell and Isabel McCaffrey
        1960    "Disengagement—a tentative theory of aging." Sociometry 23:23–35.

**15**      Cummings, Frank
    1974   "Reforming private pensions." Pp. 80–94 in Frederick R. Eisele (ed.), Political Consequences of Aging. Philadelphia: American Academy of Political and Social Sciences.

**9**       Cunningham, David A., Henry J. Montoye, Helen L. Metzner and Jacob B. Keller
    1968   "Active leisure time activities as related to age among males in a total population." Journal of Gerontology 23:551–56.

**3**       Cunningham, W. R., V. Clayton and W. Overton
    1975   "Fluid and crystallized intelligence in young adulthood and old age." Journal of Gerontology 30:53–55.

**2**       Curtis, Howard J.
    1966   Biological Mechanisms of Aging. Springfield, Illinois: Charles C. Thomas.

**9**       Curtis, Joseph E., and Dulcy B. Miller
    1967   "Community sponsored recreation in an extended care facility." Gerontologist 7:196–99.

**15**      Cutler, Neal E.
    1969   "Generation, maturation, and party affiliation: a cohort analysis." Public Opinion Quarterly 33:583–88.

**15**      Cutler, Neal E., and Vern L. Bengtson
    1974   "Age and political alienation." Pp. 160–75 in Frederick R. Eisele (ed.), Political Consequences of Aging. Philadelphia: American Academy of Political and Social Sciences.

    Cutler, Stephen J.
**1, 12**       1972a  "An approach to the measurement of prestige loss among the aged." Aging and Human Development 3:285–92.

**12, 16**      1972b  "The availability of personal transportation, residential location, and life satisfaction among the aged." Journal of Gerontology 27:383–89.

**15**          1973   "Perceived prestige loss and political attitudes among the aged." Gerontologist 13:69–75.

**17**          1973   "Voluntary association membership and life satisfaction: a cautionary research note." Journal of Gerontology 28:96–100.

**17**          1974   "The effects of transportation and distance on voluntary association participation among the aged." International Journal of Aging and Human Development 5:81–94.

**12, 16**      1975a  "Transportation and changes in life satisfaction." Gerontologist 15:155–59.

    1975b  "Age differences in voluntary association memberships." Paper presented at the meeting of the Gerontological Society in Louisville, Kentucky, October 29.

**2**       Damon, Albert
    1972   "Predicting age from body measurements and observations." Aging and Human Development 3:169–73.

**8**       Davidson, Wayne R., and Karl R. Kunze
    1965   "Psychological, social and economic meanings of work in modern society: their effects on the worker facing retirement." Gerontologist 5:129–33.

**14**      Davis, H. E.
    1973   "Pension provisions affecting the employment of older workers." Monthly Labor Review 96(4):41–45.

**7**       Davis, K.
    1973   "Hospital costs and the Medicare program." Social Security Bulletin 36(8):18–36.

    Davis, R. H. (ed.)
**16**          1972   Community Services and the Black Elderly. Los Angeles: Ethel Percy Andrus Gerontological Center, University of Southern California.

**10**          1973a  Dealing With Death. Los Angeles: Ethel Percy Andrus Gerontological Center, University of Southern California.

**6, 19**   1973b   Health Services and the Mexican-American Elderly. Los Angeles: Ethel Percy Andrus Gerontological Center, University of Southern California.

**6, 16**   Davis, R. H., and W. K. Smith (eds.)
  1973   Non-Profit Homes for the Aging: Planning, Development, and Programming. Los Angeles: Ethel Percy Andrus Gerontological Center, University of Southern California.

**16**   Davis, R. H., M. Audet and L. Baird (eds.)
  1973   Housing for the Elderly. Los Angeles: Ethel Percy Andrus Gerontological Center. University of Southern California.

Davis, Robert W.

**4**   1963   "The relationship of social preferability to self-concept in an aged population." Journal of Gerontology 18:431–36.

**4**   1967   "Social influences on the aspiration tendency of older people." Journal of Gerontology 22:510–16.

**7**   David, Z. M.
  1960   "Old-age, survivors, and disability insurance: twenty-five years of progress." Industrial and Labor Relations Review 14:10–23.

**3, 6**   Dawson, A. M., and W. R. Baller
  1972   "Relationship between creative activity and the health of elderly persons." Journal of Psychology 82:49–58.

**3, 4**   Dean, Lois R.
  1962   "Aging and the decline of affect." Journal of Gerontology 17:440–46.

**12**   DeCarlo, T. J.
  1974   "Recreation participation patterns and successful aging." Journal of Gerontology 29:416–22.

**16**   De Crow, Roger
  1975   New Learning for Older Americans: An Overview of National Effort. Washington, D.C.: Adult Education Association.

**3**   Denney, D. R., and N. W. Denney
  1973   "The use of classification for problem solving: a comparison of middle and old age." Developmental Psychology 9:275–78.

**6**   Denney, Duane, Delbert M. Kole and Ruth G. Matarazzo
  1965   "The relationship between age and the number of symptoms reported by patients." Journal of Gerontology 20:50–53.

**4**   Denney, N. W., and M. L. Lennon
  1972   "Classification: a comparison of middle and old age." Developmental Psychology 7:210–13.

Dennis, Wayne

**4**   1960   "Long-term constancy of behavior." Journal of Gerontology 15:195–96.

**3**   1966   "Creative productivity between the ages of 20 and 80 years." Journal of Gerontology 21:1–8.

**18**   Deutscher, Irwin
  1968   "The quality of postparental life." Pp. 263–68 in Bernice L. Neugarten (ed.), Middle Age and Aging. Chicago: University of Chicago Press.

**16**   Dick, Harry R.
  1964   "Residential patterns of aged persons prior to institutionalization." Journal of Marriage and the Family 26:96–98.

**3**   Dickinson, P. A.
  1974   The Fires of Autumn: Sexual Activity in the Middle and Later Years. New York: Drake Publications.

**10**   Dickstein, L. S.
  1972   "Death concern: measurement and correlates." Psychological Reports 30:563–71.

**6**     Dingfelder, Adele G.
       1969   "Chronic conditions causing activity limitation: United States, July 1963 to June 1965." Vital and Health Statistics, Series 10, No. 51.

**8**     Distefano, M. K.
       1969   "Changes in work related attitudes with age." Journal of Genetic Psychology 114:127–34.

     Donahue, Wilma

**6**       1963   "Rehabilitation of long-term aged patients." Pp. 541–65 in Richard H. Williams, Clark Tibbitts and Wilma Donahue (eds.), Processes of Aging. Volume 1. New York: Atherton Press.

**16**       1966   "Impact of living arrangements on ego development in the elderly." Pp. 1–9 in Frances M. Carp and W. M. Burnett (eds.), Patterns of Living and Housing of Middle-Aged and Older People. Washington, D.C.: United States Public Health Service.

**18**       1969   Living in the Multigenerational Family. Ann Arbor, Michigan: University of Michigan Institute of Gerontology.

**15**     Donahue, Wilma, and Clark Tibbitts (eds.)
       1962   Politics of Age. Ann Arbor, Michigan: University of Michigan Press.

**8**     Donahue, Wilma, Harold Orbach and Otto Pollak
       1960   "Retirement: the emerging social pattern." Pp. 330–406 in Clark Tibbitts (ed.), Handbook of Social Gerontology. Chicago: University of Chicago Press.

**15**     Douglass, Elizabeth B., William P. Cleveland and George L. Maddox
       1974   "Political attitudes, age, and aging: a cohort analysis of archival data." Journal of Gerontology 29:666–75.

**12**     Dowd, J. J.
       1975   "Aging as exchange: a preface to theory." Journal of Gerontology 30:584–93.

**17**     Downing, Joseph
       1957   "Factors affecting the selective use of a social club for the aged." Journal of Gerontology 12:81–84.

**8**     Drake University Pre-Retirement Center
       1968   A Program to Prepare Older Workers for Retirement and Interest Community Groups in the Pre-Retirement Planning. Des Moines, Iowa: Drake University Pre-Retirement Center.

**8**     Draper, J. E., E. F. Lundgren and G. B. Strother
       1967   Work Attitudes and Retirement Adjustment. Madison, Wisconsin: University of Wisconsin Bureau of Business Research and Services.

**12**     Dressler, D. M.
       1973   "Life adjustment of retired couples." International Journal of Aging and Human Development 4:335–49.

     Drevenstedt, J.
       1975   "Scale-checking styles on the semantic differential among older people." Journal of Gerontology 30:170–73.

**16**     Drickhamer, J.
       1971   "Rhode Island project: book reviews by older citizens." Library Journal 96: 2737–43.

**9**     Dumazedier, Joffre, and A. Ripert
       1963   "Retirement and leisure." International Social Science Journal 15:438–47.

**9**     Dunning, B. B., and A. D. Biderman
       1973   "The case of military 'retirement.'" Industrial Gerontology 17:18–37.

**9**     Durkee, Stephen
       1964   "Artistic expression in later life." Pp. 305–15 in Robert Kastenbaum (ed.), New Thoughts on Old Age. New York: Springer.

**18**     Duvall, Evelyn
         1971    Family Development. Fourth edition. Philadelphia: Lippincott.
**16**     Dye, D., M. Goodman, M. Roth, N. Bley and K. Jensen
         1973    "The older adult volunteer compared to the nonvolunteer." Gerontologist 13:
                 215–18.
**12, 17**  Edwards, John N., and David L. Klemmack
         1973    "Correlates of life satisfaction: a reexamination." Journal of Gerontology 28:
                 497–502.
         Ehrlich, I. F.
**16**     1972    "Life-styles among persons 70 years and older in age-segregated housing."
                 Gerontologist 12:27–31.
**1**      1973    "Toward a social profile of the aged black population in the United States: an
                 exploratory study." International Journal of Aging and Human Development
                 4:271–76.
**3**      Eichorn, D. H.
         1973    "The Institute of Human Development Studies, Berkeley and Oakland." Pp.
                 149–54 in L. F. Jarvik, C. Eisdorfer and J. E. Blum (eds.), Intellectual Func-
                 tioning in Adults: Psychological and Biological Influences. New York: Springer.
         Eisdorfer, Carl, and M. P. Lawton (eds.)
**19**     1968    "Patterns of federal funding for research in aging." Gerontologist 8:3–6.
**8**      1972    "Adaptation to loss of work." Pp. 245–66 in Frances M. Carp (ed.), Retire-
                 ment. New York: Behavioral Publications.
         Eisdorfer, C., and M. P. Lawton (eds.)
         1973    The Psychology of Adult Development and Aging. Washington, D.C.: Ameri-
                 can Psychological Association.
         Eisenstadt, S. N.
         1956    From Generation to Generation: Age Groups and Social Structure. Glencoe,
                 Illinois: Free Press.
**8**      Ellison, David L.
         1968    "Work, retirement and the sick role." Gerontologist 8:189–92.
**8**      Epstein, Lenore A.
         1966    "Early retirement and work-life experience." Social Security Bulletin 29(3):3–10.
**8**      Epstein, Lenore A., and Janet H. Murray
         1968    "Employment and retirement." Pp. 354–56 in Bernice L. Neugarten (ed.),
                 Middle Age and Aging. Chicago: University of Chicago Press.
**4**      Erikson, Erik H.
         1963    Childhood and Society. New York: Macmillan.
**15**     Erskine, Hazel G.
         1963    "The polls." Public Opinion Quarterly 27:137–39.
         Estes, C. L.
**16**     1973    "Barriers to effective community planning for the elderly." Gerontologist
                 13:178–83.
**16**     1974    "Community planning for the elderly: a study of goal displacement." Journal of
                 Gerontology 20:684–91.
**8**      Eteng, W. I. A., and D. G. Marshall
         1970    Retirement and Migration in the North Central States: A Comparative Analysis
                 in Wisconsin, Florida and Arizona. Population Services No. 20. Madison,
                 Wisconsin: University of Wisconsin, Department of Rural Sociology.
**6**      Euster, G. L.
         1971    "A system of groups in institutions for the aged." Social Casework 52:523–29.
**3**      Eysenck, M. W.
         1974    "Age differences in incidental learning." Developmental Psychology 10:
                 936–41.

| | |
|---|---|
| **10, 12** | Farberow, Norman L., and Sharon Y. Moriwaki<br>1975    "Self-destructive crises in the older person." Gerontologist 15:333–37. |
| **10** | Feifel, Herman, and R. Jones<br>1968    "Perception of death as related to nearness to death." Proceedings of the 76th Annual Convention of the American Psychological Association 3:545–46. |
| **15** | Feingold, Eugene<br>1966    Medicare, Policy and Politics. San Francisco: Chandler. |
| **8** | Feingold, H.<br>1971    "The effects of the meaning of work on retirement attitudes among civil servants." Industrial Gerontology 9:46. |
| **14** | Feldman, L.<br>1975    "Employment problems of older workers: a review by the International Labor Organization Advisory Committee." Industrial Gerontology 2:69–71. |
| **10** | Feldman, M. J., P. J. Handal and H. S. Barahal<br>1974    Fears Related to Death and Suicide. New York: Manuscripts Information Corporation. |
| **6, 16** | Felton, B., and E. Kahana<br>1974    "Adjustment and situationally-bound locus of control among institutionalized aged." Journal of Gerontology 29:295–301. |
| **4** | Fengler, A. P., and V. Wood<br>1972    "The generation gap: an analysis of attitudes on contemporary issues." Gerontologist 12:124–28. |
| **3** | Filer, Richard N., and Desmond O. O'Connell<br>1964    "Motivation of aging persons." Gerontologist 19:15–22. |
| | Fillenbaum, Gerda G. |
| **8, 14** | 1971a    "A consideration of some factors related to work after retirement." Gerontologist 11:18–23. |
| **8** | 1971b    "On the relation between attitude to work and attitude to retirement." Journal of Gerontology 26:244–48. |
| **8** | 1971c    "Retirement planning programs—at what age, and for whom?" Gerontologist 11:33–36. |
| **8, 14** | 1971d    "The working retired." Journal of Gerontology 26:82–89. |
| **14** | Fillenbaum, Gerda G., and G. L. Maddox<br>1974    "Work after retirement: an investigation into some psychologically relevant variables." Gerontologist 14:418–24. |
| **14** | Ferman, Louis A., and Michael Aiken<br>1967    "Mobility and situational factors in the adjustment of older workers to job displacement." Human Organization 26:235–41. |
| **4** | Finkle, A. L.<br>1973    "Emotional quality and physical quantity of sexual activity in aging males." Journal of Geriatric Psychiatry 6:70–79. |
| **10** | Fischer, H. K., and B. M. Dlin<br>1971    "Man's determination of his time of illness or death. Anniversary reactions and emotional deadlines." Geriatrics 26:88–94. |
| **3** | Fisher, Jerome<br>1973    "Competence, effectiveness, intellectual functioning and aging." Gerontologist 13:62–68. |
| **3** | Fisher, Jerome, and Robert C. Pierce<br>1967    "Dimensions of intellectual functioning in the aged." Journal of Gerontology 22:166–73. |
| **16** | Fisher, L. D., and J. R. Solomon<br>1974    "Guardianship: a protective service program for the aged." Social Casework 55:618–21. |

Fisher, Paul

7     1973     "Major social security issues: Japan, 1972." Social Security Bulletin 36(3): 26–38.

14     1975     "Labor force participation of the aged and the social security system in nine countries." Industrial Gerontology 2:1–13.

10   Flannery, R. B., Jr.
       1974     "Behavior modification of geriatric grief: a transactional perspective." International Journal of Aging and Human Development 5:197–203.

15   Foner, Anne
       1974     "Age stratification and age conflict in political life." American Sociological Review 39:187–96.

7   Fox, Alan
       1974     Earnings Replacement from Social Security and Private Pensions: Newly Entitled Beneficiaries, 1970. Washington, D.C.: Social Security Administration.

3   Fozard, James L., and Gordon D. Carr
       1972     "Age differences and psychological estimates of abilities and skill." Industrial Gerontology 13:75–96.

4   Francher, J. S.
       1973     " 'It's the Pepsi generation. . . .' Accelerated aging and the television commercial." International Journal of Aging and Human Development 4:245–55.

14   Franke, Walter H.
       1963     "Labor market experience of unemployed older workers." Monthly Labor Review 86:282–84.

10   Franklin, Paula A.
       1975     "The disabled widow." Social Security Bulletin 38(1):20–27.

16   Freeman, J. T.
       1972     "Elderly drivers: growing numbers and growing problems." Geriatrics 27(7):46–56.

16   Freund, J. W.
       1971     "The meaning of volunteer services in schools—to the educator and to the older adult." Gerontologist 11:205–08.

16   Fried, Marc
       1963     "Grieving for a lost home." Pp. 151–71 in Leonard Duhl (ed.), The Urban Condition. New York: Basic Books.

4   Friedman, Alfred S., and Samuel Granick
       1963     "A note on anger and aggression in old age." Journal of Gerontology 18:283–85.

8   Friedman, Eugene A., and Robert J. Havighurst (eds.)
       1954     The Meaning of Work and Retirement. Chicago: University of Chicago Press.

8   Friedmann, Eugene A., and Harold L. Orbach
       1974     "Adjustment to retirement." Pp. 609–45 in Silvano Arieti (ed.), American Handbook of Psychiatry. New York: Basic Books.

1   Friedrich, Douglas
       1972     A Primer for Developmental Methodology. Minneapolis: Burgess.

9   Friedsam, H. J., and C. A. Martin
       1973     "Travel by older people as a use of leisure." Gerontologist 13:204–07.

15   Fries, Victoria, and Robert N. Butler
       1971     "The congressional seniority system: the myth of gerontocracy in Congress." Aging and Human Development 2:341–48.

17   Fukuyama, Yoshio
       1961     "The major dimensions of church membership." Review of Religious Research 2:154–61.

7   Gage, F. B.
       1971     "Suicide in the aged." American Journal of Nursing 71:2153–55.

6      Gagnon, Raymond O.
       1974    "Selected characteristics of nursing homes for the aged and chronically ill:
               United States, June–August, 1969." Vital and Health Statistics, Series 12,
               No. 23.

       Gaitz, Charles M., and J. Scott
       1975    "Analysis of letters to 'Dear Abby' concerning old age." Gerontologist 15:47–50.

6      Gaitz, Charles M., M. Powell Lawton and Raymond Harris
       1968    Goals of Comprehensive Health Care in Advanced Old Age. Ann Arbor, Mich-
               igan: University of Michigan, Wayne State University Institute of Gerontology.

8      Gallaway, Lowell E.
       1965    The Retirement Decision: An Exploratory Essay. Social Security Administra-
               tion Research Report No. 9. Washington, D.C.: United States Government
               Printing Office.

10     Garfield, C. A.
       1974    "Psychothanatological concomitants of altered state experience." Unpublished
               doctoral dissertation, University of California at Berkeley (as cited in Kalish,
               1976).

6      Gelfand, Donald E.
       1968    "Visiting patterns and social adjustment in an old age home." Gerontologist
               8:272–75.

6      Geltner, Luzer
       1969    "Somatic illness: prevention and rehabilitation." Pp. 76–87 in Marjorie F.
               Lowenthal and Ariv Zilli (eds.), Colloquium on Health and Aging of the Popu-
               lation. New York: S. Karger.

10     Gerber, I., R. Rusalem, N. Hannon, D. Battin and A. Arkin
       1975    "Anticipatory grief and aged widows and widowers." Journal of Gerontology
               30:225–29.

4      Gergen, Kenneth J., and Kurt W. Back
       1966    "Cognitive constriction in aging and attitudes toward international issues."
               Pp. 322–34 in Ida H. Simpson and John C. McKinney (eds.), Social Aspects of
               Aging. Durham, North Carolina: Duke University Press.

8      Gernant, L.
       1972    "What 814 retired professors say about retirement." Gerontologist 12:349–53.

       Gerontological Society
19     1971    "Research designs and proposals in applied social gerontology: third report,
               1971." Gerontologist 11(4, part II).

19     1971    "Research proposals in applied social gerontology." Gerontologist 11(1, part
               2):2–4.

3, 4   Giambra, L. M.
       1974    "Daydreaming across the life span: late adolescent to senior citizen." Inter-
               national Journal of Aging and Human Development 5:115–40.

8      Gibson, Geoffrey
       1972    "Kin family network: overheralded structure of past conceptualizations of family
               functioning." Journal of Marriage and the Family 34:13–28.

3      Gilbert, J. G.
       1973    "Thirty-five-year follow-up study of intellectual functioning." Journal of
               Gerontology 28:68–72.

4      Gilmore, A. J. J.
       1972    "Personality in the elderly: problems in methodology." Age and Ageing
               1:227–32.

9      Giordano, Enrico A., and D. F. Seaman
       1968    "Continuing education for the aging—evidence for a positive outlook." Geron-
               tologist 8(1, part 1):63–64.

12 Gladwin, T.
1967 "Social competence and clinical practice." Psychiatry 30:30–43.
10 Glaser, B. G.
1966 "The social loss of aged dying patients." Gerontologist 6:77–80.
Glaser, B. G., and A. L. Strauss
10 1965 Awareness of Dying. Chicago: Aldine.
10 1968 Time for Dying. Chicago: Aldine.
Glenn, Norval D.
15 1969 "Aging, disengagement, and opinionation." Public Opinion Quarterly 33:17–33.
15 1974 "Age and conservatism." Pp. 176–86 in Frederick R. Eisele (ed.), Political Consequences of Aging. Philadelphia: American Academy of Political and Social Science.
15 Glenn, Norval D., and Michael Grimes
1968 "Aging, voting, and political interest." American Sociological Review 33:563–75.
15 Glenn, Norval D., and Ted Hefner
1972 "Further evidence on aging and party identification." Public Opinion Quarterly 36:31–47.
10 Glick, Ira O., Robert S. Weiss and C. Murray Parkes
1974 The First Year of Bereavement. New York: Wiley.
18 Glick, Paul C., and Robert Parke, Jr.
1965 "New approaches in studying the life cycle of the family." Demography 2:187–202.
6 Goff, Phoebe H.
1971 "Disabled beneficiary population, 1957–66." Social Security Bulletin 34(7): 32–43.
4 Goffman, Erving
1961 Encounters. New York: Bobbs-Merrill.
15 Gold, Byron D.
1974 "The role of the federal government in the provision of social services to older persons." Pp. 55–69 in Frederick R. Eisele (ed.), Political Consequences of Aging. Philadelphia: American Academy of Political and Social Sciences.
12 Golden, H. M.
1973 "The dysfunctional effects of modern technology on the adaptability of aging." Gerontologist 13:136–43.
18 Goldfarb, Alvin I.
1965 "Psychodynamics and the three-generational family." Pp. 10–45 in Ethel Shanas and Gordon F. Streib (eds.), Social Structure and the Family: Generational Relations. Englewood Cliffs, New Jersey: Prentice-Hall.
12 Goldsamt, Milton R.
1967 "Life satisfaction and the older disabled worker." Journal of the American Geriatrics Society 15:394–99.
Goldscheider, Calvin
1, 16 1966 "Differential residential mobility of the older population." Journal of Gerontology 21:103–08.
5 1971 Population, Modernization and Social Structure. Boston: Little, Brown.
Goldstein, Sidney
7, 14 1960 Consumption Patterns of the Aged. Philadelphia: University of Pennsylvania Press.
14 1965 "Changing income and consumption patterns of the aged, 1950–1960." Journal of Gerontology 20:453–61.
14 1966 "Urban and rural differentials in consumer patterns of the aged." Rural Sociology 31:333–45.

14    1968    "Home tenure and expenditure patterns of the aged, 1960–1961." Gerontologist 8:17–24.

14    1971    "Negro-white differentials in consumer patterns of the aged, 1960–1961." Gerontologist 11:242–49.

9    Goodman, M., N. Bley and D. Dye
      1974    "The adjustment of aged users of leisure programs." American Journal of Orthopsychiatry 44:142–49.

15    Goodwin, Leonard, and Joseph Tu
      1975    "The social psychological basis for public acceptance of the Social Security System." The American Psychologist 30:875–83.

5    Gordon, Gerald
      1966    Role Theory and Illness. New Haven, Connecticut: College and University Press Services.

      Gordon, Margaret S.

7    1960    "Aging and income security." Pp. 208–60 in Clark Tibbitts (ed.), Handbook of Social Gerontology. Chicago: University of Chicago Press.

8    1961    "Work and patterns of retirement." Pp. 15–53 in Robert W. Kleemeier (ed.), Aging and Leisure. New York: Oxford University Press.

7, 8    1963    "Income security programs and the propensity to retire." Pp. 436–58 in Richard H. Williams, Clark Tibbitts, and Wilma Donahue (eds.), Processes of Aging. Volume 2. New York: Atherton Press.

4    Gordon, S. K.
      1973    "The phenomenon of depression in old age." Gerontologist 13:100–05.

10    Gorer, Geoffrey
      1965    Death, Grief and Mourning. Garden City, New York: Doubleday.

      Gottesman, Leonard E.

19    1970    "Long-range priorities for the aged." Aging and Human Development 1:393–400.

6    1973    "Milieu treatment of the aged in institutions." Gerontologist 13:23–26.

16    Gottschalk, S.
      1972    "Fifty years at Moosehaven: the lessons of experience." Gerontologist 12:235–40.

8    Goudy, W. J., E. A. Powers and P. Keith
      1975    "Work and retirement: a test of attitudinal relationships." Journal of Gerontology 30:193–98.

4    Gozali, J.
      1971    "The relationship between age and attitude toward disabled persons." Gerontologist 11:289–91.

16    Grabowsky, S., and W. D. Mason
      1974    Learning for Aging. Washington, D.C.: Adult Educational Association.

7    Grad, Susan
      1973    "Relative importance of income sources of the aged." Social Security Bulletin 36(8):37–45.

12    Graney, M. J., and E. E. Graney
      1973    "Scaling adjustment in older people." International Journal of Aging and Human Development 4:351–59.

      Granick, S., and R. D. Patterson (eds.)
      1972    Human Aging II. An Eleven Year Follow-up Biomedical and Behavioral Study. Washington, D.C.: United States Government Printing Office.

6    Grauer, H.
      1971    "Institutions for the aged—therapeutic communities?" Journal of American Geriatric Society 19:687–92.

17    Gray, Robert M., and David O. Moberg
      1962    "The Church and the older person." Grand Rapids, Michigan: W. B. Eerdmans.

8              Green, Mark R., and others
                   1969    Pre-retirement Counseling, Retirement, Adjustment and the Older Employee.
                           Eugene, Oregon: University of Oregon Graduate School of Management.
16             Greenleigh Associates
                   1966    An Evaluation of the Foster Grandparent Program. New York: The Greenleigh
                           Associates.
7              Griffiths, K. A., O. W. Farley, W. P. Dean and L. L. Boon
                   1971    "Socio-economic class and the disadvantaged senior citizen." Aging and
                           Human Development 2:288–95.
               Griffitt, W., J. Nelson and G. Littlepage
                   1972    "Old age and response to agreement-disagreement." Journal of Gerontology
                           27:269–74.
10             Gruman, G. J.
                   1973    "An historical introduction to ideas about voluntary euthanasia, with a biblio-
                           graphic survey and guide for interdisciplinary studies." Omega 4(2):87–138.

               Gubrium, Jaber F.
6, 7,              1970    "Environmental effects on morale in old age and the resources of health and
12                         solvency." Gerontologist 10:294–97.
15                 1972a   "Continuity in social support, political interest and voting in old age." Geron-
                           tologist 12:421–23.
                   1972b   "Toward a socio-environmental theory of aging." Gerontologist 12:281–84.
4                  1973a   "Apprehensions of coping incompetence and responses to fear in old age."
                           International Journal of Aging and Human Development 4:111–25.
                   1973b   The Myth of the Golden Years: A Socio-Environmental Theory of Aging.
                           Springfield, Illinois: Charles C. Thomas.
10                 1974a   "Marital desolation and the evaluation of everyday life in old age." Journal of
                           Marriage and the Family 36:107–13.
                   1974b   Late Life: Communities and Environmental Policy. Springfield, Illinois:
                           Charles C. Thomas.
16                 1974c   "Victimization in old age. Available evidence and three hypotheses." Crime &
                           Delinquency, July:245–50.
18                 1975    "Being single in old age." International Journal of Aging and Human Develop-
                           ment 6:29–41.

8              Guillemard, A. -M.
                   1972    Le Retraite. Une Morte Sociale. Paris–La Haye: Mouton.
18             Gurin, Gerald, Joseph Veroff and Sheila Feld
                   1960    Americans View Their Mental Health: A National Interview Study. New York:
                           Basic Books.
4              Gutman, David L.
                   1969    The Country of Old Men: Cultural Studies in the Psychology of Later Life.
                           Ann Arbor, Michigan: University of Michigan, Wayne State University Insti-
                           tute of Gerontology.
4              Gutmann, D., L. Gottesman and S. Tessler
                   1973    "A comparative study of ego functioning in geriatric patients." Gerontologist
                           13:419–23.
9              Guttmann, D.
                   1973    "Leisure-time activity interests of Jewish aged." Gerontologist 13:219–23.
4              Haan, N., and D. Day
                   1974    "A longitudinal study of change and sameness in personality development:
                           adolescence to later adulthood." International Journal of Aging and Human
                           Development 5:11–39.
6              Hall, E. H., R. D. Savage, N. Bolton, D. M. Pidwell and G. Blessed
                   1972    "Intellect, mental illness, and survival in the aged: a longitudinal investigation."
                           Journal of Gerontology 27:237–44.

16    Hall, Gertrude H.
       1966    The Law and the Impaired Older Person. New York: National Council on the
               Aging.
      Hall, Gertrude H., and Geneva Mathiasen (eds.)
16       1968    Overcoming Barriers to Protective Services for the Aged. New York: National
                 Council for the Aging.
16       1973    Guide to Development of Protective Services for Older People. Springfield,
                 Illinois: Charles C. Thomas.
16    Hamovitch, Maurice B., and J. E. Peterson
         1969    "Housing needs and satisfactions of the elderly." Gerontologist 9:30–32.
      Handal, P. J.
         1969    "The relationship between subjective life expectancy, death anxiety, and general
                 anxiety." Journal of Clinical Psychology 25:39–42.
      Hansen, P. From (ed.)
         1964    Age with a Future. Copenhagen: Munksgaard.
14    Hanson, P. M.
         1972    "Age and physical capacity to work." Industrial Gerontology 12:20–28.
      Harris, Louis
8        1965a   "Pleasant retirement expected." Washington Post, November 28.
18       1965b   "Thoughts of loneliness haunt elderly Americans." Washington Post, Novem-
                 ber 29.
4     Harris, Louis, and Associates
         1975    The Myth and Reality of Aging in America. New York: National Council on
                 Aging.
10    Harvey, Carol D., and Howard M. Bahr
         1974    "Widowhood, morale, and affiliation." Journal of Marriage and the Family
                 36:97–106.
16    Haskell, M. A.
         1972    Income and Housing Characteristics on Delaware's Elderly Population.
                 Newark, Delaware: University of Delaware, Division of Urban Affairs.
17    Hausknecht, Murray
         1962    The Joiners: A Sociological Description of Voluntary Association Membership
                 in the United States. New York: Bedminster Press.
12    Havens, Betty J.
         1968    "An investigation of activity patterns and adjustment in an aging population."
                 Gerontologist 8:201–06.
      Havighurst, Robert J.
12       1963    "Successful aging." Pp. 299–320 in Richard H. Williams, Clark Tibbitts and
                 Wilma Donahue (eds.), Processes of Aging. Volume 1. New York: Atherton
                 Press.
12       1964    "Disengagement, personality and life satisfaction in the later years." Pp. 419–
                 25 in P. From Hansen (ed.), Age with a Future. Copenhagen: Munksgaard.
5        1971    "Social class perspectives on the life cycle." Human Development 4:110–24.
9        1972    "Life style and leisure patterns: their evolution through the life cycle." Pp. 35–
                 48 in Leisure in the Third Age. Paris: International Center for Social Gerontology.
5, 9,    1973a   "Social roles, work, leisure, and education." Pp. 598–618 in C. Eisdorfer and
14, 16           M. P. Lawton (eds.), The Psychology of Adult Development and Aging.
                 Washington, D.C.: American Psychological Association.
4        1973b   "History of developmental psychology: socialization and personality develop-
                 ment through the life span." Pp. 3–24 in Paul B. Baltes and K. Warner Schaie
                 (eds.), Life-Span Developmental Psychology: Personality and Socialization.
                 New York: Academic Press.
9     Havighurst, Robert J., and Kenneth Feigenbaum
         1968    "Leisure and life-style." Pp. 347–53 in Bernice L. Neugarten (ed.), Middle
                 Age and Aging. Chicago: University of Chicago Press.

| | |
|---|---|
| **4** | Havighurst, Robert J., and R. Glasser |
| | 1972 "An exploratory study of reminiscence." Journal of Gerontology 27:245–53. |
| **8** | Havighurst, Robert J., Bernice L. Neugarten and Vern L. Bengston |
| | 1966 "A cross-national study of adjustment to retirement: Gerontologist 6:137–38. |
| | Havighurst, Robert J., Bernice L. Neugarten and Sheldon S. Tobin |
| **12, 13** | 1963 "Disengagement, personality, and life satisfaction." Pp. 319–24 in P. From Hansen (ed.), Age with a Future. Copenhagen: Munksgaard. |
| **5** | 1968 "Disengagement and patterns of aging." Pp. 161–72 in Bernice L. Neugarten (ed.), Middle Age and Aging. Chicago: University of Chicago Press. |
| **8** | Havighurst, Robert J., Joep M. A. Munnichs, Bernice L. Neugarten and Hans Thomae |
| | 1969 Adjustment to Retirement: A Cross-National Study. New York: Humanities Press. |
| **16** | Hawkinson, W., E. P. Stanford, R. Monge and D. Dowd |
| | 1972 "Survey of gerontologists' opinions on White House Conference on Aging issues on education and training." Gerontologist 12:79–84. |
| **2** | Hayflick, Leonard |
| | 1968 "Human cells and aging." Scientific American 218(3):32–37. |
| **9, 19** | Hearn, H. L. |
| | 1971 "Career and leisure patterns of middle-aged urban blacks." Gerontologist 11(4, part 2):21–26. |
| **16, 18** | Hedden, L. J. |
| | 1974 "Intergenerational living: university dormitories." Gerontologist 14:283–85. |
| | Heidbreder, Elizabeth M. |
| **8** | 1972a "Factors in retirement adjustment: white-collar/blue-collar experience." Industrial Gerontology 12:69–79. |
| **7** | 1972b "Pensions and the single woman." Industrial Gerontology 15:52–62. |
| **5** | Heilbrun, Alfred B., Jr., and Charles V. Lais |
| | 1964 "Decreased role consistency in the aged." Journal of Gerontology 19:325–29. |
| **16** | Helling, J. F., and B. M. Bauer |
| | 1972 "Seniors on campus." Adult Leadership 21(December):203–05. |
| **16** | Hendrickson, A. (ed.) |
| | 1973 A Manual on Planning Educational Programs for Older Adults. Tallahassee: Florida State University, Department of Adult Education. |
| | Heneman, H. G. |
| **14** | 1972 "The relationship between age and motivation to perform on the job." Industrial Gerontology 16:30–36. |
| **14** | 1974 "Age discrimination and employment testing." Industrial Gerontology 1:65–71. |
| **7** | Henle, Peter |
| | 1972 "Recent trends in retirement benefits related to earnings." Monthly Labor Review 95:12–20. |
| **6** | Henry, Jules |
| | 1963 Culture Against Man. New York: Alfred A. Knopf. |
| | Henry, William E. |
| **12** | 1964 "The theory of intrinsic disengagement." Pp. 415–18 in P. From Hansen (ed.), Age with a Future. Copenhagen: Munksgaard. |
| **12** | 1971 "The role of work in structuring the life cycle." Human Development 14: 125–31. |
| **2, 3** | Heron, Alastair, and Sheila Chown |
| | 1967 Age and Function. Boston: Little, Brown. |
| **16** | Herz, Kurt G. |
| | 1968 "New patterns of social services for the aging and aged." Journal of Jewish Community Services 44:236–45. |

**1**

Hess, Beth B.
1974    "Stereotypes of the aged." Journal of Communications 24(4):76–85.

**10**

Heyman, Dorothy K., and D. T. Gianturco
1973    "Long-term adaptation by the elderly to bereavement." Journal of Gerontology
28:359–62.

Heyman, Dorothy K., and Frances C. Jeffers

**4**

1964    "Study of the relative influence of race and socio-economic status upon the
activities and attitudes of a southern aged population." Journal of Gerontology
19:225–29.

**8**

1968    "Wives and retirement: a pilot study." Journal of Gerontology 23:488–96.

Hickey, Tom

**17**

1972    "Catholic religious orders and the aging process: research, training and service
programs." Gerontologist 12:16.

**19**

1974    "In-service training in gerontology: toward the design of an effective educational process." Gerontologist 14:57–64.

**19**

Hickey, Tom, and J. W. Hodgson
1974    "Contextual and developmental issues in the evaluation of adult learning: training in applied gerontology as an example." Pp. 235–55 in Jaber F. Gubrium
(ed.), Late Life: Communities and Environmental Policy. Springfield, Illinois:
Charles C. Thomas.

**1**

Hickey, Tom, Louise A. Hickey and Richard A. Kalish
1968    "Children's perceptions of the elderly." Journal of Genetic Psychology 112:
227–35.

Hiemstra, R. P.

**16**

1972    "Continuing education for the aged: a survey of needs and interests of older
people." Adult Education 22:100–09.

**16**

1973    "Educational planning for older adults: a survey of 'expressive' versus 'instrumental' preferences." International Journal of Aging and Human Development
4:147–56.

**18**

Hill, Reuben
1965    "Decision making and the family life cycle." Pp. 113–39 in Ethel Shanas and
Gordon F. Streib (eds.), Social Structure and the Family. Englewood Cliffs,
New Jersey: Prentice-Hall.

**18**

Hill, Reuben, and R. H. Rodgers
1964    "The developmental approach." Pp. 171–211 in Harold T. Christensen (ed.),
Handbook of Marriage and the Family. Chicago: Rand McNally.

**10**

Hinton, J.
1972    Dying. Second edition. Baltimore: Penguin Books.

**7**

Hirsch, C., D. P. Kent and S. L. Silverman
1972    "Homogeneity and heterogeneity among low-income negro and white aged."
Pp. 484–500 in D. P. Kent, R. Kastenbaum and S. Sherwood (eds.), Research
Planning and Action for the Elderly: The Power and Potential of Social Science.
New York: Behavioral Publications.

**9**

Hoar, Jere
1961    "Study of free-time activities of 200 aged persons." Sociology and Social
Research 45:157–63.

**16**

Hochschild, A. R.
1973    The Unexpected Community. Englewood Cliffs, New Jersey: Prentice-Hall.

**12**

Hoffmann, H., and P. C. Nelson
1971    "Personality characteristics of alcoholics in relation to age and intelligence."
Psychological Reports 29:143–46.

15 Hollister, Robinson
    1974 "Social mythology and reform: income maintenance for the aged." Pp. 19–40 in Frederick R. Eisele (ed.), Political Consequences of Aging. Philadelphia: American Academy of Political and Social Sciences.

12 Holmes, Thomas H., and M. Masuda
    1974 "Life change and illness susceptibility." Pp. 45–72 in Barbara S. Dohrenwend and Bruce P. Dohrenwend (eds.), Stressful Life Events: Their Nature and Effects. New York: Wiley.

   Holtzman, Abraham
15  1954 "Analysis of old age politics in the United States." Journal of Gerontology 9:56–66.

15  1963 The Townsend Movement: A Political Study. New York: Bookman Associates.

7  Horlick, Max
    1973 "Supplemental security income for the aged: foreign experience." Social Security Bulletin 36(12):3–12, 24.

3  Horn, J. L.
    1966 "Integration of structural and developmental concepts of the theory of fluid and crystallized intelligence." Pp. 162–81 in R. B. Cattell (ed.), Handbook of Multivariate Experimental Psychology. Chicago: Rand McNally.

12 Horrocks, J. E., and M. C. Mussman
    1970 "Middle-scence: age-related stress periods during adult years." Genetic Psychology Monographs 82:119.

10 Howard, E.
    1974 "The effect of work experience in a nursing home on the attitudes toward death held by nurse aides." Gerontologist 14:54–56.

3  Howell, T. H.
    1949 "Senile deterioration of the central nervous system." British Medical Journal 1(4592):56–58.

16 Hoyt, George C.
    1954 "The life of the retired in a trailer park." American Journal of Sociology 59:361–70.

15 Hudson, Robert B.
    1974 "Rational planning and organizational imperatives: prospects for area planning in aging." Pp. 41–54 in Frederick R. Eisele (ed.), Political Consequences of Aging. Philadelphia: American Academy of Political and Social Sciences.

3  Hulicka, Irene M.
    1967 "Age changes and age differences in memory functioning." Gerontologist 7(2, part 2):46–54.

3  Hultsch, D. F., and R. W. Bortner
    1974 "Personal time perspective in adulthood: a time-sequential study." Developmental Psychology 10:835–37.

   Hunter, Woodrow W.
8   1968 A Longitudinal Study of Pre-Retirement Education. Ann Arbor, Michigan: University of Michigan Division of Gerontology.

17  1972 "Leadership training for pre-retirement programs in religious communities." Gerontologist 12:17–18.

7, 8 Hurwitz, Jacob C., and William L. Burris
    1972 "Terminated UAW pension plans: a study." Industrial Gerontology 15:40–51.

   Huyck, M.
    1974 Growing Older: Things You Need to Know About Aging. Englewood Cliffs, New Jersey: Prentice-Hall.

| | |
|---|---|
| **14** | International Centre of Social Gerontology |
| | 1971　Work and Aging. Second International Course in Social Gerontology. Florence —May 24–28. Paris: International Centre of Social Gerontology. |
| **9** | Irelan, Lola M. |
| | 1972　"Retirement history study: introduction." Social Security Bulletin 35(11):3–8. |
| **8** | Irelan, Lola M., and D. B. Bell |
| | 1972　"Understanding subjectively defined retirement: a pilot analysis." Gerontologist 12:354–56. |
| **6, 8** | Irelan, Lola M., and Dena K. Motley |
| | 1972　"Health on the threshold of retirement." Industrial Gerontology 12:16–19. |
| **3** | Isaacs, B., and A. J. Akhtar |
| | 1972　"The set test: a rapid test of mental function in old people." Age and Ageing 1:222–26. |
| | Jackson, Hobart C. |
| **15** | 1971　"National caucus on the black aged: a progress report." Aging and Human Development 2:226–31. |
| **19** | 1971　"National goals and priorities in the social welfare of the aging." Gerontologist 11:88–94. |
| | Jackson, Jacquelyn J. |
| | 1967　"Social gerontology and the negro: a review." Gerontologist 7:168–78. |
| **16** | 1971a　"Sex and social class variations in black aged parent-adult child relationships." Aging and Human Development 2:96–107. |
| **1** | 1971b　"The blacklands of gerontology." Aging and Human Development 2:156–71. |
| | 1971c　"Negro aged: toward needed research in social gerontology." Gerontologist 11(1, part 2):52–57. |
| **1, 16** | 1972a　"Aged negroes: their cultural departures from statistical stereotypes and rural-urban differences." Pp. 501–13 in D. P. Kent, R. Kastenbaum and S. Sherwood (eds.), Research Planning Action for the Elderly: The Power and Potential of Social Science. New York: Behavioral Publications. |
| **18** | 1972　"Social impacts of housing relocation upon urban, low-income black aged." Gerontologist 12:32–37. |
| **15** | 1974　"NCBA, black aged and politics." Pp. 138–59 in Frederick R. Eisele (ed.), Political Consequences of Aging. Philadelphia: American Academy of Political and Social Sciences. |
| **16** | Jackson, M. L., Jr. |
| | 1972　"Housing for older Americans." HUD Challenge 3(July):4–7. |
| **17** | Jacobs, Ruth H. |
| | 1969　"The Friendship Club: a case study of the segregated aged." Gerontologist 9:276–80. |
| **8** | Jacobson, D. |
| | 1972　"Willingness to retire in relation to job strain and type of work." Industrial Gerontology 13:65–74. |
| | Jaffe, A. J. |
| **8** | 1968　"Differential patterns of retirement by social class and personal characteristics." Pp. 105–10 in Frances M. Carp (ed.), The Retirement Process. Washington, D.C.: United States Department of Health, Education and Welfare. |
| **8** | 1970　"Men prefer not to retire." Industrial Gerontology 5:1–11. |
| **14** | 1971a　"The middle years: neither too young nor too old." Industrial Gerontology, September (Special Issue):1–90. |
| **8, 14** | 1971b　"Has the retreat from the labor force halted?" A note on retirement of men, 1930–1970." Industrial Gerontology 9:1–12. |

**8, 14**         1972    "The retirement dilemma." Industrial Gerontology 14:1–88.

**3**       Jarvik, Lissy F., and J. E. Blum
        1971    "Cognitive declines as predictors of mortality in twin pairs." Pp. 199–211 in Erdman Palmore and F. C. Jeffers (eds.), Prediction of the Life Span. Lexington, Massachusetts: D. C. Heath.

**19**      Jarvik, Lissy F., and D. Cohen
        1974    "Relevance of research to work with the aged." Pp. 301–31 in A. N. Schwartz and I. N. Mensh (eds.), Professional Obligations and Approaches to the Aged. Springfield, Illinois: Charles C. Thomas.

**3**       Jarvik, Lissy F., J. E. Blum and A. O. Varma
        1972    "Genetic components and intellectual functioning during senescence: a 20-year study of aging twins." Behavioral Genetics 2:159–71.

**10**      Jeffers, F. C., C. R. Nichols and C. Eisdorfer
        1961    "Attitudes of older persons toward death: a preliminary study." Journal of Gerontology 16:53–56.

**14**      Jenkins, M. M.
        1972    "Age discrimination in employment in testing." Industrial Gerontology 12:42–46.

**19**      Johnson, C. E., Jr.
        1974    "Older Americans: population projections and comparisons with the year 2000." Industrial Gerontology 1:37–44.

**16**      Johnson, S. K.
        1971    Idle Haven: Community Building Among the Working-Class Retired. Berkeley, California: University of California Press.

**3**       Jones, Harold E.
        1959    "Intelligence and problem-solving." Pp. 700–38 in James E. Birren (ed.), Handbook of Aging and the Individual. Chicago: University of Chicago Press.

      Kahana, Eva
**6**       1973    "The humane treatment of old people in institutions." Gerontologist 13:282–89.
**6, 16**      1974    "Matching environments to needs of the aged: a conceptual scheme." Pp. 201–14 in Jaber F. Gubrium (ed.), Late Life: Communities and Environmental Policy. Springfield, Illinois: Charles C. Thomas.

**18**      Kahana, Eva, and Boaz Kahana
        1971    "Theoretical and research perspectives on grandparenthood." Aging and Human Development 2:261–68.

      Kalish, Richard A.
**10**      1963a  "An approach to the study of death attitudes." American Behavioral Scientist 6:68–80.
**10**      1963b  "Some variables in death attitudes." Journal of Social Psychology 59:137–45.
**10**      1966    "A continuum of subjectively perceived death." Gerontologist 6:73–76.
**11**      1967    "Of children and grandfathers: a speculative essay on dependency." Gerontologist 7:65–69.
**11**      1969    (ed.), The Dependencies of Old People. Ann Arbor, Michigan: University of Michigan, Wayne State University Institute of Gerontology.
**10**      1971    "Sex and marital role differences in anticipation of age-produced dependency." Journal of Genetic Psychology 119:53–62.
**10**      1972    "Of social values and the dying: a defense of disengagement." Family Coordinator 21:81–94.
**1**       1974    "Four score and ten." Gerontologist 14:129–35.
**3, 4**     1975    Late Adulthood: Perspectives of Human Development. Monterey, California: Brooks/Cole.

**1, 10**   1976   "Death and Dying in a Social Context." in Robert Binstock and Ethel Shanas (eds.), Handbook of Aging and Social Sciences. New York: Van Nostrand Reinhold.

**1**   Kalish, Richard A., and Sam Yuen
   1971   "Americans of East Asian ancestry: aging and the aged." Gerontologist 11(1, part 2):36–47.

**4**   Kaplan, Howard B.
   1971   "Age-related correlates of self-derogation: contemporary life space characteristics." Aging and Human Development 2:305–13.

**16**   Kaplan, Jerome, and Gordon J. Aldridge (eds.)
   1962   Social Welfare of the Aging. New York: Columbia University Press.

**16**   Kaplan, Jerome, Caroline S. Ford and Harry Wain
   1964   "An analysis of multiple community services through the institution for the aged." Geriatrics 19:773–82.

   Kaplan, Max
**9**   1961   "Toward a theory of leisure for social gerontology." Pp. 389–412 in Robert W. Kleemeier (ed.), Aging and Leisure. New York: Oxford University Press.
**9**   1972   "Implications for gerontology from a general theory of leisure." Pp. 49–64 in Leisure in the Third Age. Paris: International Centre for Social Gerontology.

**8**   Kaplan, T. S.
   1971   "Too old to work: the constitutionality of mandatory retirement plans." Southern California Law Review 44:150–80.

**6**   Kapnick, Philip L.
   1972   "Age differences in opinions of health care services." Gerontologist 12:294–97.

**15**   Kapnick, Philip L., Jay S. Goodman and Elmer E. Cornwell
   1968   "Political behavior in the aged: some new data." Journal of Gerontology 23:305–10.

**4**   Karacan, I., C. J. Hursch and R. L. Williams
   1972   "Some characteristics of nocturnal penile tumescence in elderly males." Journal of Gerontology 27:39–45.

**18**   Karcher, C. J., and L. L. Linden
   1975   "Family rejection of the aged and nursing home utilization." International Journal of Aging and Human Development 5:231–44.

**8**   Kasschau, Patricia
   1974   "Reevaluating the need for Retirement Preparation Programs." Industrial Gerontology 1:42–59.

**16**   Kasteler, Josephine M., R. M. Gray and M. L. Carruth
   1968   "Involuntary relocation of the elderly." Gerontologist 8:276–79.

   Kastenbaum, Robert J.
   1964a   (ed.), New Thoughts on Old Age. New York: Springer.
**4**   1964b   "Is old age the end of development?" Pp. 61–71 in Robert Kastenbaum (ed.), New Thoughts on Old Age. New York: Springer.
**10**   1969   "Death and bereavement in later life." Pp. 28–54 in A. H. Kutscher (ed.), Death and Bereavement. Springfield, Illinois: Charles C. Thomas.
**12**   1971   "Getting there ahead of time." Psychology Today 5(December):52–58.
   1973   "Loving, dying and other gerontological addenda." Pp. 699–708 in C. Eisdorfer and M. P. Lawton (eds.), The Psychology of Adult Development and Aging. Washington, D.C.: American Psychological Association.
**10**   1974   "On death and dying. Should we have mixed feelings about our ambivalence toward the aged?" Journal of Geriatric Psychiatry 7:94–107.

**10**   Kastenbaum, Robert J., and R. Aisenberg
   1972   The Psychology of Death. New York: Springer.

| | |
|---|---|
| **6** | Kastenbaum, Robert J., and Sandra E. Candy |
| | 1973    "The 4% fallacy: a methodological and empirical critique of extended care facility population statistics." International Journal of Aging and Human Development 4:15–21. |
| **4** | Kastenbaum, Robert J., and Nancy Durkee |
| | 1964    "Elderly people view old age." Pp. 250–62 in Robert Kastenbaum (ed.), New Thoughts on Old Age. New York: Springer. |
| **10** | Kastenbaum, Robert J., and A. D. Weisman |
| | 1972    "The psychological autopsy as a research procedure in gerontology." Pp. 210–17 in D. P. Kent, R. Kastenbaum and S. Sherwood (eds.), Research Planning and Action for the Elderly: the Power and Potential of Social Science. New York: Behavioral Publications. |
| **8** | Katona, George |
| | 1965    Private Pensions and Individual Saving. Ann Arbor, Michigan: University of Michigan Survey Research Center. |
| **8** | Katona, George, James N. Morgan and Richard E. Barfield |
| | 1969    "Retirement in Prospect and Retrospect." Pp. 27–49 in Occasional Papers in Gerontology, No. 4. Ann Arbor, Michigan: University of Michigan, Wayne State University Institute of Gerontology. |
| **3** | Katz, M. M. |
| | 1974    "The effects of aging on the verbal control of motor behavior." International Journal of Aging and Human Development 5:141–56. |
| **11** | Kay, D. W. K., P. Beamish and Martin Roth |
| | 1964    "Old age mental disorders in Newcastle-upon-Tyne, Part I: a study of prevalence." British Journal of Psychiatry 110:668–82. |
| **16** | Kaye, I. |
| | 1973    "Transportation problems of the older American." Pp. 86–109 in J. G. Cull and R. E. Hardy, The Neglected Older American: Social and Rehabilitation Services. Springfield, Illinois: Charles C. Thomas. |
| **8** | Kelleher, C. H., and D. A. Quirk |
| | 1974    "Preparation for retirement: An annotated bibliography of literature 1965–1974." Industrial Gerontology 1:49–73. |
| **4** | Kelly, E. Lowell |
| | 1955    "Consistency of the adult personality." American Psychologist 10:659–81. |
| | Kent, Donald P. |
| **9** | 1964    "Current developments in educational programming for older people." American School Board Journal 149:1–27. |
| **16** | 1965a    Meeting the Needs of Older People at the Community Level. Washington, D.C.: United States Government Printing Office. |
| **15** | 1965b    "Government and the aging." Journal of Social Issues 21:79–86. |
| | 1968    "Aging within the American social structure." Journal of Geriatric Psychiatry 2:19–32. |
| **17** | 1971a    "The negro aged." Gerontologist 11(1, part 2):48–51. |
| **1** | 1971b    "The elderly in minority groups: variant patterns of aging." Gerontologist 11(1, part 2):26–29. |
| | Kent, Donald P., and C. Hirsch |
| | 1971    "Indigenous workers as a crucial link in the total support system for low-income, minority group aged: a report of an innovative field technique in survey research." Aging and Human Development 2:189–96. |
| | Kent, Donald P., R. Kastenbaum and S. Sherwood (eds.) |
| | 1972    Research planning and action for the elderly: the power and potential of social science. New York: Behavioral Publications. |

Kerckhoff, Alan C.

**8, 18**   1964   "Husband-wife expectations and reactions to retirement." Journal of Gerontology 19:510–16.

**18**   1965   "Nuclear and extended family relationships: a normative and behavioral analysis." Pp. 93–112 in Ethel Shanas and Gordon F. Streib (eds.), Social Structure
and the Family: Generational Relations. Englewood Cliffs, New Jersey: Prentice-Hall.

**8, 12**   1966a   "Family patterns and morale in retirement." Pp. 173–92 in Ida H. Simpson
and John C. McKinney (eds.), Social Aspects of Aging. Durham, North
Carolina: Duke University Press.

**18**   1966b   "Norm-value clusters and the strain toward consistency among older married
couples." Pp. 138–59 in Ida H. Simpson and John C. McKinney (eds.), Social
Aspects of Aging. Durham, North Carolina: Duke University Press.

Kerlinger, Fred

1974   Foundations of Behavioral Research. New York: Holt.

**4**   Kern, R. A.

1971   "Emotional problems in relation to aging and old age." Geriatrics 26(6):83–93.

**14**   Kerr, John R.

1968   "Income and expenditures: the over-65 age group." Journal of Gerontology
23:79–81.

**3, 4**   Kimmel, D. C.

1974   Adulthood and Aging: An Interdisciplinary, Developmental View. New York:
Wiley.

**10**   Kimsey, L. R., J. L. Roberts and D. L. Logan

1972   "Death, dying and denial in the aged." American Journal of Psychiatry 129:
161–66.

**8**   King, Charles E., and William H. Howell

1965   "Role characteristics of flexible and inflexible retired persons." Sociology and
Social Research 49:153–65.

**14**   Kinn, J. M.

1973   "Unemployment and mid-career change: a blueprint for today and tomorrow."
Industrial Gerontology 17:47–59.

**16**   Kistin, H., and R. Morris

1972   "Alternatives to institutional care for the elderly and disabled." Gerontologist
12:139–42.

**8**   Kleemeier, Robert W. (ed.)

1961   Aging and Leisure. New York: Columbia University Press.

Klein, R. L.

1972   "Age, sex and task difficulty as predictors of social conformity." Journal of
Gerontology 27:229–36.

**16**   Kobasky, M. G.

1974   "Educational opportunities for the elderly." Pp. 80–85 in S. M. Grabowski and
W. D. Mason (eds.), Education for the Aging. Syracuse, New York: ERIC
Clearinghouse Adult Education, Syracuse University.

**16**   Kobrin, F. E.

1973   "Household headship and its changes in the United States, 1940–1960, 1970."
Journal of American Statistical Association 68:793–800.

Kogan, Nathan

**3**   1974   "Categorizing and conceptualizing styles in younger and older adults." Human
Development 17:218–30.

1975   "Judgments of chronological age: adult age and sex differences." Developmental Psychology 11:107.

| | |
|---|---|
| 4 | Kogan, Nathan, and Michael A. Wallach<br>1961   "Age changes in values and attitudes." Journal of Gerontology 16:272–80.<br>Kohlberg, L. |
| 4 | 1973a   "Continuities in childhood and adult moral development revisited." Pp. 179–204 in Paul B. Baltes and K. Warner Schaie (eds.), Life-Span Developmental Psychology: Personality and Socialization. New York: Academic Press. |
| 4 | 1973b   "Stages and aging in moral development—some speculations." Gerontologist 13:497–502. |
| 7 | Kolodrubetz, Walter W.<br>1970   "Private and public retirement pensions: findings from the 1968 survey of the aged." Social Security Bulletin 33(9):3–22.<br>Korim, A. S. |
| 16 | 1974a   Older Americans and Community Colleges: An Overview. Washington, D.C.: American Association of Community and Junior Colleges. |
| 16 | 1974b   Older Americans and Community Colleges: A Guide for Program Implementation. Washington, D.C.: American Association of Community and Junior Colleges. |
| 16 | Kornblum, S., and I. Kaufman<br>1972   "Choice and implications of models for working with active older adults." Gerontologist 12:393–97. |
| 16 | Kostick, A.<br>1972   "A day care program for the physically and emotionally disabled." Gerontologist 12:134–38.<br>Koyl, Leon |
| 8 | 1970   "A technique for measuring functional criteria in placement and retirement practices." Pp. 140–56 in Harold L. Sheppard (ed.), Industrial Gerontology. Cambridge, Massachusetts: Shenkman. |
| 14 | 1973   Employing the Older Worker. Washington, D.C.: National Council on Aging. |
| 8 | Kratcoski, P. C., J. H. Huber and R. Gavlak<br>1974   "Retirement satisfaction among emeritus professors." Industrial Gerontology 1:78–81.<br>Kreps, Juanita M. |
| 14 | 1962   "Aggregate income and labor force participation of the aged." Law and Contemporary Problems 27:51–66. |
| 7, 8 | 1963   (ed.), Employment, Income, and Retirement Problems of the Aged. Durham, North Carolina: Duke University Press. |
| 18 | 1965   "The economics of intergenerational relationships." Pp. 267–88 in Ethel Shanas and Gordon F. Streib (eds.), Social Structure and the Family: Generational Relations. Englewood Cliffs, New Jersey: Prentice-Hall. |
| 8 | 1966   "Employment policy and income maintenance for the aged." Pp. 136–57 in John C. McKinney and Frank T. de Vyver (eds.), Aging and Social Policy. New York: Appleton-Century-Crofts. |
| 8 | 1966   (ed.), Technology, Manpower, and Retirement Policy. Cleveland, Ohio: World. |
| 14 | 1968   "Economic policy and the nation's aged." Gerontologist 8(2, part 2):37–43. |
| 8 | 1968   "Comparative studies of work and retirement." Pp. 75–99 in Ethel Shanas and John Madge (eds.), Methodology Problems in Cross-National Studies in Aging. New York: S. Karger. |
| 9 | 1968   Lifelong Allocation of Work and Leisure. Washington, D.C.: Social Security Administration. |
| 19 | 1971   "Career options after fifty: suggested research." Gerontologist 11(1, part 2): 4–8. |
| 19 | 1971   Lifetime Allocation of Work and Income. Durham, North Carolina: Duke University Press. |

Krishna, K. P.

4     1970     "Age-difference in perception of the underlying factors of student unrest." Indian Journal of Gerontology 2:63–67.

4     1971     "A study of relationship between manifest anxiety and age." Indian Journal of Gerontology 3:30–32.

Krislov, Joseph

7     1968     "Four issues in income maintenance for the aged during the 1970's." Social Service Review 42:335–43.

Krohn, Peter L. (ed.)

2     1966     Topics in the Biology of Aging. New York: Interscience.

Kubler-Ross, Elizabeth

10     1969     On Death and Dying. New York: Macmillan.

Kuhlen, Raymond G.

9     1963a     Psychological Backgrounds of Adult Education. Chicago: Center for the Study of Liberal Education for Adults.

4     1963b     "Motivational changes during the adult years." Pp. 77–113 in Raymond G. Kuhlen (ed.), Psychological Backgrounds of Adult Education. Chicago: Center for the Study of Liberal Education for Adults.

3, 4     1964a     "Developmental changes in motivation during the adult years." Pp. 209–46 in James E. Birren (ed.), Relations of Development and Aging. Springfield, Illinois: Charles C. Thomas.

4     1964b     "Personality change with age." Pp. 524–55 in Philip Worchel and D. Byrne (eds.), Personality Change. New York: Wiley.

Kutner, Bernard

18     1956     Five Hundred Over Sixty: A Community Survey of Aging. New York: Russell Sage Foundation.

1     1962     "The social nature of aging." Gerontologist 2:5–8.

Kutscher, Austin H. (ed.)

10     1969     Death and Bereavement. Springfield, Illinois: Charles C. Thomas.

Kuypers, Joseph A.

4, 5     1972a     "Changeability of life-style and personality in old age." Gerontologist 12: 336–42.

4     1972b     "Internal-external locus of control, ego functioning and personality characteristics in old age." Gerontologist 12:168–73.

4     1974     "Ego functioning in old age: early adult life antecedents." International Journal of Aging and Human Development 5:157–79.

Kuypers, Joseph A., and Vern L. Bengtson

12     1973     "Social breakdown and competence: a model of normal aging." Human Development 16:181–201.

Lacklen, C.

7, 19     1971     "Aged, black, and poor: three case studies." Aging and Human Development 2:202–07.

Lakin, Martin, and Carl Eisdorfer

4     1962     "A study of affective expression among the aged." Pp. 650–54 in Clark Tibbitts and Wilma Donahue (eds.), Social and Psychological Aspects of Aging. New York: Columbia University Press.

Lambert, Edward

8     1964     "Reflections on a policy for retirement." International Labor Review 90:365–75.

Lambing, M. L. B.

9, 19     1972a     "Leisure-time pursuits among retired blacks by social status." Gerontologist 12:363–67.

16     1972b     "Social class living patterns of retired Negroes." Gerontologist 12:285–88.

**16** Langford, Marilyn
1962 Community Aspects of Housing for the Aged. Ithaca, New York: Cornell University Center for Housing and Environmental Studies.

**5** Laufer, R. S., and V. L. Bengtson
1974 "Generations, aging, and social stratification: on the development of generational units." Journal of Social Issues 30(3):181–205.

**7** Lauriat, Patience
1970 "Benefit levels and socio-economic characteristics: findings from the 1968 survey of the aged." Social Security Bulletin 33(8):3–20.

**5** Lawrence, J. H.
1974 "The effect of perceived age on initial impressions and normative role expectations." International Journal of Aging and Human Development 5:369–91.

**8** Lawrence, Mary W.
1961 "Sources of satisfaction in the lives of working women." Journal of Gerontology 16:163–67.

**6** Lawton, Alfred H.
1965 "Accidental injuries to the aged." Gerontologist 5:96–100.

**16** Lawton, Alfred H., and Gordon J. Azar
1966 "Consequences of physical and physiological change with age in the patterns of living and housing for the middle-aged and aged." Pp. 19–26 in Frances M. Carp and W. M. Burnett (eds.), Patterns of Living and Housing of Middle-Aged and Older People. Washington, D.C.: United States Public Health Service.

Lawton, M. Powell
**6** 1968 "Social rehabilitation of the aged: some neglected aspects." Journal of the American Geriatrics Society 16:1346–63.

**16** 1969 "Supportive services in the context of the housing environment." Gerontologist 9:15–19.

**16** 1970 "Planning environments for older people." American Institute of Planners Journal 36(March):124–29.

**6** 1971 "The functional assessment of elderly people." Journal of the American Geriatric Society 19:465–81.

**3** 1972a "Assessing the competence of older people." Pp. 122–43 in Donald P. Kent, R. Kastenbaum and S. Sherwood (eds.), Research Planning and Action for the Elderly. New York: Behavioral Publications.

**12** 1972b "The dimensions of morale." Pp. 144–65 in D. P. Kent, R. Kastenbaum and S. Sherwood (eds.), Research Planning and Action for the Elderly. New York: Behavioral Publications.

**3** 1974 "Psychology of aging." Pp. 73–83 in W. C. Bier (ed.), Aging, Its Challenge to the Individual and to Society. Pastoral Psychology Series, No. 8. New York: Fordham University Press.

**16** 1975a Planning and Managing Housing for the Elderly. New York: Wiley.

**12** 1975b "The Philadelphia Geriatric Center Morale Scale: a revision." Journal of Gerontology 30:85–89.

**16** Lawton, M. Powell, and T. Byerts (eds.)
1973 Community Planing for the Elderly. Washington, D.C.: Gerontological Society.

**16** 1974 "The generality of housing impact on the well-being of the older people." Journal of Gerontology 29:194–204.

**6, 16** Lawton, M. Powell, and L. E. Gottesman
1974 "Psychological services to the elderly." American Psychologist 29:689–93.

**1, 16** Lawton, M. Powell, and M. H. Kleban
1971 "The aged resident of the inner city." Gerontologist 11:277–83.

**6** Lawton, M. Powell, and Fay G. Lawton (eds.)
1965 Mental Impairment in the Aged. Philadelphia: Philadelphia Geriatrics Center.

**12, 16**  Lawton, M. Powell, and L. Nahemow
1973    "Ecology and the aging process." Pp. 619–74 in C. Eisdorfer and M. P. Lawton (eds.), The Psychology of Adult Development and Aging. Washington, D.C.: American Psychological Association.

**18**  Lawton, M. Powell, and B. Simon
1968    "The ecology of social relationships in housing for the elderly." Gerontologist 8:108–15.

**16**  Lawton, M. Powell, Morton H. Kleban and D. A. Carlson
1973    "The inner-city resident: to move or not to move." Gerontologist 13:443–48.

**16**  Lawton, M. Powell, Morton H. Kleban and Maurice Singer
1971    "The aged Jewish person and the slum environment." Journal of Gerontology 26:231–39.

**3**  Lehman, H. C.
1953    Age and Achievement. Princeton, New Jersey: Princeton University Press.

**16**  Lehman, Virginia, and Geneva Mathiasen
1963    Guardianship and Protective Services for Older People. New York: National Council on the Aging.

**4**  Lehr, Ursula
1967    "Attitudes towards the future in old age." Human Development 10:230–38.

**16**  Lenzer, Anthony
1965    "Mobility patterns among the aged." Gerontologist 5(1, part 1):12–15.

**10**  Lester, D.
1973    "Suicide, homicide, and age dependency ratios." International Journal of Aging and Human Development 4:127–32.

**10**  Lettieri, D. J.
1973    "Suicide in the aging: empirical prediction of suicidal risk among the aging." Journal of Geriatric Psychiatry 6:7–42.

**4**  Levin, Sidney
1964    "Depression in the aged: the importance of external factors." Pp. 179–85 in Robert Kastenbaum (ed.), New Thoughts on Old Age. New York: Springer.

**18**  Le Vine, Robert A.
1965    "Intergenerational tensions and extended family structure in Africa." Pp. 188–204 in Ethel Shanas and Gordon F. Streib (eds.), Social Structure and the Family: Generational Relations. Englewood Cliffs, New Jersey: Prentice-Hall.

**4**  Lewis, Charles N.
1971    "Reminiscing and self-concept in old age." Journal of Gerontology 26:240–43.

**16**  Lewis, J. R., and R. L. Pott
1972    Programs to Aid Housing for the Elderly. Newark, Delaware: University of Delaware, Division of Urban Affairs.

**15**  Lewis, Myrna I., and Robert N. Butler
1972    "Why is women's lib ignoring old women?" Aging and Human Development 3:223–31.

**15**  Lewis, Oscar
1961    Five Families. New York: Basic Books.

Lieberman, Morton A.
**6**  1969    "Institutionalization of the aged: effects on behavior." Journal of Gerontology 24:330–40.

**16, 19**  1974a    "Relocation research and social policy." Pp. 215–34 in Jaber F. Gubrium (ed.), Late Life: Communities and Environmental Policy. Springfield, Illinois: Charles C. Thomas.

**16, 19**  1974b    "Relocation research and social policy." Gerontologist 14:494–500.

Lipman, Aaron
**18**  1961    "Role conceptions and morale of couples in retirement." Journal of Gerontology 16:267–71.

18      1962    "Role conceptions of couples in retirement." Pp. 475–85 in Clark Tibbitts and Wilma Donahue (eds.), Social and Psychological Aspects of Aging. New York: Columbia University Press.

12      1969    "Public housing and attitudinal adjustment in old age: a comparative study." Journal of Geriatric Psychiatry 2:88–101.

13      Lipman, Aaron, and Kenneth J. Smith
        1968    "Functionality of disengagement in old age." Journal of Gerontology 23:517–21.

10      Lipman, Aaron, and P. Marden
        1966    "Preparations for death in old age." Journal of Gerontology 21:426–31.

15      Lipsett, Seymour M., and Everett C. Ladd, Jr.
        1972    "The political future of activist generations." Pp. 63–84 in Philip G. Altbach and R. S. Laufer (eds.), The New Pilgrims: Youth Protest in Transition. New York: David McKay.

8      Liu, Y. H.
        1974    "Retirees and retirement programs in the People's Republic of China." Industrial Gerontology 1:72–81.

4      Livson, N.
        1973    "Developmental dimensions of personality: a life-span formulation." Pp. 97–122 in Paul B. Baltes and K. Warner Schaie (ed.), Life-Span Developmental Psychology: Personality and Socialization. New York: Academic Press.

12      Loeb, Martin B., Allen Pincus and B. J. Mueller
        1966    "A framework for viewing adjustment in aging." Gerontologist 6:185–87.

4      Loevinger, J.
        1969    "Theories of ego development." Pp. 36–58 in L. Breger (ed.), Clinical Cognitive Psychology. Englewood Cliffs, New Jersey: Prentice-Hall.

1      Long, Barbara H., Robert C. Ziller and Elaine E. Thompson
        1966    "A comparison of prejudices: the effects upon friendship ratings of chronic illness, old age, education and race." Journal of Social Psychology 70:101–09.

     Looft, W. R.

4      1972    "Egocentrism and social interaction across the life span." Psychological Bulletin 78:73–92.

4      1973a    "Socialization in a life-span perspective: white elephants, worms and will-o'-wisps." Gerontologist 13:488–97.

4      1973b    "Socialization and personality throughout the life span: an examination of contemporary psychological approaches." Pp. 25–52 in Paul B. Baltes and K. Warner Schaie (eds.), Life-Span Developmental Psychology: Personality and Socialization. New York: Academic Press.

     Lopata, Helena Z.

10      1970    "The social involvement of American widows." American Behavioral Scientist 14(September–October):41–48.

10      1971a    "Living arrangements of American urban widows." Sociological Focus 5:41–61.

18      1971b    "Widows as a minority group." Gerontologist 11(1, part 2):67–77.

18      1971c    Occupation: Housewife. New York: Oxford University Press.

14      1971d    "Work histories of American urban women." Gerontologist 11(4, part 2): 27–36.

5      1972    "Social relations of widows in urbanized countries." Sociological Quarterly 13(Spring):259–71.

10, 18      1973    Widowhood in an American City. Cambridge, Massachusetts: Schenkman.

16      1975    "Support systems of elderly urbanites: Chicago of the 1970's." Gerontologist 15:35–41.

4      Lowe, G. R.
        1972    The Growth of Personality: From Infancy to Old Age. Baltimore: Penguin Books.

Lowenthal, Marjorie F.

**19**      1964a   Lives in Distress. New York: Basic Books.

**6, 8**    1964b   "Social isolation and mental illness in old age." American Sociological Review 29:54–70.

**6**       1965    "Antecedents of isolation and mental illness in old age." Archives of General Psychiatry 12:245–54.

**12**      1971    "Intentionality: toward a framework for the study of adaptation in adulthood." Aging and Human Development 2:79–95.

**6, 8**    Lowenthal, Marjorie F., and Paul L. Berkman
            1967    Aging and Mental Disorder in San Francisco. San Francisco: Jossey-Bass.

**12**      Lowenthal, Marjorie F., and Deetje Boler
            1965    "Voluntary versus involuntary social withdrawal." Journal of Gerontology 20:363–71.

**12**      Lowenthal, Marjorie F., and David Chiriboga
            1973    "Social stress and adaptation: toward a life-course perspective." Pp. 281–310 in Carl Eisdorfer and M. Powell Lawton (eds.), The Psychology of Adult Development and Aging. Washington, D.C.: American Psychological Association.

**12, 18**  Lowenthal, Marjorie F., and Clayton Havens
            1968    "Interaction and adaptation: intimacy as a critical variable." American Sociological Review 33:20–31.

**6**       Lowenthal, Marjorie F., M. Thurnher and D. Chiriboga
            1975    Four Stages of Life. San Francisco: Jossey-Bass.

Lowy, L.

**16, 19**  1972a   "The role of social gerontology in the development of social services for older people." Pp. 20–36 in D. P. Kent, R. Kastenbaum and S. Sherwood (eds.), Research Planning and Action for the Elderly. New York: Behavioral Publications.

            1972b   "A social work practice perspective in relation to theoretical models and research in gerontology." Pp. 538–44 in D. P. Kent, R. Kastenbaum and S. Sherwood (eds.), Research Planning and Action for the Elderly. New York: Behavioral Publications.

Lozier, J., and R. Althouse

**16**      1974    "Special enforcement of behavior toward elders in an Appalachian mountain settlement." Gerontologist 14:69–80.

**8**       1975    "Retirement to the porch in rural Appalachia." International Journal of Aging and Human Development 6:7–15.

**7**       Lubove, Ray
            1968    The Struggle for Social Security: 1900–1935. Cambridge, Massachusetts: Harvard University Press.

**9**       Lucas, Carol
            1964    Recreation in Gerontology. Springfield, Illinois: Charles C. Thomas.

**4**       Ludwig, Edward G., and Robert L. Eichhorn
            1967    "Age and disillusionment: a study of value changes associated with aging." Journal of Gerontology 22:59–65.

**4**       Lynch, D. J.
            1971    "Future time perspective and impulsivity in old age." Journal of Genetic Psychology 118:245–52.

**4**       Maas, H. S., and J. A. Kuypers
            1974    From Thirty to Seventy. San Francisco: Jossey-Bass.

**5**       McCandless, B. R.
            1973    "Symposium discussion: life-span models of psychological aging." Gerontologist 13:511–12.

| | |
|---|---|
| **16** | McCaslin, R., and W. R. Calvert |
| | 1975  "Social indicators in black and white: some ethnic considerations in delivery of service to the elderly." Journal of Gerontology 30:60–66. |
| **2** | McCay, C. M., F. Pope and W. Lunsford |
| | 1956  "Experimental prolongation of the life span." Bulletin of the New York Academy of Medicine 32:91–101. |
| **14** | McConnell, John W. |
| | 1960  "Aging and the economy." Pp. 489–520 in Clark Tibbitts (ed.), Handbook of Social Gerontology. Chicago: University of Chicago Press. |
| **8** | McEvan, Peter J. M., and Alan P. Sheldon |
| | 1969  "Patterns of retirement and related variables." Journal of Geriatric Psychiatry 3:35–54. |
| | McFarland, Ross A. |
| **3** | 1968  "The sensory and perceptual processes in aging." Pp. 9–52 in K. Warner Schaie (ed.), Theory and Methods of Research on Aging. Morgantown, West Virginia: West Virginia University. |
| **8** | 1973  "The need for functional age measures in industrial gerontology." Industrial Gerontology 19:1–19. |
| **16** | McGuire, Marie C. |
| | 1969  "The status of housing for the elderly." Gerontologist 9:10–14. |
| **18** | MacIver, Robert M., and Charles H. Page |
| | 1949  Sociology: An Introductory Analysis. New York: Rinehart. |
| | McKain, Walter C., Jr. |
| **16** | 1967  "Community roles and activities of older rural persons." Pp. 75–96 in E. Grant Youmans (ed.), Older Rural Americans. Lexington, Kentucky: University of Kentucky Press. |
| **10, 18** | 1969  Retirement Marriage. Storrs, Connecticut: University of Connecticut Agriculture Experiment Station. |
| **15** | McKinney, John C., and Frank T. deVyver (eds.) |
| | 1966  Aging and Social Policy. New York: Appleton-Century-Crofts. |
| **3** | McTavish, Donald G. |
| | 1971  "Perceptions of old people: a review of research, methodologies and findings." Gerontologist 11(4, part 2):90–101. |
| **10, 18** | Maddison, David, and Agnes Viola |
| | 1968  "The health of widows in the year following bereavement." Journal of Psychosomatic Research 12:297–306. |
| | Maddox, George L. |
| **12** | 1963  "Activity and morale: a longitudinal study of selected elderly subjects." Social Forces 42:195–204. |
| **1** | 1964  "Disengagement theory: a critical evaluation." Gerontologist 4:80–82. |
| **1** | 1965  "Disengagement among the elderly: how common and with what effect?" Pp. 317–23 in Frances C. Jeffers (ed.), Duke University Council on Gerontology Proceedings of Seminars, 1961–1965. Durham, North Carolina: Duke University Regional Center for the Study of Aging. |
| **8** | 1968  "Retirement as a social event in the United States." Pp. 357–65 in Bernice L. Neugarten (ed.), Middle Age and Aging. Chicago: University of Chicago Press. |
| **1** | 1969  "Growing old: getting beyond the stereotypes." Pp. 5–16 in Rosamonde R. Boyd and C. G. Oakes (eds.), Foundations of Practical Gerontology. Columbia, South Carolina: University of South Carolina Press. |
| **19** | 1970a  "Selected methodological issues." Pp. 18–27 in Erdman Palmore (ed.), Normal Aging. Durham, North Carolina: Duke University Press. |
| **1** | 1970b  "Themes and issues in sociological theories of human aging." Human Development 13:17–27. |

Maddox, George L., and E. B. Douglass
1974    "Aging and individual differences: a longitudinal analysis of social, psycholog-
        ical, and physiological indicators." Journal of Gerontology 29:555–63.

**12**  Maddox, George L., and Carl Eisdorfer
1962    "Some correlates of activity and morale among the elderly." Social Forces
        40:254–60.

**7**   Mallan, Lucy B.
1974    "Women born in the early 1900's: employment, earnings, and benefit levels."
        Social Security Bulletin 37(3):3–25.

**6**   Marden, Parker G., and Robert G. Burnight
1969    "Social consequences of physical impairment in an aging population." Geron-
        tologist 9:39–46.

**14**  Margolius, S., P. S. Barash, V. Knauer, A. J. Jaffe, J. N. Morgan and D. A. Peterson
1969    The Aging Consumer. Occasional Papers in Gerontology, Number 8. Ann
        Arbor, Michigan: University of Michigan, Wayne State University, Institute
        of Gerontology.

**4**   Markson, E., and P. Grevert
1972    "Circe's terrible island of change: self-perceptions of incapacity." Aging and
        Human Development 3:261–71.

**3**   Markson, E. W., and G. Levitz
1973    "A Guttman scale to assess memory loss among the elderly." Gerontologist
        13:337–40.

Markus, E., M. Blenkner, M. Bloom and T. Downs
**10**  1971    "The impact of relocation upon mortality rates of institutionalized aged per-
        sons." Journal of Gerontology 26:537–41.
**10**  1972    "Some factors and their associations with post-relocation mortality among
        institutionalized aged persons." Journal of Gerontology 27:376–82.

Marshall, V. W.
1974    "The last stand: remnants of engagement in the later years." Omega 5:25–35.

**18**  Martel, Martin, and W. W. Morris
1960    Life After Sixty in Iowa. Iowa City, Iowa: Institute of Gerontology.

**9**   Martin, Alexander R.
1963    Leisure Time—A Creative Force. New York: National Council on Aging.

**19**  Martin, John B.
1970    "Gerontological challenges of the seventies." Aging and Human Development
        1:3–4.

**11**  Martin, J. David
1971    "Powers, dependence, and the complaints of the elderly: a social exchange
        perspective." Aging and Human Development 2:108–12.

**8**   Martin, John, and Ann Doran
1966    "Evidence concerning the relationship between health and retirement." Socio-
        logical Review 14:329–43.

**12**  Martin, W. C.
1973    "Activity and disengagement: life satisfaction of in-movers into a retirement
        community." Gerontology 13:224–27.

**13**  Martin, W. C., V. L. Bengtson and A. C. Acock
1974    "Alienation and age: a context-specific approach." Social Forces 53:266–74.

**4**   Mason, Evelyn
1954    "Some correlates of self-judgments of the aged." Journal of Gerontology
        9:324–37.

**8**   Masse, B. L., S. Scheiber, M. L. Lovely, H. A. Schwartz and R. Bragman
1974    "The experience of retirement." Pp. 167–83 in W. C. Bier (ed.), Aging: Its
        Challenge to the Individual and to Society. Pastoral Psychology Series, No. 8.
        New York: Fordham University Press.

**3, 18**  Masters, William H., and Virginia Johnson
    1966    Human Sexual Response. Boston: Little, Brown.

**6**  Mathis, Evelyn S.
    1973    "Characteristics of residents in nursing and personal care homes: United States, June–August, 1969." Vital and Health Statistics, Series 12, Number 19.

Maves, Paul B.

**17**    1960    "Aging, religion, and the church." Pp. 698–749 in Clark Tibbitts (ed.), Handbook of Social Gerontology. Chicago: University of Chicago Press.

**17**    1965    "Research on religion in relation to aging." Pp. 69–79 in Frances C. Jeffers (ed.), Duke University Council on Gerontology, Proceedings of Seminars 1961–65. Durham, North Carolina: Duke University Regional Center for the Study of Aging.

**6**  Mendelson, Mary A.
    1974    Tender Loving Greed. New York: Alfred A. Knopf.

**15**  Mendelson, Mary A., and David Hapgood
    1974    "The political economy of nursing homes." Pp. 95–105 in Frederick R. Eisele (ed.), Political Consequences of Aging. Philadelphia: American Academy of Political and Social Sciences.

**1**  Mercer, Jane R., and Edgar W. Butler
    1967    "Disengagement of the aged population and response differentials in survey research." Social Forces 46:89–96.

**7**  Merriam, Ida C.
    1966    "Implications of technological change for income." Pp. 166–74 in Juanita M. Kreps (ed.), Technology Manpower and Retirement Policy. New York: World.

**8**  Messer, Elizabeth F.
    1969    "Thirty years is a plenty." Pp. 5–66 in Occasional Papers in Gerontology No. 4. Ann Arbor, Michigan: University of Michigan, Wayne State University, Institute of Gerontology.

Metropolitan Life Insurance Company

**6**    1965a    "Accidental injury and death at the older ages." Statistical Bulletin of the Metropolitan Life Insurance Company 46(February):6–8.

**1**    1965b    "International trends in survival after age 65." Statistical Bulletin of the Metropolitan Life Insurance Company 46(January):8–10.

**6**    1971    "Mortality from accidents by age and sex." Statistical Bulletin of the Metropolitan Life Insurance Company 52(May):6–9.

**6**    1972    "Suicide—international comparisons." Statistical Bulletin of the Metropolitan Life Insurance Company 53(August):2–5.

**6**    1973    "Regional variations in mortality from suicide." Statistical Bulletin of the Metropolitan Life Insurance Company 54(August):2–4.

**10**    1974    "Accident mortality at the older ages." Statistical Bulletin of the Metropolitan Life Insurance Company 55(June):6–8.

**10**  Meyers, D. W.
    1973    "The legal aspects of medical euthanasia." Bioscience 23:467–70.

**10**  Miller, M. B.
    1971    "Decision-making in the death process of the ill aged." Geriatrics 26(5):105–16.

**5, 8, 9**  Miller, Stephen J.
    1965    "The social dilemma of the aging leisure participant." Pp. 77–92 in Arnold M. Rose and Warren A. Peterson (eds.), Older People and Their Social World. Philadelphia: F. A. Davis.

**8**  Mills, C. Wright
    1956    White Collar. New York: Oxford University Press.

**10**  Mishara, B. L., and R. Kastenbaum
    1973    "Self-injurious behavior and environmental change in the institutionalized elderly." International Journal of Aging and Human Development 4:133–45.

**8**

Mitchell, William L.
    1968    Preparation for Retirement. Washington, D.C.: American Association of Retired Persons.

Moberg, David O.

**17**
    1965a    "The integration of older members in the church congregation." Pp. 125–40 in Arnold M. Rose and Warren A. Peterson (eds.), Older People and Their Social World. Philadelphia: F. A. Davis.

**17**    1965b    "Religion in old age." Geriatrics 20:977–82.

**17**    1965c    "Religiosity in old age." Gerontologist 5:78–87.

**17**    1972    "Religion and the aged family." Family Coordinator 21:47–60.

**17**

Moberg, David O., and Marvin J. Taves
    1965    "Church participation and adjustment in old age." Pp. 113–24 in Arnold M. Rose and Warren A. Peterson (eds.), Older People and Their Social World. Philadelphia: F. A. Davis.

Monk, Abraham

**8**
    1971    "Factors in the preparation for retirement by middle-aged adults." Gerontologist 11(4, part 1):348–51.

**8**
    1972    "A social policy framework for pre-retirement planning." Industrial Gerontology 15:63–70.

Montgomery, James E.

**16**
    1967    "Housing for the rural aged." Pp. 169–94 in E. Grant Youmans (ed.), Older Rural Americans. Lexington, Kentucky: University of Kentucky Press.

**16, 18**    1972    "The housing patterns of older families." Family Coordinator 21:37–46.

Moore, Joan W.
    1971    "Mexican-Americans." Gerontologist 11(1, part 2):30–35.

Morgan, James N.

**8**    1962    Income and Welfare in the United States. New York: McGraw-Hill.

**7**    1965    "Measuring the economic status of the aged." International Economic Review 6:1–17.

**10**

Morison, R. S.
    1971    "Dying." Scientific American 229(3):54–62.

**4**

Moriwaki, S. Y.
    1974    "The affect balance scale: a validity study with aged samples." Journal of Gerontology 29:73–78.

**10**

Moriyama, Iwao
    1964    The Change in Mortality Trend in the United States. Washington, D.C.: National Center for Health Statistics.

**16**

Morlok, E. K., W. M. Kulash and H. L. Vandersypen
    1971    "Reduced fares for the elderly. Effects on a transit system." Welfare Review 9(5):17–24.

**12**

Morris, J. N., and S. Sherwood
    1975    "A retesting and modification of the Philadelphia Geriatric Center Morale Scale." Journal of Gerontology 30:77–84.

**12**

Morris, J. N., R. S. Wolf and L. V. Klerman
    1975    "Common themes among morale and depression scales." Journal of Gerontology 30:209–15.

**16, 19**

Morris, Robert, and Robert H. Binstock
    1966    Feasible Planning for Social Change. New York: Columbia University Press.

**16**

Morris, Robert, and Ollie A. Randall
    1965    "Planning and organization of community services for the elderly." Social Work 10:96–102.

**8**

Morse, Nancy C., and Robert S. Weiss
    1955    "The function and meaning of work and the job." American Sociological Review 20:191–98.

8    Morrison, M. H.
     1975    "The myth of employee planning for retirement." Industrial Gerontology 2:135–43.

     Motley, Dena K.
8      1972    "Health in the years before retirement." Social Security Bulletin 35(12):18–36.
6      1975    "Paying for health care in the years before retirement." Social Security Bulletin 38(4):3–22.

6    Mueller, Marjorie Smith
     1975    "Private health insurance in 1973: a review of coverage, enrollment, and financial experience." Social Security Bulletin 38(2):21–40.

6    Mueller, Marjorie Smith, and Robert M. Gibson
     1975    "Age difference in health care spending, fiscal year 1974." Social Security Bulletin 38(6):3–16.

7    Murphy, B.
     1971    "Finding the invisible elderly poor." Opportunity 1(8):2–10.

7    Murray, Janet
     1972    "Homeownership and financial assets: findings from the 1968 survey of the aged." Social Security Bulletin 35(8):3–23.

14    Murray, J. R., E. A. Powers and R. J. Havighurst
     1971    "Personal and situational factors producing flexible careers." Gerontologist 11(4, part 2):4–12.

7    Murray, Roger F.
     1968    Economic Aspects of Pensions: A Summary Report. New York: Columbia University Press.

     Myers, Robert J.
8      1954    "Factors in interpreting mortality after retirement." Journal of the American Statistical Association 49:499–509.
7      1975    "Social Security and private pensions—where do we go from here?" Industrial Gerontology 2:158–63.

8    Nadelson, Theodore
     1969    "A survey of the literature on the adjustment of the aged to retirement." Journal of Geriatric Psychiatry 3:3–20.

6    Namey, Christy, and R. W. Wilson
     1972    "Age patterns in medical care, illness, and disability." Vital and Health Statistics, Series 10, No. 70.

4    Nardi, A. H.
     1973    "Person-conception research and the perception of life-span development." Pp. 285–301 in Paul B. Baltes and K. Warner Schaie (eds.), Life-Span Developmental Psychology: Personality and Socialization. New York: Academic Press.

     National Center for Health Statistics
3      1959    Health Statistics. Series B, No. 9. Washington, D.C.: National Center for Health Statistics.
10, 18    1974    Vital Statistics of the United States, 1970. Volume 3: Marriage and Divorce. Washington, D.C.: United States Government Printing Office.

     National Council on the Aging
19      1970    The Golden Years—A Tarnished Myth. New York: National Council on Aging.
19      1971a    Directory: National Organizations with Programs in the Field of Aging, 1971. Washington, D.C.: National Council on the Aging.
16      1971b    The Older Non-Professional in Community Service: Four Professional Viewpoints. Washington, D.C.: National Council on the Aging, Senior Community Service Project.
14      1971c    Employment Prospects of Aged Blacks, Chicanos and Indians. Washington, D.C.: National Council on the Aging.

**14**       1971d   Guidelines for the Development of Employment Opportunities for Older
                     People. Washington, D.C.: National Council on the Aging, Senior Community
                     Service Project.
             1972a   Triple Jeopardy: Myth or Reality. Washington, D.C.: National Council on the
                     Aging.
**16**       1972b   Housing and Living Arrangements for Older People: A Bibliography. Washing-
                     ton, D.C.: National Council on the Aging.
**15**    National Council of Senior Citizens
             1971    Legislative Approaches to Problems of the Elderly: A Handbook of Model
                     State Statutes. Washington, D.C.: National Council of Senior Citizens.
**14**    National Industrial Conference Board
             1966    Expenditure Patterns of the American Family. New York: National Industrial
                     Conference Board.
**19**    National Retired Teachers Association and American Association of Retired Persons
             1971    Proposals for a National Policy on Aging. Washington, D.C.: National Retired
                     Teachers Association and American Association of Retired Persons.

**1**     Naus, P. J.
             1973    "Some correlates of attitudes towards old people." International Journal of
                     Aging and Human Development 4:229–43.
**16**    Naylor, H. H.
             1973    "Volunteerism with and by the elderly." Pp. 195–204 in R. R. Boyd and C. G.
                     Oakes (eds.), Foundations of Practical Gerontology. Second edition. Columbia,
                     South Carolina: University of South Carolina Press.
          Nelson, Edward E., and Bernice C. Starr
             1972    "Interpretation of research on age." Pp. 27–84 in Matilda White Riley and
                     others (eds.), Aging and Society. Volume 3: A Sociology of Age Stratification.
                     New York: Russell Sage Foundation.
**16**    Nelson, L. M., and M. Winter
             1975    "Life disruption, independence, satisfaction, and the consideration of moving."
                     Gerontologist 15:160–64.
**1**     Nesselroade, John R., and H. W. Reese (eds.)
             1973    Life-Span Developmental Psychology: Methodological Issues. New York:
                     Academic Press.
**3**     Nesselroade, John R., K. Warner Schaie and Paul B. Baltes
             1972    "Ontogenetic and generational components of structural and quantitative change
                     in adult cognitive behavior." Journal of Gerontology 27:222–28.

          Neugarten, Bernice L.
**4**        1963    "Personality changes during the adult years." Pp. 43–76 in Raymond G.
                     Kuhlen (ed.), Psychological Backgrounds of Adult Education. Chicago: Center
                     for the Study of Liberal Education for Adults.
**4**        1964    "A developmental view of adult personality." Pp. 176–208 in James E. Birren
                     (ed.), Relations of Development and Aging. Springfield, Illinois: Charles C.
                     Thomas.
**5**        1966    "The aged in American society." Pp. 167–96 in Howard S. Becker (ed.),
                     Social Problems. New York: Wiley.
             1968    Middle Age and Aging. Chicago: University of Chicago Press.
**12**       1970a   "Dynamics of transition of middle age to old age: adaptation and the life cycle."
                     Journal of Geriatric Psychiatry 4:71–87.
             1971    "Grow old along with me! The best is yet to be." Psychology Today 5(Decem-
                     ber):45–48.
**4**        1972    "Personality and the aging process." Gerontologist 12:9–15.
**19**       1973    "Patterns of aging: past, present, and future." Social Service Review 47:571–80.

**15, 19**    1974    "Age groups in American society and the rise of the young-old." Pp. 187–98 in Frederick R. Eisele (ed.), Political Consequences of Aging. Philadelphia: American Academy of Political and Social Sciences.

**1, 19**    1975    "The future and the young-old." Gerontologist 15:(1, part 2), 4–9.

**5**    Neugarten, Bernice L., and Nancy Datan

    1973    "Sociological perspectives on the life cycle." Pp. 53–69 in Paul B. Baltes and K. Warner Schaie (eds.), Life-Span Developmental Psychology: Personality and Socialization. New York: Academic Press.

**1**    Neugarten, Bernice L., and Joan W. Moore

    1968    "The changing age-status system." Pp. 5–21 in Bernice L. Neugarten (ed.), Middle Age and Aging. Chicago: University of Chicago Press.

**18**    Neugarten, Bernice L., and Karol K. Weinstein

    1964    "The changing American grandparent." Journal of Marriage and the Family. 26:199–204.

**12**    Neugarten, Bernice L., Robert J. Havighurst and Sheldon S. Tobin

    1961    "The measurement of life satisfaction." Journal of Gerontology 16:134–43.

**19**    Neugarten, Bernice L., Joan W. Moore and John C. Lowe

    1965    "Age norms, age constraints, and adult socialization." American Journal of Sociology 70:710–17.

**4, 12**    Neugarten, Bernice L., Howard Berkowitz and associates (eds.)

    1964    Personality in Middle and Late Life. New York: Atherton Press.

    Neugarten, Bernice L., Vivian Wood, Ruth J. Kraines and Barbara Loomis

    1963    "Women's attitudes toward the menopause." Vita Humana 6:140–51.

**3**    Newcomb, Theodore M., Ralph H. Turner and Philip E. Converse

    1965    Social Psychology. New York: Holt, Rinehart, and Winston.

**13**    Newell, David S.

    1961    "Social structural evidence for disengagement." Pp. 37–74 in Elaine Cumming and W. E. Henry (eds.), Growing Old. New York: Basic Books.

**6**    Newman, H. F.

    1969    "The impact of Medicare on group practice prepayment plans." American Journal of Public Health 59:629–34.

**6**    Nithman, C. J., Y. E. Parkhurst and E. B. Sommers

    1971    "Physicians' prescribing habits: effects of Medicare." Journal of the American Medical Association 217:585–87.

**16**    Oakes, C. G.

    1973    "Sociomedical fit and misfit among the elderly." Pp. 77–102 in R. R. Boyd and C. G. Oakes (eds.), Foundations of Practical Gerontology. Second edition. Columbia, South Carolina: University of South Carolina Press.

**1**    O'Donnell, C. F.

    1974    "Aging in preindustrial and in contemporary industrial societies." Pp. 3–13 in W. C. Bier (ed.), Aging: Its Challenge to the Individual and to Society. Pastoral Psychology Series, No. 8. New York: Fordham University Press.

**12**    Oliver, David

    1975    "Nutrition and Health Care." Pp. 163–84 in Robert C. Atchley (ed.), Environments and the Rural Aged. Washington, D.C.: Gerontological Society.

    Oliver, David Busch

    1971    "Career and leisure patterns of middle-aged metropolitan out-migrants." Gerontologist 11(4, part 2):13–20.

**17**    Orbach, Harold L.

    1961    "Aging and religion: a study of church attendance in the Detroit metropolitan area." Geriatrics 16:530–40.

**14**    Orbach, Harold L., and Clark Tibbitts (eds.)

    1963    Aging and the Economy. Ann Arbor, Michigan: University of Michigan Press.

| | |
|---|---|
| 8 | Orbach, Harold L., and others |
| | 1969    Trends in Early Retirement. Ann Arbor, Michigan: University of Michigan, Wayne State University Institute of Gerontology. |
| 17 | O'Reilly, Charles T. |
| | 1958    "Religious practice and personal adjustment." Sociology and Social Research 42:119–21. |
| 8 | O'Rourke, J. F., and H. L. Friedman |
| | 1972    "An inter-union pre-retirement training program: results and commentary." Industrial Gerontology 13:49–64. |
| 18 | Orthner, Dennis K. |
| | 1975    "Leisure activity patterns and marital satisfaction over the marital career." Journal of Marriage and the Family 37:91–102. |
| 8 | Owen, John P., and L. D. Belzung |
| | 1967    "Consequences of voluntary early retirement: a case study of a new labour force phenomenon." British Journal of Industrial Relations 5:162–89. |
| | Owens, William A. |
| 3 | 1953    "Age and mental abilities: a longitudinal study." Genetic Psychology Monographs 48:3–54. |
| 3 | 1966    "Age and mental abilities: a second adult follow-up." Journal of Educational Psychology 57:311–25. |
| | Palmore, Erdman |
| 7 | 1964a    "Work experience and earnings of the aged in 1962: findings of the 1963 survey of the aged." Social Security Bulletin 27(6):3–14. |
| 8 | 1964b    "Retirement patterns among aged men: findings of the 1963 survey of the aged." Social Security Bulletin 27(8):3–10. |
| 8 | 1965    "Differences in the retirement patterns of men and women." Gerontologist 5:4–8. |
| 8 | 1967    "Employment and retirement." Pp. 89–108 in Lenore Epstein (ed.), The Aged Population of the United States. Washington, D.C.: United States Government Printing Office. |
| | 1970    (ed.), Normal Aging: Reports from the Duke Longitudinal Study, 1955–1969. Durham, North Carolina: Duke University Press. |
| 8 | 1971a    "Why do people retire?" Aging and Human Development 2:269–83. |
| 1 | 1971b    "Attitudes toward aging as shown by humor." Gerontologist 11:181–86. |
| 8 | 1972    "Compulsory versus flexible retirement: issues and facts." Gerontologist 12:343–48. |
| 6 | 1973a    "Social factors in mental illness of the aged." Pp. 41–52 in E. W. Busse and E. Pfeiffer (eds.), Mental Illness in Later Life. Washington, D.C.: American Psychiatric Association. |
| 19 | 1973b    "Potential demographic contributions to gerontology." Gerontologist 13:236–42. |
| 1 | 1974    "The brighter side of four score and ten." Gerontologist 14:136–37. |
| 8 | 1975a    The Honorable Elders. Durham, North Carolina: Duke University Press. |
| | 1975b    "What can the USA learn from Japan about aging?" Gerontologist 15:64–67. |
| 1 | 1975c    "The status and integration of the aged in Japanese society." Journal of Gerontology 30:199–208. |
| | Palmore, Erdman, and Frances C. Jeffers |
| 6 | 1971    "Health care in a longitudinal panel before and after Medicare." Journal of Gerontology 26:532–36. |
| | Palmore, Erdman, and K. Manton |
| 1 | 1973    "Ageism compared to racism and sexism." Journal of Gerontology 28:363–69. |
| 1 | 1974    "Modernization and status of the aged: international correlations." Journal of Gerontology 29:205–10. |

**1**
Palmore, Erdman, and F. Whittington
1971 "Trends in the relative status of the aged." Social Forces 50(September):84–91.

**9**
Parker, Edwin B., and William Paisley
1966 Patterns of Adult Information Seeking. Stanford, California: Stanford University Institute for Communications Research.

Parkes, C. M.

**10**
1970 " 'Seeking' and 'finding' a lost object." Social Science and Medicine 4:187–201.

**10**
1972 Bereavement. New York: International Universities Press.

Parsons, Talcott (ed.)

**5**
1942 "Age and sex in the social structure of the United States." American Sociological Review 7:604–16.

**10**
1972 "Death in American experience." Social Research 39:367–567.

**16**
Patnaik, B., M. P. Lawton, M. H. Kleban and R. Maxwell
1974 "Behavioral adaptation to the change in institutional residence." Gerontologist 14:305–07.

**10**
Peck, R. C.
1968 "Psychological developments in the second half of life." Pp. 88–92 in Bernice L. Neugarten (ed.), Middle Age and Aging. Chicago: University of Chicago Press.

**4**
Peters, George R.
1971 "Self-conceptions of the aged, age identification, and aging." Gerontologist 11(4, part 2):69–73.

Peterson, D. A.

**7**
1972a The Crisis in Retirement Finance: The Views of Older Americans. Occasional Papers in Gerontology, No. 9. Ann Arbor, Michigan: University of Michigan, Wayne State University Institute of Gerontology.

**7**
1972b "Financial adequacy in retirement: perceptions of older Americans." Gerontologist 12:379–83.

Pfeiffer, Eric, and G. C. Davis

**5, 9**
1971 "The use of leisure time in middle life." Gerontologist 11(3, part 1):187–95.

**3**
1972 "Determinants of sexual behavior in middle and old age." Journal of the American Geriatric Society 20:151–58.

**15**
Philibert, Michel
1970 "La politique nationale de la vieillesse en France." Gerontologie November: 10–13.

**12**
Phillips, Bernard S.
1957 "A role theory approach to adjustment in old age." American Sociological Review 22:212–17.

**10**
Phillips, D. P., and K. A. Feldman
1973 "A dip in deaths before ceremonial occasions: some new relationships between social integration and mortality." American Sociological Review 38:678–96.

**12**
Pierce, R. C., and M. M. Clark
1973 "Measurement of morale in the elderly." International Journal of Aging and Human Development 4:83–101.

**10**
Pihlblad, C. Terence, and D. L. Adams
1972 "Widowhood, social participation and life satisfaction." Aging and Human Development 3:323–30.

**12, 18**
Pihlblad, C. Terence, and Robert L. McNamara
1965 "Social adjustment of elderly people in three small towns." Pp. 49–73 in Arnold M. Rose and Warren A. Peterson (eds.), Older People and Their Social World. Philadelphia: F. A. Davis.

**6, 12, 16**
Pihlblad, C. Terence, Richard Hessler and Harold Freshley
1975 The Rural Elderly, 8 Years Later: Changes in Life Satisfaction, Living Arrangements and Health Status. Columbia, Missouri: University of Missouri.

18  Pineo, Peter
    1961    "Disenchantment in the later years of marriage." Marriage and Family Living 23:3–11.

15  Pinner, Frank A., Paul Jacobs and Philip Selznick
    1959    Old Age and Political Behavior: A Case Study. Berkeley, California: University of California Press.

4  Plutchik, R., H. Conte and M. Bakur-Weiner
    1973    "Studies of body image. III. Body feelings as measured by the semantic differential." International Journal of Aging and Human Development 4:375–80.

7  Polinsky, Ella J.
    1969    "The position of women in the Social Security System." Social Security Bulletin 32(7):3–19.

8  Pollak, Otto
    1956    The Social Aspects of Retirement. Homewood, Illinois: R. D. Irwin.

    Pollman, A. William

8      1971a    "Early retirement: a comparison of poor health to other retirement factors." Journal of Gerontology 26:41–45.

8      1971b    "Early retirement: relationship to variation in life satisfaction." Gerontologist 11(1, part 1):43–47.

8  Pollman, A. William, and A. C. Johnson
    1974    "Resistance to change, early retirement and managerial decisions." Industrial Gerontology 1:33–41.

15  Polner, Walter
    1962    "The aged in politics: a successful example, the NPA and the passage of the Railroad Retirement Act of 1934." Gerontologist 2:207–15.

6  Posner, J.
    1974    "Notes on the negative implications of being competent in a home for the aged." International Journal of Aging and Human Development 5:357–64.

15  Post, J. M.
    1973    "On aging leaders: possible effects of the aging process on the conduct of leadership." Journal of Geriatric Psychiatry 6:109–16.

1  Powers, Edward A., and G. L. Bultena
    1972    "Characteristics of deceased dropouts in longitudinal research." Journal of Gerontology 27:530–35.

8, 14  Powers, Edward A., and Willis H. Goudy
    1971    "Examination of the meaning of work to older workers." Aging and Human Development 2:38–45.

10, 18  Powers, Edward A., Patricia Keith and Willis H. Goudy
    1975    "Family relationships and friendships." Pp. 67–90 in Robert C. Atchley (ed.), Environments and the Rural Aged. Washington: Gerontological Society.

15  Pratt, Henry J.
    1974    "Old age associations in national politics." Pp. 106–19 in Frederick R. Eisele (ed.), Political Consequences of Aging. Philadelphia: American Academy of Political and Social Sciences.

1  Press, I., and M. McKool, Jr.
    1972    "Social structure and status of the aged: toward some valid cross-cultural generalizations." Aging and Human Development 3:297–306.

4  Preston, Caroline E., and Karen S. Gudiksen
    1966    "A measure of self-perception among older people." Journal of Gerontology 21:63–71.

16  Preston, Caroline E., and S. Helgerson
    1972    "An analysis of survey data obtained by a service agency for older people." Gerontologist 12:384–88.

10  Preston, Caroline E., and R. H. Williams
    1971    "Views of the aged on the timing of death." Gerontologist 11:300–04.

6       Preston, S. H.
        1974    "Effect of mortality change on stable population parameters." Demography
                11:119–30.
8       Pyron, H. Charles, and U. Vincent Manion
        1970    "The company, the individual, and the decision to retire." Industrial Geron-
                tology 4:1–11.
        Quirk, Daniel A.
14      1974    "Public policy note: age discrimination on employment—some recent develop-
                ments." Industrial Gerontology 1:77–80.
7       1975    "Public policy note in defense of the Social Security System: the white paper."
                Industrial Gerontology 2:164–66.
14      Quirk, Daniel A., and J. H. Skinner
        1973    "Physical capacity, age, and employment." Industrial Gerontologist 19:49–62.
15      Ragan, Pauline K., and James J. Dowd
        1974    "The emerging political consciousness of the aged: a generational interpreta-
                tion." Journal of Social Issues 30:137–58.
4       Ramamurti, P. V.
        1971    "Attitude towards personal futurity: a cross-sectional analysis of age span 20–
                70." Indian Journal of Gerontology 3:33–35.
16      Randall, Ollie A.
        1965    "Some historical developments of social welfare aspects of aging." Geron-
                tologist 5:40–49.
3       Reese, H. W.
        1973    "Life-span models of memory." Gerontologist 13:472–78.
        Reichard, Suzanne, Florine Livson and Paul G. Petersen
4       1962    Aging and Personality. New York: Wiley.
8       1968    "Adjustment to retirement." Pp. 178–80 in Bernice L. Neugarten (ed.), Middle
                Age and Aging. Chicago: University of Chicago Press.
16      Reingold, J., and R. L. Wolk
        1974    "Gerontological sheltered workshops for mentally impaired aged: some tested
                hypotheses." Industrial Gerontology 1:1–11.
        Reno, Virginia P.
8       1971    "Why men stop working at or before age 65." Social Security Bulletin 34(4):
                3–17.
8       1972    "Compulsory retirement among newly entitled workers: survey of new bene-
                ficiaries." Social Security Bulletin 35(3):3–15.
7       1973    "Women newly entitled to retired-worker benefits: survey of new beneficiaries."
                Social Security Bulletin 36(4):3–26.
7       Reno, Virginia P., and Carol Zuckert
        1971    "Benefit levels of newly retired workers." Social Security Bulletin 34(7):3–31.
1       Reston, J.
        1971    "On the nobility of old age." Journal of American Geriatric Society 19:460–61.
4, 10   Reynolds, D. K., and R. A. Kalish
        1974    "Anticipation of futurity as a function of ethnicity and age." Journal of Geron-
                tology 29:224–31.
6       Reynolds, Frank W., and Paul C. Barsam
        1967    Adult Health: Services for the Chronically Ill and Aging. New York: Macmillan.
18      Rheinstein, Max
        1960    "Duty of children to support parents." P. 442 in E. W. Burgess (ed.), Aging in
                Western Societies. Chicago: University of Chicago Press.
1, 12,  Ricciardelli, Sister R. M.
13      1973    "King Lear and the theory of disengagement." Gerontologist 13:148–52.

Riegel, Klaus F.

**4**    1959    "Personality theory and aging." Pp. 797–851 in James E. Birren (ed.), Handbook of Aging and the Individual. Chicago: University of Chicago Press.

**3, 4**    1973a    "On the history of psychological gerontology." Pp. 37–68 in C. Eisdorfer and M. P. Lawton (eds.), The Psychology of Adult Development and Aging. Washington, D.C.: American Psychological Association.

**3**    1973b    "Language and cognition: some life-span developmental issues." Gerontologist 13:478–82.

Riegel, Klaus F., and R. M. Riegel

**9**    1972    "Development, drop, and death." Developmental Psychology 6:306–19.

Riley, Matilda W.

**5**    1971    "Social gerontology and the age stratification of society." Gerontologist 11(1, part 1):79–87.

**1**    1973    "Aging and cohort succession: interpretations and misinterpretations." Public Opinion Quarterly 37(Spring):35–49.

Riley, Matilda W., and Anne Foner

1968    Aging and Society. Volume 1: An Inventory of Research Findings. New York: Russell Sage Foundation.

Riley, Matilda W., Marilyn Johnson and Anne Foner

**5**    1972    Aging and Society. Volume 3: A Sociology of Age Stratification. New York: Russell Sage Foundation.

Riley, Matilda W., John W. Riley, Jr. and Marilyn E. Johnson

1969    Aging and Society. Volume 2: Aging and the Professions. New York: Russell Sage Foundation.

**7**    Robbins, Ira S.

1971    Housing the Elderly. Washington, D.C.: White House Conference on Aging.

**4**    Robin, Ellen Page

1971    "Discontinuities in attitudes and behaviors of older age groups." Gerontologist 11(4, part 2):79–84.

**16**    Robinson, P. B., Jr.

1972    "Socio-cultural characteristics of senior citizen participants in adult education." Adult Leadership 20:234–36, 258.

**10**    Robson, K. S.

1974    "Clinical report: letters to a dead husband." Journal of Geriatric Psychiatry 7:208–32.

**2**    Rockstein, Morris

1968    "The biological aspects of aging." Gerontologist 8:124–25.

**8, 16**    Rogers, T. W.

1974    "Migration of the aged population." International Migration 12:61–70.

**18**    Rollins, Boyd C., and Kenneth L. Cannon

1974    "Marital satisfaction over the family life cycle: a re-evaluation." Journal of Marriage and the Family 36:271–82.

**18**    Rollins, Boyd C., and Harold Feldman

1970    "Marital satisfaction over the family life cycle." Journal of Marriage and the Family. 32:20–28.

**12, 13**    Roman, Paul, and Philip Taietz

1967    "Organizational structure and disengagement: the emeritus professor." Gerontologist 7:147–52.

Rose, Arnold M.

**17**    1960    "The impact of aging on voluntary associations." Pp. 666–97 in Clark Tibbitts (ed.), Handbook of Social Gerontology. Chicago: University of Chicago Press.

**12, 13**    1964    "A current issue in social gerontology." Gerontologist 4:45–50.

**388**    References

| | | |
|---|---|---|
| **1, 8** | 1965a | "The subculture of aging: a framework for research in social gerontology." Pp. 3–16 in Arnold M. Rose and Warren A. Peterson (eds.), Older People and Their Social World. Philadelphia: F. A. Davis. |
| **6** | 1965b | "Physical health and mental outlook among the aging." Pp. 201–09 in Arnold M. Rose and Warren A. Peterson (eds.), Older People and Their Social World. Philadelphia: F. A. Davis. |
| **6** | 1965c | "Mental health of normal older persons." Pp. 193–99 in Arnold M. Rose and Warren A. Peterson (eds.), Older People and Their Social World. Philadelphia: F. A. Davis. |
| **15** | 1965d | "Group consciousness among the aging." Pp. 19–36 in Arnold M. Rose and Warren A. Peterson (eds.), Older People and Their Social World. Philadelphia: F. A. Davis. |
| **15** | 1966 | "Class differences among the elderly: a research report." Sociology and Social Research 50:356–60. |

Rose, Arnold M., and Warren A. Peterson (eds.)

| | | |
|---|---|---|
| **8** | 1965 | Older People and Their Social World. Philadelphia: F. A. Davis. |

Rose, Charles L., and John M. Mogey

| | | |
|---|---|---|
| | 1972 | "Aging and preference for later retirement." Aging and Human Development 3:45–62. |

Rosenberg, George S.

| | | |
|---|---|---|
| **18** | 1968 | "Age, poverty and isolation from friends in the urban working class." Journal of Gerontology 23:533–38. |
| **8, 16** | 1970 | The Worker Grows Old. San Francisco: Jossey-Bass. |

Rosenberg, Morris

| | | |
|---|---|---|
| **8** | 1964 | Society and the Adolescent Self-Image. Princeton, New Jersey: Princeton University Press. |
| | 1968 | The Logic of Survey Analysis. New York: Basic Books. |

Rosenblatt, Aaron

| | | |
|---|---|---|
| **16** | 1966 | "Interest of older persons in volunteer activities." Social Work 11(3):87–94. |

Rosenblum, M.

| | | |
|---|---|---|
| **8** | 1975 | "The last push: from discouraged worker to involuntary retirement." Industrial Gerontology 2:14–22. |

Rosenfelt, Rosalie H.

| | | |
|---|---|---|
| **1** | 1965 | "Elderly mystique." Journal of Social Issues 21:37–43. |

Rosenheim, Margaret K.

| | | |
|---|---|---|
| **18** | 1965 | "Social welfare and its implications for family living." Pp. 206–40 in Ethel Shanas and Gordon F. Streib (eds.), Social Structure and the Family: Generational Relations. Englewood Cliffs, New Jersey: Prentice-Hall. |

Rosow, Irving

| | | |
|---|---|---|
| **1** | 1962 | "Old age: one moral dilemma of an affluent society." Gerontologist 2:182–91. |
| **18** | 1964 | "Local concentrations of aged and intergenerational friendships." Pp. 478–83 in P. From Hansen (ed.), Age with a Future. Copenhagen: Munksgaard. |
| **18** | 1965 | "The aged, family and friends." Social Security Bulletin 28(11):18–20. |
| **16** | 1966 | "Housing and local ties of the aged." Pp. 47–64 in Frances M. Carp and W. M. Burnett (eds.), Patterns of Living and Housing of Middle-Aged and Older People. Washington, D.C.: United States Public Health Service. |
| **16, 18** | 1967 | Social Integration of the Aged. New York: Free Press. |
| **9** | 1969 | "Retirement, leisure, and social status." Pp. 249–57 in Frances C. Jeffers (ed.), Duke University Council on Aging and Human Development: Proceedings of Seminars, 1965–1969. Durham, North Carolina: Duke University Center for the Study of Aging and Human Development. |
| **4** | 1973 | "The social context of the aging self." Gerontologist 13:82–87. |
| **5** | 1974 | Socialization to Old Age. Berkeley, California: University of California Press. |

| | |
|---|---|
| **4** | Ross, B., S. R. Greenwald and M. W. Linn<br>1973    "The elderly's perception of the drug scene." Gerontologist 13:368–71. |
| **16** | Ross, Hugh<br>1968    "Protective services for the aged." Gerontologist 8(1, part 2):50–53. |
| **16** | Rossiter, C. M.<br>1970    "Chronological age and listening of adult students." Adult Education 21:40–43. |
| **8** | Rowe, A. R.<br>1972    "The retirement of academic scientists." Journal of Gerontology 27:113–18. |
| **17** | Rubenstein, Daniel<br>1971    "An examination of social participation found among a national sample of black and white elderly." Aging and Human Development 2:172–88. |
| **18**<br>**18** | Rubin, Isadore<br>1965    Sexual Life after Sixty. New York: Basic Books.<br>1968    "The 'sexless older years'—a socially harmful stereotype." Annals of the American Academy of Political and Social Sciences 376:86–95. |
| **7** | Rubin, Leonard<br>1973    "Late entitlement to retirement benefits: findings from the survey of new beneficiaries." Social Security Bulletin 36(7):3–20. |
| **14** | Rusalem, Herbert<br>1963    "Deterrents to vocational disengagement among older disabled workers." Gerontologist 3:64–68. |
| **10** | Russell, O. Ruth<br>1975    Freedom to Die: Moral and Legal Aspects of Euthanasia. New York: Human Sciences Press. |
| **16** | Sainer, J. S., and F. K. Kallan<br>1972    "SERVE: a case illustration of older volunteers in a psychiatric setting." Gerontologist 12:90–93. |
| **16** | Sainer, J., and M. Zander<br>1971    "Guidelines for older person volunteers." Gerontologist 11:201–04. |
| **10** | Sainsbury, Peter<br>1963    "Social and epidemiological aspects of suicide with special reference to the aged." Pp. 153–75 in Richard H. Williams, Clark Tibbitts and Wilma Donahue (eds.), Processes of Aging. Volume 2. New York: Atherton Press. |
| **16** | Saltz, R.<br>1971    "Aging persons as child-care workers in a foster-grandparent program: psychosocial effects and work performance." Aging and Human Development 2:314–40. |
| **4** | Sanford, A. J., and A. J. Maule<br>1973    "The concept of general experience: age and strategies in guessing future events." Journal of Gerontology 28:81–88. |
| **19** | Sax, Sidney<br>1967    "The goals of gerontology." Gerontologist 7:153–60. |
| **3**<br><br>**3**<br><br>**1**<br>**1** | Schaie, K. Warner<br>1958    "Rigidity-flexibility and intelligence: a cross-sectional study of the adult life span from 20 to 70 years." Pp. 1–26 in Psychological Monographs: General and Applied 72, No. 9, No. 462.<br>1960    Manual for the Test of Behavioral Rigidity. Palo Alto, California: Consulting Psychologists Press.<br>1967    "Age changes and age differences." Gerontologist 7:128–32. |
| | Schaie, K. Warner, G. V. Labouvie and T. J. Barrett<br>1973    "Selected attrition effects in a fourteen-year study of adult intelligence." Journal of Gerontology 28:328–34. |

3     Schaie, K. Warner, G. V. Labouvie and B. U. Buech
       1973    "Generational and cohort-specific differences in adult cognitive functioning: a fourteen year study of independent samples." Developmental Psychology 9:151–66.

1     Schlesselman, J. J.
       1973    "Planning a longitudinal study. I. Sample size determination. II. Frequency of measurement and study duration." Journal of Chronic Diseases 26:553–70.

15     Schmidhauser, John
       1968    "The political influence of the aged." Gerontologist 8(1, part 2):44–49.

12     Schmidt, John F.
       1951    "Patterns of poor adjustment in old age." American Journal of Sociology 57:33–42.

14     Schneider, Betty V. H.
       1962    The Older Worker. Berkeley, California: University of California Institute for Industrial Relations.

8     Schneider, Clement J.
       1964    Adjustment of Employed Women to Retirement. Unpublished doctoral dissertation, Cornell University, Ithaca, New York.

12     Schooler, Kermit K.
       1969    "The relationship between social interaction and morale of the elderly as a function of environmental characteristics." Gerontologist 9:25–29.

        Schorr, Alvin L.
18     1960    Filial Responsibility in the Modern American Family. Washington, D.C.: Social Security Administration.

18     1962    "Filial responsibility and the aging, or beyond pluck and luck." Social Security Bulletin 25(5):4–9.

7     Schottland, C. I.
       1965    "Poverty and income maintenance for the aged." Pp. 227–39 in Margaret S. Gordon (ed.), Poverty in America. San Francisco: Chandler.

16     Schreiber, M. S.
       1972    "The multi-purpose senior center: a vehicle for the delivery of services to older people." Pp. 19–26 in Senior Centers: A Focal Point for Delivery of Services to Older People. Washington, D.C.: National Institute of Senior Centers, National Council on Aging.

        Schuchat, T.
8     1971    "Postponed retirement under the Social Security Act." Industrial Gerontology 11:20–22.

7, 8     1973    "The impact of private pension plan terminations." Industrial Gerontology 17:72–74.

7     1974    "Pension reform: limits and accomplishments." Industrial Gerontology 1:26–33.

7     1975    "Report of the sixth advisory council on Social Security." Industrial Gerontology 2:167–71.

16     Schulz, D. A.
       1972    A Survey of Delaware's Elderly Living in Public Housing for the Elderly. Newark, Delaware: University of Delaware, Division of Urban Affairs.

        Schulz, James H.
7, 16     1967    "Some economics of aged home ownership." Gerontologist 7:73–74.

7     1968    The Economic Status of the Retired Aged in 1980: Simulated Projections. Washington, D.C.: United States Government Printing Office.

7     1970    Pension Aspects of the Economics of Aging: Present and Future Roles of Private Pensions. Washington, D.C.: United States Senate Special Committee on Aging.

14     1973    "The economic impact of an aging population." Gerontologist 13:111–18.

**8**    1974    "The economics of mandatory retirement." Industrial Gerontology 1:1–10.
**14**    1976    The Economics of Aging. Belmont, California: Wadsworth.
**7**    Schulz, James H., and others
     1974    Providing Adequate Retirement Income. Hanover, New Hampshire: Brandeis University Press.
**4**    Schwartz, Arthur N., and Robert W. Kleemeier
     1965    "The effects of illness and age upon some aspects of personality." Journal of Gerontology 20:85–91.
**10**    Scott, F. G., and R. M. Brewer (eds.)
     1971    Confrontations of Death: A Book of Readings and a Suggested Method of Instruction. Eugene, Oregon: Oregon Center for Gerontology.
**16**    Sears, D. W.
     1974    "Elderly housing: a need determination technique." Gerontologist 14:182–87.
**4**    Secord, Paul F., and Carl W. Backman
     1964    Social Psychology. New York: McGraw-Hill.
**8**    Seguin, M. M.
     1973    "Opportunity for peer socialization in a retirement community." Gerontologist 13:208–14.
**19**    Seltzer, Mildred M.
     1974    "Education in gerontology: an evolutionary analogy." Gerontologist 14:308–11.
     Seltzer, Mildred M., and Robert C. Atchley
**1**    1971a    "The concept of old: changing attitudes and stereotypes." Gerontologist 11:226–30.
**9, 13**    1971b    "The impact of structural integration into the profession on work commitment, potential for disengagement, and leisure preferences among social workers." Sociological Focus 5:9–17.
**19**    1974    Developing Educational Programs in the Field of Aging. Oxford, Ohio: Scripps Foundation.
**8**    Serwer, A. M.
     1974    "Mandatory retirement at age 65—a survey of the law." Industrial Gerontology 1:11–22.
     Shanas, Ethel
**18**    1960    "Family responsibility and the health of older people." Journal of Gerontology 15:408–11.
**6, 11**    1962    The Health of Older People: A Social Survey. Cambridge, Massachusetts: Harvard University Press.
**18**    1964    "Family and household characteristics of older people in the United States." Pp. 449–54 in P. From Hansen (ed.), Age with a Future. Copenhagen: Munksgaard.
**6**    1965    "Health care and health services for the aged." Gerontologist 5:240, 276.
**5, 18**    1967    "Family help patterns and social class in three countries." Journal of Marriage and the Family 29:257–66.
**4**    1968    "A note on restriction of life space: attitudes of age cohorts." Journal of Health and Social Behavior 9:86–90.
**6**    1971a    "Measuring the home health needs of the aged in five countries." Journal of Gerontology 26:37–40.
**8**    1971b    "Disengagement and work: myth and reality." Pp. 109–19 in Social Gerontology, International Centre of Social Gerontology.
**8**    1972    "Adjustment to retirement: substitution or accommodation?" Pp. 219–44 in Frances M. Carp (ed.), Retirement. New York: Behavioral Publications.
**18**    Shanas, Ethel, and Gordon F. Streib (eds.)
     1965    Social Structure and the Family: Generational Relations. Englewood Cliffs, New Jersey: Prentice-Hall.

| | |
|---|---|
| **1, 8,** <br> **18** | Shanas, Ethel, Peter Townsend, Dorothy Wedderburn, Henning Friis, Poul Milhøj and Jan Stehouwer <br> 1968    Older People in Three Industrial Societies. New York: Atherton Press. |
| **9** | Shapiro, E. <br> 1974    "Guidelines for a creative newspaper written by and for residents of homes for aged." International Journal of Aging and Human Development 5:365–68. |
| **1** | Sheldon, Henry D. <br> 1960    "The changing demographic profile." Pp. 27–61 in Clark Tibbitts (ed.), Handbook of Social Gerontology. Chicago: University of Chicago Press. |
| **16** | Sheley, J. F. <br> 1974    "Mutuality and retirement community success: an interactionist perspective in gerontological research." International Journal of Aging and Human Development 5:71–80. |
| **4** | Shenkin, A. <br> 1964    "Attitudes of old people to death." Pp. 171–77 in William F. Anderson and B. Isaacs (eds.), Current Achievements in Geriatrics. London: Cassell. |
| **14** | Sheppard, Harold L. <br> 1970    Industrial Gerontology. Cambridge, Massachusetts: Schenkman. |
| **8** | Sheppard, Harold L., and Michel Philibert <br> 1972    "Employment and retirement: roles and activities." Gerontologist 12(2, part 2): 29–35. |
| **14** | Sherman, E. M., and M. R. Brittan <br> 1973    "Contemporary food gatherers: a study of food shopping habits of an elderly urban population." Gerontologist 13:358–64. |
| **7** | Sherman, Sally R. <br> 1973    "Assets on the threshold of retirement." Social Security Bulletin 36(8):3–17. |
| | Sherman, Susan R. <br> 1971    "The choice of retirement housing among the well-elderly." Aging and Human Development 2:118–38. |
| **16** | 1975a  "Patterns of contacts for residents of age-segregated and age-integrated housing." Journal of Gerontology 30:103–07. |
| **16** | 1975b  "Mutual assistance and support in retirement housing." Journal of Gerontology 30:479–83. |
| **9** | 1975c  "Leisure activities in retirement housing." Journal of Gerontology 29:325–35. |
| **16** | Sherman, Susan R., Wiley P. Mangum, Jr., Suzanne Dodds, Rosabelle Walkley and Daniel M. Wilner <br> 1968    "Psychological effects of retirement housing." Gerontologist 8:170–75. |
| **4** | Sherwood, S., and T. Nadelson <br> 1972    "Alternate predictions concerning despair in old age." Pp. 408–44 in D. P. Kent, R. Kastenbaum and S. Sherwood (eds.), Research Planning and Action for the Elderly. New York: Behavioral Publications. |
| **6** | Sherwood, S., J. Glassman, C. Sherwood and J. N. Morris <br> 1974    "Pre-institutionalization factors as predictors of adjustment to a long-term care facility." Journal of Aging and Human Development 5:95–105 |
| | Shock, Nathan W. (ed.) |
| **2** | 1962    Biological Aspects of Aging. New York: Columbia University Press. |
| **2** | 1966    Perspectives in Experimental Gerontology. Springfield, Illinois: Charles C. Thomas. |
| **2** | Shock, Nathan W., and A. H. Norris <br> 1970    "Neuromuscular coordination as a factor in age changes in muscular exercise." Pp. 92–99 in D. Brunner and E. Jokl (eds.), Physical Activity and Aging. New York: S. Karger. |

| | |
|---|---|
| 4 | Shukin, Alexey, and Bernice L. Neugarten<br>1964    "Personality and social interaction." Pp. 149–57 in Bernice L. Neugarten and others (eds.), Personality in Middle and Late Life. New York: Atherton Press. |
| 7 | Shulman, Harry<br>1969    "Beneficiaries with minimum benefits: their characteristics in 1967." Social Security Bulletin 32:3–20. |
| 1 | Siegel, S., and William E. O'Leary<br>1973    "Some demographic aspects of aging in the United States." Current Population Reports, Series P-23, Population Estimates, No. 43. Washington, D.C.: United States Bureau of the Census. |
| 10 | Silverman, P. R.<br>1972    "Widowhood and preventive intervention." Family Coordinator 21:95–102. |
| 1 | Simmons, Leo W.<br>1945    The Role of the Aged in Primitive Society. New Haven, Connecticut: Yale University Press. |
| 1 | 1960    "Aging in preindustrial societies." Pp. 62–91 in Clark Tibbitts (ed.), Handbook of Social Gerontology. Chicago: University of Chicago Press. |
| 14 | Simpson, Ida H.<br>1973    "Problems of the aging in work and retirement." Pp. 157–72 in R. R. Boyd and C. G. Oakes (eds.), Foundations of Practical Gerontology. Columbia, South Carolina: University of South Carolina Press. |
| 8, 15,<br>16, 18 | Simpson, Ida H., and John C. McKinney (eds.)<br>1966    Social Aspects of Aging. Durham, North Carolina: Duke University Press. |
| 8 | Simpson, Ida H., Kurt W. Back and John C. McKinney<br>1966a    "Continuity of work and retirement activities, and self-evaluation." Pp. 106–19 in Ida H. Simpson and John C. McKinney (eds.), Social Aspects of Aging. Durham, North Carolina: Duke University Press. |
| 8 | 1966b    "Exposure to information on, preparation for, and self-evaluation in retirement." Pp. 90–105 in Ida H. Simpson and John C. McKinney (eds.), Social Aspects of Aging. Durham, North Carolina: Duke University Press. |
| 8 | 1966c    "Orientation toward work and retirement, and self-evaluation in retirement." Pp. 75–89 in Ida H. Simpson and John C. McKinney (eds.), Social Aspects of Aging. Durham, North Carolina: Duke University Press. |
| 6 | Singer, E.<br>1974    "Premature social aging: the social-psychological consequences of a chronic illness." Social Science and Medicine 8:143–51. |
| 6 | Sirrocco, Alvin<br>1972    "Services and activities offered to nursing home residents: United States, 1968." Vital and Health Statistics, Series 12, No. 17. |
| 4 | Slater, Philip E., and Harry A. Scarr<br>1964    "Personality in Old Age." Genetic Psychology Monographs 70:228–69. |
| 8 | Slavick, Fred<br>1966    Compulsory and Flexible Retirement in the American Economy. Ithaca, New York: Cornell University Press. |
| 8 | Slavick, Fred, and Seymour L. Wolfbein<br>1960    "The evolving work-life pattern." Pp. 298–329 in Clark Tibbitts (ed.), Handbook of Social Gerontology. Chicago: University of Chicago Press. |
| 3 | Smith, A. D.<br>1975    "Aging and interference with memory." Journal of Gerontology 30:319–25. |
| | Smith, B. K.<br>1973    Aging in America. Boston: Beacon Press. |

18     Smith, Harold E.
      1965     "Family interaction patterns of the aged: a review." Pp. 143–61 in Arnold M. Rose and Warren A. Peterson (eds.), Older People and Their Social World. Philadelphia: F. A. Davis.

18     Smith, Joel
      1966     "The narrowing social world of the aged." Pp. 226–42 in Ida H. Simpson and John C. McKinney (eds.), Social Aspects of Aging. Durham, North Carolina: Duke University Press.

15     Smith, Joel, and others
      1962     "Understanding local political behavior: the role of the older citizen." Law and Contemporary Problems 27:280–98.

        Smith, John M.
14     1969     "Age and occupation: a classification of occupations by their age structure." Journal of Gerontology 24:412–18.

14     1973     "Age and occupation: the determinants of male occupational age structures—hypothesis H and hypothesis A." Journal of Gerontology 28:484–90.

14     1974     "Age and occupation: a review of the use of occupational age structures in industrial gerontology." Industrial Gerontology 1:42–58.

12     Smith, K. J., and A. Lipman
      1972     "Constraint and life satisfaction." Journal of Gerontology 27:77–82.

4     Smith, Madorah E., and Calvin Hall
      1964     "An investigation of regression in a long dream series." Journal of Gerontology 19:66–71.

8     Smith, P. C., and others
      1969     The Measurement of Satisfaction in Work and Retirement: A Strategy for the Study of Attitudes. Chicago: Rand McNally.

        Smith, Stanley H.
      1967     "The older rural negro." Pp. 262–80 in E. Grant Youmans (ed.), Older Rural Americans. Lexington, Kentucky: University of Kentucky Press.

16     Snyder, L. H.
      1973     "An exploratory study of patterns of social interaction, organization, and facility design in three nursing homes." International Journal of Aging and Human Development 4:319–33.

7     Social Security Administration
      1972     "Annual Statistical Supplement." Social Security Bulletin.

3     Soliday, S. M.
      1974     "Relationship between age and hazard perception in automobile drivers." Perception and Motor Skills 39:335–38.

12     Solomon, Barbara
      1967     "Social functioning of economically dependent aged." Gerontologist 7:213–17.

1     Sontag, Lester W.
      1969     "The longitudinal method of research: what it can and can't do." Pp. 15–25 in Frances C. Jeffers (ed.), Duke University Council on Aging and Human Development: Proceedings of Seminars 1965–1969. Durham, North Carolina: Duke University Press.

5     Sontag, Susan
      1972     "The double standard of aging." Saturday Review 55(39):29–38.

9     Spain, Nola
      1969     "Recreational programs for the elderly. Pp. 180–90 in Rosamonde R. Boyd and C. G. Oakes (eds.), Foundations in Practical Gerontology. Columbia, South Carolina: University of South Carolina Press.

18     Spanier, Graham B., Robert A. Lewis and Charles L. Coles
      1975     "Marital adjustment over the family life cycle: the issue of curvilinearity." Journal of Marriage and the Family 37:263–75.

**4**       Sparks, P. M.
           1973    "Behavioral versus experiential aging: implications for intervention." Geron-
                   tologist 13:15–18.

**16**      Spear, Mel
           1968    "Paramedical services for older Americans." Journal of the American Geriatrics
                   Society 16:1088–94.

**12**      Spreitzer, E., and E. E. Snyder
           1974    "Correlates of life satisfaction among the aged." Journal of Gerontology
                   29:454–58.

**4**       Staats, S.
           1974    "Internal versus external locus of control for three age groups." International
                   Journal of Aging and Human Development 5:7–10.

**14**      Stagner, R.
           1975    "Boredom on the assembly line: age and personality variables." Industrial
                   Gerontology 2:23–44.

           Stanford, E. P. (ed.)
**8**       1971    "Retirement anticipation in the military." Gerontologist 11:37–42.
           1974    Minority Aging: Institute on Minority Aging Proceedings. San Diego: Center
                   on Aging, School of Social Work, San Diego State University.

**7**       Staples, Thomas G.
           1973    "Supplemental security income: the aged eligible." Social Security Bulletin
                   36(7):31–35.

**6**       Starkey, P. D.
           1968    "Sick-role retention as a factor in nonrehabilitation." Journal of Counseling
                   Psychology 15:75–79.

**18**      Stehouwer, Jan
           1965    "Relations between generations and the three-generation household in Den-
                   mark." Pp. 142–62 in Ethel Shanas and Gordon F. Streib (eds.), Social Struc-
                   ture and the Family. Englewood Cliffs, New Jersey: Prentice-Hall.

**9**       Steiner, Gary A.
           1963    The People Look at Television. New York: Alfred A. Knopf.

**7**       Steiner, Peter O., and Robert Dorfman
           1957    The Economic Status of the Aged. Berkeley, California: University of Cali-
                   fornia Press.

**16**      Stephens, J.
           1975    "Society of the alone: freedom, privacy, and utilitarianism as dominant norms
                   in the SRO." Journal of Gerontology 30:230–35.

**10**      Stern, Karl, Gwendolyn M. Williams and Miguel Prados
           1951    "Grief reactions in later life." American Journal of Psychiatry 108:289–94.

           Sterne, R. S., J. E. Phillips and A. Rabushka
           1974    "The urban elderly poor: racial and bureaucratic conflict." Lexington, Massa-
                   chusetts: D. C. Heath.

**14**      Stewart, C. D.
           1974    "The older worker in Japan: realities and possibilities." Industrial Gerontology
                   1:60–75.

**18**      Stinnett, Nick, Linda M. Carter and James E. Montgomery
           1972    "Older persons' perceptions of their marriages." Journal of Marriage and the
                   Family 34:665–70.

**8**       Stokes, Randall G., and George L. Maddox
           1967    "Some social factors in retirement adaptation." Journal of Gerontology
                   22:329–33.

**5**       Stone, K., and R. A. Kalish
           1973    "Of poker, roles, and aging: description, discussion, and data." International
                   Journal of Aging and Human Development 4:1–13.

4     Storck, P. A., W. R. Looft and F. H. Hooper
         1972    "Interrelationships among Piagetian tasks and traditional measures of cognitive abilities in mature and aged adults." Journal of Gerontology 27:461–65.

8     Strain, R. M.
         1974    "Retirement among priests and religious." Pp. 145–63 in W. C. Bier (ed.), Aging: Its Challenge to the Individual and to Society. Pastoral Psychology Series, No. 8. New York: Fordham University Press.

2     Strehler, Bernard L.
         1962    Time, Cells, and Aging. New York: Academic Press.

    Streib, Gordon F.

8          1956    "Morale of the retired." Social Problems 3:270–76.

8, 18          1958    "Family patterns in retirement." Journal of Social Issues 24:46–60.

         1965a    "Are the aged a minority group?" Pp. 311–28 in Alvin W. Gouldner (ed.), Applied Sociology. New York: Free Press.

18          1965b    "Intergenerational relations: perspectives of the two generations on the older parent." Journal of Marriage and the Family 27:469–76.

13          1968    "Disengagement theory in sociocultural perspective." International Journal of Psychiatry 6(1):69–76.

1     Streib, Gordon F., and Harold L. Orbach
         1967    "Aging." Pp. 612–40 in P. E. Lazarsfeld and others (eds.), The Uses of Sociology. New York: Basic Books.

8, 12     Streib, Gordon F., and Clement J. Schneider
         1971    Retirement in American Society. Ithaca, New York: Cornell University Press.

    Streib, Gordon F., and Wayne E. Thompson

8          1958a    "Situational determinants: health and economic deprivation in retirement." Journal of Social Issues 14(2):18–34.

8          1958b    (eds.), "Adjustment in Retirement." Journal of Social Issues 14(2):1–63.

8     Streib, Gordon F., Wayne E. Thompson and E. A. Suchman
         1958    "Family Patterns in Retirement." Journal of Social Issues 14:46–60.

10     Sudnow, David
         1967    Passing On: The Social Organization of Dying. Englewood Cliffs, New Jersey: Prentice-Hall.

    Sussman, Marvin B.

18          1955    "Activity patterns of post-parental couples and their relationship to family continuity." Marriage and Family Living 17:338–41.

18          1965    "Relationships of adult children with their parents in the United States." Pp. 62–92 in Ethel Shanas and Gordon F. Streib (eds.), Social Structure and the Family: Generational Relations. Englewood Cliffs, New Jersey: Prentice-Hall.

    Sussman, Marvin B., and Lee Burchinal

         1962a    "Parental aid to married children: implications for family functioning." Marriage and Family Living 24:320–32.

18          1962b    "Kin family network: unheralded structure in current conceptualizations of family functioning." Marriage and Family Living 24:231–40.

1     Suzuki, Peter T.
         1975    "Minority group aged in America: a comprehensive bibliography of recent publications on Blacks, Mexican-Americans, Native Americans, Chinese, and Japanese." Council of Planning Librarians Exchange Bibliography, No. 816. Monticello, Illinois: Council of Planning Librarians.

10     Swenson, W. M.
         1961    "Attitudes toward death in an aged population." Journal of Gerontology 16:49–52.

**19**     Taber, Merlin
           1965    "Application of research findings to the issues of social policy." Pp. 367–79 in Arnold M. Rose and Warren A. Peterson (eds.), Older People and Their Social World. Philadelphia: F. A. Davis.

**14**     Taggart, Robert
           1973    The Labor Market Impacts of the Private Retirement System. Studies in Public Welfare, Paper Number 11. Washington, D.C.: United States Congress, Subcommittee on Fiscal Policy, Joint Economic Committee.

           Taietz, Philip
**16**     1966    "Community structure and aging." Pp. 375–78 in Proceedings of the 7th International Congress of Gerontology, VI. Vienna: Wiener Medizinischen Akadamie.

**16**     1975a   "Community complexity and knowledge of facilities." Journal of Gerontology 30:357–62.

**16**     1975b   "Community facilities and social services." Pp. 145–56 in Robert C. Atchley (ed.), Environments and the Rural Aged. Washington, D.C.: Gerontological Society.

**17**     Taietz, Philip, and Olaf F. Larson
           1955    "Social participation and old age." Rural Sociology 21:229–38.

**3**      Talland, George A. (ed.)
           1968    Human Aging and Behavior. New York: Academic Press.

**13**     Tallmer, Margot, and Bernard Kutner
           1969    "Disengagement and the stresses of aging." Journal of Gerontology 24:70–75.

**3**      Taub, H. A.
           1975    "Mode of presentation, age, and short-term memory." Journal of Gerontology 30:56–59.

**6**      Taube, Carl A.
           1965    "Characteristics of patients in mental hospitals: United States, April–June, 1963." Vital and Health Statistics, Series 12, No. 3.

**8**      Taylor, Charles
           1972    "Developmental conceptions and the retirement process." Pp. 75–116 in Frances M. Carp (ed.), Retirement. New York: Behavioral Publications.

**14**     Tellier, R. D.
           1974    "The four-day workweek and the elderly: a cross-sectional study." Journal of Gerontology 29:430–33.

           Templer, D. I.
**10**     1971    "Death anxiety as related to depression and health of retired persons." Journal of Gerontology 26:521–23.

**10**     1972    "Death anxiety in religiously very involved persons." Psychological Reports 31:361–62.

**10**     Templer, D. I., C. Ruff and C. Frank
           1971    "Death anxiety: age, sex, and parental resemblance in diverse populations." Developmental Psychology 4:108.

**16**     Terris, Bruce J.
           1972    Legal Services for the Elderly. Washington, D.C.: National Council on the Aging.

**4**      Thaler, Margaret
           1956    "Relationships among Wechsler, Weigl, Rorschach, EEG findings and abstract-concrete behavior." Journal of Gerontology 11:404–09.

**7**      Thomas, G.
           1973    "Regional migration patterns and poverty among the aged in the South." Journal of Human Resources 8:73–84.

Thompson, Gayle B.

8    1973    "Work versus leisure roles: an investigation of morale among employed and retired men." Journal of Gerontology 28:339–44.

14    1974    "Work experience and income of the population aged 60 and older, 1971." Social Security Bulletin 37(11):3–20.

6    1975    "Blacks and social security benefits: trends, 1960–73." Social Security Bulletin 38(4):30–40.

Thompson, Wayne E.

8    1956    The Impact of Retirement. Unpublished doctoral dissertation, Cornell University, Ithaca, New York.

8    1958    "Pre-retirement anticipation and adjustment in retirement." Journal of Social Issues 14:35–45.

Thompson, Wayne E., and Gordon F. Streib

8    1958    "Situation determinants: health and economic deprivation in retirement." Journal of Social Issues 14:18–34.

Thompson, Wayne E., Gordon F. Streib and John Kosa

8, 12    1960    "The effect of retirement on personal adjustment: a panel analysis." Journal of Gerontology 15:165–69.

Thorson, J. A.

1    1975    "Attitudes toward the aged as a function of race and social class." Gerontologist 15:343–44.

Thorson, J. A., L. Whatley and K. L. Kancock

1    1974    "Attitudes toward the aged as a function of age and education." Gerontologist 14:316–18.

Thune, Jeanne M.

4    1967    "Racial attitudes of older adults." Gerontologist 7:179–82.

Thune, Jeanne M., Sebastian Tine and F. E. Booth

16    1964    "Retraining older adults for employment in community services." Gerontologist 4:5–9.

Thune, Jeanne M., C. R. Webb and L. E. Thune

4    1971    "Interracial attitudes of younger and older adults in a biracial population." Gerontologist 11:305–10.

Thurnher, M.

8    1974    "Goals, values, and life evaluations at the preretirement stage." Journal of Gerontology 29:85–96.

Thurstone, L. L., and T. G. Thurstone

3    1949    Examiner manual for the SRA primary mental abilities. Chicago: Science Research Associates.

Tibbitts, Clark

1    1960    (ed.), Handbook of Social Gerontology. Chicago: University of Chicago Press.

15    1962    "Politics of aging: pressure for change." Pp. 16–25 in Wilma Donahue and Clark Tibbitts (eds.), Politics of Age. Ann Arbor, Michigan: University of Michigan Press.

1    1964    "The future of research in social gerontology." Pp. 139–45 in P. From Hansen (ed.), Age with a Future. Copenhagen: Munksgaard.

19    1969    "Manpower needs in the field of aging." Aging (173–174):3–5.

Tibbitts, Clark, and Wilma Donahue (eds.)

19    1962    Social and Psychological Aspects of Aging. New York: Columbia University Press.

Tissue, Thomas L.

12    1968    "A Guttman Scale of disengagement potential." Journal of Gerontology 23:513–16.

7    1970    "Downward mobility in old age." Social Problems 18:67–77.

| | |
|---|---|
| **7** | 1971a "Old age, poverty and the central city." Aging and Human Development 2:235–48. |
| **12** | 1971b "Disengagement potential: replication and use as an explanatory variable." Journal of Gerontology 26:76–80. |
| **16** | 1971c "Social class and the senior citizen center." Gerontologist 11:196–200. |

Tissue, Thomas L., and L. Wells
1971    "Antecedent lifestyles and old age." Psychological Reports 29:1100.

| **12** | Tobin, Sheldon S., and Bernice L. Neugarten |
| | 1961    "Life satisfaction and social interaction in the aging." Journal of Gerontology 16:344–46. |

| **14** | Tomika, K. |
| | 1975    "Counseling middle-aged and older workers." Industrial Gerontology 2:45–52. |

Townsend, Peter
| **18** | 1957    The Family Life of Old People: An Inquiry in East London. Glencoe, Illinois: Free Press. |
| **1** | 1964    "The place of older people in different societies." Lancet 1:159–61. |
| **6** | 1964    The Last Refuge. New York: Routledge. |
| **18** | 1965    "The effects of family structure on the likelihood of admission to an institution in old age: the application of a general theory." Pp. 163–87 in Ethel Shanas and Gordon F. Streib (eds.), Social Structure and the Family: Generational Relations. Englewood Cliffs, New Jersey: Prentice-Hall. |
| | 1968    "Problems in the cross-national study of old people in the family: segregation versus integration." Pp. 41–60 in Ethel Shanas and John Madge (eds.), Methodology Problems in Cross-National Studies in Aging. New York: S. Karger. |

| **7, 14,** | Townsend, Peter, and Dorothy Wedderburn |
| **15** | 1965    The Aged in the Welfare State. London: Bell. |

| **6** | Travis, Georgia |
| | 1966    Chronic Disease and Disability. Berkeley, California: University of California Press. |

Trela, James E.
| **15** | 1971    "Some political consequences of senior center and other old age group membership." Gerontologist 11(2, part 1):118–23. |
| **15, 17** | 1972    "Age structure of voluntary associations and political self-interest among the aged." Sociological Quarterly 13:244–52. |

| **12** | Trenton, Jean-Rene |
| | 1963    "The concept of adjustment in old age." Pp. 292–98 in Richard H. Williams, Clark Tibbitts and Wilma Donahue (eds.), Processes of Aging. Volume 1. New York: Atherton Press. |

Troll, Lillian E.
| **18** | 1970    "Issues in the study of generations." Aging and Human Development 1:199–218. |
| **10, 18** | 1971    "The family of later life: a decade review." Journal of Marriage and the Family 33:263–90. |
| **4, 12** | 1973    "The onus of 'developmental tasks' and other reactions to Duvall's Family Development in its fourth edition." International Journal of Aging and Human Development 4:67–74. |

| **1** | Troll, Lillian E., and N. Schlossberg |
| | 1971    "How 'age biased' are college counselors?" Industrial Gerontologist 10:14–20. |

Tuckman, Jacob, and Irving Lorge
| **8** | 1953    Retirement and the Industrial Worker: Prospect and Reality. New York: Columbia University Teachers College. |
| **4** | 1954    "Classification of the self as young, middle-aged, or old." Geriatrics 9:534–36. |

| **4** | Tuckman, Jacob, Irving Lorge and F. D. Zeman |
| | 1961    "The self-image in aging." Journal of Genetic Psychology 90:317–21. |

| | | |
|---|---|---|
| 15 | | Turk, Herman, Joel Smith and Howard P. Myers |
| | 1966 | "Understanding local political behavior: the role of the older citizen." Pp. 254–76 in Ida H. Simpson and John C. McKinney (eds.), Social Aspects of Aging. Durham, North Carolina: Duke University Press. |
| 15 | | Turner, Barbara F., and Robert L. Kahn |
| | 1974 | "Age as a political issue." Journal of Gerontology 29:572–80. |
| 14 | | Turner, R. G., and W. M. Whitaker |
| | 1972 | "The impact of mass layoffs on older workers." Industrial Gerontology 16:14–21. |
| 18 | | Tyhurst, James S., Lee Salk and Miriam Kennedy |
| | 1957 | "Mortality, morbidity, and retirement." American Journal of Public Health 47:1434–44. |
| | | United Nations |
| 14 | 1973 | Demographic Yearbook: 1973. New York: United Nations. |
| | 1975 | The Aging: Trends and Policies. New York: United Nations, Department of Economic and Social Affairs. |
| | | United States Bureau of the Census |
| 17 | 1958 | Current Population Reports, Series P-20, No. 79. Washington, D.C.: United States Government Printing Office. |
| 15 | 1965 | "Voter participation in the national election, November, 1964." Current Population Reports, Series P-20, No. 143. Washington, D.C.: United States Government Printing Office. |
| 1 | 1968 | "Lifetime migration histories of the American people." Current Population Reports, Series P-23, No. 25. Washington, D.C.: United States Government Printing Office. |
| 1, 19 | 1970 | "Projections of the population of the United States, by age and sex (interim revisions): 1970 to 2020." Current Population Reports, Series P-25, No. 448. Washington, D.C.: United States Government Printing Office. |
| 1 | 1971a | "Projections of the population of the United States, by age and sex: 1970–2020." Current Population Reports, Series P-25, No. 470. Washington, D.C.: United States Government Printing Office. |
| 7 | 1971b | "Characteristics of the low-income population, 1970." Current Population Reports, Series P-60, No. 81. Washington, D.C.: United States Government Printing Office. |
| 1 | 1972 | "Projections of the population of the United States by age and sex: 1972 to 2020." Current Population Reports, Series P-25, No. 493. Washington, D.C.: United States Government Printing Office. |
| 15 | 1973a | "Voting and registration in the election of November 1972." Current Population Reports, Series P-20, No. 253. Washington, D.C.: United States Government Printing Office. |
| 14 | 1973b | "Employment status and work experience." Census of Population: 1970. Subject Report PC(2)-6A. Washington, D.C.: United States Government Printing Office. |
| 1 | 1973c | Census of Population: 1970. Volume 1, Characteristics of the Population, Part I, United States Summary, Section 1. Washington, D.C.: United States Government Printing Office. |
| 10 | 1973d | Census of Population: 1970. Subject Reports, Final Report PC(2)-4B, Persons by Family Characteristics. Washington, D.C.: United States Government Printing Office. |
| 15 | 1974 | Statistical Abstract of the United States: 1974. Washington, D.C.: United States Government Printing Office. |
| 7 | 1975 | "Money income in 1973 of families and persons in the United States." Current Population Reports, Series P-60, No. 97. Washington, D.C.: United States Government Printing Office. |

**16**      United States Department of Health, Education, and Welfare, Office of Aging
1965    Foster Family Care for the Aged. Washington, D.C.: United States Government Printing Office.

**14**      United States Department of Health, Education, and Welfare, Office of Consumer Affairs
1973    An Approach to Consumer Education for Adults. Washington, D.C.: Office of Consumer Affairs.

**16**      United States Department of Health, Education, and Welfare, Social and Rehabilitation Service, Administration on Aging
1971    Transportation and Aging: Selected Issues. Washington, D.C.: United States Government Printing Office.

United States Department of Health, Education and Welfare, Social Security Administration, Office of Research and Statistics

**7, 8**    1971a   Resources after Retirement. Report No. 34. (By Edna C. Wentworth and Dena K. Motley.) Washington, D.C.: Office of Research and Statistics.

**7**       1971b   Resources of People 65 or Over. Washington, D.C.: Office of Research and Statistics.

**6**       1971c   Posthospitalization Use of Home Health Services under Medicare, 1967. H1-29. Washington, D.C.: Office of Research and Statistics.

**7**       1972    Economic Resources of Institutionalized Adults: 1967 Survey of Institutionalized Adults. Report No. 3. (By Philip Frohlich.) Washington, D.C.: Office of Research and Statistics.

**7**       1973    Income of the Aged Population: 1971 Money Income and Changes from 1967. Note No. 14. (By Gayle B. Thompson.) Washington, D.C.: Office of Research and Statistics.

1974a   Earnings Replacement from Social Security and Private Pensions: Newly Entitled Beneficiaries, 1970. Report No. 13. (By Alan Fox.) Washington, D.C.: Division of Retirement and Survivors Studies.

**7**       1974b   Effects of the OASDI Benefit Increase in March, 1974. Note No. 14. (By Barbara A. Lingg.) Washington, D.C.: Office of Research and Statistics.

1975a   Demographic and Economic Characteristics of the Aged, 1968 Social Security Survey. (By Lenore E. Bixby, Wayne W. Kolodrubetz, Patience Lauriat and Janet Murray.) Washington, D.C.: Office of Research and Statistics.

**6**       1975b   Age Differences in Health Care Spending, Fiscal Year 1974. No. 6. Washington, D.C.: Office of Research and Statistics, Division of Health Insurance Studies.

**16**      United States Department of Health, Education, and Welfare, Welfare Administration
1966    Planning Welfare Services for Older People. Washington, D.C.: United States Government Printing Office.

United States Department of Housing and Urban Development

**16**      1968    Housing for the Physically Impaired: A Guide for Planning and Design. Washington, D.C.: United States Government Printing Office.

**16**      · 1971  Population, Housing and Income: The Federal Housing Programs. Washington, D.C.: United States Government Printing Office.

**6, 16**   1973    Older Americans: Facts about Incomes and Housing. HUD 359-S. Washington, D.C.: United States Government Printing Office.

United States Department of Labor

**14**      1965    The Older American Workers Age Discrimination in Employment. Washington, D.C.: United States Department of Labor.

**14**      1975    Manpower Report to the President. Washington, D.C.: United States Government Printing Office.

**8**       United States Department of Labor, Labor Management Services Administration
1969    The 100 Largest Retirement Plans: 1960–1968. Washington, D.C.: United States Government Printing Office.

**16**     United States Senate Committee on the District of Columbia
        1974    All About Age in the Greater Metropolitan Washington Community. Washington, D.C.: United States Government Printing Office.
    United States Senate Special Committee on Aging

**14**     1965    Frauds and Deceptions Affecting the Elderly. Washington, D.C.: United States Government Printing Office.

**19**     1968    Long-Range Program and Research Needs in Aging and Related Fields, Part I. Washington, D.C.: United States Government Printing Office.

**6**     1969a    Health Aspects of the Economics of Aging. Washington, D.C.: United States Government Printing Office.

**7**     1969b    Economics of Aging: Toward a Full Share of Abundance. Washington, D.C.: United States Government Printing Office.

**6**     1971a    Trends in Long-Term Care. Parts 12 and 13—Chicago, Illinois. Hearings before the Subcommittee on Long-Term Care, 92nd Congress, 1st Session. Washington, D.C.: United States Government Printing Office.

**1**     1971b    Elderly Cubans in Exile: A Working Paper. Prepared for the Special Committee on Aging, United States Senate, 92nd Congress, 1st Session. Washington, D.C.: United States Government Printing Office.

**19**     1971c    Developments in Aging, 1970. Washington, D.C.: United States Government Printing Office.

**16**     University of Delaware, Division of Urban Affairs
        1972    Delaware's Elderly: Findings and Recommendations. Newark, Delaware: University of Delaware, Division of Urban Affairs.

**18**     Updegraff, Sue G.
        1968    "Changing role of the grandmother." Journal of Home Economics 60:177–80.

**6**     Van Zonneveld, Robert J.
        1962    The Health of the Aged. Baltimore, Maryland: Williams and Wilkins.

**16**     Vessey, Wayne
        1968    "Organization of community social services for the aging." Gerontologist 8(2, part 2):54–56.

**18**     Verwoerdt, Adriaan, Eric Pfeiffer and Hsioh-Shan Wang
        1969    "Sexual behavior in senescence: changes in sexual activity and interest in aging men and women." Journal of Geriatric Psychiatry 2:168–80.

**2**     Verzar, F.
        1957    "The aging of connective tissue." Gerontologist 1:363–78.

**15**     Vinyard, Dale
        1972    "The Senate Special Committee on Aging." Gerontologist 12:298–303.

**8**     Vogel, Bruce S., and Robert E. Schell
            1968    "Vocational interest patterns in late maturity and retirement." Journal of Gerontology 23:66–70.

**2**     Walford, Roy L.
        1964    "The immunologic theory of aging." Gerontologist 4:195–97.

**2**     Walford, Roy L., and Gary M. Troup
        1966    "Auto-immunity theories." Pp. 351–58 in Nathan W. Shock (ed.), Perspectives in Experimental Gerontology. Springfield, Illinois: Charles C. Thomas.

**12**     Walker, D. W.
        1968    "A study of the relationship between suicide rates and age in the United States (1914 to 1964)." Pp. 408–20 in Proceedings of the Social Statistics Section. Washington, D.C.: American Statistical Association.

**10**     Walker, J. V.
        1968    "Attitudes to death." Gerontologia Clinica 10:304–08.

**8**

Walker, J. W., and K. F. Price

1974    "The impact of vesting, early retirement, rising cost of living and other factors on projected retirement patterns: a manpower planning model." Industrial Gerontology 1:35–48.

**6, 8**

Wan, T.

1972    "Social differentials in selected work-limiting chronic conditions." Journal of Chronic Diseases 25:365–74.

**3**

Waugh, Nancy C., James L. Fozard, George A. Talland and Donald E. Erwin

1973    "Effects of age and stimulus repetition on two-choice reaction time." Journal of Gerontology 28:466–70.

**4**

Webber, I. L., D. W. Coombs and J. S. Hollingsworth

1974    "Variations in value orientations by age in a developing society." Journal of Gerontology 29:676–83.

**7**

Wedderburn, Dorothy

1968    "Cross-national studies of income adequacy." Pp. 61–74 in Ethel Shanas and John Madge (eds.), Methodology Problems in Cross-National Studies of Income Adequacy. New York: S. Karger.

**6**

Weinstock, C., and R. Bennett

1971    "From 'waiting on the list' to becoming a 'newcomer' and an 'old timer' in a home for the aged: two studies of socialization and its impact upon cognitive functioning." Aging and Human Development 2:46–58.

**1**

Weinberger, L. E., and J. Millham

1975    "A multidimensional, multiple method analysis of attitudes towards the elderly." Journal of Gerontology 30:343–48.

Weisman, Avery D.

**10**    1972    On Dying and Denying. New York: Behavioral Publications.

**10**    1974    "On death and dying. Does old age make sense? Decisions and destiny in growing older." Journal of Geriatric Psychiatry 7:84–93.

**3**

Weiss, Alfred D.

1959    "Sensory functions." Pp. 503–42 in James E. Birren (ed.), Handbook of Aging and the Individual. Chicago: University of Chicago Press.

**16**

Weiss, Joseph D.

1969    Better Buildings for the Aged. New York: Hopkinson and Blake.

Welford, Alan T.

**3**    1958    Ageing and Human Skill. London: Oxford University Press.

**3**    1959    "Psychomotor performance." Pp. 562–613 in James E. Birren (ed.), Handbook of Aging and the Individual. Chicago: University of Chicago Press.

**4**    1964    "Aging and personality: age changes in basic psychological capacities." Pp. 60–66 in P. From Hansen (ed.), Age with a Future. Copenhagen: Munksgaard.

Welford, Alan T., and James Birren (eds.)

**3**    1965    Behavior, Aging and the Nervous System. Springfield, Illinois: Charles C. Thomas.

**3**    1969    Decision Making and Age. New York: S. Karger.

**7**

Wendell, Richard F.

1968    "The economic status of the aged." Gerontologist 8(2, part 2):32–36.

**8, 14**

Wentworth, Edna C.

1968    Employment after Retirement: A Study of Post-entitlement Work Experience of Men Drawing Benefits under Social Security. Washington, D.C.: United States Government Printing Office.

Wershow, Harold J.

1964    "The older Jews of Albany Park—some aspects of a subculture of the aged and its interaction with a gerontological research project." Gerontologist 4:198–202.

6     Wessen, A. F.
       1964    "Some sociological characteristics of long-term care." Gerontologist 4:72–75.

7     West, Howard
       1971    "Five years of Medicare—a statistical review." Social Security Bulletin 34(12): 17–27.

9     Whiskin, Frederick E.
       1964    "On the meaning and function of reading in later life." Pp. 300–04 in Robert Kastenbaum (ed.), New Thoughts on Old Age. New York: Springer.

6     White, E. L., and T. Gordon
       1969    "Related aspects of health and aging in the United States." Pp. 27–44 in Marjorie F. Lowenthal and Ariv Zilli (eds.), Colloquium on Health and Aging of the Population. New York: S. Karger.

4     White, Robert W.
       1959    "Motivation reconsidered: the concept of competence." Psychological Review 66:297–333.

19    White House Conference on Aging
       1971    Report of the Delegates from the Conference Sections and Special 'Concerns Sessions. Washington, D.C.: White House Conference on Aging.

      Wilder, Charles S.
6       1971    "Chronic conditions and limitations of activity and mobility: United States, July 1965 to June 1967." Vital and Health Statistics, Series 10, No. 61.

5       1973    "Limitation of activity due to chronic conditions: United States, 1969 to 1970." Vital and Health Statistics, Series 10, No. 80.

6       1974    "Acute conditions: incidence and associated disability: United States, July 1971 to June 1972." Vital and Health Statistics, Series 10, No. 88.

6     Wilder, Mary H.
       1972    "Home care for persons 55 years and over: United States, July 1966 to June 1968." Vital and Health Statistics, Series 10, No. 73.

17    Wilensky, Harold
       1964    "Life cycle, work situations and participation in formal associations." Pp. 213–42 in Robert W. Kleemeier (ed.), Aging and Leisure. New York: Oxford University Press.

      Williams, Richard H.
5       1960    "Changing status, roles and relationships." Pp. 261–97 in Clark Tibbitts (ed.), Handbook of Social Gerontology. Chicago: University of Chicago Press.

10      1973    "Propaganda, modification, and termination of life: contraception, abortion, suicide, euthanasia." Pp. 80–97 in R. H. Williams (ed.), To Live and to Die: When, Why, and How. New York: Springer.

12    Williams, Richard H., and Martin B. Loeb
       1968    "The adult's social life space and successful aging: some suggestions for a conceptual framework." Pp. 379–81 in Bernice L. Neugarten (ed.), Middle Age and Aging. Chicago: University of Chicago Press.

1, 12,   Williams, Richard H., and Claudine Wirths
13      1965    Lives Through the Years. New York: Atherton Press.

      Williams, Richard H., Clark Tibbitts and Wilma Donahue (eds.)
       1963    Processes of Aging. Volumes 1 and 2. New York: Atherton Press.

16    Wilner, Daniel M., and Rosabelle P. Walkley
       1966    "Some special problems and alternatives in housing for older persons." Pp. 221–59 in John C. McKinney and F. T. deVyver (eds.), Aging and Social Policy. New York: Appleton-Century-Crofts.

16    Wilner, Daniel M., Susan R. Sherman, Rosabelle P. Walkley, Suzanne Dodds and Wiley P. Mangum, Jr.
       1968    "Demographic characteristics of residents of planned retirement housing sites." Gerontologist 8:164–89.

| | |
|---|---|
| **17** | Wingrove, C. Ray, and Jon P. Alston<br>1971 "Age, aging, and church attendance." Gerontologist 11(4, part 1):356–58. |
| **6, 16,**<br>**19** | Winiecke, L.<br>1973 "The appeal of age segregated housing to the elderly poor." International Journal of Aging and Human Development 4:293–306. |
| **8** | Withers, W.<br>1974 "Some irrational beliefs about retirement in the United States." Industrial Gerontology 1:23–32. |
| **6, 7** | Witkin, E.<br>1971 The Impact of Medicare. Springfield, Illinois: Charles C. Thomas. |
| **9** | Wittels, I., and J. Botwinick<br>1974 Survival in relocation. Journal of Gerontology 29:440–43. |
| **14** | Wolfbein, Seymour L.<br>1963 "Work patterns of older people." Pp. 303–12 in Richard H. Williams, Clark Tibbitts and Wilma Donahue (eds.), Processes of Aging. Volume 2. New York: Atherton Press. |
| **10** | Wolff, K.<br>1971 "The treatment of the depressed and suicidal geriatric patient." Geriatrics 26(7):65–69. |
| **16** | Wolk, R. L., and R. B. Wolk<br>1971 "Professional workers' attitudes toward the aged." Journal of American Geriatric Society 19:624–39. |
| **5** | Wood, V.<br>1971 "Age-appropriate behavior for older people." Gerontologist 11(4, part 2): 74–78. |
| **4** | Woodruff, D. S., and J. E. Birren<br>1972 "Age changes and cohort differences in personality." Developmental Psychology 6:252–59. |
| **16** | Woodward, H., R. Gingles and J. C. Woodward<br>1974 "Loneliness and the elderly as related to housing." Gerontologist 14:349–51. |
| **6** | World Health Organization<br>1959 "Mental health problems of aging and the aged: sixth report." World Health Organization Technical Report Series 171:3–51. Paris: World Health Organization. |
| **16** | Wray, R. P.<br>1971a An Interdisciplinary Non-Credit Community Course in Adult Development and Aging. Bethesda, Maryland: ERIC Document Reproduction Service. |
| **19** | 1971b "Gerontology: interdisciplinary and intercollegiate." Gerontologist 11:261–63. |
| **6** | Wunderlich, Gooloo S.<br>1965 "Characteristics of residents of institutions for the aged and chronically ill: United States, April–June, 1963." Vital and Health Statistics, Series 12, No. 2. |
| **4** | Wylie, R. W.<br>1971 "Attitudes toward aging and the aged among black Americans: some historical perspectives." Aging and Human Development 2:66–70. |
| | Youmans, E. Grant |
| **14** | 1966 "Objective and subjective economic disengagement among older rural and urban men." Journal of Gerontology 21:439–41. |
| **13** | 1967a "Family disengagement among older urban and rural women." Journal of Gerontology 22:209–11. |
| | 1967b (ed.), Older Rural Americans: A Sociological Perspective. Lexington, Kentucky: University of Kentucky Press. |
| **1** | 1971 "Generation and perceptions of old age: an urban-rural comparison." Gerontologist 11:284–88. |

**4**

1973     "Age stratification and value orientations." International Journal of Aging and Human Development 4:53–65.

**4**

1974     "Age group, health and attitudes." Gerontologist 14:249–54.

**12, 13**

Youmans, E. Grant, and Marian Yarrow

1971     "Aging and social adaptation: a longitudinal study of old men." Pp. 95–103 in Samuel Granick and Robert D. Patterson (eds.), Human Aging II: An Eleven-Year Followup. Washington, D.C.: United States Government Printing Office.

**18**

Young, Michael, and Peter Willmott

1957     Family and Kinship in East London. London: Routledge & Kegan Paul.

**6**

Zarit, S. H., and R. L. Kahn

1975     "Aging and adaptation to illness." Journal of Gerontology 30:67–72.

**4, 16**

Zatlin, C. E., M. Storandt and J. Botwinick

1973     "Personality and values of women continuing their education after thirty-five years of age." Journal of Gerontology 28:216–21.

**9**

Zborowski, Mark

1962     "Aging and recreation." Journal of Gerontology 17:302–09.

**1**

Zelinsky, Wilbur

1966     "Toward a geography of the aged." Geographical Review 56:445–47.

**12**

Zimberg, Sheldon

1974     "The elderly alcoholic." Gerontologist 14:221–24.

**4**

Zola, Irving K.

1962     "Feeling about age among older people." Journal of Gerontology 17:65–68.

**3**

Zuckerman, Harriet, and Robert K. Merton

1972     "Age, aging, and age structure in science." Pp. 292–356 in Matilda W. Riley, Marilyn Johnson and Anne Foner (eds.), Aging and Society. Volume 3: A Sociology of Age Stratification. New York: Russell Sage Foundation.

# Index

**A**

activities of older people, 75, 92–93
activity:
  as drive, 60
  restriction of, 98, 99, 105, 106–09, 207, 208, 212, 214–15, 219
  in retirement, 145, 146, 158–59
activity theory of adjustment, 26-27, 170, 219
adaptation:
  to aging, 207–24 (See also aging, adaptation to)
  defined, 214
adaptive tasks, 214–17
adjustment:
  personal, 160–61, 162–64
  social, 156–57 (See also aging, adaptation to; retirement, adjustment to)
Administration on Aging (AOA), U.S., 243, 256, 317–18
adolescence, 10, 199, 301
adulthood, 199–200
afterlife, 182, 281, 282
age discrimination. See discrimination, age
Age Discrimination Employment Act (1967), 238
age grading, 23
ageism, 20-21
age stratification theory, 23–24
aging:
  adaptation to, 77, 207–24

aging (cont.):
  biological aspects of, 5, 33–39
  problems of the, 12–23, 251, 252–59
  processes of, 4–5
  psychological aspects of, 5, 40–66
  social aspects of, 23–27
  sociopsychological aspects of, 67–83
Aid for the Aged, 134, 258
alcoholism, 110–11, 217–18, 219
American Association of Retired Persons, 253, 268, 276, 287
Anderson, Barbara G., 201–05, 214–17, 220–23, 281, 299, 312, 317
anomie, 70, 191
Area Agencies on Aging (AAA), 258, 259, 262–63, 265, 269
arthritis, 241–42
Atchley, Robert C., 79, 170, 191, 192–93
"autoimmunity" theory of senescence, 35

**B**

balance, sense of, 44–45
Baltes, Paul B., 52–53
beliefs, 72 (See also religion)
Berardo, Felix, M., 190–91, 192–94
bereavement, 185–86
Bible reading, 281–82, 283
biological renewal, 302–03
birth rates, 305

black older people, 129, 284 (*See also* minority-group older people)
boredom, 64–65
Bucks County (Pennsylvania) Department of Adult Services, 269–70

**C**

career tracks, 91
Carp, Frances M., 229
Catholics, 280, 283–84
childhood, 10, 198–199
children, adult:
  contacts with, 252, 276, 299
  relations with older parents, 204, 296, 297, 299–300
China, imperial, status of aged in, 94
chronological age, 8–10, 11, 90
church:
  attendance, 280–81
  programs for aged, 284–85
Clark, Margaret, 201–05, 214–17, 220–23, 281, 299, 312, 317
closure, 46, 80
cognitive functioning, 78
"collagen" theory of senescence, 35
community, 261–78 (*See also* social services)
  agencies, 201, 204, 243, 269
  facilities, 263–64
  participation in, 101–02, 190, 245–46, 261–62, 275, 279–88
  programs, 113, 204, 258, 264–70
  urban-rural, 263–64, 306
companionship, 294, 296
competence, 217 (*See also* leisure competence)
Comprehensive Service Amendments (1973), 258
concept formation, 55–56
congregate meals, 264–65
conservatism, political, 246
consolidation of commitments, 212
consumer role, 239–43
continuity theory of aging, 27, 171, 173, 217, 230, 286
Cottrell, W. Fred, 170, 171
counseling service, 269–70
couplehood, 213
couples, 162, 291–95, 297–99
Cousins, Norman, 174
craftsmanship, 140
creativity, 57–58
Cumming, Elaine, 92–93, 228–29, 230, 231

**D**

day care, 269, 270
Dean, Lois R., 64–65
death:
  attitudes toward, 18, 25–26, 181–86, 281, 283
  causes of, 38, 180, 181
  defined, 179–80
decision demand, 91
Democrats, 248
dependency, 80, 97–98, 155, 197, 203–06, 243, 299–300
depression, 112, 156, 218
development, definition of, 214
developmental theory of aging, 214–17
disability, 80, 98, 99, 105, 107–08, 155, 204, 208, 209
discrimination, age, 25, 146–47, 148, 149, 238
disengagement, 209–11, 212, 213
  forced, 210–11
  individual, 26–27, 209–11, 228–29, 229–32
  societal, 25–26, 227–32
  theory of, 170, 219, 227–32
divorce, 291, 292, 293, 297
DNA, 35–36
drives, 58–60
drug abuse, 218, 219
dying trajectory, 179, 183, 184

**E**

earnings, 127, 136
economic cycle in life course, 89–90
economic roles, 17, 234–44 (*See also* finances; income)
education:
  inequality of, 20–21
  for leisure, 174
  obsolescence of, 18
  for retirement, 146, 275–76, 319
educational level, 245–46, 247, 306
ego psychology, 73, 76
Eliminate Poverty in California, 256
emotional response, 61, 64–65
Employee Retirement Income Security Act (1974), 131
employment, 139, 235–39, 265, 268, 319–20
  equal opportunity for, 148
"empty nest," 207, 208, 290, 292
energy, declining, 204, 207, 208, 209, 210, 212, 214

engagement, 210, 211 (*See also* disengagement)
entry criteria, 95
"error" theory of senescence, 36
escape from aging, 217–19
ethnicity, 251–52, 254
expectancies, 58

**F**

familism, 213
family, 17, 116, 239, 290–309
   cycle, 89–90, 290, 305, 306
   of orientation, 290, 291, 304
   of procreation, 290, 291, 304
   relations, 296, 301, 305–09
   roles, 187–88, 189, 228, 231, 234–35, 304–05
   services, 307, 308–09
   structure, 162, 304–05
   values, 305–07
Filer, Richard N., 62–63
finances, 125–38 (*See also* income)
   in retirement, 144, 145, 150, 152, 160–61, 163
financial independence, 200, 201
financial resources, 127–34, 194, 285–86, 293–94, 295
food, 134, 135
foster grandparent program, 267–68
foster home care, 269, 270
fraud against the aged, 239–43
friendship, 188, 309–12
funeral business, preneed, 241

**G**

geriatrics, 4n
gerontology, 4–5 (*See also* social gerontology)
Golden Age clubs, 100, 284, 286
Gottesman, Leonard E., 121
government programs, 134, 254–59, 262–63, 321
grandparent role, 301, 302–03, 305
Gray Panthers, 253
great-grandparent role, 301, 304, 305
Green Thumb, 268
group identity, 251–52, 254

**H**

Havighurst, Robert J., 168, 170, 175, 219–20
health, 104–123, 201, 207, 208, 218, 285, 286
   care and services, 112–15, 119–20, 121–22, 135–36, 320
   defined, 104–05

health *(cont.)*:
   and retirement, 145, 149, 150, 152
hearing, 43–44, 204
Henry, William E., 92–93, 228–29, 230, 231
heredity, 37
HEW. *See* U.S. Department of Health, Education, and Welfare
home care, 113, 204, 269, 270
homemaker services, 204, 265, 269, 270, 272
home ownership, 132, 133, 273–75, 295
housewives, 140, 191, 193
housing, 200–01, 272–75
   characteristics of, 272, 273, 320
   expenditures, 135
   programs, 134, 284, 320
hunger as drive, 58–59

**I**

identity, 171, 173, 190, 191, 192
identity continuity, 171, 173 (*See also* continuity theory of aging)
identity crisis theory, 169–70, 172, 173
illness, 80, 116, 118, 155–56, 204, 231
immune system, 36
income, 320 (*See also* finances; retirement)
   adequacy of, 159, 163, 164, 173, 187, 189, 191, 207, 208, 239
   counseling, 265
   inequality, 20–21
   sources, 127–34
independence, 197–206, 220, 272–75, 301 (*See also* dependency)
India, status of aged in, 94
individualism, 141
industrialization, 12, 17–18, 24, 141–42, 234–35
inflation, 137
Institute for Lifetime Learning, 276
institutionalization:
   attitudes toward, 62–63, 102, 116, 118, 204–05
   and role changes, 98–99, 204–05, 208, 209
institutions, 116–21 (*See also* mental institutions)
   mortality rates in, 118
   population of, 117
   types of, 115, 118–19, 272, 273, 283
insurance, 114–15, 127
intelligence, 49–51, 52–53
intelligence quotient (IQ), 49–50
interiority, 76–78, 209
interpersonal relationships, 184, 289–314
intimacy, alternate sources of, 193–94

involvement, minimal, 213 (*See also* engagement)
irritation, 64–65
isolation, social, 110–11, 136, 156, 157–58, 194, 203, 213, 218, 263, 296, 310–11

**J**

Japan, older workers in, 142
Jews, 280, 283
Job, 61–62, 139, 140, 142 (*See also* employment; work)
  dissatisfaction, 150, 152
  roles, 157, 168, 234–39
  skills and transference to leisure, 170–71
Johnson, Virginia, 59–60, 298

**K**

Kahana, Eva, 120, 121
Kalish, Richard A., 179, 182, 183, 184–85, 197
Kansas City Study of Adult Life, 3–4, 64–65, 92–93, 317
Kerckhoff, Alan C., 162, 305–06
kinship, 291, 296, 297, 305 (*See also* family, extended)
Kosa, John, 160–61
Kübler-Ross, Elizabeth, 183–84
Kuhlen, Raymond G., 60–61
Kuhn, Margaret, 253

**L**

labor force, 17, 18–19, 235–39 (*See also* employment; work)
Langley Porter Institute Studies on Aging, 317
late adulthood, 214
later maturity, 10, 11
learning, 51, 52
leisure, 168–77, 286
  competence, 174–75
  participation in retirement, 150, 152, 158–59, 171–74, 217, 229
  roles, 100, 168–77, 276
Lewis, Oscar, 251
liberalism, political, 246
life:
  course, 10–11, 22, 88–91
  expectancy, 13
  satisfaction, 156–57, 218–20, 271, 283
  space, 210, 214, 215, 271
  styles, 140, 212–13
limitations, instrumental, 214–15
living, level of, 134–36

living arrangements, 191–92, 193, 213, 231, 307–08, 310–11
living fully, 213–14
living wills, 184
loneliness, 65, 187, 190, 218, 296
Lowenthal, Marjorie F., 110–11

**M**

Manton, Kenneth, 20–21
marital satisfaction, 292, 293, 294
marital status, 291–97
marriage, 291–95, 297–99
Masters, William H., 59–60, 298
Meals-on-Wheels, 122, 264, 272
Medicaid, 115, 134
medical care. *See* health care
Medicare, 114, 115, 121, 134, 137, 253, 254, 255–56, 258
memory, 54–55
menopause, 37–38, 59, 298
mental faculties, 73n
mental functioning, 49–58
mental illness, 109–12, 156, 281
mental institutions, 120–21, 267
mental sets, 58
methodology in gerontology, 325–28
middle age, 10–11
migration, 160–62, 173, 261–62
milieu therapy, 121
Miller, Stephen J., 169–70, 171, 172, 173
minority group, the aged as, 25
minority-group older people, 129, 253, 254, 284
mobility, 201, 271
  geographic, 141, 171
morale, 156, 203, 210, 211
mortality rates, 141, 180–81, 305
motivation, 60–61, 62–63
Mott Foundation, 276
"mutation" theory of senescence, 35–36

**N**

National Caucus on the Black Aged, 253
National Council on Aging (NCOA), 253, 256, 268
National Council of Senior Citizens (NCSC), 253, 268
National Institute on Aging (NIA), 11, 318, 319
National Retired Teachers Association, 253, 268
neighborhoods, 16
neighbors, 309–12
Nesselroade, John R., 52–53

Neugarten, Bernice L., 76–78, 79, 83, 209, 219–20, 302–03
neuroses, 111
Newell, David S., 227–29
norms, 68–70, 90–91, 151–53, 211, 263 (*See also* socialization)
nucleated family cluster, 306
nutrition, 38, 122, 135
 programs, 134, 269, 270, 320

**O**

occupational cycle in life course, 89–90
occupational inequality, 20–21
occupational level, 163
 and family relations, 306
 and retirement attitudes, 144, 158, 170–71, 292–93
O'Connell, Desmond O., 62–63
Office of Aging (HEW), 256
old age, 10, 11
Older Americans Act (1965), 317
Older Americans Comprehensive Service Amendments (1973), 262
older persons, definitions of, 4–5, 258, 326
opportunity, atrophy of, 229–32
outreach services, 265, 267

**P**

Palmore, Erdman B., 20–21
parent-child relationships, 97, 299–300, 305–307 (*See also* children, adult)
Pension Benefit Guarantee Corporation, 131
pensions, dual, 132
 private, 128, 129–31, 137, 197
 public, 128–29, 131–32
perception, 45–46
personal action system, 220
personality, 67, 73, 76–82, 219
physical therapy, 269
physician visits, 113
policy on aging, national, 319–22
political participation, 99, 245–50, 254
political power, 25, 26, 250–54
politics and aging, 245–60
Pollman, A. William, 152
population:
 growth, 12–13
 older, 12–13, 322
poverty, 125, 136, 148, 149, 159, 187, 204, 208
power elite, gerontocratic, 251, 253
pressure group, older people as, 250–54

principled thinking, 68–69
privacy, 65
problem solving, 56–57
protective services, 266–67, 269, 270
Protestants, 280, 283
psychogenic disorders, 110–11
psychomotor performance, 46–49
psychoses, 111

**Q**

quackery, 241–43

**R**

Railroad Retirement, 128, 131, 243
"rate-of-living" theory of senescence, 35
reaction time, 47–48
referral services, 265, 269–70
rehabilitation, 122
religion, 99, 182, 279–85, 320
remarriage, 187, 194, 293–95
Republicans, 248
retired person, 19–20, 151–53
Retired Senior Volunteer Program (RSVP), 268, 269, 270
retirement, 139–66, 319–20
 adjustment to, 145–46, 162–64
 attitudes toward, 143–44, 149, 160–61, 162, 292–93
 communities, 160, 161, 251–52, 276–77
 consequences of, 100, 101, 155–64, 207, 208, 217, 299
 defined, 139–40
 early, 136, 147, 148, 152, 232
 evolution of, 141–43, 151, 164
 financing of, 128–34, 238–39, 243
 mandatory, 147–49, 164, 169, 170, 238
 policies, 17–18, 146–49, 150
 preparation for, 144–46
 reasons for, 146–51, 152
 right to, 140, 141–43
 roles in, 69–70, 71, 80, 95–96, 97, 151–53, 163–64, 168–77, 192–93, 230, 231
rigidity, mental, 58
rinethesis, 45
RNA, 36
role:
 loss, 79–80, 81–82, 93, 193, 201, 212, 228–29
 performance, 81, 82
roles, social, 69, 79–81, 91–102, 183
Roman, Paul, 230
Rose, Arnold, 251–52
Rosow, Irving, 70, 81–82, 310–11

**S**

Schaie, K. Warner, 52–53
Scripps Foundation, 170–72
self-assertiveness, 76–77
self-concept, 67, 74–75, 78–82, 186–87, 214, 216,
    220
  defined, 78
  in retirement, 156, 157, 169, 170
self-esteem:
  age changes in, 78–79, 80–82
  defined, 78–79
  and independence, 202
  and religion, 282–83
  in retirement, 157
self-image, 74–75, 159, 282–83
self-respect in leisure roles, 168–69, 173
self-stability, 81–82
self-sufficiency, 197–202 (*See also* independence)
  changes in age, 200, 202
  mental, 201
senescence:
  defined, 33
  results of, 37–38
  theories of, 34–37
senility, 33
senior centers, 258, 265–66, 269, 270, 272, 275,
    276, 286
Senior Companion Program, 268
sensory:
  experience, 40
  loss, 207, 208–09
  processes, 40–45
  threshold, 40–41, 47
Service Corps of Retired Executives (SCORE),
    268
sex:
  as drive, 59–60
  ratio, 293–94, 318
  roles, 292, 293
sexuality, 218, 297–99
siblings, 304, 305
Sinclair, Upton, 256
single older person, 129, 296–97
situational changes, 101, 285 (*See also* social
    situation)
  in retirement, 159–62
smell, sense of, 45
social:
  change, 12, 19–23
  class, 24, 174, 175, 189, 276, 292–93, 297
  criticism, 7–8
  gerontology, 5–10, 23–29, 256–57, 316–23
  interaction, 61–62, 157–58, 228, 311

social *(cont.)*:
  learning theory, 76
  services, 113, 204, 258, 264–70, 321
  situation of older people, 87–103, 317
  status, 24–25, 94–95
socialization, 67–73, 198–200, 306–07
Social Security, 127, 128–29, 132, 133–34, 137,
    142, 145, 164, 239, 252–53, 254, 255–56,
    257, 258, 326–27
society:
  changing demands of, 214, 217
  response of to older people, 210–11, 227, 229,
    231–32, 262–63
spending patterns, 134–36
spouse, loss of, 186–94
stereotypes of older people, 72–73, 74–75, 164
stigma of old age, 18–19
stimulus generalization, 55
Streib, Gordon F., 160–61
stress situations and disengagement, 231
subculture, older people as, 24, 251–52, 253
substitution for loss, 212, 214, 215–17, 219
suicide, 218, 219, 295
Supplemental Security Income (1974), 133–34, 137

**T**

Taietz, Philip, 230
taste, sense of, 45
telephone reassurance, 265
television, 100, 174
terminal patients, 120
thinking, 55–56
Thompson, Wayne E., 160–61
Tibbitts, Clark, 5
Tobin, Sheldon S., 219–20
Townsend Movement, 256
transportation, 175, 201, 271–72, 286, 321

**U**

unions, 243, 287
United Auto Workers, 287
urbanization, 12, 13–17, 141
U.S. Department of Health, Education, and Wel-
    fare (HEW), 243, 256, 317–18
U.S. Department of Labor, 130, 131, 268
U.S. Senate Special Committee on Aging, 256, 257

**V**

values:
  defined, 71–72
  family, 305–07

values *(cont.)*:
  reintegration of, 214, 216
vision, 41–43
visitor programs, 265
voluntary associations, 99, 100, 253, 285–87
volunteer work, 229, 268–69
voting behavior, 246–48, 249, 254

## W

"waste-product" theory of senescence, 35
"wear-and-tear" theory of senescence, 34–35
Wechsler Adult Intelligence Scale (WAIS), 49–51
Weinstein, Karol K., 302–03
welfare, 231, 243, 258, 284
White House Conference on Aging (1971), 253, 262, 318, 319–22
widowhood, 129, 186–94, 291, 293, 295–96
  adaptations in, 208, 209, 218, 231

widowhood *(cont.)*:
  roles of, 80, 96–97, 301
  situational changes in, 118
Williams, Richard H., 212–14, 220
Williams, Senator Harrison, 242
Wirths, Claudine, 212–14, 220
work, 139, 140 (*See also* employment; job)
  orientation, 169, 170–71
  return to, 162–63
  roles, 228, 229, 230
  view of as temporary, 171–73
workers:
  black, 129
  older, 238
World of Work life style, 212–13

## Y

young adulthood, 10
youth, needs of, 255